D1282735

RIVERSIDE TEXTBOOKS IN EDUCATION

EDITED BY ELLWOOD P. CUBBERLEY
DEAN OF THE SCHOOL OF EDUCATION
LELAND STANFORD JUNIOR UNIVERSITY

We can look upon the junior college movement which is now spreading throughout the United States as the most wholesome and significant occurrence in American education in the present century. —

RAY LYMAN WILBUR

WILLIAM RAINEY HARPER
1856–1906
President of the University of Chicago, 1891–1906
"Father of the Junior College"

THE JUNIOR COLLEGE

BY

WALTER CROSBY EELLS

Professor of Education
Leland Stanford Junior University
Editor, Junior College Journal

HOUGHTON MIFFLIN COMPANY

BOSTON · NEW YORK · CHICAGO · DALLAS

ATLANTA · SAN FRANCISCO

The Riverside Press Cambridge

The Riverside Press
CAMBRIDGE · MASSACHUSETTS
PRINTED IN THE U.S.A.

TO MY WIFE

NATALIE SOULES EELLS

SEVEREST BUT KINDEST OF CRITICS

EDITOR'S INTRODUCTION

THE school is by nature a conservative institution, and those who guide and direct it tend to hold to traditional attitudes. As a result, progress in educational organization tends to lag behind national needs, coming by slow evolution rather than by any marked revolutionary advance. In consequence, those fundamental educational reorganizations which at times are demanded in the interests of national progress and are called for to meet new national needs take place but slowly. Often too, what is being evolved is only partially understood by those who live and work at the time a fundamental reorganizing movement is under way. Especially is this true, if one is a part of an organization that is being gradually changed or superseded. What is, seems fixed, and what is to be, often seems visionary and impossible. Perhaps, on the whole, it is well that this is the case, as it insures conservative progress rather than radical change.

While the historical development of American education has been characterized by a slow and gradual evolution rather than by any radical upheavals, certain fundamental and far-reaching changes and reorganizations have nevertheless from time to time taken place which have fundamentally changed and redirected the character of the instruction provided. The rise of state control, with the consequent abolition of the rate bill, the pauper school, and sectarian aims in instruction, in time completely altered the type of education provided and made a substantial common school education the birthright of every American boy and girl. The slow rise of professional school-supervision and the gradual development of a science of educational organization and administration changed the public school from a local and largely political affair to an institution, national in character and importance. The slow but gradual expansion of the original common school of our pioneer agricultural days to include the public high school, with a curriculum of studies better adapted to the growing needs of the nation, was an event of great educational as well as national significance. The creation and firm establishment of the state university, to provide leadership and to establish standards for the enterprises of democracy, was another forward educational step that did much to promote national well-being. The evolution of the public normal school and the creation of a body of professionally educated and trained teachers for our schools did much to reshape the instruction provided and gave a new character to the teaching staff. The recent development of a broad and comprehensive system of vocational education, to supplement intellectual and cultural courses and to train those who work with their hands as well as their heads, not only provided a type of education calculated to meet the needs of a great manufacturing and exporting nation, but clearly marked, as well, a fundamental redirection of educational aims and purposes.

The change from the poorly taught and very limited common school of the forties to the eight-year elementary school of the eighties represented a fundamental reorganization and development of the whole field of elementary education, and it took place so slowly and so gradually that many did not realize the character or the importance of the movement. The American high school of the eighties, with its common three-year course of study — including subjects now taught exclusively in the upper grades of the elementary school became, by gradual evolution, the four-year high school of today with its varied offerings — cultural, scientific, vocational — coupled with its great expansion in number of schools, instructors, and students. This has been a change of great significance to popular education in the United States, and one that has done much, not only to advance the educational and cultural standards of the American people, but one that also has enabled our colleges and universities to advance their work to a higher level. The multiplication in number of our high schools and the advance of their instruction has also permitted our colleges and universities to dispense with their former "academic" or "preparatory" departments (once the chief end of their instructional activities). The advance of the high schools in length of course and character of their instruction has enabled the colleges, in turn, to pass down to them most of what, in the eighties and the nineties, was taught in the freshman year.

Probably the most fundamental reorganization of public education, within the past two decades, has been the rather general reorganization of the work of the public school system from an 8-4 type of organization to that of a 6-3-3 type, through the organization of the new junior high school, the better to adapt the curriculum of the seventh, eighth, and ninth grades to the new instructional needs which changing social and economic conditions have brought about. The fundamental ideas underlying this reorganization of our public school work has been to make better provision for the peculiar psychological needs of early adolescence through intelligent placement, flexible grouping, differentiated study, failure prevention, training in moral values and the right type of habit reactions, better citizenship training, the development of personality under good conditions, and vocational guidance. The junior high school represents the creation of a new and intermediate type of educational institution, devised to meet the special needs — physical, mental, social, and moral — of young people in their early teens. As this fundamental reorganization of school work has been instituted in our cities the instruction in both the junior and senior high school has been advanced to meet the new needs of a rapidly advancing people.

Almost wholly within the past two decades still another

fundamental reorganization in American education has been slowly evolving, and another new institution of large future importance has gradually been shaping its work and its future. The history, classification, functions, organization and administration, plant and equipment, finance, form, place, and future of this new division of the American educational ladder — the junior college — form the subject matter of the present number in this series of textbooks. That the author has provided us with an excellent presentation of the organization and work of the junior college, and its position in the educational scheme, will be recognized by all who read or use this volume. Well organized as a textbook, its reasoning based on concrete data, and interestingly and forcefully written, it makes a contribution of first importance to our educational literature and one certain to find a place of great usefulness as a textbook in courses on the organization and administration of the junior college, as well as a general reference book for those interested in the development and place and purpose of this new educational creation.

Just what form of organization will best fit this new institution into the existing school systems, public and private, and just what relation to existing institutions of higher education it will in time assume, cannot now be foretold with exactness. Probably the form and the relationship will be different in various parts of the country and with different institutions. So far as its position in the public school system is concerned, the author's strong arguments for a 6–3–3–2 form of organization, as contrasted with the 6–4–4 form, have convinced the editor that where it can be effected this is the better type of development. Time and experience alone can determine its final position, however, and it is not unlikely that more than one form of organization will be found fitted to the needs of different communities.

That the general effect on existing higher institutions, both public and private, will be good, viewed from the standpoint of the further development of American education as a whole, does not seem to be in doubt. Fifty years ago the colleges were very fearful that if they abolished their thriving and often profitable two-year academic and preparatory departments, and depended on the rising high schools for the preparation of their students, it would mean the lowering of standards and the disorganization of collegiate instruction. Finally these departments were abolished, but with much misgiving as to the outcome. The result was the making of both the high schools and the colleges. There is reason now to think that within the next decade or two, a similar step upward will be attended with equally happy results, and be the making of the real American college and university — in the older cultural colleges a three-year course of training leading to the master's degree, and in the larger universities a group of professional schools radiating from the beginning of the junior year. One cannot read the present volume without the feeling that this desirable development is probably nearer at hand than we, as a people, now realize.

ELLWOOD P. CUBBERLEY

PREFACE

No book has appeared, since the publication of Koos's *The Junior College Movement* in 1925, which has attempted to give a comprehensive view of the entire junior college field. Yet in this brief time, the number of junior colleges has more than doubled, widespread public interest has been greatly intensified, and the literature in the field has increased at an astonishing rate. Prior to 1925 not a single course on the junior college had been offered in any American university. By 1930 such a course had been given in at least twenty universities, with a total class enrollment in excess of 900 students. Additional universities have announced the introduction of such a course in 1931 for prospective junior college administrators and instructors. There is need, therefore, for an up to date text presenting a systematic survey of the entire field for the use of university students, junior college executives, and the general educational public. Such a course has been given, by the author, at Stanford University in the School of Education, twice annually, since the spring of 1928. This volume is an outgrowth of that course.

Although the junior college movement is very recent in American education, the literature dealing with it is already extensive. A bibliography prepared by the author, and published in 1930 by the United States Office of Education, includes 1600 titles, totaling nearly 13,000 pages of printed material. In the present volume an effort has been made to digest this material. What is presented here is not, however, a mere summary or glorified bibliography; on the contrary, it represents a rigorous selection of only the most significant matter, which has been unified, organized, and interpreted. Where controversial issues are involved or differences of opinion exist, the author has tried to present both sides of the argument. No effort is made to settle every question; such an effort would be futile in a field so full of experimental problems and uncertainties of development as the junior college; nor is it desirable in a volume designed primarily as a textbook.

No textbook can give all the information needed, or represent all points of view. It is essential, especially in graduate work, that reading should extend beyond the limits of any single textbook. Great care, therefore, has been used in the selection of the lists of suggested readings given at the close of each chapter. These are not meant to be exhaustive, but selective and suggestive.[1] Usually they represent a careful selection from several times as many available titles. They are from sources most likely to be available in university libraries, and represent the writer's best judgment of the supplementary material which he would like to have read by a class under his instruction to secure a comprehensive view of the entire field. A half-dozen of the most important and outstanding references are starred in each list.

The author will feel that the book is successful if the body of material proves to be presented in such a way as to arouse interest, encourage thought, and impel to further investigation. With this in mind, much care has been devoted to the formulation of suggested questions and problems at the close of each chapter.

Many statistical and objective data are given, usually in tabular or graphic form. No apology is required for this. In the modern scientific study of education, progress and policies must be based upon a knowledge of facts. There is little value, however, in a mere array of facts. In many cases only the most significant summaries have been reproduced from ex-

[1] For exhaustive study of any topic, reference should be made to the extensive annotated bibliography described in Appendix I.

tensive tables in original studies. An effort has been made to evaluate and interpret these facts critically but sympathetically.

As stated above, this volume is intended primarily as a textbook for courses on the junior college, but it is hoped that it may be helpful to several other classes of readers as well. It presents a summary of facts and investigations which should prove useful for convenient ready reference to active administrators in the junior colleges of the country. It should be stimulating to junior college instructors who are interested in the relation of their own instructional work to the larger problems of the institution and movement of which they are a part. It should be valuable for library reference and for supplementary reading in courses on secondary and higher education where only incidental reference is made to the junior college aspect. Research workers in the field may find it helpful in many ways.

The body of the book is arranged in three main divisions. Part One is devoted to the *Development of the Junior College.* Chapters I and II present a general view of the extent and variety of the junior college as it exists today; the ten chapters following are devoted to an effort to answer how and why it has reached its present state of development — history, standards, and functions.

Part Two deals with the *Organization and Administration of the Junior College.* In a series of eleven chapters, consideration is given to such topics as the staff, buildings, library, curriculum, finance, criteria for establishment, publicity, tests, and student activities.

In Part Three, after the specific discussion earlier of the development, existence, and operation of the junior college in actual practice, the more general question of *The Place of the Junior College in American Education* is discussed. Various types of educational reorganization, such as the six-four-four plan, are evaluated. The relation of this new educational unit, the junior college, to standard colleges and universities is considered. A final chapter deals with the prospects of this new institution.

The information and ideas contained in this book have developed very largely from stimulating association with successive classes in Junior College Administration at Stanford University. The arrangement of the material for class presentation has resulted from repeated experiments with these groups. To the many graduate students who have been members of these classes and whose questions, discussions, and reactions have aided so largely, although often unconsciously, in its development, the author would first express his appreciation. His obligation is great in every chapter. It is particularly so in Chapter XXI, in which the work there reported could not have been done without the aid of many students.

Public school officials and junior college executives in many states have answered numerous letters of inquiry. J. E. Hollingsworth made the detailed investigation summarized in Chapter XVIII. Commissioner William John Cooper has kindly allowed the reproduction of material which forms a considerable part of Chapter XXV. Publishers and authors have given permission to quote briefly from their works. Specific acknowledgment of such quoted material will be found throughout the text. To all of those who have thus contributed to this book the author wishes to express his sincere thanks.

He would also express his gratitude to President J. B. Lillard, of the Sacramento Junior College, for a critical reading of the manuscript of Chapters XXVI and XXVII; and to his colleague, Dr. William M. Proctor, for a similar service with Chapters XXIV, XXV, XXVI, and XXVII. Especially great is the author's obligation to three persons who have read the entire manuscript with searching discrimination: to his friend,

Reginald Bell, whose penetrating criticisms and constructive suggestions have been invaluable; to his son, Kenneth Walter Eells, who, while typing the manuscript, detected many inconsistencies and ambiguities; and to his wife, Natalie S. Eells, whose partnership in this, as in many other interests and activities, has been unceasingly helpful.

Finally would the author essay the impossible in attempting to express his appreciation of the helpfulness of the editor of the Riverside Textbooks in Education, Dr. Ellwood P. Cubberley, at whose suggestion the work was undertaken. His friendly interest has been a constant encouragement; his personal example of fine scholarship and skillful technique in educational research has been a source of unfailing inspiration.

Walter Crosby Eells

School of Education
Stanford University

CONTENTS

Part One

DEVELOPMENT OF THE JUNIOR COLLEGE

Part Two

ORGANIZATION AND ADMINISTRATION OF THE JUNIOR COLLEGE

Part Three

PLACE OF THE JUNIOR COLLEGE IN AMERICAN EDUCATION

LIST OF FIGURES

LIST OF TABLES

THE JUNIOR COLLEGE

∴

PART ONE
DEVELOPMENT OF THE JUNIOR COLLEGE

THE JUNIOR COLLEGE

CHAPTER I

CLASSIFICATION OF JUNIOR COLLEGES

Convinced by the amazing increase in enrollments of the colleges and universities that our people are awake to the needs of school training beyond the age of childhood, we commend the addition of junior colleges as an integral part of the public school system. — Resolutions of the Department of Superintendence, National Education Association, February, 1929.

Contents of this chapter. Seven possible bases for useful classifications of the junior colleges are outlined briefly. One of these, control and support, is selected as fundamental, and is made the basis of a more detailed subdivision into eight types of junior colleges which are found in different parts of the country.

What is a junior college? "The junior college is an institution offering two years of instruction of strictly collegiate grade."[1] Such was the simple definition of the junior college adopted by the American Association of Junior Colleges at its second annual meeting at Memphis, Tennessee, in 1922. As it has developed, however, the junior college is by no means as simple a unit structure as this definition would imply. In fact it is a rather complex institution, and can be classified in many ways. While it is impossible to set up clear-cut boundaries between the different varieties in every case, yet a number of different types may be clearly recognized.

Possible bases of classification. There are at least seven

[1] Printed in the *Proceedings* of Third Annual Meeting of American Association of Junior Colleges, p. 65, and reprinted in the *Proceedings* of the fourth to ninth annual meetings.

possible bases for useful classifications of junior colleges, the last one of which will be taken as fundamental and outlined in detail in this chapter. The seven bases suggested are the following:

1. By sex admitted; coeducational, men, women.
2. By length of course; one, two, three, four, or six years in length.
3. By function; terminal or preparatory.
4. By size of enrollment.
5. By age; date of foundation.
6. By method of origin.
7. By method of control and support.

1. *By sex admitted.* The great majority of junior colleges are coeducational, especially the public institutions; but a considerable number of the private colleges are for women, particularly in the Eastern and Southern states. There are a few for men, most frequently military schools. The numerical frequency and geographical distribution of junior colleges on this basis of classification will be shown in the next chapter.

2. *By length of course.* The typical junior college at the present time is a two-year institution, sometimes organized entirely independently, but more frequently administered in more or less close association with an academy or high school course. There is considerable sentiment in some quarters in favor of four-year "junior colleges" in which the last two years of the standard high school course and the freshman and sophomore years of the college are welded together into a unified institution, but as yet only a few institutions are actually organized on this basis. This type of organization will be discussed in Part III. There are occasional one-year institutions, usually, but not always, on the way to becoming two-year colleges;[1] or three-year institutions on the way to four-

[1] Muskogee, Oklahoma, limited itself to a one-year college curriculum for eight years, until 1928. Springfield, Massachusetts, has a one-year curriculum only.

year degree-granting colleges. The six-year high school, including two collegiate or junior college years, was tried for a time but is not common as such under that name today. In many places, however, small junior colleges are so closely associated with the high school in instruction and administration as to secure in effect almost a single six-year course of study in a single institution.

3. *By function.* Many junior colleges, especially the smaller institutions, confine their work almost exclusively to preparation of students for upper-division work in the universities. A few, however, mainly state junior colleges, are definitely organized as terminal institutions, aiming to prepare students by means of a two-year course for positions of usefulness to society, particularly in the so-called semi-professions. More frequently, however, a junior college recognizes an obligation to perform both of these functions at the same time, and others as well. It offers courses adapted to various types of students, or plans to do so as soon as increase in enrollment and resources will permit. On the whole, this functional classification pertains to work within the college, or to types of students served, rather than to types of junior colleges, themselves. The functions of the junior college will receive fuller treatment in Chapters VIII to XII.

4. *Size of enrollment.* Junior colleges are prevailingly small institutions, the majority of them at the present time having less than one hundred students; only a few have enrollments in the thousands. Classification on this basis is of interest, but has little fundamental value since enrollments are constantly changing.

5. *By age.* Junior colleges are generally young institutions, the majority of them being less than ten years old. Valuable as age data are for the student of the history of the movement, they offer no significant basis for classification.

6. *By method of origin.* The four principal ways in which

junior colleges have developed, historically, as discussed in Chapter III, will be found very illuminating in understanding more fully the reasons for the existence of the varieties of junior colleges described in the remainder of this chapter.

7. *By method of control and support.* This is the fundamental and most useful method of classification of the junior college. It will be treated in detail, since it will be used constantly throughout this volume. The chief features of a division on this basis are exhibited in Figure 1. The colleges are first divided into *public* and *private* institutions.

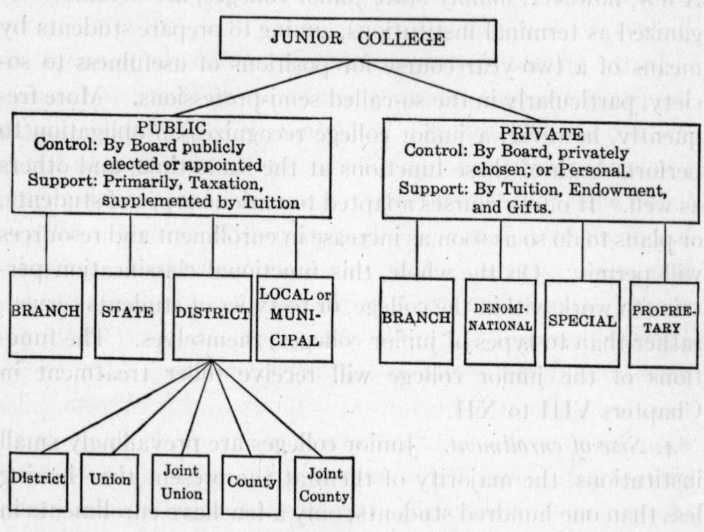

FIG. 1. FUNDAMENTAL CLASSIFICATION OF JUNIOR COLLEGES

The control of public junior colleges is vested in a *board* (variously known as a Board of Regents, Board of Trustees, Board of Education, School Board, etc.), elected by the voting public, or appointed by the governor or other public official. In the better established and more successful public junior colleges the support is predominantly from public funds, as is the case in California, although in some states substantial tuition charges or other fees received from students are an important supplement to these funds, as in Texas. In states where there is yet no express legal authorization of public junior colleges, and where they exist only because demanded by the public, a substantial tuition charge forms the principal basis of support. Thus, in the State of Washington, a tuition of $100 a year, or in one case $150, is charged and used for instructional salaries. In such states, where the plant and equipment are usually shared with the local high school, non-instructional expenses usually are absorbed in the high school budget.

In the private institutions the control is most frequently in the hands of a board, usually known as the Board of Trustees, selected in various ways. Sometimes it is self-perpetuating, in whole or in part; sometimes elected by the church organization under whose auspices it exists; sometimes chosen in other ways, but never by public vote. Sometimes, the private institution is purely a private venture, on a commercial basis, the entire control being in the hands of the founder, who is likely to be also the president or dean of the college. Support of the private institutions comes in varying proportions from tuition fees, from interest on endowment funds, and from gifts. Tuition is the most important source of income in many of the private institutions and in some it is practically the only source of revenue. Historically the private antedate the public institutions. As will be shown in the next chapter, there are also more private institutions, although the number of students attending them is less than in the public.

PUBLIC JUNIOR COLLEGES

Branch junior colleges. Four types of public junior colleges should be distinguished: *branch*, *state*, *district*, and *local*. Branch junior colleges may be thought of as those that are administratively an integral part of the state university, subject to the financial and educational control of the faculty and board of regents. In its closest form, the separation of the freshman and sophomore work administratively from that of the junior and senior years, may be thought of as a junior college of the university, even though it may be known by another name. Thus the Lower Division of the University of California, the Experimental College of the University of Michigan, and the Lower Division of the University of Minnesota are examples of junior college organization, on the actual campus and under the control of the state university. Establishment of the junior college of the University of Idaho is a very recent example where the name "junior college" is used. True, the lower division of the university is not ordinarily thought of as a junior college, when discussing the junior college movement. The difference, however, is in degree rather than in principle, and has important relations to the independent junior colleges, especially when, as at the University of Utah, as well as at several private universities, proposals are under consideration for the complete elimination of lower division or junior college work on the university campus. It is but a step, furthermore, from the branch junior college on the university campus, to the branch junior college off the university campus, which is more commonly recognized as a junior college. Thus the University of Tennessee Junior College is an integral part of the university, although operated at Martin, 275 miles distant from the University of Tennessee. The Southern Branch of the University of Idaho (formerly Idaho Technical Institute) at Pocatello, is located over 300 miles in a straight line, and much farther by rail, from the main seat of the state university of which it is a part. Other examples are afforded by the Cebu and Vigan junior colleges of the University of Manila, with more branch junior colleges contemplated on other islands of the archipelago.

Two state junior colleges in Texas, North Texas Junior Agricultural College, at Arlington, and John Tarleton College at Stephenville, are nominally under the control of the State Agricultural and Mechanical College.

State junior colleges. State junior colleges have usually been established by act of the legislature, are supported in whole or in large part by state funds, are controlled by state-appointed boards, and are open to all students in the state on equal terms. The branch junior colleges mentioned in the previous section, even when located on separate campuses, are almost always state institutions. Usually the state junior colleges are technical institutions of some sort, such as the Agricultural and Mechanical colleges of Arkansas or Texas, the California Polytechnic School, or the New Mexico Military Institute. They are for the most part definitely or prevailingly terminal institutions where the essentials of technical and agricultural occupations on the semi-professional level are adequately given. Two-year normal schools have sometimes been classed as state junior colleges, in states in which only two years of work in advance of high school are required for teachers' certificates, and there is no real reason why they should not be so considered, since they are quite definitely terminal institutions offering a professional course of two years' duration. They have not ordinarily been so considered, however. The normal school has had a century or more of independent existence, name, function, and consciousness, and it may be permitted to retain this feeling of independence of the junior college movement, probably with advantage to both sides. The marked tendency for normal schools to develop into four-year teachers' colleges, thus placing education on a truly professional, rather than semi-professional basis, is one that should be encouraged as rapidly as possible.[1]

[1] For possible development of combination teachers' colleges and junior colleges, see Chapter XXVIII.

District junior colleges. The real glory and contribution of the public junior college movement has been in the popularization of collegiate education in smaller local institutions. Thus it is the district and local institutions which are decidedly the most significant groups to be considered. The district junior colleges constitute California's unique contribution to the junior college movement. The exact conditions under which they may be organized will be presented more in detail in Chapter IV. With organization independent of the local school district or high school district, although related to it, with the frank recognition of collegiate education, even in local districts, as a distinct state function, evidenced by liberal state support, with sufficient local taxable wealth required to assure adequate supplementary funds for efficient work, the sixteen district institutions which have developed in California during the last decade have set a standard of high grade junior colleges which suggest what the general movement may become under suitable encouragement, guidance, and support. The new Texas junior college law of 1929 provides for a very similar system of district junior colleges in Texas. The Texas law, for example, requires an assessed valuation of $12,000,000 and an average daily attendance in the high schools of the proposed district of 400 students, before a district junior college can be formed.[1] It further requires an election to determine the question of formation.

Classes of district junior colleges. Figure 1 shows five subdivisions of the district type of college as found in California. In the ordinary district type, the junior college district is coterminous with the local high school district, although this itself may be a union high school district made up of several elementary school districts. The union district consists of two

[1] Until 1929 the California law required $10,000,000 assessed valuation and a high school average daily attendance of 400 students. These figures have been changed to $25,000,000 and 1000 students by the California law of 1929, but no new institutions have yet been organized under its provisions.

or more contiguous high school districts which unite their strength to support a single larger and better junior college, administered more economically than either could afford to support alone. Examples of this type in California are Marin Junior College at Kentfield in Northern California, and San Bernardino Valley Junior College at San Bernardino in Southern California. The joint union district is the same as the union, except that the component districts are in different counties, necessitating special financial provisions. The county type covers the area of a county not already organized into a junior college district. The only one at present existing, Yuba County (Marysville), includes the entire county. The joint county type provides where desired for the union of two or more counties to form a single district for junior college purposes. None such exist at present in California, but several are to be found in Mississippi, under the new policy recently inaugurated in that state. Thus it will be seen that there is a high degree of flexibility permitted in the organization of junior college districts, and a desire to encourage units large enough to be efficient, while retaining at the same time local interest and initiative. The Texas law of 1929 provides for four of the five types of districts shown in the diagram — all except the Joint Union district.

Local or municipal junior colleges. Most of the public junior colleges are purely local institutions, locally organized, administered, and supported. Conditions for organization vary, but in many cases there are not sufficient restrictions to insure collegiate vitality. In California any high school board, without a vote of the people, may, by resolution, establish such a local junior college provided the district has an assessed valuation of $3,000,000. This is known technically as a high school junior college course. In many other states there is not even the safeguard of minimum assessed valuation to prevent community pride and local enthusiasm from starting a local junior college. In some states, such as Iowa or Kansas, an election is required. In others, such as Montana and Louisiana, there is not even this restriction. In still others, such as Washington and Arkansas, where there is no provision by law, junior colleges have been organized without legal authority, in response to local demand, and exist by sufferance. In Arkansas, the attorney-general has ruled that there is nothing in state law to prevent such an extension of the high school. Usually these high school junior college courses receive support on the basis of high schools, but in some cases it has been ruled that they are not to be so considered, and in this event all support for the so-called "public" junior college is met by tuition charged the students. Although there is probably no legal warrant for it, and it could doubtless be stopped by court action, local sentiment in many states permits the use of the local high school plant, building and equipment, library and laboratories, and in some cases part of the time of the administrative force, without segregating the portion properly chargeable to the junior college. Ultimately such subterfuges and artifices will be corrected by suitable laws providing conditions under which junior colleges may be organized, either as local units, or in districts, and providing suitable support for them This has already happened in several states, in the past two or three years. Meanwhile, it is striking testimony to the virility of the junior college idea, and to the eagerness of many local communities to take advantage of its acknowledged function in furnishing college education to their youth, that they resort to all sorts of makeshifts to secure its advantages, pending the time that slower-moving state legislatures shall catch up with more progressive local sentiment. The local or municipal junior college is an institution which has the advantage of being more directly and immediately responsive to changes in public opinion than any other class of junior colleges.

PRIVATE JUNIOR COLLEGES

Branch junior colleges. The branch junior colleges under private control (see Figure 1) are exactly analogous to those of the public type already considered, except that they are branches of private universities instead of public ones. Historically the most outstanding example is the junior college of the University of Chicago, probably the first institution ever to actually bear that name. President Harper's early influence at Chicago will be treated in a later chapter.

Other universities of greater significance for the present status of the junior college movement are Stanford and Johns Hopkins. While not called junior colleges, the freshman and sophomore work of these universities has been separately organized and administered (organization of "Lower Division" at Stanford dates from 1920). This organization is of special interest now because of the announced policies of these two institutions gradually to abolish this work entirely, leaving the field of lower collegiate instruction entirely to the independent junior colleges.[1] Stanford, however, has offered sites on its campus to a public and to a private junior college, where such work may be done under the influence of the university but not under its control. This offer has already been accepted by the private institution, Menlo Junior College.

The decentralization type is represented by the action of Columbia University, in 1928, when it established Seth Low Junior College at Brooklyn as a branch junior college of Columbia University. A proposal for a second branch at a site on the Hudson has also been under consideration, but the plans for it have lapsed, at least temporarily.

Considerable prominence has been given recently to the three junior colleges established by the University of Pittsburgh. In three communities in the western part of Pennsylvania — Johnstown, Uniontown, and Erie — local junior

[1] For history and progress of this abolition, see Chapters III and XXVIII.

colleges have been established under the complete management of the University of Pittsburgh. These have sometimes been called public junior colleges, since the local public school board furnishes the buildings and equipment; but the faculty is appointed by the university, and in some cases faculty members live at the university, giving only part-time to the junior colleges; the curriculum is prescribed by the university; students' record cards are kept at the registrar's office at Pittsburgh; and transfer is freely permitted from the local unit to the central one. Thus it seems to be essentially a decentralization of the university, the lower division work being given by the university at three local centers in addition to Pittsburgh. The arrangement seems to be working satisfactorily, but the time has been too brief to determine whether it will be permanent, or whether the local units will ultimately demand greater freedom from university dominance. There is danger that university control may tend to hamper and hinder freedom of development along progressive lines in the local branches. This will depend much upon local sentiment, and upon the type of constructive leadership furnished by the university.

A further example of the branch idea in the junior college field, and of a still different type, is afforded by two Southern Methodist colleges in Mississippi, which have recently united in forming the "Millsaps-Whitworth Collegiate System." Whitworth College, a long-established high-grade junior college for women, located ninety miles from Millsaps College, has joined with it to form a senior-junior college system. Under the arrangement, the president of Whitworth becomes the associate president of the system. At Millsaps, boarding women will not be received below the junior year, although they will continue to be received locally as day students. All boarding women are to be sent to Whitworth for their freshman and sophomore years. Those who desire to continue further may then transfer to the senior unit of the system, Millsaps.

The outcome of this experiment, the first of its type in the denominational junior college field, will be watched with interest.

Denominational junior colleges. A large group of private junior colleges are organized under denominational influence and auspices, and in many cases under direct denominational control. In some cases the boards of trustees, or a portion of them, are elected by the regional church organization; in others it is required that they, or a majority of them, be members of the controlling denomination. In some cases, regular annual appropriations for support are made by the local or national church bodies; in others, dependence for gifts, both for endowment and running expense, is placed upon the members of the supporting church. The foregoing is especially true of the colleges under Protestant auspices. The Catholic junior colleges are usually controlled and supported in accordance with the special customs and regulations of the various orders sponsoring them. The strength of the denominational junior colleges is in Missouri, Texas, and other Southern states. The leading denominations are the Methodist and the Baptist. While denominational in control, they are usually not narrowly sectarian, but are broadly Christian in administration and open to students of any belief, although the student bodies as might be expected are usually predominantly of the supporting denomination. In the Principia, at St. Louis, however, attendance is limited to the sons and daughters of members of the Christian Science Church.

Special types of junior colleges. For want of a better name there is classified under special types of junior colleges a considerable group of schools similar to the denominational group, in that they are governed by a board of trustees or similar responsible body, rather than by a single individual. They often have considerable income aside from tuition, either the gift of some single benefactor, as in the case of Sarah Lawrence

College, of New York, or the backing of some non-denominational group or organization. Of the latter type may be mentioned the half-dozen Y.M.C.A. junior colleges in Ohio, Colorado, and Illinois; Cottey College in Missouri, sponsored by the P.E.O. Sisterhood; or the Junior College of the Polish National Alliance in Pennsylvania. Some are exceptionally wealthy, like National Park Seminary, Forest Glen, Maryland, near the national capital, with a plant valued at $5,000,000. Some have been founded to work out special experiments in the junior college field. Thus Menlo Junior College, California, is experimenting with the four-year unit for men, while Sarah Lawrence College is devoting itself to a two-year cultural terminal course for women.

Proprietary, or personal. Finally there is a group of junior colleges organized on a purely private, commercial, or proprietary basis. In these there is no board of trustees or other governing body. The founder, who is usually the administrative head, is in entire control. Usually they are junior college departmental extensions of existing proprietary secondary schools; but sometimes they have been independently established and maintained. On the whole they have had a rather brief and precarious existence, although a few are on a firm basis and doing excellent work. It is significant of the strength of the junior college name, however, that a considerable group of men and women are willing to undertake such work with no financial backing, and that parents will support them by the relatively high tuition charges necessary, in order to secure the advantages of the superior work, closer personal contacts, and other advantages claimed for the small private junior college.

Summary. Such are the principal types of junior colleges that may be distinguished at the present time.[1] It may not

[1] Still another type sometimes appears in lists of junior colleges given by various accrediting agencies. Weak four-year colleges, in some instances, are *accredited* for the first two years only, and listed with regular junior colleges. They are not, however, true junior colleges.

always be possible to classify a particular institution unmistakably in any one class. In particular, the branch junior colleges tend to overlap somewhat with other classes. In spite of this possible difficulty in individual cases, however, the eight main types here pointed out are clearly distinguishable groups, and the distinctions between them are important as the basis for a clear understanding of the junior college movement. It is evident that the junior college is a complex affair. Generalizations are likely to be misleading, in many cases. What is characteristic of one group is not at all applicable to another. There are marked and essential differences between the California district college and the denominational college of the Southern states. The problems of the public junior college are different in many vital respects from those of private control. The weak and the strong, the rich and the poor, the large and the small, the efficient and the counterfeit, the conservative and the progressive are all part of the general junior college movement, and too often they are thought of without discrimination by the public. It is evident, however, that there is no such thing as *the* junior college; there is a wide diversity of junior colleges. The careful student of the movement should have clearly in mind, at the outset, the essential characteristics of the different main types.

QUESTIONS AND PROBLEMS

1. List and classify all the junior colleges in your state, or in an assigned group of states, under the eight general groups given in Figure 1. Are there any which will not fit into this classification?
2. Find, if possible, at least five junior colleges of each of the eight main types outlined in Figure 1 in the United States, or in an assigned portion of it.
3. Make a diagram showing the classification used by Koos (see references below) and compare with that of the text.
4. Classify the junior colleges in your state, or any state or region, according to Koos's classification.
5. Make a diagram showing the classification outlined by Houston (see reference below), and compare with that given in the text.

6. Classify the junior colleges in your state, or any state or region, according to Houston's classification.
7. Are there four-year colleges, not universities, in which there is an administrative distinction in organization of the first two years, corresponding to lower division or junior college? If so, name them.
8. Outline, preferably in graphic form, a classification of junior colleges in which the primary basis of division is the sex of the students admitted.
9. Should two-year normal schools, requiring high school graduation for entrance, be classified as junior colleges? Why? Or why not?
10. Should business colleges, schools of pharmacy, industrial institutes, engineering schools, schools of design, etc., offering a two-year course of study beyond the high school period be classified as junior colleges? If so, under what restrictions?
11. For all colleges listed in the latest Directory of the American Association of Junior Colleges as "Church," find, by consulting their catalogues, under what denominational auspices they are conducted.
12. For all colleges listed in the latest Directory of the American Association of Junior Colleges as "Private," find which might be classified as "Special" and which as "Proprietary," by finding from their catalogues or other sources whether they are controlled by boards of trustees. Determine, if possible, how these boards are chosen, and the number and terms of office of the trustees.
13. List all of the "Branch" junior colleges that you can.
14. Look up the exact relationship of the University of Pittsburgh to the junior colleges at Erie, Johnstown, and Uniontown. Are they public or private? Could they be classified as local or district institutions? If you classify them as "Branch" junior colleges, what changes would be necessary to remove them from such classification?
15. Should district and local junior colleges be permitted or encouraged to exist simultaneously in the same state?
16. What changes would be required in the law of any particular state to authorize the establishment of district junior colleges, similar to those in California?

SUGGESTED READINGS

Note: Before attempting to make use of the following readings the student should refer to the bibliographical materials described in Appendix I, pages 805–10.

*Koos, Leonard V. *The Junior College Movement*, pp. 1–10, 313–73; or *The Junior College*, pp. 1–8, 535–72.
Types of junior colleges described and evaluated.

*Houston, G. D. "The Junior College of the Future"; *Education*, vol. 48, pp. 401-09. (March, 1928.)

Four types of junior colleges defined.

*Campbell, D. S. "Directory of the Junior College, 1931"; *Junior College Journal*, vol. 1, pp. 223-34. (January, 1931.)

Lists and data on the different types.

*Hurt, H. W. *The College Blue Book* (second edition), pp. 194-247. Hollywood-by-the-Sea, Florida, 1928.

Lists and data on the different types.

*Whitney, F. L. *The Junior College in America*, pp. 220-53.

Lists and data on the different types.

Paul, A. G. "Address of Welcome." *Bulletin of the Pacific Coast Association of Collegiate Registrars. Proceedings of the Fourth Annual Convention at Riverside, and Claremont, California*, pp. 15-16. (March, 1929.)

Describes five types of junior colleges within visiting distance of the convention.

Frazier, C. R. "The Junior College"; *Journal of Education*, vol. 65, pp. 92-98. (February, 1923.)

Economical plan for one-year junior college.

Hills, E. C. "Shall the College be Divided?" *Educational Review*, vol. 65, pp. 92-98. (February, 1923.)

Result of questionnaires to 28 universities.

The Junior College in California, Bulletin No. G-3, pp. 21-26, 30-48. State Department of Education, Sacramento, California, 1928.

Types of public junior colleges in California. Changed in some respects by modifying legislation adopted in 1929.

Shockley, F. W. "The Proposed Johnstown Junior College of the University of Pittsburgh"; *School Review*, vol. 35, pp. 483-85. (September, 1927.)

Crawford, S. C. "Junior Colleges in Pennsylvania"; *American Association of Junior Colleges, Ninth Annual Meeting, 1928*, pp. 108-09.

Morris, J. T. "The University of Pittsburgh and its Junior Colleges"; *University of Pittsburgh Bulletin*, vol. 25, pp. 7-96. (January 15, 1929.)

Slawson, S. J. "The 6-4-4 Plan in Johnstown, Pennsylvania"; *Seventh Yearbook, Department of Superintendence, National Education Association*, pp. 233-34. (February, 1929.)

Shockley, F. W. "The Junior College Plan of the University of Pittsburgh"; *American Association of Junior Colleges, Tenth Annual Meeting, 1929*, pp. 46-57.

The last five references deal with the branch colleges of the University of Pittsburgh. That by Morris is the most comprehensive, if available.

CHAPTER II

PRESENT STATUS OF THE JUNIOR COLLEGE

The development of the junior college movement is so rapid that it is scarcely possible to present a study which reflects its status accurately. By the time data have been gathered and organized for publication, new junior colleges have been organized, some have been discontinued, while others have undergone changes in size and in organization. — DOAK S. CAMPBELL.[1]

Contents of this chapter. The object of this chapter is to give a general picture of the present status of the junior college movement in America, using the latest available information from the best sources obtainable. This information is presented under the following heads: (1) total number and enrollment; (2) size; (3) number and enrollment according to type of control; (4) comparison, as to number and enrollment, of coeducational institutions with those for men or women exclusively; (5) geographical distribution; (6) enrollment by classes; (7) number of graduates; (8) instructors; (9) accreditation; (10) high school relationship; (11) age; (12) curriculum; (13) Negro junior colleges; (14) legal status. The treatment of these topics is not complete or exhaustive. Some of them will be taken up more in detail in succeeding chapters. The object here is to provide, as a basis for later discussion, a comprehensive view of essential features of the junior college movement as a whole, as it exists today.

Sources of data used. Unless otherwise stated, all numerical data in this chapter have been secured from the March, 1930, *Directory* of the American Association of Junior Colleges, compiled by its secretary, Doak S. Campbell of George Peabody College, Nashville, Tennessee. These are undoubtedly the most complete and recent data obtainable, but even they

[1] Campbell, D. S. *A Critical Study of the Stated Purposes of the Junior College.* George Peabody College: Contribution to Education, no. 70, p. ix. 1930.

have many shortcomings of which probably no one is more conscious than the compiler himself. As shown in the preceding chapter there is a great variety of institutions classified as junior colleges, without any common responsibility to a central body. Accurate reports on a comparable basis are very difficult to obtain. The author has not hesitated to supplement this directory by other information when he could secure it. Thus he has added twenty-one colleges to those listed in the *Directory* of the American Association of Junior Colleges, but only on the authority of a letter from the administrator of the college concerned or from a responsible state educational authority. These changes are indicated in footnote 2 on this page.[1] Additional information is provided by the reports of the United States Office of Education, by Hurt's *College Blue Book*, and by Whitney's *The Junior College in America*, but none of these are as complete, accurate, and recent as the Junior College Association *Directory.* Detailed information for Texas and California are available in official reports of their respective state departments of education.

TOTAL NUMBER AND ENROLLMENT

Number. According to the best information the writer was able to secure there were, in 1930, at least 450 junior colleges in the United States.[2] They are found in all but five

[1] The *Directory*, however, publishes but a single summary of the data contained in it, for total number of institutions and enrollment by states. The author is responsible for the various classifications and analyses of the data given in this chapter.

[2] The *Directory* lists 429, to which 9 public and 12 private have been added by the author, as follows:

Public: California: Antelope Valley; Georgia: Middle Georgia A. & M.; Mississippi: Copiah-Lincoln, Holmes, Kemper County, Newton County, Tate County; North Carolina: State Normal School (colored); Washington: Yakima Valley.

Private: Colorado: Denver (Y.M.C.A.); Connecticut: Hillside School; District of Columbia: Gunston Hall; Minnesota: Redwing Seminary; Mississippi: Chickasaw College; Missouri: Will Mayfield; South Carolina: Ashley Hall, Hailey Military Institute, Bishop England, Carlisle School, Porter Military Academy, Summerland College.

states, California and Texas leading with 49 and 47 institutions, respectively. In addition there is a considerable group of Negro institutions, only 14 of which are listed in the *Directory*. The author has a list of 19 other Negro institutions,[1] but 18 of these have not been included, because of lack of definite information regarding their present existence and status. Nor are two junior colleges in the Philippine Islands, two in Canada, one in China, and one in Greece, included. On the other hand, the names of a few may be found in the *Directory* which have ceased to exist or have changed to a four-year status. It is probable, however, that there were approximately 475 institutions in this country in 1930 doing some junior college work.[2]

Enrollment. Enrollment data are available for 428 institutions. The total enrollment in this group is 69,497, an average of 162 per institution. Those for which enrollment data are not furnished are probably somewhat smaller schools, at least as far as the number of junior college students is concerned; but, if they average only 25 students each, the total number of junior college students in the country would be over 70,000.

SIZE

The junior college shows a great variation in size, from institutions which report only a half dozen students or less, of junior college grade, to Crane Junior College, Chicago, with an enrollment of 4000. Four others reported enrollments in excess of 1000, namely, Sacramento, 1800;[3] Kansas City, Missouri, 1744; Los Angeles, 1369; and Pasadena, 1045 (in the upper two years of the four-year institution). Ninety-three are

[1] Compiled by the registrar of Birmingham-Southern College, Alabama.

[2] The *Directory* states: "The list is meant to be inclusive rather than exclusive, and, therefore, it contains the names of many schools which are doing very little junior college work."

[3] Evidently an early estimate; stated as 2211 in the official California state report, for 1928–29.

reported with enrollments of less than 50, and 124 with enrollments between 50 and 100. A classification of public and private junior colleges according to size of enrollment is shown in Table 1. The largest of the private group is Cleveland Y.M.C.A. (850); the largest of the women's junior colleges is Stephens College, Missouri (586).

Table 1. Distribution of Public and Private Junior Colleges, According to Enrollment (1929–30)

	Total	Public	Private
Total number	**428**	**163**	**265**
0– 24	36	6	30
25– 49	58	19	39
50– 74	81	19	62
75– 99	43	16	27
100– 124	44	21	23
125– 149	29	10	19
150– 174	29	15	14
175– 199	11	5	6
200– 224	20	9	11
225– 249	11	4	7
250– 274	8	1	7
275– 299	11	3	8
300– 399	15	10	5
400– 499	13	10	3
500– 599	6	4	2
600– 699	3	2	1
700– 799	1	1	0
800– 899	3	2	1
900– 999	1	1	0
1000–1999	4	4	0
2000–2999	0	0	0
3000–3999	0	0	0
4000–4999	1	1	0

NUMBER AND ENROLLMENT BY TYPE OF CONTROL

By states. In Table 2 is shown, for each state, the number of public and private junior colleges, and the enrollment in each type of institution. There are only 5 states in which no

TABLE 2. NUMBER AND ENROLLMENT, JUNIOR COLLEGES OF UNITED STATES, BY TYPE OF CONTROL (1929-30)

STATE	TOTAL		PUBLIC		PRIVATE	
	Number	Enrollment	Number	Enrollment	Number	Enrollment
Total	**450**	**69,497**	**171**	**39,095**	**279**	**30,402**
Alabama	5	292	1	30	4	262
Arizona	2	550	1	422	1	128
Arkansas	11	1,956	7	1,363	4	593
California	49	13,922	35	13,392	14	530
Colorado	5	467	2	134	3	333
Connecticut	5	336	0	..	5	336
Delaware	0	..	0	..	0	..
District of Columbia	8	330	0	..	8	330
Florida	3	224	1	150	2	74
Georgia	13	1,435	4	640	9	795
Idaho	2	897	1	667	1	230
Illinois	18	6,514	6	4,767	12	1,747
Indiana	3	287	0	..	3	287
Iowa	28	1,858	21	1,177	7	681
Kansas	19	2,232	10	1,178	9	454
Kentucky	17	1,664	1	107	16	1,557
Louisiana	5	219	1	..	4	219
Maine	3	139	0	..	3	139
Maryland	5	689	0	..	5	689
Massachusetts	8	621	1	35	7	586
Michigan	9	2,046	7	1,949	2	97
Minnesota	11	1,403	7	1,216	4	187
Mississippi	18	1,396	11	563	7	833
Missouri	23	5,554	7	2.517	16	3,037
Montana	2	142	1	..	1	142
Nebraska	9	805	2	159	7	646
Nevada	0	..	0	..	0	..
New Hampshire	2	92	0	..	2	92
New Jersey	2	123	0	..	2	123
New Mexico	1	207	1	207	0	..
New York	11	1,087	0	..	11	1,087
North Carolina	18	2,439	3	306	15	2,133
North Dakota	2	350	2	350	0	..
Ohio	6	1,724	1	..	5	1,724
Oklahoma	14	1,744	11	1,591	3	153
Oregon	2	112	0	..	2	112
Pennsylvania	9	1,000	0	..	9	1,000
Rhode Island	0	..	0	..	0	..
South Carolina	8	312	0	..	8	312
South Dakota	4	219	0	..	4	219
Tennessee	13	1,680	1	151	12	1,529
Texas	47	8,886	19	4,755	28	4,131
Utah	6	1,026	1	112	5	914
Vermont	0	..	0	..	0	..
Virginia	12	1,586	0	..	12	1,586
Washington	5	424	3	295	2	129
West Virginia	5	426	2	262	3	164
Wisconsin	2	82	0	..	2	82
Wyoming	0	..	0	..	0	..

junior colleges are found. Public colleges are found in 30 states, private, in 42.[1] The leading states from the standpoint of public junior colleges (six in number), including those having 10 or more institutions, are California (35), Iowa (21), Texas (19), Oklahoma (11), Mississippi (11), and Kansas (10). The eight states leading in the number of private junior colleges having 10 or more institutions, are Texas (28), Kentucky (16), Missouri (16), North Carolina (15), California (14), Illinois (12), Tennessee (12), and Viginia (12). From the standpoint of enrollment, however, the ranking of the principal states with reference to public junior colleges is: California, Illinois, Texas, Missouri, Michigan, and Kansas; with reference to private junior colleges Texas, Missouri, North Carolina, Illinois, Ohio, and Virginia.

Summary of enrollment. The number of junior colleges, total enrollment, and average enrollment for those reporting are summarized in Table 3 for the principal types of public and private junior colleges.[2] The most significant features from

TABLE 3. SUMMARY OF NUMBER AND ENROLLMENT OF JUNIOR COLLEGES, BY TYPES (1929–30)

Type	Number	Enrollment Reported	Average for Colleges Reporting Enrollment
Total	**450**	**69,497**	**162**
Public	**171**	**39,095**	**240**
Local	128	23,045	189
District (California)	16	10,010	626
State	27	6,040	242
Private	**279**	**30,402**	**115**
Denominational	196	21,308	112
Special	43	6,453	150
Proprietary	40	2,641	75

[1] Including the District of Columbia.

[2] Dr. Campbell, secretary of the American Association of Junior Colleges, using a somewhat different classification found the following frequencies for

this table are exhibited in Figure 2. This presents vividly the greater average strength of the public junior college. While the public institutions constitute only 38 per cent of the junior colleges of the country, they enroll 56 per cent of the students.

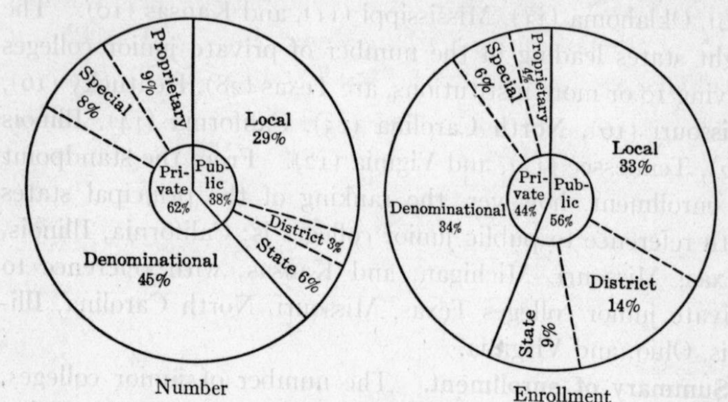

FIG. 2. NUMBER AND ENROLLMENT, PUBLIC AND PRIVATE JUNIOR COLLEGES, 1929–30

Average enrollment. The average enrollment in the public junior colleges is more than twice as large as in the private colleges. In the California district colleges it is 626, over three times as large as in local public institutions. The smallest average enrollment is found in the proprietary group.

Denominational junior colleges. A more detailed analysis of the group of 196 denominational junior colleges will be of

seven classes of junior colleges existing in 1929. (*A Critical Study of the Stated Purposes of the Junior College,* George Peabody College: Contribution to Education, no. 70, p. 6.)

TYPE OF CONTROL	FREQUENCY
1. Directly by state	24
2. Jointly by state and local tax unit	36
3. Local tax unit	19
4. Jointly local tax unit and patrons	73
5. Private, but not for profit	38
6. Proprietary	59
7. Denominational	155
Total	404

interest.[1] This is shown in Table 4 giving number, total enrollment, and average enrollment for reporting institutions for the different denominations. Over half of this group are Methodist, Baptist, and Catholic institutions. Of the denominational group, 25 are for men only (10 of them Catholic and 10 Lutheran), and 68 are for women only (18 Catholic, 16 Methodist, 13 Baptist, and 9 Presbyterian).

TABLE 4. SUMMARY OF NUMBER AND ENROLLMENT OF DENOMINATIONAL JUNIOR COLLEGES (1929-30)

Denomination	Number	Enrollment Reported	Average for Colleges Reporting Enrollment
Total	**196**	**21,308**	**112**
Methodist	43	5,640	134
Baptist	39	6,108	157
Catholic	29	2,151	77
Lutheran	23	1,525	73
Presbyterian	17	1,389	82
Christian	11	1,472	134
Episcopal	7	272	45
Latter Day Saints	7	1,490	213
Congregational	5	372	74
Seventh Day Adventist	4	256	64
Mennonite	2	77	38
Others[1]	9	556	62

[1] One each of Brethren, Brothers in Christ, Christian Science, Friends, Nazarene, Pilgrim Holiness, Swedenborgian, Swedish Evangelical, and United Brethren.

Y.M.C.A. junior colleges. The only group of special junior colleges of sufficient number and importance to justify separate report is the group of five Y.M.C.A. institutions, with a total enrollment of 2218, an average of 442 per institution.

Distribution of private junior colleges. The distribution of private junior colleges, according to the three main types, with

[1] Many of these are inadequately classified in the *Directory*, being reported as "church" or "private." By comparison with several standard reference works and the catalogues of institutions, these have been classified by denominations, as far as possible. Probably a few others which are included in the special or proprietary groups are actually denominational.

subdivisions for the principal denominational groups, is shown in Figure 3.

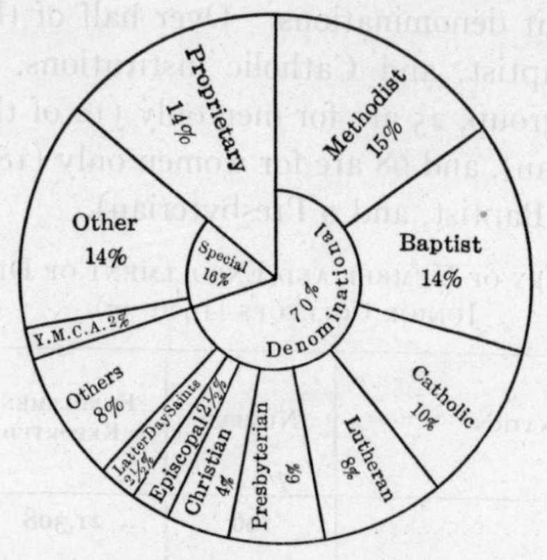

FIG. 3. DISTRIBUTION OF PRIVATE JUNIOR COLLEGES, 1929-30

COMPARISON, AS TO NUMBER AND ENROLLMENT, OF COEDUCATIONAL INSTITUTIONS WITH THOSE FOR MEN OR WOMEN EXCLUSIVELY

All but three of the 171 public junior colleges are coeducational. These three are for men.[1] There is a marked differentiation, however, in the case of the private institutions. Less than half of the private junior colleges are coeducational, but these tend to have somewhat larger enrollments than those for men or women exclusively. The coeducational institutions comprise 65 per cent of all in the country, with 78 per cent of the enrollment. The number and enrollment of the private junior colleges in the three groups, coeducational, men, and women, is shown in Table 5 and illustrated in Figure 4. The coeducational institutions comprise 45 per cent of the private

[1] For men: California Polytechnic, New Mexico Military Institute, and Oklahoma Military College. Howard Seminary, Massachusetts, and Paris Junior College, Texas, are erroneously reported in the *Directory* as public institutions for women only. Howard is for women, but private; Paris is public, but coeducational.

group, with 52 per cent of the enrollment. Most of the men's institutions are military or technical schools.

TABLE 5. SUMMARY OF PRIVATE JUNIOR COLLEGES ACCORDING TO SEX OF STUDENTS (1929–30)

	Number	Enrollment Reported	Average for Colleges Reporting Enrollment
Total	**279**	**30,402**	**115**
Coeducational	125	15,948	129
Men	41	3,491	100
Women	113	10,963	102

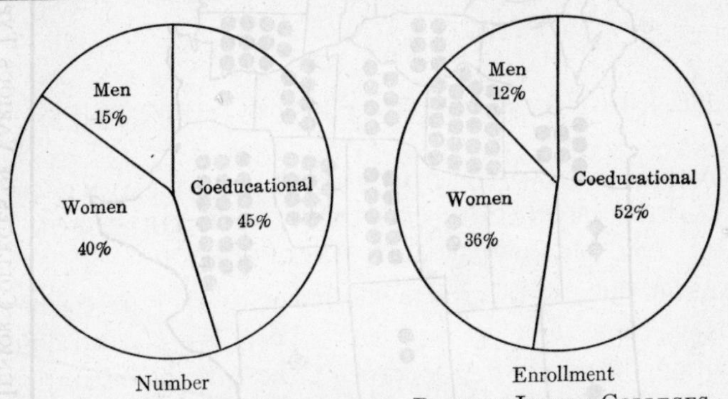

FIG. 4. NUMBER AND ENROLLMENT, PRIVATE JUNIOR COLLEGES, ACCORDING TO SEX OF STUDENTS ATTENDING, 1929–30

GEOGRAPHICAL DISTRIBUTION

Public. The geographical distribution, by states, of the public junior colleges of the country, both state and local, is shown on the map of Figure 5, which summarizes in different form some of the information in the last two sections. This map, of course, is statistical, not geographical. It shows only the number in each state, not their location. It is seen at once that the strength of the public junior college movement is in the Middle West and in California. There are scattered institutions, however, in many of the Eastern and Southern states.

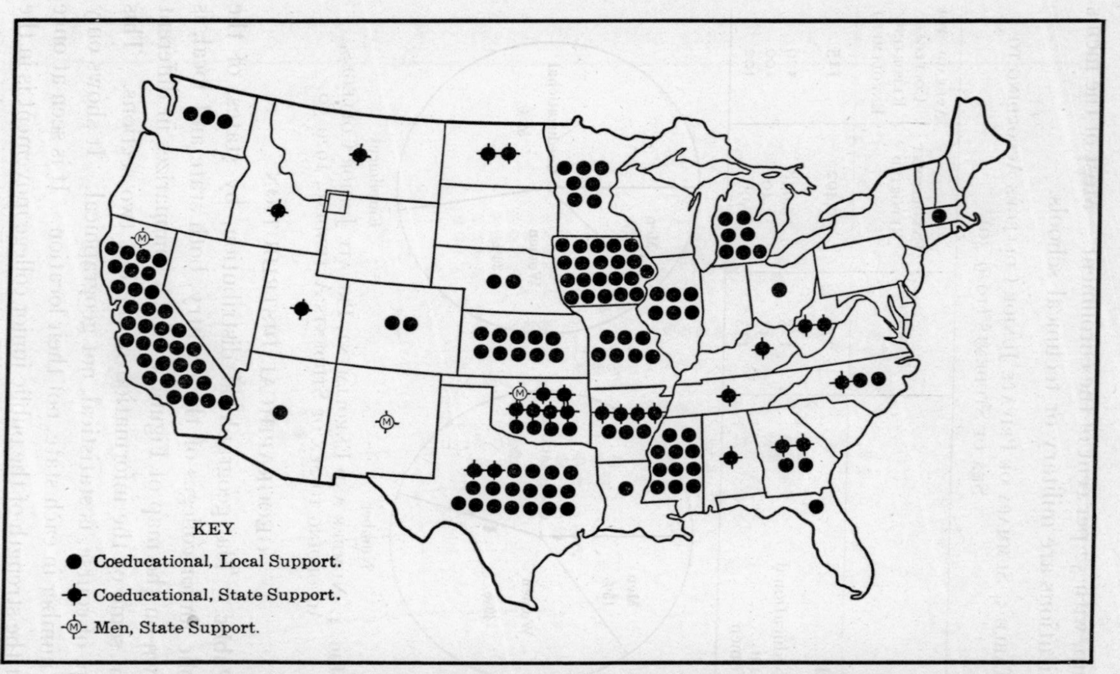

FIG. 5. NUMBER OF PUBLIC JUNIOR COLLEGES OF VARIOUS TYPES IN THE UNITED STATES, 1930

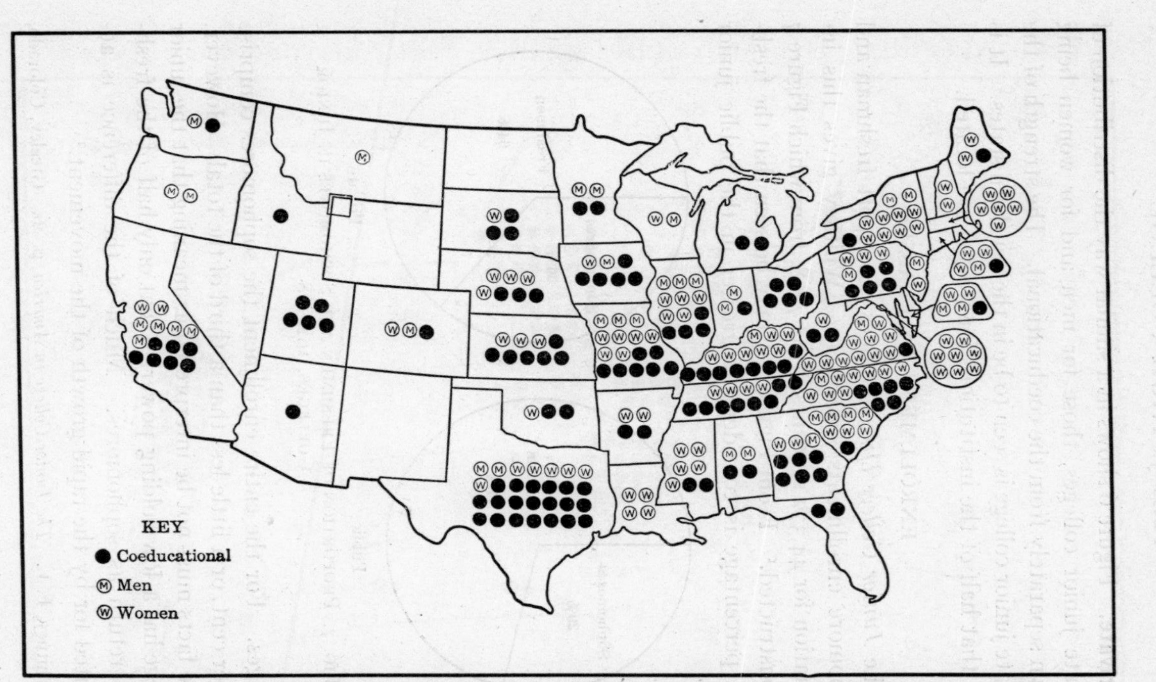

Fig. 6. Number of Private Junior Colleges of Various Types in the United States, 1930

Private. Figure 6 shows in a similar way the distribution of private junior colleges, those for men and for women being shown separately from the coeducational. The strength of the private junior college is seen to be in the Southern states. It is here that half of the institutions for women are located.

ENROLLMENT BY CLASSES

The *Junior College Directory* does not report freshman and sophomore enrollments separately. Whitney gives this information for 44,372 students in 1927–28, from which Figure 7 is constructed.[1] From Figure 7 it may be seen that the freshman percentage is considerably greater in the public junior

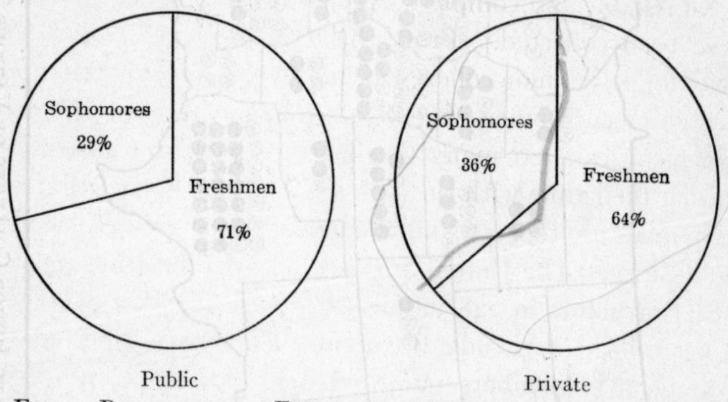

FIG. 7. PROPORTION OF FRESHMEN AND SOPHOMORES IN JUNIOR COLLEGES, 1927–28

colleges. For the entire enrollment the sophomores comprise 32 per cent, or a little less than a third of the total. However, these facts must not be interpreted as meaning that the junior college has a low holding power — that only half of the freshmen return as sophomores. Much of the difference is accounted for by the rapid growth of the movement.[2]

[1] Whitney, F. L. *The Junior College in America*, p. 26. Greeley, Colorado, 1928.

[2] This feature is discussed later (p. 231), where the two factors of survival and growth are separated.

NUMBER OF GRADUATES

The *Junior College Directory* does not report the number of graduates. Whitney reported for 1926–27, 3253 graduates in 146 public junior colleges, or 59 per cent of the sophomores; and 4342 graduates from 236 private junior colleges, or 70 per cent of the sophomores.[1] If these proportions and those of the last section are assumed to hold for the 69,497 students reported for 1929–30, it may be estimated that there were approximately 6650 graduates from the public institutions, and 7600 from the private in 1930, or a total of over 14,000.[2]

INSTRUCTORS

No reliable and complete data on the number of instructors have been collected. From the data in Hurt's *College Blue Book* for 295 junior colleges in 1927–28, it is found that 2211 men and 2449 women were reported as members of junior college faculties. So many of these are part-time instructors, sharing their time with the high school, that the fact that 4660 individuals are reported, an average of 16 per college, has little significance. The United States Office of Education reported 3484 instructors in 248 junior colleges in 1928, an average of 14 per college. A study at Stanford University [3] showed over 4000 faculty members named in 200 catalogues, averaging approximately 20 per college. Using the smallest of these figures, 14 per college, would lead to an estimate of over 6000 instructors, part-time or full-time, in all the junior colleges in the country for 1930.

[1] Whitney, F. L. *The Junior College in America*, pp. 22, 26. Greeley, Colorado, 1928.

[2] Public: 59 per cent of 29 per cent = 17 per cent of total enrollment.
Private: 70 per cent of 36 per cent = 25 per cent of total enrollment.

[3] Discussed more fully in Chapter XV.

ACCREDITATION

Of the entire list of 429 institutions reported in the *Junior College Directory*, 83 per cent are reported as "accredited" by some accrediting agency, national, regional, or local. Eighteen per cent are reported as accredited by one agency only, 20 per cent by two, 21 per cent by three, 18 per cent by four, and 6 per cent by five. These facts are summarized in Figure 8.

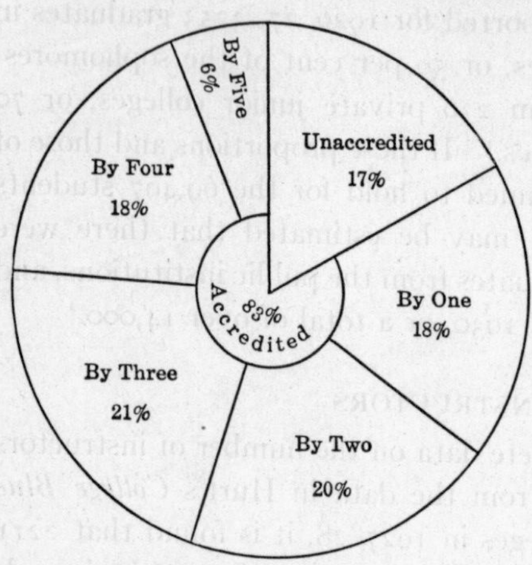

Fig. 8. Proportion of Junior Colleges Accredited by One or More Accrediting Agencies, 1930

Of the public institutions, 89 per cent are accredited by some agency; of the private ones, 79 per cent.[1]

HIGH SCHOOL RELATIONSHIP

No exact information is available as to the number of institutions that are more or less intimately connected with high schools, and the number that exist entirely independent of high school connections. The *Junior College Directory* reports for each institution enrollment in college and in high school. Where no high school enrollment is reported it may be assumed that the junior college is administratively distinct from the high school. In the case of the 412 institutions for which enrollment is reported, 80, or approximately one fifth, report no high school enrollment. In over a hundred of those

[1] More complete discussion of the entire matter of accreditation will be found in Chapter VI.

reporting both junior college and high school enrollment, the junior college enrollment, although representing only two years, is larger than the high school enrollment.

AGE OF JUNIOR COLLEGES

Public. How old are the junior colleges in the country? A graph giving the number founded each year and still surviving will be found in the next chapter, Figure 13. The average age of the public institutions existing in 1930 was 6.8 years. One third of them were three years of age or less. Only a quarter of them were ten years of age or more. The public junior college is essentially a very young institution.

Private. For the private institutions it is much more difficult to get reliable data. Many junior colleges in earlier investigations that have been reported by Koos, Whitney, Hurt, and others give the date of founding *as an institution,* not the date of *first real junior college work.* This carries some of them well back into the early part of the nineteenth century, dates that are quite misleading as far as any true significance for the junior college movement is concerned. In compiling the 1930 *Junior College Directory,* a special effort was made to secure the date of first junior college work.[1] In spite of that effort twenty-four private institutions reported dates prior to 1900. To secure a reasonable approximation to the average age, all with dates given prior to 1900 have been ignored.[2]

[1] In a letter of May 20, 1930, Secretary Campbell writes: "Last October, I wrote personally to the president of each junior college, asking that he check the item of the date. The following paragraph was inserted: 'In filling the blank regarding the date of organization as a junior college, be sure to indicate the year in which junior college work *was actually begun* in your institution.'"

[2] As shown in the next chapter, there were two or three private junior colleges in Texas in 1898. A statement from Mrs. C. L. Graves (see p. 58) indicates that some of the girls' seminaries in the last century were probably doing the equivalent of junior college work, although hardly recognized as such at the time. If some of these should be credited with a date prior to 1900, they are more than offset by the institutions organized subsequent to that date which did not begin real junior college work until several years after organization, as far as computation of an average age for the private institutions is concerned.

With this assumption, the average age of the private junior colleges in the country in 1930 is 9.8 years. One third of them were five years old or less, while a quarter were fourteen years of age or over. It is doubtful whether many of the 18 listed as beginning between 1900 and 1910 actually gave any junior college work at that time. If they were omitted the average age of the remaining group would be 7.8 years.

Summary. From any reasonable standpoint, therefore, the junior college is a young institution, averaging considerably less than ten years of age for both private and public institutions, and with not over three years difference in average age between the two groups. Very few indeed have given junior college work for longer than twenty years, although many private colleges date their origin as institutions far back into the nineteenth century.

CURRICULUM

Corresponding to variety of type and size, the junior colleges of the country offer a wide variety of curricula in varying amounts. While prevailingly of the academic or college preparatory type, many so-called terminal or semi-professional courses are found in commercial, agricultural, and engineering lines. Some two thirds of the work offered, however, is of the academic type. In quantity, the curricula of almost three hundred two-year junior colleges which have been carefully analyzed, vary from a bare fifty or sixty semester hours for the two-year course, allowing no freedom of choice, to institutions where the student has an opportunity of electing from a varied offering of over a thousand semester hours.[1] In something less than half of the junior colleges of the country the academic curriculum may be considered adequate as judged by reasonable standards,[2] while in the others it is too meager for satis-

[1] The nature and extent of the curriculum will be presented in greater detail in Chapter XVIII.

[2] See Chapter XVIII for a statement of "reasonable standards."

factory college work with sufficient latitude of choice to fit varying capacities and needs of different students. There is a decided tendency, however, especially in the older junior colleges, to offer much more adequate and varied terminal curricula.

NEGRO JUNIOR COLLEGES

Of possibly over thirty junior colleges for Negroes, data relating to only fifteen are available.[1] Seven of these are in Texas, three in North Carolina, two in West Virginia, and one each in Alabama, Florida, and Kentucky. Ten are private, and five are public institutions. Of the private institutions all are denominational, four being Methodist, two Baptist, two Congregational, one Presbyterian, and one Episcopal. Four of the public are state institutions, the only local one being at Houston, Texas, with the largest enrollment of any of the entire group, 225. The average enrollment reported for the private colleges is 86, with two exceeding 100; for the public, 117. Six are reported as first giving junior college work during 1926 or 1927. Only three have the name "junior college." Three are for women, the other twelve are coeducational. A movement is on foot, endorsed by the American Association of Junior Colleges at its meeting at Atlantic City in 1929, to organize a national association of Negro junior colleges.

LEGAL STATUS

In at least nineteen states the public junior college has been recognized by law. In twelve of these such legislation may be

[1] Hurt's *Blue Book* lists only nine Negro junior colleges, including one in Texas. Reid's State Department Bulletin on Texas Municipal Junior Colleges lists eight in that state alone. The American Association of Junior Colleges lists fourteen. A list furnished by the registrar of Birmingham-Southern College, Alabama, gives the names of 33, including institutions in Arkansas, Delaware, Georgia, Maryland, Mississippi, Pennsylvania, Tennessee, and Virginia in addition to the states named above. Sixteen were reported at the meeting of the American Association of Junior Colleges in Atlantic City in 1929. Klein, in his *Survey of Negro Colleges and Universities* (United States Bureau of Education Bulletin, 1928, no. 7), reports in detail on seven junior colleges.

classified as *general*, in the sense that it defines conditions under which junior colleges may be organized in the form of enabling laws. In others it has been limited to specific bills establishing particular junior colleges, usually of the state type. The general legislation varies all the way in amount and detail from simple statements that junior colleges may be formed as parts of the public school system, to the extensive detail of the laws found in California, Mississippi, and Texas. A fuller statement of the legal conditions under which junior colleges may be established will be found in tabular form in Chapter XX.

In this chapter it is desired only to summarize the states in which legislation has been passed, with the dates of passage of the various laws.[1] These are indicated on the map, Figure 9. As far as known, states in which legislation has been proposed but failed of passage by the legislature or approval by the governor, are indicated by the letter *P*. Much care, study, and correspondence have been devoted to the preparation of Figure 9 in the effort to make it as accurate as possible. It does not agree in several particulars, however, with the statements regarding the legislative status of the junior college as given by the United States Office of Education and by Dr. Whitney. In some cases a difference of interpretation as to what constitutes "junior college legislation" may cause the variation. In several cases officials of the state departments of education have stated that no legislation has been passed, meaning thereby general legislation only. While the complete accuracy of the map cannot be guaranteed in view of conflicting statements found, yet it is believed to be an essentially accurate portrayal of the situation in 1930.

That public junior colleges exist in many states without express legal sanction can be easily seen from a comparison of Figure 9 and Figure 5. In such cases, as already explained in

[1] More detailed information regarding the legislative situation in many of the states will be found in Chapter V. See also Supplementary Note, p. 43.

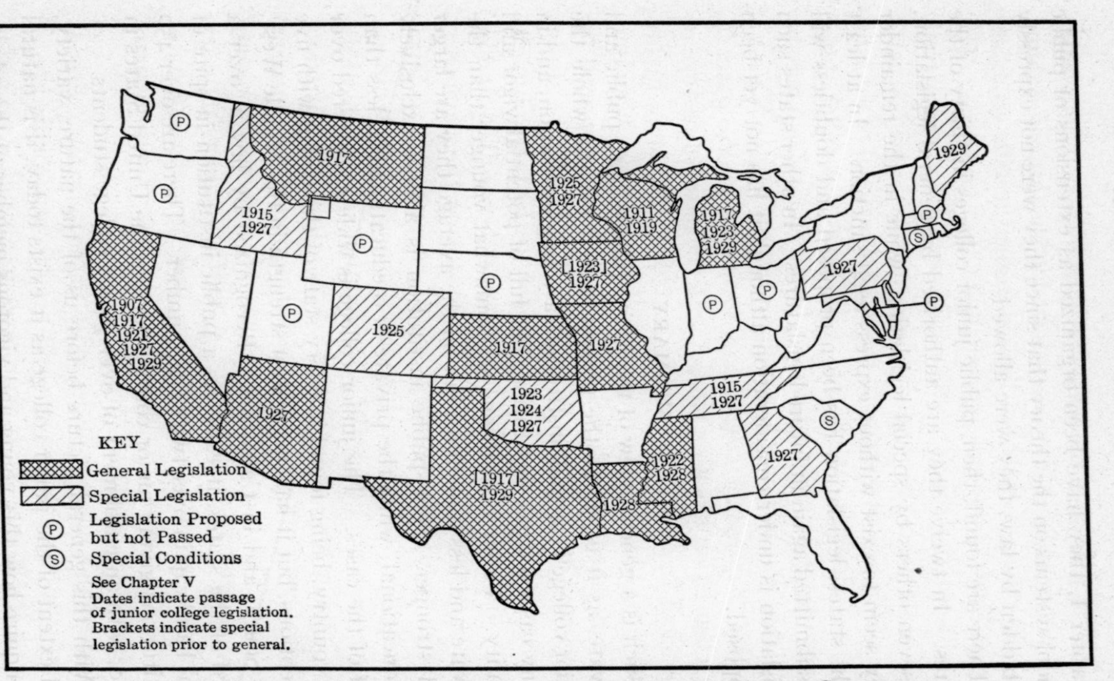

FIG. 9. STATUS OF JUNIOR COLLEGE LEGISLATION IN THE UNITED STATES, 1930

Chapter I, they have been organized as extensions of public school systems on the theory that since they were not expressly forbidden by law, they were allowed.

There are found, then, public junior colleges in thirty of the states. In twelve they are authorized by general legislation, in seven others by special legislation, while in the remainder they seem to exist without express legal sanction. In at least eight states, legislation has been proposed and doubtless will be submitted again in future legislatures. In other states such legislation is under consideration although it has not yet been proposed.

SUMMARY

Such is a general view of the junior college, both public and private, as it exists at the present time. On the whole the junior college is a small institution, a young institution, and in many cases a weak institution, but full of potential vigor and vitality. Public institutions are somewhat younger than the private and less numerous, but on the average they are larger and stronger. The public institution is almost exclusively coeducational, while the private is coeducational in less than half of the cases. The junior college is widely scattered over the country, being found in every state of the Union with five exceptions, but it has its greatest strength in the Middle West, the South, and in California. Recognized by law in over a third of the states, it exists as a public institution in spite of legal handicap in over twice that number. There are over 450 institutions giving junior college work in the United States in 1930, with an enrollment of over 70,000 college students.

With this general picture before us of the nature, variety, and extent of the junior college as it exists today, it is natural to inquire how this young and vigorous member of the educational family has so suddenly come into existence, almost entirely within the twentieth century. What has been its historical development? What are the forces that have caused its birth and rapid development in such varied forms in different parts of the country. How is it defined? What are its chief functions? The next ten chapters will be devoted to answers to these questions.

QUESTIONS AND PROBLEMS

1. Make a table showing, in two parallel columns, the principal facts for public and private junior colleges as summarized in this chapter or easily derived from the tables given.
2. From the latest *Directory* of the American Association of Junior Colleges (later than 1930), compile data to bring up to date any of the tables or figures in this chapter which are based upon it.
3. What are the ten leading states in junior colleges, if both public and private ones are considered as a single group, judging both by number and by enrollment? Exhibit by bar diagrams.
4. Make a bar diagram showing the ten states having the greatest average enrollment per college.
5. Account for the difference in rank of the states for public and private junior colleges, when arranged according to number of colleges, or according to total enrollment.
6. To what extent do public and private junior colleges tend to be strong in the same states? Are they supplementary or antagonistic?
7. How does the distribution of coeducational, men's, and women's private junior colleges compare with a similar distribution of four-year colleges and universities?
8. How does the enrollment in junior colleges in any state compare with the freshman and sophomore enrollment in the four-year colleges and universities of the state? Make a comparison over a period of several years, if possible.
9. What is the ratio of freshman to sophomore enrollment in selected four-year colleges and universities? How does this compare with freshman-sophomore ratio in the junior colleges? Why the difference?
10. Compute the junior college enrollment per thousand population for each state, according to the 1930 Census. How does it compare with a computation of the same type for the four-year colleges and universities of the country?
11. Look up the educational policies of some of the stronger denominations, and see to what extent they explain the denominational facts shown in Table 4.
12. On an outline map of the United States, show the distribution of

denominational junior colleges, using different symbols (e.g., initials, letters in circles) for each of the principal denominations.
13. Make a detailed analysis of the main facts regarding the junior colleges of any particular denomination, as found from their catalogues and from denominational reports. (Detailed surveys are available for the Lutherans, Disciples, and Brethren.)
14. Does the number of public junior colleges in any state tend to have a relationship to the date of first passage of junior college legislation in the state?
15. How does the number of public junior colleges in states having junior college legislation compare with the number in states without it?
16. Add other data to the map of Figure 9 regarding legislation, proposed or adopted subsequent to 1930.
17. Examine the advertising pages in the educational section of the *Red Book Magazine*, the *Cosmopolitan Magazine*, or similar publications, and list all institutions which advertise as junior colleges. Compare this list with that given in the current issue of the *Junior College Directory*.

SUGGESTED READINGS

Note: It is obviously impossible to suggest any readings on the present status of the junior college movement which will not be out of date soon after publication. The "present status" is not a fixed thing in education, but constantly changing, and with surprising rapidity in the junior college field. The few titles suggested below refer to regular publications, which should be consulted to secure the latest facts regarding the movement.

American Association of Junior Colleges. *Annual Directory of the Junior College.* Office of the Secretary, Peabody College, Nashville, Tennessee.

Until 1930 this was a separate publication. Beginning with the 1931 issue, it is planned to print it as part of one issue of the *Junior College Journal*, but with separate reprints which will be available.

United States Office of Education. *Educational Directory.* Published annually as Bulletin no. 1 for the current year.

Available about April of each year. This gives a list of presidents of junior colleges, with name of institution and location by states. Although not complete it is of value. The 1930 edition listed 277 institutions.

United States Office of Education. *Statistics of Universities, Colleges and Professional Schools.*

This is a bulletin of advance sheets from the regular Biennial Surveys of Education. It is later incorporated in the bound volumes comprising the Biennial Survey. The latest Bulletin, 1929, no. 38, gives statistics of junior colleges for 1927–28. The bulletin tabulates data regarding public and private individual institutions of higher education separately, but junior colleges are distributed alphabetically with other institutions. Data are given for each junior college on date of founding, number and sex of professors and students.

Hurt, H. W. *The College Blue Book.* Hollywood-by-the-Sea, Florida, 1928. (Publication office moved to New York.)

This standard college statistical reference book gives a wider variety of information regarding junior colleges than any other reference work. It is planned to reissue it at two or three year intervals. The second edition (1928) endeavored to give for each of 383 junior colleges in 41 states information on accreditation, control, date of foundation, status, dates of opening and closing, required entrance units, fees and other expenses, resources including endowment, buildings, and equipment; enrollment and faculty by sex, and name of executive officer with year of his appointment. The location of all institutions is also shown by colored symbols on a series of state maps. In addition similar data is given for a group of Negro junior colleges.

Sargent, Porter E. *Handbook of Private Schools*, thirteenth edition, Boston, 1929.

An annual publication. Gives brief information about many private institutions, including some which give only a small amount of work but which are not included in other lists. Statistical data usually is not segregated for the junior college department. Chiefly of value, therefore, for location, name of principal, and type of control.

Education Index. H. W. Wilson Company, New York City.

This invaluable publication covering the education field since 1929 in the same detailed and exhaustive way that the well-known *Readers' Guide* of the same company has covered the general periodical field for so many years, is indispensable for securing the latest references to all publications in journals and periodicals dealing with the latest developments in the junior college field.

Junior College Journal. Stanford University Press, Stanford University, California.

In the monthly issues of this journal an effort is made to continue the annotated bibliography described in Appendix I of this book, and to furnish other recent information on the status of the junior college movement.

SUPPLEMENTARY NOTE. In 1931 the legislatures of North Dakota and Nebraska passed general junior college enabling bills, and the legislature of Utah passed special junior college legislation. If added to the map, Fig. 9, these additions would make a total of 22 states with junior college legislation in 1931. See *Junior College Journal*, May and June, 1931.

CHAPTER III

HISTORICAL DEVELOPMENT: GENERAL

The junior college has shown flashes of promise rather than uniformly demonstrated strength. These tokens of greater possibilities of service are sufficient to warrant a sanguine faith in its future fulfillment of all its functions, while, to the one who insists on accomplished facts, there are already convincing achievements enough to justify the distinctive place which it has come to hold in higher education. — F. W. THOMAS.[1]

Contents of this chapter. This chapter traces in broad outline the origin and growth of the junior college from four standpoints — university amputation, high school elongation, college decapitation, and independent creation. Its development is then summarized in a few statistical tables and figures; the legislative history is considered briefly; the development of junior college organizations and associations is sketched, and the situation in other countries is mentioned. The next chapter will outline the history of the movement in California, and the following one its development and status in other states.

Introductory. Three distinct aspects of the origin of the junior college movement may be distinguished. These were admirably summarized by Dr. A. F. Lange, of the University of California, when, referring to the legendary highwayman of Attica, Procrustes, and his famous iron bed so ill-fitted to his victims, he suggested three questions:[2]

1. Shall the American university have its legs cut off, and, if so, where?
2. Shall the American four-year high school be stretched, and, if so, how much?
3. Shall certain American colleges have their heads cut off, and, if so, by whom?

[1] Thomas, F. W. "The Functions of the Junior College"; in Proctor, W. M. (editor): *The Junior College: Its Organization and Administration*, p. 159. Stanford University, California, 1927.

[2] Lange, A. F. "The Junior College as an Integral Part of the Public School System"; in *School Review*, vol. 25, p. 465. (September, 1917.)

Each of these questions suggests an important phase of the junior college movement which will be treated in this chapter. Later, a fourth aspect will also be considered.

UNIVERSITY AMPUTATION

The first question. "Shall the American university have its legs cut off, and if so, where?" That the work being done by the first two years of the university was not well fitted to it, was pointed out almost a half-century before anything was done toward the amputation or even segregation of the lower two years. A feeling was gradually developing that freshman and sophomore work was distinctly secondary in character, and different in purpose, content, organization, and method from the scholarly specialization, professional preparation and pure research of the university; that sophomore work might properly mark the close of general or cultural education, and the junior year the beginning of true university specialization.

Early opinions on the question. Perhaps the first specific suggestion for this change in American education was contained in the inaugural address of Henry P. Tappan as president of the University of Michigan, in 1852. In this he suggested the advisability of the transfer of the work of the secondary departments of the university to the high schools.[1]

Likewise, W. W. Folwell, in his inaugural address as president of the University of Minnesota, in 1869, suggested the great desirability of transferring the "body of work for the first two years in our ordinary American colleges" to the secondary schools.[2] President James, of the University of Illinois, in the early eighties, made an unsuccessful attempt to interest the authorities of the University of Pennsylvania in a similar plan. About the same time (1883) the University of

[1] Hinsdale, B. A. *History of the University of Michigan*, p. 43. Ann Arbor, Michigan, 1906. For quotations from President Tappan's *University Education*, published in 1851, see Koos, L. V., *The Junior College*, pp. 342–43.

[2] Folwell, W. W. *University Addresses*, pp. 37–38. Minneapolis, 1909.

Michigan differentiated between the upper and lower two years of undergraduate work by giving upper classmen a chance to specialize along the lines of major and minor work and requiring a thesis for graduation. The plan was abandoned a few years later, however, chiefly on account of administrative difficulties. Something of the same sort was in existence at Western Reserve University prior to 1896.[1] President James, in his inaugural address at the University of Illinois, in 1905, recommended modification of the work of the university by a "continued growth at the top and a lopping off at the bottom."[2] He said:

> My own idea is that the university ought not to be engaged in secondary work at all, and by secondary work I mean work which is necessary as a preliminary preparation for the pursuit of special professional, that is, scientific, study. Consequently our secondary schools, our high schools, and our colleges will be expected to take more and more of the work which is done in the lower classes of the different departments of the university as at present constituted, until we shall have reached a point where every student coming into the university will have a suitable preliminary training to enable him to take up, with profit and advantage, university studies in a university spirit and by university methods.

None of these efforts of university administrators to differentiate lower division work seem to have had any permanent effect.[3] They are of historic interest as indicating early convictions on the part of a few educators that there should be a greater differentiation of functions of the so-called lower divi-

[1] Brush, H. R. "The Junior College and the Universities"; in *School and Society*, vol. 4, p. 358. (September 2, 1916.)

[2] Lewis, E. E. "The Junior College and the Public Schools"; in *Bulletin of the School of Education of Indiana University*, vol. 4, no. 4, pp. 13–20. (March, 1928.)

[3] An exception to this statement, perhaps, should be made in the case of the University of Michigan. Although the differentiation was abandoned there after a brief trial, as stated, it was the direct seed from which later sprang the extensive junior college development in California. See p. 91.

sion, if indeed not entire separation of it from the university proper.

Segregation of the junior college. The first real separation came with the opening of the reorganized University of Chicago in 1892, under William Rainey Harper, sometimes called the "father of the junior college." President Harper's influence was a major element in all three phases of the junior college situation suggested by the three questions with which this chapter began. His influence on other aspects will be considered later. At present it should be noted that he made the freshman and sophomore work a distinct division which he called the "Academic College" while the upper two years were called the "University College." These names were awkward, did not suggest the real difference in nature of the two groups, and did not receive ready acceptance. In 1896, the happier designations "junior college" and "senior college" were adopted, and have been used at Chicago ever since. As far as known this is the first use of the term "junior college," although it was not until a few years later that it was used, also by President Harper, to designate an institution entirely distinct from the university. The University of Chicago conferred a title of Associate in Arts. In his first decennial report, covering the period closing July 1, 1902, President Harper discusses in a most illuminating manner the experience of the university with the junior colleges. He considers the philosophy back of them, and the resulting advantages and problems. The report includes an extensive discussion, from many standpoints, of the advantages and disadvantages of separation of the sexes in the junior college. He points out that the results, in his opinion, would be fivefold: [1]

(1) Many students will find it convenient to give up college work

[1] Harper, W. R. "President's Annual Report, University of Chicago, July, 1902"; in *Decennial Publications of the University of Chicago*, vol. 1, p. xcvi. Chicago, 1903.

at the end of the sophomore year; (2) many students who would not otherwise do so, will undertake at least two years of college work; (3) the professional schools will be able to raise their standards for admission, and in many cases, many who desire a professional education will take the first two years of college work; (4) many academies and high schools will be encouraged to develop higher work; (5) many colleges which have not the means to do the work of the junior and senior years will be satisfied under this arrangement to do the lower work.

In later years this separate administrative organization has been made in a considerable number of universities, although the designation "junior college" has been reserved, as a rule, except at Chicago, for separate institutions, and the terms lower division and upper division are more common for the university organization. This segregation, more or less complete, has been accomplished in at least eight large universities, although in none of them has there yet been complete abolition of the lower division.

Progress toward lower division abolition. In two institutions, however, a policy of complete elimination has been definitely announced, and is in process of gradual accomplishment. Unquestionably it will be adopted by others in time. At two leading American universities, widely separated by distance, Johns Hopkins on the eastern coast, and Stanford University on the western, the process of gradual progressive amputation of the lower limbs has actually begun. At Stanford University this was advocated as early as 1907, when Dr. David Starr Jordan, in the President's Report, recommended that Stanford University abolish freshman and sophomore work by 1913. This was before a single junior college existed in the state of California. This report contains a discussion of the function of the college as distinguished from the university. At least three years earlier, however, he had discussed the same subject, stating that "The college is part of the dividing trunk, of which the university represents the fruiting branches."[1] Again in 1908 he recommended the separation of the "junior college" at Stanford University as a temporary measure, and its complete discontinuance by 1914. There was not sufficient development of independent junior colleges in California by 1908, however, to justify such abolition at that time. Dr. Jordan has shown very recently[2] that its founder, Senator Stanford, as early as 1892 looked forward to a time when the institution should limit itself to upper division or graduate work entirely. Writing in 1929, he further said:[3]

In the proposed elimination of the freshman and sophomore classes, first officially formulated by me in 1907 as an inevitable step, Stanford will take her rightful position as one of our highest (not only higher) institutions of learning. With the rapid increase in the number of excellent junior colleges she ought no longer to have to dissipate her best strength in preparing young students for their true university work. The day has now arrived when, like most of the universities of Europe, she should stand above the ordinary routine of the college, properly so called.

Later developments at Stanford. The policy thus initiated by Dr. Jordan was cordially adopted by President Ray Lyman Wilbur, who in his First Annual Report, in 1916, sketched the rapid growth of junior colleges in California and suggested that Stanford could therefore stress university and graduate work more. In his 1920 Report he discussed the relation of the junior colleges to the newly established "lower division." In the next few years he wrote and spoke frequently on the desirability of leaving this work entirely to the junior colleges, "shock-absorbers," as he termed them, between the high school and the university. In 1926, in his

[1] Jordan, D. S. "Actual and Proper Lines of Distinction between College and University Work"; in *Proceedings of Association of American Universities*, vol. 5, p. 32. (1904.)

[2] Jordan, D. S. "Regarding Aims"; in *Stanford Illustrated Review*, vol. 30, p. 510. (July, 1929.)

[3] *Idem*, p. 510.

Alumni Day address, he definitely advocated the abolition of the lower division, and in a way that indicated it as an immediate issue.[1] This was at once the stimulus for an extensive alumni controversy which was waged with much heat and some light for two or three years. On the whole, alumni sentiment, harking back to the "good old days," was opposed to the proposed change, although a considerable number favored it as a progressive move. The number of men entering the lower division annually was reduced first to 450, and in 1927 from 450 to 350, with the expectation that similar reductions would be made until none would be admitted by 1934 or 1935. The Board of Trustees was not quite ready to set a definite date for final abolition. At their meeting June 23, 1927, the following resolution was passed:

Resolved, that the Board of Trustees approve the recommendation of the President of the University that there be a further reduction in the number of students to be admitted to the Lower Division at the University, and that the President be authorized to carry out this policy, at such rate and to such extent as may, from time to time, be authorized by this Board, and that no determination be made at this time of the question of the elimination of the Lower Division at any specific period.[2]

The present situation at Stanford. In the absence of Dr. Wilbur from the university, as Secretary of the Interior, no further action has been taken. The statement just quoted, however, means, in the opinion of Dr. Wilbur, that Stanford University is now on the way to further development of its Upper Division and graduate work as its responsibilities for Lower Division work are reduced. In his latest *President's*

[1] Wilbur, R. L. "President Wilbur Outlines the Future"; in *Stanford Illustrated Review*, vol. 27, pp. 440–41. (May, 1926.)

[2] Wilbur, R. L. "Limitation of Students"; in *Twenty-Fourth Annual Report of the President of Stanford University. Stanford University Bulletin*, fifth series, no. 41, p. 7. (November, 1927.)

Annual Report, reviewing the development of ten years, President Wilbur states:[1]

In general, our students come at a somewhat more advanced stage and stay with us for longer periods, and the wastage from other sources, including poor scholarship, is less. In other words, Stanford University is gathering together a faculty and a student body of high quality doing more and more work of university grade. Much of the elementary college work is passing into the hands of numerous institutions, the majority of them state supported.

In 1928–29 the lower division constituted 29.6 per cent of the student body, while three years earlier, 1925–26, it was 39.2 per cent of it.

Johns Hopkins University. The change to upper division and graduate basis has been determined upon and is being accomplished with much less controversy and commotion in the case of Johns Hopkins University, where the emphasis on graduate work has been a major factor ever since its foundation. In one way there was much less justification for the action at Hopkins than at Stanford, because there are comparatively few junior colleges in the eastern part of the country. President Goodnow, in his commemoration day address at Johns Hopkins in February, 1925, proposed to abolish instruction in most subjects in the freshman and sophomore years. He said:[2]

The instruction in the first two college years has probably always been in essence what is known as secondary rather than advanced instruction. On that account it has no proper place in a university as distinguished from a college. Under present conditions, where this kind of instruction is given to masses of somewhat immature minds in probably the largest school of the modern American university, the development of the best kind of advanced work is made difficult if not impossible. The only justification for the

[1] Wilbur, R. L. "Trend of the University"; in *Twenty-Sixth Annual Report of the President of Stanford University. Stanford University Bulletin*, fifth series, no. 81, p. 2. (November, 1929.)

[2] Goodnow, F. J. "President Goodnow's Commemoration Day Address"; in *Johns Hopkins Alumni Magazine*, vol. 13, pp. 239–40. (March, 1925.)

giving of secondary instruction by the American university is historical. But the recent development of the idea of the junior college, which in many instances is attached to the high school, is an indication of a movement, which if continued will both remedy the present situation and as well bring American secondary and higher education more into accord with European practice.

The official announcement of the plan on the part of the university authorities reads in part:[1]

> The President, the Trustees, and the Faculties of the Johns Hopkins University believe that the time has come and the opportunity is ripe for a reorganization in this field of higher education. To this end they contemplate the adoption of a plan proposed by the president of the University by which (1) only such students will be attracted and selected as may possess the necessary mental endowment and equipment for research; (2) more intensive training will be given such students, unhampered and unimpeded by the deadening weight of numbers. The first steps in this plan are... that the University cease to provide those courses ordinarily given during the first two years of the American college.

On account of charter provisions, the proposal required approval by the state legislature, but this was granted in 1927. Actual abolition, however, has not yet been entirely accomplished.

HIGH SCHOOL ELONGATION

The second question. "Shall the American four-year high school be stretched, and, if so, how much?" Not only has there been a long continued effort on the part of university leaders to eject the freshman and sophomore work, but there has been, during the same period, a strong influence in many high schools to extend their work upward to include the two years unwelcomed by the universities. There are those who would trace the beginning of the junior college movement, in this sense, back to the Renaissance, to the prolonged secondary school of

[1] Quoted in *Proceedings of Seventh Annual Meeting*, American Association of Junior Colleges, Jackson, Mississippi, November 29–30, 1926, p. 29.

Sturm at Strassburg, in the sixteenth century. While there is some analogy, the casual connection is very remote, if indeed any real influence can be traced. The American four-year high school is one of the most uniquely distinctive American educational institutions. Any modification of it must be looked for in causes much nearer home. The reasons for the development of the junior college from below, from the standpoint of economy, home conditions, enlarged functions, overcrowding of the universities, etc., will be considered more in detail in a subsequent chapter. At present it is desired only to point out some of the early junior college work accomplished in connection with both public and private secondary schools.

President Angell of Yale stated, in 1915, that the immediate motivation for the junior college came not so much from the universities, however much they may have served the cause through occasional educational leaders and occasional agitation of educational ideals, but rather from the secondary schools and from the intelligent public that supports them.[1]

Beginnings in Michigan. The first work of this sort in the United States seems to have been done in Michigan.[2] In the early nineties the University of Michigan was accepting one year of college work done by the stronger high schools. By 1895, the East Side High School of Saginaw gave freshman college work in Latin, algebra, trigonometry, English, and history. By 1897, eight students with such work had graduated at the university in three years after entrance. Later, however, this work was discontinued.

[1] Angell, J. R. "The Junior College Movement in High Schools"; in *School Review*, vol. 23, pp. 289–302. (May, 1915.)

[2] Even much earlier, it is interesting to observe that du Pont de Nemours, in a French treatise written in 1800 on *National Education in the United States of America* (an English translation of the second, 1812, French edition was published by the University of Delaware Press, Newark, Delaware, 1923, 161 pages), outlined a plan for national education which represented the joint work of himself and Thomas Jefferson. His outline of secondary schools has many striking similarities to the present junior colleges of the country.

The first permanent public junior college. It is of some interest to note the first public junior college still in existence. This distinction belongs to the Joliet Junior College, Illinois, which began operation in 1902.[1] It was due directly to the influence of President Harper, in his effort to encourage the development of the lower two years of college in connection

[1] There is some confusion in the literature regarding the date of the earliest existing public junior college at Joliet. G. F. Winfield states that full college freshman and sophomore work was given in 1900 (*Journal of Education*, vol. 94, p. 238). An editorial in the same issue of the *Journal of Education* also gives 1900. Whitney (*Junior College in America*) gives 1901. Hurt's *College Blue Book*, Koos's *Junior College*, United States Bureau of Education, and the *Directory* of the American Association of Junior Colleges give 1902. Hines, in the *Educator Journal* (vol. 18, p. 180, December, 1917), gives 1903. City School Reports of Joliet from 1897 to 1903 make no mention whatever of junior college work. J. Stanley Brown, who organized it, stated in 1920 that it was established in 1902 with five or six students (United States Bureau of Education, Bulletin no. 19, p. 27, 1922). See also article by T. M. Dean in *Junior College Journal*, vol. 1, pp. 429–32. (April, 1931.)

That essentially junior college work was given before this date at Joliet, however, is clearly indicated by a quotation from remarks made by J. Stanley Brown, at the dedication of the present plant, April 4, 1901, when he said: "Our own great University of Illinois, whose distinguished president addresses us this evening, admits our recommended graduates into the sophomore class without condition and enables them to complete a four-year course in three years." (Quoted in Haggard, W. W. "An Early Upward Extension of Secondary Education," in *School Review*, vol. 38, p. 431, June, 1930.) Haggard also gives in detail five-year and six-year courses of study which were offered in 1903.

Joliet's claim to being the first junior college was disputed at the first meeting of the American Association of Junior Colleges by T. C. Burgess, of Bradley Polytechnic Institute at Peoria, Illinois. He stated that a junior college was established as a part of that institution when it was founded in 1897, five years prior to Joliet. He claims that Lewis Institute in Chicago and the junior college of Goshen, Indiana, may also claim equal antiquity or possibly an earlier beginning. (United States Bureau of Education, Bulletin no. 22, p. 53, 1919.) In a personal letter in February, 1928, G. N. Carman, director of Lewis Institute, stated that Lewis Institute opened as a junior college in 1896, and was listed as such by the North-Central Association until 1917, when it changed to four-year status. Neither Bradley nor Lewis Institutes are public institutions, however, and the only claim made for Joliet is that it is the first public institution still in existence. Even earlier than Goshen can be mentioned Saginaw, Michigan, if defunct institutions are to be considered. Further, neither Lewis nor Bradley have remained junior colleges, so that neither can claim to being the oldest private junior college still functioning as a junior college. For the earliest institutions of this type see pages 57 and 63.

with the high schools. The superintendent of Joliet, J. Stanley Brown, was a strong Baptist, as also was Dr. Harper. It was while they were together at Baptist conventions that they talked over plans for educational progress, and Dr. Harper succeeded in inspiring Brown with some of his zeal and enthusiasm for educational reorganization which was the real inspiration for the organization of the work at Joliet, Illinois, at such an early date — almost ten years before the second one now existing appeared in California. Brown says:[1]

The public junior college was established in Joliet, Illinois, in 1902. Joliet takes no particular credit for it, but concedes it to the man of vision, Dr. William R. Harper, the first president of the University of Chicago.

The Chicago Conference. At the Conference of the Academies and High Schools Affiliated with the University of Chicago, in 1902, President Harper made his famous proposals for reorganization all along the line from the elementary school through the university, including the six-year high school, and three committees of seven each were appointed to consider the proposals from the standpoint of elementary, secondary, and higher education. This was vigorously discussed during the next two years. Brown was chairman of the high school committee.

Other early public junior colleges. Similar work was organized at Goshen, Indiana, in affiliation with the University of Chicago, possibly even earlier than at Joliet, and continued very successfully for several years, but was discontinued for local reasons. At the 1904 Conference, J. Stanley Brown reported that Philadelphia; Muskegon and Saginaw, Michigan; St. Joseph, Missouri; Goshen, Indiana; Joliet, Illinois; and eighteen semi-public institutions in different sections of the

[1] Brown, J. S. *The Growth and Development of the Junior Colleges in the United States;* United States Bureau of Education, Bulletin no. 19, p. 27. Washington, D.C., 1922.

country were working out the six-year plan, giving collegiate work in connection with the high school.

University of Missouri recommendations. As early as 1907, the annual conference of teachers in accredited schools in the University of Missouri recommended giving college credit for one or two years of college work done in high schools of larger cities. The matter of expense prevented the high schools from taking advantage of the plan until 1915, when Hannibal, Kansas City, and St. Joseph organized junior colleges in connection with their high schools. Other early institutions beginning such work included both Crane and Lane High Schools in Chicago. Crane, which began junior college work in 1911, has continued to the present and is now the largest junior college in the country enrolling over 4000 students. Lane also began in 1911 with 50 students. Others organized prior to 1916 and still in existence include Grand Rapids, Michigan (1914), and Rochester, Minnesota (1915).

Junior college work in two large cities. In 1915, Kansas City, Missouri, and Detroit were the two largest cities in the country in which there were no large four-year institutions offering collegiate work. At Kansas City it happened quite naturally, therefore, that a considerable number of high school graduates, not having any college or university in the immediate vicinity, returned to the high school in the fifth year to take subjects which had not been taken in their regular courses. Many of these wanted to go on to college, but found they could receive no credit for this fifth year. The board of education had built a new building for the high school, and in September, 1915, opened a junior college in the old building, with E. M. Bainter as principal. The University of Missouri formally approved the faculty and proposed courses of study before the institution opened. The junior college in Kansas City was thus purely an outgrowth of a definitely felt local need of high school extension, and the community felt it was right and proper to give a partial college education to public school students who needed or wanted it. It is now the third largest junior college in the country. A similar need led to the organization of a junior college in Detroit, but in the latter case it expanded, in 1923, to a four-year municipal college. Detroit also began, in 1915, with 33 students, which rapidly increased by 1920 to 700 regular students and 300 special students.

Recent growth. The rapid development of the public junior college has come in the past decade. In the period from 1915 to 1920, 22 were established, which still continue; in the next five-year interval, 56; and in the last, 74. The increase in number of institutions is shown graphically in Figure 13 (p. 74).

The high school motive. Thus a very strong motivation for the junior college came from the high schools themselves, and from the intelligent public supporting them. The high school has long been known as the "people's college" — a designation frequently attached to it, with too little justification in many cases aside from its tremendous enrollment. With the addition of the junior college, however, it seems destined in many cases to fulfill this popular designation of it.

The stretching process in private institutions. Junior college work developed by the stretching process not only in public institutions, but also in private ones. Unquestionably the earliest instance is to be found at Newton, Maryland, where the first Catholic "college" in what is now the United States was opened in 1677. It might be called the earliest junior college, since in addition to secondary work it did not carry its students beyond the freshman year in college. Its students who wished further education were then sent to St. Omer's in Belgium to complete their studies.[1]

In recent years many academies, seminaries, institutes, finishing schools, and similar institutions of general secondary

[1] Kirchgessner, F. "The Junior College"; in *The Catholic Educational Review*, vol. 22, p. 157. (March, 1924.)

grade, especially in the Southern States, have added two years of junior college work to their courses of studies, but it is difficult to give exact dates of such changes, nor are they of much significance.

In the East, as well as in the South, such junior college beginning is rather characteristic. Thus, Mrs. C. L. Graves, former head of Bradford Academy and Junior College in Massachusetts, says: [1]

> In the East, then, the movement is a development of the private institution for the education of women. In the majority of cases, the institution brought a two-year course for high school graduates into existence as far back as seventy-five or one hundred years ago. In several, the present junior college course represents the last part of what was formerly a five or six-year secondary course of a general cultural character, usually including music, home economics and art, with sometimes a secretarial course. In 1920, when Bradford Academy took the name, "Junior College," only four others were so listed: Packer Collegiate Institute, the Springfield High school, Mount Ida, and an industrial or reform school for girls in Massachusetts. By the end of 1930, if plans now under way mature, there will be over fifty in this northeastern section, including Washington City.

This method of origin accounts for most of the junior colleges of the proprietary type, as well as for some of the denominational institutions which developed from earlier denominational academies. Many of the denominational junior colleges had quite a different origin, however, as is pointed out in the next section.

Horizontal development. Another way in which junior college work has been developed has been neither upward nor downward, but sideways. This represents the case where two-year normal schools have added junior college curricula not

[1] Graves, Mrs. C. L. "Problems of Standards for Eastern Junior Colleges"; in *Proceedings of Tenth Annual Meeting of American Association of Junior Colleges, Atlantic City, 1929*, p. 145. Atlantic City, 1929.

designed especially for teacher training. The best example of this was in Wisconsin, where the legislature, in 1911, passed a law providing that:

> The board of normal school regents may extend the course of instruction in any normal school so that any course, the admission to which is based upon graduation from an accredited high school or its equivalent, may include the substantial equivalent of the instruction given in the first two years of a college course. Such course of instruction shall not be extended further than the substantial equivalent of the instruction given in the first two years of such a college course without the consent of the legislature.[1]

A somewhat similar plan in California has been in operation in some of the California teachers' colleges, notably San José, whose junior college work will be described later (p. 103).

COLLEGE DECAPITATION

The third question. "Shall certain American colleges have their heads cut off, and if so, by whom?" Advocacy of such college decapitation represented the third great plank in President Harper's educational platform. He urged that many weak, struggling, four-year colleges, especially denominational ones, with inadequate financial resources, should give up attempting relatively expensive junior and senior work, often with questionable efficiency, and should concentrate on two years of really effective work. His plan was to have both extended high schools and decapitated junior colleges affiliated with the University of Chicago, which, after suitable inspection, would admit the graduates of such institutions to the University for senior college and graduate work. This phase of his plan was not so successful. The small colleges for the most part feared loss of identity and absorption by the vigorous and rapidly expanding university on the shores of Lake Michigan; denominational pride and zeal and local rivalry also

[1] For subsequent abolition of this arrangement, and reasons for it, see p. 157.

tended to keep them going. They were not yet ready for such a move, nor did they clearly see the logic of it. A few church colleges, but not many, ceased giving the bachelor's degree and became affiliated with the University of Chicago. Perhaps the earliest to make this arrangement definitely was Hardin Junior College, a Baptist institution at Mexico, Missouri, under President J. W. Million.

President Harper's junior college prophecy. In a famous analysis of the small college at a National Education Association meeting at Charleston, South Carolina, July 10, 1900, President Harper said:[1]

> Strong academies are needed side by side with the high schools of the state, just as strong colleges and universities, founded by private means, are needed to work side by side with the universities of the state. While therefore 25 per cent of the small colleges now conducted will survive, and be all the stronger for the struggle through which they have passed, another 25 per cent will yield to the inevitable, and, one by one, take a place in the system of educational work which, though in one sense lower, is in a true sense higher. It is surely a higher thing to do honest and thorough work in a lower field than to fall short of such work in a higher field. Another group of these small institutions will come to be known as junior colleges. I use the name "junior college," for lack of a better term, to cover the work of the freshman and sophomore years.... It is not until the end of the sophomore year that university methods of instruction may be employed to advantage.... There are at least two hundred colleges in the United States in which this change would be desirable.

He pointed out that such institutions were found, not only in the West and South, but in New York, Pennsylvania, Ohio, Indiana, Illinois, and Michigan. The reduction of such institutions to junior colleges, he said, would accomplish six results:

1. The money now wasted in doing the higher work superficially could be used to do the lower work more thoroughly.

[1] Harper, W. R. "The Small College — Its Prospects"; in *Proceedings of National Education Association, Charleston, South Carolina, 1900*, pp. 67–87. Chicago, 1900.

2. The pretense of giving a college education would be given up, and the college would become an honest institution.
3. The student who was not really fitted by nature to take the higher work could stop naturally and honorably at the end of the sophomore year.
4. Many students who might not have the courage to enter upon a course of four years' study would be willing to do the two years of work before entering business or professional school.
5. Students capable of doing the higher work would be forced to go away from the small college to the university. This change would in every case be most advantageous.
6. Students living near the college whose ambition it was to go away to college could remain at home until greater maturity had been reached — a point of the highest moment in these days of strong temptation.

These reasons are almost equally valid for all types of junior colleges, and form a remarkable Bill of Rights or Magna Charta for the junior college, given in the opening year of the twentieth century by the great educational statesmen to whom the movement owes so much.

In the early suggestions regarding junior college work in high schools, preceding those of President Harper which have been mentioned in this chapter, there was no clear recognition of the junior college as a separate institution. The passage just quoted contains the first use of the term "junior college," in the sense of an independent institution, which has been discovered by the author.

Writing in the report of the United States Commissioner of Education for 1902, President Harper says:[1]

> President Jordan, of the Leland Stanford Junior University, has suggested to me that among the various important movements of the year is the disposition of small colleges to become junior colleges. ... Within my own observation, many facts pointing in this direction have occurred.

[1] Harper, W. R. "The Educational Progress of the Year 1901–02"; in *Report of the Commissioner of Education for the Year 1902*, p. 663. Washington, D.C., 1903.

Yet on the whole this observation on the part of both President Jordan and President Harper at this time seemed to be more hope than realization. President Harper's untimely death in 1906, before he reached the age of fifty, deprived the educational world in general and the junior college field in particular of one of its great leaders.

Why President Harper's plan was not successful. In part because he spoke of "coöperation" with public high schools, but of "affiliation" with private academies and colleges, President Harper's plan was not successful. In the minds of many, "affiliation" suggested depriving an institution of its independent existence. Yet such fears were not well founded. President Harper believed thoroughly in the small college, and was perhaps one of the best friends that it ever had. In his first decennial report he said:[1]

> The existence of the smaller colleges is not only a desirable thing; it is a necessity in the intellectual growth of the great sections of the country which make up the West, the Northwest, and the South, and the greatest calamity which could possibly befall the cause of higher education in the United States would be the extinction, or even a considerable deterioration, of the small college.

Verification of Harper's 25-50-25 per cent prophecy. While Dr. Harper's policy was not immediately successful, it has been partially so, in Texas, in Missouri, and in other parts of the country in the quarter-century since his death. It is of interest to try to verify it. One of the author's students endeavored to do so,[2] using the 203 colleges listed by the United States Bureau of Education as having 150 or more students in 1900–01. While inadequate and incomplete reports, changes of name and location, and other factors made an exact check impossible, yet it was possible to determine

[1] Harper, W. R. *Decennial Publications of the University of Chicago*, vol. 1, p. lxvii. Chicago, 1903.

[2] A. G. Nelson, in a term paper, 1929.

that approximately 37 per cent had perished, 49 per cent survived in 1924–26 as four-year institutions, and 14 per cent, or 28, had become junior colleges. Undoubtedly there is room for a much larger number of the weaker four-year colleges still existing to transform themselves and improve themselves by so doing, as President Harper advised thirty years ago.

Decapitation of Baptist colleges in Texas. While the decapitation of small colleges was never widely realized, under the leadership of the University of Chicago, it was accomplished in two states, Texas and Missouri, in somewhat systematic form. Perhaps Harper's influence was a strong factor in causing such action.

Missouri has commonly been given credit for the first systematic correlated group of private junior colleges affiliated with a university, but the work of Dr. F. Eby, of the University of Texas, has shown that Texas developed such a system over a decade before it was begun in Missouri.[1] He states that the first system of correlated colleges incorporating the junior college principle, although not calling themselves junior colleges because this term had not yet been invented by President Harper, was established in Texas in 1897–98. The Baptists in this state shortly before this time awoke to the fact that they had a number of weak, competing institutions, which when combined were not worth as much as their total indebtedness. Under the heroic leadership of the Reverend J. M. Carroll, a state-wide Educational Commission was authorized by the state convention, and a plan of correlating all the schools of the denomination in the state was adopted. Under this plan, formulated by the American Baptist Education Society, Baylor University at Waco became the head of the affiliated system; Baylor College at Belton, a senior college, and three junior colleges, Decatur Baptist College, Rusk

[1] Eby, F. "Shall We Have a System of Public Junior Colleges in Texas?" in *Texas Outlook*, vol. 11, pp. 20–24. (January, 1927.)

Baptist College, and Howard Payne College, Brownwood, completed the group. The junior colleges agreed to end their work with the sophomore year, and in consideration of this concession their graduates were given full admission to the junior classes at Baylor University and Baylor College. Further developments in Texas will be outlined in Chapter V.

The earliest junior college. Thus Decatur Baptist College seems to deserve the distinction of being the first established junior college in the United States, which is still in existence as a junior college. It antedates by four years the earliest public institution, still existing, at Joliet.[1]

Decapitation in Missouri. The best known and most frequently quoted example of reduction of a group of denominational four-year colleges to stronger junior colleges is found in the State of Missouri, where the change took place under the leadership of the University of Missouri. The situation is thus described by the President of the University:[2]

In Missouri we had a lot of colleges that were trying to be four-year colleges and many of those, under our advice and assistance and some of them under grave necessity without any advice or assistance, reduced to what they honestly were, what they could honestly do, namely, the first two years of the college work. In 1911 we began our coöperation with these colleges, persuading several alleged four-year colleges that their own interest and honesty in education required them to devote all of their resources to two years instead of four years of work. The results in those colleges have been very satisfactory to them. They have actually increased their attendance. Parents who could not be persuaded to send their children to a small college for four years, could be induced to send them to a junior college near at home for two years, pro-

[1] Rusk College has been discontinued, while Howard Payne has become a four-year institution. It is possible that some of the institutions vaguely referred to by Mrs. Graves on page 58 deserve credit as the first private junior college still existing. No such claims, however, seem to have been put forward for any specific institution.

[2] Brooks, S. D. "The Growth of Junior Colleges"; in *Transactions and Proceedings of the National Association of State Universities*, vol. 26, pp. 150–51. Washington, D.C., 1928.

vided transfer to the university without loss of credit could then be made. Devoting their entire financial resources to the first two years enabled most of these colleges to reach a standard justifying credit for two full years.... At the present time we have in Missouri 25 junior colleges, 18 of which are accredited colleges, this is, giving the full 60 hours of accredited work, seven are on the certificate plan, meaning that a part only of their work is accepted.[1]

In Missouri the private junior colleges for women all have residence halls, whereas such accommodations are limited, if they exist at all, in the state institutions. This feature of residence halls has been a chief argument presented by the private junior colleges to their patrons, and accounts in part also for their large enrollment and general success.

Before 1915 arrangements had been made with private colleges, not only at the University of Missouri, but also at the University of Texas, whereby the latter became junior colleges with certain approved standards and could send their graduates into the junior year of the universities. Similar experiments were tried in Wisconsin even earlier.

Opportunity in the South. That the Southern States presented an unusual opportunity for junior college development from existing institutions labeling themselves as "colleges," was pointed out in 1914 by a Southern educational leader, Miss E. A. Colton. The South is preëminently the field for the private junior college. Miss Colton says:[2]

We have 380 institutions claiming to be colleges or universities, only 31 of which are recognized by the Southern College Association; 35 or 40 others approximate the minimum standard college requirement. Of the remaining 350 there are perhaps 50 or 60 others which might improve their equipment and do two years of real college work.

[1] The following Missouri institutions were accredited by the University of Missouri as junior colleges prior to 1915. March, 1913: Hardin, Lindenwood, Stephens; June, 1914: Christian, Cottey.

[2] Quoted in Rivers, W. W. "The Present Status of the Junior College"; in *Southern Baptist Educational Association, Select Papers,* Baylor Bulletin, vol. 14, no. 4, p. 49. Waco, Texas, 1916.

By 1916 she could report at the Southern Association:[1]

Over sixty nominal colleges in the South have within the past six years adopted the name "junior college."

The action of church boards. Church boards of education began to give recognition to junior colleges, especially in the South, as early as 1912, when the Southern Baptist Convention mentioned the junior college as deserving consideration at the hands of the board of education. In the same year, also, the secretary of the Board of Education of the Methodist Episcopal Church, South, listed the junior colleges in that denomination, and two years later the general conference of the church gave legal status to the junior colleges under its jurisdiction. The commission on education defined the junior college and listed nine institutions which met the requirements. This number had increased to twenty-five by 1920. The Presbyterian Church officially recognized the junior college as early as 1916.

Results of the decapitation policy. Thus, the development of the junior college movement, especially in the private field, has come about, as expressed by President Angell, of Yale University, "through a process of retraction and condensation as a result of which a formerly thin and emaciated four-year course has been reconstructed into a fairly robust and well-nourished two-year program."[2]

INDEPENDENT CREATION

A fourth possibility. There is, however, a fourth way in which modern educators have attempted to fit the educational Procrustean bed. Not by amputation, stretching, or decapitation, but by the creation of a new institution, designed to fit

[1] Colton, E. A. "The Junior College Problem in the South"; in *Proceedings of the Twenty-Second Annual Meeting of the Association of Colleges and Secondary Schools of the Southern States*, pp. 96–100. (1916.)

[2] Angell, J. R. "Problems Peculiar to the Junior College"; in *School Review*, vol. 25, p. 387. (June, 1917.)

exactly. In some parts of the country the effort has been made to create an entirely new educational unit, like Athene springing full-formed from the head of Zeus, disassociated in every way from the high school below or the university above, fitted to perform its educational function as a collegiate institution, giving true college education in the sense of general cultural education, somewhat higher than the restrictions of the high school, and somewhat lower than the scholarly specialization of the university. This has found its best and fullest development in California, with the legal provisions for the establishment of independent institutions in separately organized junior college districts. These will be described in the next chapter. This class of institution, however, is not confined to California. An outstanding example of this type recently organized on the other side of the continent is Sarah Lawrence College in New York, organized as a junior college *de novo*.

Early attempts and plans. It might be maintained that in some of the early state systems of education it was contemplated that there should be institutions doing work now being done by junior colleges, that is, supplementing the general training of the secondary schools and preparing students for later specialization in the university. Thus the educational system of Virginia as conceived in the original plans for the University of Virginia, and the first Education Act of Missouri, contemplated a number of collegiate institutions which would serve as connecting schools between the public schools and the university. As a matter of fact these contemplated middle schools were never established.

State junior colleges independently established — Centipede theory. Many of the state type of junior colleges, agricultural and mechanic arts colleges, and polytechnic schools have been organized as junior colleges, while others have been adjusted (either upward or downward) to this basis.

Another type of created junior college is the branch institution. Some universities, so far from being ready to "cut off their legs," seem to have adopted the centipedal or decentralizing theory of multiplication of their lower extremities. Examples are furnished by the University of Pittsburgh with its three branch junior colleges at Johnstown, Uniontown, and Erie; Columbia University, with Seth Low Junior College, and perhaps others to follow; or, on the other side of the world, by the University of the Philippines with its branch junior colleges at Cebu and Vigan. It is highly questionable whether America, with its long history and tradition of local initiative and independence, will generally accept this type of junior college. It is questionable even in communities such as the Pennsylvania group, where the arrangements seem to be working with entire satisfaction to all concerned, whether it will be a permanent one. Absentee administration is hardly consistent with as intensely local an institution as the junior college should be in its fullest development.

The four phases. Thus the junior college has developed in these several ways: high schools have been raised to junior colleges; small colleges, especially denominational ones, have been cut down to junior colleges; independent junior colleges have been established *de novo*; and the whole movement has been aided and accompanied by the segregation or elimination of lower division work in the universities. A college course worthy of the highest respect and of cordial approval can be given in the junior college today which will be equal to if not in many respects superior to the average college course of a half-century ago.

GROWTH STATISTICALLY CONSIDERED

It is desirable to picture the development of the junior college by certain statistical summaries, as far as these can be secured in reliable form. This is difficult to do, since the statistics are not entirely comparable when collected by different agencies at different periods. Five agencies may be considered, however: the United States Bureau (Office) of Education, the American Association of Junior Colleges, and Koos, Whitney, and McDowell. The earliest collection of the number of junior colleges, historically considered, was made by McDowell who reported 132 institutions, only 39 of them public.

Koos's comparisons. Dr. Koos made his celebrated Commonwealth Study of the junior colleges of the country in 1922. In 1927 he made a careful effort to gather comparable data from those then in existence to show the progress in the five-year period. Unusual care was used to make the two results comparable from various standpoints. In an effort to locate existing junior colleges, inquiries were sent to all state departments of education, state universities, and junior colleges already known. Essential features of the two comparisons are shown below:

	1927	1922	Per cent Increase
Total junior colleges	**325**[a]	**207**	**57**
Public	105	46	128
State	31	24	19
Private	189	137	38
Total students	**35,630**	**16,121**	**121**
Public	16,382	5,163	217
State	3,763	3,276	15
Private	15,485	7,682	102

[a] Includes 19 announced to open in fall of 1927.

Koos comments, "judged by the increment both in numbers and in enrollment the public junior college is more dynamic than the private junior college." It is notable that the public junior college more than doubled in size and tripled in enrollment during the short five-year period between the two studies, while the state type changed but slightly.

Whitney's study. Whitney, in his study of 1927–28, a year later than that of Koos, found 382 in the country, an increase of 18 per cent over Koos's figure for the previous year, and of 85 per cent over 1922.

Latest data. The latest figures available, those of the American Association of Junior Colleges, supplemented by the author and as used in the last chapter, show 450 in the country in 1929–30. This is an increase of 117 per cent in the seven-year period — truly a remarkable growth.

Statistics by the Federal Bureau. The United States Bureau of Education published statistics showing the growth of junior colleges over a ten-year period, which are reproduced in Table 6. (The last column is added by the writer.)

TABLE 6. GROWTH OF JUNIOR COLLEGES (1918–28) [1]

	Number of Schools	Number of Instructors	Number of Students	Average Number of Students
All junior colleges				
1928	248	3,484	44,855	181
1926	153	2,762	27,122	171
1924	132	1,758	20,559	156
1922	80	1,554	12,124	148
1920	52	988	8,102	156
1918	46	557	4,504	98
Public junior colleges				
1928	114	1,919	28,437	249
1926	47	953	13,859	295
1924	39	699	9,240	237
1922	17	404	4,771	281
1920	10	207	2,940	294
1918	14	172	1,367	98
Private junior colleges				
1928	134	1,565	16,418	123
1926	106	1,809	13,236	125
1924	93	1,059	11,319	122
1922	63	1,150	7,353	117
1920	42	781	5,162	123
1918	32	385	3,137	98

These figures are far from complete. For example, in 1928, the American Association of Junior Colleges Directory showed 408, instead of 248. In 1920, Table 6 shows only ten public

[1] *United States Bureau of Education*, Bulletin no. 38, p. 1. (1929.)

junior colleges in the country, when there were 18 in California alone that year. In spite of these limitations it is probably fairly comparable for the different years, it covers a longer period than any other set of comparable data available, and it is the only table that gives the number of instructors. It is noticeable from these figures that enrollment in public and private junior colleges ran almost parallel until 1926, when the public institutions slightly passed the private, and in the next two years more than doubled. All institutions show a marked increase in average enrollment of 82 per cent in the seven years, with the public colleges again in the lead, but the average is much smaller than it should be for efficiency. Koos points out as an extraordinary fact that the junior college, virtually within a period of twenty years, has increased in number to half the total number of institutions of higher education in the United States founded in the three centuries since the establishment of Harvard College in 1636.

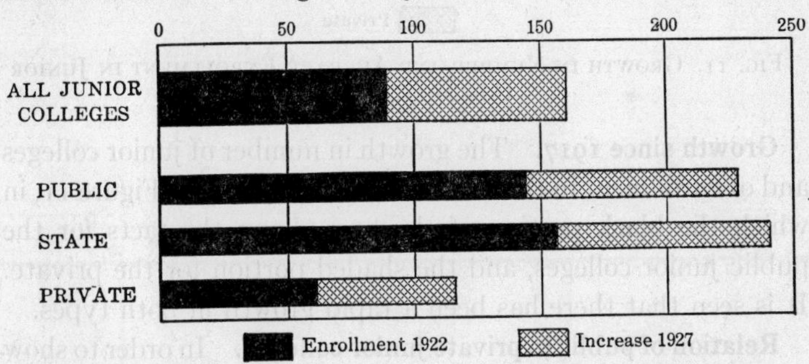

FIG. 10. CHANGE IN AVERAGE ENROLLMENT IN JUNIOR COLLEGES, 1922–27

Change in average enrollment. The change in average enrollment in seven years has been as follows:

	1929	1922	INCREASE (per cent)
All junior colleges	**162**	**89**	**82**
Public	228	143	59
State	242	156	55
Private	115	61	89

This change is shown more vividly in Figure 10. The private institutions show the greatest proportional, but least actual, increase.

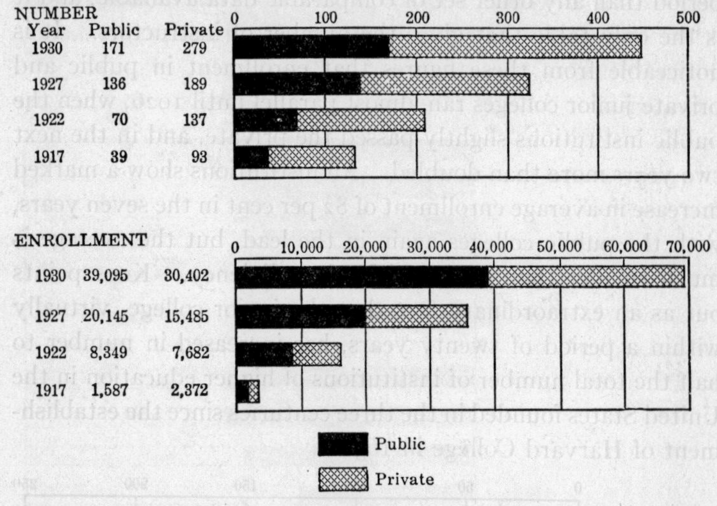

FIG. 11. GROWTH IN NUMBER AND AVERAGE ENROLLMENT IN JUNIOR COLLEGES, 1917-30

Growth since 1917. The growth in number of junior colleges and of enrollment in them is summarized briefly in Figure 11, in which the black portion of the bars shows the facts for the public junior colleges, and the shaded portion for the private. It is seen that there has been a rapid growth in both types.

Relation of public to private junior colleges. In order to show more clearly the increasing importance of the public junior college since 1917, Figure 12 has been constructed. This shows the way in which the number of public junior colleges is approaching the fifty per cent line, while in enrollment they have already reached and passed it.

Foundation of existing junior colleges. Figure 13 is an historical graph showing the number of junior colleges, in existence in 1930, which were in existence at five-year intervals preceding that date. Dates are taken from the *Directory* of the American Association of Junior Colleges, which endeavors to show, for 430 junior colleges, the date of beginning of actual junior college work. Figure 13, then, does not include institutions existing for a time but dying or changing their status prior to 1930.

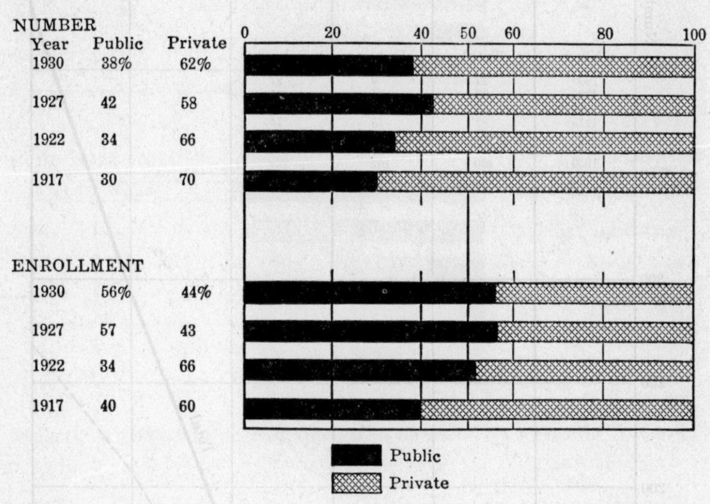

FIG. 12. CHANGE IN PROPORTION OF PUBLIC AND PRIVATE JUNIOR COLLEGES, 1917–30

DEVELOPMENT OF LEGISLATION

The earliest legislation authorizing junior colleges was passed in California in 1907, and this basic legislation has been modified at intervals since that time. It was not until ten years later, 1917, that two other states, Michigan and Kansas,[1] passed general junior college legislation. In the same year California enacted a new law, still in force. Special legislative action, establishing particular state junior colleges, was found

[1] In 1911 Wisconsin passed legislation, as indicated earlier in this chapter, authorizing establishment of junior colleges in normal schools, but it has been a dead letter since 1922.

as early as 1915 in Idaho and Tennessee. The dates of original and subsequent legislation, either special or general, have been given on the map of Figure 9, page 39. It will be noted that most of the legislation has been enacted subsequent to 1925.

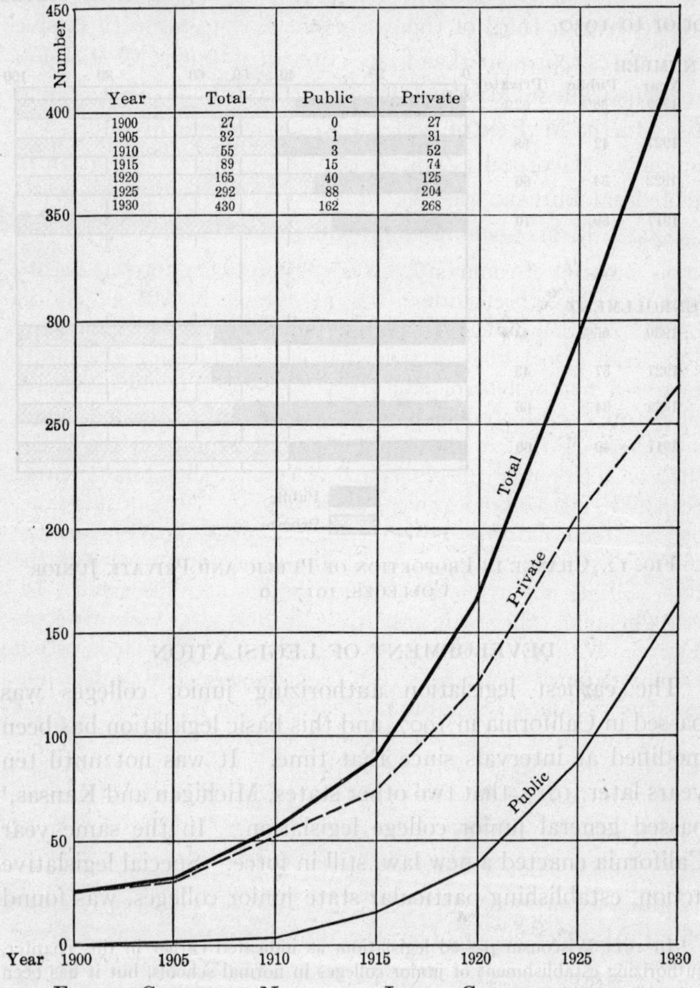

Year	Total	Public	Private
1900	27	0	27
1905	32	1	31
1910	55	3	52
1915	89	15	74
1920	165	40	125
1925	292	88	204
1930	430	162	268

FIG. 13. GROWTH IN NUMBER OF JUNIOR COLLEGES, 1900–30

JUNIOR COLLEGE ORGANIZATIONS

St. Louis Conference of 1920. Commissioner of Education P. P. Claxton called a meeting of junior college representatives at St. Louis, where a two-day meeting was held June 30 and July 1, 1920. Thirty-four members were present at this conference, over a third of them from Missouri, but with twelve other states represented as well. President James M. Wood of Stephens College, Missouri, was chairman of the meeting, and Miss Martha M. Reid of William Woods College, Missouri, was secretary. George F. Zook, specialist on higher education in the federal bureau, was the educational leader directing the meeting. In his opening statement, he said:[1]

It is a matter of common knowledge that during the last twenty years there have been formed a large number of national educational associations, and even a larger number of sectional and state educational associations, at which questions affecting the future welfare of our system of education have been freely discussed. Among the questions which have received no little consideration in recent years is that of the function and the future of the junior colleges. The junior colleges have been commanding this attention because they have been growing tremendously. Up to this time, however, there has been no gathering of representatives from the junior colleges themselves at which the place and function of the junior colleges in our system of education has been discussed. Indeed, the junior colleges are practically the only large body of people concerned with a definite type of education which so far have not held any national conferences. It, therefore, occurred to the Commissioner of Education and to me that it would be highly desirable for the Bureau of Education to call a meeting of representatives from the junior colleges of the country for a full and frank discussion of their mutual interests and problems. This, in brief, is the occasion for this conference.

At the St. Louis Conference a decision was reached to organize a national association of junior colleges. Dean David MacKenzie, of Detroit Junior College, was elected

[1] *National Conference of Junior Colleges, 1920*; United States Bureau of Education, Bulletin no. 19, p. 1. Washington, D.C., 1922.

president; T. W. Raymond, Mississippi Synodical College, vice-president; and Miss Reid, secretary. At the meeting in Chicago, February 16–17, 1921, more than seventy schools were represented. This is generally considered the first meeting of the American Association of Junior Colleges, for at this time a constitution was adopted and permanent committees appointed. According to the constitution the object was stated as:

To define the junior college by creating standards and curricula, thus determining its position structurally in relation to other parts of the school system; and to study the junior college in all of its types (endowed, municipal, and state) in order to make a genuine contribution to the work of education.

Provision was made for active, institutional, associate, and individual membership.

Summary of officers and meetings. The date and place of the eleven annual meetings of the Association held since the St. Louis Conference, and the principal officers have been as follows:

Year and Date	Place of Meeting	President	Secretary
1921 Feb. 16, 17	Chicago, Ill.	David MacKenzie	Martha McKenzie Reid
1922 March 24, 25	Memphis, Tenn.	Geo. F. Winfield	Martha McKenzie Reid
1923 Feb. 27, 28	Cleveland, Ohio	James M. Wood	Doak S. Campbell
1924 Feb. 26, 27	Chicago, Ill.	James M. Wood	Doak S. Campbell
1925 Feb. 20, 21	Cincinnati, Ohio	Louis E. Plummer	Doak S. Campbell
1926 March 17, 18	Chicago, Ill.	H. G. Noffsinger	Doak S. Campbell
1926 Dec. 3, 4	Jackson, Miss.	L. W. Smith	Doak S. Campbell
1928 March 12, 13	Chicago, Ill.	Edgar D. Lee	Doak S. Campbell
1928 Dec. 3–5	Fort Worth, Texas	J. Thomas Davis	Doak S. Campbell
1929 Nov. 19, 20	Atlantic City, N.J.	John W. Barton	Doak S. Campbell
1930 Nov. 18, 19	Berkeley, Cal.	J. B. Lillard	Doak S. Campbell
1932 Feb.	Kansas City, Mo.	Richard G. Cox	Doak S. Campbell

It has been the general policy of the Association to alternate the presidency between public and private junior colleges, although this has only been strictly followed since 1924. All the presidents are living and active now with the exception of Dean David MacKenzie, who died in 1925.[1]

[1] For sketch of his life, see *Junior College Journal*, March, 1931. For photographs of all living ex-presidents, see *Junior College Journal*, February, 1931.

Growth of the Association. Some features of the growth of the Association are epitomized in Table 7, which shows the number of pages in the published proceedings including papers and addresses given and the number of members both active and associate, each year.

TABLE 7. GROWTH OF THE AMERICAN ASSOCIATION OF JUNIOR COLLEGES (1920–29)

Meeting	Date	Pages in Proceedings	Membership	
			Active	Associate
Preliminary	1920	47	34	..
First	1921	24	..	..
Second	1922	10	..	..
Third	1923	68	..	..
Fourth	1924	84	67	12
Fifth	1925	117	87	7
Sixth	1926	93	95	8
Seventh	1926	84	101	9
Eighth	1928	93	133	12
Ninth	1928	153	168	14
Tenth	1929	176	210	26

[a] No papers published.

Location of conventions. Until 1929, meetings were always held in the Middle West or South. In 1929 the experiment was tried of taking it to the extreme East, where the junior college has had much less development. Some fears were expressed at planning an independent meeting so far from the majority of the junior college organizations, but the attendance was almost as large at Atlantic City as when the meetings were held in the Middle West, and the sessions served to bring the junior college vividly to the attention of a great section of the country where it was little known. Then, in 1930, the place was changed to the extreme Pacific Coast, at Berkeley, California. In view of the many junior colleges in California there was no question of attendance, but it was gratifying to find the large group of Eastern and Middle Western junior college men who took the opportunity to visit California and its junior colleges. With the successful Atlantic City and Berkeley meetings the nationalization of the American Association of Junior Colleges may be said to be complete. It has become national in fact as well as in name.

Activities of the Association. Without doubt the American Association of Junior Colleges has been the most powerful single influence tending to unify the junior college movement and to give it a feeling of independent self-consciousness. In 1929 Secretary Campbell, of the Association, characterized its activities as follows:[1]

The activities of the Association have been rather varied and interesting. At first, I think we should characterize them as defensive. We came together, a small group, seemingly for the purpose of defending this child which appeared to be greatly in need of defense just at that time. A little later, this defense program turned from the defensive to a forward movement, a promotional program. These aspects can be quite freely found in the early literature of the Association. There then followed those conscious attempts to define objectives. There was courage even to overlook traditions at times and efforts to find frontiers where logical development of the junior college might be wrought out. I somehow believe that the Association is somewhere on the outskirts of this latter phase today.

Nature of the meetings. Reports of proceedings have been printed annually. These have contained not only the formal papers and addresses, but stenographic reports of all the discussions as well, thus forming an excellent mirror of the progress of the junior college movement during the decade. Many of the discussions have been concerned with standards. These are mentioned in Chapter VI. Other subjects which have been considered and discussed from time to time include relationship to other educational organizations and to standardizing

[1] Campbell, Doak S. "A Brief Study of the Development of the Junior College Movement"; in *Proceedings of Tenth Annual Meeting of American Association of Junior Colleges*, p. 15. Atlantic City, 1929.

agencies, coöperative advertising, honor scholarship societies, publicity, etc. The professional papers and addresses have been given by members of the Association and by outside authorities from the universities and from the business world. Many of them have been of a high order, and mark a real advance in junior college thinking. The research committee has made several outstanding reports. The Association sponsored the extensive bibliography mentioned in Appendix I, which was printed at its request by the United States Office of Education, and more recently the establishment of the *Junior College Journal.*

The *Junior College Journal*. A national journal seems to have been first suggested at the fourth meeting of the Association at Chicago, in 1924, when J. P. Craft, of Averett College, Virginia, raised the question whether the Association was strong enough to be thinking of an official publication, monthly or quarterly. Again in 1928, at Fort Worth, a proposition was made to have the Association subscribe for the quarterly organ of the National High School Inspectors' Association, and be guaranteed a certain amount of space in each issue, but the proposal did not meet with favor.

At the Atlantic City meeting a definite proposal was laid before the Association, from the Stanford University Press, for the publication of a monthly *Junior College Journal* under the joint editorial control of the American Association of Junior Colleges and the School of Education of Stanford University. This proposal was accepted, and a four-year contract entered into by which the Stanford University Press assumed the financial management and major financial responsibility. Walter C. Eells, of Stanford University, was the first editor, and Doak S. Campbell, secretary of the Association, associate editor. There was a national advisory board of twenty leaders in the junior college field, including, *ex-officio*, the members of the executive committee of the Association. The first issue appeared in October, 1930, consisting of 64 pages. This journal should be a powerful factor in giving greater unity and consciousness to the junior college movement and in promoting its growth and development.

Other national organizations. In 1925, the Department of Secondary School Principals of the National Education Association established a regular junior college section, and amended their constitution to provide that the Executive Committee should have a junior college representative upon it, who is also the chairman of the section. The first program meeting was at Cleveland, in 1929, under the chairmanship of F. L. Bacon, of Evanston, Illinois, when there were two sessions of the section, with eight addresses by national leaders. In 1930, at Atlantic City, J. W. Harbeson, of Pasadena, California, was chairman, and there were six addresses given at two sessions. For 1930–31, E. E. Oberholtzer, of Houston, Texas, was chairman and four major addresses were given at two sessions.

At the meeting of the American Association of Collegiate Registrars at Memphis, Tennessee, in 1930, a junior college section was established.

At the meeting of the American Library Association in Los Angeles, in June, 1930, a junior college conference section was organized. Miss Ermine Stone, librarian of Sarah Lawrence College, was chosen chairman for 1931.

A national organization of Negro junior colleges had been discussed in 1929, as stated on page 37, but had not been effected by the spring of 1931.

Regional associations. The only regional junior college association organized, covering more than a single state, seems to be the New England Junior College Council, organized in 1929, with E. E. Cortright and G. M. Winslow as first president and secretary, respectively.

Other organizations, state and local. In California there are four junior college organizations. The first to be organized was the Southern California Junior College Association (1925), followed by the Northern California Junior College Association (1928), and the Central California Junior College Association (1929). Each of these holds meetings semi-annually where professional addresses are given. Attendance is largely confined to administrators, but in the Central Association students as well as faculty attend, with a general session for all, followed by separate section meetings, and an intercollegiate athletic event. Finally there was organized, in 1929, a Federation of California Junior College Associations with A. C. Olney as first president. The object of this was to coördinate the work of the three constituent associations, and particularly to promote research and dissemination of information. Meetings are held annually.

The Missouri Junior College Union was the first state organization to be formed, sometime prior to 1915, with seven members, but it ceased to function several years ago, primarily because it was merely an organization of private institutions, several of which have since gone out of existence.

Numerous other state organizations exist, either independently or as sections or divisions of state teachers' associations. In addition to professional organizations there are several athletic organizations or conferences. Among the professional organizations, may be mentioned the Junior College Section of the Iowa State Teachers' Association, the Kansas Public Junior College Association, the Oklahoma Association of Junior Colleges, the Texas Junior College Association, the Michigan Association of Junior Colleges, the Georgia Junior College Association, and the Minnesota Junior College Deans' Association.

THE JUNIOR COLLEGE IN OTHER COUNTRIES

Canada. In Canada, interest has recently developed in certain phases of the junior college movement. In 1927,

Sandiford reported a general survey of conditions and developments in the United States, with special application to conditions in Canada. He also referred to the 21 virtual junior colleges under Catholic control in Quebec, and to the upward extension of high school work planned for Ontario.[1] Two years later G. H. Ferguson, premier of Ontario, announced his intention of attempting to reform the educational system of the province. One phase of his plan involved giving the first year of university work in the public high schools.[2] There are two junior colleges of the Seventh Day Adventist denomination in Canada.

Philippines. In the Philippine Islands a branch junior college of the University of the Philippines was established at Cebu, in 1918. It had 120 students in 1926–27, which had increased to 174 by 1927–28. By 1925 another branch had been authorized at Vigan. There would seem to be considerable room for growth of this type of institution in meeting the higher educational needs of other scattered islands of the archipelago.[3]

China. In China there has been, for several years, a considerable number of competing four-year colleges, supported by the various denominational boards doing missionary work there. The situation was analogous to that found in Missouri or Texas before the demotion of some of the four-year colleges, existing in those states, to junior college status. At a recent conference, composed of representatives of most of the denominations concerned, it was recommended that several of them become junior colleges. At least one has already ac-

[1] Sandiford, Peter. "Junior High Schools and Junior Colleges or The Reorganization of Secondary Education"; in *Queen's Quarterly*, vol. 34, pp. 367–83. Kingston, Ontario, April–June, 1927.

[2] "Education in Ontario"; in *School and Society*, vol. 29, p. 768. (June 15, 1929.)

[3] Monroe, Paul (chairman). *A Survey of the Educational System of the Philippine Islands, 1925*, pp. 105, 610, 621. Manila, 1925.

cepted this recommendation and others will probably do so in the near future. The junior college seems to be a happy remedy for some of the unnecessary denominational rivalry in higher education found in some parts of China.

Japan. S. A. Stewart, for ten years head of Hiroshima School for Girls, states that up to about five years ago the government had made no provision for the college education of women in Japan, with the single exception of two normal schools for training women teachers. Recently, however, the tendency has been growing to add two or three years of special training to the high school course for girls, and in some cases to establish special schools for them. These, he says, are what would be ranked as junior colleges in America. In 1929 the government maintained twenty-seven such schools, and fifty-seven were privately maintained.[1] In 1931, E. A. Knight, of the University of North Carolina, was asked to visit Japan and make a special study of the junior colleges there.

Greece. The American Junior College for Girls was established at Old Phaleron, near Athens, in 1923, by Miss Minnie B. Mills, formerly of Iowa. In 1929 it was offered by the Greek government, through the influence of Premier Venizelos, a splendid site of thirty acres at Elleniko on Phaleron Bay, opposite Salamis, and plans were being matured in 1930 for removal to the new site.

QUESTIONS AND PROBLEMS

1. For any one or more of the twenty individuals named below, state his significance for the junior college movement, and, if still living, his present location and relation to the junior college field: J. Stanley Brown, Doak S. Campbell, Marion Coats, Elizabeth A. Colton, William J. Cooper, William R. Harper, Merton E. Hill, David Starr Jordan, Leonard V. Koos, A. F. Lange, F. M. McDowell, A. C. Olney, William M. Proctor, L. W. Smith, F. L. Whitney, Ray Lyman Wilbur, George F. Winfield, J. M. Wood, Will C. Wood, George F. Zook.

---

[1] Stewart, S. A. "Modern Education for the Japanese Women of Today"; in *Alumni Register of Duke University*, p. 160. (May, 1930.)

2. Are the reasons given by President Harper, in 1903 (*School Review*, vol. 11, pp. 1-3), still valid today? The committee proposed by him, in its report the next year (*School Review*, vol. 12, pp. 15–28), indicated the work that should be done to prepare students to enter the junior year of a standard college. Compare this with current practice.
3. Is separation of the sexes desirable in the lower division of a university? (See President Harper's Annual Report, in *Decennial Publications of the University of Chicago*, p. xcvii *et seq.*)
4. Find to what extent President Harper's 25–50–25 per cent recommendation has been carried out in practice in the United States.
5. Is there any evidence of use of the term "junior college" before it was used by President Harper? When and where did he first use it?
6. What would probably have been the effect on the junior college movement had President Harper lived twenty years longer?
7. "It is the opinion of your Commission that these questions are of a kind that may not be settled on *a priori* considerations; that in this field as in others, the inductive method must be employed and many experiments undertaken; and, still further, that only after a considerable period of time will it be possible to reach results that may be regarded as well tested and satisfactory." (Commission of Twenty-One. *School Review*, vol. 13, p. 24, 1905.) What progress in results that "may be regarded as well tested and satisfactory" has been made since 1905 in answering the six questions stated by the Commission?
8. Study the affiliation agreement between the University of Chicago and the six-year high school at Goshen, Indiana. (*School Review*, vol. 13, pp. 19-23, January, 1905.) Does it destroy the independence of the junior college? Should such an agreement be modified in any way today?
9. Why were the six-year high schools at Goshen, Philadelphia, and other places discontinued?
10. By what claims do Lewis Institute and Bradley Polytechnic Institute consider themselves to be the first junior colleges?
11. Study in detail the history of the junior college movement in any single state.
12. What have become of the Southern colleges which Miss Colton suggested might well become junior colleges?
13. Compare the reasons for the abolition of the lower division as given at Johns Hopkins and Stanford Universities. Why has the Stanford proposal aroused greater alumni opposition?
14. Tabulate all the universities having a separate lower division organization, showing type of organization, date of adoption, degree of segregation, etc.

15. How many private junior colleges now in existence are decapitated four-year colleges? Where are they located?
16. To what extent have the existing state type of junior colleges actually been created as independent junior colleges *de novo*? To what extent have they developed otherwise, and how?
17. "In the midst of these difficult problems, comes the junior college, almost completely unsoiled by the touch of educational research, born Venus-like, full blown without any childhood, much less adolescence." (G. D. Stoddard, in *School Executives Magazine*, vol. 49, p. 356, April, 1930.) Discuss the truthfulness of this characterization of the junior college.

SUGGESTED READINGS

*American Association of Junior Colleges. *Preliminary Conference and First Meeting*. United States Bureau of Education, Bulletin no. 19. (1922.)

Angell, J. R. "The Junior College Movement in High Schools"; in *School Review*, vol. 23, pp. 289–302. (May, 1915.)
Paper before North Central Association giving early history of the movement, and its status in 1915.

Blauch, L. E. "Reorganization on European Lines Appears Imminent"; *School Life*, vol. 9, pp. 77–79. (December, 1923.)
Traces junior college influences back to the Renaissance.

Brooks, S. D. "The Growth of Junior Colleges"; in *Transactions of National Association of State Universities*, vol. 26, pp. 149–57. Washington, 1928.
Development in Missouri described by the president of the State university.

Brush, H. R. "The Junior College and the Universities"; in *School and Society*, vol. 4, pp. 357–65. (September 2, 1916.)

Bunker, F. F. *Reorganization of the Public School System*. United States Bureau of Education, Bulletin no. 8. (1916.)
Chapters III and IV (especially pp. 56–60) contain excellent summary of the early movement started by President Harper for six-year high school, in 1902.

*Campbell, D. S. "A Brief Study of the Development of the Junior College Movement"; in *Proceedings of the Tenth Annual Meeting of the American Association of Junior Colleges*, pp. 11–15.
Deals especially with early evidences.

Canada, S. W. "The Relationship of the State University and Junior Colleges in Missouri"; in *Bulletin of American Association of Collegiate Registrars*, vol. 2, pp. 191–99. (July, 1926.)
Excellent statement of Missouri junior college history by Registrar of University of Missouri.

Confrey, A. "Annual Meeting of the American Association of Junior Colleges"; in *Catholic Educational Review*, vol. 28, pp. 20–24. (January, 1930.)

Eby, F. "Shall We Have a System of Public Junior Colleges in Texas?"; in *Texas Outlook*, vol. 11, pp. 20–24. (January, 1927.)
Excellent history of junior colleges in Texas.

Goodnow, F. J. "The Future Policy of the Johns Hopkins University"; in *School and Society*, vol. 21, p. 618. (May 23, 1925.)

*Harper, W. R. "The Situation of the Small College"; chapter 23 of *The Trend in Higher Education*, Chicago, 1905. Also in *Proceedings of the National Education Association*, Charleston, South Carolina, 1900, pp. 67–87.
Contains his 25–50–25 per cent prophecy.

Harper, W. R. "The High School of the Future"; in *School Review*, vol. 11, pp. 1–3. (January, 1903.)
Proposals for a six-year high school at Chicago conference.

*Harper, W. R. "President's Decennial Report"; in *Decennial Publications of the University of Chicago*, vol. 1. (Chicago, 1903.) "Affiliation and Coöperation" (pp. lxvi–lxxi); "The Junior Colleges" (pp. xciv–cxiv).
One of President Harper's great reports. Contains much of historical importance and of present interest in connection with junior colleges.

Hill, A. R. "The Junior College Movement"; in *Educational Problems in College and University*, pp. 188–98. Ann Arbor, 1921.
Discussion of the history and philosophy of the junior college by president of University of Missouri at the inauguration of M. L. Burton as president of University of Michigan.

"Junior College Movement: Land Grant College Heads in Conference"; in *American Educational Digest*, vol. 47, pp. 167, 172–73. (December, 1927.)
Reports of attitudes and progress in many different states.

*Koos, L. V. "The Present Status of the Junior College"; in Hudelson, E., *Problems of College Education*, pp. 118–27. (Minneapolis, Minnesota, 1928); also in *School Review*, vol. 36, pp. 256–66. (April, 1928.)

"Length of the Baccalaureate Course"; in *Proceedings of National Education Association*, p. 489 ff. Boston, 1903.
A series of addresses by E. E. Brown, W. R. Harper, N. M. Butler, etc.

*McDowell, F. M. "The Junior College"; in United States Bureau of Education, Bulletin no. 35, pp. 10–70. (1919.)
Excellent general survey of early history of the movement.

Pierce, E. C. "How Far Should the High School do College Work?"; in *School Review*, vol. 5, pp. 117–21. (1897.)
An early address before Michigan Schoolmasters' Club.

"Report of the Commission of Twenty-One"; in *School Review.* (January, 1903) Appointment; (January, 1904) First Report; (January, 1905) Second Report.
President Harper's proposals for a six-year high school and reports of the Commission to study it.

Sandiford, P. "Junior High Schools and Junior Colleges"; in *Queen's Quarterly*, vol. 34, pp. 367-83. (April–June, 1927.)
Conditions and development in Ontario and Quebec.

Smith, L. W. "Current Conditions in Junior College Development"; in *Proceedings of the Tenth Annual Meeting of the American Association of Junior Colleges*, pp. 57–87. Atlantic City, 1929.
Extensive report by research committee of 1928 questionnaire to 120 colleges.

Walker, N. W. "The Significance of the Junior College Movement"; in *Proceedings of the Seventh Annual Meeting of the American Association of Junior Colleges*, pp. 28–32. Jackson, Mississippi, 1926.
Discusses Johns Hopkins and Stanford Universities.

Whitney, F. L. *The Junior College in America.* Chapter II. Greeley, Colorado, 1928. 258 pp.

Wilkins, E. H. "The Relation of the Senior College and the Graduate School"; in *Bulletin of American Association of University Professors*, vol. 13, pp. 107–21. (February, 1927.) Also in *Proceedings of Twenty-Eighth Annual Conference of American Universities*, pp. 59–70. Chicago, 1926.

Winfield, G. F. "The Junior College Movement in America"; in *Journal of Education*, vol. 94, pp. 227–28. (September 15, 1921.)
Historical summary by former President of American Association of Junior Colleges, who wrote first master's thesis in the country on the private junior college.

Zook, G. F. "Model Junior College Legislation"; in *Proceedings of the Tenth Annual Meeting of the American Association of Junior Colleges*, pp. 40–46. Atlantic City, 1929.

CHAPTER IV

HISTORICAL DEVELOPMENT: CALIFORNIA

> It is natural that the movement should reach its first demonstrable position in that state of immense distances, immense resources, and immense initiative — California. Thanks to the efforts and achievements of this progressive state, the junior college is no longer a theory to be discussed pro and con; but an actual accomplishment, a movement which is growing even more rapidly than the public consciousness can take it in. — STANWOOD COBB.[1]

Contents of this chapter. California has proved to be an exceptionally fertile field for the growth of the junior college. McDowell found, in 1919, that over half of the public institutions in the country were within its borders. In this chapter, therefore, the development of this new institution in California is sketched from its earliest beginnings, through the periods of infancy, adolescence, and manhood; statistics of growth are given; the causes of its phenomenal advance in the state are presented; the principal features of the various laws are summarized; and the significance of the most recent legislation is discussed.

Introductory. In his discussion of the junior college movement in California,[2] Dr. W. J. Cooper happily divides the life of the junior college into three periods, as follows:

1. Birth and infancy (1907–17).
2. Adolescence (1917–21).
3. Early manhood (1921–29).[3]

[1] Cobb, Stanwood. *The New Leaven*, p. 325. John Day Company, New York, 1928.

[2] Cooper, W. J. "The Junior College Movement in California"; in *The Junior College in California*, Bulletin G–3, pp. 5–16. State Department of Education, Sacramento, California, 1928; also in *School Review*, vol. 36, pp. 409–22. (June, 1928.)

[3] Cooper says 1928, the date of publication of the monograph.

BIRTH AND INFANCY

The first junior college law. The first law permitting junior college work, although not then known by that title, was passed in California in 1907.[1] This law was worded as follows:[2]

> The board of trustees of any city, district, union, joint union or county high school may prescribe post-graduate courses of study for the graduates of such high school, or other high schools, which courses of study shall approximate the studies prescribed in the first two years of university courses. The board of trustees of any city, district, union, joint union, or county high school wherein the post-graduate courses of study are taught may charge tuition for pupils living without the boundaries of the district wherein such courses are taught.

Thus simply in two brief sentences the junior college idea, a tiny infant, was legally ushered into the world in California. No one could have had the faintest idea of the vigorous growth which lay ahead of it.

The origin of the law. The idea which thus eventuated in legislation in 1907 was the result of gradual growth over many years. The bill just quoted was introduced and sponsored in the legislature by Senator Anthony Caminetti, of Amador County, who had been long interested in progressive educational legislation. Twenty years earlier he had been responsible for the "Caminetti Act" authorizing the establishment of high schools in the state as upward extensions of the grammar school. The further upward extension of the high school in 1907 was thus but the logical sequel of the law which he had sponsored two decades before.

Influence of University of California and Stanford University. No positive evidences of the reasons that caused

[1] Erroneously given in the *First Biennial Report of the State Board of Education* (1913–14) as 1911 (p. 98); in Whitney's *Junior College in America*, as 1917 (p. 47); in *Educational Review* (vol. 49, p. 215, February, 1915), as 1911; and in *Proceedings of Fifth Annual Meeting of American Association of Junior Colleges* (p. 36), as 1910.

[2] Chapter 69, Statutes 1907, p. 88.

Senator Caminetti to introduce this bill at this time have come to light, but it may be surmised that the influence of the University of California and Stanford University were potent contributing factors. For fifteen years the University of California had been trying to reshape itself toward a separation of the upper and lower division. A leader in this movement at the state university and in the development of junior college sentiment through the state was Dr. Alexis F. Lange, Professor of English from 1890 to 1907, and subsequently Professor of Education and Dean of the School of Education until his death in 1924. For years he spoke, wrote, and urged the junior college idea in the state. He was ably seconded by the President of Stanford University, Dr. David Starr Jordan, to whom credit is due for the introduction and popularization of the term "junior college" in California. The influence of the University of California and of Dr. Jordan, in the period preceding and immediately following the law of 1907, were thus summarized by Dr. Lange in an address before the National Education Association at Oakland, in 1915:[1]

The University of California has been trying, since 1892, to reshape itself around two organizing ideas, "one and inseparable." One was and is that, for theoretical and practical considerations alike, the university proper should begin in the middle of the inherited four-year college scheme; the second was and is that the work of the first two years, as a matter of history and fact, is all of a piece with secondary education and should, therefore, be relegated as soon and as far as practicable to secondary schools.

This trend of thought and preaching and practice resulted *gradatim* in the junior certificate, to mark the distinction between university and secondary education, in the policy of placing all professional schools on a basis of not less than two years of non-

[1] Lange, A. F. "The Junior College with Special Reference to California"; in *Proceedings of the National Education Association* (Oakland, 1915), pp. 119–24; also in *Educational Administration and Supervision*, vol. 2, pp. 1–8 (January, 1916); also in *The Lange Book*, pp. 118–25. Trade Publishing Company, San Francisco, 1927.

professional college training, in making the studies of the last two years of the high school and the first two years of the college largely interchangeable, and, last but not least, in publicly exhibiting the requirements for the junior certificate in terms of unified six-year curricula. By 1908 the high school teachers of the state had become generally aware of the fact that what was to be known soon as the junior college idea had been put into practice at Berkeley and several of them were trying to utilize locally the precept and example of the State university.

But this propaganda would probably not have gathered momentum very fast without President Jordan's dynamic articles and addresses urging the amputation of freshman and sophomore classes to prevent university atrophy and urging the relegation of these classes to the high school. His advocacy of its upward extension made the public "sit up and take notice" and thought and prodded schoolmen into taking the initiative. What had been a Berkeley idea at the beginning had become a California idea, and the spectacle of Berkeley and Stanford climbing the Golden Stairs together, hand in hand, made its appeal with great persuasiveness. Moreover, while Berkeleyans had been in the habit of speaking of six-year high schools, Dr. Jordan gave general currency to the name junior college, and this proved much more potent in suggestible communities.

Influence of University of Michigan. The idea of separation of the lower division, however, was not original at the University of California, but may be traced directly to the influence of the University of Michigan. We have seen that the first official recognition of the distinction between early and later years of university work was found in the "University System" at the University of Michigan in 1883. Dr. Lange was a student at Michigan during the very years it was on trial there. It was soon abandoned, and apparently forgotten. The young student who received his master's degree in Michigan in 1885, came to California in 1890 as Assistant Professor of English. He says that the Michigan conception of functions at the junior level "was carried literally and bodily as a beneficently potent bacillus, so to speak, to the University of

California." In Michigan the idea had failed and been forgotten by all in authority, but the chance influence on one student, thus transferred to the California soil, gradually inoculated the youthful state university. With a feeble beginning in 1892, the separation was completed in 1903 for the cultural colleges when provision was made for giving the junior certificate at the end of the sophomore year. The same principle was extended to the technical colleges in 1909.

It was the growing consciousness of the significance of this transformation on the part of the high school teachers of the state, that is referred to by Dr. Lange in the quotation just given.

For a number of years prior to 1907 many of the stronger high schools in the state, situated at a distance from the two leading universities, had been giving so-called post-graduate work to students who could not go to the universities. The law of 1907 simply legalized this practice and endeavored to place it on a more strictly collegiate basis, where formerly most of it had consisted of courses not already taken in the regular high school course. In this sense it represented a gradual evolution rather than a sudden birth of a new type of institution. Thus encouraged by the universities from above, by the high schools from below, and with the legislature as a unifying factor, the brief law marking the legal genesis of the junior college came into being in California. It was merely permissive. There had been no demand for it on the part of any particular community. It lay unused on the statute books for three years before the first community took advantage of its provisions.

The first junior college, at Fresno. In the spring of 1910 C. L. McLane, then superintendent of schools at Fresno, in the heart of a rich agricultural district in the San Joaquin valley, began to investigate junior college possibilities. He sent out a circular letter explaining it to school patrons. Over two hundred replies were received — not a single one unfavorable to the idea. Plans for an organization took form rapidly as a result. On May 6, 1910, the Board of Education adopted a report, in part, as follows:

1. That the Board of Education authorize the establishment of a two years' post-graduate course.
2. That mathematics, English, Latin, modern languages, history, economics and technical work be the general courses offered for the first year.
3. That a competent person be secured as the dean or head, with such assistants as the attendance and courses desired may justify.

There is no institution of higher education within two hundred miles of Fresno where students may continue their studies beyond the regular high school courses. Many of our high school graduates are but seventeen or eighteen years of age and parents are frequently loath to send these young people so far from home. Many who desire to continue their studies cannot afford the expense necessary to college attendance where the items of room and board mean so much. Authorities in the University of California and Stanford University have been consulted in this matter and seem much interested in the project. Both have promised such assistance as they may be able to render in planning courses and securing instructors.

Attitude of the universities toward the Fresno experiment. Cordial encouragement was received from the two leading universities. President Jordan of Stanford University wrote:[1]

I am looking forward, as you know, to the time when the large high schools of the state, in conjunction with the small colleges, will relieve the two great universities from the expense and from the necessity of giving instruction of the first two university years.

Dr. A. F. Lange of the University of California said:[2]

Farsighted and progressive educators are agreed that the establishment of "junior colleges" denotes a necessary development in

[1] McLane, C. L. "The Junior College, or Upward Extension of the High School"; in *School Review*, vol. 21, pp. 166–67.

[2] *Ibid.*, p. 167.

the right direction. The state university has stood for the junior college plan for more than fifteen years, and its policy is to further the establishment of junior colleges in every way possible. The city of Fresno is to be congratulated on being the first city in the state to establish a junior college.

Beginnings at Fresno. Frederick Liddeke, a Harvard graduate of 1891, who had just finished a year of graduate work at Berlin in 1910, was secured as the first principal of the high school and junior college. Junior college work was begun in the autumn of 1910.[1] Three teachers were selected for the first year, devoting part time to high school work. One was given the title "Dean of the Junior College," probably used for the first time in the sense of chief administrative officer of a junior college.

Mr. McLane says:[2]

A separate faculty, with one of the number chosen as dean, was selected; it being the purpose to have a separate student body, and in every way possible endeavor to impress upon students and the public at large the fact that serious work of distinctive college standard is being undertaken.

The enrollment for the first year was at least fifteen.[3] A tuition charge of $4 per month was made to non-residents. In the first year, work was done in agriculture as well as in the ordinary freshman subjects. In September, 1911, the Fresno State Normal School was established, housed temporarily in the high school building, and operated in conjunction with the

[1] Erroneously given as 1911 in *Report of California Special Legislative Committee on Education*, p. 73 (1920); error repeated in *Education*, vol. 37, p. 83.

[2] McLane, C. L. *Op. cit.*, p. 166.

[3] There are various conflicting statements as to the opening enrollment in California's first junior college. Superintendent Cooper states that the enrollment the first year was fifteen. F. Liddeke, the principal, writing in 1914, says that it was twenty-eight. (*School Review*, vol. 10, p. 410.) Gray, in his master's thesis in 1915, said that it started with twenty students. (*School Review*, vol. 23, p. 466.)

junior college. By 1912–13, the junior college faculty had increased from three to eight.

Use of term "junior college" in California. Although it was ten years later that the phrase "junior college" first occurred in California legislation, it is interesting to note that this term was associated with Fresno from the very beginning. In a letter to the high school principals and students in the vicinity of Fresno in May, 1910, announcing plans for instituting the new work in the autumn, it was spoken of as a "two-year" post-graduate or "junior college" course, and on July 15, 1910, there appeared an article in the now long-defunct *California Weekly*, entitled "The Fresno Junior College," in which Superintendent McLane said, in his opening sentence:[1]

> The above title may appear rather high-sounding; yet when one contemplates the purpose of the act of the legislature of 1907 authorizing the establishment of post-graduate high school courses "which shall approximate the studies prescribed for the first two years of university courses," the title, "junior college" may not seem inappropriate.

Other communities follow Fresno's lead. While the junior college idea was slow in getting a start on California soil, after Fresno set the example, it nevertheless grew rapidly. Mr. A. C. Olney, who had been principal of the Fresno High School in 1909–10, had made the detailed plans in conjunction with Mr. McLane for starting the work at Fresno in the autumn of 1910. Instead, however, he accepted a position as principal of the high school at Santa Barbara, carrying with him the junior college "bacillus." He immediately began to organize a junior college department which began there in the autumn of 1911, the second one in the state. The next two were established at Hollywood and Los Angeles, in 1911–12. In the autumn of 1913, three others began work at Bakersfield

[1] McLane, C. L. "The Fresno Junior College"; in *California Weekly*, vol. 2, p. 539. (July 15, 1910.)

(Kern County), Fullerton, and Long Beach. The next year there were three more, San Diego, Sacramento, and Placer, followed in 1915 by Santa Ana and Citrus (at Azusa), and in 1916 by five others. The enrollment in them exceeded 1100 students. Beside the sixteen which were in existence when the legislature of 1917 met, a number of others had offered post-graduate or junior college work, including Yreka, and Santa Monica.

ADOLESCENCE OF THE JUNIOR COLLEGE

Weakness of the 1907 law. There were two serious weaknesses in the 1907 law, however — lack of standards, and inadequate support. As a result several high schools reported "junior college departments" with enrollments of one, two, or three students. The junior college work had been maintained entirely at local district expense. At the 1909 session of the legislature a bill was passed providing substantial state aid for such schools as desired to take advantage of junior colleges, but the governor vetoed it on grounds of economy. When the legislature of 1917 met there were at least sixteen high schools in the state, definitely interested in promoting legislation to provide state and county funds for them. The question now became, should such aid be given without more definite standards for organization? If the work were made financially more attractive there would doubtless be many more high schools, regardless of need, standards, or ability, which would begin such work. Action was also stimulated by an unfavorable ruling of the attorney-general in 1915.

An important statement of junior college principles. The significance of these various elements is admirably summarized by Will C. Wood, commissioner of secondary schools, in his report for September, 1916. He said in part:[1]

[1] Wood, Will C. "The Junior College"; in *Second Biennial Report of the State Board of Education of California*, pp. 163–64. Sacramento, California, 1916.

The law under which junior college departments have been organized was approved in 1907. This law is somewhat vague and indefinite, and there is need for amendment at the approaching session of the legislature.... It will be observed that no specific provision for maintenance is made in the law. Practically all the districts which have established post-graduate courses have raised the expense of maintenance by district taxation. In 1915, the Attorney General gave an opinion that students enrolled in such courses cannot be counted in making apportionments out of the state high school fund.... The time has arrived when the graduate or junior college department should be placed on a more satisfactory financial basis. A more comprehensive law concerning the organization of post-graduate courses should be placed upon the statute books and this law should contain the provision that the average daily attendance of students enrolled in such courses shall be counted in estimating the amount of state and county high school revenues. Apportionments should be made on account of attendance on post-graduate courses in the same manner as apportionments are made on account of attendance on regular high school courses. Provision should also be made that wherever students residing in a county where junior college privileges are not provided attend post-graduate courses maintained in a school of an adjoining county, the attendance of such pupils shall be reported to the county superintendent of schools of the county in which such students reside, and the county superintendent shall include in the estimate of county high school fund required an amount computed at $60 for each student so attending. This amount should be transferred to the credit of the school in which the students are enrolled. If such provision is made, the clause relating to the payment of tuition should be stricken out. *The junior college is part of our public school system and tuition therein should be free.*[1]

In making provision for state and county contributions to the support of post-graduate or junior college courses, we should guard against the organization of such courses in districts which cannot adequately support them. The first duty of a community in educational affairs is to provide adequately for the support of its elementary schools. Its next duty is to provide adequately for the support of its high school. Until the elementary and high schools are adequately provided for, a post-graduate or junior college course

[1] Italics are not in the original.

should not be established. The establishment of weak junior college departments will hinder the development of the junior college movement and will work injury to the elementary and high schools. After investigation, the Commissioner recommends that the law provide that a post-graduate course shall not be established in any high school district having an assessed valuation, exclusive of operative property, of less than $7,500,000. It should also provide that no post-graduate course shall be established unless at least fifteen qualified students apply therefor. The law should contain a provision that whenever the average daily attendance in the post-graduate department for any school year is less than ten, the post-graduate department shall be suspended and shall not be reëstablished until at least fifteen post-graduate students petition for such reëstablishment.

This statement is remarkable for its early enunciation of such fundamentally sound educational principles regarding the relation of elementary schools, secondary schools, high schools, and junior colleges — freedom of tuition, and desirable types of safeguards to secure efficient institutions. Not all these recommendations were enacted into law in 1917, but the germs of much of the legislation of 1921 may be found in them.

With this type of encouragement from the state department, and with the demand of so many high schools for more adequate legislation, the legislature in 1917, under the leadership of Senator Ballard, passed the Ballard Act,[1] embodying some of the recommendations of Mr. Wood. It provided for state and county support on the same basis as that for high school students, and restricted organization of junior college courses to districts with a valuation of $3,000,000, a much lower limit than recommended. The provisions of this act are given more in detail in Table 9, pages 117–19.

Further organization of junior colleges. In the next four years, eleven new junior college departments were organized

[1] Known subsequently as Section 1750b of the Political Code. Erroneously referred to several times as law of 1915 by W. C. Wood, in *Proceedings of the Fifth Annual Meeting of the American Association of Junior Colleges*, pp. 63–64.

under the provisions of this law. In the same period a half dozen of those existing in 1917 suspended operations. Three of these were in or near Los Angeles, where their places were taken by the establishment of the Southern Branch of the University of California at Los Angeles, which was authorized in 1919, and at first offered only junior college work. In three others, the attendance was too small to justify continuation. The war depleted enrollments and increased costs, with resultant mortality to some of the weaker institutions. At the close of this four-year period of adolescence there were eighteen junior college departments of high schools in the state, with an enrollment of approximately 1500, in addition to the University of California branch at Los Angeles. This was a net increase of only two institutions over the 1917 situation.

Inadequate support. Another vital fact was standing out more and more clearly — a financial one. Junior college work, of standard collegiate grade, was much more expensive than high school work, and the units in many cases were too small. Further legislation was needed before the junior college in California was to attain the full stature of vigorous manhood. Nevertheless the law of 1917 still remains on the statute books, and 18 institutions were existing under it in 1930. F. W. Thomas, in his doctor's dissertation, in 1926, thus summarized the junior college development in the state up to the close of the "period of adolescence": [1]

After the early wave of enthusiasm which was responsible for the rapid spread of these organizations,... there was a period in which little headway was made. High school graduates were not inclined to regard them as "real colleges," and many preferred to wait in the hope of attending a larger institution rather than become identified with the unappreciated junior college which seemed to them a mere appendage on the high school, even lacking the high school life and attractiveness. The Fresno junior college, for example, in 1919,

[1] Thomas, F. W. *A Study of Functions of the Public Junior College and the Extent of Their Realization in California*, p. 77. Stanford University, 1926.

almost ten years after its establishment, enrolled only 129 of the more than 600 high school pupils who had been graduated in the adjacent community during the preceding two years. By the year 1920, almost half of the junior colleges organized prior to that time, had been discontinued. Up to 1925 there were in all 22 such discontinuations.... The year 1921 seems to mark the turning point in the struggle of the junior colleges for general acceptance and prestige in their own communities.

MANHOOD OF THE JUNIOR COLLEGE

Work of the Legislative Committee on Education of 1919. The legislature of 1919 provided for a special Legislative Committee on Education, of which Senator H. C. Jones was chairman. This committee made a careful study of the entire educational organization and presented a noteworthy report of ninety-six pages, which was the basis of several pieces of constructive educational legislation in 1921. The University of California had reorganized on a basis of upper division and lower division, with the award of the junior certificate at the close of the lower division, and in 1920 Stanford had adopted a similar division of undergraduate work. The committee made a careful study of the whole trend in higher education in the state and in the country, and recommended the development of junior colleges in connection with each of the state normal schools, as well as the development of a series of supplemental junior colleges. These recommendations were stimulated in large part by the overcrowded conditions at the state university and the failure of a constitutional amendment which had proposed as a relief a large tax for additional facilities and development at the university. Their report, written for the Committee by Ellwood P. Cubberley, Dean of the School of Education at Stanford University, states:[1]

By developing the junior colleges, as is recommended in this report, a large and expensive and largely unsatisfactory develop-

[1] *Report of the Special Legislative Committee on Education*, p. 78. Sacramento, 1920.

ment in buildings and teaching staff at Berkeley can be avoided, and Lower Division education in this state can at the same time be carried to different parts of the state and to more young people by the development of a number of smaller and less expensive units. This Committee therefore recommends that the Legislature, at the coming session, decide this question of state educational policy, that the lines of future development may be determined and educational and financial waste be avoided.

The report recommended that the existing law of 1917 be amended to require an assessed valuation of at least $10,000,000, a population of 15,000 in the district, state aid to the extent of $100 per student in average daily attendance the previous year, and provisions for accreditation, courses of study, etc. The figure of $100 was based upon an assumed cost of $250 for freshman and sophomore instruction as determined at the University of Washington, with the idea that $150 might properly be raised locally.

The district law of 1921. The substance of these recommendations was embodied in the district junior college law of 1921,[1] the most foresighted and influential piece of constructive junior college legislation ever passed in the state, placing the junior college for a number of years on a stable foundation, financially and educationally. It provided for junior college districts of three types: (1) district, coterminous with a high school district, (2) union, composed of two or more contiguous high school districts, and (3) county, composed of all territory in a county not already in a high school district. No district could be organized until it had an assessed valuation of $10,000,000 and an average daily high school attendance of 400 during the previous year. Establishment was contingent upon a special vote of the people of the proposed district, after approval by the state board of education. State aid was provided to the extent of $2000 per year for each junior college,

[1] Act 1477, Deering.

and $100 per student in average daily attendance the previous year. Various other administrative procedures were provided in this comprehensive bill, other details of which are shown in Table 9. Under the wise encouragement of this legislation the development of the junior college has gone forward by leaps and bounds.

District junior colleges organized. The first institution to take advantage of the new law was the Modesto Junior College, which was organized *de novo*, entirely independent of high school connections, in October, 1921. It was followed a few weeks later by Riverside, which changed over from the high school departmental organization under which it had existed since 1917. In 1922, San Mateo organized as a new junior college district, and four other institutions changed over from the high school type, the oldest of which, Fullerton, had existed since 1913.[1] In 1926, the first two union junior college districts were organized, the Marin Junior College at Kentfield in Northern California, and the San Bernardino Valley Junior College at San Bernardino in the southern part of the state. The first county junior college, and the only one to date (1930), was organized at Marysville in Yuba County, in 1928, after a year's previous existence under the 1917 law. Up to 1930, sixteen district junior colleges had been organized, seven of them *de novo*, and nine by transformation from the high school departmental type. Eighteen are of the high school departmental type, one is a state institution and

[1] The dates of approval by the State Board of petitions for establishment of the first eight district junior colleges are as follows:

Modesto	September 22, 1921
Riverside	September 30, 1921
Sacramento	November 14, 1921
Fullerton	January 12, 1922
Santa Ana	January 12, 1922
Chaffey	February 17, 1922
San Mateo	March 9, 1922
Pasadena	January 8, 1924

fifteen are private, bringing the total number in 1930 up to fifty.[1]

State teachers' college type. The 1921 law contained a provision stating that the governing board of any junior college, or any junior college department of a high school, might contract with a teachers' college for the maintenance of junior college courses of instruction. Under this provision junior college work at once was instituted in six of the seven state teachers' colleges — all but San Francisco. In the majority of cases this did not seem to work well. It was abandoned by Arcata in 1926, after a five-year trial, and by San Diego and Chico in 1927, when the law authorizing such arrangement was repealed. Santa Barbara continued for another year under special local arrangement before giving up this form of organization. At San José, however, the people proceeded to form a junior college district under the provisions of the law, but arranged with the local state teachers' college for the use of buildings and facilities, and for a common administration of the two institutions. This has been a very satisfactory arrangement, and seems to be mutually advantageous to both junior college and teachers' college divisions. In practice, the differentiation between the two institutions is minimized and to all intents and purposes it is administered as a single institution, although the support comes from different sources. At Fresno, the first junior college in the state, arrangement was made in 1921, with the adoption of the new law, for the local teachers' college to handle the junior college work on contract. With the abolition of this provision of the law, in 1927, a similar arrangement was continued, the junior college department of the high school paying the salaries of sufficient instructors in the Fresno State Teachers' College to

[1] The tables in Chapter II show 49 junior colleges in the state in 1929–30. The California School of Mechanical Arts in San Francisco announced the opening of a junior college department in the autumn of 1930.

give instruction to the "non-recommended" junior college students attending it. Legally, then, only two of the seven state teachers' colleges now administer junior colleges as a part of themselves. However, with the strengthening of the teachers' college curricula, much of the professional work has been placed in the last two years or upper division, since four years of work are now required even for elementary school credentials, and much of the lower division work is devoted to subject matter courses in language, literature, science, history, and mathematics. These courses can be taken also by students who are not preparing to become teachers. Practically, therefore, these teachers' colleges are still functioning to a considerable extent as junior colleges for the localities in which they are found, and students in them are frequently referred to locally, though unofficially, as "junior college" students. In all cases except Fresno and San José they are entirely state supported and state controlled, and thus are in effect, although not legally, state junior colleges.

Affiliation with state university. Provision for safeguarding the standards of the newly authorized independent institutions was contemplated in the law of 1921 by authorizing affiliation of such institutions with the University of California. The law provided that "the courses in such junior college whose purpose is to prepare for advanced university standing shall be visited, inspected, and accredited by said university, and that the qualifications of teachers in such courses shall be recommended by said university." Under the provisions of this act in the first year or two, five junior college departments of state teachers' colleges and three junior college departments of high schools, affiliated with the university. For a year or two the state university maintained a special official junior college coördinator, in addition to inspection by many individual faculty members. The arrangement was only moderately satisfactory; there was more or less friction and misunderstanding, and gradually it was allowed to fall into disuse. In 1925, there were only four affiliated institutions. As the junior colleges proved themselves to be dependable institutions with proper collegiate standards, the possible desirability for university domination to maintain standards vanished, if, indeed, it ever existed. All that could have been accomplished by law was better accomplished by friendly advice and coöperation. Dean Kemp, of the School of Education of the University of California, said, in 1924:[1]

> The university has come to realize the permanency of the junior college as an independent unit of our public school system. The question now arises as to the need of indefinitely prolonging the policy of affiliation. I believe I am safe in saying that affiliation *is not* regarded as a permanent policy by the university.

Legislation of 1927. In 1927, several changes were made in the 1921 basic law. One of these provided for joint county junior college districts, of two or more adjacent counties, and for joint union districts composed of high school districts located in different counties. No institutions of either type have yet been organized. The provision for contractual relationship with state teachers' colleges was repealed at this time.

State junior college. Only a single "state" junior college exists, the junior college division of which was established not by legislation, but by the State Board. In 1927, the State Board of Education authorized the addition of a junior college department of the California Polytechnic Institute, located at San Luis Obispo. The first year there were seventy-seven students, with small increases each year since. Only a few of the students take the college preparatory course. Most of

[1] Kemp, W. W. "The Junior College Movement in California"; in *Eighth Yearbook of the National Association of Secondary School Principals*, p. 94. Berwyn, Illinois, 1924.

them are taking semi-professional vocational courses of collegiate grade, largely in electricity and aeronautics.

Need of surveys. In the spring of 1928 Dr. Leonard V. Koos, assisted by Dr. F. J. Weersing, made a preliminary survey of secondary education in the state, at the request of the State Department of Education. They made a careful analysis of many phases of the junior college situation, and recommended further extensive investigations of district organization, curriculum, finance, and other phases of the entire junior college independently and in its relation to the larger program of secondary education in the state. As a result of this survey, a lay commission of nine members was appointed by the governor to study the educational problems of the state. The commission early expressed itself as dissatisfied with the existing insecure basis of state aid to junior colleges. It was to submit its report early in 1931.

Private junior colleges. Private junior colleges have played a very minor rôle in the development of the movement as a whole in California. Los Angeles Pacific College, under the auspices of the Free Methodist Church, organized in 1904, seems to have given its first junior college work in 1911, only a year after the organization of the public work at Fresno. If others were organized prior to 1918 they have not survived. Only five of the fifteen existing in 1930 had given junior college work for more than three years. The total enrollment in 1929–30 was slightly over 500, less than that in any one of ten public district colleges. The total number of graduates in 1929 was only 67. The principal junior colleges of the private type are Holmby (1924) and Cumnock (1927) at Los Angeles, both for women; and Menlo Junior College (1927), for men. The last, under the unofficial influence of Stanford University, is experimenting with a six-four-four type of organization.

General evaluation in 1928. Writing in 1928, Will C. Wood, former State Superintendent of Public Instruction, who has

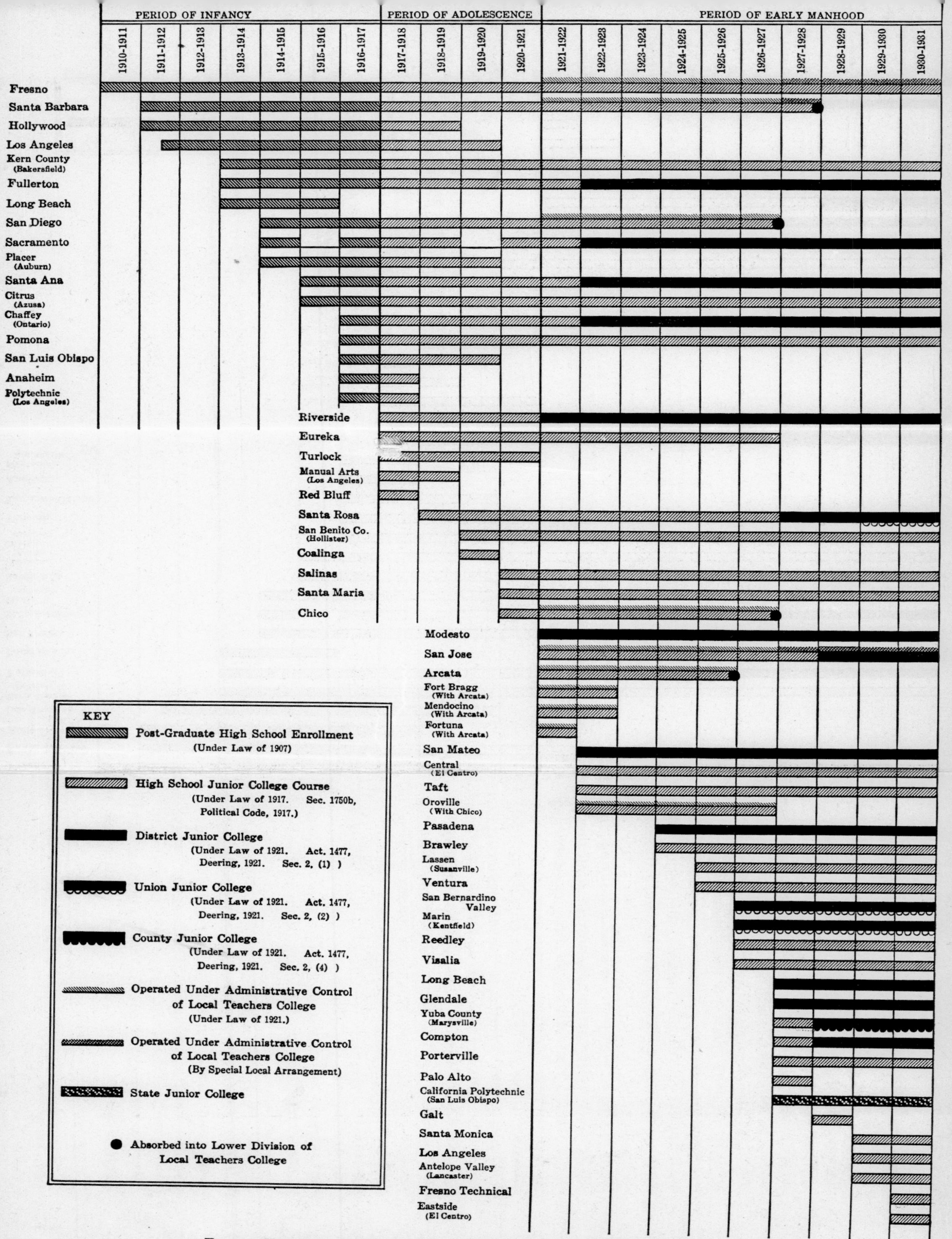

FIG. 14. HISTORICAL CHART OF THE PUBLIC JUNIOR COLLEGES OF CALIFORNIA

had more to do with the development of the junior college in California than any other state official, said:[1]

> The junior college is with us. In fact, it is so much with us here in California that discussion of its desirability is simply discussion *ex post facto*.... It would require a public upheaval to uproot any established junior college in the state.... The original intent of the junior college laws, all of which I drafted, was that the state board of education should work out a regional plan for junior college development, allowing one junior college for each of about fifteen regions into which the state was to be divided. It was thought that this would assure a limited number of strong institutions, each enrolling a thousand or more students. However, the state board, in approving applications, soon got away from the regional idea. The development since 1921 indicates that the state is now committed to approve the establishment of a junior college in each community that wants the institution, provided the community has students enough to justify it, wealth enough to support it, and a will strong enough to have it. I am inclined to the belief that the plan that developed after the passage of the law is better than the original plan.

STATISTICS

Increase in number and enrollment. Certain features of the growth of the junior college in California are summarized in Table 8 and in Figure 14. Figure 14 shows the period of existence of each public junior college in the state, under the various forms of organization, during the three periods. Table 8, and Figure 15 based upon it, emphasize the growth in enrollment in these junior colleges, both public and private. There was a gradual rise in number of students during the period of infancy, a slump during the period of adolescence due to the World War and the establishment of the Southern Branch of the State University at Los Angeles, and then, following the passage of the noteworthy law of 1921, a remarkable increase of total enrollment from year to year. In the

[1] Wood, W. C. "The Junior College Justifies Itself"; in *Woman's City Club Magazine*, pp. 13–14. San Francisco, August, 1928.

TABLE 8. NUMBER AND ENROLLMENT, CALIFORNIA JUNIOR COLLEGES, 1910–11 TO 1929–30

Year	Total		High School		District		Private		State	
	No.	Enrollment	No.	Enrollment	No.	Enrollment	No.	Enrollment	No.	Enrollment
1910–11....	**1**	**15**	1	15						
1911–12....	**5**	**70**	4	70			1			
1912–13....	**5**	**247**	4	247			1			
1913–14....	**8**	**509**	7	509			1			
1914–15....	**11**	**732**	10	732			1			
1915–16....	**13**	**1,104**	12	1,104			1			
1916–17....	**17**	**1,259**	16	1,259			1			
1917–18....	**22**	**1,561**	21	1,561			1			
1918–19....	**20**	**1,255**	18	1,255			2			
1919–20....	**20**	**1,096**	17	2,096			3			
1920–21....	**21**	**1,442**	14	1,442			4			
1921–22....	**27**	**2,259**	21	2,013	2	246	4			
1922–23....	**29**	**2,888**	18	1,416	7	1,427	4	45		
1923–24....	**28**	**4,054**	17	1,618	7	2,391	4	45		
1924–25....	**31**	**5,433**	18	2,023	8	3,323	5	87		
1925–26....	**33**	**5,865**	20	2,293	8	3,479	5	93		
1926–27....	**36**	**8,178**	21	2,488	10	5,585	5	105		
1927–28....	**44**	**11,038**	20	2,729	13	7,981	10	251	1	77
1928–29....	**46**	**14,080**	16	1,777	16	11,716	13	487	1	100 *
1929–30....	**49**	**21,213**	18	4,404	16	16,157	14	531	1	121

* Estimated.

last decade the number of junior colleges in existence has more than doubled, while the enrollment in them has increased no less than thirteen-fold.[1] For the five latest years for which statistics are available the increase has been over three thousand per year. A glance at Figure 15 shows that this phenomenal increase has been almost exclusively in the district junior college, where the increase in average daily attendance during the past seven years has averaged 40 per cent each year. "During the past two years," said Walter Morgan, chief of the State Bureau of Research and Statistics, at the Atlantic City

[1] While the increase in enrollment has been phenomenal, it cannot justify the enthusiasm shown by the *American Educational Digest*, which says: "California has 32 junior colleges... with a total registration of sixty thousand students"! (Vol. 47, p. 172, December, 1927.)

meeting of the National Education Association in 1930, "the increase was 52 per cent and 64 per cent. Similar increases are expected during the next few years. A continuance of the present policy of junior college expansion and of stressing the

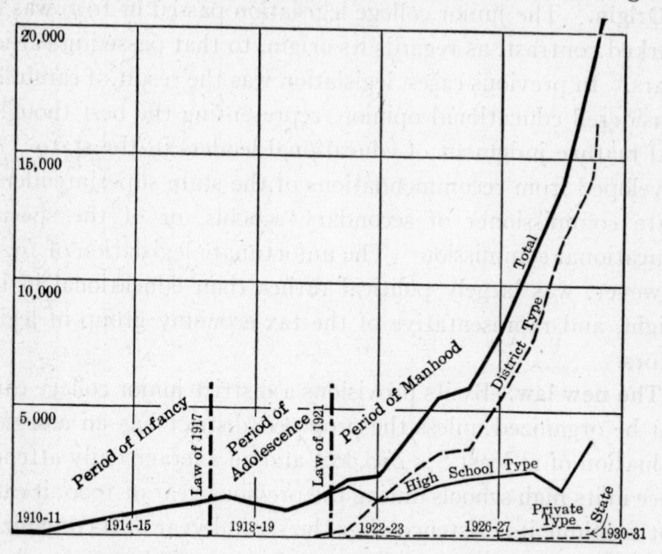

FIG. 15. ENROLLMENT IN CALIFORNIA JUNIOR COLLEGES, 1910–30

secondary school character of the junior college may possibly result, for a time at least, in an accelerated rate of increase in these institutions." Certainly the rapid upward climb of the curve shows little or no signs of diminution either in rate or amount as yet. It cannot rise indefinitely, but there seems to be little reason to suppose that it will not continue to rise for some time. Figure 15 shows vividly that the private junior colleges and the single state institution play only a minor rôle in determining total enrollment. The marked rise in the high school type for the last year shown is due very largely to the new Los Angeles Junior College, organized as a temporary expedient in this form, but essentially of the district type, and change to the district form of organization was voted by the people of Los Angeles at a special election in March, 1931.

REACTIONARY LEGISLATION OF 1929

Origin. The junior college legislation passed in 1929 was in marked contrast, as regards its origin, to that passed in earlier years. In previous cases, legislation was the result of carefully considered educational opinion, representing the best thought and mature judgment of educational leaders in the state. It developed from recommendations of the state superintendent, state commissioner of secondary schools, or of the special educational commission. The unfortunate legislation of 1929, however, was largely political rather than educational in its origin, and representative of the tax-economy group of legislators.

The new law. By its provisions a district junior college cannot be organized unless the proposed district has an assessed valuation of at least $25,000,000, and an average daily attendance in its high schools during the previous year of 1000; it cannot continue its existence after the second year of its organization unless its average daily attendance exceeds two hundred students.

Development under the old law. It has been under the stimulating encouragement of the law of 1921 that the most significant development of junior colleges in California has taken place. In the short period since 1921, nine of the old high school departments have reorganized as junior college districts, and seven new institutions have organized without any previous high school connections. By 1930, sixteen vigorous and flourishing district junior colleges were rendering noteworthy educational service to their communities, and several of them were known nationally. Meanwhile many of the weak, struggling junior college departments of high schools have perished of malnutrition, or have been absorbed by other institutions or replaced by them. Thus, of forty-six departmental junior colleges which have come into existence since 1910 in California, only sixteen survive today in that form of organization. Several of these have been planning to change to the district type in the near future, some through the annexation of adjacent territory necessary to meet the $10,000,000 requirement.

Significance of the district junior college. The vigorous development and stimulating leadership of the junior college movement in the state has come from the district institutions. It is significant that not a single one established on this basis has ever been discontinued. All have been growing rapidly. The number and enrollment of district junior colleges each year since 1921 have already been shown in Table 8. The contrast between the two types of institutions is strikingly shown in the following table of average daily attendance per institution of the two types:

Year	District Type	High School Type
1921-22	123	96
1922-23	204	79
1923-24	342	95
1924-25	415	112
1925-26	435	115
1926-27	558	118
1927-28	614	130
1928-29	732	111

The high school type, closely connected with the high school, on the whole has remained small, local, unimportant. The really efficient institution, educationally and financially, demands a very much larger attendance than one hundred.

Effect of the new legislation. The law of 1917, which allowed high schools to serve their communities by creating junior college departments, was very useful at the time. It was an important step in the evolution of a significant educational experiment, but it has long since served its purpose, and should have been repealed in 1921 when the new law was enacted, as was specifically recommended by the legislative committee at that time. Educational leaders in the state have felt that everything possible should be done to discourage the less efficient high school departments, and to encourage the development of the district type of institution. It is highly questionable whether the 1929 legislation will have this result. By raising the standards, both as regards assessed valuation and attendance, to two and one half times their previous amounts, it becomes difficult if not impossible for many meritorious localities to organize such institutions. This is strikingly shown by the fact that if this law had been in existence previously, seven of the sixteen district junior colleges in the state in 1929 could not have been organized. These seven had assessed valuations varying from $13,000,000 to $22,000,000, averaging $19,000,000. The average enrollment of the six existing in 1927–28 was 626;[1] average number of graduates, 64. Both figures are larger than corresponding *averages* for *all* district junior colleges in the state! This is the type of vigorous, useful, community junior college which will be prevented from further organization under the provisions of the new law.

Several junior college departments of high schools which had been planning reorganization on the district basis found it impossible to do so. Another high school department, although it had an assessed valuation of over $65,000,000, had a high school enrollment of less than 1000 and so could not qualify under the terms of the new law. One isolated county in the extreme northern part of the state, 250 miles from another district junior college and over 300 miles from the state university, had an assessed valuation of $22,000,000. Some

[1] The seventh, newly established, Yuba County, had 109.

of its people were agitating a county junior college for its youth so far distant from higher educational advantages, but it became impossible to organize it under the new law. The California requirements were already the highest in the country. It seems, therefore, a sad blow at educational progress in the junior college field to have such a statute enacted. While it might be argued that it will force consolidation and stronger regional junior colleges, it seems more likely that it will force the organization of many more small, inefficient junior college departments of high schools — just the type that should be discouraged.

Explanation of the new legislation. The explanation of this new legislation is to be found in terms of financial short-sightedness and expediency, not of educational vision and statesmanship. The measure was not initiated by educators or by the State Department of Education, but by the State Department of Finance. The state support of junior colleges comes from leases on federal oil and mineral lands. Up to 1927–28, these were more than sufficient each year to meet the demands made upon them by junior colleges, but with the increase in attendance, in that year, the annual federal fund was insufficient, and only $96 was actually received by the junior colleges for each student in average daily attendance, instead of the $100 provided by law. To prevent the recurrence of this situation, a law was introduced in the 1929 legislature providing that the necessary difference between money from federal sources and $100 per student should hereafter be made up from the state treasury, up to a maximum of $30. This was an excellent measure, and had the support of educational forces.

Late in the session, however, the new provisions changing the standards and requirements for organization of junior college districts, sponsored by the State Department of Finance, were added to this bill as amendments, and the entire bill was rushed through in the jam of final legislation before adjournment of the legislature. It is doubtful whether many of the educators of the state knew what was happening or appreciated its significance. In view of these facts another change in requirements is highly significant. The 1921 law provided for an election to determine the organization of a junior college district, only after a petition for it signed by 500 voters had been approved by the *State Board of Education.* The 1929 law required that this petition must have the approval not only of the State Board of Education, but also of *the State Department of Finance!* It is not difficult to see the dangerous possibilities inherent in this provision. It would be perfectly easy to throttle the organization of any more district junior colleges, regardless of local need or demand for them.

Prospects of further changes. Even more vicious than prevention by unnecessarily high requirements was the provision for suspension. Many reasons, temporary in character, such for example as a world war, might temporarily reduce the average daily attendance below two hundred, and no option but suspension and sale of property would remain. Again, an isolated county might be able to maintain an average daily attendance of 190, far greater than in half the junior colleges of the country, but would not dare risk going to the expense of organizing and equipping an institution.

As soon as the educational forces of the state began to understand the significance of the new legislation, a strong sentiment developed for a change. Various proposals were made by different groups and committees, and modifying legislation of some sort with reference to the organization of junior colleges was certain to be brought up before the 1931 legislature. The requirements as set up were arbitrary, and not the result of any careful study of real requirements. It is doubtful whether satisfactory and fair minimum requirements can be set up which will be just in all conditions and localities. A proposal that has much merit has been made that after certain minimum requirements have been met, the organization of a junior college district shall be contingent upon a careful scientific survey under the auspices of the State Department of Education, with subsequent approval of its findings by the State Board of Education. If such a survey can be conducted on a high educational plane, and not be determined by political expediency, it will have real value. The 1929 legislation, however, is not consistent with the period of manhood. It probably would be too strong to characterize it as marking the beginning of an age of senility, but at any rate it represents an unfortunate period of backsetting illness in the life of this vigorous California product.

SUMMARY OF LEGISLATION

Need for clear distinctions. Unfortunately there have been many misstatements and much confusion regarding the organization of the various public junior colleges in California, and their status at different times. Much publicity has been given to the provisions of the District Law of 1921, and many writers, not only in other parts of the country, but even in California, have confused the two types, or have tacitly or expressly assumed that all existing ones came under the provision of this one law. It is hoped that the presentation of their status in Figure 14, the map on page 116 (Figure 16), and the tabulation of the chief features of the various laws as given in Table 9 (pages 118–20) will serve to clarify the situation.

A dual system of junior colleges. It must be borne in mind that California has today, and has had for the past decade, a dual system of public junior colleges, entirely different in mode of organization, administration, support, and official status. The law of 1907 was superseded by the law of 1917, which is still in existence and over half the public junior colleges in the state are administered under it. The law of 1921 expressly stated that it did not affect in any way the law of 1917. The law of 1921 also holds today, as modified by legislation of 1927 and 1929, and under it exist the other group of public junior colleges. The institutions of one group are, technically, merely additional courses of high schools; those of the other are independent self-contained collegiate institutions. Most students of California conditions agree that it was unfortunate that the legislature saw fit, against the express recommendation

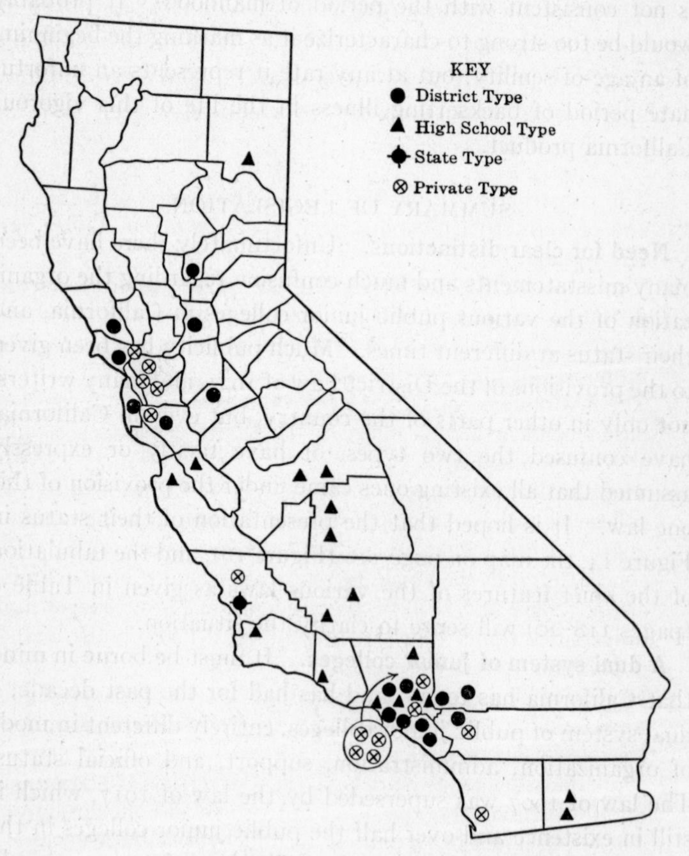

FIG. 16. LOCATION OF JUNIOR COLLEGES IN CALIFORNIA, 1930

of the Legislative Commission of 1919–20, to retain the earlier law and the weaker departmental type of college, when the district type of institution was authorized.

THE GROWTH OF CALIFORNIA JUNIOR COLLEGES

The vigorous growth of the junior college in the state has been exhibited in many ways. California has less than 5 per cent of the population of the United States, but she has over 11 per cent of the junior colleges in the country; and over 20 per cent of the junior college students. Why this phenomenal growth of the junior college in the state? The following may be thought of as important factors which have been more or less unique to California:

1. The constructive leadership of the University of California and of Stanford University, and especially of Dr. Lange and Dr. Jordan.
2. The constructive leadership of the state superintendents of public instruction and of their subordinates in the state department, especially in the formation of statesmanlike proposals for improved legislation.
3. The favorable constructive legislation, especially in formation of independent junior college districts with generous state aid and encouragement.
4. The size of the state, combined with the concentration of college and university opportunities in two areas, 400 miles apart. Until rather recent years, these opportunities were concentrated in the single region in the vicinity of San Francisco. Since the bulk of the students in most colleges and universities come from a relatively small local radius, many population centers were entirely unserved.
5. Favorable climate and an extensive system of paved highways, making daily transportation over considerable distances feasible for many students.
6. The admission requirements of the University of California, Stanford University, and other institutions of high standards. The requirement of 15 units of recommending grade (A or B) automatically disqualifies from half to two thirds of all high

Table 9. Summary of Chief California Junior College Laws

Type of Junior College	Junior College Departments of High Schools		Independent Junior College Districts	
Date of Legislation	1907	1917	1921 and 1927 (1921 except as indicated)	1929
Extent and status.	Very brief. Two sentences, eight lines. Repealed by law of 1917.	Fifty-six lines. Still in force.	Seventeen pages. Still in force, except as modified by 1929 legislation.	Still in force, supplementing laws of 1921 and 1927.
Type of work provided for.	"Post-graduate courses of study for high school graduates."	"Junior college courses of study including not more than two years of work."	"Junior college courses of study, including not more than two years of work."	
Course of study.	Shall "approximate the studies prescribed in first two years of university courses."	May include "junior certificate courses of University of California, and mechanical and industrial arts, household economy, agriculture, civic education, and commerce," subject to approval of State Board of Education.	May provide "instruction to prepare for higher institutions; also agricultural, civic, industrial, commercial, home-making, and other courses."	
Type of district.	(Part of the high school district.)	(Part of the high school district.)	District (coterminous with high school district). Union (two or more high school districts). County. Joint union 1927 (two or more high school districts in different counties). Joint county 1927 (two or more counties).	
Control.	(High school board.)	(High school board.)	Junior college board with same membership as high school board in District type. Special junior college board of five members in all other types.	

TABLE 9 (*continued*)

Type of Junior College	Junior College Departments of High Schools		Independent Junior College Districts	
Date of Legislation	1907	1917	1921 and 1927 (1921 except as indicated)	1929
Requirements for organization.	Any high school district.	High school district with assessed valuation of $3,000,000.	Assessed valuation of $10,000,000. High school average daily attendance of 400 in previous year.	Assessed valuation of $25,000,000. High school average daily attendance of 1000 in previous year. (For county districts, 500.)
Method of organization.	Vote of board of high school district.	Vote of board of high school district.	Petition by 500 voters, approval of State Board of Education, vote of electors of district, and petition of majority of high school board in each high school district.	Same as law of 1921, with addition of approval by the State Department of Finance.
Requirement for suspension.	None.	None.	If average daily attendance is not over 75 after second year.	If average daily attendance is not over 200 after second year.
Support.	(Local taxation implied.) May charge tuition for non-resident students.	On same basis as high school students ($30 per student in average daily attendance from state; $60 from the county, plus local taxation).	(1) From state; (from funds from federal oil and mineral lands). $2000 per year, and $100 per student in average daily attendance if similar amount raised by local taxation. (2) Net cost from county of residence for non-resident students. (3) Local district tax.	(1) If federal funds are insufficient, deficit up to $30 per student to be made up from state treasury, (2) in addition to net cost, $65 per student for use of buildings and equipment for non-resident students.
Admission requirements.	Not stated.	High school graduation *or* over 21 years of age with recommendation of principal of junior college. (Modified in 1929.)	High school graduation *or* over 18 years of age with recommendation of principal of junior college.	Modified law of 1917 to 18 years instead of 21 years for special students.
Graduation requirements.	Not mentioned.	Sixty semester hours.	Sixty semester hours.	

TABLE 9. (*continued*)

TYPE OF JUNIOR COLLEGE	JUNIOR COLLEGE DEPARTMENTS OF HIGH SCHOOLS		INDEPENDENT JUNIOR COLLEGE DISTRICTS	
Date of Legislation	1907	1917	1921 and 1927 (1921 except as indicated)	1929
Provisions for annexation of additional territory.			Initiative with territory to be annexed.	Initiative with the junior college district.
Miscellaneous			Provisions for voluntary affiliation with University of California. Provision for state teachers' colleges to contract with district for junior college work (Repealed in 1927.)	Dormitories may be built at county or joint county junior colleges.
Junior colleges 1930 existing under each act, with date of original organization.		Fresno (1910) [a] Kern County (1913) Citrus (1915) Pomona (1916) San Benito County 1919 Salinas 1920 Santa Maria 1920 Central 1922 Taft 1922 Brawley 1924 Lassen 1925 Ventura 1925 Reedley 1926 Visalia 1926 Porterville 1927 Santa Monica 1929 Los Angeles 1929 Antelope Valley 1929	Modesto 1921 [b] Riverside (1917) 1921 Chaffey (1916) 1922 Fullerton (1913) 1922 Sacramento (1914) 1922 Santa Ana (1915) 1922 San Mateo 1922 Pasadena 1924 San Bernardino (Union) 1926 Marin (Union) 1926 Glendale 1927 Long Beach 1927 Santa Rosa (1918) 1927 (Union in 1929) San José (1921) 1928 Yuba County (County) (1927) 1928 Compton (1927) 1928	None.

[a] Date of organization under the law of 1907.
[b] Dates given are those of organization under the district law. Dates in parentheses refer to original organization as high school departments.

school graduates in the state. Further numerical restriction on entrance at Stanford University. Relief to the overcrowded universities.

7. The relatively small number of small colleges, especially denominational ones. Excessive denominational enthusiasm for founding colleges, largely characteristic of Middle Western States, did not extend to California.
8. The large number and proportion of high school students in the state.
9. The holding power of the high school. In 1923–24, there were 51,000 regular first-year high school students enrolled. Four years later there were 25,000 graduates, or 49 per 100. Corresponding figures for the nation are 45 per 100.
10. The average age of employment of minors in regular jobs is relatively high. Prevalence of Japanese and Mexican labor.
11. The compulsory attendance law requiring a student to stay in school until age 16, unless already a high school graduate.
12. The ability of the state to support education. Superiority in wealth and income. Favorable economic conditions in the state. In 1926, California ranked third in the country in percentage of its estimated income spent for education, second in amount of wealth per child of elementary school age, and first in annual income per child of elementary school age.
13. Large royalties from mineral lands, collected by the Federal Government and devoted by the state to junior college expenses, thus giving the state ability to support extensive junior college development without tapping regular sources of income.
14. The lack of educational conservatism and tradition. Strong attitude of liberal state support for elementary and secondary education.
15. The propensity of Californians to "boost" their communities and advertise their wares. The Chamber of Commerce spirit.
16. Sufficient capable instructors in the high schools to carry on junior college work. Especially applicable in the high school departmental type. All high school instructors must have had at least one year of graduate work.
17. Reasonable minimum standards for establishment of district junior colleges. None have ever failed. All have grown and prospered.

18. The success of graduates of the junior college who have transferred to the upper divisions of the universities. (See Chapter IX.)

QUESTIONS AND PROBLEMS

1. Trace the development of the junior college idea in California prior to 1907. How did Senator Caminetti become interested in the plan? The University of California? Dr. David Starr Jordan?
2. Compare the recommendations of the Special Legislative Committee on Education (H. C. Jones, chairman; E. P. Cubberley, secretary) with the junior college legislation actually adopted. In what respects were they not followed? Were the changes fortunate or unfortunate?
3. Examine the affiliation agreement between the University of California and junior colleges. What provisions might not be agreeable and feasible? (Printed in *Proceedings of the National Association of State Universities*, vol. 20, pp. 58-61, 1922.)
4. Evaluate the influence on junior college development in the state, of Will C. Wood and William J. Cooper, while they were state superintendents of public instruction.
5. Trace the influence of President Ray Lyman Wilbur on the development of the junior college in California.
6. Compare Cooper's division of the history of the junior college to that of Proctor into permissive, recognition, and affiliation stages, and stage of assured permanence.
7. Investigate all legislation dealing in any way with the junior college in the state which has been introduced in the legislature, but failed of passage, and give reasons, if possible, for the failures.
8. Collect and summarize all recommendations regarding junior colleges made by state officials in their official printed reports.
9. Trace and evaluate the influence of the University of California in the development of the junior college in California.
10. Do the same for Stanford University.
11. Do the same for the University of Southern California.
12. Why has the development of the private junior college in the state been so slight?
13. Of the reasons suggested in the text for the growth of the junior college in the state, select the five most important ones and justify your choice.
14. Of the same reasons, select the five least important ones and justify your choice.
15. Find additional supporting evidence to justify any of the suggested reasons for the growth of junior colleges, or to disprove any of them.
16. Are there other significant reasons for the growth of the junior college in California, not listed in the text?

17. What California junior colleges should probably be discontinued or combined with others?
18. Examine the predictions of the growth of the junior college in California made in 1928 (*California Quarterly of Secondary Education*, vol. 4, pp. 59-69, October, 1928) and see to what extent they have been realized to date.

SUGGESTED READINGS

Biennial Reports of the California State Department of Education since 1910, and of the California State Board of Education since 1913-14.

Reports and recommendations by Will C. Wood, A. C. Olney, N. Ricciardi, W. J. Cooper, and others.

*Cooper, W. J. "The Junior College Movement in California"; in *School Review*, vol. 36, pp. 409-22. (June, 1928.) Also in *The Junior College in California*, Bulletin G-3, pp. 5-16. State Department of Education, Sacramento, California, 1928.

Authoritative outline of the history of the movement in the state. Bulletin G-3 contains other valuable historical matter as well.

Diether, R. O. "The Los Angeles Junior College"; in *California Quarterly of Secondary Education*, vol. 5, pp. 365-68. (June, 1930.)

*Eells, W. C. "Trends in Junior College Enrollment"; in *California Quarterly of Secondary Education*, vol. 4, pp. 59-69. (October, 1928.)

Summarizes trends since 1920, and ventures predictions up to 1940.

Eells, W. C. "The Early History of California Public Junior Colleges"; in *California Quarterly of Secondary Education*, vol. 4, pp. 214-22. (April, 1929.)

Founding, enrollment, and early history of 18 public junior college departments prior to 1917.

Eells, W. C. "Private Junior Colleges in California"; in *California Quarterly of Secondary Education*, vol. 5, pp. 82-86. (October, 1929.)

History, organization, and enrollment of the 13 private junior colleges in the state in 1928-29.

*Eells, W. C. "The New California Junior College Law"; in *School and Society*, vol. 30, pp. 65-68. (July 13, 1929.)

Unfavorable comments on the 1929 legislation.

Gray, A. A. "The Junior College in California"; in *School Review*, vol. 23, pp. 465-73. (September, 1915.)

*Jones, H. C. *Report of the Special Legislative Committee on Education.* 96 pp. Sacramento, 1920.

Review of junior college development in the state and recommendations which were the basis of the district junior college law of 1921.

Kemp, W. W. "The Junior College Movement in California"; in *Eighth Yearbook of the National Association of Secondary School Principals*, pp. 82-94. (1924.)
Outline of historical development to 1924, and relationship to state university. Includes substance of various laws.

*Koos, L. V., and Weersing, F. J. *Secondary Education in California; Report of a Preliminary Survey.* 128 pp. Sacramento, 1929.
Contains late data and analyses of many phases of the junior college situation in the state, and recommendations for changes or further study.

*Lange, A. F. "The Junior College, With Special Reference to California"; in *Proceedings of the National Education Association*, pp. 119-24. (Oakland, 1915.) Also in *Educational Administration and Supervision*, vol. 2, pp. 1-8. (January, 1916.)
Excellent sketch of original causes and development by many persons influential in its early history.

McLane, C. L. "The Fresno Junior College"; in *California Weekly*, vol. 2, pp. 539-40. (July 15, 1910.)
First published description of plans for the first junior college in the state, published the summer before it opened.

*McLane, C. L. "The Junior College or Upward Extension of the High School"; in *School Review*, vol. 21, pp. 161-70. (March, 1913.)
Account of conditions leading to the organization of the Fresno junior college and its early development.

*Morgan, W. E. "Recent Developments in the Junior College Movement in California"; in *Fourteenth Yearbook of the Department of Secondary School Principals of the National Education Association.* Bulletin no. 30, pp. 229-42. (March, 1930.) Also in *Junior College Journal*, vol. 1, pp. 64-73. (November, 1930.)
Latest discussion of trends and desirable developments in the junior college situation in the state.

Proctor, W. M. "The Junior College in California"; in *School Review*, vol. 31, pp. 363-75. (May, 1923.)
Detailed report of a survey of the 27 junior colleges in the state in 1921-22.

*Proctor, W. M. "California's Contribution to the Junior College Movement"; Chapter 1 of his *Junior College: Its Organization and Administration*, pp. 1-10. Stanford University, 1927.
General summary of historical development in four periods, relation to university, and costs to state

Ricciardi, N. "Vital Junior College Problems in California"; in *Junior College Journal*, vol. 1, pp. 24-27. (October, 1930.)

CHAPTER V

HISTORICAL DEVELOPMENT: OTHER STATES

The junior college is the product of a variety of local ferments and hence is different, both in form and purpose, in the various areas in which it has sprung up. — S. P. CAPEN.[1]

Contents of this chapter. This chapter presents a brief summary by states of the beginnings, significant development, and present status of the junior college. Where states have already been discussed in Chapter III only supplementary information will be given here. Statistical data and dates are taken in large part, but not exclusively, from the 1930 Directory of the American Association of Junior Colleges. Information on laws was secured largely by letters of inquiry to each state department of education. Many other sources have also been consulted. The emphasis will be placed on the development of public junior colleges, but the private institutions will not be ignored. The states are arranged alphabetically.

ALABAMA

Alabama has a few private but no public junior colleges, except one for Negroes. A committee of the State Educational Association, in 1930, recommended against public junior colleges for the state until more adequate provision could be made for placing elementary and secondary education on a satisfactory financial and professional basis. The strongest private institution is Marion Institute, founded in 1887, a military school, with a long record of excellent work.

ALASKA

There are no junior colleges in Alaska, and only one institution of higher learning in that territory. As a result, many of

[1] Capen, Samuel P. "The Reorganization of the American Educational System"; in *School and Society*, vol. 27, p. 510. (April 28, 1928.)

the young people travel hundreds or thousands of miles to secure collegiate education in the states. Lester D. Henderson, for twelve years Commissioner of Education in Alaska, has made a careful analysis [1] on the basis of which he recommends the establishment of two public junior colleges at Juneau and Ketchikan, which would meet the needs of a large proportion of the population. His recommendations have been embodied in a bill to be presented to the territorial legislature.

ARIZONA

Arizona has a single public junior college, begun at Phœnix, in 1920, without legal sanction. The establishment of junior colleges was legalized in a bill passed in 1927, providing that local boards of education may establish such institutions in districts having an average daily attendance of 100 or more in high school, and an assessed valuation of at least $5,000,000. The bill originally provided for state aid, but this provision was eliminated in the legislature, and now requires local support exclusively. No new institutions have been organized under the provisions of the bill. Gila College (1922) is under the auspices of the Latter Day Saints. Some information regarding the policy of this church with reference to its colleges will be found under Utah.

ARKANSAS

Arkansas has twelve junior colleges, including four of the state type, the earliest dating from 1909, three state Agricultural and Mechanical Colleges, and the Polytechnic College. There is no junior college legislation although there are several municipal junior colleges recently organized and operating in connection with the public school systems in various parts of the state. Little Rock and El Dorado both opened in 1927.

[1] In an unpublished master's thesis at Stanford University. 1930. (Summarized in an article in the *Junior College Journal*, April, 1931.)

Tuition is charged in all cases, presumably sufficient to meet the cost of instruction. The buildings, equipment, and materials are furnished by the public schools. The attorney-general of the state has ruled that such a procedure is permissible. The junior college at Little Rock received a noteworthy bequest of $2,000,000 in 1929. This recognition by a private individual of the permanence and worth of the public local junior college is remarkable. Central College, at Conway (1922), was for several years under the presidency of Doak S. Campbell, secretary of the American Association of Junior Colleges. The Federal Bureau's survey of education in Arkansas, in 1922, recommended that many of the denominational four-year colleges be changed to junior college status.

CALIFORNIA

Chapter IV is devoted entirely to the development of the junior college in California.

COLORADO

No general junior college legislation has been passed in Colorado. By special enactment, junior colleges were established in Trinidad and Grand Junction in 1925, and small appropriations of $2500 made to each "to beautify the grounds." Otherwise they have been local in character, organization, and support.

Since the establishment of these two institutions a lively legislative battle has been waged in the state for general legislation to maintain and equip these and similar colleges. The existing state institutions of higher learning were united in their opposition to the proposed legislation because it provided for state support from the same general tax fund and in the same manner in which the existing institutions of higher learning were maintained. They felt that none of the existing institutions were adequately supported, and they would be still less so under the proposed legislation. In both the sessions of 1927[1] and of 1929 the issue was fought on both sides with intense bitterness, and loomed larger than almost any other question. In the 1929 legislature a bill was introduced, modeled on the California law, but it was killed in committee. The matter was not settled, and another bitter fight was predicted in the 1931 legislature.

CONNECTICUT

Outstanding work in making the coeducational junior college better known in Connecticut and in the entire New England area has been accomplished through the establishment of the Junior College of Connecticut at Bridgeport. It was chartered as an independent private institution on a two-year basis by the State Legislature in 1927. Its president, E. E. Cortright, has been instrumental in securing recognition of the junior college movement on the part of the New England Association. Two well known girls' schools, Marot and Miss Porter's, at Thompson and Farmington, have junior college divisions, the former dating from 1923.

DELAWARE

There are no junior colleges, nor is there any junior college legislation in the state of Delaware.

DISTRICT OF COLUMBIA

Several private junior colleges for women have flourished for a number of years under the attractions of the national capital. Most of these are girls' seminaries of long standing which have recently added junior college work. Mount Vernon Seminary dates from 1875. National Park Seminary is an outstanding institution to which reference will be made later. It is just outside the limits of the District, but is practi-

[1] See Whitney, F. L.: *The Junior College in America*, p. 174, for text of the law proposed in 1927.

cally a Washington institution. A public junior college for the District was proposed in joint resolutions in both the House and the Senate in 1926, but nothing came of it. Representative Arentz introduced a bill in 1929, endorsed by the City Board of Education, for a junior college on government land adjoining Rock Creek Park, but no action was taken.

FLORIDA

There is no junior college legislation in Florida, although there is one public junior college at St. Petersburg, and two or three private institutions, including Bethune-Cookman, founded by the Methodist church in 1923, for colored students.

GEORGIA

There are twelve or more junior colleges, both public and private, in Georgia. The private institutions are largely denominational. A letter from G. G. Singleton, director of the Division of Information and Statistics of the State Department of Education, states:

> The junior colleges in Georgia are not provided for in a general act. State-owned and maintained junior colleges are each created individually and each is a part of the University of Georgia and its branches. An act is required for the establishment of each institution. Each junior college has its own board of trustees and the General Assembly makes an appropriation to each unit college. There are not any laws governing private and denominational junior colleges as distinguished from the law governing all colleges. The junior colleges are not a part of the public school system.

The two state junior colleges at Cochran and Douglass are branches of the University of Georgia in name only. They are virtually independent institutions. The local institutions at Augusta (1925) and Waynesboro (1927) were in each case established by the county boards of education.

IDAHO

At Pocatello, in southeastern Idaho, is the Southern Branch of the University of Idaho, a junior college which was organized in 1927, the successor of the Idaho Technical Institute. The latter was a state institution of junior college rank established by law in 1915.[1] There are as yet no local junior colleges in the state, but there has been much discussion pertaining to general junior college legislation. It was expected that measures concerning their establishment would be introduced in the 1931 legislature. Ricks College was established by the Latter Day Saints at Rexburg in 1917. Its development is described in connection with the system of church schools in the Utah section of this chapter.

ILLINOIS

Although Illinois has the earliest public junior college, Joliet (1902),[2] which is still in existence, there has been no enabling legislation in the third of a century since its organization, nor has the public junior college grown as rapidly as expected by President Harper and President James. The latter said, in his inaugural address in 1905:

> Surely it is true that the work done at present in the freshman and sophomore years at the University of Illinois may just as well be done at any one of fifty or one hundred centers in the state of Illinois as at Urbana.

Yet there were only half a dozen such public institutions in the entire state in 1929. Concerning their official legal status, the superintendent of the State Department of Education states that:

> Illinois has enacted no legislation regarding junior colleges. We have a number of junior colleges supported by public taxation. They are treated as a continuance of the public school system.

[1] The Idaho Technical Institute, in turn, developed from the State Academy of Idaho, established in 1901.

[2] For this date see page 54.

They are operated by common consent of the taxpayers of the school district and not under any special legislative act.[1]

There are also a dozen private junior colleges in the state, some of which have carried out President Harper's original plan of affiliation with the University of Chicago.

INDIANA

Indiana to date has passed no junior college legislation, nor are there any public junior colleges in the state, although some of the earliest in the country were established there, including Goshen before 1900. These institutions, however, had stormy careers, and, due to lack of funds, competition, politics, and various other causes, were forced to discontinue their junior college work. Other high schools, as at Gary and Indianapolis, introduced junior college work, but legal right to continue such courses was seriously questioned following a decision by the attorney-general in 1921, and the experiment was abandoned. The idea was much discussed, however, culminating in a bill which was introduced in the legislature in 1927. It provided that junior colleges might be established in any district where there was a school population of 2000. It was passed in the Senate, but indefinitely postponed in the House, "fortunately for the public education of Indiana," says Dr. Foster, of Indiana University, in a detailed analysis of the bill before the high school principals' conference in Indiana in 1927.[2] He felt that the standards were not high enough, and that they would have permitted a junior college, often weak or useless, in every county in the state, of which there are nearly one hundred. He feels, however, that "the junior college is coming in Indi-

[1] Whitney states that public junior college legislation appeared in Illinois in 1927 (p. 47), but the state superintendent in a letter of May 15, 1930, says, "There is no legislation in Illinois relating to the establishment of junior colleges."

[2] Foster, I. O. "Some Phases of the Junior College Movement with Special Reference to Indiana"; in *Bulletin of the School of Education, Indiana University*, vol. 4, no. 4, p. 31. (March, 1928.)

ana." A bill authorizing Fort Wayne to establish a district junior college was passed by the legislature but vetoed by the governor, in 1929. There are several private junior colleges in the state. Vincennes University, established in 1806, became a junior college in 1924.

IOWA

The first public junior college in Iowa was established at Mason City, in 1918. The number had increased to ten by 1926–27, although only two offered two years of work. The enrollment in most of them was small, averaging only 65 students. The next year the number jumped to twenty. All of them were organized without express authorization of state law before standards were prescribed by the State Department of Education. They are supported exclusively by tuition. The average enrollment was only 56, even smaller than the inadequate average enrollment reported two years earlier. Only three were in excess of 100. Although Iowa ranks second in number of public junior colleges in the country, she ranks ninth in number of students enrolled in them. Iowa is an unfortunate example of local enthusiasm, in some cases, overcoming sound judgment when minimum standards are not established by law. In 1923 a law was passed requiring cities of over 20,000 inhabitants which maintained a junior college, to charge tuition for instruction therein "at such an amount as will fully cover the cost of maintenance of such school of a higher order." But this applied to only two cities in which junior colleges were located, Mason City and Burlington. It was not until 1927 that a general law was passed requiring approval of the State Department of Education and a vote of the electors of the district. Professor F. C. Ensign, of the State University of Iowa, states the situation thus:[1]

[1] Ensign, F. C. "What One State is Doing with the Junior College"; in *Epsilon Bulletin, Phi Delta Kappa*, vol. 10, pp. 1, 12. (November, 1929.)

Since Mason City launched the experiment in 1919, it has extended to other centers, until now almost a third of our counties have within their boundaries a public junior college. This movement has developed in a typical Iowa fashion without much direction and with practically no legal control. Indeed, not until some twenty-four junior colleges had been organized, was there a scrap of legal authority for their existence. Finally, in 1926,[1] a very general law was enacted giving the state superintendent of public instruction a small measure of authority in determining whether or not a community could organize a junior college, and empowering that official to regulate, to some extent, the curriculum. The result has been what might have been expected. Public junior colleges are found in a few communities that are, no doubt, abundantly able to support them; they have, also, been established in small communities with very limited economic resources, and with no very large body of high school graduates from which to draw junior college students. Some of the junior colleges maintain an excellent corps of instructors on a fairly liberal salary schedule. Others are forced to pay the college staff less than the salary provided for high school teachers in a neighboring town or city of greater economic resources. I think all will agree that it is time now for us in Iowa to examine with care the laws and standards worked out, and the results achieved in the state which has undoubtedly been the leader thus far in the junior college movement — California.... As it is we have 28 public junior colleges, about seven of which meet, or come near meeting the minimum requirements now laid upon communities in California.

Professor Stoddard of the University of Iowa says: [2]

In Iowa alone, twenty-five junior colleges are in operation and four or five more are voted to begin next year. We are in the midst of an epidemic; no town boasting as many as 2000 inhabitants and a strong Chamber of Commerce is immune.

The tentative standards set up by the State Department of Education in 1928 for communities desiring to establish junior

[1] Whitney and the United States Bureau of Education give this date as 1927.

[2] Stoddard, G. D. "The Articulation of High School and College Subject Matter"; in *School Executives Magazine*, vol. 49, p. 356. (April, 1930.)

colleges, in accordance with the 1927 law, while none too high, have had a healthy effect in preventing the organization of new ones. They require, for instance, a prospective enrollment of twenty-five in a one-year or fifty in a two-year junior college. Ten now existing have enrollments below fifty. No financial support comes from the state or locality (except for use of high school building). Instructional costs are met by tuition. Therefore it is easy for the people to vote to establish a college. Tuition varies from $60 to $120 a year. It is significant that since the adoption of the standards no new institutions have been organized as compared with the ten which sprang into existence in 1927.

KANSAS

The development of the public junior college in Kansas is in marked contrast with that in the neighboring state of Iowa, although it covers practically the same period. The first junior colleges now existing in Kansas were established at Fort Scott and Garden City in 1919.[1] The state, however, passed her enabling legislation before the junior colleges developed, not after they were all in existence. California was the only state to pass a general law in an earlier year than Kansas. The Kansas law of 1917 required an election for the establishment of a junior college, authorized a special tax levy to support it, and gave the State Board of Education power to prescribe the course of study and to inspect the institution. The influence of the University of Kansas was excellent, especially in the surveys made by Dr. F. P. Obrien, dealing with the desirability of establishment of junior colleges at Atchison (1923), Chanute (1924), and Hutchinson (1925).[2] These surveys were

[1] This is the date given by Koos, Whitney, and the Junior College Directory. Hughes, however, in a recent detailed study, says Fort Scott began in 1918. See Hughes, R. J., "The Public Junior Colleges in Kansas"; in *School Review*, vol. 38, pp. 450–55. (June, 1930.)

[2] See Chapter XX, Readings, for reference to these surveys.

pioneer efforts to determine by careful study of facts and conditions the probability of success of a junior college prior to its proposed establishment. Kansas set an excellent example in the decade from 1920 to 1930 of how junior colleges should be established, while Iowa was furnishing an equally good example of how it should not be done. Wellemeyer, in 1926, made a valuable study of student opinion in the eight public junior colleges existing at that time.[1]

Legislation was introduced in 1925 providing for state support to the extent of $100 per student enrolled in institutions having 100 students, but unfortunately it failed by a very narrow margin. The first two public institutions to be established at Holton (1917) and at Marysville (1918) were abandoned. The 1917 law was sponsored by the people of Holton, where Campbell College, a denominational institution, had ceased to function, being succeeded by a private junior college for two years. It opened with an enrollment of thirteen, just at the outbreak of the World War, on account of which it lasted but two years. The average enrollment was 178 in the ten junior colleges existing in 1928–29 with only one falling below 100.

KENTUCKY

Kentucky has a large group of private denominational junior colleges, most of them of recent origin, but only one public institution, which is for Negroes. The private junior colleges are subject to standards for accrediting which were adopted by the Association of Kentucky Colleges and Universities in 1915. Sixteen private institutions are reported in the state, half of them coeducational. At least ten have begun their junior college work since 1920.

[1] Wellemeyer, J. F. "The Junior College as Viewed by its Students"; in *School Review*, vol. 34, pp. 760–67. (December, 1926.)

LOUISIANA

Interest in the public junior college in Louisiana is very recent, and unfortunately has not had the most auspicious beginning. Three local institutions had been established and recognized by the State Board of Education by 1927, and in 1928 a law was passed authorizing and regulating their organization. The first one was established at Hammond, being quickly followed by Homer and Haynesville. The latter two were discontinued in 1928 for lack of adequate financial support. The two towns were only fourteen miles apart, and not large enough to justify two junior colleges in the same parish. It was another case in which community spirit and enterprise acted as the chief incentive and without regard for educational need. The law of 1928 limited a parish to one junior college. Since the two towns could not agree on a junior college at either, both were discontinued. The Hammond Junior College, after two or three years' existence, developed four-year ambitions and succeeded in 1928 in having the state legislature make it into the Southeast Louisiana State College.

MAINE

There are no public junior colleges in Maine, but there are three or four small private ones known as seminaries or institutes. The oldest is Westbrook Seminary and Junior College at Portland (1925). These may receive state aid in accordance with the new law passed in the state in 1929. This provides for per capita aid from the state treasury on a graduated scale on the basis of enrollment, institutions having enrollments of 20–40 receiving $20 per capita; 41–60, $18; 61–80, $16; 81–100, $14; 101–150, $12; 151–200, $10; and over 200, $8. Institutions having incomes of over $2500 from invested funds may not receive this per capita allowance.

MARYLAND

No public junior colleges have been organized in Maryland.

The most outstanding private one is National Park Seminary, established in 1894, in the suburbs of Washington, and described more fully in Chapter XVI. Charlotte Hall Academy and St. Charles College are Catholic institutions with substantial junior college enrollments.

MASSACHUSETTS

Unusual interest in the public junior college was stimulated by the extensive survey of higher education in Massachusetts, made in 1923 by the United States Bureau of Education under the direction of George F. Zook. The survey commission discovered that by the establishment of twelve junior colleges approximately 90 per cent of the population of the state would be within approximately fifteen miles of one of them. Zook, in 1923, recommended an excellent system of junior colleges for Massachusetts. He proposed that the local district should furnish the buildings and equipment and provide for the operating expense, but that the state should pay 90 per cent of the instructional and administrative salaries, and that tuition should be free. While the plan had much merit, it did not meet with the unanimous approval of the survey commission, and was not adopted.

The only public junior college in the state is the one year of collegiate work maintained by the Central High School at Springfield. There are several private junior colleges for women. The oldest of them, Bradford Academy and Junior College, dates as an Academy from 1803, although its junior college work did not begin until 1920. Under the leadership of Miss Marion Coats, a broadened collegiate curriculum was developed along the lines of culture, leisure, and activities, which became the prototype, in some respects, for the new Sarah Lawrence College organized by Miss Coats (now Mrs. Graves) in New York in 1926. Lasell Seminary, at Auburndale, has a collegiate enrollment of 250, the largest junior college in the state.

MICHIGAN

It has already been pointed out that the first public junior college work in the country recognized by a state university was in Michigan, possibly at Saginaw. The oldest public institution in the state, still existing, Grand Rapids, was organized in 1914. Michigan was one of the first states, also, to pass a junior college law. It was passed in 1917 at the instigation of Detroit, to make secure the legal basis of the Detroit Junior College, organized two years earlier.[1] In 1923 the Detroit Junior College developed into a four-year municipal college. The 1917 law limited the establishment of junior colleges to cities of 30,000 or over. In 1923 this limit was changed to 25,000 and in 1929 to 18,000. The seven public junior colleges in Michigan form a rather strong group, with average enrollment of 278, none dropping below 100. The attitude of the University of Michigan has been one of constructive leadership and helpfulness. The committee on inspection of junior colleges reported, in 1925:[2] "The university welcomes the establishment of junior colleges... and rejoices that the movement is growing so rapidly here in Michigan." Noteworthy later action came under President Little in separation of the lower division and organization of it as a "University College," with a diploma granted on completion of its course. The constructive leadership and coöperation of the state university in Michigan contrast with the open hostility of the state institutions in Colorado and the lukewarm attitude in some other states.

[1] A. M. Stowe, in his report of a survey of Detroit and Grand Rapids Junior Colleges in 1921 (United States Bureau of Education, Bulletin no. 19, p. 65, 1922), states that Detroit Junior College began to offer a one-year course in 1913 which was extended to a two-year course in 1917. The date given above is based upon the statement of David MacKenzie, dean of the Detroit Junior College, in 1920. (*Ibid.*, p. 29.)

[2] Frayer, W. A. (chairman). "Junior Colleges"; in *The President's Report* for 1923–24, in University of Michigan Bulletin, new series, vol. 26, no. 43, p. 180. (April 25, 1925.)

MINNESOTA

The public junior college movement began early in Minnesota also, the first institution being established at Rochester (1915), closely followed by Hibbing (1918) and Eveleth (1918). Its first law, however, was not passed until 1925. This expressly legalized junior colleges then existing, and provided that new ones could be organized in any independent or special school district of the state, when authorized by a three-fourths vote of the district. In practice the State Department of Education recommends that junior colleges shall be maintained only in districts with an assessed valuation in excess of $3,000,000. In 1927 an additional law was passed permitting cities of 50,000 or over to establish junior colleges, by vote either of a majority of the school board or of the people of the district. In 1928–29, the seven public junior colleges in the state had an average enrollment of 174.

MISSISSIPPI

Mississippi, in 1921, had five junior colleges which were recognized by the State Board of Education and whose graduates were granted teaching licenses. The first junior college legislation was passed in 1922. At the special session of the legislature, in 1928, a very extensive and detailed law was passed. It incorporates most of the standards suggested by national and state accrediting agencies, including standards as to definition, criteria for organization, arrangements for inspection and control, arrangements for accrediting, entrance requirements, curricula, standards for faculty, standards for levels of students' work, graduation requirements, library and laboratory standards, records, and material aspects.

One of the most important provisions of the law was the creation of the "Legalized Commission" on Junior Colleges. This commission has made a detailed survey of the entire state, including such features as number and standards of the elementary schools, number and standards of the high schools, number of high school graduates and per cent attending college, potential resources of the proposed zone, minimum of $20,000,000 assessed valuation, possibility of minimum junior college enrollment of 150 students, and proximity to other colleges and transportation facilities.

As a result of their comprehensive study of the state, they set up in 1928, twelve zones, varying in assessed valuation from $25,000,000 to $94,000,000, which "represent the Commission's best judgment for a working basis, and they recommend that they be adhered to in the organization and development of a safe system of public junior colleges." Since most of the municipalities are not large, the commission rather favors establishing junior colleges which may have groups of counties as the taxing basis.

The Mississippi junior colleges are based in part upon the existing county agricultural high schools. The agricultural high schools in Pearl River County and Hinds County undertook first-year junior college work in 1922, adding a second year two or three years later. Two others began in 1926. By 1928–29, 19 counties were coöperating in the support of twelve junior colleges, with plants valued at over $3,000,000. In one case there is a tri-county college, in another, four counties support a single college, while in three others two adjacent counties have combined. The total enrollment for 1928–29 was 878, a 54 per cent increase over the previous year. The Mississippi junior colleges seem well adapted to agricultural conditions in what is essentially an agricultural state. Mr. Broom, state supervisor, says that "It is probable that as many again counties will be coöperating in the support of these institutions within the next twelve months."

An honest effort appears to have been made to profit by all previous experience in other states, and to establish a statewide system on a carefully planned basis, well-adapted to local needs and conditions. The movement is only in its infancy, and it is too early to do much prediction of results, but if the Commission continues to approach its problems in a professional rather than a political attitude, Mississippi ought in the next decade to have one of the outstanding progressive public junior college systems of the country.

There are also several strong private junior colleges for women. Hillman College opened in 1910; the Mississippi Synodical College (Presbyterian), in 1916; Gulf Park College, in 1921; and Whitworth College (Methodist), in 1928. Whitworth has formed the working agreement with Millsaps, which has already been mentioned in Chapter III.

MISSOURI

The early development of the movement in Missouri, through the accrediting of private junior colleges by the state university, has already been outlined.[1] The public junior college history is much more recent, the law having been passed in 1927 permitting the organization of junior college courses in any public school district in the state with a fully accredited high school, "on the approval of and subject to the supervision of the state superintendent of schools." At least five public junior colleges had been organized before this, the earliest of which were St. Joseph (1914) and Kansas City (1915). The latter is the third largest in the country with an enrollment in 1928–29 of 1744. Two new institutions were organized in 1927. The state is supplied with a large number of four-year colleges as well as private junior colleges.[2]

MONTANA

In 1917, Montana passed a law providing that any accredited and approved high school in the state might establish junior

[1] See pages 64–65.

[2] In addition to those summarized in Chapter II, the 1929–30 *State Educational Directory* lists three others, Kidder and Rockhurst as private and Caruthersville as public.

college courses, provided such courses should conform to such requirements and regulations as might be prescribed by the Chancellor of the University of Montana.[1] No junior colleges have been established under the law, however. With Montana's great distances, somewhat similar to those found in California, and her well-organized system of county high schools, it would seem that there would be a distinct need for junior college work in some localities far distant from the state university. Only one public institution is reported, the Northern Montana School at Havre, which is a branch of the University of Montana, carrying the first two years of university work exactly as at the university, under the same rules and regulations, and financed in the same manner.

NEBRASKA

There is no junior college legislation in Nebraska.[2] Bills were introduced at the sessions of the legislature in 1927 and 1929, but were killed in each case. The 1929 bill was patterned after the California law. Two public junior colleges are in existence, McCook (1926) and Norfolk (1928), the students being required to pay tuition. They are not legalized, but the communities are so much in favor of them that no one has contested the right of the boards of education to set them up. There are also seven private junior colleges in Nebraska, three Lutheran and four Catholic institutions.

NEVADA

There are no junior colleges of any type in Nevada, nor has any legislation regarding them been proposed.

NEW HAMPSHIRE

There is no junior college legislation in New Hampshire, but regulations of the State Board of Education for accrediting

[1] Whitney (*Junior College in America*, p. 47) gives 1927 as the date of the first legislation in Montana.

[2] See Supplementary Note, p. 43.

junior colleges have the force of law. The State Board has accredited two private junior colleges, the Colby School for Girls at New London (1928) and Stoneleigh School at Rye Beach (1926).

NEW JERSEY

One of the early public junior colleges in the country was organized at Newark, New Jersey, in 1918, but it ceased operation in 1922, and there has been no public junior college in existence since that time. Two small private institutions are found.

NEW MEXICO

New Mexico has but a single junior college, the New Mexico Military Institute at Roswell, with a faculty of twelve, organized in 1918. It is supported for the most part by a special land grant, and by fees of students from without the state. It enrolls over two hundred students. There has been no general junior college legislation of any sort in the state.

NEW YORK

New York has no junior college legislation, the Board of Regents of the State of New York having all jurisdiction. There are no public junior colleges. There are several under private control, mostly outgrowths of long-established girls' finishing schools. Two outstanding junior colleges of different types that have been recently founded are Sarah Lawrence College (1926) at Bronxville, and Seth Low Junior College (1928) at Brooklyn under the control of Columbia University.

Since New York State students must take pre-law, pre-dental, and pre-medical courses in college, the logical place to take any of these courses would seem to be in a junior college. In 1925 there was some discussion of superimposing such junior colleges on some of the high schools in New York City where it could be done with little change, since many of the teachers were well qualified for college teaching and the newer high school buildings were well fitted with laboratories, libraries, assembly halls, and the like, but nothing of this sort has yet been done.

The University of the State of New York has adopted regulations for registration of junior colleges, requiring them to be equivalent to a standard college except in three items, where the standards are reduced one half, namely, a junior college must have a minimum productive endowment of at least $250,000; a library of at least 4000 volumes; and at least four full-time, salaried instructors.

NORTH CAROLINA

North Carolina has had a considerable group of junior colleges, mostly of the private type, many of them of long existence as institutions. These are largely denominational — Baptist, Presbyterian, and Methodist being most frequent. Louisburg College is the oldest, founded as an institution in 1802.

Two local public junior colleges have been established, the College of Asheville at Asheville (1926), and the Buncombe County Junior College at Biltmore (1927). There is no junior college legislation in the state, but the State Department of Education administers the standards adopted by the North Carolina College Conference in 1927 for the purpose of issuing teachers' certificates to graduates of accredited institutions.

In the spring of 1930 the attorney-general handed down a decision that the Asheville Board of Education could not legally use school funds for carrying on a junior college. As a result the College of Asheville was compelled to close at the end of the year. This decision will doubtless stimulate legislation to authorize public junior colleges.[1]

[1] For a later decision of the state Supreme Court see *School Review*, December, 1930, or *Junior College Journal*, January, 1931.

NORTH DAKOTA

No general junior college legislation has been passed or proposed in North Dakota.[1] Only two junior colleges are reported, and they are both of the state type. They were not planned as such, but have "just happened." Many years ago the state legislature created a State School of Science at Wahpeton, and a State School of Forestry at Bottineau. Because there was no need of the specialized training given by such schools, they gradually drifted into junior college work.

OHIO

Ohio has not yet established a system of public junior colleges, although in 1921 the need for them was pointed out by a special legislative committee on administrative legislation. It recommended authorization and possible state aid to public junior colleges in the state as a relief to the overcrowded state university, but nothing came of it. A bill was introduced in the 1927 General Assembly authorizing any city boards of education to extend the curriculum of high schools of the first grade to two years of junior college work, but it failed of passage. In 1929 there was introduced a similar bill, but even more general, authorizing any board of education to establish a junior college, if approved by the state department of education. It, too, failed of passage.[2] After Dr. Zook left the Federal Bureau to become the President of the University of Akron, in 1925, he began to point out the need of junior colleges in Ohio. Speaking before the Ohio College Association in 1927, he emphasized the fact that although Ohio had a large number of colleges, most of them were not near the centers of population. For the twenty-five largest cities, each with a population in excess of 25,000, he found that only eight had any kind

[1] After its introduction it was amended to require a property valuation of $50,000,000 for organization of a junior college. Another bill in 1931 also failed to pass.

[2] A general junior college law was passed by the 1931 Legislature. See *Junior College Journal*, May, 1931.

of college facilities, either in the cities themselves or within a radius of ten miles. The following year, 1928, as chairman of a committee on junior colleges he recommended the promotion of legislation authorizing them. Young, in 1930, for his doctor's dissertation at Ohio State University, made a careful study of the junior college movement in relation to higher education in Ohio.

Ohio has a small group of private junior colleges. One of the oldest of these was Glendale College, which for financial reasons closed its doors in 1929 after a notable career of three quarters of a century. A type of junior college which has had its widest development in Ohio is the Y.M.C.A. junior college. There are three of these in the large centers, Columbus (1925), Cleveland (1927), and Youngstown (1927), all doing excellent work.

OKLAHOMA

When Koos made his study in 1922, he reported but a single junior college in Oklahoma, the private Oklahoma Presbyterian College for Girls. In 1930, thirteen were reported, both private and public, the latter both local and state. The first public junior college seems to have been at Muskogee (1920). While there are several other small public colleges reported, Muskogee is the only municipal junior college recognized by the state department. There are several vigorous state institutions.

There has been no general legislation in the state, but special acts of the legislature in 1923, 1924, and 1927 established various state junior colleges. Oklahoma Military College was thus authorized in 1923.

OREGON

Oregon has no public junior colleges, and only one or two private ones. There is a considerable group of denominational four-year colleges in the Willamette Valley, some of which could well be made into junior colleges, as were many of the Missouri colleges. Prior to 1925 a bill was introduced in the legislature providing that any high school district, with a valuation of at least $4,000,000 and an average attendance of 300 high school students, might establish a junior college. The bill was not passed, however.

PENNSYLVANIA

Pennsylvania has been chiefly known in the junior college field for its unique development of branch junior colleges in the western part of the state. There are three such, at Johnstown (1927), Erie (1928), and Uniontown (1928), all branches of the University of Pittsburgh. In these centers, as already explained, the buildings and upkeep are furnished by the local school boards (public), but the instruction and control is entirely in the hands of a private university. This makes them hybrids — private institutions operating in public school plants. To meet this situation special legislation in 1927 permitted public school districts to lease property to private universities for junior college purposes. No general junior college legislation has been enacted or proposed.

RHODE ISLAND

Rhode Island is one of the five states in which no junior college is found. No legislation has been introduced, nor does there seem to be any need of it in this smallest state in the Union — smaller than many California and Texas counties, in which junior colleges thrive.

SOUTH CAROLINA

There are no public junior colleges in South Carolina, and those that are private are of very recent origin. In 1928, Summerland College, previously operated by the Lutheran Church as a four-year institution for women, decapitated itself, reorganizing as a junior college. In 1929, the General

Assembly authorized a change in the charter of Bailey Military Institute, a privately owned secondary school for boys, under which it was permitted to give junior college work. Anderson College began junior college work in 1930, advertising itself as the first junior college in the state. The State Department of Education, however, reports eight private institutions listed as junior colleges.

There has been some spasmodic agitation for upward extension of the public high school to include the freshman year of college, but this has gone no farther than occasional newspaper discussions.

SOUTH DAKOTA

There are four or five denominational junior colleges in South Dakota, the oldest being Wessington Springs Junior College, a free Methodist institution, founded in 1887, and beginning junior college work in 1918.

TENNESSEE

Koos found eight private junior colleges in Tennessee in 1922, half of them under the control of the Methodist Church. There were no public institutions at that time. In 1930 the private junior colleges had increased to twelve. One of the strongest of these is Ward-Belmont School for women (1913), with a collegiate enrollment of 499 in 1929. A state institution, Tennessee Polytechnic Institute, was organized in 1915 by special act of the legislature. In 1927 a branch of the University of Tennessee was organized as a junior college at Martin, in northwestern Tennessee, over three hundred miles from the University of Tennessee at Knoxville, with an enrollment in 1928–29 of 151. In 1929 special arrangements were made for closer coördination of work between Tennessee Wesleyan Junior College and the University of Tennessee, the precursor of an arrangement in Tennessee as satisfactory as that in Missouri between the state university and the private junior colleges.

TEXAS

Summary of development. The largest state in the Union has next to the largest number of junior colleges, being surpassed by California alone. When Koos made his study, he found fifteen private institutions in Texas, but only four under public control. The only municipal junior college was established at El Paso in 1920. In the next decade, however, sixteen municipal junior colleges came into existence. In 1920, the sentiment in favor of public local control of junior colleges was scarcely apparent except in two or three centers. By 1926, favorable sentiment had spread throughout the state, and by 1929 there was a state-wide interest in the publicly controlled institution, which came to a climax in the legislation exacted in that year. Texas now ranks third in the number of public junior colleges in the country, being outranked only by California and Iowa. In enrollment, however, she far outnumbers Iowa.

The junior college at Hillsboro has achieved considerable notice through its assertion that it is the first four-year junior college in the country still in existence. It was organized in 1923.[1]

The junior college of El Paso was operated as a separate institution until 1927, when it was consolidated with the branch of the University of Texas known as the Texas School of Mines and Metallurgy. The city agreed to meet the expenses of a department of education in the school, all other expense to be met by state appropriations.

The 1929 law. The general law of 1929, modeled on the California district law, provides for local junior colleges in districts with assessed valuation of $12,000,000 or more — a legislative compromise between $6,000,000 and $25,000,000 — and a high school average daily attendance of 400 or more. It does not, however, provide for state aid to the junior colleges, but the district may levy a tax for support. All municipal junior colleges existing in 1929 could change to the dis-

[1] See p. 735 for further information on Hillsboro Junior College.

trict status as soon as desired. The law also provided for union junior colleges and county and joint county institutions. It is a progressive law, but inadequate in that it throws the whole burden of support on the local district, supplemented only by tuition from the local students.

State junior colleges. According to Dr. Eby,[1] the state junior colleges grew out of an agitation for the establishment of a new agricultural college in western Texas. President W. B. Bizzell, who from student days at Baylor University had been familiar with the plan of correlated junior colleges in effect there, endeavored to modify the movement by advocating a junior college under the control of the Agricultural and Mechanical College. Pursuant to this suggestion, the Texas legislature, in 1917, took over the John Tarleton College at Stephenville and also created the Grubbs Vocational School at Arlington, later the North Texas Agricultural School. Both of these were placed under the management of the Board of Regents of the State Agricultural and Mechanical College, forming a group of correlated junior colleges.

University of Texas experiment with a branch junior college. The University of Texas carried on some experimental work in organizing junior colleges, similar to the University of Pittsburgh plan, before the municipal institutions developed extensively. Dr. Splawn, President of the university, thought that the university might sponsor development of junior colleges in the state. The experiment was undertaken in 1925 at San Antonio, the local board of education furnishing building, equipment, janitor service, etc., the university outlining the course of study, employing the faculty, and being responsible for their salaries. It was expected that this expense, however, would be largely met by local tuition fees without permanent use of university funds. The faculty was employed as mem-

[1] Eby, F. "Shall We Have a System of Public Junior Colleges in Texas?" in *Texas Outlook*, vol. 11, pp. 20–24. (January, 1927.)

bers of the university faculty, but with the understanding that their work would be at San Antonio. The arrangement seemed at first to be quite successful and satisfactory from an educational point of view. After a year, however, it became necessary to transfer the selection of the faculty and the financing of its salaries to the local school board as a municipal junior college; this change was made because of the opinion of the attorney general that such work could not legally be undertaken by the state university. In the first year, because the high school building was used during the day, all junior college work was carried on from four in the afternoon until nine at night. Even under such conditions the enrollment the first year was about 300, and the university lost only $600 on the experiment.

Private Institutions. The early history of private junior colleges, and the development of the Baptist system of senior and junior colleges in Texas, has already been sketched in Chapter III.[1] During the next twenty years the private junior college movement in Texas developed slowly. In 1908, Burleson College, which for ten years had struggled to maintain senior college rank, joined the Baptist correlated system as a junior college. In 1913, Wayland Baptist College also became a member of the system, and similarly the newly founded College of Marshall in 1917. Meanwhile, the Board of Education of the Methodist Episcopal Church South decided to classify all the Methodist institutions under its jurisdiction as universities, senior colleges, junior colleges, and academies. Four in Texas were classified as junior colleges by 1917. In

[1] See page 63. Of the independent junior colleges in Texas it is quite difficult to determine the first to be established. "Decatur college, established in 1891 — the oldest junior college west of the Mississippi river" and "Westminster College, opened in 1895 — the oldest junior college in Texas"; if their catalogues may be credited. There is no evidence that they were doing real junior college work at that time, however. Others were founded earlier, as in other states, but make no junior college claims for their early existence. Decatur College (1898) seems to have the best claim to first organization on a distinctively junior college basis.

1916, Colonel L. C. Perry became convinced that the junior college was a permanent institution in American education and showed his faith by establishing the Texas Military College at Terrell as a private enterprise. In 1917, the state legislature of Texas recognized the private junior colleges by accepting their work for teachers' certificates, greatly increasing their prestige and usefulness. From this time on the private junior colleges began to multiply rapidly in number until in 1930 there were at least 28, seven of which were for Negroes.

Private college mortality. Deaths as well as births have been frequent in the private junior college ranks in Texas. Since the World War, maintenance and support in many cases have been on an unsatisfactory basis. The physical equipment of the denominational colleges is, in most cases, inadequate. Many, in their excessive effort to protect themselves from the "inroads of modernism, so prevalent in higher institutions of learning" have become reactionary and lost ground. Within the ten-year period following the World War, at least a score of church junior colleges gave up the struggle for existence, due to insufficient funds and inadequate student bodies. Five closed in the one year, 1928–29. Probably others are facing a similar fate. Unwise denominational rivalry led, in several cases, to the establishment of two or three institutions in the same town by competing denominations. Nowhere have the unfortunate effects of excessive denominational rivalry been better shown than in some Texas communities. Recently the Baptist Convention withdrew support from a group of such colleges and renounced all obligation for further indebtedness. Only three were reported in 1929, with endowments, the largest of which was $75,000.

UTAH

Types in Utah. Utah has two types of junior colleges, state and private. Westminster College at Salt Lake City is controlled denominationally by six coöperating Protestant groups. Weber College at Ogden; Snow College at Ephraim; Dixie College at St. George, and the Latter Day Saints College at Salt Lake City, are all units of the general system of church schools maintained by the Church of Jesus Christ of Latter Day Saints. The branch Agricultural College was established in 1913 at Cedar City in southern Utah as a branch of the Utah Agricultural College, but had existed since 1897 as a normal school and branch of the state university.

Educational policy of the Latter Day Saints. The Latter Day Saints colleges were founded as church academies at varying dates from 1888 to 1911. Weber, Snow, and Dixie colleges in Utah, Ricks in Idaho, and Gila in Arizona were expanded into junior colleges during the World War, primarily to train teachers for the public schools when there was a war shortage. Furthermore, the state was increasingly being supplied with public high schools, and it was felt that the junior colleges would fill a public need which the state was not legally prepared to meet. Even as far back as 1912, however, a feeling had been developing among church leaders that their available funds could be better devoted to religious rather than to secular education. By 1928–29, when church appropriations to these five institutions amounted to a total of $224,335 for a total enrollment of slightly over 1300 pupils,[1] sentiment had crystallized along two or three lines. It was thought that the

[1] It is interesting to note the actual contribution of the Church to the five junior colleges under its control for 1927–28 and 1928–29:

College	Church Appropriation 1927–28	Church Appropriation 1928–29	Total Receipts 1927–28	Total Enrollment 1927–28
Ricks (Idaho)	$47,400	$47,400	$63,170	354
Weber	56,000	56,000	68,075	306
Snow	39,500	37,000	48,435	215
Dixie	42,700	46,135	61,010	252
Gila (Arizona)	31,000	37,500	35,687	216
Total	$216,600	$224,035	$276,377	1,343

public in Arizona, Idaho, and Utah was as well able to maintain junior colleges as the Church. The need for the colleges was unchanged, but they should no longer be maintained on a missionary basis. Legal provision should be made for taking over the existing junior colleges by the public in the same way that seventeen church academies at an earlier decade had been taken over as public high schools. It was felt that even if the provision were not made by the public to take them over, the Church should cease its contributions, and they should be closed as church institutions. As a result, early in 1929, the General Board of Education of the Church announced that it would retire from the field of junior college education, and that, after 1930, it would make no appropriation to existing institutions of this type.

The legislature was in session at the time this unexpected announcement was made, so that time was lacking for the formulation of any unified or careful policy by those interested in state education. Local interests and special groups introduced conflicting bills. One of these provided for the establishment of local or union junior colleges when the assessed valuation was $14,000,000 and the high school attendance 500 or more, authorized tuition not exceeding $54 per year, and provided at the same time for a state contribution of $100 per student in attendance for a semester or more. Another bill proposed junior colleges at Ephraim and Ogden which should be an integral part of the University of Utah, and be controlled by it. With lack of unity among friends of the junior college as to proper procedure, the legislature adjourned without action.[1] Following its adjournment, the governor and the State Board of Education appointed a survey committee to investigate the problem. Definite legislation, presumably

[1] The secretary of the State Education Association writes: "There is but little doubt in my mind that had the school people been united upon a well-thought-out plan, the recent legislature would have done something of constructive nature along the lines proposed."

better coördinated, was sure to be introduced in the 1931 legislature.[1]

VERMONT

Vermont is one of the five states in which no junior college of any type exists, nor has there been any legislation on the subject.

VIRGINIA

In Virginia there are no public junior colleges, but a dozen under private control, usually denominational, most of them founded as institutions in the years soon after the Civil War. All but one are colleges for women, with fairly large enrollments. While most of the institutions now organized as junior colleges have been in operation for many years, it is only since 1913 that an attempt has been made to adjust organization to meet the requirements for standard junior colleges set up earlier by the Virginia State Board of Education. In 1913, standards for junior colleges were adopted by the Virginia Association of Colleges and Schools for Girls. By 1916, eleven institutions had been accredited as junior colleges in the state. In 1926, the state supervisor of teacher training, T. B. Eason, stated that:[2]

The average of the junior college work does not appear to be equivalent [to the first two years of standard colleges] though, with the tremendous improvement that is now being accomplished in junior colleges it soon should be. The practice of conducting under the same management a junior college, a high school, and a special school of music and art, has a tendency to divert attention from the college department. If the existence of junior colleges depends on the operation of a sort of three-ring educational circus, the junior colleges should coördinate the three enterprises sufficiently to satisfy the college people that the work of college grade is receiving due emphasis.

[1] See Supplementary Note, p. 43.

[2] Eason, T. B. "Articulation of Junior Colleges in Virginia with the Schools Above and Below"; in *Proceedings of the Seventh Annual Meeting of the American Association of Junior Colleges*, p. 17. Jackson, Mississippi.

He further says:

The fact that Virginia is already supporting a large number of higher institutions, the need of additional funds for education below the college level, and the further fact that but little serious study has been directed toward the junior college movement in Virginia — all conspire to prolong the time until the municipal junior college will find a place in the educational system of the Commonwealth.

WASHINGTON

The first public junior college work in Washington was given in connection with the high school at Everett in 1916, and was accepted at full value at the University of Washington. With a change of administration at Everett, however, subsequent to 1922, it was dropped. Of those now existing, the first was opened at Centralia in 1925 by C. L. Littel, as a part of the high school, but supported on a tuition basis. It was followed in 1926 by Mount Vernon, and in 1928 by Yakima. All three exist without legal authority, largely supported by charges of $100 or $150 tuition per year.

The legislature of 1929 passed a bill authorizing public junior colleges in districts with an assessed valuation of $10,000,000 and an average daily high school attendance of 500. All resident students were to be required to pay a tuition of $25 per quarter. Unfortunately, however, this law was vetoed by a reactionary governor, so that the three public institutions in the state exist only because of local sentiment favorable to them. New local junior colleges which were planned under the proposed law have postponed organization. It is reported that the governor, who appoints the regents of the state university, has requested them to "inform" the university that it is to accredit no new junior colleges. There has been discussion of new public institutions at Raymond and Aberdeen. There are three private junior colleges, in the state, two of them Lutheran.

WEST VIRGINIA

The Potomac and New River state schools are classified as public junior colleges, and there are three small denominational institutions. No legislation has been enacted. The secretary of the State Board of Education states that West Virginia is looking forward with much hope to the development of public junior colleges in the state. The recent Cavins survey of education recommends consideration of local junior colleges, and suggests the desirability of Parkersburg, Charleston, and possibly Wheeling as locations for them. It also recommends that the two existing state junior colleges be changed to local institutions.

WISCONSIN

There are only two small private junior colleges in Wisconsin. In 1911 the legislature authorized the normal schools to offer general courses on the junior college level, as already mentioned.[1] Such courses were given until 1922 in at least six normal schools. Concerning them, E. G. Doudna, secretary of the State Board of Normal Regents, says: [2]

> One or two colleges apparently forgot they were training teachers — gave practically all their time to developing the college work. There was considerable reaction from the superintendents of the state and as a result of this, in July, 1922, the Board of Regents repealed the rules under which the college courses had been authorized. Since that time there has been no junior college work given as such in the schools.

In 1919, the legislature of the State of Wisconsin passed a bill permitting cities to organize junior colleges and to appropriate a small sum of money to cover the expense, but no city has taken advantage of the law.

[1] See pages 59 and 756.

[2] In a letter to the author, May 17, 1930.

WYOMING

Wyoming has no junior college institutions of any type. A number of unsuccessful attempts have been made by the state legislature to establish state supported junior colleges in various parts of the state. The proposed plans met with the opposition of many Wyoming educators. A committee of the State Teachers' Association went on record in 1929 as definitely opposed to state-supported and state-controlled junior colleges, and briefly outlined the conditions that they felt should be met by any school district before being allowed to establish a local junior college.[1] Further legislation in accordance with their recommendation is anticipated.

QUESTIONS AND PROBLEMS

1. For any state given in this chapter, expand as much as possible the brief historical treatment. Look up all references to the state in the Eells bibliography, examine files of the state education journal, read the state law, and read the historical statements in catalogues of junior colleges located within the state.
2. In which states has the junior college development been most satisfactory, i.e., in accordance with sound educational principles and practice? Why?
3. In which states has the junior college development been least satisfactory? Why?
4. You are chairman of the state educational association committee on future junior college policy of a particular state. Outline the proposed report of your committee.
5. In which states has the development of public junior colleges been most significant? Of private junior colleges? Of state junior colleges?
6. In what states have public junior colleges been established prior to legal sanction for them? In which states have they existed the longest time without legal sanction? Is there any significance in a comparison of the two groups of states?
7. In what states has special legislation for the establishment or support of a particular institution or institutions preceded more general legislation?
8. Select five states in which you feel there is the greatest possibility of significant constructive development and action regarding junior colleges in the next five or ten years. Why?

[1] Printed in *The Junior College Journal*, vol. 1, pp. 51–52. (October, 1930.)

9. Which five states have the largest junior college enrollment in proportion to their population? Restrict this question, if desired, to public or to private junior colleges.
10. Which five states are strongest from the standpoint of denominational junior colleges?
11. Write a short editorial for a local newspaper, showing the need for junior college legislation in the next legislature in the state of publication.
12. Outline desirable methods of stimulating interest in the junior college in any special state.

SUGGESTED READINGS

See the Eells bibliography for suggested readings on most of the states. These are given in the index under the names of states, with cross-references to institutions located in them. The general works of McDowell, Koos, and Whitney contain much information on the junior college development in individual states. Hurt's *College Blue Book*, the *Directories* of the American Association of Junior Colleges, and the *Reports* of the United States Office of Education should also be consulted.

Special Bulletins published by the State Departments of California, Texas, Iowa, Louisiana, and Mississippi will be found valuable for those states.

The latest editions of State School Laws should also be available for reference.

The *Junior College Journal* contains a series of articles on junior college developments and needs of various states.

CHAPTER VI

DEFINITIONS AND STANDARDS

> The junior college is, as yet, in that interesting stage where there is nothing standardized about it — not even its name.... The term has become generic, like church or education, covering a multitude of experiments on the border line between so-called secondary and higher education. — MARION COATS.[1]

Contents of this chapter. This chapter offers and discusses various definitions of the junior college; it traces the development of standards by the various accrediting agencies; compares old and new standards of the American Association of Junior Colleges; analyzes and summarizes in tabular form the principal features of a large group of standards; presents the present status of standardization; and discusses the limitations and dangers of standardization.

WHAT IS A JUNIOR COLLEGE?

Difficulty of definition. The term "college" in itself is as difficult to define in America as the term "gentleman." The difficulty is accentuated when "junior college" is under consideration. Junior colleges, especially private ones, go under the name of seminary, institute, school, academy, hall, and even university.[2] Chapter II has shown the wide variety of institutions in fact as well as in name that are included in the junior college movement. Is there a basic underlying definition sufficiently broad and comprehensive to cover all types?

[1] Coats, Marion. "The Junior College"; in *Forum*, vol. 80, p. 82. (July, 1928.)

[2] The catalogue of "Vincennes University — a Junior College," says: "Consult the catalogue of the *college* you intend to enter after finishing at Vincennes *University*, so that you may be sure to qualify for conditional entrance to its junior class"! (Italics not in the original.) The catalogue of Urbana University (Ohio) states that it "is a coeducational liberal arts junior college."

Shall it be defined in terms of length of course, character of work, entrance requirements, or what?

Two well-known definitions. The American Council on Education has formulated the most widely accepted definition:

> The junior college is an institution of higher education which gives two years of work equivalent in prerequisite, scope, and thoroughness to the work done in the first two years of a college as defined elsewhere by the American Council on Education.

The junior college, according to this conception, is merely a slice of a four-year college. Somewhat broader, in that it apparently at least permits other types of college work, is that of the North Central Association:

> A standard junior college is an institution of higher education with a curriculum covering two years of college work which is based upon and continues or supplements the work of secondary instruction as given in any accredited four-year high school.

It is interesting to compare this definition with one given by P. P. Claxton, when he was United States Commissioner of Education, in which quality of work is emphasized:[1]

> A junior college is a college which requires for admission four full years of high school education or its equivalent, and gives only two years of college work, centering all of its energies and means on doing the best possible work in these two lower classes.

Definition of the junior college association. An interesting combination of fact, aspiration, and prophecy is found in the definition which for four years was accepted by the American Association of Junior Colleges. It was characterized by Dr. Farrington as "of the machine-gun variety, intended to bring down all game within range, or whatever may come within range, for it is delightfully vague in the forward-looking statements" which it contains. It was:

> The junior college is an institution offering two years of instruc-

[1] Robertson, D. A. "Standard Terminology in Education — Junior College"; in *Educational Record Supplement*, vol. 8, p. 22. (January, 1927.)

tion of strictly collegiate grade. This curriculum may include those courses usually offered in the first two years of the four-year college; in which case these courses must be identical, in scope and thoroughness, with corresponding courses of the standard four-year college. The junior college may and is likely to develop a different type of curriculum, suited to the larger and ever changing civic, social, religious, and vocational needs of the entire community in which the college is located.

This prophetic element, however, is lacking from the new definition of the institution adopted at the Atlantic City meeting of the Association in 1929, as given on page 167.

The real definition. The real definition of the junior college, however, is much broader and more extensive than those quoted above. It is found in terms of the standards for the junior college which have been set up by various standardizing or accrediting agencies. The remainder of this chapter will be devoted to a discussion of these standards — constituting the most significant working definition of this new member of the American educational family.

STANDARDS OF ACCREDITING AGENCIES

American Council on Education. The most influential set of junior college standards is that adopted by the American Council on Education, in 1924. It has been adopted *in toto* by the Northwest Association, by the State Department of Education of Maryland, and by others, and has been the basis of those adopted by many other agencies. A committee of the Council first recommended standards in March, 1921. J. H. Kirkland was chairman of the committee. Its recommendations were extensively discussed at the 1923 meeting, with the decision to delay action still longer. They were finally adopted at the meeting in 1924. Because of their wide influence and importance, they are reproduced below:

Definition. The junior college is an institution of higher education which gives two years of work equivalent in prerequisites, scope, and thoroughness to the work done in the first two years of a college as defined elsewhere by the American Council on Education.

1. *Admission of students.* The requirement for admission should be the satisfactory completion of a four-year course of study in a secondary school approved by a recognized accrediting agency or the equivalent of such a course of study. The major portion of the secondary school course of study accepted for admission should be definitely correlated with the curriculum to which the student is admitted.

2. *Graduation requirements.* Requirements for graduation should be based on the satisfactory completion of 30 year hours or 60 semester hours of work corresponding in grade to that given in the freshman and sophomore years of standard colleges and universities. In addition to the above quantitative requirements, each institution should adopt qualitative standards suited to its individual conditions.

3. *Faculty.* Members of the teaching staff in regular charge of classes should have a baccalaureate degree and should have had not less than one year of graduate work in a recognized graduate school; in all cases efficiency in teaching, as well as the amount of graduate work, should be taken into account.

4. Teaching schedules exceeding 16 hours per week per instructor, or classes (exclusive of lectures) of more than 30 students, should be interpreted as endangering educational efficiency.

5. *Curricula.* The curricula should provide both for breadth of study and for concentration and should have justifiable relations to the resources of the institution. The number of departments and the size of the faculty should be increased with the development of varied curricula and the growth of the student body.

6. *Enrollment.* No junior college should be accredited unless it has a registration of not less than 50 students.

7. *Income.* The minimum annual operating income for the two years of junior college work should be $20,000, of which not less than $10,000 should be derived from stable sources other than students, such as public support or permanent endowments. Increase in faculty, student body, and scope of instruction should be accompanied by increase of income from such stable sources. The financial status of each junior college should be judged in relation to its educational program.

8. *Buildings and equipment.* The material equipment and upkeep of a junior college, including its buildings, lands, laboratories, apparatus, and libraries, and their efficient operation in relation to its educational program, should also be considered when judging the institution.

9. *Inspection.* No junior college should be accredited until it has been inspected and reported upon by an agent or agents regularly appointed by the accrediting organization.

Summary for regional accrediting agencies. Campbell has made a detailed study of the proceedings of the regional accrediting agencies for matter dealing with the junior college. He gives the following summary of dates of first mention of the junior college, and date of first adoption of standards.[1]

	First Mention	First Standards
North Central Association	1903	1917
Northwest Association	1920	1922
Southern Association	1913	1923
Middle States and Maryland	1919	1927
New England Association	1925	1929

North Central Association. The North Central Association discussed many phases of the junior college movement for over a decade before the first formal standards for accrediting were adopted, in 1917, when the names of eight junior college members were published. These standards were revised at various times during the next ten years. In 1927, special permission was granted Stephens College to deviate from these standards in some respects in order to experiment with a four-year junior college.[2] Until 1930, accrediting of junior colleges had always been under the Commission on Higher Education. In that year a significant change was proposed looking toward cooperation of the Commission on Higher Education and the

[1] Campbell, D. S. *A Critical Study of the Stated Purposes of the Junior College*, p. 39.

[2] For a detailed study of the relation of the North Central Association to the junior college movement, see Campbell, D.S., *op. cit.*, pp. 39–47.

Commission on Secondary Schools — thus recognizing the dual collegiate-secondary nature of the junior college accrediting problem. A joint committee of the two commissions was appointed to report at the annual meeting of the association in March, 1931.

Southern Association. Miss E. A. Colton (chairman), at the meeting of the Southern Association in 1914, reported extensive studies of the junior college situation and needs, especially with reference to existing four-year colleges which were not of standard grade. She recommended at that time standards under which junior colleges might be admitted to membership. It required a decade of intermittent discussion in the Southern Association, however, before working standards were adopted at the Richmond meeting in 1923, and two years more before the first two junior colleges, Ward-Belmont (Tennessee) and Virginia Intermont, were actually accredited and admitted to membership in the association. The 1923 standards were further revised in 1927.[1]

Other regional associations. The Northwest Association of Secondary and Higher Schools adopted the standards of the American Council on Education, as recommended by its Commission on Higher Institutions in 1922, and has admitted two junior colleges to membership.[2] In 1927, the Association of Colleges and Secondary Schools of the Middle States and Maryland adopted the same standards, but reported that there were so many problems of a general nature requiring further study that they deemed it inadvisable at that time to accredit individual institutions, although several junior

[1] See Campbell, D. S., *op. cit.*, pp. 47–53, for discussion and evolution of the junior college idea in the Southern Association.

[2] Subsequently the Northwest Association modified these standards making them distinctly lower in some particulars. For example, the new regulations permit 18 to 22 teaching hours per week, instead of 16, and require an income of only $10,000 instead of $20,000. See *Proceedings of the Twelfth Annual Meeting*, April, 1930, pp. 38–39. Spokane, Washington.

colleges had applied for membership. Various problems relating to the junior college had been considered beginning with 1919. At the meeting of the New England Association, December, 1928, a set of standards was submitted, but was considered so much higher than those in effect elsewhere that action was delayed until December, 1929, when the standards as summarized later in Figure 17, were adopted. In this case they are standards for membership rather than for accrediting.[1] Thus, after fifteen years, all the regional accrediting associations have officially recognized junior colleges and adopted standards for them.[2]

STANDARDS OF THE JUNIOR COLLEGE ASSOCIATION

First standards in 1922. At its second meeting, in 1922, at Memphis, the American Association of Junior Colleges, after a day and a half of lively debate, adopted tentative standards dealing with definition, admission, graduation, equipment, faculty, support, and recognition.[3] These were revised at Cincinnati in 1925, and again at Atlantic City in 1929. Several meetings of the Association have been occupied in part with long and earnest debates over the matter of standards. Unlike most of the others adopted, the standards of the American Association of Junior Colleges are not standards for accredit-

[1] In a letter of May 17, 1930, W. B. Jacobs, secretary of the Association, wrote: "This association does not accredit colleges, junior colleges, or secondary schools. In order to understand the action of the association this should be kept carefully in mind. On December 7, 1929, the Association passed a 'Standards for Junior Colleges,' a copy of which I enclose. No junior college has as yet been admitted to membership in the association, although presumably one or two will be admitted in the near future. The attitude of this association towards the junior college movement is in no sense hostile. It recognizes that it is a new movement in New England, and that the institutions claiming to be junior colleges vary very greatly in form and attitude."

[2] See Campbell, D. S., *op. cit.*, pp. 53–56, for further details, especially on the Association of the Middle States and Maryland.

[3] Printed in *Proceedings of the Fourth Annual Meeting of the American Association of Junior Colleges*, pp. 79–81. (Chicago, 1924.)

ing; rather they are standards which institutions seeking membership in the Association should reasonably be expected to meet. The constitution of the Association provides that the active membership shall be made up of standardized junior colleges. The state or regional accrediting organization has been recognized as the proper accrediting agency where it exists. The Association's standards have been used for recognition of junior colleges in states where the regional associations do not accredit them, e.g., in New England and the Middle States.

Progress in junior college thought. A study of the successive standards adopted by the American Association of Junior Colleges reveals the progress of the best thought on the part of the junior college executives themselves as to the desirable standards their institutions should reach. All the other standards set up have been primarily written by men not directly engaged in the junior college field — they have been standards imposed from without the movement, rather than developed from within.

Old and new standards. A comparison of the old standards of the American Association of Junior Colleges, adopted at the fifth annual meeting at Cincinnati, February 21, 1925, with the new standards adopted at the tenth annual meeting at Atlantic City, November 20, 1929, are shown below in parallel columns. Changes are shown by italics.

OLD	NEW
Definition.	*Definition.*
The junior college is an institution offering two years of instruction of strictly collegiate grade. This curriculum may include those courses usually offered in the first two years of the four-year college; in which case these courses must be identical, in scope and thorough-	*The junior college, as at present constituted, comprises several different forms of organization; first, a two-year institution embracing two years of collegiate work in advance of the completion of what is ordinarily termed the twelfth grade of an accredited secondary school; sec-*

ness, with corresponding courses of the standard four-year college. The junior college may, and is likely to, develop a different type of curriculum suited to the larger and ever changing civic, social, religious and vocational needs of the entire community in which the college is located. It is understood that in this case also the work offered shall be on a level appropriate for high school graduates.

Entrance Requirements.

The requirements for admission shall be the satisfactory completion of a standard four-year course of study of not fewer than fifteen units in an accredited high school or academy approved by any recognized accrediting agency. The major part of the secondary school course accepted for admission should be definitely correlated with the curriculum to which the student is admitted.

Requirements for Graduation.

For graduation from a junior college, a student must complete a minimum quantitative requirement of thirty-session hours of credit (or the equivalent in semester hours, quarter hours, etc.) with such scholastic qualitative requirements adapted by each institution to its conditions. This work shall correspond in grade to that given in the freshman and sophomore years of standard colleges and universities. A session hour is defined as a credit given for a class which meets one

ondly, the institution embracing two years of standard collegiate work integrated with one or more contiguous years of fully accredited high school work administered as a single unit. The aims of the curriculum in either case are to meet the needs of the student for maximum growth and development, to further his social maturity, and to enable him to make his greatest contribution as a member of society.

Entrance Requirements.

For entrance to the two-year junior college fifteen standard units are required. The requirements for admission to the four-year junior college shall be the satisfactory completion of seven standard units from an accredited secondary school (junior or senior high school). For entrance to other types of organizations proportioned number of units shall be required. The student should maintain a continuity of interest in the selection of his studies throughout his junior college course.

Requirements for Graduation.

For graduation from a junior college *of any type as defined above, the student must complete in addition to the amount of work required for the completion of the traditional standard four-year high school sixty semester hours during the last two years of the course or thirty session hours*, with such scholastic qualitative requirements adapted by each institution to its conditions. A session hour is defined as a credit given for a class which meets at least one sixty-minute period (*in-*

sixty-minute period weekly for lecture, recitation or test for a session of thirty-six weeks (thirty-four weeks exclusive of holidays), two hours of laboratory work being counted as the equivalent of one hour of lecture, recitation or test. Students shall not carry for credit more than eighteen hours per week.

Degrees.

No junior college shall confer a bachelor's degree.

Number of College Departments.

The number of separate departments maintained shall not be less than five (English, social science, foreign languages, mathematics, science) and the number of teachers not less than five employed specifically for college instruction giving the major part of their time to this instruction.

Training of the Faculty.

The minimum preparation of teachers shall not be less than the equivalent of one year of work satisfactorily completed in a gradu-

cluding ten minutes for change of classes) weekly for lecture, recitation or test for a session of thirty-six weeks, two hours of laboratory work being counted as the equivalent of one hour of lecture, recitation or test. *A student shall not carry for credit more than sixteen hours per week, unless his work averages ninety or more, in which case he may carry for credit as many as eighteen hours.*

Length of Session.

A junior college shall be in session at least thirty-four full weeks each year exclusive of all holidays.

Permanent Records Kept.

A system of permanent records showing clearly all credits (including entrance records) of each student shall be carefully kept. The original credentials filed from other institutions shall be retained by the junior college.

Number of College Departments.

The number of separate departments maintained shall not be less than five (English, social science, foreign languages, mathematics, science) and the number of teachers not less than five employed specifically *for instruction in the upper level of the junior college, and* giving the major portion of their time to such instruction.

Training of the Faculty.

The minimum preparation of teachers shall not be less than the equivalent of one year of work satisfactorily completed in a graduate school of recognized standing, it being assumed that teachers already hold the baccalaureate degree. Efficiency of teaching, as well as training, both general and specific in the subject to be taught, shall also be taken into account.

Number of Class Room Hours for Teachers.

The average number of class hours per week for each instructor shall not exceed eighteen. Where some time is given to teaching below the college level, as many as twenty class hours per week may be allowed.

Number of Students in Classes.

The number of students in a class shall not exceed thirty (except for lectures). It is recommended that the number in a class in foreign language and English Composition should not exceed twenty-five. The number of students in laboratory section shall not exceed the number for which desk space and equipment have been provided.

Support.

The minimum annual operating income for the two years of junior college work should be $20,000.00 of which ordinarily not less than $10,000.00 should be derived from stable sources other than students such as public or church support or

ate school of recognized standing, it being assumed that teachers already hold the baccalaureate degree.

Number of Class Room Hours for Teachers.

The average number of class hours per week for each instructor shall not exceed eighteen, *fifteen is recommended as a standard load.*

Number of Students in Classes.

The number of students in a class shall not exceed *thirty-five* (except for lectures). It is recommended that the number in a class in foreign language and English Composition should not exceed twenty-five. The number of students in laboratory section shall not exceed the number for which desk space and equipment have been provided.

Registration.

No junior college shall be accredited that has fewer than sixty students in its upper two years of regular work.

Support.

The minimum annual operating *expenditure of the two-year junior college* should be $20,000.00 *or $30,000.00 for a four-year junior college*, of which ordinarily not less than $10,000.00 should be derived from stable sources other than permanent endowment. Increase in student body, faculty and scope of instruction should be accompanied by increase of income from such stable sources. The financial status of each junior college shall be judged in relation to its educational program.

Library.

A working library, adequately catalogued, of not less than 2,500 volumes, exclusive of public documents, with appropriate current periodicals shall be maintained and there shall be a reading room in connection with the library which is open to the students throughout the day. A trained librarian shall be in charge of the library. A definite annual income for the support of the library shall be provided.

Laboratories.

The laboratories shall be adequately equipped for individual work on the part of each student, and an annual income shall be provided. It is recommended that the school with limited income be equipped for good work in one or two sciences and not attempt work in others.

students, such as public or church support or permanent endowment. Increase in student body, faculty and scope of instruction should be accompanied by increase of income from such stable sources. The financial status of each junior college shall be judged in relation to its educational program. *A community with less than $10,000,000 assessed property valuation should be discouraged from establishing a public junior college.*

Library.

A working library, adequately catalogued, *modern and well distributed*, of not less than *3,500* volumes, exclusive of public documents, with appropriate current periodicals shall be maintained and there shall be a reading room in connection with the library which is open to the students throughout the day. A trained librarian shall be in charge of the library. A definite annual *appropriation* for the support of the library shall be provided. *It is recommended that this shall not be less than $500.00.*

Laboratories.

The laboratories shall be adequately equipped for individual work on the part of each student, and an annual income shall be provided. It is recommended that the school with limited income be equipped for good work in one or two sciences and not attempt work in others.

Separation of College and High School Classes.

Where a junior college and high school are maintained together, it is required that students be taught in separate classes.

High School Accredited.

Where a junior college and high school are maintained together, the high school shall be accredited by an authorized accrediting agency before the junior college shall be accredited.

Proportion of Regular College Students to the Whole Student Body.

At least 75 per cent of the students in the junior college shall be pursuing courses leading to graduation.

General Statement Concerning Material Equipment.

The location and construction of the building, the lighting, heating and ventilation of the rooms, and the nature of the laboratories, corridors, closets, water supply, school furniture, apparatus and methods of cleaning shall be such as to insure hygienic conditions for teachers and students.

General Statement Concerning Curriculum and Spirit of Administration.

The character of the curriculum, the efficiency of instruction, the system of keeping students' records, the spirit and atmosphere of the institution, the nature of its publicity, and its standing in the educational world shall be factors in determining its rating.

General Statement Concerning Material Equipment.

The location and construction of the building, the lighting, heating, and ventilation of the rooms, and the nature of the laboratories, corridors, closets, water supply, school furniture, apparatus and methods of cleaning shall be such as to insure hygienic conditions for teachers and students.

General Statement Concerning Curriculum and Spirit of Administration.

The character of the curriculum, the efficiency of instruction, the system of keeping students' records, the spirit and atmosphere of the institution, the nature of its publicity, and its standing in the educational world shall be factors in determining its rating.

Extra Curricula Activities.	*Extra Curricula Activities.*
Athletics, amusements, fraternities and sororities, and all other extra-curricular activities shall be properly administered and shall not occupy an undue place in the life of the college.	Athletics, amusements, fraternities, and sororities, and all other extra-curricular activities shall be *administered under faculty supervision* and shall not occupy an undue place in the life of the college. *In judging the standing of a junior college account shall be taken of the existence of and the influence upon the students of such extra-curricular activities as: Student government, student publications, literary societies, debating teams, current event, scientific, musical, artistic, and foreign language clubs, religious and social service organizations. Such activities properly conducted develop leadership and enrich college experiences.*
	Entrance to Terminal Courses.
	For entrance to terminal courses the criterion shall be the capacity of the individual to profit by the instruction offered.

ANALYSIS OF STANDARDS

Previous analyses. Two very detailed and comprehensive analyses have been made of the standards of the various accrediting agencies, state, regional, and national. Chamberlain,[1] in 1927, analyzed the standards set up by seven state,

[1] Chamberlain, L. M. "An Analysis of Junior College Standards"; in *Bulletin of the School of Education of Indiana University*, vol. 4, pp. 34–59, 125. (September, 1927.) He includes American Association of Junior Colleges, American Council on Education, the Southern Association, Association of Texas Colleges, North Central Association, Northwest Association, State Association of Mississippi Colleges, Methodist Episcopal, and Methodist Episcopal South churches; State universities of Illinois, Iowa, Kansas, Kentucky, Michigan, Minnesota, Missouri, South Dakota, and Wyoming, and State departments of Minnesota, North Carolina, Utah, and Virginia.

regional, and national education associations, two church boards of education, nine state universities, and our state departments of education. These are summarized and discussed under twenty-seven different topics. Whitney,[1] in 1928, made an extensive analysis of the standards of two regional and two national associations, and of local agencies in twenty-four states. An extensive summary of fifty-two items reports the most approved practice on various features. One of the limitations of both studies is that the different agencies which have various standards cannot always be identified. All, whether state, regional, or national, are tacitly assumed to be of equal weight, and results are stated in terms of number or percentage of the agencies having the given standards. The standards of the University of Kentucky are given the same weight as those of the American Council on Education. They are, however, very valuable and extensive studies, covering twenty-seven and thirty-five pages respectively. The student of this phase of the subject should be thoroughly familiar with these two tables and summaries. Koos made a detailed study of the standards of eleven different agencies which were available in 1922,[2] and compared them with the conditions as he had found them in the institutions which he had visited in his survey. Still earlier, McDowell[3] devoted a chapter to a study of accrediting standards, by states.

Summary of existing standards. In 1926, the United States Bureau of Education in its bulletin, *Accredited Higher Institutions*,[4] published in detail the standards adopted by fourteen agencies — two national, two regional, six university, three state board, and one church — and referred to several others.

[1] Whitney, F. L. *Junior College in America*, pp. 57–91. Also in *School Review*, vol. 36, pp. 593–603. (October, 1928.)

[2] Koos, L. V. *The Junior College*, pp. 625–42.

[3] McDowell, F. "The Junior College"; in *United States Bureau of Education*, Bulletin no. 35, pp. 71–97. (1919.)

[4] *United States Bureau of Education*, Bulletin no. 10. (1926.)

Unfortunately, in later revisions of this bulletin[1] only the national and regional associations are included. The chief features of the various organizations listed in the 1926 bulletin are summarized in Figure 17 (pages 176–83). In the case of four organizations[2] where later standards have been adopted the tabulation is based upon these revised standards. From this chart it is easy to see at a glance the standards prescribed with reference to any topic—e.g., "admission requirements"—by reading it vertically; or the principal requirements of any agency, by reading it horizontally. This includes all of the important national and regional accrediting agencies which have adopted junior college standards and widely representative state agencies of various types. For more detailed analyses the reader is referred to the works of Chamberlain and Whitney.

PRESENT STATUS OF ACCREDITATION

The directory of the American Association of Junior Colleges gives the different agencies by which a junior college is accredited, under eight different heads. The Association does not act as an accrediting agent except in those areas where no authorized agency takes account of the junior college. All

TABLE 10. NUMBER OF JUNIOR COLLEGES ACCREDITED BY VARIOUS AGENCIES (1929–30)

	TOTAL	PUBLIC	PRIVATE
American Association of Junior Colleges	230	88	142
American Council on Education	3	2	1
North Central Association	43	24	19
Southern Association	23	6	17
Association of Middle States and Maryland	4	0	4
State Departments of Education	288	125	163
State University	181	23	158
State College Associations	105	36	69

[1] *United States Bureau of Education*, Bulletins no. 41 and no. 7. (1927, 1929.) Bulletin no. 19 (1930) again contains complete information.

[2] American Association of Junior Colleges, New England Association, North Carolina State Department of Education, and Association of Texas Colleges.

FIG. 17. JUNIOR COLLEGE STANDARDS

Accrediting Organization	*Admission Requirements*	*Minimum Number of Faculty*	*Minimum Preparation of Faculty*	*Teaching Schedule (hours per week)*
American Council on Education. 1924.	Completion of four-year course in approved secondary school.	Not specified.	Bachelor's degree and one year graduate work; and teaching efficiency.	Over sixteen "endangers educational efficiency."
Association of Colleges and Secondary Schools of Southern States. 1923.	Completion of four-year course of fifteen units in approved secondary school.	Five, giving major part of time.	Bachelor's degree and one year graduate work.	Average not over sixteen.
North Central Association of Colleges and Secondary Schools. 1926.	Completion of fifteen units in approved secondary school correlated with curriculum to be taken	Not specified.	Bachelor's degree and one year graduate work.	Eighteen permitted; but fifteen recommended as a maximum.
New England Association of Colleges and Secondary Schools. 1929.	Graduation from four-year accredited secondary school or equivalent; correlated with curriculum to be taken.	Five full time. Ratio of faculty to students to be less than one to twenty.	One year graduate study; and experience or teaching efficiency.	Eighteen, including work in other institutions.
Northwest Association of Secondary and Higher Schools. 1930.	Graduation from four-year course in approved secondary school.	Not specified.	Bachelor's degree and one year graduate work; and teaching efficiency.	Eighteen; twenty-two, if part-time.
American Association of Junior Colleges. 1929.	Completion of fifteen standard units.	Five, giving major part of time.	Bachelor's degree and one year graduate work in subject taught.	Eighteen permitted; but fifteen recommended as a standard.
University of Illinois.	Same as admission requirements of University of Illinois.	Not specified.	Bachelor's degree and one year graduate work. New members must have A.M. or Ph.D. degree.	Twenty.
University of Kentucky. 1925.	Same as for University of Kentucky. Fifteen acceptable units.	Five.	Bachelor's degree. Seventy-five per cent should have master's degree (except Manual Arts).	Over sixteen "endangers educational efficiency."
University of Indiana.	Graduation from a commissioned high school.	Five full time.	College or Normal graduate and one year graduate work for heads of departments.	Twenty permitted; but sixteen desirable.

University of Michigan.	Same as for University of Michigan.	Not specified.	Approximately that of instructors in Univ. of Michigan. One year graduate study and Ph.D. as soon as circumstances permit, and two years' teaching experience.	Sixteen; but twenty when junior college and high school combined.
University of Missouri.	Equivalent to University of Missouri, including English — three units, Mathematics — one unit, Foreign Language — two units.	"Sufficient number."	Four years in standard college and one year of graduate work "desirable."	Not specified.
North Carolina College Conference and State Department of Education. 1927.	Completion of four-year course in approved secondary school, or equivalent; correlated with curriculum to be taken.	Five, each giving at least half time.	"Must" have bachelor's degree. "Should" have one year of graduate work and teaching efficiency.	Eighteen; or twenty-two if not all in the junior college.
Mississippi State Law and Accrediting Commission. 1929.	Fifteen units.	Four full time, or five major time.	A.B. for all. One year graduate work for instructors of sophomores.	Eighteen permitted; sixteen standard.
Association of Texas Colleges. 1928.	Graduation from four-year course, including fifteen units, "affiliated by state department of education."	Five, each giving full time to one department.	Bachelor's degree. Three department heads with master's degree. Other department heads working for master's.	Twenty-one.
Utah State Department of Public Instruction.	Fifteen scholastic units in accredited secondary school.	Not specified.	Master's degree or equivalent.	Twenty. Count five in high school equal four in junior college when combined.
Virginia State Board of Education.	Completion of accredited four-year high school course of sixteen units.	Five, giving major part of time.	Bachelor's degree and one year of graduate work; and teaching efficiency.	Eighteen; but twenty if part in high school or preparatory department.
Methodist Episcopal Church, South, Board of Education. 1925.	Fifteen units in four-year course in accredited secondary school.	Seven, exclusive of art, music, or expression; of whom three must give full time.	"Must" have bachelor's degree. "Should" have one year of graduate work.	Eighteen; but twenty-two if secondary school included.
University of California and State Law, etc.	Equivalent of University of California, for transfer students.	Not specified.	"Should" have bachelor's degree and two years' graduate work. Normally M.A. in subject taught.	Not over fifteen hours. Five of high school equivalent to three hours junior college.

FIG. 17. JUNIOR COLLEGE STANDARDS (*continued*)

Accrediting Organization	*Minimum Enrollment*	*Maximum Class Size*	*Minimum Number of College Departments*	*Curricula*
American Council on Education. 1924.	Fifty.	Thirty, except in lectures.	Not specified.	Provide for breadth of study and concentration.
Association of Colleges and Secondary Schools of Southern States. 1923.	Sixty regular students.	Thirty, except in lectures. In foreign languages twenty-five recommended. In laboratory not over desk space and equipment.	Five, including English, History, Foreign Language, Mathematics and Science.	"Character of curriculum" to be considered.
North Central Association of Colleges and Secondary Schools. 1926	Sixty, of which one third should be in second year.	Over thirty, except in lectures, "endangers educational efficiency."	Not specified.	Two years of college work. Sixty semester hours.
New England Association of Colleges and Secondary Schools. 1929.	Not specified.	Thirty in recitation or laboratory sections.	Five, including English, Mathematics, Foreign Language, Social Science, and Natural Science.	May have terminal courses. Preprofessional must be sufficient to enable graduate to enter junior year of standard colleges.
Northwest Association of Secondary and Higher Schools. 1930.	Fifty; twenty-five for one year institutions.	Thirty in recitation or laboratory sections.	Five.	Equivalent in scope and thoroughness to first two years of standard college.
American Association of Junior Colleges. 1929.	Sixty as standard.	Thirty-five, except for lectures. Recommend twenty-five in foreign language and English composition.	Five, including English, Social Science, Foreign Language, Mathematics, and Science.	Usual courses of first two college years. May meet civic, social, and vocational needs also.
University of Illinois.	Fifty.	Thirty in recitation and laboratory sections.	Six.	One half prescribed. Six hours Rhetoric, six hours History, six hours Foreign Language, sixteen hours Mathematics and Science.
University of Kentucky. 1925.	Thirty.	Over thirty, except in lectures, "endangers educational efficiency."	Five.	Of grade corresponding to standard colleges and universities.

University of Indiana.	Not specified.	Forty-five permitted; but thirty preferable.	Not specified.	Not specified.
University of Michigan.	Not specified.	Not specified.	Not specified.	Not specified.
University of Missouri.	Not specified.	"No overcrowding of classes."	Not specified.	Must include six hours English, five hours History, ten hours one Foreign Language, three hours Mathematics or Logic, ten hours Science.
North Carolina College Conference and State Department of Education. 1927.	Approximately fifty.	Thirty in recitation or laboratory classes.	Five.	"Should provide for breadth of study" of standard college grade.
Mississippi State Law and Accrediting Commission. 1929.	Thirty-five for two year institutions. Twenty for one year institutions.	Thirty, except in lectures.	Require Agriculture, Home Economics, Commercial, Mechanic Arts.	Equivalent to that of standard colleges.
Association of Texas Colleges. 1928.	Sixty, of which twenty should be in second year.	Not specified.	Five.	Should offer two years of college work.
Utah State Department of Public Instruction.	Sixty.	Not specified.	Four.	Offer four college courses, including three of Language, Social Science, Biological Science, Exact Science, and Education.
Virginia State Board of Education.	Approximately fifty.	Thirty, except in lectures. In foreign languages, twenty-five. In laboratory not over desk space.	Five, including English, History, Foreign Language, Mathematics, Science.	"Instruction of strictly collegiate grade."
Methodist Episcopal Church, South, Board of Education. 1925.	Not specified.	Thirty in recitation or laboratory classes.	Not specified.	College work should be essential part of the curriculum.
University of California and State Law, etc.	Seventy-five in A.D.A. after second year (200 by 1929 law) in District Junior Colleges. No restrictions in high school departmental type.	Not specified.	Five, including English, History, Mathematics, Foreign Language, and Science.	Equivalent to Junior Certificate of University of California. Must have English, History, Mathematics, Foreign Language, and Science.

FIG. 17. JUNIOR COLLEGE STANDARDS (*continued*)

Accrediting Organization	*Graduation Requirements (semester hours)*	*Student Program Limitation (hours per week)*	*Library*	*Laboratories*
American Council on Education. 1924.	Sixty and qualitative standards.	Not specified.	Subject to inspection.	Subject to inspection.
Association of Colleges and Secondary Schools of Southern States. 1923.	Sixty. Must not grant degrees.	Not specified.	2500 volumes, exclusive of government documents. Annual income of $500.	Adequately equipped for individual instruction; and annual income for upkeep.
North Central Association of Colleges and Secondary Schools. 1926.	Not specified.	Not specified.	3000 selected volumes, exclusive of government documents. Annual income of $800.	Fully equipped to illustrate each course announced.
New England Association of Colleges and Secondary Schools. 1929.	Sixty and qualitative requirements.	Not specified.	4000 volumes, exclusive of government documents. Annual appropriation.	Sufficient to insure efficient operation.
Northwest Association of Secondary and Higher Schools. 1930.	Sixty and qualitative requirements.	Not specified.	Efficient in relation to educational program.	Efficient in relation to educational program.
American Association of Junior Colleges. 1929.	Sixty and appropriate qualitative requirements.	Normally sixteen; but eighteen permitted if work averages over ninety.	3500 volumes, and periodicals and reading room. Annual appropriation of $500.	Adequately equipped for individual work; and annual income.
University of Illinois.	Sixty.	Sixteen, exclusive of physical training and military science.	5000 volumes, and periodicals and public documents. $600 annually for new books.	Equipment valued as follows: Physics, $3000; Chemistry, $2500; Biology, $2500.
University of Kentucky. 1925.	Sixty, exclusive of physical training and military science.	Sixteen, exclusive of physical training and military science.	2000 volumes, exclusive of periodicals and public documents. $200 per year for books.	Sufficient for equivalent of first two years of a standard college.

University of Indiana.	Two years of thirty-six weeks each.	Sixteen of fifty minutes each.	4800 volumes, exclusive of public documents, and trained librarian and room.	"Adequate."
University of Michigan.	Not specified.	Not specified.	Standards approved by University Committee of Inspection.	Standards approved by University Committee of Inspection.
University of Missouri.	Sixty units, equivalent to first two years of University of Missouri.	Sixteen.	"Adequate."	Must be adequate for individual work in physical and biological sciences.
North Carolina College Conference and State Department of Education. 1927.	Sixty and qualitative requirements.	Not specified.	2000 volumes, exclusive of public documents. Annual appropriation and "professionally administered."	"Adequate" — about $2000 for each science; and annual appropriation.
Mississippi State Law and Accrediting Commission. 1929.	Sixty.	Not specified.	1500 volumes, exclusive of public documents, for 2 years; 1000 for 1 year; and $5 per student annual appropriation.	Aggregate value $2000; $250 annually for each science.
Association of Texas Colleges. 1928.	Sixty.	Fifteen and music and fine arts.	2000 volumes, bearing specifically upon subjects taught.	"Sufficient laboratory equipment." and annual appropriation.
Utah State Department of Public Instruction.	Sixty.	Not specified.	5000 volumes, exclusive of public documents. Annual purchase of new books.	"Equipment necessary to meet college standards."
Virginia State Board of Education.	Sixty and qualitative requirements.	Not specified.	2500 volumes and periodicals. Reading room open all day. Librarian and annual income.	"Adequate"; and annual appropriation.
Methodist Episcopal Church, South, Board of Education. 1925.	Sixty and qualitative requirements.	Not specified.	2000 volumes, exclusive of public documents. Annual appropriation for new books.	Adequate — at least $1500 for each science; and annual appropriation.
University of California and State Law, etc.	Equivalent of Lower Division of University of California — or sixty-four hours, including English, six; Physical Education, four; Social Science, six; science or mathematics, six.	Normally twelve to eighteen units per semester.	"Adequate" and budgetary provision for regular growth.	"Adequate" for all science courses offered.

Fig. 17. Junior College Standards (*continued*)

Accrediting Organization	*Annual Operating Income*	*Independent of Organization*	*Miscellaneous*
American Council on Education. 1924.	$20,000, of which $10,000 is from stable sources, other than students.	Not specified.	Must be inspected by regular accrediting agency.
Association of Colleges and Secondary Schools of Southern States. 1923.	$20,000, of which $10,000 is from stable sources, other than students.	Classes must be separate from high school classes.	Seventy-five per cent of students must be taking courses leading to graduation.
North Central Association of Colleges and Secondary Schools. 1926.	$20,000, of which $10,000 is from stable sources, other than students.	Must be organized on a college, not a high school basis.	Inspection after sophomore year in operation at least one full year.
New England Association of Colleges and Secondary Schools. 1929.	$350 per student. Should total at least $50,000 as soon as possible.	Not specified.	
Northwest Association of Secondary and Higher Schools. 1930.	$10,000, of which $5000 is from stable sources, other than students.	Not specified.	
American Association of Junior Colleges. 1929.	$20,000, of which $10,000 is from stable sources, other than students.	Not specified.	Sessions of thirty-four weeks per year required.
University of Illinois.	$10,000.	Should be separate administrative organization, with Dean; separate building, library, and laboratories.	
University of Kentucky. 1925.	$20,000, of which $5000 is from stable sources, other than students.	Complete segregation in classes. Separate administrative organization with Dean.	Must be inspected before accrediting.

University of Indiana.	Endowment of $300,000, or fixed income of $15,000 other than tuition.	Not specified.	
University of Michigan.	Not specified.	Not specified.	Inspection by University committee of three.
University of Missouri.	Not specified.	Not specified.	
North Carolina College Conference and State Department of Education. 1927.	$10,000, of which $5000 is not from tuition.	Not specified.	Related high school must be accredited.
Mississippi State Law and Accrediting Commission. 1929.	$15,000 from stable sources.	Must be organized on a college, not a high school basis.	High school department must be approved. Not over fifteen per cent special departments.
Association of Texas Colleges. 1928.	Not specified.	Students may take both college and preparatory work under certain restrictions.	
Utah State Department of Public Instruction.	Not specified.	By special permission, high school seniors may take junior college work.	
Virginia State Board of Education.	$20,000, of which $10,000 is not from tuition.	College classes must be taught separate from high school classes.	Athletics, fraternities, etc., must not occupy undue place. Seventy-five per cent of students must be taking courses leading to graduation.
Methodist Episcopal Church, South, Board of Education. 1925.	$10,000, of which $5000 is not from tuition.	Must publish in Catalogue instructors and students separate from other instructors and students.	
University of California and State Law, etc.	For district junior college, $2000, and $100 per student in A. D. A. from state. Local tax to provide at least $100 per student additional.	Not specified.	$25,000,000 assessed valuation for junior college districts; $3,000,000 for high school departments, required for organization.

schools which are members of the Association are listed as accredited by it. Other classifications are self-explanatory. The number of junior colleges accredited by each association or type of agency is summarized in Table 10 (page 175), based upon the data of the directory.

LIMITATIONS OF STANDARDIZATION

There are several limitations and possible dangers in the standards as summarized in this chapter.

Danger of one-sidedness. They have been written, almost exclusively, from the university-preparatory point of view. All organizations except the American Association of Junior Colleges have been interested primarily in setting up standards that will insure adequate preparation of students for university entrance. The broader possibilities of the junior college for the great mass of students, who may and probably should never enter the university, but who are entitled to more than a high school education, are usually ignored or barely suggested. It should be borne in mind, therefore, that they have not attempted to be complete, but only partial definitions. For the most part the two objectives are not inconsistent. When, however, an agency requires that at least 75 per cent of the students shall be pursuing courses leading to graduation, it is sacrificing the possibility of wider usefulness to the exclusively preparatory aspect of the junior college.[1]

They are largely written by college men. This has its advantages, but also its disadvantages. The junior college has important secondary as well as collegiate aspects. Both should be considered in formulation of definitions and standards. The action of the North Central Association in this respect is hopeful and possibly prophetic. Shall standards be imposed from without, or developed from within?

Danger of mistaking the shadow for the substance. Stand-

[1] See Southern Association or Virginia standards, Figure 17.

ards are necessarily mechanical, expressed in quantitative terms. The junior college, if it is to be truly successful and realize its highest mission, must maintain a high quality of work. It is likely that this will follow the quantitative standards, but not necessarily so. A junior college should meet these standards, but should not be satisfied merely with this. There are standards of curriculum, of teaching method, of morale, and of character which must be attained, even if not stated by any standardizing agency. If the junior college standards encourage, stimulate, vitalize — they are successful.

Danger of university comparisons. The implication that the junior college is educationally safe if it is equal in quality to the college or university, is another possible danger. The university is frequently criticized for mass education, for dehumanized education, for lecture method, for mechanical and lifeless teaching. Shall the junior college be satisfied to come up to (or down to!) the standard of some (not all) university teaching?

Danger of quantitative standards. There is danger that standards will be retained, because they are expressed in quantitative terms. There is no concrete evidence that "over 30 endangers education efficiency," in all classes alike; that teaching schedules should never exceed 16 hours per week; that there should be a library of 5000 volumes. These and similar figures may be too high — they may be too low. It is probable that they are not right, certainly not in every case. For the most part they represent committee judgment. The scientific method should replace the committee method where possible.

The danger of stagnation. The glory of the junior college now, and probably for another quarter of a century, if not longer, is that it is an experimental institution. Any standards which restrict its growth, which tend to prevent full and free experimentation, are to be deplored. It is true that certain minimum standards should be maintained, but they should be flexible and subject to frequent change. That standards of some agencies are the same now as when adopted ten or fifteen years ago is a sign not of strength, but of weakness and stagnation. They should be subject to constant revision. The effort of certain enthusiasts of one form of organization to define it exclusively in terms of a four-year institution, for example, is to be deplored, as is also that of other enthusiasts who would limit it by definition to a two-year institution. The latest formulation of the American Association of Junior Colleges properly permits both types to be called junior colleges. The best friends of the junior college will be those who insist upon sufficient flexibility in definition to fit different conditions in different parts of the country. If junior college standards are so drawn as to encourage experimentation, they will be a blessing; if to stifle, cramp, solidify, they will be a curse. It is a healthy sign that the American Association of Junior Colleges has revised its definitions and standards completely three times in less than ten years. A pragmatic, not a static philosophy, must be the genius of the junior college.

Value of standards. With all their limitations, the standards summarized in this chapter have been a powerful influence in helping the junior college to find itself, and to become established in the confidence of higher institutions and of the general public. Rightly used, progressively interpreted, and constructively revised, they will continue to be a potent stimulus to constant improvement.

QUESTIONS AND PROBLEMS

1. Select or formulate a satisfactory definition of "junior college."
2. What progress is shown between the 1925 and 1929 standards of the American Association of Junior Colleges? Why were certain standards dropped? Do you approve of changes made?
3. What further changes in the standards of the American Association

of Junior Colleges are likely to be made during the next five-year period?

4. Compare American Association of Junior Colleges standards for 1925 as given in the text, with those adopted by same organization at Memphis in 1922. (See *Accredited Higher Institutions*; United States Bureau of Education Bulletin no. 10, pp. 29–30, 1926.) What significant changes are found? Why were these changes made?
5. Should standards adopted by the American Association of Junior Colleges be higher or lower than those of a regional accrediting agency? (See Oppenheimer.)
6. Should the American Association of Junior Colleges limit active membership to "accredited" or standard junior colleges?
7. Look up the standards of other agencies, not included in Figure 17, and make a similar chart for them; e.g., State Association of Mississippi Colleges, and University or State Department of Iowa, Kansas, South Dakota, Wyoming, Minnesota, Oklahoma, New York, etc.
8. Should either state departments or state universities adopt distinct junior college standards of their own?
9. What are the strong points and what the weak points of the methods of analysis of junior college standards followed by Chamberlain and Whitney?
10. Should junior college standards be formulated by junior college executives, by leaders in the field of secondary education, or by leaders in the four-year college and university field?
11. Should standards be established for junior colleges in their terminal and popularizing functions as defined in the next chapter? If so, who should do it?
12. Formulate a tentative set of standards for the junior college as a terminal institution.
13. Formulate a tentative set of standards for the junior college as a popularizing institution.
14. Take any standard and study it in detail in the statements of all the different accrediting agencies.
15. Should accrediting standards for the junior college be uniform throughout the nation? If so, what agency should formulate and apply them?
16. Study in detail the development of junior college accreditation in any of the regional associations.
17. A junior college executive writes: "The demand of regional and national accrediting associations that the high school and college be kept separate in its organization and operation places a heavy burden on the junior college. The biggest items of added expense are found in separate libraries, laboratories, classrooms, equipment, etc., for high school and college." Discuss this statement.

SUGGESTED READINGS

*_Proceedings of Annual Meetings of the American Association of Junior Colleges_, especially Fourth (Chicago), pp. 68–71; Fifth (Cincinnati), pp. 41-62, 90-93; Sixth (Chicago), pp. 38-45; Seventh (Jackson), pp. 33-42. Eleventh (Berkeley), pp. 332-35.

*Campbell, D. S. _A Critical Study of the Stated Purposes of the Junior College._ George Peabody College: Contribution to Education, Number 70, pp. 38-57. Nashville, Tennessee, 1930.

*Chamberlain, L. M. "An Analysis of Junior College Standards"; in _Bulletin of the School of Education of Indiana University_, vol. 4, pp. 34-59. (September, 1927.)

Colton, E. A. "Standards of Southern Colleges for Women"; in _School Review_, vol. 20, pp. 458-75. (September, 1912.)
Discusses standards of junior colleges in Missouri and Kentucky.

Colton, E. A. (chairman). "Report of the Committee on the Junior College Problem"; in _Proceedings of Twentieth Annual Meeting of the Association of Colleges and Secondary Schools of the Southern States_, pp. 17-18, 40-49. (1914.)

Craft, J. P. "Report of Fraternal Delegate to Southern Association"; in _Proceedings of the Sixth Annual Meeting of the American Association of Junior Colleges, Chicago, 1926_, pp. 75-78. See also _Proceedings of the Thirtieth Annual Meeting of the Southern Association_, pp. 348-55. Charleston, South Carolina, 1925.

*Farrington, F. E. "How to Define the Term 'Junior College'"; in _Proceedings of the Sixth Annual Meeting of the American Association of Junior Colleges_, pp. 101-02. Fort Worth, Texas, 1928.

*Graves, Mrs. C. L. "Problems of Standards for Eastern Junior Colleges"; in _Proceedings of the Tenth Annual Meeting of the American Association of Junior Colleges_, pp. 143-52. Atlantic City.

Kirkland, J. H. "Report of the Committee on Standards"; in _Educational Record_, vol. 5, pp. 126-27, 202-04 (July, 1924). See also _School Review_, vol. 29, pages 403-04 (June, 1921); and _Educational Record_, vol. 2, pp. 68-69. (April, 1921).
Adoption of standards by American Council on Education.

*Koos, L. V. Chapter 40, "Junior College Standards and Other Administrative Problems"; in _The Junior College_, pp. 625-42.
Discussion of standards in 1922.

McDowell, F. M. Chapter 5, "Accrediting of Junior Colleges"; in _The Junior College_, United States Bureau of Education, Bulletin no. 35, pp. 71-97. (1919.)
A detailed study by states in 1919.

Oppenheimer, J. J. "The Necessity of Maintaining our Standards as High as those of the Regional Accrediting Agency"; in *Proceedings of the Sixth Annual Meeting of the American Association of Junior Colleges*, pp. 50-54. Chicago, 1926.

*Ratcliffe, E. B. *Accredited Higher Institutions.* United States Bureau of Education, Bulletin no. 10, 105 pp. (1926.) Also Bulletin no. 19, 156 pp. (1930.)

*Whitney, F. L. Chapter V, "Junior College Standards and Standardizing Agencies"; in *The Junior College in America*, pp. 57-91.

Whitney, F. L. "Present Standards for Junior Colleges"; in *School Review*, vol. 36, pp. 593-603. (October, 1928.)
A condensation of above, with special reference to public junior colleges.

CHAPTER VII

REASONS FOR THE JUNIOR COLLEGE

Despite the very various motives which have contributed to the inauguration of the junior college movement and despite the wide divergence of type represented in the institutions now being administered under this title, there is underlying the whole situation a deep and widespread body of interests to which the new organization promises to give far fuller expression than has hitherto been possible. The movement is certainly in its main lines consonant with our best educational opinion, and it ought to receive, as no doubt it will, the most sympathetic opportunities to demonstrate its peculiar values.[1] — JAMES R. ANGELL.

Contents of this chapter. This chapter defines the four commonly recognized functions of the junior college. Under these four functions it groups a considerable number of reasons for the junior college and discusses them briefly; it summarizes studies of McDowell, Koos, and Whitney based upon catalogues and other literature, and considers statements of various groups of students as to their own reasons for attending junior colleges.

THE FUNCTIONS OF THE JUNIOR COLLEGE

Method of determination. In his doctor's dissertation (1926) F. W. Thomas first systematically determined the basic functions of the junior college, and established the terminology which has been rather generally accepted in later articles in referring to them. In discussing the need for such a determination, he says:[2]

One of the most vital of the issues involved in the junior college movement is that concerning the legitimate functions of this type

[1] Angell, J. R. "Problems Peculiar to the Junior College"; in *School Review*, vol. 25, p. 397. (June, 1917.)

[2] Thomas, F. W. "The Functions of the Junior College"; in Proctor, W. M. *The Junior College; Its Organization and Administration*, p. 11.

of educational institution. It seems obvious that the form of organization, the range and character of courses offered, the regulations and requirements, and similar matters must ultimately be determined in the light of their relation to the appropriate functions of the junior college.

In order to make the selection of functions reliable, he proposed three basic criteria by which to judge them, viz., history, need, and authority:

a. Has the proposed function played any influential part as a recognized aim in the establishment of existing junior colleges?
b. Does there exist a marked social or educational need, not met by other institutions, which would be satisfied through the fulfillment of the proposed function?
c. Has this function been advocated or approved by educators of sufficient standing and familiarity with college problems to merit consideration on such grounds?

He concludes that there are four basic functions which meet these criteria, which he designates as the popularizing, preparatory, terminal, and guidance functions. These may be briefly defined and characterized as follows:

Popularizing function. To give the advantage of college education of a general nature to high school graduates who could not otherwise secure it for geographical or economic reasons; and to give similar benefits to mature residents of the community.

Preparatory function. To give two years of work locally, equivalent to that given in the freshman and sophomore years of standard universities, which will adequately prepare students for upper division specialization in the university.

Terminal function. To give specific preparation by vocational courses for specific occupations on the semi-professional level, qualifying students who finish them for immediate place in a definite life occupation.

Guidance function. "This assumes a scientific interest in the individual traits and ability and the personal welfare of young students, in training them to think, in organizing their studies effectively, in supervising their teaching, and in making the college experience of each profitable to him to an optimum degree." [1]

A chapter will be devoted to each one of these functions later, especially to a consideration of the success which has been attained in each. In this chapter it is proposed to group under these four general heads the chief reasons which have been suggested for the existence of junior colleges, and to discuss them in concise form.

REASONS RELATED TO THE POPULARIZING FUNCTION

Democratization of college education. Is education above the high school to be the privilege of the classes or the boon of the masses? Going to college has become the great American habit. The junior college should be the "people's college" and available to all. It should provide collegiate opportunity for the mass of high school graduates who can't, won't, or shouldn't become university students.

Be it resolved that it is the unanimous sentiment of this conference, that the junior college is an integral part of the California state system of secondary schools, and that, as such it must be considered as a part of the common educational heritage of all California youth; and that this conference believes it to be essential, in the meeting of the State's obligations to its youth of secondary school age, that an adequate policy be developed which will eventuate in the establishment of public junior colleges which shall be available to all of the secondary school youth of the state. — Junior College Conference, Los Angeles, California, January 31, 1930.

Over 30 years ago an Illinois principal wrote: [2] "The offering of college courses in the high schools would open to all the added opportunity for intellectual growth and culture which so many are urged to obtain by going away to college."

[1] Whitney, F. L. *The Junior College in America*, p. 46.

[2] Pierce, E. C. "How Far Should the High School do College Work?"; in *School Review*, vol. 5, p. 118. (1897.)

University opportunity denied in some states. In states where the state university is not open to all high school graduates, the junior college furnishes an opportunity for public college education to those who would otherwise be deprived of it.

In California, Washington, New Mexico, New Jersey, Wisconsin, and Maine, entrance to the state university is definitely limited to the superior high school graduate, as determined by various criteria. Over half the graduates of California high schools have been unable to meet the entrance requirements of the University of California or Stanford University for this reason. In many other states there is some restriction on admission. Shall such students be deprived of all college opportunity? The junior college is the answer in the case of thousands of such youth.

"To thousands of our young people — modest in brain power — the four-year universities are closed because high school grades have not measured up to an arbitrary standard. To these the junior college means opportunity — opportunity to show their worth, if worth they have, and to enter the upper division of the university; opportunity to try again under teachers whose sympathies are human and understanding great."[1]

Geographical. The junior college, as a local institution, enables many youth to attend college who could not otherwise do so. Distance is a strong deterrent to college attendance.

Studies have shown that 90 per cent of the students in the average college come from within a radius of 100 miles. The homes of 50 per cent of University of California students are within 30 miles of Berkeley. Koos found that 41 per cent of the enrollment in 39 four-year colleges came from within a radius of 25 miles and that 27 per cent came from the immediate community. Green found that 96 per cent of the students in public junior colleges came from within a radius of twenty miles. Koos found in California that in counties having junior colleges the freshman enrollment was 71 per cent of the high school graduates; in counties without junior colleges or other higher institutions, it was 38 per cent.

[1] Boren, F. J. "The Junior College: A Community Asset"; in *Teachers' Journal of Northern California*, vol. 3, p. 4. (September 24, 1928.)

Financial. The junior college, as a local public institution, enables the student to secure two years of college education, at much less cost to himself.

He saves by living at home, with consequent reduction in cost of board and room, and other living costs; he has no traveling expenses; in many cases he has little or no tuition to pay. It has been estimated that the average student attending college away from home spends from $750 to $1500 per year. Much of this can be saved by living at home. This reason does not apply, as a rule, to the private junior college.

The Dean of Clarendon junior college, Texas, states that it would cost the people of the town $54,790 per year to send its seventy junior college students away to the university.

"An incontrovertible principle in all industry is that goods, wares, and merchandise in everyday demand, those in use by the multitudes, should be transported by the producer or manufacturer in quantities to, as nearly as possible, the very door of the consumer. This economic law is the basis for carload shipments.... Freshman and sophomore college advantages could be extended to Texas youths by the establishment of junior colleges at strategic points throughout the state, that could be operated at less than half the present cost per capita to the state for the same grade of work, done in the state's institutions, and at about one third the present cost to patrons."[1]

State obligation. The state has an obligation to furnish higher education which can be discharged more efficiently and more economically in scattered local units for the first two years than when concentrated in a single large university.

This obligation has been implied in the organization of state universities. Efficiency and economy are not easily proved, but there are many facts pointing in that direction.[2] Decentralized collegiate education usually is a considerable saving over concentrated university education for the first two years, as far as cost to

[1] Allison, A. A. "Junior Colleges"; in *Texas Outlook*, vol. 12, page 10. (June, 1928.)

[2] For discussion of relative costs in junior college and university, see Chapter XIX.

the state treasury is concerned, because a large part if not all of the cost of the junior colleges is met locally. Proctor estimates the cost to the state as less than one-fourth in California. Whether the cost per student to society is less, may be questioned. Doubtless the total cost is greater because so many more students will attend the local junior college. The state would save money by helping to support the junior college rather than bearing the whole expense in the lower division of the state university. Some elements ought to be less expensive, e.g., less elaborate and expensive equipment and facilities are necessary. On the other hand, there is greater duplication of equipment.

Adult education. The junior college can give additional cultural training to adults who are prepared to profit by it.

"The new junior college will take over the functions of the old liberal arts college and will extend the benefits of such college training to adults in their hours of leisure.... There will be classes in history, economics, finance, international affairs, etc., for those citizens who have had earlier benefits of high school and college education."[1]

As early as 1905 President James of the University of Illinois expressed his belief that the junior college would relieve the university of the burden of extension work and do it more economically and effectively.

Citizenship. The junior college can give training in better citizenship to a far greater number than can the regular colleges and universities.

The California law of 1917 authorized junior colleges to give courses in "civic education," and this phase of the work was stressed by Dr. Lange in an address before the National Education Association in 1915, "A junior college department of civic education." Commissioner Cooper says that such courses will be taken by citizens who "will be men and women of highly specialized colleges such as law, medicine, dentistry, nursing, who wish to inform themselves in subjects they could not study in college or in which they wish to keep up to date. Such citizens feel an obligation to

[1] Cooper, W. J. "Adult Education in the Junior College Program"; in *California Quarterly of Secondary Education*, vol. 4, p. 36. (October, 1928.)

devote at least a part of their leisure time to preparing themselves to discharge more wisely the responsibilities of American citizenship." [1]

Such courses may also be taken by the regular student, to prepare the youthful student for the activities of life — to participate in and enjoy these activities on a higher intellectual level as socially efficient citizens, and so achieve the civic, social, and cultural aims of our public school system.

An economic asset. The junior college is an economic asset to the community in which it is located.

Money that would be spent by students at the distant university is kept in the local community for two years. Additional students are attracted from nearby communities, with consequent increased spending power. Faculty salaries and other administrative expenses are a financial asset to the community. An educational institution is a good thing for a community, tending to make it a better place to live and raise families.

Mr. Boren, superintendent of the San Mateo Junior College District, recently said:[2]

The city or town which boasts a junior college gives tangible evidence of its exceptional interest in the welfare of its adolescents and its willingness to back its interest with its dollars. More than one community has found itself in the educational spotlight through its sponsorship of this institution. Of course taxpayers grumble at times because of costs, but Chambers of Commerce — composed for the most part of men who pay and men who see — are real boosters. If you want to hear a storm of protest, suggest to the Chamber of Commerce, the Rotarians, and the Kiwanians that the junior college now in the community should be abandoned. These men know its value, they know it to be a magnet which draws to their locality people that are worth drawing, and who will help to add to its material prosperity and its spiritual wealth.

Cultural asset. The junior college is a cultural asset to the community in which it is located. The faculty is qualified and

[1] Cooper, W. J., *op. cit.*, p. 32. [2] Boren, F., *op. cit.*, p. 4.

willing to take a leading part in the social and intellectual life of the community.

"The most important contributions, however, of the junior college to the State of California, can not be stated in terms of money cost or money economy. The presence of thirty-one public junior colleges, not to mention ten or twelve private junior colleges, means that there are scattered throughout the state just that many cultural and higher educational centers which tend to raise the standards of living and thinking in those communities."[1]

This may be accomplished by plays, concerts, lectures, addresses, entertainments, church and other organizations, and in less tangible ways.

Local adjustment possible. The junior college can adjust its work to special needs of the local community.

Diversities of climate and industry call for special educational adjustments. There are special opportunities for agricultural courses in a farming community, for horticultural courses in a fruit belt, for commercial courses, industrial work, forestry, oil, and other special types of work in other communities.

Proportion of high school students desiring college education. An increasingly large number of students are looking forward to collegiate education, upon graduation from high school.

The Utah committee investigating junior college needs in the state in 1929–30 sent questionnaires to all junior and senior high school students in the state. Replies tabulated from 49 of the 68 high schools (the missing schools included but one of any size) showed the following expression of intention on the part of 5688 students:

Fully expect to go to college	45 per cent
Will probably go to college	27 per cent
Quite undecided	22 per cent
Do not expect to go to college	6 per cent[2]

[1] Proctor, W. M. *The Junior College: Its Organization and Administration*, p. 10. Stanford University, 1929.

[2] Millikin, B. E. "Need of Public Junior Colleges in Utah," in *Junior College Journal*, vol. 1, p. 349. (March 1931.)

REASONS RELATED TO THE PREPARATORY FUNCTION

Nature of lower division work. Lower division work is not suited to the university, which is primarily interested in specialization, research, and professional work.

The work of the first two years is "secondary" or better "general," giving the broad basis of languages, literature, history, and science essential as a well rounded foundation for university specialization. This argument has been repeatedly stated by many writers on the junior college, since its enunciation by President Tappan of the University of Michigan in 1852.

Broad cultural foundation. The junior college may furnish a broad foundation for later specialization in the university.

"The junior college may well be an opportunity to provide that elusive cultural background of wide sympathies which Europeans say we so lack here in America. Instructors in the greater universities are interested primarily in specialized research work, and justly so. Often they are not particularly interested in stimulating immature adolescents to find their way into the realms of Plato, Sophocles, Dante, or Shakespeare from a broad humanistic viewpoint. Still more often they are not suited temperamentally to talk over human values in general with the patience that is necessary. The result is that even in the Lower Divisions, there is the permeating odor of narrow research and specialization taking the place of the linguistic, literary, and appreciative backgrounds that should precede specialization. I can recall that, as a freshman, most of my time in one course was spent on an exhaustive report on Studies of Negro Intelligence. And yet now I regret to confess that I never have read Homer through, nor the Divine Comedy, joys that I should have been guided into instead of thumbing over dusty reports on Negro Intelligence. The hue and cry ordinarily used against the junior college is that in it one loses contact with the older students of the university. In many ways this is desirable, for university students should be and usually are specializing intensively, while college students are still laying the broader foundations, for which the influence of enthusiastic specialists is not always healthy."[1]

[1] John Read, in a student report at Stanford University.

Free university resources. The junior college can free the limited university resources for more advanced upper division and graduate work.

This is especially significant in the case of private universities with only limited endowment and income. Privately controlled colleges and universities comprise 85 per cent of the 780 institutions of higher learning in the country and enroll approximately two-thirds of the students. Lack of funds for needed expansion has compelled the policy of exclusion and restriction with resulting dissatisfaction and hardship on those refused admission. Junior colleges can and should help to solve the problem — whether the private universities ultimately eliminate their lower division work or not. In New England, in 1926, a study of twenty colleges and universities showed that the number of applicants for admission that were accepted ran as low as 20 per cent and in no case exceeded 80 per cent.

University preparation at home. The junior college enables the student to take at home two years of work thoroughly satisfactory for university entrance.

Evidence is found in the case of many universities. Many of these are indicated in Chapter IX. "In the university the student goes through more school; in the junior college more school may go through the student."

Relief to the university. The junior college can help to take care of the greatly increased number of American youth who want a university education.

Even if the lower division is not abolished, the great increase in the number of students desiring university courses is overwhelming the universities and threatening them with educational indigestion. America wants to go to college. Will the decentralized and localized junior college solve the problem and relieve the universities of an impossible task? Since 1890 the growth of the college and university has been five times as fast as the growth of the population. In California, in a single year, 1928, 29,000 graduated from high school. The principal universities of the state cannot begin to take care of them all. In one year in the University of California the enrollment of freshmen dropped off 500, while the enrollment in the district junior colleges increased 2400. "What is to become of all the youths of both sexes who strive unsuccessfully to enter the sacred precincts of the college?... The halls of learning being packed to the doors, and thousands still clamoring for admittance, it becomes necessary to hold overflow meetings. Where shall these be held?"[1] "The junior colleges will tend to prevent annual cloudbursts of freshmen and sophomores from drowning the university proper."[2]

Pre-professional courses. The junior college can give satisfactorily many "pre-professional" courses.

Many universities and professional schools require two years of work for entrance to professional training. The junior college can in many cases give adequate pre-legal, pre-medical, pre-engineering, pre-commercial courses.

As a "shock-absorber." The junior college acts as a sorting and sifting agency for the university; as a "shock-absorber," as phrased by President Ray Lyman Wilbur.

The universities are constantly complaining of the inability of students to do work of university calibre. Let the junior colleges try their hands at the double job of preparing better the ones who enter the upper division, and discouraging others from going to the university at all. Not all students graduating from the high school, or entering the university as freshmen, should take a full university course. The tendency is to keep on, once having entered the university, or be marked as a failure. The junior college forms a logical stopping point for many who should not go farther. It is a try-out institution. The superior students are selected and recommended for further university specialization.

Student mortality. There is excessive student mortality in the university; this can be greatly reduced in the junior college, with benefit to the student and to society.

[1] Cobb, Stanwood. *The New Leaven: Progressive Education and its Effects upon the Child and Society*, p. 324. John Day Company, New York, 1928.

[2] Lange, A. F. "The Junior College"; in *Sierra Educational News*, vol. 16, p. 483. (October, 1920.)

Over 50 per cent of the freshmen in a large middle western university failed in one or more courses. Probation and dismissal are far too common. A university president reports that 58 per cent of the freshman class drops out before the end of the junior year.

Decapitated four-year colleges. Weak, small, and insufficiently supported four-year colleges, can do adequately junior college preparatory work of the first two years with full satisfaction to the university, and with profit and strength to themselves.

This has been pointed out in the case of Texas, Missouri, and other states where many denominational colleges voluntarily "decapitated" themselves.

Financial possibilities. The junior college makes a full college education financially possible for many students who could not otherwise secure it.

The student and his parents, in many cases, can save enough money while he is living at home to make possible two years of more expensive education at the university, where the expense of four years of non-resident education would be prohibitive.

Overlapping of courses. There is great overlapping of courses between the present high school and the first two years of the university.

Koos has studied this in detail for many different subjects with results showing marked duplication of work. This can be partially eliminated through a closer coördination of high school and junior college work.

A salvaging institution. The junior college is a salvaging institution. In states where "unrecommended" high school graduates cannot enter the university, it gives another chance to the bright academic mind that has been slumbering.

This is an exceedingly important reason in some states. Many a student in high school has an off-year, fails to find himself, gets into courses for which he is not well prepared, is hindered by illness or home duties, falls in love, spends too much time in student activities or in earning his way, and so fails to meet arbitrary university standards. Yet he has the stuff in him, when he wakes up under additional incentive, to be excellent university timber, if he had another chance. The junior college gives him that chance. What shall we do with the unrecommended student? President Lillard of Sacramento Junior College says, "We shall accept him and we shall give him, to the limit of our ability, what he wants and needs. We may salvage him for the upper division work, or we may equip him, as far as possible, for his life work while he is in the junior college."[1]

Superior instruction. The smaller junior college may give superior instruction because classes are smaller than in the university.

Freshman lecture courses of hundreds or a thousand are not known in the junior college. Recent experiments at the University of Minnesota and elsewhere have tended to show, although they have not proved, that larger classes may be quite as efficient as smaller ones. Even if this should be substantiated, however, there have been, are yet, and will continue to be for a long time in the future many parents and others who *feel* that small classes with opportunity for individual instruction are superior, and will wish their children to go to an institution where such classes are possible. As one of the author's students expressed it: "I went to the University of —— for a year, but I never got close enough to the professor in elementary economics to tell whether he was bald-headed or used wax on his hair."

Superior instructors. The junior college may give better instruction because it tends to have better instructors and tends to emphasize the teaching function.

On the whole instructors in the well-directed junior college have had more preparation, more experience in teaching, more professional preparation in education, than many of the university lower division instructors who often are graduate students whose primary interest is not in teaching but in research. The junior college

[1] Lillard, J. B. "What Shall We Do with the Unrecommended Student?" in *California Quarterly of Secondary Education*, vol. 5, pp. 69–70. (October, 1929.)

instructor is chosen primarily for his teaching ability; the permanent university instructor, primarily for his ability and promise in research. To teach students at the junior college level is more important than to teach subjects. "The President of Ohio State University said to your committee that freshmen at the university were being given work under teachers less qualified and conditions less favorable than they left last year in their high schools."[1]

A college dean in a large university in the Mississippi valley says:[2] "The combination of good teachers and research men is rare. We do not want any man in the college of liberal arts who is not a productive scholar. The question arises: Can a pure teacher keep pace? No. The universities should not keep a pure teacher more than five years. We should keep the good research man, however, whether he can teach or not."

REASONS RELATED TO THE TERMINAL FUNCTION

Need for semi-professional training. Many students who go to the university or standard college are unable to profit by the course of instruction they receive there. They could profit more by proper "terminal" or "semi-professional" courses.

There are a large number of occupations above the trade level but below the professional level, for which a two-year course beyond the work of the high school is adequate training. Many students, especially a large proportion of the unrecommended ones, could take such courses with profit and success. These courses are discussed in detail in Chapter X.

Gap in the educational ladder. There is a distinct need for semi-professional training in public junior colleges to fill a gap now existing in the educational ladder.

The public school system now gives adequate preparation for many trades in technical high schools and vocational schools, and for professions in universities and technical schools. The field of semi-professions has not been adequately covered, but left very

[1] *Report of the Joint Committee on Administrative Reorganization*, p. 391. Columbus, Ohio, 1921.

[2] In *Second Yearbook of the National Association of Secondary School Principals*, p. 58. (1919.)

largely to private initiative and capital to furnish such training, through correspondence schools or local institutions — often with distressingly high mortality and excessive cost.

Coöperative education possibilities. The junior college furnishes an excellent opportunity for "coöperative" education in connection with many courses.

Engineering, nursing, banking, and other courses have been carried on successfully in the junior college with students spending half time in the institution and the other half in industry, with financial advantage and increased incentive.

Preparation for teaching. The junior college gives preparation for the teaching profession.

The work of the teacher should be classed as professional, not semi-professional. In the states with the highest standards, graduation from a four-year college is a prerequisite for all teachers for every grade or type of certificate. This is none too high. In a large part of the country, however, the requirement as yet is for only two years' training in advance of the high school — thus placing it on a semi-professional basis. In such states the junior college when it gives sufficient professional courses in education is functioning as a teacher training institution. There are 37 states in which two years' work beyond high school qualify for teachers' certificates of a sufficiently attractive type to justify the establishment of teacher training curricula in the junior colleges.

Occupational extension course. In some cases the junior college can offer occupational extension courses for those now employed in some trade.

Thus, an intelligent carpenter can take courses in economics, accounting, psychology, and management, that will prepare him better to be a contractor; a bookkeeper can prepare himself as an accountant; a stenographer as a private secretary.

Opportunities for girls. The junior college is particularly helpful in the education of girls for professional and semi-professional work.

"The girl who is looking forward to earning her own living shortly can often be saved for a profession if she can spend only two years in professional training. A profession today almost connotes a monied class, so expensive is the training for it. Again, a girl whose heart is set on a vocation can often be persuaded to wait and take a two-year course which will give her more background, when she would resolutely decline to consider a full four-year course." [1]

Non-professional terminal courses. The junior college can give a non-professional terminal course for students who do not wish to take a full four-year course, but wish a general cultural background on a higher level than the high school.

Sarah Lawrence College, New York, has been organized as an experimental institution with this object in view. Girls are discouraged from entrance who wish to continue their studies in four-year colleges after graduation.

Need for more than technical training. Roger Babson has asserted that "More failures are due to lack of character than to lack of skill or technical knowledge." The junior college is adapted to the giving of this proper balance to the strictly vocational type of training.

The private business college, semi-technical or trade school, and such schools aim at the strictly "bread and butter" phase. The graduate is guaranteed a job (in the advertisements). The junior college can give this same training at public expense and combine with it the broader understanding of "human relationships or job wisdom." A combination of skill, technical knowledge, and good citizenship or social understanding is needed for success in a vocation.

REASONS RELATED TO THE GUIDANCE FUNCTION

Home influence. The junior college permits a continuation of home influence during immaturity.

The average freshman is only seventeen or eighteen years of age. In many cases he could profitably and safely remain at home for

[1] Coats, Marion. "The Junior College in the Education of Girls"; in *Red Book Magazine.* (February, 1923.)

two years more until he has developed more judgment, balance, and maturity. "How many boys and girls seventeen years of age can safely enter a large university where there are a thousand or more freshmen and there depend almost entirely upon their own wisdom for the solution of the complex moral and social problems with which they are confronted daily?" [1] Not all youths need to continue at home. For many, a change is desirable. Let them go away from home. But for many others an added two years at home is their salvation. The great majority are scarcely mature enough to be thrust abruptly into the atmosphere of the large university, before they reach social and moral maturity.

Dormitory supervision. The junior college may offer to the student, who is away from home, the advantage of being under careful dormitory supervision.

This is stressed by many of the smaller residential private junior colleges especially those for women. "Segregation for girls in the junior college for women exclusively is excellent. The first taste of freedom, of absence from home, is unsettling at best; and the small group, living in daily association with older women who are interested but wise in their interference, becomes stronger in scholarship, and in principles of life." [2]

Guidance and understanding. There is a lack of individual guidance and of sympathetic understanding of the problems of the freshmen in many universities.

"The freshman enters an environment wholly different from anything he has experienced. He is a stranger in a strange land — new classmates, new teachers, new subjects, new methods, and perchance new aspirations. He needs advice. He needs encouragement. He needs sympathy. He needs the magnetic touch of personality. And under the conditions that necessarily obtain, these are the things most difficult to give or to get. In his freshman

[1] Cox, R. G. "The Junior College"; in *Hearst's International Cosmopolitan Magazine*, p. 1. (August, 1928.)

[2] Coats, M. "The Junior College in the Education of Girls"; in *Red Book Magazine*. (February, 1923.)

year the college student craves and needs more help and more consideration than at any later time."[1]

Dr. W. L. Smith, president of Washington and Lee University, says:[2] "What the American freshman generally gets during the critical and formative first year of campus life is: (1) Individual indifference, neglect, and contempt; (2) Organized enmity, tyranny, and cruelty; (3) The poorest, least trained, and cheapest teachers; (4) The most crowded classes and laboratories and the least individual attention and guidance; (5) and the most rigid and wholesale discipline and dismissal by the faculty officers." It is to be hoped that the picture is not as black as here painted. But if it is only gray instead of black, it suggests that the junior college has a remarkable opportunity to throw more high lights into the composition. The university is for mature men and women, not for immature boys and girls. The junior college is chiefly concerned with the student as a developing individual — the university with subject matter, scholarship, and research. Guidance is a personal matter.

Home coöperation. In the junior college closer coöperation is possible between home and college.

In the smaller local community the administrator is likely to have a better opportunity to become acquainted with the parents and to coöperate in the extra-classroom training and guidance of the immature freshman.

Religious training. Religious and moral training can be and in many cases are emphasized in the junior college.

This reason is frequently stressed by many of the private junior colleges — less so in the case of the public institutions.

Personal contacts. In the junior college there are greater opportunities for helpful outside personal contacts with the men and women of the faculty than in the large university.

[1] Christensen, D. H. "The Junior College"; in *Utah Educational Review*, vol. 23, pp. 386–87, 412–14. (April, 1930.)

[2] "Junior Colleges Steadily Increasing in Favor"; in *School Life*, vol. 11, pp. 150–51. (April, 1926.)

Even in our complex modern civilization "Mark Hopkins and the log" still remain in many ways the ideal of faculty-student relations, both intra- and extra-classroom.

Development of leadership. The junior college offers many opportunities for the development of leadership and responsibility.

In the four-year institution most such positions go to juniors and seniors. In the junior college such responsibilities come earlier and more frequently. In the junior college the student may be a big fish in a little puddle, in the university a little fish in a big puddle. The junior college is more likely to bring out the latent ability of the backward student — the slow, the shy, the awkward.

Try-out for university. The junior college gives the student an opportunity to try-out at home his aptitude for university work at less expense and with less chagrin if he proves to be not fitted for it.

As already pointed out, freshman mortality in the university is shockingly high. The human wastage is far too great. One American university announced in the middle of the year that 1700 freshmen out of a class of 2900 would not be permitted to enter as sophomores.[1] Another institution dropped 300 of a class of 800 freshmen. One of the large middle western universities reports that 51 per cent of the freshman class failed to do satisfactory work. Thomas says that many freshmen in California were sent home in humiliation from the university when their previous records justified the most sanguine expectation of success, until the general impression spread over the state that the freshman year at the University of California was an "extra-hazardous" venture, both from an educational and from a social standpoint.[2] President Ray Lyman Wilbur says that when something like 60 per cent of those admitted to our colleges fail to graduate, the collective disappointment is prodigious. What is wrong? Is it the freshman? Is it the institution? Is it something we do to the freshman? Is it some-

[1] *American Educational Digest*, vol. 47, p. 312. (March, 1928.)

[2] Thomas, F. W. *A Study of Functions of the Public Junior College and the Extent of their Realization in California*, p. 96. Stanford University, California. 1926.

thing we don't do to him? Are our colleges playing fair with their freshmen? Let the ambitious student test himself in the local junior college, where conditions may be more favorable, success more likely, failure less disastrous.

A transition institution. The junior college is an institution making the transition easier from high school restrictions and methods to university freedom and independence.

Just as the junior high school eliminated the classic gap between the grade school and high school, so the junior college, higher than the high school, lower than the university, tends to close the high-school-university gap. A difficult jump is reduced to two easier steps.

STATEMENTS OF REASONS BY ADMINISTRATORS AND PARENTS

Several rather extensive studies of reasons for the existence of junior colleges, stressing different phases and made at different times, are of sufficient importance to be summarized and compared.

McDowell's study. McDowell asked administrators to check the controlling reasons for the organization of their junior colleges among a suggested list of eleven such reasons. His results are summarized in Table 11.[1]

McDowell's study represents the reasons for the organization of junior colleges as viewed by the administrators themselves. There is a marked difference, as might be anticipated, between the replies from the private and from the public junior college men. The rank order correlation between the two is .09 ± .20. The three reasons in which the greatest difference in emphasis is found are: (1) the desire of parents to keep their children at home, and (2) geographical remoteness, which were important reasons in the public institutions, but much less so in the pri-

[1] McDowell, F. M. *The Junior College.* United States Bureau of Education, Bulletin no. 35, pp. 28, 35, 107. Washington, D.C., 1919.

Table 11. Summary of Reasons for Organization of Public and Private Junior Colleges According to McDowell, in 1919

Suggested Reason	Public Junior Colleges (21)		Private Junior Colleges (54)	
	Number	Rank	Number	Rank
Desire of parents to keep children at home	20	1	17	9
To provide a completion school for those who cannot go farther	17	2	36	2
Desire of students to secure college work near home	14	3	25	4
To meet specific local needs	10	4	22	5
Geographical remoteness from a standard college or university	9	5	10	11
To meet the entrance requirements of professional schools	9	5	22	5
To provide vocational training more advanced than high school work	5	7	20	7
Financial difficulty in maintaining a four-year course	5	7	26	3
To provide additional opportunities for teacher training	2	9	19	8
To secure the segregation of the sexes	1	10	14	10
To provide opportunities for higher education under church control	1	10	38	1

vate ones; and (3) the religious motive which was the predominant one in the private institutions, but was at the bottom of the list for those under public control.

Koos's investigations. Koos studied the "special purposes" for the existence of junior colleges as stated in two different sources: (1) an analysis of the reasons given in twenty-two published articles and addresses, which had appeared within the previous decade; and (2) an analysis of statements found in the catalogues or bulletins of 56 junior colleges, 23 public and 33 private. Some fifty different reasons were condensed into 21 "more or less distinct purposes" which were presented in five groups. These 21 reasons have been widely quoted, and junior colleges have sometimes been judged by the extent to which they were fulfilling them. They are given in Table 12.[1]

[1] Koos, L. V. *The Junior College Movement*, p. 21. Ginn and Company, Boston, 1925.

TABLE 12. SPECIAL PURPOSES OF THE JUNIOR COLLEGE, AS DETERMINED BY ANALYSIS OF EDUCATIONAL LITERATURE AND JUNIOR COLLEGE CATALOGUES ACCORDING TO KOOS, IN 1922

	Percentage of Purposes in		
	Educational literature (per cent)	Public junior college catalogues (per cent)	Private junior college catalogues (per cent)
I. Affecting education in the two years under consideration			
1. Offering two years of work acceptable to colleges and universities	15	22	31
2. Completing education of students not going on	10	5	4
3. Providing occupational training of junior college level	12	12	16
4. Popularizing of higher education	18	15	10
5. Continuing home influence during immaturity	18	4	4
6. Affording attention to the individual student	8	5	10
7. Offering opportunities for training in leadership	0	0	2
8. Offering better instruction in these school years	2	1	0
9. Allowing for exploration	1	0	1
II. Affecting the organization of the school system			
10. Placing in the secondary school all work appropriate to it	11	2	0
11. Making the secondary school period coincide with adolescence	8	0	0
12. Fostering the evolution of the system of education	9	0	0
13. Economizing time and expense by avoiding duplication	5	0	0
14. Assigning a function to the small college	7	0	1
III. Affecting the university			
15. Relieving the university	8	0	0
16. Making possible real university functioning	10	0	0
17. Assuring better preparation for university work	4	2	0
IV. Affecting Instruction in the high school			
18. Improving high school instruction	4	0	0
19. Caring better for brighter high school students	1	0	0
V. Affecting the community of location			
20. Offering work meeting local needs	9	4	0
21. Affecting the cultural tone of the community	6	0	0

The articles and addresses stress many different functions, as indicated in the table. In the catalogues of the 56 institutions, however, only four reasons are mentioned in ten or more catalogues: offering two years of work acceptable to colleges and universities; providing occupational training of junior college grade; popularizing higher education; and affording attention to the individual student. Koos concludes, after his study of these purposes:[1]

These aspirations outline an ambitious program for this new unit

[1] Koos, L. V. *The Junior College Movement*, p. 28. Ginn and Company.

— so ambitious, indeed, that the special purposes as catalogued cannot be accepted forthwith. However, they furnish a cross-section of the educational consciousness which has given rise to the movement, and at the same time they supply a set of tentative criteria, the validity of which is scrutinized in subsequent portions of this volume.

Koos also asked the parents of over 600 junior college students in nine junior colleges in Minnesota, Michigan, Texas, and California why their sons and daughters were attending the local junior college rather than a college or university elsewhere. Replies were received from 199, giving reasons which were classified as follows: [1]

	Number	Per cent of Total
Attendance at junior college less expensive	143	71.9
Home influence extended	118	59.3
Training received as good or better	63	31.7
More attention to individual	47	23.6
Preference of student	7	3.5
Duty to patronize local junior college	6	3.0
Gap between high school and college bridged	5	2.5
Student needed at home	5	2.5
General and miscellaneous	29	14.6

The first four are the only important reasons given; economy and home influence are the only ones mentioned by over half the parents.

Whitney's study. Whitney made an extensive analysis, in 1927–28, of the objectives of the junior college, based upon an analysis of published statements in the college catalogues and replies in a questionnaire to the question, "Please give the reasons for the organization of your junior college and its special purpose." He used Koos's classification, slightly modified. He did not differentiate between the two types of sources, grouping them all together, first with a discussion of private colleges and then of public colleges. His results are summarized in Table 13 for 294 institutions.

[1] Koos, L. V. *Junior College*, p. 124.

TABLE 13. A COMPARISON OF THE PERCENTAGE OF STATEMENTS RECOGNIZING THE SPECIAL PURPOSES OF PUBLIC AND PRIVATE JUNIOR COLLEGES (1927-28)

(162 private, 132 public)

	PRIVATE (per cent)	PUBLIC (per cent)
I. Affecting education in the two years under consideration		
1. Furnishing moral and religious training	45.7	0.0
2. Providing occupational training of junior college grade	43.2	24.2
3. Completing education of students not going on	35.2	22.7
4. Popularizing higher education	29.0	76.5
5. Affording attention to the individual	25.3	8.3
6. Offering two years of work acceptable to colleges and universities	23.5	19.7
7. Continuing home influence during immaturity	17.3	45.4
8. Offering better opportunities for training in leadership	9.3	0.8
9. Offering better instruction in these school years	8.0	14.4
10. Allowing for exploration	4.3	1.6
II. Affecting the organization of the school system		
1. Fostering the evolution of the system of education	3.1	5.3
2. Economizing time and expense by avoiding duplication	1.2	0.0
3. Placing in the secondary school all work appropriate to it	0.6	0.8
4. Making the school period coincide with adolescence	0.0	2.3
5. Assigning a function to the small college	0.0	0.8
III. Affecting the university		
1. Assuring better preparation for university work	8.0	4.6
2. Relieving the enrollment in the university	5.6	8.3
3. Making possible real university functioning	1.2	0.0
IV. Affecting instruction in the high school		
1. Improving high school instruction	0.6	0.0
2. Providing better department heads	0.0	0.8
3. Raising standards and putting equipment to use	0.0	0.8
V. Affecting the community of location		
1. Offering work meeting local needs	24.7	9.9
2. Affecting the cultural tone of the community	2.4	4.6
3. Keeping local money at home	0.0	0.8
4. Cutting down the number leaving the community permanently	0.6	0.8

Comparisons of Koos and Whitney. In both Whitney's and Koos's studies the classification is necessarily somewhat subjective. General statements of purpose are especially difficult to analyze and classify under the headings given. As Koos points out:[1]

> Mention should be made of some difficulties met with in the attempts at classification. In studies of this sort meanings shade into one another almost imperceptibly; one cannot be certain that violence has not sometimes been done by placing a particular statement under some particular category, thus to some extent misrepresenting the meaning intended by the author. It is also at times impossible to take account of all interrelationships of purposes, expressed or implied.

This difficulty of classification of course is greatly accentuated when different men at different times classify such material. Whitney studied seven years' development in junior college objectives by comparing his percentages with those of Koos. It is doubtful whether such a comparison has much validity, when the difficulties of classification are so great. It would be instructive to have several different men classify the same body of material, and measure the reliability of the classification. Until some such guarantee of reliability is available, such comparisons as Whitney makes, showing the progress in seven years, should be accepted with considerable caution.[2]

With these reservations, it is interesting to quote Whitney's general conclusions in comparing the two periods. Concerning the development of special purposes of private junior colleges, he finds that:[3]

(1) Three times the proportion of private junior colleges are now

[1] Koos, L. V. *The Junior College Movement*, pp. 18–19. Ginn and Company.

[2] For example, Whitney classifies all statements bearing on the lowering of the cost of education under the topic "popularizing higher education," and states that 29 per cent of the private colleges in 1927–28 mentioned it, but none of them did in 1920–21. Did Koos use this vague phrase in exactly the same sense? As already shown in the various reasons listed under the popularizing function, many interpretations of this phrase are possible.

[3] Whitney, *op. cit.*, p. 41.

offering curriculums organized with a view to terminal opportunities; (2) over one fourth, as compared to none, aim to popularize higher education; (3) a few, as compared to none, offer improved instruction and exploratory courses; and (4) the "small college" idea seems to have dropped out since 1920.

For the public institutions he finds the following significant progress, in the same period:[1]

(1) Secondary education as offered in the local system is fast breaking away from the age-old domination of higher education; (2) but one half the proportion of junior colleges are now offering vocational curriculums; (3) in the modern junior college there is but about one third the emphasis on individual education; (4) there is renewed emphasis on better instruction.

Campbell's study. Campbell, in 1930, published by far the most extensive study of this type that has been made, his doctor's dissertation, covering 126 pages in published form. He summarized the stated purposes found in 343 junior college catalogues; and in 349 general articles dealing in any way with purposes and objectives. He found 35 different purposes stated in the catalogues, the eleven most frequently mentioned, and the per cent of catalogues in which they were found, being as follows:[2]

1. Preparation for college or university........ 43 per cent
2. Give individual attention to students........ 32
3. Economy of time and money................ 29
4. Provide smaller classes..................... 22
5. Continue home influence.................... 22
6. Provide occupational training............... 21
7. Provide suitable try-out for college.......... 18
8. Offer completion education................. 14
9. Develop leadership......................... 12
10. Further training for high school graduates.... 12
11. Meet local needs.......................... 10

[1] Whitney, *op. cit.*, p. 43.

[2] Campbell, Doak S. *A Critical Study of the Stated Purposes of the Junior College.* George Peabody College, Contributions to Education, Number 70. Nashville, Tennessee, 1930.

Similarly the functions given in 10 per cent or more of the general articles were found to be:[1]

1. Preparation for college or university	66 per cent
2. Completion of education	37
3. Providing educational training	33
4. Completion of secondary education	29
5. Economy of time and expense	25
6. Popularizing higher education	25
7. Meeting local needs	22
8. Fitting the school to adolescence	19
9. Relieving the universities	18
10. Continuing home influence	17
11. Assigning function to smaller college	12
12. Democratization of higher education	12
13. Giving individual attention to students	10

Campbell's general conclusions as to the relative importance of the reasons analyzed are:[2]

Judged by frequency of mention in the catalogues studied, those responsible for the program of the junior college attach more importance to the preparatory function and purpose than to all other functions and purposes combined.

Other studies. Other briefer studies by Proctor and Wood, based on junior college administrators' opinions, are referred to in the suggested problems at the close of the chapter.

STUDENT REASONS FOR ATTENDING JUNIOR COLLEGES

Introductory. A few studies of considerable significance have been made from an entirely different angle by asking not administrators, educators, or parents, but the students themselves their reasons for attending junior colleges. These reasons may lack the breadth of the administrator-educator type of study, but they have the advantage of showing how the different reasons actually appeal to the person most concerned — the student himself. It is very significant to know why the

[1] Campbell, D. S., *op. cit.*, p. 30. [2] *Ibid.*, p. 19.

student actually attends the junior college — or at least what he says in reply to such a question.

Brand's California study. The most extensive study of student opinion has been made by Brand, at Stanford University,[1] who summarized the answers given by over three thousand students in twenty-eight junior colleges in California who were asked to indicate which of eleven suggested reasons had an influence upon their attending junior college, and which single reason was the most important one. They were also asked to insert other reasons, if the suggested ones were not applicable. A summary for the entire group of students is exhibited in Figure 18 (p. 218) where the different reasons are arranged in the order of frequency of mention. The entire length of a bar represents the number of times a reason was mentioned, while the solid black part indicates the number of times it was designated as the most important, or dominant, reason. "To save money" and "to prepare for work in the university" were mentioned most frequently. They are the only reasons given by more than one half of the students. It is interesting to find that "to secure advantage of small classes" stands third in frequency. The large number of students who attend junior college because of "lack of university entrance credits" is explained by the fact that in California entrance to the University of California and to Stanford University is denied to students who have not secured in the high school fifteen "recommending" units (units of A or B grade), while the junior college is open by law to all high school graduates. "To prepare for a vocation" is another reason frequently given. These five are the reasons of outstanding importance; the others were given less frequently but still in considerable

[1] Unpublished master's thesis at Stanford University. Published in summary form: "Student Opinion in Junior Colleges in California"; in *School Review*, vol. 38, pp. 176–90 (March, 1930); and in *Proceedings of the Tenth Annual Meeting of American Association of Junior Colleges*, pp. 126–42. Account in this chapter is condensed from *School Review* article.

numbers. An additional reason, "to be at home," was inserted so frequently as to warrant inclusion in the figure.

When the dominant reasons are considered, the four of outstanding importance are among the five most frequently

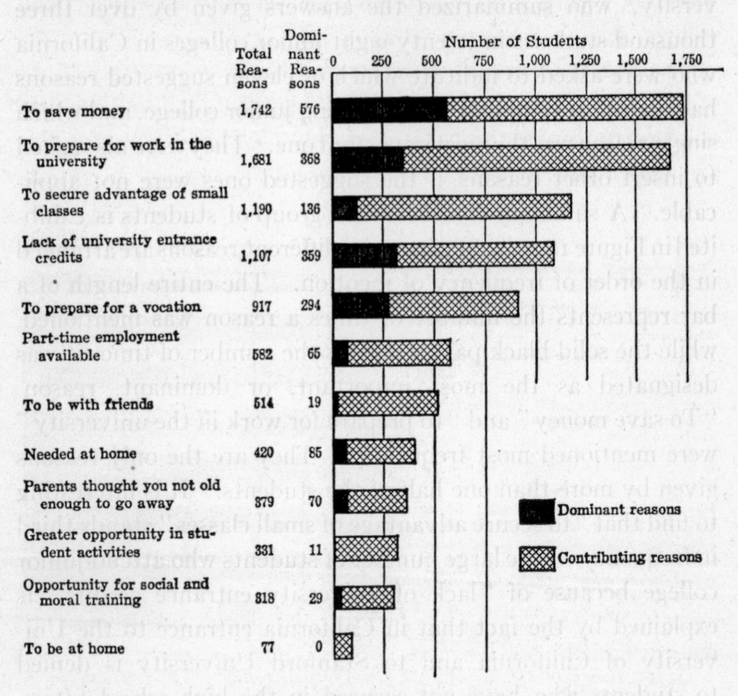

FIG. 18. REASONS GIVEN BY 3058 CALIFORNIA STUDENTS FOR ATTENDING JUNIOR COLLEGE

mentioned. The marked difference is in "to secure advantage of small classes," which was indicated much less frequently as the dominant reason but still was given as such by 136 students. Every suggested reason was indicated as the dominant one by some students, even "greater opportunity in student activities" being indicated by eleven. The rank-order correlation between dominant reasons and total reasons is .88

"To be at home" was mentioned by seventy-seven students, and doubtless would have been mentioned more frequently had the parents been consulted. Approximately the same order of importance is found to be assigned to the different reasons when the results are studied from the point of view of type of college, sex, or class.

The questionnaire also contained seven important questions of opinion to be answered by "Yes" or "No," all but the first one bearing upon the subject of this chapter. The answers are shown graphically in Figure 19. As shown by the replies

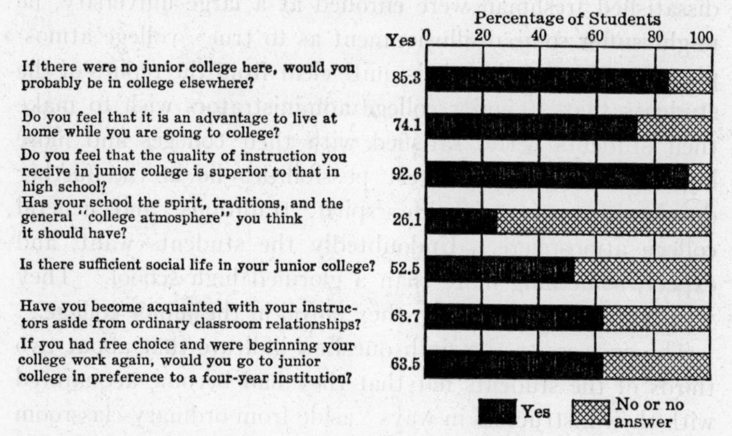

FIG. 19. REPLIES OF CALIFORNIA JUNIOR COLLEGE STUDENTS TO SEVEN QUESTIONS REGARDING THEIR COLLEGE LIFE AND RELATIONSHIPS

to the second question, approximately three fourths (74.1 per cent) of the students felt that it was a distinct advantage to live at home while going to college, at least for the first two college years.

There was a greater degree of unanimity in the answers to the third question ("Do you feel that the quality of instruction you receive in junior college is superior to that in high school?") than in the answers to any other question in the entire study. Ninety-three per cent of the students felt that junior college instruction was superior. It would be highly interesting if a similar comparison could be made with lower-division instruction in the universities.

The answers to the fourth and fifth questions are by no means so favorable to the junior college. Only one fourth of the students felt that their college had the spirit, traditions, and general college atmosphere that it should have, and only slightly more than one half felt that the social life was sufficient. It is possible that there was some halo effect; distance usually lends enchantment to the view. Possibly, if the dissatisfied freshman were enrolled at a large university, he might suffer some disillusionment as to true "college atmosphere." Nevertheless, it is quite clear from the replies of the students that, if junior college administrators wish to make their students better satisfied with their colleges and more loyal to them, the greatest possibilities lie in the further development of social life, spirit, traditions, and general college atmosphere. Undoubtedly the students want, and expect, something more than a glorified high school. They want real college life when they enroll in the junior college.

The answers to the sixth question indicate that about two thirds of the students felt that they had become acquainted with their instructors in ways "aside from ordinary classroom relationships." It should be noted, too, that 40 per cent of the students concerned were attending junior colleges of more than four hundred students.

The last question was, to a considerable extent, a summary of the entire study — "If you had free choice and were beginning your college work again, would you go to junior college in preference to a four-year institution?" Doubtless many could not have changed, even if they had wished, because of financial, home, or other conditions. For them alone, perhaps, the junior college is worth while. Nevertheless, two thirds of the entire group of students stated that, if they had had free choice (which, of course many would not have had) they would have chosen the junior college again.

Brand not only secured from the students checks on a suggested list of reasons, but he also secured their subjective personal evaluation by asking them to state, in their own words, what they considered the outstanding advantages and disadvantages of the junior college. In many cases the items listed indicated careful consideration of both favorable and unfavorable features as seen through student eyes. On account of their great variety, the replies could not be treated as objectively as those previously reported, but much time and care were spent in a careful classification and analysis of them. Altogether, forty-four advantages were distinguished; these were mentioned 6638 times by the students in twenty-seven of the twenty-eight colleges involved. A summary of the advantages, arranged in eight general groups, is presented in Table 14. So far as feasible, the student phrasing is retained.

TABLE 14. ADVANTAGES OF THE JUNIOR COLLEGE AS EXPRESSED BY 2918 JUNIOR-COLLEGE STUDENTS IN CALIFORNIA (1929)

	FREQUENCY OF MENTION
Instructional:	
Small classes	1021
Individual help from instructors	736
Better instructors: teachers not specialists	54
More recitation and class discussion	53
More studying done in junior college	37
Students trained to study	30
Less danger of failing in courses	19
Junior college accredited by university	13
Easier to make good marks	7
Total	1970
Financial:	
Possible to save money: no tuition, board, or room	1149
Easier to get work	150
Free textbooks	12
Total	1311

	Frequency of Mention
Size of institution:	
Personal contacts with faculty possible	405
More friendships possible: know everyone	376
Small school	82
All students in similar environment; no fraternities or cliques	26
Total	889
Home and community:	
Possible to live at, or be near, home: help at home	709
Friendships of high school, community, and family unbroken	44
Home influence: parents' advice, home training	38
Inadvisable to leave home because of youth	37
Acquainted in community, environment, church: small town	31
Community loyalty to a local institution	13
Total	872
Increased educational opportunity:	
Unrecommended students can go to college	188
More people able to go to college	169
High-school failures can be made up	79
Vocational training available	31
Popularizes higher education	29
Provides terminal education	28
Easy to enter junior college	18
College failures can be made up	8
Total	550
Preparation for continuing education:	
Makes transition easier	214
Prepares better for upper-division work	169
Opportunity to find one's self, one's ability, vocation, interests	76
Introduction to college	46
Background for specialization at the university	10
Total	515
Development through activity:	
Greater opportunity for extra-curricular activities	221
More social life in school, community, and home	85
More athletic opportunities	64
Individual development: talents brought out	61
Opportunity for development of leadership	46
Total	477
Miscellaneous advantages:	
Fewer distractions	21
Supplies moral training	15
Eliminates those unfit for university work	14
Fewer temptations	4
Total	54
Grand total	6638

Student opinion in Arizona. In 1930, H. A. Cross used a slight modification of the Brand questionnaire with over three hundred students in the Phœnix (Arizona) Junior College. Results are available only in mimeograph form. He found that the reasons most frequently indicated were "to save money" and "to prepare for work in the university," with "preparation for a vocation" a poor third.

Student opinion in Kansas. In 1926, Wellemeyer reported the results of a questionnaire answered by 469 students in eight public junior colleges in Kansas. Replies are summarized in Table 15.

TABLE 15. REASONS FOR JUNIOR COLLEGE ATTENDANCE GIVEN BY 469 JUNIOR COLLEGE STUDENTS IN EIGHT KANSAS JUNIOR COLLEGES (1926)[1]

	TOTAL	MEN	WOMEN
To save money	172	81	91
To better self	121	53	68
Wanted at home	78	32	46
To continue education	53	26	27
To get a teachers' certificate	22	3	19
To prepare for college	15	8	7
To back a community project	14	2	12
To obtain more individual attention	14	8	6
Inconvenient to go elsewhere	13	9	4
Small college better	8	4	4
Too young to work or to go away	6	1	5
Part time employment	4	3	1
To keep from loafing	3	3	..
Uncertain or no answer	17	8	9

Student opinion in Iowa. In Iowa, in 1927, 587 junior college students in nine public junior colleges gave as their most important reasons for attending junior college rather than a distant four-year college: expense, 319; nearness to home, 285; individual instruction, 80.[2]

[1] Wellemeyer, J. F. "The Junior College as Viewed by Its Students"; in *School Review*, vol. 34, p. 762. (December, 1926.)

[2] Weaver, E. L. *et al.* *A Study of Junior Colleges in Iowa.* Bulletin no. 2 of the Educational Council of the Iowa State Teachers' Association, p. 5. Des Moines, December, 1927.

QUESTIONS AND PROBLEMS

(The first ten questions refer to the list of 42 reasons given and briefly discussed in the first part of this chapter.)

1. Choose any one of the reasons given, and elaborate supporting evidence.
2. Which might be considered reasons against the junior college?
3. Which lose their force in a large junior college — one of a thousand or more students?
4. Which of the suggested reasons are given or implied in the catalogue of some particular junior college?
5. Which reasons would be most likely to appeal to a prospective student?
6. Which reasons would be most likely to appeal to parents?
7. Which reasons would be most likely to appeal to professional educators?
8. You are to make a fifteen-minute address to a luncheon club on the reasons for a junior college. Which reasons will you stress?
9. An election to establish a junior college is before the tax-payers of the community. Which reasons would you stress in the publicity favoring it?
10. Which of the suggested reasons should be eliminated, or combined with others, in the list?
11. Read President Harper's argument for the small college, list the reasons he gives, and see to what extent they are commonly given as reasons for the junior college.
12. Compare Koos's designations for the main functions of the junior college with those given by Thomas. Which are preferable, and why?
13. The seal of the Duluth Junior College contains the three words "Culture, Democracy, and Vocation." Are they a suitable epitome of the functions of the junior college? Can you suggest an improvement?
14. Write a page for a public or private junior college catalogue setting forth the reasons for its existence.
15. Discuss the relative advantage of asking for a suggested list of purposes to be checked (McDowell's method), or of asking for an individual statement of special purpose (Whitney's method), or of using both (Brand's method).
16. Do you agree with Whitney's major conclusions as to tendencies in junior college objectives in a seven-year period?
17. In Whitney's list, Table 13, compute the rank order correlation between the importance of reasons for public and private institutions. What does it mean?
18. Compute the rank order correlation for importance of purposes as

given in Koos's list for public as compared with private junior colleges. What does it mean?

19. Compare the reasons given by McDowell, Koos, Whitney, and Campbell, in this chapter with those secured by J. M. Wood from 53 junior college administrators. (See *Seventh Yearbook of Department of Superintendence of National Education Association*, pp. 302-13. February, 1929.)
20. Compare the important reasons given by students for junior college attendance in California, Kansas, Arizona, and Iowa.
21. Discuss the significance of the following statement by President Lowell of Harvard University: "One of the merits of the junior college is to keep out of college, rather than to lead into it, those who have no natural taste for higher education." (*Effective College*, p. 281.)

SUGGESTED READINGS

Andrews, A. "How the Junior College Serves the Community"; in *Thirteenth Yearbook of Department of Secondary School Principals of National Education Association*, pp. 340-47. (March, 1929.)

Campbell, D. S. *A Critical Study of the Stated Purposes of the Junior College.* George Peabody College Contributions to Education, no. 70. 126 pp. (1930.)
Ph.D. thesis at Peabody College.

Christenson, D. H. "Arguments in Favor of the Junior College"; in *School Review*, vol. 37, pp. 404-06. (June, 1929.)
General arguments, and special application to Utah.

Cobb, S. *The New Leaven; Progressive Education and its Effect upon the Child and Society.* 340 pp. John Day Company, New York, 1928.
Chapter 16, "The Junior College — A Solution," presents many reasons for the junior college development.

Cox, R. G. "Junior College Objectives from the Standpoint of the Private Junior College"; in *Proceedings of the Ninth Annual Meeting of the American Association of Junior Colleges*, pp. 92-96. Fort Worth, 1928.

*Eells, W. C., and Brand, R. R. "Student Opinion in Junior Colleges in California"; in *School Review*, vol. 38, pp. 176-90. (March, 1930.) Also in somewhat different form as "California Junior Colleges Through the Eyes of their Students"; in *Proceedings of the Tenth Annual Meeting of the American Association of Junior Colleges*, pp. 126-42. Atlantic City, 1929.

Fitzpatrick, E. A. "The Case for Junior Colleges"; in *Educational Review*, vol. 65, pp. 150-56. (March, 1923.)
Junior college as a relief to the overcrowded universities. University enrollments in 1930 and 1950 predicted.

Ganders, H. S. "Junior College Movement"; in *American Educational Digest*, vol. 46, pp. 460-61. (June, 1927.)
Seven reasons favorable to development of junior colleges.

Hale, W. W. "Attitude of Junior College Graduates"; in *Junior College Journal*, vol. 1, pp. 255-61. (February, 1931.)

Harbeson, J. W. "The Place of the Junior College in Public Education"; in *Educational Review*, vol. 67, pp. 187-91. (April, 1924.)
Gives eight reasons for the junior college as a local project.

*Harper, W. R. "The Small College — Its Prospects"; in *Proceedings of National Education Association*, pp. 67-87. Charleston, South Carolina, 1900.
Lists both advantages and disadvantages of it.

Judd, C. H. "Adapting the Curriculum to the Psychological Characteristics of the Junior College"; in *Junior College Curriculum* (Gray, W. S., editor), pp. 1-13. Chicago, 1929.

*Koos, L. V. *The Junior College*, pp. 42-43; or *The Junior College Movement*, pp. 16-28; similar in *School Review*, vol. 29, pp. 520-29. (September, 1921.)

Lillard, J. B. "What shall We Do with the Unrecommended Student?" in *California Quarterly of Secondary Education*, vol. 5, pp. 69-70. (October, 1929.)

Million, J. W. "Advantages of the Junior College"; in United States Bureau of Education, Bulletin no. 19, pp. 6-9. (1922.)

O'Brien, F. P. "Junior College and College Standards"; in *American Educational Digest*, vol. 45, pp. 58-61. (October, 1925.)
Junior college offers many distinctive opportunities. States many of them.

*Thomas, F. W. "The Functions of the Junior College"; in *The Junior College; Its Organization and Administration* (Proctor, W. M., editor), pp. 11-25. Stanford University, California, 1927.

Way, W. W. "The Objectives of the Church Junior College"; in *Proceedings of the Ninth Annual Meeting of the American Association of Junior Colleges*, pp. 97-100. Fort Worth, 1928.

Weersing, F. J. "Misconceptions Regarding the Junior College"; in *Junior College Journal*, vol. 1, pp. 363-69. (March, 1931.)

Wellemeyer, J. F. "The Junior College as Viewed by its Students; in *School Review*, vol. 34, pp. 760-67. (December, 1926.)

*Whitney, F. L. *The Junior College in America*, pp. 31-46. Similar in *North Central Association Quarterly*, vol. 3, pp. 289-97. (September, 1928.)

CHAPTER VIII

THE POPULARIZING FUNCTION

Education for all the people is America's noblest contribution to civilization. The old ideal of training a few for leadership has been superseded by the modern idea of universal education to increase national harmony and unity of action. — CALVIN COOLIDGE.

Contents of this chapter. Is the junior college succeeding in its popularizing function? Is it making collegiate education available to the masses, as well as to the classes? If so how, and to what extent? These are the questions that this chapter attempts to answer. It presents first, evidence of the popularization of higher education for regular full-time students, with respect to: (1) number and enrollment, (2) age of students, (3) uniqueness of college opportunity, and (4) retention. The last part of the chapter deals with so-called extension education, particularly adapted to the needs and desires of the adults in the community in which the junior college is located. This phase is discussed with respect to: (1) correspondence work, (2) extension courses, (3) summer schools, and (4) institutes.

POPULARIZATION FOR REGULAR STUDENTS

Number and enrollment. There is no more convincing general evidence of the fact that the junior college is popularizing higher education than the growth of the movement, as already outlined in the previous chapters. The increase in junior colleges from 132 to 450 in a period of only twelve years, and the increase of students from less than four thousand to seventy thousand in the same period, is striking evidence that the junior college is rapidly becoming the "people's college" at least in extent. In California, during the last decade the total junior college enrollment has more than doubled every three years, as was shown by Table 8 (p. 108).

Age of students. The junior college is popularizing college education in giving the local student an opportunity to go to college at a somewhat younger age than that of university freshmen. Koos concluded, on the basis of comparisons of ages of junior college students with those of University of Minnesota freshmen, that the presence in the local community of a college tends to lower the average age at entrance by as much as six to nine months, and conversely that the absence of such opportunity tends to delay entrance that long. This is accounted for, in part, by the feeling of many parents that their children are too young to leave home, and in part by the necessity of earning the money necessary for the more expensive college education at a distance.

Uniqueness of opportunity. Does the junior college offer a unique opportunity for college education to a considerable group? How many would be deprived of all opportunity of such education if the junior college did not furnish it? Several direct answers have been given to this question by various groups of junior college students and administrators; there is also indirect evidence which bears upon it.

Evidence from deans. Thomas secured replies from the deans of twelve California junior colleges as to the percentage of their students who would have been unable to attend college at all had it not been for the existence of the local institution. These varied from 25 to 80 per cent, with a median of 50 per cent. Some were based upon estimates, and some upon detailed inquiries from the students themselves. The highest percentage, 80, was from the Kern County Junior College, and was based upon individual student statements. "The fact that three fourths of the officials reporting are convinced, either from complete surveys or individual conferences, that not less than 50 per cent of their students would be unable to attend college at all if it were not for the local institution, is of significance." [1]

Evidence from students. In Kansas, in 1926, 469 students in eight public junior colleges were asked the question, "If there were no junior college here, would you be in school?" "Yes" was the answer of 47 per cent, while 37 per cent said "No." The remaining 16 per cent were doubtful or non-committal.[2]

Green, in 1929, secured data from 3825 students in public junior colleges in eight states in answer to a similar question. The replies were distributed as follows:

	Per cent
Yes	44
No	22
Perhaps	12
Not this year	10
Doubtful	8
Don't know	4

It is highly probable that most of those in the last four groups would not have been in college elsewhere. Both Wellemeyer's and Green's results show that less than one half of the students were confident that they would be in college elsewhere. On the other hand, as shown in Figure 19 (p. 219), Brand found in California, when over 3000 students were asked the same question in a form which necessitated an answer of either "Yes" or "No," that 85 per cent answered "Yes."

At the Phœnix Junior College, in 1929, the same question (with only two answers permitted) was answered "Yes" by 83 per cent of the students; the previous year when the form of answer was optional, similar to Green's above, the per cent

[1] Thomas, F. W. *A Study of Functions of the Public Junior College and the Extent of Their Realization in California*, p. 89. Stanford University, 1926.

[2] Wellemeyer, J. F. "The Junior College as Viewed by its Students"; in *School Review*, vol. 34, pp. 760–67. (December, 1926.)

answering "Yes" was 64.[1] It is likely that the result would have been similar in the larger California group, had the question been arranged to provide for various grades of uncertainty.

Indirect evidence. The junior college has been established for a long time in California — in terms of youthful student memory. In many localities it has come to be accepted as such a normal part of the educational equipment of the community that the young people of college age cannot really imagine themselves in the situation that would exist if no junior college were available. Even if 85 per cent were honest in *thinking* that they would be in college elsewhere, it is very doubtful that they would be. Nor is this a matter of opinion, alone. Data recently collected show that in eight junior college districts in California the enrollment, in 1929, was three times as great per thousand high school pupils as the enrollment of freshmen and sophomores in all other classes of collegiate institutions in the state. The evidence also seems to suggest that from one third to one half of the students are enjoying college privileges and opportunities which would not be theirs if the junior college were not giving it to them. It is to be remembered, too, that more than half of the high school graduates in California have been unable to enter the state university due to insufficient recommending units. When the new Los Angeles Junior College was opened, in 1929, there was an enrollment the first year of over seventeen hundred, 85 per cent of whom could not have entered the university for this reason.[2]

[1] Green found (p. 71) that from 194 high schools in cities without any type of college, 31 per cent were enrolled in the first two years of higher institutions; while from 63 high schools in cities having public junior colleges, 51 per cent were so enrolled.

[2] Koos found that from high school graduating classes where there were no junior colleges, but 38 per cent of the graduates went to any college, whereas from high schools where there was a nearby junior college, 70 to 75 per cent of the graduates entered some college.

Retention of students in the junior college. The junior college has enrolled a large number of students, but to what extent has it held them? How great has been the freshman mortality? Four answers may be given to this question, two from general statistics available, and two from specific studies of this feature by Hanna and by Hale.

The only recent enrollment figures for the country, by classes, are those given by Whitney, as follows:

	Freshmen	Sophomores
1926–27	13,404	5,489
1927–28	17,701	7,076

For either year it may easily be computed that the sophomore enrollment was approximately 40 per cent of the freshmen enrollment. From this fact the deduction has been made by some that there is a 60 per cent shrinkage in the sophomore year — rather a heavy mortality. This method of reasoning, however, is in error where the freshman enrollment is changing rapidly from year to year. The fairer comparison is to compare the sophomore enrollment of 1927–28 with the freshman enrollment of the *previous* year. When this is done for the country as a whole, with the figures given above, it is seen that the sophomore enrollment is 53 per cent of the freshman. The freshman enrollment, too, in many cases, includes special students, mid-year entrants, and other factors which make this method not entirely valid. Many students classified as freshmen in 1926–27 were doubtless classified as freshmen again the next year. The 53 per cent figure probably means that at least that percentage of freshmen returned the next year — but perhaps a great many more.

Analogous data for the district junior colleges of California are available for a longer period, as exhibited in Table 16. The most significant feature in this table is the marked increase in holding power, as shown in the last column. Where the sophomore enrollment in 1925–26 was only half that of the

TABLE 16. ANALYSIS OF ENROLLMENT IN CALIFORNIA DISTRICT JUNIOR COLLEGES (1924-25 TO 1928-29)

YEAR	TOTAL ENROLLMENT	FRESHMEN	SOPHOMORES	SPECIALS	GRADUATES	PERCENTAGE SOPHOMORE ENROLLMENT IS OF FRESHMAN OF PREVIOUS YEAR
1924-25....	3,327	1,506	541	1,280	243	..
1925-26....	3,479	1,883	790	806	385	52
1926-27....	5,585	2,239	1,134	2,212	548	61
1927-28....	7,981	3,779	1,340	2,662	776	69
1928-29....	11,716	5,419 *	2,796 *	3,501 *	1,309	74

* Basis of classification changed from previous years, but figures given are believed to be approximately comparable.

previous year's freshman class, three years later it had increased to almost three fourths — certainly a marked improvement. Both of these sets of figures, however, are only approximations to the truth because, as already pointed out, it is impossible to tell to what extent identical students are dealt with in the two different years. A study is needed which will take account of individual students, not annual totals alone.

Such a study has been made by Hanna,[1] in which he studied student retention in 36 junior colleges in the Middle West, South, and Far West. Data were secured on three successive entering and graduating classes from 1923 to 1927. Participating colleges submitted lists of names of entering and graduating students, so that the results were based upon checking of individual names. Hanna, however, was not studying retention of freshmen until second year enrollment, but until final graduation — a severer standard. Of a total of 7737 students in three successive classes, 36 per cent were graduated from the institution in which they had matriculated. The variability between institutions was very great, varying from

[1] Hanna, J. V. *Retention and Elimination in Thirty-Six Junior Colleges.* Unpublished doctor's dissertation at New York University, 1929, 137 pp. Summarized in *Journal of Educational Research,* vol. 22, pp. 1-8. (June, 1930.)

only 9 per cent to 86 per cent. There was little or no relation between size of institution and holding power. Approximately 19 per cent of the entering students transferred to some other institution for their second year, making a total retention for the two years of 55 per cent. Private junior colleges excelled the public ones. It is probable that this is partly due to the comparative youth of the public junior college. The increase in three years in the California institutions tends to substantiate this supposition.

Unfortunately, Hanna does not give similar data for comparison from four-year colleges and universities. This lack, however, is supplied in a study made by W. W. Hale, registrar of Birmingham Southern College, Alabama.[1] He took all junior colleges for which catalogues of two successive years were available in the Stanford University library, in which the roster of students was given by years, and checked the names of all students for one year who came back as freshmen or sophomores the following year. Such data were available for 38 colleges, 11 public and 27 private. For comparison he did the same thing with 19 four-year colleges, 14 of them selected alphabetically from the first ones containing the necessary information, and five because of special interest in the institutions.[2] Of a total of 3303 freshmen in these junior colleges he

[1] Hale, W. W. "Comparative Holding Power of Junior Colleges and Regular Four-Year Colleges"; in *Phi Delta Kappan*, vol. 13, pp. 69–74. (October, 1930.)

[2] *Junior colleges — public:* Branch Agricultural College, Utah; Southern Branch University of Idaho; LaSalle-Peru-Oglesby; New Mexico Military Institute; North Dakota School of Forestry; North Texas Agricultural College; Paris Junior College; Santa Ana; Sheldon; Branch of University of Tennessee; Virginia (Minnesota). *Junior colleges — private:* Alliance; Bethel; Bluefield; Blue Ridge; Central; Chesbrough Seminary; Christian; Dixie; Hardin; Hesston; Hiwassee; Jacksonville; Louisburg; Mansfield: Monticello Seminary; Nasson; Packer; Palmer; St. John's; St. Paul's; Southwest Baptist; Stephens; Trevecca; Weaver; Westminster; Whitworth; William Woods. *The four-year colleges were:* Adelphi; Agnes Scott; Albion; Alfred; Allegheny; Alma; Amherst; Antioch; Aurora; Bates; Baldwin-Wallace; Bethany; Birmingham-Southern; Bridgewater; California Institute of Technology; Mississippi Agricultural and Mechanical; Oberlin; Whitman; and Whittier.

found that 54.3 per cent returned the following year, 48.8 per cent of them as sophomores, 5.5 per cent as freshmen again. The general averages found and the variability in each case are shown for the four-year colleges and for the two types of junior colleges, in Table 17.

TABLE 17. HOLDING POWER OF JUNIOR COLLEGES AND STANDARD COLLEGES

GROUP	NUMBER OF COLLEGES	FRESHMAN ENROLLMENT	MEAN PER CENT RETURNED NEXT YEAR AND PROBABLE ERROR OF MEAN	NUMBER OF COLLEGES WITH OVER 70 PER CENT RETURNED
Four-year colleges				
Total	19	5576	66.0 ± 1.3	7
Range		36-536	51-81	
Junior colleges				
Total	38	3303	54.3 ± 1.6	5
Range		13-329	31-84	
Public				
Total	11	1293	52.7	0
Range		23-259	36-62	
Private				
Total	27	2010	55.4	5
Range		13-329	31-84	

The variability is great in both groups of institutions, the best of the junior colleges being better than any of the four-year institutions and the poorest being likewise poorer than any of the four-year colleges. On the whole the four-year institutions show a significant superiority, the difference being about six times its probable error. However, there are eight of the junior colleges (over one fifth) which have a greater holding power than the average of the four-year colleges. The private junior colleges make a slightly better showing than the public. It is unfortunate that more public junior colleges do not publish catalogues that will make such studies possible. Thus only one of the entire group of California public junior colleges could be included. The data of Table 16 indicate that many of them would certainly raise the average, with the crude figure of 74 per cent there shown. Hale's study suggests that it would be fair to add 5.5 per cent for freshmen returning as freshmen again. If this were done, the holding power of the California institutions would average approximately 80 per cent — a very favorable figure indeed — showing that in the older and better established junior colleges the retention may approach and even exceed that of many of the better four-year colleges. California Institute of Technology, for example, showed 73.3 per cent returning; Oberlin, 74.5 per cent; and Amherst, 79.3 per cent — to select three well-known institutions in the East, Middle West, and West.

Summary. Thus the popularizing function works to the extent of at least a 50 per cent return the second year in most junior colleges, and reaches 75 per cent, or higher, in the more stable institutions, comparing very favorably with the standard four-year colleges in this respect. The junior college is giving standard college education to a large group of students who would otherwise, because of distance, cost, inability, or other factors, not be able to enjoy it. Thus it is popularizing higher education for the *regular* student. What is it doing for the *special* student and the adults in the community of which it is a part?

SERVICE OF THE JUNIOR COLLEGE TO THE COMMUNITY

Introduction. The second important aspect of the popularizing function relates to its effort to meet community needs, as distinguished from those of the youth who compose its regular student body. This is a rich field of service in which the junior colleges may lift, in a most wholesome way, the cultural standards of their communities. At the organization meeting of the American Association of Junior Colleges, in 1920, Dean MacKenzie, of the Detroit Junior College, said:[1]

I think that it is a great mistake to limit the scope of the junior college.... If democracy is to be preserved by education it will be by bringing education down to the masses. There are many intelligent people in large communities who are capable of profiting by college work but who are in no way fitted for college according to the typical entrance examinations. The junior college ought to offer a large number of courses that will appeal to such persons. The community as a whole supports the junior college. Is it justifiable, then, to give only those courses which appeal to those who are going on to larger colleges, or should the community be helped by raising the general intelligence?... The junior college in large cities is going to appeal to thousands when it offers courses of this character and particularly courses in the evening. This, I believe is going to be the saving grace of democracy.

This is a field as yet largely untouched, except by a small number of the junior colleges of the country. Yet it is full of possibility, of opportunity, and of promise. What has been done in a few places is only a suggestion of the vast service the junior college can render in innumerable ways in raising the entire cultural level of the country. No longer need there be a few great centers of culture. There may be instead a myriad of smaller cultural centers, leavening the whole lump, tending to cause it to rise equally instead of irregularly.

A general survey. In 1928 L. R. Alderman, specialist in adult education in the Federal Bureau of Education, made an extensive survey of what the colleges and universities of the country were offering in the way of helps in adult education.[2] He found such work, of one type or another, being given by 31 junior colleges in 16 different states. He lists 13 types of extension activities, in all but one of which the junior colleges

[1] MacKenzie, D., in United States Bureau of Education, Bulletin no. 19, pp. 20–21. (1922.)

[2] Alderman, L. R. *College and University Extension Helps in Adult Education.* United States Bureau of Education, Bulletin no. 3. 35 pp. (1928.)

were represented. These were as follows, for the 31 junior colleges:

Public lectures and lyceums	16
Institutes, conferences, and short courses	13
Class instruction outside of institution	10
Promotion of debates	10
Correspondence courses	8
Community drama	7
Parent-teacher's association or other club service	5
Community center	4
Radio	4
Publications educational in nature	3
Public information (including package library service)	2
Visual instruction	2
Home reading courses	0

Many of the types of activity listed by Alderman are not of great significance, but a few of them deserve more extended treatment.

Correspondence study courses. Alderman reports correspondence study courses given as follows:

Georgia: Southern Georgia Agricultural and Mechanical College — English, Education, History.

Iowa: Graceland College — Commercial subjects, Education, English, History, Latin, Mathematics, Religion.

Kansas: Hesston College — College preparatory courses in Algebra, Bible, English, German, History, Latin.

Kentucky: Sacred Heart Junior College — Advanced German, College Rhetoric and Composition, Latin, European History.

Texas: Kidd-Key College — Algebra, Bible, Education, History, Latin.

Texas: John Tarleton Agricultural College — Algebra, Advanced American History, Composition, Economics, Education, English, Geology, History of Modern Europe, Latin, Mechanical Drawing, Sociology, Solid Geometry, Spanish, Trigonometry.

Utah: Snow — Agriculture, American Literature, Education, Engineering, Health, School Organization and Supervision.

According to President F. P. Keppel, of the Carnegie Corporation, there are over 3,000,000 people enrolled in correspondence schools in the country,[1] many of them in private schools with substantial fees. Most of the work is doubtless not of college grade, but much of it is, and could be done by the local institution, either by correspondence, or still better in many cases in extension courses, with the added advantages of class stimulus and personal contacts with instructor and with fellow students.

Extension courses. Alderman reports the following extension courses as offered in the junior colleges:

Arizona: Phœnix — Constitution, General Psychology, Pharmacy, Principles of Education, Public Speaking, Short Story.

California: Pasadena — Art, Commerce, English, Home Economics, Languages, Science, Social Sciences.

California: Sacramento — Applied Art, Art Appreciation, Dramatics, French, History of Education, Italian, Music, Public School Art, Public Speaking, School Law, Spanish.

Iowa: Graceland — Bible, Character Education, Home Building, Modern Religious Thought.

Kansas: Hesston — Economics.

Texas: El Paso — Accounting, Chemistry, Industrial Arts, Engineering, English, Home Economics, Psychology, Public School Methods, Public Speaking, Sociology, Typewriting.

Texas: John Tarleton — Classes upon demand.

Texas: Lon Morris — Bible, Education.

Utah: Snow — Child Welfare, Coöperative Marketing, Feeds and Feeding.

Hollingsworth[2] found that 36 of 279 junior colleges offered extension courses in their catalogues. The total number of units offered was 1617, an average of 45 per college, indicating that some institutions are paying much attention to such work.

This is the greatest opportunity for the junior college systematically to meet community needs, and it is in this field that the greatest strides have been made in a few institutions, even

[1] *Current History*, vol. 27, pp. 513–15. (January, 1928.)

[2] In an unpublished study at Stanford University, described more fully in Chapter XVIII.

in the short period since that represented by Alderman's data. It will be worth while, therefore, to report in detail what is being done in a few typical cases. Extension courses for the adults of the community (also known as extra-hour courses, evening courses, etc.) have been of two general types — vocational and cultural.

Agricultural courses at Chaffey. Outstanding vocational work for adults in a local institution has been done at Chaffey Junior College, in California. Its catalogue states:

> The junior college derives the greater part of its income from its own district, and its first obligation is to the people of the Chaffey district. The primary consideration, therefore, is that of service to the local community. In rendering this service every effort is made to serve also those students who expect to continue their collegiate work with the object in view of securing an academic degree from a higher institution.

Located in the heart of the citrus belt of Southern California, Chaffey maintains an experimental farm for research and demonstration purposes. Numerous experiments have been carried on in the use of fertilizers, pruning, budding, development of new varieties, thinning, spraying. The farm is a laboratory for the students of the school, but it is a community laboratory as well.

> In all of the agricultural work there is constant correlation with the farms and farmers of the community. Classes for adults are a part of each year's work. Night classes are held during the winter for farmers, where courses are given in entomology and general horticulture. In these classes the practical phases of the work are emphasized in order to instruct those growers who might not be interested in the purely scientific aspects of the phases treated. During the year 1926–27 the Chaffey junior college had 776 adults in various types of extension courses, a practical demonstration of its success in catering to community interests and needs. [1]

[1] Hill, Merton E. "Administrative Problems of the Large Rural Junior College"; in Proctor, W. M. (editor), *The Junior College; Its Organization and Administration*, p. 95. Stanford University, California, 1927.

Cultural courses for adults. Many people, past normal school age, are hungering for so-called cultural courses more than for practical or vocational ones. An outstanding junior college in which this type of extension work has been emphasized is the one at Sacramento, California. In 1928–29 almost half of the enrollment (1076 of 2211) was composed of special liberal arts students. Sacramento regularly scheduled, in 1929, many "extra-hour" courses, at 4 to 6, or 7 to 9, for the benefit of teachers and others interested in self-advancement and collegiate training. College credit was given for most of them at the rate of one unit per hour per week of attendance. The following were definitely scheduled for specific times, places, and instructors, and others were promised if there were sufficient demand:

Biography, Botany, Color and Design, Constitution, Dante, Drama, Economic History of the United States, Principles of Economics, Beginning French, Advanced French, German, Great Humorists, History of Art, Interior Decoration, Modern Language Pronunciation, Music Appreciation, Musical Masterpieces, Music, Orchestra and Instruments, Pen and Ink, Philosophy, Pottery, Psychology and Mental Hygiene for Nurses, General Psychology, Public School Art, Recreation, Elementary Spanish, Advanced Spanish.

San Bernardino's program. The recently organized (1926) union junior college at San Bernardino, California, has an ambitious program of community helpfulness. It published, in September, 1929, a special bulletin of 32 pages dealing exclusively with extension courses. The main purpose of the extension service is to contribute to the cultural growth of those in the community who do not expect to continue in regular college work, and who desire inspirational rather than credit courses. However, certain courses are provided whereby teachers and others who are high school graduates may receive college credit. The following list of courses is presented:

Geology, Studies in Plant Life, Physics, Anthropology, Chemistry, Biology and its Makers, Psychology, Art, including Theory of Color and Design; Art Appreciation, Zoölogy, Unified Mathematics, French, Spanish, Public Speaking, Mines and Minerals, Physical Education for both men and women, Thermodynamics, Literature and Composition, Liberal Thought in English Literature, Economics, World Culture, and Music.

The course in Economics is given under the auspices of the Riverside chapter of the American Institute of Banking.

Western Pennsylvania. In one sense the three junior colleges in western Pennsylvania at Erie, Johnstown, and Uniontown may be thought of as extension departments of the University of Pittsburgh. They give both regular college work during the day and special courses in the evening. The enrollment of special students for the evening courses in two of the centers is more than double that of the day work. The following enrollment figures are for 1929–30:

	Regular	Evening
Johnstown	209	566
Erie	186	407
Uniontown	157	157
Totals	552	1130

Other examples of extension courses. Grand Rapids Junior College, in Michigan, has an "Evening Institute" in which it offers English, French, German, Spanish, Economics, Psychology, Accounting, Music, Applied Art, Practical Art, and other courses. "The work is developing, and this is a field in which the junior college is to render distinct service," says Arthur Andrews, the president.

Modesto, California, not only has extension work in the city, but also throughout the county. Their catalogue states:

During the current year numerous citizens of Modesto and neighboring towns have availed themselves of the opportunity to enroll in special subjects offered by the college in extension division classes. The subjects offered during the past years include Home Gardening, Educational Measurements, Home Economics, History of Education, Child Psychology, Curriculum Building, Logic, Art and Astronomy. It is anticipated that the extension work for the coming year will be enlarged, and that additional courses in Astronomy, History, Education, and Commerce will be offered at various points in the county where there may be a sufficient number interested to warrant giving the work.

Hesston College, Kansas, provides three types of work in its newly organized extension department: correspondence courses in thirteen subjects; special courses in neighboring affiliated schools; and local evening classes.

Kansas City, Missouri, offers to give evening courses in any of the junior college subjects described in the catalogue, provided at least thirty persons desire any single course.

The universities and extension work. Extension work up to now has been for the most part in the hands of the large universities. There are many reasons to think that this work can be done more efficiently and more conveniently from a number of local centers, the junior colleges. As early as 1905, President James, of the University of Illinois, expressed his belief that the junior colleges would relieve the universities of the burden of extension work, and do it more effectively and without the deterrent costs entailed by distance from the localities in need of such service. In 1927, President Butler, of Columbia University, in his *Annual Report* stated that the junior college was the direct outcome of the theory of higher education which underlay the plan of organization adopted by Columbia in 1890. He recommended the development of junior colleges at centers of population through the university extension department, under university direction and control.

Extension course methods. Extension work in the junior colleges is still largely in the experimental stage. A technique of adult education at the college level must be developed.

Shall it be the pure lecture method, conferences, problems, or some combination of these? That lectures alone are inadequate is the opinion of Commissioner Cooper: [1]

The traditional organized classes, listening to a lecturer and turned loose to survive or perish, will not serve the purpose. A new conference technique, adapted to men and women of differing degrees of previous formal schooling must be developed. I think the effect of such work on the development of teaching skill will be a great blessing to the junior college itself. Let us do some experimenting here in California under the leadership of our great universities, and make some real contributions to the solution of this serious problem.

Summer schools. A substantial beginning has also been made in summer school work by the junior colleges. From the latest statistics on colleges and universities of the United States Bureau of Education [2] it is found that at least 53 junior colleges in 18 states had summer schools in 1927, enrolling almost eight thousand students. The leading state was Texas, with 20 colleges, and almost three thousand students. There is no legal provision in California permitting summer schools in the public junior colleges, but neither is it expressly forbidden. Summer school work was undertaken by Marin Junior College in the summer of 1930 with an enrollment of 35, and was so successful that it was planned to continue and expand it. Doubtless similar work will be undertaken by other colleges in the state. The Pasadena four-year junior college had a summer school for lower division students only, in 1930; and has announced one without such restrictions in 1931. The fee will be $2.50 per unit.

The principal facts regarding summer school work for various types of colleges are shown in Table 18.

[1] Cooper, W. J. "Adult Education in the Junior College Program"; in *California Quarterly of Secondary Education*, vol. 4, p. 36. (October, 1928.)

[2] United States Office of Education, Bulletin no. 38. Tables 25 and 28. (1929.)

TABLE 18. SUMMARY OF NUMBER OF JUNIOR COLLEGES HAVING SUMMER SCHOOLS, AND ENROLLMENT IN THEM (1927)

	Total	Public		Private
		State	Local	
Number of colleges	53	9	12	32
Number of states	18	6	4	12
Enrollment	7926	2566	2125	3235
Men	2512	720	930	862
Women	5414	1846	1195	2373

Leadership institutes. Snow College, in Utah, has developed a unique type of community work, covering an experience of several years, and known as leadership institutes. Suggested by the specialized teachers' institute, the people of a large surrounding district gather at the college to receive a week's training in leadership for various lines of activity in their home communities. The attendance at them has varied from a few hundred to two or three thousand. The institute has been divided into sections, under the leadership of the college faculty, for such work as training recreational leaders, scoutmasters, civic betterment, pageantry, farm and home, home management, religious education, genealogy, art, and science. President Knudsen, in 1926, thus described the method of the institute, which covered a week's time:[1]

All our work is carried on as distinct class work. We discourage lecture courses. There is only one session each day where lectures are given, and that is in a general assembly. In this general assembly we have a short musical program, and then a very excellent lecture to take up some topic of general interest. The lecturer may choose his own topic or if the people have suggested some definite line of work, we may assign this topic to this period to be treated by an expert in lecture form. We never permit the lecture to run over one hour. We do not want to tire the people. Often we have as high as a thousand people gathered into a big hall to hear the

[1] Knudsen, M. H. "Leadership Institutes"; in *Proceedings of the Seventh Annual Meeting of the American Association of Junior Colleges*, p. 46. Jackson, Mississippi, 1926.

lecture. This gathering is the only big gathering of our entire institute and meets once each day only. We have found that we can do more good by having our people divided up into smaller groups where there is more of a personal contact and the discussion can partake of the round table type.

Terminal courses as evidence of popularizing function. In one sense all the development of so-called terminal or semi-professional courses in junior colleges may be looked upon as evidence of further popularization of junior college work.[1] This feature is so important, however, and has come to be looked upon as such a distinct function, that a separate chapter will be devoted to it.

QUESTIONS AND PROBLEMS

1. What is the effect of the four-year private college and of the state university in popularizing higher education? (See Green's study.)
2. Study the relation of freshman and sophomore enrollments for a group of four-year colleges, to compare with the retention in California junior colleges as computed in Table 16.
3. Compare the retention of students in junior colleges in some other state, with that given in the text for California.
4. How may the holding power of a junior college be improved?
5. How has the age of students entering college changed? (See Brown, E. E. *Proceedings of the National Education Association*, pp. 489-95. 1903.)
6. Make a study of a group of four-year colleges in a form to be comparable with Hanna's study.
7. Suggest other types of evidence, than those given in the text, to answer the question of whether students would probably be in college if a local junior college were not available.
8. Is there any way of determining the probable educational destiny of various groups of students who do not answer unequivocally "Yes" or "No," in such studies as those of Green and Wellemeyer?
9. If a group of parents of junior college students were asked whether their sons or daughters would be in college if there were not a junior college available, how would the results compare with those reported from students themselves in this chapter?

[1] Koos treats the features discussed here under the heads of popularizing and terminal functions under the single caption, the "Democratizing Function."

10. Make a plan for a "Leadership Institute" for a junior college in a particular community with which you are familiar.
11. What are some of the experiments which could be conducted under the auspices of "our great universities" for the solution of the problems of adult education, as suggested by Commissioner Cooper?
12. Why do junior college students withdraw before graduation?
13. Should the success of a junior college be judged by the proportion of students who enroll as sophomores? Should it be judged by the proportion who graduate?
14. "It is the ambition of practically every father and mother that the son or daughter should have the practical and cultural advantages of a college education. Under the existing educational machinery this has been reserved almost exclusively for an intellectual or a social aristocracy. Under the proposed reorganization, the liberal arts college itself would open its doors in every community now able to maintain a junior college." — President J. M. Wood. (Quoted in Cobb, Stanwood, *The New Leaven*, pp. 330–31.) Discuss the validity and significance of this statement.
15. How should the faculty be secured and compensated for extension and extra-hour courses in the junior college?
16. Study more in detail the popularizing function as it has been worked out at Chaffey, Sacramento, Modesto, Grand Rapids, or Snow Junior Colleges.
17. In which of the thirteen types of adult education activities listed by Alderman do you think junior colleges in general should engage? A particular junior college?
18. The junior college standards of the Virginia State Board of Education require that 75 per cent of the students must be taking courses leading to graduation. What is the relation of this requirement to the popularizing function as discussed in this chapter?
19. What types of community work, not mentioned in this chapter, have been or could well be undertaken by a junior college?
20. Should junior colleges have summer sessions? If so, under what circumstances?
21. Should junior colleges admit any adult student to extension courses, or should they require high school graduation as a prerequisite? Why?

SUGGESTED READINGS

Alderman, L. R. *College and University Extension Helps in Adult Education*. United States Bureau of Education, Bulletin no. 3. 35 pp. (1928.)

Allison, A. A. "Junior Colleges"; in *Texas Outlook*, vol. 12, pp. 9–10, 26. (June, 1928.)
A Texas farmer shows the value of the junior college to the community.

*Andrews, A. "How the Junior College Serves the Community"; in *Thirteenth Yearbook of the Department of Secondary School Principals, of the National Education Association*, pp. 340-47. (March, 1929.)

Based on experience at Grand Rapids, Michigan.

Bowman, L. E. "The Educational Barrier Smasher"; in *School Executives Magazine*, vol. 50, pp. 118-20, 148-50. (November, 1930.)

States four ways in which the junior college is popularizing college education.

*Cooper, W. J. "Adult Education in the Junior College Program"; in *California Quarterly of Secondary Education*, vol. 4, pp. 34-36. (October, 1928.)

*Green, R. E. "Is the Public Junior College Popularizing Higher Education?"; in *School Executives Magazine*, vol. 49, pp. 70-72. October, 1929.)

Harbeson, J. W. "Organization and Administration of the Public Junior College"; in *California Quarterly of Secondary Education*, vol. 1, pp. 426-30. (June, 1926.)

Treats briefly adult education in the junior college.

Hill, M. E. "Community Relations of the Junior College"; in Proctor, W. M. (editor), *The Junior College; Its Organization and Administration*, p. 93.

Description of the work at Chaffey Junior College.

*Knudsen, M. H. "Leadership Institutes"; in *Proceedings of the Seventh Annual Meeting of the American Association of Junior Colleges*, pp. 42-48. Jackson, Mississippi, 1927.

Lange, A. F. "A Junior College Department of Civic Education"; in *School and Society*, vol. 2, pp. 442-48. (September 25, 1915.)

"A tentative sketch of what a department of civic education might be, and should do."

Thomas, F. W. "The Curriculum as a Means to Wider Community Service" in Proctor, W. M. (editor), *The Junior College; Its Organization and Administration*, pp. 63-65.

CHAPTER IX

THE PREPARATORY FUNCTION

The junior college has begun also a most desirable decentralization of the "freshman flood" that has inundated our larger universities. — LEONARD V. KOOS.[1]

Contents of this chapter. In this chapter an effort is made to evaluate the success of the junior college as an institution preparing for the university. After a brief discussion of the curriculum in its preparatory aspect, answers are given to the questions: How many junior college students want to go on to university or other advanced work? How many actually do so? How successful are they when they actually enter the university? The latter question is answered with concrete evidence of success in several universities and four-year colleges in seven different states. Student opinion on the advantages and disadvantages of the junior college as a preparatory institution are then presented, and some of the dangers and objections discussed.

Importance. The preparatory function[2] has been emphasized from the first. The junior college, in its experimental stage, was anxious to measure its product against previously existing definite standards, namely, upper division university work. The university was somewhat skeptical of its new ally, in some cases, and proceeded to set up various standards,

[1] Koos, L. V. "We Need Junior Colleges"; in *World's Work*, vol. 56, pp. 201–02. (June, 1928.)

[2] Koos designates this function as the "Isthmian" function. The connotation of this word hardly suggests the significance of this phase of junior college work. An isthmus is merely incidental, connecting two really important and significant bodies. The junior college is too important in this aspect of its work to be reduced to the incidental status of an isthmus. As well call the high school an isthmus between elementary school and college. Junior high school, senior high school, junior college, university — each represents an important step in the educational process.

definitions, and accreditation which stressed almost exclusively the preparatory function, and the junior college spent its first energies in an effort to meet these. An institution which was not giving courses of real college grade could not expect long to survive.

Curriculum for the preparatory function.[1] With the exception of a few technical colleges every type of junior college, both public and private, offers a curriculum or group of courses that is directly preparatory to junior standing in the universities. In a number of states the law expressly provides that the courses so given shall be the equivalent of freshman and sophomore work as given in the state university. If other types of work are given, they are supplementary to the preparatory curriculum, not a substitute for it.

In general such courses are of the liberal arts type, stressing a broad general preparation in history, science, language, and literature. Those who finish them are qualified to enter the arts course in most standard American colleges and universities. In addition, however, many institutions give courses more specifically designed as preparation for certain professional schools, especially in states where entrance to these has been rather definitely placed at the junior level, as in Missouri. Thus we have courses listed as pre-legal, pre-medical, pre-engineering, pre-commercial, and other pre-professional courses specifically outlined to prepare students to enter legal, medical, engineering, commercial, and other professional schools of the university.

AMOUNT OF JUNIOR COLLEGE TRANSFER TO THE UNIVERSITY

To what extent have junior college students actually gone on to further work in college and university? To what extent

[1] A more detailed discussion of the curriculum in its various aspects will be found in Chapter XVIII.

do they desire to do so? Evidence on the latter question will be given first.

Student intention. When over 3000 students in California junior colleges were asked the question, in 1929, "Will you go beyond the junior college in your education?" 90 per cent of them answered in the affirmative. Of the sophomores, 17 per cent expected to return to the junior college to complete their courses; 70 per cent of the remainder expected to enter the university the same autumn, and 14 per cent expected to go to work, in many cases, doubtless, to earn money for later university courses. At Phœnix junior college, in 1930, 73 per cent of the sophomores were planning on college or university the following year, and 20 per cent on going to work.

On a much more extensive scale, over nine thousand students in junior colleges in California in 1929 were asked whether they expected to continue their education after junior college, and if so, where. Their answers were studied and summarized by Miss Jones, for various groups. She found not only the number expressing an intention of going to universities, but also their average scores on the Thurstone and Iowa tests.[1] She found that 80 per cent were intending to attend some higher institution, 15 per cent were uncertain, and only 5 per cent were definitely not intending to do so. There was only slight difference between classes, 79 per cent of the freshmen and 82 per cent of the sophomores expressing definite intention of further education. The principal institutions or groups of institutions represented are shown in Figure 20.

Thus there is ample evidence that the junior college is succeeding in the first step of its preparatory function, namely, in giving its students an ambition to go on to further work in the university. In fact there are many reasons to suppose it is

[1] Eells, W. C., and Jones, H. F. "Higher Educational Aspirations of California Junior College Students"; in *California Quarterly of Secondary Education*, vol. 6, pp. 239–44. (April, 1931.) The tests used are more exactly defined in Chapter XXII.

succeeding too well in this respect, a point which will be discussed later. The data so far given, however, indicate only student hope, ambition, expectation. To what extent are these aspirations realized? How many actually go to college? Unfortunately, published data on this point are not very plentiful. There have been very few follow-up studies of junior college students to find what they do and how well they do it after graduation or withdrawal from college.

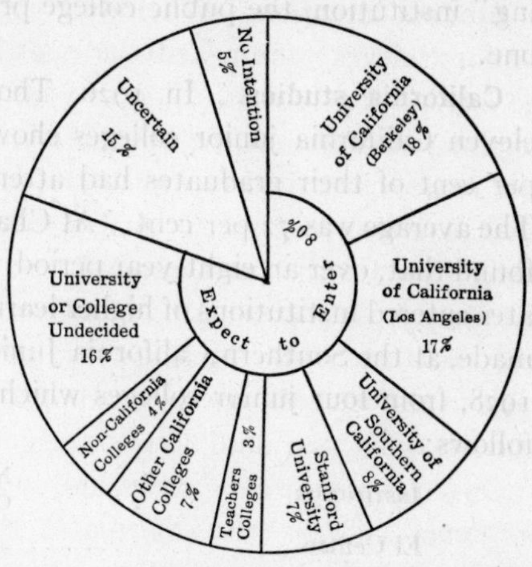

FIG. 20. INTENTION OF UNIVERSITY ENTRANCE AS EXPRESSED BY 9232 CALIFORNIA JUNIOR COLLEGE STUDENTS

McDowell's findings. The first study of this sort was made by McDowell, who reports the number of graduates and the proportion of them continuing their education for three different years, as follows:

YEAR	NUMBER OF GRADUATES	PER CENT CONTINUING EDUCATION
12 *public junior colleges*		
1915	59	80
1916	127	79
1917	184	67
53 *private junior colleges*		
1915	649	40
1916	793	42
1917	783	40

Almost twice as large a proportion went from public as from private junior colleges. Over half of the public junior colleges studied by McDowell were in California. At that period the private junior college was prevailingly a completion or "finishing" institution, the public college prevailingly a preparatory one.

California studies. In 1926, Thomas gave reports from eleven California junior colleges showing that from 50 to 80 per cent of their graduates had attended higher institutions. The average was 72 per cent. At Chaffey Junior College, Hall found that, over an eight-year period, 74 per cent of the graduates entered institutions of higher learning. Brief reports were made, at the Southern California Junior College Association in 1928, from four junior colleges which may be summarized as follows:

Institution	Number of Graduates	Per cent to Other Institutions
El Centro	32	81
Pomona	66	67
Riverside	317	74
Santa Ana	59	71
Total	474	73

These four institutions of various sizes and types show a fairly uniform proportion going on to higher institutions. If they can be taken as typical of the larger California groups reported above, they indicate a shrinkage between aspiration and realization from 80 per cent to 73 per cent. The percentage going to college in California is probably higher than in the country as a whole, if Hanna's study can be taken as typical.

Hanna's study. Hanna, in a study of 2812 graduates of 36 junior colleges in the Middle West, South, and Far West, in 1925–27, found that 44 per cent of them actually entered other institutions the following autumn, as far as junior college officials could determine. This may be taken as a minimum figure. There is no record of the number entering after a longer interval, but from the California and Phœnix data it is not unlikely that 10 per cent more entered later. If the total entry was 55 per cent of the graduating class, there was a great difference between aspiration of 80 per cent and realization. The 80 per cent, however, refers to quite a different group. Hanna found a somewhat higher record for public than for private junior colleges. Fifty-three per cent of graduates from public institutions, as compared with 37 per cent of those from the private, entered other institutions immediately for a third year of work. He found that 70 per cent of the graduates of junior colleges for men, 45 per cent of those from coeducational institutions, and 35 per cent of those from junior colleges for women entered higher institutions. His findings may be compared with a more extensive study by Campbell.

Campbell's study. Doak S. Campbell collected information from 83 junior colleges, showing the number of graduates in 1927–28 who continued their studies in four-year colleges or universities the following year. His results are summarized in Table 19, for four types of institutions.

TABLE 19. AVERAGE PERCENTAGE OF JUNIOR COLLEGE STUDENTS GRADUATING AND CONTINUING THEIR EDUCATION IN 83 JUNIOR COLLEGES[1]

Type	Number of Colleges	Average Enrollment, 1927–28	Per cent of Graduates	Per cent Continuing Education in 1928–29
Denominational	33	140	18	50
State	4	600	14	55
Public	26	228	15	63
Private	20	95	25	60

Transfer of non-graduates. So far data have been given regarding the transfer of junior college *graduates* to the university. To what extent do junior college students expect to transfer to the university and actually do so before they

[1] Campbell, D. S. *A Critical Study of the Stated Purposes of the Junior College.* George Peabody College: Contributions to Education no. 70, pp. 22–26. Nashville, Tennessee. (1930.)

finish the junior college? For the same groups already mentioned, of 1689 California junior college freshmen, 13 per cent said they were planning to go to the university the next year; at Phœnix, 19 per cent. Dean Cross, says, however, that this is so with each succeeding class at Phœnix, although usually at the end of the freshman year most of them have changed their minds and remain another year. At Chaffey, over a period of several years, one fifth of the students transferred to other institutions before graduation. In the 36 junior colleges studied by Hanna, 19 per cent of the students transferred to other institutions for the second year of work.

SUCCESS OF JUNIOR COLLEGE TRANSFERS

How successful is the junior college transfer who enters the university? Does his work stand up in comparison with that of students who have had their previous training in the university? This is the acid test of the success of the preparatory function. A variety of evidence is available in answer to this question, based upon the experience of several colleges and universities in different states. In some cases very careful and detailed scientific studies have been made; in others, rather vague generalities must suffice. Some of the results are meager. In many cases they are only suggestive and may be misleading. They have been made between groups that were not strictly comparable — e.g., junior college entrants with freshman entrants, or with all students in the university; junior college entrants at several institutions with advanced students at a single one; first semester grades only, during period of adjustment to new conditions; or junior college transfers with one semester or more of credit, instead of the real junior college product — the graduate who transferred as a junior.

Koos's study. The earliest study of this matter was made by Koos, who studied graduates of junior colleges in 1919,

1920, or 1921. He secured the records of 95 junior college graduates who entered thirteen universities and six colleges, and compared them with the records of 75 juniors at the University of Minnesota. The median mark of the junior college group was 80.6; of the Minnesota group, 79.8 — a slight superiority for the junior college. This difference is not significant, however, in view of the small number concerned and the difficulty of comparing marks in 19 different institutions, where marking systems as well as standards varied widely. Koos concluded that there was no appreciable difference in the two groups. His is the only general study, covering more than one institution, and it is quite inadequate. In another chapter Koos makes an extensive study of mental test data, from which he concludes: [1]

> The most obvious point of significance in the findings just presented as to the mental character of junior college students is that the authorities in higher institutions, more especially our state universities, have little or no grounds for the fear that the junior college in its present state of development brings into their upper years a flood of mentally incompetent students. These data make clear that junior college students are in this respect about on a par with students of the same classification in most colleges and universities.

The most extensive studies of the success of junior college transfers have been made in different California universities.

Stanford University. A brief study made of 30 junior college transfers in 1923–24, and of 44 junior college transfers in 1924–25, showed almost exact identity of grades in comparison with all other advanced students. The number of cases, however, was too small, and the comparisons too crudely made, to be of much significance.

A more extensive investigation at Stanford, made by the present writer in 1927, dealt with a group of 80 junior college

[1] Koos, L. V. *The Junior College*, pp. 103–04.

transfers from 1923 to 1926.[1] This, however, was superseded by the same author's much more comprehensive and reliable study made in 1928, which is discussed below in greater detail.

The most extensive and detailed statistical study yet made of junior college transfers was completed by the author in 1928, and reported in various publications. It dealt with transfers from three distinct types of public junior colleges in California: (1) independent junior colleges, organized in separate junior college districts, (2) junior college departments of high schools, and (3) junior college departments connected with six of the state teachers' colleges.[2]

During the five years from 1923–24 to 1927–28, inclusive, Stanford University received 510 students by transfer from junior colleges: 212 from nine independent junior colleges in California, 40 from eight junior colleges in California of the high school type, 210 from six junior colleges in California of the teachers' college type, and 48 from fourteen non-California junior colleges scattered from Alabama to Washington. Of these 510 students, 317 had completed their courses in the junior college, and therefore entered Stanford University with full upper-division or junior-year standing. Since this smaller group was more nearly homogeneous and more truly representative of the complete junior college product, it was used as the basis of study. The group consisted of 264 men and 53 women. Comparisons were made of ability, and of accomplishment.

Ability. Since 1921 a satisfactory score on the Thorndike Intelligence Examination for high school graduates had been required of all undergraduate students entering Stanford University. Table 20 summarizes the essential data by sexes

[1] Eells, W. C. "The Junior College Transfers in the University"; in Proctor, W. M., *The Junior College: Its Organization and Administration*, pp. 170–87.

[2] The third classification has recently been abolished, but this change does not affect the students considered in the study here reported.

for the different junior college groups, and for two other groups used for comparison. This table shows the number of students, the mean score on the Thorndike test, and the reliability of this score.

TABLE 20. SCORES ON THE THORNDIKE INTELLIGENCE EXAMINATION BY TYPE OF SCHOOL AND SEX FOR JUNIOR COLLEGE TRANSFERS AT STANFORD UNIVERSITY (1923–24 TO 1927–28)

	MEN			WOMEN		
	Number	Mean Score	Probable Error of Mean Score	Number	Mean Score	Probable Error of Mean Score
Type of junior college attended by students:						
Independent district	115	80.4	1.0	25	79.5	2.0
High school type	18	80.4	2.4	6	88.7	4.2
Teachers' college type	103	80.1	1.0	18	81.6	2.4
Non-California	25	83.4	2.0	4	68.5	5.0
Total	261	80.6	0.6	53	80.5	1.4
Groups for comparison:						
Native Stanford students*	492	72.3	0.45	87	69.1	1.0
Students from four-year colleges †	290	79.8	0.7	100	78.4	0.9

* All students in the upper division of Stanford University in the autumn quarter of the school year 1925–26 who entered the University direct from high school and for whom scores on the Thorndike test were available.

† All students from four-year colleges and universities in the United States who entered Stanford University as undergraduates from October, 1923, to June, 1926, with eighty-seven or more quarter-units of advanced credit and for whom scores on the Thorndike test were available.

No significant differences were found between the students from the different types of junior colleges, but very significant differences were found between the junior college students as a whole and the two groups used for comparison. The groups of junior college transfers, both men and women, show marked superiority over the corresponding groups of native Stanford students, and slight superiority over the upper division students transferring from standard four-year colleges. Similar results were found when the previous academic records were used as a measure of ability.

Accomplishment. Four distinct measures of the actual accomplishment of the junior college transfers were used.

1. *Records for successive quarters of all junior college transfers.* The academic accomplishment at Stanford University of each junior college transfer was computed for each quarter of residence. The results are summarized in Table 21. The

TABLE 21. AVERAGE GRADE-POINT-RATIO FOR SIX SUCCESSIVE QUARTERS OF JUNIOR COLLEGE TRANSFERS AT STANFORD UNIVERSITY

	First Quarter	Second Quarter	Third Quarter	Fourth Quarter	Fifth Quarter	Sixth Quarter	Six Quarters: Average	Six Quarters: Probable Error of Average
Men:								
All junior colleges	1.40	1.56	1.62	1.66	1.71	1.75	1.58	.01
Independent type	1.38	1.55	1.59	1.58	1.54	1.62	....	....
High school type	1.35	1.66	1.62	1.64	1.76	1.81	....	....
Teachers' college type	1.49	1.61	1.71	1.74	1.81	1.82	....	....
Non-California	1.19	1.28	1.36	1.60	1.77	1.75	....	....
Group for comparison: Native Stanford students	1.46	1.44	1.47	1.48	1.46	1.49	1.46	.02
Women:								
All junior colleges	1.78	1.91	1.92	1.81	1.83	1.98	1.86	.03
Independent type	1.74	1.84	1.86	1.77	1.74	2.04	....	....
High school type	1.94	2.65	2.48	2.41	2.44	2.24	....	....
Teachers' college type	1.88	1.89	2.01	1.94	1.75	1.86	....	....
Non-California	1.29	1.66	1.06	1.44	1.73	1.33	....	....
Group for comparison: Native Stanford students	1.73	1.64	1.72	1.86	1.87	1.89	1.78	.03

group of native Stanford men used for comparison represented an alphabetical sample of 200 men who entered Stanford University as freshmen in the autumn of 1922, 137 of whom graduated. The group of native Stanford women represented a similar sample of 51 women from the same class.

The most important information in Table 21 is shown in Figure 21. The numbers below each line indicate the number of grades averaged for the group each quarter. It should be noted that these numbers cannot be taken as a measure of elimination since many of the students were still in the university when the study here reported was made.

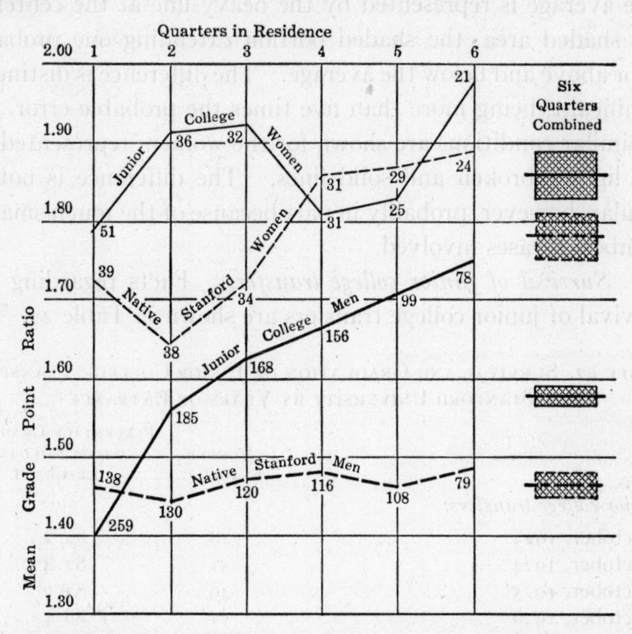

FIG. 21. AVERAGE GRADES FOR SIX SUCCESSIVE QUARTERS OF JUNIOR COLLEGE TRANSFERS AT STANFORD UNIVERSITY, AND OF NATIVE STANFORD STUDENTS

Figure 21 is a highly significant and illuminating graph, particularly with respect to the men, where the number of cases is large enough to give stability and regularity to the results. The heavy broken line, which represents native Stanford men, maintains practically the same level for all six quarters of the junior and senior years. The heavy solid line, which represents junior college men, while starting lower than the line for the native Stanford men, rises steadily and constantly, showing distinct and constantly increasing superiority of accomplishment for the junior college group. The averages of the grades for all six quarters and their probable errors are shown by the shaded areas at the extreme right of the figure. The average is represented by the heavy line at the center of the shaded area, the shaded portion extending one probable error above and below the average. The difference is distinctly significant, being more than five times the probable error.

Similar conditions are shown for the women, represented by the lighter broken and solid lines. The difference is not so regular, however, probably in part because of the much smaller number of cases involved.

2. *Survival of junior college transfers.* Facts regarding the survival of junior college transfers are shown in Table 22. The

TABLE 22. SURVIVAL AND GRADUATION OF JUNIOR COLLEGE TRANSFERS AT STANFORD UNIVERSITY BY YEARS OF ENTRANCE

	Number Entering	Percentage Graduating or Still in Residence
Junior college transfers:		
October, 1923	28	82.1
October, 1924	51	82.4
October, 1925	49	83.7
October, 1926	71	88.7
Total	199	84.9
Native Stanford groups for comparison:		
Entering as Juniors in 1923-24	284	94.0
Entering as Juniors in 1924-25	281	88.6
Entering as Juniors in 1925-26	326	87.7
Entering as Juniors in 1926-27	341	91.2

significant information in this table is that practically 85 per cent of those entering have survived, and the percentage of survival has increased each year during the four-year period studied. The native Stanford groups used for comparison have only slightly better survival records, and the superiority may be accounted for by the fact that they had had two previous years in the institution. First-year mortality in an institution is always the highest. Even with their transition and adjustment, the junior college groups make almost as good a record for survival as do native Stanford students who have gone through their severest testing and weeding-out two years earlier. The record of the junior college transfers entering in October, 1926, is particularly high.

3. *Graduation honors won by junior college transfers.* High scholastic attainment is recognized at Stanford University by conferring honors at graduation on the upper 15 per cent of the graduating class. The bachelor's degree is conferred "with great distinction" on the upper 5 per cent and "with distinction" on the next 10 per cent. Figure 22 summarizes the facts

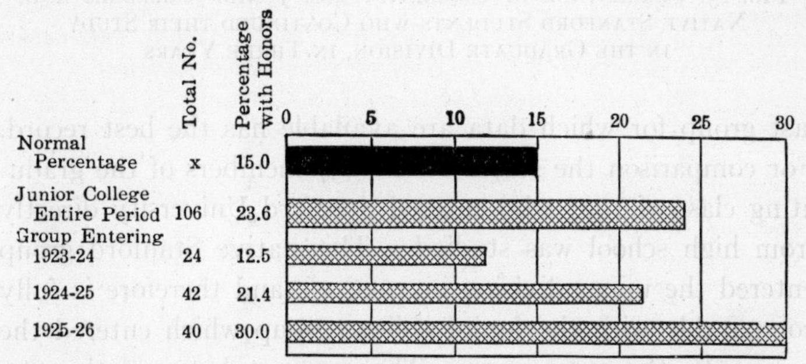

FIG. 22. PERCENTAGE OF STUDENTS FROM JUNIOR COLLEGES WHO RECEIVED GRADUATION HONORS AT STANFORD UNIVERSITY, IN THREE YEARS

with regard to the graduation honors won by junior college transfers. Where normally 15 per cent of the graduates receive honors, 23.6 per cent of the junior college transfers graduating achieved this distinction. Superiority is shown by all groups, whether classified by year or by sex. The superiority for the group entering in 1925–26 is particularly striking, exactly twice the expected number of students achieving both "distinction" and "great distinction."

4. *Junior college transfers in graduate work.* The percentage of junior college transfers who have undertaken graduate work at Stanford University is shown in Figure 23. Here, also, the

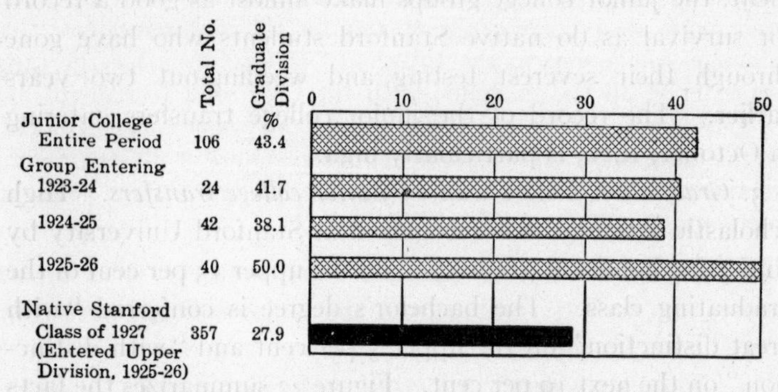

FIG. 23. PERCENTAGE OF STUDENTS FROM JUNIOR COLLEGES AND NATIVE STANFORD STUDENTS WHO CONTINUED THEIR STUDY IN THE GRADUATE DIVISION, IN THREE YEARS

last group for which data are available has the best record. For comparison the status of the 357 members of the graduating class of 1927 who entered Stanford University directly from high school was studied. This native Stanford group entered the upper division in 1925–26, and therefore is fully comparable with the junior college group which entered the university the same year. The contrast between the two records is striking. While almost one half of the graduates who have come from junior colleges have gone into graduate work at the university, only slightly more than one fourth of the native Stanford group have done so. Apparently the chance of securing students for the graduate division from among junior college transfers is almost twice as great as the chance of securing graduate students from among those who were admitted to the university as freshmen.

University of California (Berkeley). Several early studies were made before the major one of Ruch, Baker, and Ryce.

1. *Gray's study.* Gray, in 1915, in the first master's thesis ever written on the junior college, reported that:[1]

> The twenty-four junior college students who entered the university in August, 1913, took on an average 16.4 semester hours and made an average grade of 2.15 for the first semester. The average scholarship in the University of California for the same semester of all the freshmen from the California accredited high schools is 2.35, much lower than that of the junior college students in the university. When admitted to sophomore or junior standing in the university, the junior college student more than holds his own, and seemingly without difficulty.

The comparison was not entirely valid, however, since sophomores and juniors coming from the junior colleges were compared with freshmen.

2. *Thomas's report.* A better study than Gray's, from the standpoint of comparability, was reported by Thomas in 1926:[2]

> An investigating committee of the California Senate, appointed for the purpose of studying junior colleges, found that the scholarship attained in the university by the third and fourth year students, whose first two years of college work were done in junior colleges, was superior to that of those whose lower division work was done in the university.

In 1925, the following data[3] were compiled for 1923–24:

Group	Number	Average Grade
All upper division students	574	2.68
Upper division junior college transfers	58	2.78
Selected lower division students (Those who had completed 15 units of work)	641	2.87
All junior college transfers (Includes those with only one semester of junior college work)	124	2.91

[1] Gray, A. A. *The Junior College*, pp. 139–40. Berkeley, California, 1915. An average of "1" is equivalent to "A"; of "2" to "B"; etc. Thus the lower the grade average, the higher the scholarship.

[2] Thomas, F. W. *A Study of Functions of the Public Junior College and the Extent of their Realization in California*, p. 64. Stanford University, California, 1926.

[3] Thomas, F. W., *op. cit.*, pp. 65–68. Again the lower grade represents the higher scholarship.

The full-fledged junior college product entering the university as juniors made records midway between the upper division and lower division students.

3. *Study by Ruch, Baker, and Ryce.* A very comprehensive study was made at Berkeley in 1929 by Ruch, Baker, and Ryce, comparable in many respects with the Stanford study already discussed. It is based upon comparisons of 157 junior college transfers who entered the university in August, 1926, and 175 "native" California students who entered the university two years earlier. One limitation of the study was that about one third of the junior college transfers were not junior college graduates. The number of cases is less, also, than in the Stanford study, since it is restricted to the entries for a single year, but this tends to make it more homogeneous. Unfortunately, intelligence-test records were not available for the California groups. Essentials of their study are found in Table 23 and Figure 24 which, for the sake of comparison, are made analogous to Table 21 and Figure 21 as exhibited for Stanford University.[1]

TABLE 23. AVERAGE GRADE-POINT RATIOS FOR FOUR SUCCESSIVE SEMESTERS OF JUNIOR COLLEGE TRANSFERS AT UNIVERSITY OF CALIFORNIA (BERKELEY)

	First Semester	Second Semester	Third Semester	Fourth Semester	Four Semesters	
					Average	Probable error of average
Men						
Junior College	1.28	1.50	1.58	1.67	1.50	.05
Native California	1.19	1.26	1.38	1.46	1.31	.04
Women						
Junior College	1.08	1.24	1.41	1.65	1.30	.04
Native California	1.52	1.57	1.68	1.70	1.62	.04

[1] Figure 24 is redrawn from Figure 2 of the University of California study. For full reference see Suggested Readings at close of chapter.

The junior college men show an even more striking superiority to the native men than was the case at Stanford. Unlike Stanford, where the junior college men were lower in the first quarter, at California they were higher even the first semester

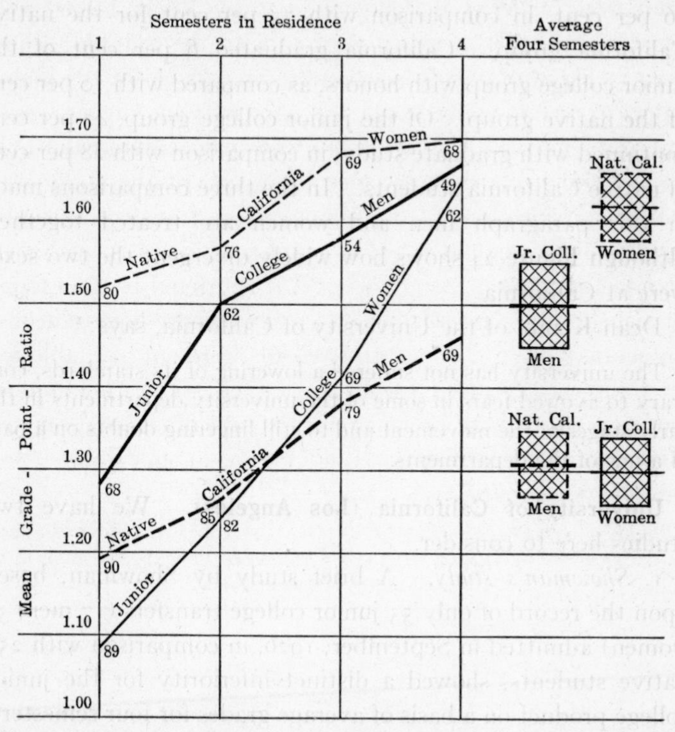

FIG. 24. AVERAGE GRADES FOR FOUR SUCCESSIVE SEMESTERS OF JUNIOR COLLEGE TRANSFERS AT THE UNIVERSITY OF CALIFORNIA, AND OF NATIVE CALIFORNIA STUDENTS

and maintained and increased this superiority in later semesters. In the case of the women, however, for whom entrance limitations are not as severe at California as at Stanford, the case was strikingly different. The junior college women made the lowest record of all the groups the first semester. The interesting feature in their case, however, is the rapid increase from semester to semester, finishing almost on a par with the native California women.

The per cent of junior college student transfers who graduated or were still in residence when the study was made was 66 per cent, in comparison with 75 per cent for the native California group. California graduated 6 per cent of the junior college group with honors, as compared with 10 per cent of the native group. Of the junior college group, 42 per cent continued with graduate study, in comparison with 28 per cent of native California students. In the three comparisons made in this paragraph men and women are treated together, although Figure 24 shows how widely divergent the two sexes were at California.

Dean Kemp, of the University of California, says:[1]

> The university has not suffered a lowering of its standards, contrary to avowed fears in some of the university departments in the early stages of the movement and to still lingering doubts on a part of a few of the departments.

University of California (Los Angeles). We have two studies here to consider.

1. *Showman's study.* A brief study by Showman, based upon the record of only 53 junior college transfers (17 men, 36 women) admitted in September, 1926, in comparison with 250 native students, showed a distinct inferiority for the junior college product on a basis of average grades for four semesters. His figures are as follows:

Men	
Junior College	1.30
Native California	1.53
Women	
Junior College	1.33
Native California	1.54

[1] Kemp, W. W. "The Junior College Movement in California"; in *Eighth Yearbook of the National Association of Secondary School Principals*, p. 666. Berwyn, Illinois, 1924.

The number of cases is too small, however, to be more than suggestive. Unlike the situation in the northern institution at Berkeley, there are no marked sex differences in either the junior college or the native groups.

2. *Jones and Robison study.* This study covered the records of 409 junior college transfers from 1923–27, but is concerned largely with the differences between different junior colleges. It shows a median grade point-ratio of 1.13 for the junior college group, as compared with 1.22 for a native group of 538 students.[1] The authors state that "the significant finding of these studies is not the difference between the work of the whole group of junior colleges... and of the university... so much as the great difference existing between the junior colleges themselves." Thus 24 different junior colleges, having from one to 70 transfers each, have mean grade-point ratios varying from 1.7 to 0.7.

University of Southern California. 1. In 1926, in reply to the question "How do you find that the graduates of junior colleges compare in scholarship with students who have had their lower division work with you?" the registrar replied, "The same."

2. *Watt and Touton study.* In 1930 appeared the last of the group of California statistical studies patterned somewhat upon the Stanford study which has been reported in greater detail.[2] It was based upon the records of 234 transfers from junior colleges, 1922 to 1928, of whom 128 were junior college graduates. A group of 100 native upper-division students, decreasing to 50 in the fourth semester, was used for comparison. Data for men and women were not given separately,

[1] The probable error of the difference is not given, but may be estimated as .04.

[2] Watt, R. R. G., and Touton, F. C. "Relative Scholastic Achievement of Native Students and Junior College Transfers at the University of Southern California"; in *California Quarterly of Secondary Education*, vol. 5, no. 3, pp. 243–48. (April, 1930.)

nor was any statement of the number of each. The results of this study are summarized in Table 24. Probable errors are not given, but the probable error of the difference may be estimated as .06.

TABLE 24. AVERAGE GRADE-POINT RATIO FOR FOUR SUCCESSIVE SEMESTERS OF JUNIOR COLLEGE TRANSFERS AT UNIVERSITY OF SOUTHERN CALIFORNIA

	Number First Semester	First Semester	Second Semester	Third Semester	Fourth Semester	Four Semesters: Average	Four Semesters: Probable error of average
With two years' previous work							
Junior college......	128	1.46	1.51	1.47	1.49	1.48*	.04 †
Native U.S.C....... (With five or more semesters)	100	1.28	1.37	1.48	1.75	1.43 ‡	.05
With one year junior college work							
Junior college......	68	1.32	1.47	1.29	1.31	1.39 ‡	
Native U.S.C....... (With three or more semesters)	61	1.32	1.40	1.57	1.73	1.46 ‡	

* Given as 1.45, but evidently in error, since it is less than for any of the four semesters.
† Estimated from given data.
‡ Computed as weighted average from data given.

The significant feature of Table 24 is the opportunity it gives to study the difference between junior college graduates, and those transferring with only one year of junior college credit. The graduates excel the native group by .05, but the one-year group fall below their comparable native group by .07. The junior college graduate makes an average record for each semester superior to the one-year transfer, the average for the four semesters being .09 in favor of the graduate. In distinction to the studies summarized in other California universities, however, the junior college students make a slightly lower record in their senior year than in their junior year, while the native students climb steadily upward. The authors conclude their study with the observation:[1]

On the whole the junior college seems to be carrying on effectively its function of preparation for advanced university work, and the university has been able so to organize course presentations as to allow transfers to attain scholarship success approximately equal to that of native students.

University of Chicago. 1. *The* 1923 *tabulation.* In a study made of the records of 220 junior college transfers for 1917–22, from three private and five public junior colleges, the following results were secured.[2]

	Number of Schools	Number of Students	Average Grade-Point Ratio
University of Chicago	1	100	3.2
Illinois four-year colleges	7	173	2.91
Junior colleges	8	220	2.74

The best record was made by 26 Joliet Junior College students with an average of 3.0.

2. *The* 1929 *tabulation.* In 1929 information on transfers from ten junior colleges was furnished by the recorder as follows: (Individual records are given only for junior colleges furnishing twelve or more students.)

	Number of Students	Average Grade-Point Ratio
Total	**468**	**3.05**
Crane	349	3.1
Joliet	34	3.5
North Park	21	3.0
Francis Shimer	20	3.0
Medill	15	2.9
Kansas City	12	2.4

While no groups were available for comparison, it is evident that the junior college product had shown a marked improvement in the interval between the two reports.

[1] Watt, R. R. G., and Touton, F. C., *op. cit.*, p. 248.

[2] Submitted to the Board of Admissions of the university, February 3, 1923.

3. *Miss Sloan's study.* Miss Sloan [1] studied the average scholastic standing of students in the university in the winter quarter, 1927–28. The 128 junior college students included came from Crane, Joliet, Kansas City, and La Salle. In all, 785 students had entered with advanced standing. Her results are summarized in Table 25.

TABLE 25. SCHOLASTIC STANDING OF VARIOUS GROUPS AT UNIVERSITY OF CHICAGO, WINTER QUARTER, 1927–28

Group	Number	Mean Grade-Point Ratio	Probable Error of Mean *
All students	2,447	2.81	.02
All junior college transfers	128	3.23	.08
All non-junior college transfers	657	3.05	.03
Normal school and teachers' colleges	110	3.43	.08
Universities	250	3.02	.06
Colleges	191	2.95	.05
Miscellaneous	106	2.92	.09

* Estimated from the author's data.

This study shows a marked superiority of the junior college transfers over all other groups, except those coming from normal schools and teachers' colleges.

University of Colorado. Superintendent R. E. Tope, in charge of the Grand Junction Junior College, reported, in 1928: [2]

Students have gone to ten different institutions of higher learning. All of these students, with one exception, have made good. Most of the students who have gone to other institutions are in the University of Colorado. In the first quarter of this year these students were enrolled in twenty-three courses in the sophomore and junior

[1] Sloan, Mary E. *A Statistical Study of the Records of 2447 Students in the Colleges of Arts, Literature and Science at the University of Chicago.* Unpublished master's thesis, 1927. Summarized in President's *Annual Report*, vol. 28, no. 26, p. 54. (October 15, 1927.)

[2] From a mimeographed address before spring conference, University of Colorado, April 5, 1928.

years of the university. In all these courses, with only two exceptions, they rank considerably above the general university average, the general university average being 76.7, and the average of the Grand Junction Junior College group in the same work 80.4. Junior college students do make good.

University of Iowa. In a study at the University of Iowa of 136 students coming from public junior colleges in the state, Weaver reported[1] that there was a slight advantage on the side of the junior college in three of the four groups compared.

University of Michigan. 1. Michigan was probably the first state university to receive transfers from public junior colleges. It will be recalled, from Chapter III, that in the early nineties the university was accepting students with one year of work from Saginaw and other high schools and graduating them in three years, although there is no record of their standing in comparison with other Michigan students.

2. In the President's Report in 1926, Dean M. E. Cooley reported that students from junior colleges were equal to those having taken their entire course at the university; and, in 1929, Associate Dean Paterson stated, in a personal letter, that "our records continue to show that students from junior colleges, admitted to advanced standing, do as satisfactory work as those who enter as freshmen."

3. *Congdon's study.* A much more extensive study was made as a doctor's dissertation by Congdon, in 1929, similar in nature to some of the California studies. This is unique among all of the studies reported in that it deals not with a general university group but with those in a professional school, namely, the School of Engineering of the University. He compared the scholastic success of 258 students who entered the engineering school from public junior colleges in the

[1] Weaver, E. L. "A Study of Junior Colleges in Iowa"; in *Bulletin of Iowa State Teachers' Association*, no. 2, p. 7.

state, from 1923 to 1928, with 1048 native Michigan students, on the basis of various average marks, of their disciplinary records due to poor scholarship, of economy of time in finishing their engineering course, of their persistence in residence, of the percentage of fifth-semester entrants graduated, and of the percentage of graduates taking honors. The weight of cumulative evidence yielded through these different lines of inquiry showed that the junior college students did better work, both before entering the Engineering College and during their two years of study in it, during which they were competing on a par with students who had had all their training at the University of Michigan.[1]

Mississippi colleges and universities. Dean O. A. Shaw, of the University of Mississippi, at the seventh meeting of the American Association of Junior Colleges, gave the following information regarding the success of junior college students in that state. Of 56 graduates of Hillman junior college who had gone to higher institutions, every one maintained a satisfactory class standing. Three fourths of 96 students who had graduated from Pearl River County Junior College had gone to other colleges; they ranked from B to A in their studies at the end of their first year in the institution to which they went. The registrars of several Mississippi institutions reported as follows: Mississippi College: "Judging from the type of students coming from the junior colleges, they are doing the first two years of college work very successfully." Mississippi State College for Women: "No complete failures. By the type of work done, I would consider the junior college a success." Millsaps College: "The young people coming to us from junior colleges in this state, which we have recognized, have maintained themselves in an acceptable manner." University of

[1] Congdon, W. *Tendencies as to the Scholastic Success of Junior College Transfers at the University of Michigan.* Unpublished doctor's dissertation, 540 pp. 1929. Summarized briefly in University of Michigan School of Education, Bulletin no. 1, pp. 29–30. (November, 1929.)

Mississippi: "Going over the entire number of young people taken at the university last year I found only two failures in possibly a hundred subjects there. There were three E's, which means a complete failure. They possibly made a B or an A in other subjects."

University of Texas. The *Report* of the Texas Educational Survey Commission, published in 1924, gave studies of the records of 100 upper-division junior college students at the University of Texas, in comparison with 100 students who had had their freshman and sophomore work at the University. It was found that the junior college transfers were distinctly inferior to the native group. Their median scholastic index was 57, while that for "native" students was 73.[1] Only a quarter of the junior college students surpassed the median of the native group. The Commission commented:[2]

> The conclusion seems justified by the facts, that, in so far as preparation for advanced college work of a high grade is concerned, the standard of work in junior colleges is low and inadequate. This leads to two conclusions: In the first place, there is need on the part of the state for closer supervision of existing institutions to protect students from ultimate failure in advanced college work. In the second place, there must be close supervision and control in standards adopted for public and state-supported junior colleges.

Baylor University. In a report made before the Association of Texas Colleges in 1930, by Dean W. S. Allen, the records of 330 junior college graduates from twenty-six junior colleges, from 1910 to 1929, at Baylor University, were studied. The average grade was 83.4. For a random sample group of 330 students with four years at Baylor the average was 83.5,

[1] In the plan used, a scholastic index had the following equivalents, D being the lowest passing grade: A = 133, B = 100, C = 67, and D = 33.

[2] Judd, C. H. *Texas Educational Survey Report*, vol. 3, pp. 45. Austin, Texas, 1924.

virtually the same. For the junior colleges sending twenty or more students, records were as follows:

	Number	Average Grade
College of Marshall	30	84.2
Rusk	34	83.6
Burleson	85	83.2
Decatur	104	83.1
Wayland	23	82.5

These five are all private (Baptist) institutions, whereas the groups at the state university were prevailingly from public junior colleges.

Conclusion. These studies vary widely in character and reliability. Some are little more than bare statements of opinion; some are based upon a careful statistical treatment of adequate data. On the whole they show marked success for the junior college in the exercise of the preparatory function. The University of Texas and the University of California seem to be the only institutions where there is a marked inferiority, and in the latter case there was distinct superiority on the part of the men. It is quite significant of the success of the junior college in its preparatory function that there is such a variety of judgment and evidence in its favor.

Unfortunately the studies are not strictly comparable with one another. This should be remedied to a large extent when an extensive investigation now under way is completed. Mr. Wyatt Hale, registrar of Birmingham Southern College, Alabama, and first recipient of the national Phi Delta Kappa fellowship, as a part of the National Survey of Secondary Education, began an extensive study of junior college graduates, on a nation-wide basis, in 1930. His study contemplated securing (1) data from every junior college on every graduate who has entered a university or college over a three-year period; (2) data from the registrar of each institution receiving such graduates; and (3) data by means of an individual questionnaire from each individual concerned. The study will cover over 6000 graduates of more than 100 junior colleges. Statistical evaluation, of course, will be made on a comparable basis for the entire group, as far as possible. The study was to be completed by the autumn of 1931.

STUDENT OPINION OF THE PREPARATORY FUNCTION

Student evaluation. Some light on the success of the preparatory function can be secured by studying the opinions of students who have gone to the junior college. "If you had free choice and were beginning your college work again, would you go to junior college in preference to a four-year institution?" This is the question that was asked over 3000 junior college students in California. Sixty-four per cent of the students answered "Yes." At Phœnix 66 per cent answered "Yes." At Chevy Chase School for Girls at Washington, D.C., the percentage was the same.

These replies are interesting as indicating the opinion of junior college students while they are still in the institution; although they lack sufficient background and experience, of course, to make an entirely valid comparison. It would be better if opinion could be secured from junior college graduates who have continued their courses in the university. In his class in Introduction to Education, at Stanford University, given for juniors and seniors, the writer has had from 15 to 30 junior college transfers enrolled each year for the past three years. Each year he has asked them the same question, "Would you go to junior college again?" and has been surprised to find with what constancy approximately two thirds of those in each class gave an affirmative answer and one third a negative one.

Hall's inquiry. Hall asked the opinion of 154 graduates and 43 non-graduates of Chaffey Junior College, all of whom transferred to universities, as to whether their junior college work was superior to that in the university or not. Their replies are given in Table 26.

TABLE 26. OPINIONS OF 154 GRADUATES AND 43 NON-GRADUATES, OF CHAFFEY JUNIOR COLLEGE WHO ENTERED UNIVERSITIES AS TO THE RELATIVE MERITS OF ACADEMIC WORK IN THE TWO INSTITUTIONS[1]

OPINION	TOTAL GROUP (per cent)	GRADUATES (per cent)	NON-GRADUATES (per cent)
Junior college was			
Decidedly better	24	28	12
Slightly better	18	18	19
No difference	37	32	51
Slightly worse	17	18	16
Decidedly worse	4	4	2

It is noticeable that the graduates, the full-fledged junior college product, rank it decidedly better than the drop-outs. Eighty-four per cent of the students had gone to California universities. The students as a whole were satisfied with the junior college work as preparation for upper division.

Brand and Hale studies. In his study of 3000 junior college students in California, Brand asked the students to state in their own words the advantages and disadvantages of the junior college. Among the advantages from an academic or preparatory standpoint most frequently given were small classes, individual help from instructors, better teachers, more class discussion and recitation, better training in study methods, and less danger of failing in courses. Among the limitations most often stated were limited range of courses, poor instructors, lack of prestige — only a secondary school, too informal, lack of contacts with specialists, too much work under one professor, teaching by high school methods, provincialism, and lack of broadening contacts. Most of these limitations lose their force as the small junior college increases to one of moderate size.

[1] Hall, W. A. *A Follow-up Study of Chaffey Junior College Students.* Unpublished master's thesis at University of Southern California, 1929.

When Hale's study is completed, authentic information on an extensive scale will be secured as to the opinion of junior college transfers regarding the success of the preparatory function. Meanwhile a tentative conclusion may be made that about two thirds of them are fairly well satisfied, and would choose to repeat the experience if they had the opportunity. In addition, of course, are the large number who would have to take the junior college or nothing, for the first two years, on account of geographical, economic, or scholastic limitations.

REASONS FOR SUCCESS

The evidence presented in this chapter shows that on the whole the university has received, from the junior college, students who easily hold their own with the university trained lower-division product, and in many cases surpass them. Such seems to be the fact, fairly well substantiated by a variety of evidence. Statistics furnish us a statement of the fact, but offer no explanation of the cause of it. In the opinion of the writer, there are two major reasons for this superiority as shown: (1) better selection, and (2) better instruction.

Better selection. As to better selection, the tendency for the university freshman and sophomore is to continue to the end of the course leading to the bachelor's degree. It is true, there is heavy mortality along the way, but there is no logical place for the student to stop short of the bachelor's degree without being stamped as more or less of a failure. In the junior college it is different. Junior college graduation forms a logical and an honorable stopping point. Transfer to the university requires new purpose, effort, and adjustment. The junior college instructor and administrator should, and in many cases does, discourage many students from attempting university work who might otherwise have entered and managed to survive to the junior year. The junior college can and does act as a sorting device, a protective sieve, a bumper, tending to select only the superior student for further university work. It may be questioned whether this selective process is working as well as it should, however, when 75 per cent or more of the junior college graduates actually go on to the university. This selection has taken place, however, at the end of the freshman year as well, as witness the 30 to 40 per cent of freshmen who do not reënter as sophomores, and the entering sophomores who fail to graduate. The junior college, from the preparatory standpoint, is carrying on the winnowing process constantly, and not at a single time and place only. With better operation of the guidance function, it is possible that this process will be carried out even more effectively.

Better instruction. The second method of explanation is superior instruction. Koos visited 111 junior college classes, and 41 college and university classes for approximately one full period each. As a result he reported, "In skill in teaching, the group of junior college instructors tends to be somewhat superior."[1] Dean Lange, of the University of California, in 1917 said:[2]

> At the University of California the scholarship average of those coming from junior colleges is found to be several fractions higher than the general university average — a fact not wholly accounted for, to be sure, by the scholarly fitness of junior college teachers. The junior college year is longer by at least a month. Hitherto the classes have been small. They have been homogeneous, and so have been able to start in on a higher level than is possible for the heterogeneous mass of university-college freshmen. They have been in charge, not of the least, but of the most experienced teachers of their respective institutions.

While the junior college is often handicapped by inferior facilities in the way of library, laboratories, etc., it is still true that the all-important element in instruction is the instructor. In spite of some individual exceptions, all studies seem to show

[1] Koos. *The Junior College*, p. 230.
[2] Lange, A. F. *School Review*, vol. 25, p. 476. (September, 1917.)

that the teaching ability of the junior college instructor on the average is superior to that of the average lower-division university instructor.[1] With superior professional preparation, with prime interest in teaching rather than in research, with emphasis upon personality and interest in students in smaller and more intimate groups, better teaching on the whole ought to be done in the smaller (but not too small) junior college. The junior college instructor may not have as great a breadth of view as the university professor; but he may have greater insight into the problems of the student. When the junior college is more interested in students than in subjects, when it discourages the inapt for university work, and when it sends the apt to the university with a better instructional foundation, then it will have reached the acme of success from the standpoint of the preparatory function.

OBJECTIONS AND DANGERS

Present dangers. There is danger that studies that have been made, especially studies such as that at Stanford, showing marked superiority of the junior college product, will lull the junior college administrator into a false sense of security and satisfaction. The junior college, as a young institution, has been on its mettle to make good. Only the better class of students have been encouraged to go to the university. Will the junior college rest on its laurels and tacitly assume that all junior college graduates can be encouraged to go on to the university and will make good there? Eternal vigilance is the price of safety, educationally as well as otherwise. After a careful evaluation of the various functions in California junior colleges, Thomas reached the conclusion that there was a probability that the preparatory function is being unduly emphasized, and that the junior colleges are not only preparing many students in an excellent manner for advanced university work,

[1] See Chapter XV for several such studies.

but are perhaps encouraging others to attempt that work who might more wisely pursue terminal courses on a semi-professional level.[1]

The junior college will need to continue to maintain high standards of instruction and of selection in order to keep the reputation which it has gradually established in so many universities during the period when its product has been looked upon with doubt and skepticism on the part of many university administrators. It has made good, as a preparatory institution so far — it must continue to do so. This generalization is true of the junior college movement as a whole, but not of every junior college. While the group as a whole has made good, there are as strikingly great "individual differences" in junior colleges as the psychologist has discovered among individual students. There are many weak and inefficient institutions whose graduates have made exceedingly unsatisfactory records, far below the university average. There is danger then that the poorer junior colleges will attempt to ride to success on the superior average record of the entire group. The average is a convenient and necessary device for summarizing; it has a marvelous power to reveal truth for a group as a whole, but it has a dangerous power to conceal truth with regard to the individuals which compose the group. The individual junior college must not be allowed to hide under the protecting cloak of the average.

QUESTIONS AND PROBLEMS

1. In what way could quantitative data be gathered to investigate the cause of superiority of junior college students in universities in which such superiority has been found?
2. Discuss the relative merits of the terms "Isthmian" or "Preparatory." Is some other term still better?

[1] Thomas, F. W. *A Study of Functions of the Public Junior College and the Extent of Their Realization in California*, p. 75. Stanford University, California, 1926.

3. Find junior colleges in which the preparatory function is stressed little, or not at all.
4. Investigate Sarah Lawrence Junior College, from the standpoint of the preparatory function.
5. From their catalogues, make a list of junior colleges offering definite pre-legal, pre-medical, pre-engineering, and other pre-professional types of junior college curricula. Can any generalizations be made from standpoints of distribution, size, type, or location?
6. How much value is there in student opinion with reference to success of the preparatory function? Limitations? Bias? Halo effect?
7. Is it possible to determine what proportion of junior college graduates should be expected to enter the university? If so, how?
8. Is there any evidence in the high school on the difference between intention of students with reference to university entrance, and actual entrance?
9. Why should percentage of university attendance be greater from public junior colleges than from private ones?
10. In studying junior college transfers to a university, what are the advantages or disadvantages of including one-year transfers with graduates?
11. Make a careful comparative study of the methods, limitations, and results of the various studies of California universities, summarized in this chapter, from the original studies as published in the *California Quarterly of Secondary Education*.
12. Why might junior college transfers be expected to make lower marks in their first semester or quarter of university residence? Do other students tend to do the same? If so, to what extent?
13. Some universities have evaluated the junior college product in terms of the first semester record, exclusively. What, if any, are the objections to this method?
14. What is the advantage of including probable errors in studies of the type reported in this chapter?
15. Suggest other objections and dangers than those mentioned in the last section of this chapter.
16. Analyze the curriculum of any junior college as given in its catalogue to see what proportion of it can be classified as preparatory. How does it compare with the lower division work of the state or other leading university, in the same state? How does it compare with the curriculum recommended by Koos as satisfactory for preparatory work? (Koos, *Junior College Movement*, pp. 45-49.)
17. Examine the curricula preparatory to a group of several universities in some junior college catalogue. Are they so different in character that a small junior college will have difficulty in offering preparatory courses for all of them?

SUGGESTED READINGS

Allen, W. S. "University Success of Junior College Graduates"; in *Junior College Journal*, vol. 1, pp. 147–48. (December, 1930.)

*Eells, W. C. "University Records of Students from Junior Colleges" (published in various forms, with some variation); in *California Quarterly of Secondary Education*, vol. 3, pp. 301–17 (June, 1928); *Proceedings of the Ninth Annual Meeting of the American Association of Junior Colleges*, pp. 3–21 (Fort Worth, Texas, 1928); condensed in *Bulletin of the American Association of Collegiate Registrars*, pp. 362–85 (April, 1928); and in *School Review*, vol. 37, pp. 187–97 (March, 1929).

A study of 510 junior college transfers at Stanford University.

Eells, W. C., and Jones, H. F. "Higher Educational Aspirations of California Junior College Students"; in *California Quarterly of Secondary Education*, vol. 6, pp. 239–44. (April, 1931.)

Jones, A. H., and Robison, C. H. "Studies Based on Scholarship of Students Transferring from Junior Colleges to the University of California at Los Angeles"; in *California Quarterly of Secondary Education*, vol. 4, pp. 313–18. (June, 1929.)

Koos, L. V. "Junior College Instruction — III. The Success of Junior College Graduates"; in *The Junior College*, pp. 233–38.

*Koos, L. V. "The Junior College in Its Isthmian Function"; in *The Junior College Movement*, pp. 29–49.

*Ruch, G. M., Baker, D. C., and Ryce, E. "A Comparison of the Scholarship Records of Junior College Transfers and Native Students of the University of California"; in *California Quarterly of Secondary Education*, vol. 4, pp. 201–13. (April, 1929.)

Shaw, O. A. "The Junior College Movement in Mississippi"; in *Proceedings of the Seventh Annual Meeting of the American Association of Junior Colleges*, pp. 1–6. Jackson, Mississippi, 1926.

Showman, H. M. "Junior College Transfers at the University of California at Los Angeles"; in *California Quarterly of Secondary Education*, vol. 4, pp. 319–22. (June, 1929.)

Watt, R. R. G., and Touton, F. C. "Relative Scholastic Achievement of Native Students and Junior College Transfers at the University of Southern California"; in *California Quarterly of Secondary Education*, vol. 5, pp. 243–48. (April, 1930.)

CHAPTER X

THE TERMINAL FUNCTION

> The junior colleges do not seem to me a menace to the good American college, but on the contrary a benefit.... One of the merits of these new institutions will be keeping out of college, rather than leading into it, young people who have no taste for higher education. — A. LAWRENCE LOWELL.[1]

Contents of this chapter. This chapter endeavors to answer in order, several important questions: What are terminal or semi-professional courses? What semi-professions are of junior college grade? Why should they be given in the junior college? What terminal courses are actually given? How are they given? How successful are these courses in actual practice? What occupations are junior college students actually preparing for? What is the future of terminal courses in junior colleges?

WHAT ARE TERMINAL OR SEMI-PROFESSIONAL COURSES?

To answer this question, "What are terminal or semi-professional courses?" it is necessary to define three occupational levels, which is done by Koos, as follows:[2]

Profession: An occupation for which the training should be that given by an institution requiring for entrance at least graduation from an accredited secondary school, and offering a course of college grade of no less than four years in length culminating in an appropriate and recognized degree.

Semi-Profession: An occupation in order to enter upon which one should prepare himself with a course of training approximately two years in length, with a high school education or its equivalent as a prerequisite.

[1] Lowell, A. L. "The Outlook for the American College"; in Kelly, R. L. (editor), *The Effective College*, p. 283. Association of American Colleges.

[2] Koos, L. V. *Junior College*, p. 153.

Trades or Clerical Occupations: Those occupations in order to enter upon which one should be trained in a public or private high school, trade school, commercial school, or other institution which presupposes a knowledge of the common-school subjects and gives education on a level of less than college grade.

This presupposes that there is a definite group of occupations for which two years of collegiate training is necessary and sufficient; that a person who has taken suitable terminal or culminal courses is prepared to take his place in society as a producer in one of those semi-professions or middle-level occupations.

WHAT SEMI-PROFESSIONS ARE OF JUNIOR COLLEGE GRADE?

Dr. Leonard's opinion. Dr. R. J. Leonard, in a notable address before the American Association of Junior Colleges in 1925, listed a considerable number of occupations which in his judgment belonged to the "middle level," suitable for the junior college: pharmacy; optometry; nursing; commercial, including nearly all types of salesmanship, accounting, secretarial work, passenger and mercantile traffic; public-service occupations by the score; most of the so-called engineering occupations; the great majority of agricultural pursuits; and foremanship in industry. "To make a very long story short," he says, "the middle-level occupations are all potentially open to junior colleges. They represent permanent and distinctive fields for which junior colleges alone can best train prospective workers. It remains for administrators of vision and imagination to demonstrate what can be done."[1]

Composite opinion of experts. Koos, in 1922, secured the composite judgment of a considerable group of expert judges

[1] Leonard, R. J. "The Contributions of a Study of Occupational Levels to Junior College Policy"; in *Proceedings of the Fifth Annual Meeting of the American Association of Junior Colleges*, pp. 99–100. Cincinnati, Ohio, 1925.

in three important fields regarding the suitability of certain occupations as semi-professions suitable for junior college training. From a variety of sources he listed over two hundred occupations in the fields of commerce, engineering, and agriculture which had been suggested as suitable for the junior college level. These were submitted to deans of colleges of commerce, engineering, and agriculture, with the request that they classify them in accordance with the definition given at the beginning of this chapter. A summary of their judgments is given in Table 27.

TABLE 27. SUMMARY OF JUDGMENTS ON SEMI-PROFESSIONS IN COMMERCIAL, ENGINEERING, AND AGRICULTURAL OCCUPATIONS BY KOOS'S EXPERT JUDGES

Occupation	Number of judges	Total number of occupations judged	Number judged semi-professional by over 50 per cent of the judges	Number judged semi-professional by over 33 per cent of the judges but less than 50 per cent
Commercial......	23	57	14	21
Engineering.....	84	104	43	22
Agricultural....	36	48	12	25
		209	69	68

The principal occupations of the fourteen commercial occupations, judged as semi-professional by over half of the deans of colleges and heads of departments of commerce, were: loan and stock-brokers, city department-store buyers, chief clerks, credit men, commercial designers, insurance agents and adjusters, jobbing and wholesale merchants, statistical clerks, shipping department heads, and storekeepers with large concerns. Among the 43 engineering semi-professions placed on the list by over half of the deans of colleges of engineering were: cement testers, chemical-laboratory workers, general contractors in building trades, draftsmen of various sorts (mechanical, structural, architectural, topographical, mining, etc.), electricians, inspectors, superintendents, and surveyors. Among the twelve agricultural occupations (including forestry) selected by over half of the deans of colleges of agriculture, were: florists, foremen on truck farms, managers of butter and cheese factories, makers of butter and cheese or ice cream, testers for cow-test associations, poultrymen, lumber salesmen, forest rangers, woods superintendents.[1]

Such composite opinions are valuable. Probably no better judges could be selected, yet one cannot but be impressed with the diversity of judgment shown even more than by the community of opinion. For example, there was only one occupation, of the two hundred and more submitted for judgment, on which over three fourths of the judges agreed in their judgment. This amount of agreement was found (79 per cent) in the case of mining draftsman, although for eight other varieties of draftsmen the agreement was less than 75 per cent, and in one case, draftsmen in building trades, it fell below 60 per cent. The highest percentage of agreement in the commercial group was 65 per cent for city department-store buyer; in the agricultural group it was 68 per cent for a tester for a cow-testing association! Such wide variability in judgment, and in failure to agree, causes one to accept the results of such judgments, interesting and suggestive as they are, with some reservations.

Bennett's determination of semi-professions. Bennett, in his doctor's dissertation at the University of California, 1925 (published in 1928), endeavored to secure a valid list of occupations of junior college grade by a combination of two methods, viz., an examination of about 500 catalogues of

[1] Koos also suggested other possible semi-professions, upon which no effort was made to obtain expert consensus of opinion, as follows:

Home Economics: Cafeteria manager, dietician, professional shopper.

Art: Art-glass worker, decorative modeler, designer, engraver, commercial illustrator, interior decorator, map maker.

Miscellaneous: chiropodist, dental mechanic, veterinarian, masseur, pharmicist, teacher, welfare worker, musician.

institutions, some 100 of which were found to be offering curricula of approximately junior college grade in preparation for specific occupations. Using this as a basis, with various further modifications, he developed a list of 106 occupations, which was then sent to ten different classes of experts in vocational education throughout the country, asking them to indicate those of true junior college grade. Lists were received from 205 such men. Finally the catalogue lists and those of the judges were compared, and ultimately a list of 28 occupations was derived which Bennett made the subject of detailed analysis and study in his dissertation.[1]

He groups the 28 occupations of junior college grade, thus selected, with estimated number of new men needed for them annually, as follows:

Profession — technicists	29,000	*Agriculture — technicists*	73,000
Chiropractor	2,000	Buyer and shipper of farm produce	3,000
Detective	1,000	Dairy farmer	7,000
Librarian	3,000	Landscape gardener and florist	1,000
News reporter	2,000	Large-scale general farmer	39,000
Nurse	15,000	Large-scale single-crop farmer	15,000
Optometrist	2,000	Orchardist	4,000
X-ray operator	4,000	Stock-raiser	4,000
Commerce — technicists	62,000	*Industry — technicists*	26,000
Accountant	7,000	Builder and contractor	4,000
Bank teller	3,000	Commercial artist	2,000
Café manager	5,000	Draftsman	4,000
Hotel-keeper	3,000	Photographer	2,000
Railway station agent	2,000	Printer and linotypist	8,000
Stenographer-secretary	10,000	Surveyor	3,000
Storekeeper	32,000	Watchmaker	3,000

WHY SHOULD TERMINAL COURSES BE GIVEN IN THE JUNIOR COLLEGE?

Chapter VII has already explained in part why terminal courses should be given in the junior college. Society has an

[1] Bennett, G. V. *Vocational Education of Junior College Grade.* University Research Monographs, no. 6, p. 35. Baltimore, 1928.

obligation to train its citizens at public expense for positions of usefulness in the social body. This has been long recognized in practice in the training for trades and clerical occupations given in hundreds of general and technical high schools; for the professions of law, medicine, engineering, and others in the universities; but the field of semi-professions has been left almost exclusively to private enterprise. Most of it has been done in schools established on a purely commercial or proprietary basis, without sufficient inspection, regulation, or guarantee that standards will be maintained, or value received for the tuition fees demanded.

Opinion of authorities on vocational education. On the basis of a detailed analysis of occupations by states, Bennett estimates that to supply the need in 28 semi-professions which he studied, 190,000 new recruits would be required annually, and that to maintain such a number of graduates would require an enrollment each year in two-year junior colleges of 471,000 students.[1] Almost 200,000 young people are entering these occupations each year, but only a small percentage of them are receiving their training in the junior college.

McDowell found, when he made his study, that "to provide a completion school for those who can go no further" was the reason second in importance for the existence of junior colleges. Koos, in his more extensive investigation of reasons, found that "providing occupational training of junior college grade" ranked fourth in importance.

Dean Lange wrote, in 1920:[2]

It is coming to be a notorious fact that those who seek or should seek vocations occupying the middle ground between those of the artisan type and the professions are as yet nowhere and nohow aimfully provided for in our scheme of public schooling.... I am

[1] Bennett, G. V. *Vocational Education of Junior College Grade.* University Research Monographs, no. 6, p. 134. Baltimore, 1928.

[2] Lange, A. F. "The Junior College"; in *Sierra Educational News*, vol. 16, pp. 484-85. (October, 1920.)

more than skeptical about the educational success of any junior college with only non-vocational departments.

President Ray Lyman Wilbur speaks of the junior college as providing particularly for that class of men who are mechanically minded, and of women who are domestically minded, the opportunity to improve their abilities. The late Dr. Leonard, of Columbia University, said:[1]

In so far as universities concern themselves with professional education, their efforts will be confined to the higher and highest levels. Those are the permanent university fields. No other institutions can perform these services satisfactorily. And, in so far as junior colleges concern themselves with occupational education, their efforts will be confined to the middle level and, in like manner, this will be their permanent field.

The vocational expert of the California State Department of Education, Dr. Ricciardi, said, in 1928, that 60 per cent of the 9000 junior college students then in the state could best be trained through terminal courses. As pointed out in Chapter VIII, the junior college has popularized education. It is rapidly becoming the people's college. Where a local junior college is established, probably the number of people who "go to college" is at least doubled. It would be unwise and unfortunate if all of these tried to enter a university and prepare for professions which in most cases are already overcrowded, and for which their talents and abilities in many cases do not fit them. Federal census figures indicate that less than ten per cent of the population of the country is required for the professions. The junior college must offer something more than a simple university preparatory course, if it is to live up to its true destiny. The development of the terminal function is an essential corollary of the success of the popularizing function.

[1] Leonard, R. J. "Professional Education in Junior Colleges"; in *Teachers College Record*, vol. 26, p. 729. (May, 1925.)

TERMINAL COURSES ACTUALLY GIVEN

What terminal courses are actually being given in the junior colleges of the country and what is the nature of them? A few general facts will first be given, and then seven groups of courses briefly discussed.

a. GENERAL SURVEYS

Junior college catalogue offerings. In a detailed analysis of the courses offered in the catalogues of 279 junior colleges in the country, reported more fully in Chapter XVIII, Hollingsworth found the number of colleges offering certain courses which may be thought of as terminal in nature, and the average number of semester hours in each, as shown in Table 28. While it is not maintained that these are all strictly terminal, they nevertheless constitute the raw material out of which terminal courses may be built.

TABLE 28. NUMBER OF JUNIOR COLLEGES OFFERING CERTAIN COURSES AND AVERAGE NUMBER OF SEMESTER HOURS FOR EACH

(Total colleges examined, 279)

SUBJECT	NUMBER OF COLLEGES	AVERAGE NUMBER SEMESTER HOURS
Education	180	16
Music	160	31
Commerce	134	30
Home Economics	131	21
Art	124	15
Engineering	109	21
Agriculture	46	23

Vocational junior colleges. There are a few junior colleges, all of the state type, definitely organized on the vocational basis. Whitney classified fourteen of this type, including agricultural schools, a school of forestry, a school of mines, and a polytechnic school, and made a detailed analysis of their course offerings.[1] While for some of their students the

[1] These fourteen institutions, limited to five states, are as follows: *Arkansas:* Arkansas Polytechnic College at Russelville, and the four Agricultural and

work is doubtless in preparation for advanced work in the same field in universities or technical schools, for the most part the students are taking true terminal or finishing courses. The average number of semester hours offered in general and special courses, as summarized by Whitney, may be classified roughly as vocational and academic, as follows:

Vocational		Academic	
Engineering	39.4	Science	39.8
Agriculture	33.8	Modern Languages	18.2
Commerce	33.7	Mathematics	15.6
Home Economics	27.1	Social Studies	14.4
Education	23.9	Ancient Languages	13.3
Music	23.4	English	11.4
Art	8.5	Psychology	5.2
		Physical Education	4.7
		Public Speaking	3.7
Total	189.8	Total	126.3

It is thus seen that approximately 60 per cent of the offerings may be classified as prevailingly vocational in nature, and doubtless many of the subjects classified as academic, such as mathematics, have many vocational aspects.

The junior college division of the California Polytechnic, organized in 1927, offers college work in agriculture, engineering-mechanics, aeronautics, architectural drafting, civil engineering, electrical engineering, mechanical drafting, and mechanical engineering.

Mechanical Colleges at Magnolia, Monticello, Jonesboro, and Pine Bluff. *California:* California Polytechnic at San Luis Obispo. *Oklahoma:* Cameron State School of Agriculture at Lawton, Northeastern Oklahoma Junior College at Miami, Murray State School of Agriculture at Tishomingo, Connor State School of Agriculture at Warner, and Eastern Oklahoma College at Wilburton. *Texas:* North Texas Junior Agricultural College at Arlington, and John Tarleton Agricultural College at Stephenville. *North Dakota:* State School of Forestry at Bottineau. It is doubtful whether the last-named school should be included. It was organized as a state school of forestry, but there proved so little need for such an institution that it gradually drifted into an academic junior college. It was offering barely ten hours of instruction in forestry in 1928. The Northeastern Oklahoma Junior College retained very largely its courses offered in its former status as the Miami School of Mines. Aside from the California Polytechnic, all the others were classified as agricultural institutions.

The state junior college, however, is not the typical junior college of the country. What is the situation in other types of institutions?

Private junior colleges. Terminal work of vocational character is not common in most of the private institutions. In many of the junior colleges for women, considerable work is given in home economics, art, music, and secretarial training, which in many cases is doubtless vocational in character, while in others it is of general cultural nature. In the small group of five or six Y.M.C.A. evening junior colleges the work is largely of a vocational type.

Municipal or local junior colleges. The offerings of vocational work are rather extensive in the public junior colleges of the country, but the proportion of it of a terminal character is very meager if conditions in fifteen public junior colleges which are members of the North Central Association are typical. In a study reported in 1928, Cross found that 86 per cent of the 166 curricula offered in these schools were vocational, as follows: Engineering, 32; Education, 24; Business, 18; Medical, 12; Legal, 11; Dental, 10; Music, 9; Agriculture, 8; Home Economics, 6; Pharmacy, 6; Journalism, 3; Nursing, 3; Library, 2. Only 8 per cent, or 14, of the entire group of curricula as offered could be classified as terminal or completion. These represent the better type of schools in the North Central Association territory. Doubtless the terminal work would be much less in the non-member junior colleges. Crane Junior College, the largest in the country, has frequently been referred to as offering terminal courses. The great emphasis at Crane, however, has been upon engineering courses preparatory to further engineering work in the University of Illinois. Of the eight curricula which they offer, only one, Commerce and Administration, is definitely terminal in character.

The most outstanding opportunity to develop terminal work in a municipal junior college is to be found in the new Los

Angeles Junior College. The academic needs of the city of Los Angeles can be largely cared for by the two large institutions, University of Southern California, and University of California at Los Angeles. When the Los Angeles Junior College opened, in 1929, some 85 per cent of its 1370 entering freshmen were of the "non-recommended" group; that is, not eligible for entrance at the state university. Here is probably the finest opportunity in the country to secure a large, homogeneous group of students, the majority of whom probably should never look forward to university work, and to work out curricula adapted to their needs. It is too early to evaluate the success of such courses, but a beginning has been made toward providing them. "These curricula are designed to meet the needs of those who desire to spend not more than two years beyond high school for cultural courses or for such courses as will fit them for vocational or semi-professional work." The semi-professional curricula offered for 1930–31 included art, aviation, banking, civic health (doctors' and dentists' assistants), drama, electrical technology, civil engineering, mechanical engineering, music, journalism, nursing, recreational leadership, registrars' assistants, secretarial, general business, and social arts.

District junior colleges: San José. The most extensive offering of terminal courses is probably to be found in the district junior colleges of California, a few of which have done outstanding work of a terminal nature. The most extensive offering of detailed curricula of definite type is that found at San José where 26 distinct courses are outlined, as follows:

Commerce: secretarial, stenographic, accounting, bookkeeping, merchandising, clerical.

Home-making: hotel operation, catering, governess's work, costume design, home-making.

Art: sculpture and pottery, home decoration, illustration, crafts, painting, design, commercial art, photography.

English: journalism.
Speech Arts: stage manager.
Library: library assistants.
Music: professional musician.
Natural science: landscaping and nursery.
Engineering: radio technical engineering, general engineering.

The prescriptions in 23 of these courses, amounting in all to some 2200 quarter units of work, may be classified approximately as follows:

General academic work (English, public speaking, physical education, hygiene, language, etc.)	20 per cent
Specific requirements of strictly vocational type	65
Electives	15

The specific requirements vary in different courses from 31 of the 96 required units in library training, to 87 in radio engineering and general engineering, and 90 in painting. This may seem to be a very extensive offering, and to require an unusually large faculty to give such a number of courses. There is much overlapping between many of these curricula, however, and a core of English and physical education is common to all of them. As a matter of fact, the entire offering of separate courses is less than 500 term hours, of which about half are in subjects of the regular academic curriculum, and half are special courses in the vocational fields. If a teaching load of 15 hours per week be assumed, all of the extra-vocational courses necessary to give the curricula as outlined could be handled by 6 or 8 additional instructors. Most of it is found in the four departments of commerce, home-making, industrial education, and music.

Other California colleges. Terminal vocational courses in a few other district junior colleges may be briefly summarized as follows:

Chaffey: Agriculture, Commerce, Home Economics, Mechanic Arts.

Compton: General Arts and Sciences, General Business, Practical Engineering, Practical Home-Making, Journalism and Writing, Mechanic Arts, Pre-Nursing.

Fullerton: General Business, Secretarial, Mechanic Arts.

Glendale: Commerce and Business, Bookkeeping and Accounting, Stenographic, Practical Engineering, Home Economics, Liberal Arts, Mechanical Arts, Vocational Music, Pre-Nursing.

Long Beach: Architectural, Art, Engineering, General Business, Home Economics, Journalism, Liberal Arts, Pre-Nursing, Secretarial.

Pasadena: Art, Commerce, Household Science and Art, Building Practice and Design, General Mechanics, Music, Landscape Gardening.

Riverside: Engineering, Nursing, Library Work, Architecture, Home-Making, Hotel Management.

b. COMMERCIAL COURSES

The most extensive and recent study of the elements to consider in building junior college terminal curricula in the commercial field has been made by E. W. Barnhart, chief of the commercial education service of the Federal Board for Vocational Education. The statements in this paragraph are drawn from his illuminating and thoughtful discussion.

Curriculum making for the terminal commercial courses is truly creative; indeed curriculum making for these courses is an adventure into new fields of education, of business, of citizenship, and of community building. Approximately 75 per cent of the graduates of commercial courses of a junior college do not go to higher schools of business or to any other school. Two thirds of the graduates of commercial courses remain in their home town or return to it. These statements are based upon a study of the commercial curricula in 131 junior colleges, made by La Dow at Iowa. In planning curricula for junior college terminal commercial courses the size of the community is a vital factor. The problem is different in the large city and in the small community. For the large city junior college its greatest opportunity lies in developing courses preparatory for entrance into the semi-business professions, such as credit managers, traffic agents, purchasing agents, executive secretaries, life underwriters, managers or owners of small retail stores, hotels, restaurants, and a host of similar minor executive and managerial positions. However, the ease with which purely high school short hand, typewriting, and bookkeeping can be taught apparently has prevented the large metropolitan junior colleges of commerce from pioneering in these needed fields. The small community junior college, for whom the temptation to reproduce the high school commercial courses is great, and apparently too often prevails, will ultimately be forced to offer curricula for other occupations. It will have to widen its field of commercial offerings, rather than specialize in particular lines for which the local community has relatively small demand. Its offerings must be based upon a detailed study of local employment opportunities.

Commercial course at Crane Junior College. In contrast with these principles, may be mentioned the single general business curriculum offered at Crane, Chicago, as training for general business, accountants, secretarial work, advertising, and credit and collection service.

FIRST YEAR

First Semester	Hours	*Second Semester*	Hours
Commercial Geography	3	Economic History of the United States	3
Accounting	3	Accounting	3
Public Speaking	2	Rhetoric	3
Rhetoric	3	Public Speaking	2
Electives	4–7	Electives	4–7
Total	15–18	Total	15–18

Electives Open to Freshmen

English, European history, mathematics, chemistry, engineering drawing, foreign languages.

SECOND YEAR

First Semester	Hours	*Second Semester*	Hours
Economics	5	Banking and Finance	3
American Government	3	Business Administration	3
Business Correspondence	3	Electives	9–12
Electives	4–7	Total	15–18
Total	15–18		

Possible electives in the commercial field include accounting, advertising, business law, geography and resources, statistics, banking and finance, labor problems, personnel work, market structures, foreign trade, and railway transportation.

In a detailed evaluation of the success of the graduates of the commercial curriculum of the Fullerton Junior College, it was found that these courses taken were actually functioning in the business vocations entered, and that there was a demand for more advanced commercial courses at the junior college level. Ferris Institute, Big Rapids, Michigan, yearly sends out many graduates into the several branches of the commercial field.

Two important conferences were held in Los Angeles in November, 1929, and January, 1930, looking toward greater development of junior college business curricula in the state. A series of criteria for evaluating each subject in the curriculum was set up. Further important results were anticipated from a continuation of these conferences.

c. ENGINEERING

Engineering courses at General Motors Institute of Technology. An outstanding address on engineering education at the junior college level was given at the 1929 meeting of the American Association of Junior Colleges by R. H. Spahr, of the General Motors Institute of Technology. He stated that probably at least one hundred junior colleges are now giving engineering courses. An extensive study had shown that the technical staff positions in industry were fairly well supplied by engineering college graduates, but that production positions were very inadequately recruited. An investigation of over 15,000 men in technical positions showed an almost complete neglect of training of men for supervisors and technicians for industrial production, of contractors, jobbers, and builders, and of plant operation and maintenance personnel for technical services — all of which may be called semi-professional positions of business and industry. Mr. Spahr stated that practically sixty of every hundred students entering the four-year engineering colleges leave for employment at various stages before graduation; from 45 to 50 per cent of them leave from the junior college levels; only one fiftieth as many men of the two-year level of training are now being produced as industries think is needed; two to three men trained on the junior college level can be absorbed for every man needed on the four-year graduate level of engineering. Mr. Spahr says:[1]

I know of but one place where definite experiments are in progress looking toward employability at various terminal points in a four-year engineering curriculum.[2] I am firmly convinced that there is opportunity for considerable development in this direction, and, at the same time not sacrifice necessary fundamentals. The following shows the first two years of a four-year coöperative engineering course with definitely planned terminal points:

FIRST YEAR ENGINEERING

First Semester	Hours per week	*Second Semester*	Hours per week
Engineering Mathematics	5	Engineering Mathematics	5
Mechanical Drawing	8	Mechanical Drawing	8
Chemistry	7	Physics	7
Machine Shop Practice	8	Machine Shop Practice	8
Machine Shop Methods	2	Machine Shop Methods	2
Manufacturing Methods	4	Manufacturing Methods	4
Engineering English	2	Engineering English	2
Coördination	2	Coördination	2
	38		38

[1] Spahr, R. H. "Engineering Education on the Junior College Level"; in *Proceedings of the Tenth Annual Meeting of the American Association of Junior Colleges*, pp. 113–14. Atlantic City, 1929.

[2] The General Motors Institute of Technology, Flint, Michigan.

SECOND YEAR ENGINEERING

First Semester	Hours per Week	*Second Semester*	Hours per Week
Engineering Mathematics	5	Engineering Mathematics	5
Machine Drawing	6	Machine Design	6
Tool or Die Design	4	Tool or Die Design	4
Physics	7	Chemistry	7
Machine Shop Practice	8	Machine Shop Practice	8
Machine Shop Methods	1	Machine Shop Methods	1
Industrial Development	3	The Factory Organization	3
Engineering English	2	Engineering English	2
Coördination	1	Coördination	1
	37		37

This course has been planned carefully and arranged with due consideration to instructional results, administration, and employability of the student.

The first two years have been organized to provide training of such a nature that the student who ends his course at the end of this period may be prepared immediately for work of a technical nature, and in some cases for skilled mechanical, or minor supervisory positions.

Attention has also been given in the organization of the curriculum for the first year in order to provide the student ending his course at this point with a well-rounded training, of practical value, for employment in mechanical, operating, and, in some instances, detail drafting work in the plants.

Notwithstanding the facts that the usefulness of the student in employment is given consideration and that the curriculum is organized to create effective terminal points at the end of each year, the course is, at the same time, arranged to provide a program of consecutive years in which each builds on the foundation laid by the preceding year. The fundamentals of engineering are included each year in the necessary amounts as direct preparation for more advanced study in engineering either in or out of school.

Opinion of California engineers. Thomas submitted Koos's list of 43 engineering occupations on the semi-professional level and the 32 on the professional level, without distinguishing them, to 84 prominent officials in 14 of the major engineering corporations in California, and secured from them a classification of over a thousand men holding positions in their companies. He found that 72 per cent of the total number were employed in positions on the semi-professional level, agreeing closely with Spahr's more extensive studies along the same line.

Types of engineering courses offered. The chief types of courses offered in this line are aeronautical, civil, electrical, mechanical, mining, industrial, and general engineering courses. Two such courses will be given in detail, as samples of such work.

Aeronautics. A good example of a strong course in aeronautics is found at the California Polytechnic School. Quoting from its catalogue:

The junior college course in aeronautics at the California Polytechnic has two aims: first, to provide every student with training sufficient to allow him to obtain either or both of two airplane licenses: the airplane-engine mechanic's license and the airplane mechanic's license; second, to provide a technical foundation in aeronautics so that each graduate can advance to a position in the airplane industry superior to that of the ordinary mechanic.

FIRST YEAR

First Semester			*Second Semester*		
	Periods			Periods	
Subject	Class	Lab.	Subject	Class	Lab.
Engines	5	8	Engines	5	8
Ship Construction		8	Ship Construction		8
Analytic Geometry	5		Differential Calculus	5	
Strength of Materials	5		Strength of Materials	5	
Aero Drafting		4	Aero Drafting		6
Physical Education		5	Physical Education		5
Assembly		1	Assembly		1

SECOND YEAR

Subject	Class	Lab.	Subject	Class	Lab.
Aerodynamics	5		Aerodynamics	5	
Stress Analysis	5		Stress Analysis	5	
College Physics	3	4	College Physics	3	4
Engines	3		Engines	3	
Meteorology and Navigation	4		Meteorology and Navigation	4	
Engines or Shop		10	Engines or Shop		10
Aero Drafting		6	Aero Drafting		4
Physical Education		5	Physical Education		5
Assembly		1	Assembly		1

Prerequisites

Mathematics, 4 units (2 units of algebra, 1 of plane geometry, and ½ each of solid geometry and trigonometry advised); high school physics, 1 unit; mechanical drawing, 1 unit; wood shop, ½ unit; forge, ½ unit; welding, ½ unit; machine shop, 1½ units; high school chemistry strongly advised, but not required.

Civil engineering. A typical course in civil engineering, as given at Los Angeles Junior College, is as follows:

FIRST YEAR

First Semester	Units	*Second Semester*	Units
English	3	English	3
Mathematics	3	Mathematics	3
Drawing	2	Drawing	2
Physics	4	Physics	4
Surveying	3	Surveying	3
Physical Education	½	Physical Education	½
Health	1	Health	1
	16½		16½

SECOND YEAR

Social Science	3	Social Science	3
Mathematics	3	Drawing	3
Descriptive Geometry	3	Structural Design	2
Materials of Construction	2	Applied Mechanics	3
Advanced Surveying	3	Engineering Calculations	3
Strength of Materials	3	Elementary Hydraulics	3
Physical Education	½	Physical Education	½
	17½		17½

d. AGRICULTURE

The state agricultural junior colleges, already mentioned, of course give extensive courses in agriculture. Of the other types which provide agricultural instruction, probably the work at Chaffey Junior College is the oldest, strongest, and most extensive. Located in the heart of the Southern California fruit belt, it has seized the opportunity to do an outstanding piece of work in connection with the academic and commercial work of the institution. Courses in agriculture include botany, citriculture, economic entomology, principles of marketing, coöperative marketing, and general horticulture.[1]

e. EDUCATION

In the opinion of leading educators, education should not be classed as a semi-profession, but as a profession requiring at least four years of work beyond high school for adequate preparation. Other states, however, have not reached the California standard, which requires a bachelor's degree for elementary teachers and a year of graduate work for high school teachers.[2] In some of them, therefore, the junior college plays a most important part as a terminal institution preparing teachers for state certification or credentials. The amount and character of the courses required vary considerably, being determined very largely by the requirements for credentials in the different states. Whether it is desirable or not, the country over, probably the junior college is training more students for the teaching field than any of the other semi-professional fields considered.

It is interesting to note that Arkansas, Georgia, and Kentucky specifically mention junior colleges in the list of higher institutions from which graduation (including professional training) qualifies for certain types of teachers' certificates.

Hollingsworth's study showed a larger number of junior colleges giving terminal vocational courses in education than in any of the other fields under which he classified the catalogue offerings.[3]

Mangum examined 101 junior college catalogues from 24 states, and found that 72 of them listed teacher training

[1] For further discussion of work at Chaffey, see p. 339.

[2] See United States Bureau of Education, Bulletin no. 19 (1927), for certification requirements in the different states.

[3] See page 489.

courses.[1] That these teacher-training courses represent a serious attempt on the part of junior colleges to provide real professional training is evidenced from the fact that 35 different education courses were listed by one or more institutions. Educational psychology, for example, was listed by all 72 schools as a part of the teacher training curriculum. Mangum found also that 38 junior colleges of Texas furnish each year approximately one thousand teachers for the Texas schools.

f. MEDICAL

In this field there are a number of occupations for which training may not require more than two years beyond the high school. Dental technicians, pharmacists, veterinarians, nurses, hospital assistants, and medical secretaries are some that have been suggested. Following is a semi-professional curriculum in civic health as offered at Los Angeles Junior College:

FIRST YEAR

First Semester	Units	*Second Semester*	Units
English	3	English	3
Chemistry	4	Chemistry	4
Biology	3	Biology	3
Community Health	1	Community Health	1
First Aid	1	Electives	4
Electives	3	Physical Education	½
Physical Education	½	Health	1
Health	1		16½
	16½		

SECOND YEAR

Social Science	3	Social Science	3
Physiology	3	Anatomy	3
Nursing	2	Nursing	2
Psychology	3	Psychology	3
Bacteriology	3	Bacteriology	3
Electives	2	Electives	2
Physical Education	½	Physical Education	½
	16½		16½

[1] Mangum, W. A. *Teacher Training in the Junior College.* Colorado State Teachers' College, Greeley, Colorado, 1928.

An interesting example of fitting a course to a distinct community need is furnished by the junior college of Rochester, Minnesota, the home city of the famous Mayo clinic. In response to a local demand a course for medical secretaries has been given. Over a hundred medical secretaries were found to be employed locally, and a course for training new ones was worked out to include shorthand, typewriting, rhetoric and composition, science, and German in the first year; technical vocabulary, medical German, Latin and Greek roots and prefixes, anatomy, and office practice in the second year. A high standard of selection is maintained for prospective students in the course.[1]

g. WOMEN'S SEMI-PROFESSIONAL COURSES

Most of the fields described so far have been for men, or in some cases for both sexes. There are certain semi-professional fields, however, open almost exclusively to women. Among those for which junior colleges give definite terminal training are catering, costume designing, interior decoration, painting, photography, commercial art, library assistants, musicians, nursing, and others. Space is lacking to give details of the curricula worked out in various institutions for these and other occupations on the middle-occupational level which are especially adapted to women.

h. GENERAL CULTURE COURSES

General culture is a legitimate objective for some students who do not expect to continue in the university, but wish the broadening influence of a general knowledge of the so-called humanities, enabling them to be better citizens and to live richer and more abundant lives, without necessarily training them to make a living. This objective was definitely recognized in the California law of 1921 creating district junior col-

[1] For nursing, usually given as a coöperative course, see page 306.

leges, when they were authorized to "provide for the civic and liberal education of the citizens of the community." "Culture" perhaps has been somewhat overworked in educational discussions. There is danger that in an excessively practical age its real value may be overlooked. In a very real sense the junior college may provide this breadth of cultural background for a large number of students who could not otherwise have their lives thus enriched. Sarah Lawrence College is an outstanding example of a junior college organized with this as its prime motive. It discourages students from entering who are planning on later entering a four-year college or university; it offers no strictly vocational or "practical" courses; it is not preparatory, it is not vocational; but in a very real sense it is terminal, culturally terminal. The first president says:[1]

> The course is intended to give two or three years of liberal arts work to students who do not intend to matriculate for the A.B. degree. The work is a unit in itself, its value consisting in its intrinsic worth, rather than in its reference to something further on.

Many other women's junior colleges have a similar function, although not organized so definitely as an experiment in this particular direction as Sarah Lawrence.

HOW ARE SEMI-PROFESSIONAL COURSES GIVEN?

For the most part, semi-professional courses are given in the same way as other courses, by regular class work, supplemented by laboratory experience, when the nature of the subject permits. One special type, however, deserves special mention — coöperative courses.

Coöperative work. Coöperative work, that is, half-time in school and half-time in industry, is well known in the educational world through the pioneer work done by the University of Cincinnati and by Antioch College. It is, however, pecu-

[1] Coats, Marion. "A New Type of Junior College"; in *Journal of the National Education Association*, vol. 18, p. 5. (January, 1929.)

liarly applicable to the junior college field, with its course of study only two years in length. In the period covered by the normal four-year college course the coöperative student can take the junior college course and have two years of supplementary remunerative experience in the occupation in which he is securing training. The most outstanding work of this sort has been carried out not in a large city, but in a city of only 30,000, Riverside, California, with a total junior college enrollment of less than 400 students. A few extracts from the Riverside catalogue will give the essentials of the plan as carried out there:

Riverside Junior College offers a special type of education for the professions of Engineering, Nursing, Library Work, Architecture, etc., on the "Coöperative Plan." It involves symmetrical development along a number of different lines — intellectual, practical, social, and æsthetic, and requires close coördination between the school and a number of leading organizations of Southern California, including the Southern Sierras Power Company, the Riverside Community Hospital, the Riverside Public Library, the Edison Electric Appliance Company, and the Riverside Portland Cement Company. Preparation for leadership in several professional fields is made available for a limited number of students selected on the basis of character, ambition, and ability above the average.

Experience is fully as important as any other factor in education, and the "Coöperative Plan" is unique in providing experience in as large a measure as classroom instruction. Each student spends in technical work, under the supervision of the College, every alternate six weeks throughout the year. The employment is arranged by coördinators on the college staff, who assign students to specific positions and arrange with the coöperating employers to change the work at intervals to give the widest possible experience. Starting at the bottom the student works up to positions of responsibility during the coöperative course, and finishes as a semi-professional worker or as a recommended entrant to a larger institution, where he takes the last part of a university course.

Due to the fact that the coöperative student spends alternate periods acquiring technical experience, the usual first-year academic work is ordinarily completed in two years. At the end of that time some students transfer to regular status, entering the sophomore class either at the junior college or at some other institution. However, with the opportunities for study during the working periods, a large proportion finish the junior college program entirely on the coöperative basis. On the other hand, many prefer to remain for four years in the coöperative course to make the most of the opportunity for technical work under exceptionally advantageous conditions.

Admission to the Coöperative Course must be limited to those who are qualified to make the best use of the opportunity. Coöperating employers have received in the past intelligent and consistent service from student employees above the average in industry, interest, and initiative, and they have a right to expect the standard to be maintained. The course is designed primarily for the development of leaders in the professions, and applicants are required to give evidence of above average performance throughout the high school course. Selection of coöperative students, then, is based on superior ability in scholarship and in practical work, with due attention to character and personality.

Coöperative work began at Riverside in 1922 with an enrollment of 12 students; in 1930 there were 51 students enrolled in these courses.

Other coöperative work. Coöperative work in foreign and domestic trade began in 1928 at Marin Junior College, in coöperation with certain banks, steamship companies, and railroads in San Francisco.

The North Texas Agricultural College gives a coöperative course in agriculture designed especially to enable boys to work half-time on the farm, either on the college farm or at home, as financial conditions necessitate. In this way, two brothers can attend for alternate six weeks periods. The course of study is an abbreviated one of practical essentials, from the standpoint of actual problems that confront the farmer. The course can therefore be finished on the coöperative basis in two years.

Coöperative work in training of nurses is also found in the

junior colleges at Sacramento, San Bernardino, Kansas City (Missouri), and Grand Rapids.

In the junior college department of the Textile Industrial Institute of Spartanburg, South Carolina, the students earn their way by working every other week in the cotton mill.

SUCCESS OF TERMINAL COURSES

Considerable space has been devoted to a consideration of the various types of semi-professional, terminal, or culminal courses that are offered by the junior colleges. How successful are they in actual practice? Is the *taking* as extensive as the *offering*, or do they exist too largely on paper? Definite information on an extensive scale is lacking to answer such a question, important as it is. The actual extent of the terminal function, its operation and success, should be studied more extensively than has yet been done. On the whole, however, it has not been as successful as it might or as it should be. Many junior colleges give no such courses. The examples given in this chapter are exceptional rather than typical. They show what can be done, not what is commonly done.

Even in California, where terminal courses have had their best development, Dr. Kemp, of the University of California, said in 1924:[1]

> I believe, and firmly so, that the development of the vocational and community functions of these institutions is just as important — possibly more so. To any careful observer, however, it is perfectly evident that California's junior colleges, with the few exceptions I have previously cited, have done no more than make initial gestures along these lines.

That the situation had changed but little in six years, is apparent from data of the California State Department of Educa-

[1] Kemp, W. W. "The Junior College Movement in California"; in *Eighth Yearbook of the National Association of Secondary School Principals*, p. 94. Berwyn, Illinois, 1924.

tion, giving the enrollment for 1929–30. This shows that only 16 per cent of the students were enrolled either in short-unit vocational courses or in two-year vocational curricula, largely the latter. This was less than one sixth of the students in the junior colleges of the state, where, according to Dr. Ricciardi, probably 60 per cent of the students should be taking such courses.

The only detailed study of the success of terminal students has been made at Chaffey Junior College.[1] Of over three hundred Chaffey graduates, three fourths entered universities. Of the remainder, one third were found to be teaching, one fifth in agricultural work, one sixth in commercial work, and one seventh were housewives. The remainder were scattered in over thirty other occupations.

WHAT IS THE FUTURE OF THE TERMINAL COURSE?

It is not surprising that the terminal courses have been slower in coming into their own than preparatory courses. The latter were first emphasized in most of the junior colleges, particularly those that developed from high schools. Accrediting agencies have all stressed the preparatory function. Laws, when passed, have often specified that work shall be given equivalent to the freshman and sophomore work in the university. The junior college has been a small institution, in many cases too small to justify more than a single curriculum, and that must needs be of the preparatory type. Terminal work is relatively expensive, and necessarily requires larger institutions before differentiation of curricula is economically or educationally justifiable. Preparatory work was the pioneer stage, but it is time now to advance to another stage.

Judging from the engineering data of Mr. Spahr, and other similar studies, there is probably need for three or four times as

[1] Hall, W. A. *A Follow-up Study of Chaffey Junior College Students*, 354 pp. University of Southern California, Los Angeles, California, 1929.

many people on the semi-professional basis as on the professional one. It will require missionary work to make the terminal courses successful. Unfortunately, a stigma has been attached to them in many institutions. The emphasis in student thinking, often encouraged by the faculty, has been on preparatory work. Especially in California, with its university distinction between certificate and diploma students, those who can take preparatory courses do — those who can't, don't — but are ignominiously shunted into the "dumb-bell" courses.

In many cases, however, students are gradually finding out that it requires real ability to succeed in some of the engineering and commercial courses. As already pointed out, Los Angeles has an excellent opportunity to popularize a fine type of terminal work. The stigma must be removed. The inferiority complex too often attached to them must be changed. For a while, terminal courses must be more than offered; they must be made attractive. Students cannot be forced to take them, it is true, but perhaps they can be led, enticed, attracted. Mr. Kersey, state superintendent of schools of California, has definitely announced a program of expansion of junior college courses in commercial, vocational, and other semi-professional lines.

It is not necessary that a single junior college should offer a great array of terminal courses. Bennett feels that terminal courses should be limited to cities of 25,000 or more that can prepare for all 28 of the occupations he discusses. This standard, however, is a Utopian ideal that will wait long for realization, and it is doubtful if it will ever be realized. It would be better for a junior college to offer a few strong courses, especially adapted to the needs of the surrounding community. Chaffey has done signal work in commercial and agricultural terminal courses; had it waited until it could give 28 it would not yet be giving any. In fact it is desirable that junior colleges specialize somewhat in this respect. Even a large state would never need a dozen or more institutions giving complete courses in optometry, but it could use one or two to excellent advantage.

The outstanding achievement of the past decade in the junior college world has been the development and success of the preparatory function; the outstanding achievement of the next decade should be similar achievement and success of the terminal function. It, too, must be popularized, standardized, and recognized.

QUESTIONS AND PROBLEMS

1. The designation "terminal course" has been objected to. Why? What would you suggest as a substitute?
2. List all occupations in the groups not treated in detail by Koos which are of proper semi-professional grade; i.e., education, medical, home economics.
3. Compare the lists of semi-professions suitable for junior college training as given by Koos and Bennett. Are all of Bennett's included in Koos's longer list?
4. Are there not occupations in which 75 per cent or more of competent judges should agree in classifying them as semi-professional?
5. Based upon occupational analysis methods, Patty gives a list of 133 "occupations suggested tentatively as worthy of consideration of junior colleges." (Bulletin of the School of Education, Indiana University, vol. 4, no. 1, pp. 120–22, September, 1927.) Compare his list with those given by Koos and Bennett.
6. List semi-professions suitable for women.
7. From census reports find the ratio of number of persons in semi-professional occupations to those in professions. Compare with the ratios found by Spahr for the engineering occupations.
8. Discuss, for any particular state, the validity of Bennett's table of annual need of new recruits in 28 semi-professions.
9. Do you agree with Douglass's diagnosis of the reasons for the lack of success of the terminal function? List the reasons that he presents.
10. Compare Douglass's and Bush's diagnoses of the situation regarding terminal courses.
11. To what extent will the attitude of the universities affect the spread of terminal courses in the junior colleges?
12. Make definite suggestions for the popularization of terminal courses for a junior college in a particular locality.

13. "Evidently they (the vocational junior colleges) are groping about among the complex possibilities of what they might and can offer hoping to discover eventually by trial and error what will be most acceptable to their clientèle, using in the meantime their enrollment numbers as approval and success indices." (Whitney, F. L. *Industrial Arts Magazine*, vol. 18, p. 420. November, 1929.) Do you agree with this generalization? Why, or why not?
14. Should terminal or semi-professional courses be left to private schools; e.g., detective, chiropractic, etc.?
15. "In our orange packing houses an important part of the equipment is machinery for the separation and grading of the fruit. The best is given the 'Sun-kist' rating and commands the highest prices.... Now the junior colleges do a great piece of work in grading and separating the students who enter. The 'Sun-kist' ones, they send on to the universities; the others, they market through other channels, if I may be permitted to continue the orange-packing analogy. There are some 'culls,' but the percentage is far less than it is where the grading is done in the wholesale manner that prevails in the big university." (E. P. Clarke, in Bulletin of Pacific Coast Association of Collegiate Registrars, p. 27. March, 1929.) Discuss the validity of this analogy.
16. Make a plan for the investigation of the success of the terminal function to date.
17. Make a follow-up study of the students in a particular junior college who have completed terminal courses in it.
18. What are the principal limitations and difficulties in maintaining coöperative courses?
19. In what other subjects besides those described would it be desirable to organize coöperative courses?
20. Compare Barnhart's discussion of principles for junior college commercial curricula with those actually offered in some particular junior college.
21. On the basis of Barnhart's recommendations, determine a suitable commercial curriculum for a junior college in a specific city.
22. Is a general engineering terminal curriculum better than a series of more specific curricula in the different engineering fields?
23. Should junior colleges give courses in teacher training, or should such courses be limited to normal schools and teachers' colleges?
24. Sadler says: "The demand today in the various professions is for something more than mere technicians. They should have a certain amount of cultural background." Is there danger that semi-professional courses, especially in engineering, may be too narrowly technical? If so, how may the danger be met?
25. Compare the aims and methods of terminal courses in junior colleges with those of the Folk High Schools of Denmark.

SUGGESTED READINGS

Andrews, A. "How the Junior College Serves the Community"; in *Bulletin of the Department of Secondary School Principals of the National Education Association* (*Thirteenth Yearbook*), pp. 340-47. (March, 1929.)

Terminal courses at Grand Rapids Junior College.

Barnhart, E. W. "Making Commercial Curriculums for the Junior College"; in *Yearbook of the Eastern Commercial Teachers' Association*. New York, 1929.

Barton, J. W. "Education for Life as One of the Objectives of the Junior College"; in *Proceedings of the Ninth Annual Meeting of the American Association of Junior Colleges*, pp. 47-52. Fort Worth, Texas, 1928.

Contains many excellent quotations on the importance of the terminal function.

*Bennett, G. V. *Vocational Education of Junior College Grade*. University Research Monograph, no. 6, 244 pp. Warwick and York, Baltimore, 1928.

Bennett, G. V. "A State Two-Year College of Technology"; in *California Quarterly of Secondary Education*, vol. 5, pp. 77-81. (October, 1929.)

Need for such an institution in Southern California.

Bush, R. H. "Curricular Problems in the Junior College"; in *California Quarterly of Secondary Education*, vol. 5, pp. 87-92. (October, 1929.)

Recommends change of policy on part of the universities.

Castle, D. W. "Terminal Engineering Courses in the Junior College"; in *Industrial Education Magazine*, vol. 32, pp. 77-79. (September, 1930.)

Cross, H. A. "What are the Predominant Objectives of Junior Colleges as They Are Reflected in Junior College Curricula"; in *Proceedings of the Ninth Annual Meeting of the American Association of Junior Colleges*, pp. 132-34. Fort Worth, Texas, 1928.

*Douglass, A. A. "Curricular Determinants in the Junior College"; in *California Quarterly of Secondary Education*"; vol. 4, pp. 37-44. (October, 1928.)

Terminal courses have not come up to expectations. Why?

Hall, W. A., and Touton, F. C. "A Follow-up Study of Chaffey Junior College Students"; in *California Quarterly of Secondary Education*, vol. 5, pp. 331-39. (June, 1930.)

*Koos, L. V. "The Junior College and Training for Semi-Professions"; in *The Junior College*, pp. 144-66.

*Leonard, R. J. "Professional Education in Junior Colleges"; in *Teachers*

College Record, vol. 26, pp. 724-33 (May, 1925); also in *Proceedings of the Fifth Annual Meeting of the American Association of Junior Colleges*, pp. 94-101. Cincinnati, Ohio, 1925.

Nelson, T. H. "Education Within Education"; in *Independent Education*, vol. 2, pp. 18-22. (February, 1929.)
Work of the Y.M.C.A. junior colleges.

Oppenheimer, J. J. "Terminal Courses in High Schools and Junior Colleges"; in *Fourteenth Yearbook of the Department of Secondary School Principals of the National Education Association*, Bulletin no. 30, pp. 185-95. (March, 1930.)
Need for further experimentation and work in progress at Stephens College, Missouri.

Patty, W. W. "Junior College Curricula"; in Bulletin of the School of Education of Indiana University, pp. 79-124. (September, 1927.)

Paul, A. G., and Bliss, H. H. "Coöperative Part-Time Work in the Junior College"; in Proctor, W. M. (editor), *The Junior College; Its Organization and Administration*, pp. 141-54.
Description of the work at Riverside Junior College.

*Ricciardi, N. "The Need for Terminal Courses in the Junior College"; in *California Quarterly of Secondary Education*, vol. 3, pp. 145-54 (January, 1928); also in Bulletin no. C-3, State Department of Education, 14 pp. Sacramento, California, 1928.

Sadler, H. C. "The Junior College Curriculum in Engineering Schools"; in Gray, W. S. (editor), *The Junior College Curriculum*, pp. 93-103.

*Shields, H. G. "Economics and Business Education on the Junior College Level"; in *Proceedings of the Tenth Annual Meeting of the American Association of Junior Colleges*, pp. 16-24. Atlantic City, New Jersey, 1929.

*Snyder, W. H. "The Real Function of the Junior College"; in *Junior College Journal*, vol. 1, pp. 74-80. (November, 1930.)
Based on experiences and plans at Los Angeles Junior College.

*Spahr, R. H. "Engineering Education on the Junior College Level"; in *Proceedings of the Tenth Annual Meeting of the American Association of Junior Colleges*, pp. 106-18. Atlantic City, New Jersey, 1929.

*Sproul, R. G. "Certain Aspects of the Junior College"; in *Junior College Journal*, vol. 1, pp. 274-80. (February, 1931.)
Amplification of a portion of his inaugural address as President of the University of California.

Thomas, F. W. "Terminal Curricula"; in Proctor, W. M. (editor), *The Junior College: Its Organization and Administration*, pp. 65-72.

*Whitney, F. L. "Vocational Courses in Junior Colleges"; in *Industrial Arts Magazine*, vol. 18, pp. 417-20. (November, 1929.)

Zook, G. F. "Junior College"; in *Journal of Engineering Education*, vol. 16, pp. 333-37. (December, 1925.)

CHAPTER XI

THE GUIDANCE FUNCTION

When the junior college student is ready to go on to the university or to take up his vocation he will have some insight into his opportunity as an individual not only "to live, but to live well," intellectually, physically, and emotionally. — L. McNutt.[1]

Contents of this chapter. The subject of guidance is too large to be treated adequately in a chapter. Many books have been written on the whole field of guidance; numerous textbooks for freshman orientation courses have appeared; and an entire volume dealing with guidance problems and methods, largely at the junior college level, is in preparation. This chapter points out the importance and significance of the guidance function; indicates the unique opportunity of the junior college to solve problems of student guidance; states the objectives of a guidance program; discusses different methods of guidance; summarizes the present practice in the guidance field; and suggests future needs.

THE IMPORTANCE OF THE GUIDANCE FUNCTION

Not a unique function. Unlike the other three functions so far considered, the guidance function is not separate and distinct from the others; rather it is the foundation upon which all the others rest. Effective guidance underlies and permeates all the other functions. It is essential in all sizes of institutions, but increasingly so as the enrollment expands and the personal element becomes harder to retain.

Standards lacking. Standards for definite evaluation of the success of the guidance function are lacking. The necessity of

[1] McNutt, L. "Psychiatric Social Work in the La Salle-Peru-Oglesby Junior College"; in *Mental Hygiene*, vol. 13, p. 277. (April, 1929.)

meeting university entrance requirements furnishes a criterion by which to measure the success of the preparatory function; the additional population given college facilities measures the popularizing function; commonly accepted vocational practices and needs furnish standards for judging the terminal function; but Thomas's observation, made in 1926, still holds true:[1]

> When we search for well-defined standards by which to estimate the efficiency of the means used in the guidance of the immature student who is essaying higher education, we enter a field in which pioneering is still in progress and landmarks are not yet fully established.

Consequently, this chapter is necessarily restricted to a report of various methods that are under trial, rather than to evidence of the ultimate success of any of them.

Wrenn[2] refers to a variety of immature practices that:

> cause college administrators to view vocational guidance programs cautiously. The factors concerned in a career decision are too many and too intricate to be treated by any but the most careful and thoughtful of measurements, and the interrelations are too delicate to demand any but the most respectful consideration. Educational theory leads us to reverence self-determination. Educational science warns us to be chary of drawing exact conclusions when our premises are not precise.

Guidance not a simple matter. Guidance at any level is a difficult matter. It is particularly so in the junior college field. There is no patent formula that can be applied to all cases. One could wish that it were as simple and clear-cut as advertised in the catalogue of one junior college in one of the largest cities in the country; but one may be pardoned a slight hesita-

[1] Thomas, F. W. *A Study of Functions of the Public Junior College and the Extent of Their Realization in California*, p. 127. Ph.D. thesis, Stanford University, California, 1926.

[2] Wrenn, C. G. "Career Information for College Students"; in *School and Society*, vol. 31, pp. 827–28. (June 21, 1930.)

tion in accepting without some reservations the following comprehensive promise of aid:

> The Personnel Service Bureau maintains a complete guidance service for the use of college students. It is prepared to give accurate information and advice in regard to choosing, preparing for, entering, and succeeding in any occupation. It gives to the individual who is in doubt about the choice of an occupation a complete vocational analysis. A fee of two dollars is charged for the latter service.

This fee is a very modest one, indeed, for such service as this!

UNIQUE OPPORTUNITY OF THE JUNIOR COLLEGE

One of our greatest universities reports that the faculty adviser spends an average of fifteen minutes per month with each student. It would not be impossible to find institutions where the time spent is even less! As indicated in Chapter VII, there are many influences of fundamental importance (such as home relations, immaturity, educational plans, vocational ambitions) that offer an opportunity for constant informational and inspirational guidance for the average junior college student whose intellectual, vocational, and social horizons are broadening so rapidly.

The opportunity of the junior college. There are several reasons why the junior college has a unique opportunity to do a more successful piece of guidance work than the four-year college or university.

1. *Its size.* While there are a few junior colleges that are surpassing in enrollment some of the smaller universities, the junior college nevertheless is characteristically a small institution. Guidance is essentially a matter of dealing with individuals, not masses; and the individual is far easier to isolate in a college of three hundred than in one of three thousand or more.

2. *Its emphasis.* The true emphasis of the junior college,

as already stated, is or should be on the student, whereas the university emphasis is more likely to be on the subject matter — and guidance is a matter of personality.

3. *Home coöperation.* The typical junior college student still lives at home, and many opportunities for coöperation between home and college are available which are not possible when he is at a distance from home influences and environment.

4. *Virgin territory.* The junior college, as a new educational unit, is untrammeled by tradition; it has an opportunity to blaze a new trail in a region as yet largely unexplored — in a region where personality and individuality are the chief aspects to be emphasized. For these reasons the junior college has a unique opportunity to help the student to discover his talents, problems, and interests, and to direct them in ways that will help him to meet the complex social, educational, and vocational adjustments which he must face in his transition from boyhood to manhood.

OBJECTIVES OF GUIDANCE

The objective of all guidance work is, briefly, to enable the student to find himself, and to find his place in the complex society of which he is a part. More specifically it is to give information and counsel along four different lines, failure in any one of which may spell disaster and unhappiness for years to come. These four are:

Vocational. To furnish information about himself and about vocations which will enable him more intelligently to make a choice of a life work for which he is fitted and in which he will be successful and happy.

Educational. To assist him in correct choice of courses in the junior college, with due regard to immediate value in securing a well-balanced education, and to future training which he may undertake in some more advanced institutions.

Social. To further desirable types of social choices, adjustments, and attitudes; to stimulate effective leadership, democratic participation, and wholesome standards in social organizations, athletics, and other activities.

Physical. To assist him in the necessary physical adjustments to secure and maintain good health.

METHODS OF GUIDANCE

Variety of methods. The methods of guidance in practice are almost as numerous as the junior colleges practicing them. In some colleges the guidance offered is largely a matter of class work, in a special guidance or orientation course; in others it is entirely extra-class; in others varying combinations of the two plans are employed. In some the guidance function is delegated to one or two responsible counselors; in others, committees or groups of the faculty handle it, more or less incidentally; in a few it is everybody's business, and it is to be feared, as a result, all too often nobody's business. Methods and machinery necessarily differ vitally in large and small junior colleges. The informal methods most helpful in a college of a hundred students are utterly inadequate in one of two thousand. Conditions differ in public and in private junior colleges; in local ones and residence institutions; and in military schools for men, and in boarding schools for women! These methods may best be illustrated by reporting somewhat in detail the actual practice in a few institutions of different types.

Pasadena's plan. The largest junior college in the country to work out an extensive and carefully planned guidance system is the four-year junior college at Pasadena. It is based upon the class system, but with an extensive supplementary organization to secure personal contact outside of class. Mr. Harbeson, the principal, describes it as follows:[1]

The guidance program of the Pasadena four-year junior college

[1] Harbeson, J. W. "Orientation Courses in Junior Colleges"; in *Thirteenth Yearbook of the Department of Secondary School Principals of the National Education Association*, Bulletin no. 25, pp. 352–53. (March, 1929.)

is centered in a department of personnel. This department is conducted by a dean who is trained in educational psychology and personnel procedure and is a member of the administrative staff of the college. He is assisted by 15 specially selected instructors each giving four fifths of his time to instruction and one fifth to counseling. Each counselor is responsible for 200 students, all of whom, with the exception of some unavoidable transfers, he has had in the course in group counseling. There is a suite of counseling offices adjacent to the office of the dean of personnel and each counselor maintains an office hour daily.

The orientation course forms the very foundation of the guidance program. Besides the three classes taught in his own department, each counselor teaches an eleventh grade group counseling class each semester with an enrollment of approximately 30 students. This makes a total of 60 students per year, who, if they remained in school for the entire four years would comprise a counseling group of 240 students. The drops during the four years, however, bring the group down to approximately 200 students. These students feel free to visit their counselor with personal and educational problems.

The chief advantages of the plan are first, that the guidance program is held to a reasonable cost and secondly, the fact that the counseling rests both upon adequate objective data, such as that of test scores, academic records, etc., and upon a personal acquaintance of counselor and pupil. Fifteen counselors giving one fifth of their time to the guidance program are the equivalent of three full term counselors, which for a college of 3000 students do not entail an unreasonable expense. Inasmuch, moreover, as the counselor has had practically all of his 200 students in class he has a personal knowledge regarding them, which, coupled with the objective data, make him a wise and trustworthy guide.

La Salle-Peru-Oglesby plan. In striking contrast to the Pasadena plan, based upon orientation courses, is the concentrated individual plan successfully followed in the smaller La Salle-Peru-Oglesby Junior College, in Illinois. For a junior college of one hundred students and a high school of eight hundred, there is a bureau of educational counsel in charge of a director, with an assistant and a secretary. It was established in 1923, and is claimed to be the first complete and systematic personnel department organized in any public school for normal and supernormal students. Its objects are to study intensively the individual needs of students, to estimate their native abilities and disabilities, to discover their occupational bents and aspirations; to plan their school courses; and to indicate the vocations and careers they may reasonably follow. Its method is a careful study of the individual student. General emphasis falls on the study of behavior, the development of personality, and the adjustment of emotional conflicts common to adolescent life. The principal aspects of the program include educational, vocational, health, social, and ethical guidance. Although the work is essentially educational and ethical in scope, advanced mental hygiene is the chief instrument of research and psychiatric social work is the technique employed. Adviser service is secured from the Illinois Institute of Juvenile Research in Chicago.

Special attention has been devoted to superior students of high general scholarship and special ability. The bureau definitely provides individual attention for every student, with a minimum service of an intelligence test, a forty-five-minute interview, and health talks. Although the bureau reaches all students, it places the major emphasis on the study of superior ones, feeling that larger attention may properly be devoted to those potential leaders from whom society will expect and demand most. Such a program does not exclude the problem case nor the difficult student, but the results of available time and energy are felt to bring greater returns when more help is given the student of keen intellect, good foresight, and ability to coöperate.

Fullerton's plan. The catalogue of the Fullerton Junior College (California) lists a five-fold approach to the problem of vocational guidance, as follows:

First. A vocational guidance director who is also chairman of the Vocational Guidance Committee of the faculty.

Second. A provision by which the study program of each student is carefully inspected by an instructor who has definite knowledge concerning the field selected for a major.

Third. The use of special shelves in the library which carry books defining various occupations, methods of study, and problems confronting the college student.

Fourth. The maintenance of a placement service, both for students desiring part-time work and those desiring full-time employment after completing a course of study.

Fifth. Arrangement for each student to have one or more personal conferences with the director during the year.

Tests at San José. San José is distinctive in its extensive use of a wide variety of tests, required of all entrants. These include intelligence, achievement, special aptitude, and personality tests. Normally sixteen different tests are required of each student. Together with a variety of personnel data collected, they are constantly used by the counselors in their guidance work. The tests used in 1930 included: Thorndike Intelligence Test (complete form, three parts), Moss Social Intelligence Test, MacQuarrie Mechanical Aptitude Test, Iowa Chemistry Aptitude Test, Iowa Mathematics Aptitude Test, Allport Ascendance-Submission Test, Seashore Musical Test of Memory, New Stanford Achievement Test, Staffelbach Geography Test, Courtis Geography Test, Ayres Handwriting Scale (Gettysburg Edition), Columbia Research Bureau History Test, Staffelbach Arithmetic Test, Whipple College Reading Test, and Almack Civics Test. This battery of tests is required of every entering student, freshman or transfer. It should be noted that the junior college is virtually coterminous with the lower division of the Teachers' College, so that these tests serve a double purpose: they seek to select good teacher-training material, and they seek to redirect the material rejected for teacher-training. Even such an extensive battery of tests as outlined above is felt to be incomplete, especially in the field of aptitude testing. A special need is felt in the fields of artistic aptitude and commercial aptitude.

San Mateo's organization. At San Mateo the counseling is organized on a subject-matter basis, by departments, so that one counselor may happen to have two or three times as many students in his care as another. The supervisor of the plan is known as the Guidance Director, whose function is to centralize, coördinate, and equalize the activities of the counselors and to aid the student in selecting his interest group.

The counselors are faculty members, each of whom advises a student group that is interested in his particular field. They aim to give the student good sound advice, coupled with personal interest and sympathy. These advisers check programs for requirements for graduation and for upper-division standing in the senior college, and review the college rules and regulations with the students of their group. Also, they keep in touch with the student's failures and work with him to improve his standing. They try to discover the reasons for failures, and to aid him in removing the cause wherever it is possible to do so. In their entire relation with the student, they make every effort to stimulate his initiative and independence. They look upon him as a responsible individual who is attending junior college with a purpose, and they are simply what the name implies, counselors. The final decision regarding program, course, or vocational aim rests in each case with the student.

The Graceland experiment. At Graceland Junior College, in Iowa, an interesting experiment was carried out with 250 students in an effort to "help each student achieve at the level of his ability," ability being determined by scores in seven tests, and achievement by quarterly and semester grade reports. The essential personnel services as carried out at Graceland are eleven in number, as listed by Jones:[1] faculty

[1] Jones, L. "A Project in Student Personnel Service at the College Level"; in *School and Society*, vol. 28, pp. 765–68. (December 15, 1928.)

coöperation, freshman days, a class in methods for freshman students, letters to parents, student interviews, time budgets, study of class attendances and absences, supervision of rooming quarters, health supervision, provision of extra-curricular activities, adjustment of student difficulties. The experiment as carried out is said to have focused the attention of the faculty upon the student as an individual, rather than upon the average tendencies of students as a mass.

Orientation courses. The term "orientation course" unfortunately is used in two rather distinct senses:

1. As a general survey course in social science, or natural science like "Contemporary Civilization," at Columbia University; "The Nature of the World and of Man," at the University of Chicago; or survey courses in the humanities, and natural and social sciences, at Stephens College.

2. As a course aiming more directly to orient the student in his immediate collegiate environment.

In the former sense the courses are essentially reorganizations of the curricular material, and belong under a consideration of the curriculum; but the primary aim of the second type is guidance. This latter is the only sense in which orientation courses are considered in this chapter. J. W. Harbeson has made a study of this type of orientation course, based upon a questionnaire to 31 representative public junior colleges, of which 18 were in California, which was reported at the 1928 meeting of the Department of Superintendence.[1]

Wrenn[2] found that the orientation courses in California junior colleges gave more attention to mental hygiene and vocational orientation than did a nation-wide group of standard colleges, as studied by Fitts and Swift. He thinks this due to the nature of the terminal function of the junior college, where

[1] Harbeson, J. W. "A Survey of Orientation Courses Given at Public Junior Colleges"; in *Sixth Yearbook of Department of Superintendence of National Education Association*, pp. 256-65. Washington, D.C., 1928.

[2] In an unpublished term paper at Stanford University. (March, 1929.)

more emphasis is needed on orientation to proper study and mental habits and to the vocational possibilities of the world for the student who will go no further in school.

Opinions of administrators. A group of 39 junior college administrators stated the following as the desirable aims of a course in guidance and orientation in the junior college. They are given in order of importance as determined by frequency of mention.[1] The first one was given by 28 administrators, the last by 14. Adjustment to college environment and life; improvement of technique of study; self-knowledge and self-development (including an elaborate standardized testing program, followed by group and individual counseling); educational guidance; training in use of library; training in thinking; vocational and avocational guidance (including aptitude tests and counseling); training in the scientific method; training in note-taking; training in silent rapid reading; a study of our social heritage and problems involved in modern human relations; looking forward to increased social efficiency; physical and mental hygiene.

The same administrators were asked whether the writing of a term paper should be required in an orientation course. Thirteen advised it, suggesting such topics as a report on some college or university of national standing; formal paper on one of the topics treated in the course; autobiographical sketch; best-liked high school subject; my plans for the next seven years; desirable vocation or avocation based on study of one's self in relation to social group and nature and demand of work chosen; what is college education all about; chief obstacles to a successful time program; value and use of opinion; health and scholarship; my life work.

Harbeson concludes, as a result of his survey:[2]

> The orientation course appears to be the logical method of putting over a counseling program for college freshmen. Only four colleges

[1] Harbeson, J. W., *op. cit.*, p. 257. [2] *Ibid.*, p. 265.

reporting maintain a counselor apart from the orientation staff. A well-balanced use of group and individual counseling, however, has not been worked out. The possibilities of using orientation courses in counseling have hardly been touched.

The orientation course at Compton. An excellent orientation course is given at Compton Junior College. It meets two hours a week for a year, and is largely devoted to problems of personal college adjustment. The topics considered include the following:

PROBLEMS OF COLLEGE ADJUSTMENT

Division I, General: The nature and purpose of an orientation course; origin and development of European colleges and universities; beginnings of American higher education; modern colleges and universities; and the junior college and the educational system of California.

Division II, Personal: The choice of a college; getting acquainted with college requirements; getting acquainted with the subject matter of college courses; individual adjustment to college life; the mechanism of college work and study; the marks of college men and women; planning your future college work and career; your contributions to college life and society; college financial hygiene; and developing a genuine philosophy of life.

Extensive references are given for each topic, the purpose being to entice the student to perform most of the activities of the course. Occasional lectures are given by faculty members and outside speakers, but these are in addition to regular class hours. The course is problematic and practical in nature.

Use of tests. Definite measurement of aptitudes, both special and general, of achievement in various lines, of physical, social, and personality traits, and of special interests are highly desirable in any well coördinated guidance program. Comparatively few junior colleges, however, are giving such tests, and still fewer are systematically using their results in their guidance work. This is partly due to lack of counselors, with the necessary psychological and statistical background to interpret them. Used mechanically or slavishly such tests are of course dangerous, like other edged tools, but used with care and discrimination, and in connection with all other pertinent data, they furnish supplemental evidence that is too valuable to be disregarded in any guidance program that makes any pretense at being scientific. The extensive program at San José has already been outlined. In Chapter XXII will be reported the results obtained by giving a psychological test and an achievement test to over ten thousand students in California junior colleges.

Harbeson found that the following tests were actually in use in the different colleges he studied: Terman, Otis, Thorndike College Entrance, Stenquist Mechanical Ability, Cross English Test, Inglis Vocabulary Test, McQuarrie Mechanical Ability, Seashore Musical, Pressey X–O, Laird Introvert, Downey Will-Temperament, Army Alpha, Miller, American Council on Education (Thurstone), Robock Superior Adult, Raubenheimer Overstatement, Ayres Handwriting and Spelling. Harbeson recommends a testing program to cover approximately three or four weeks of class time in an orientation course.

GUIDANCE PRACTICE

Thomas's study. Thomas, in 1924, listed six types of guidance procedure and collected data from 18 California junior colleges, with the following results, showing the number of institutions in which each was then used:

Directed extra-curricular activities	18
Special advisers or counselor	16
Orientation courses	7
Aptitude tests	6
Pre-registration contacts	1
Coöperative relations in coöperative courses	1

It will be noted that the first two were the only procedures in use by more than half of the colleges reporting.

Thomas reached the conclusion that:[1]

> A critical analysis of the current practices of the junior college in regard to guidance reveals somewhat contradictory facts. In the matter of facilities for guidance as these are being worked out by the universities, we find a comparatively favorable showing. The fair inference is that the junior colleges are doing the same type of guidance as most of the universities, but under more favorable conditions and probably with better effect. But in the matter of their own peculiar problems and the outstanding guidance needs of their particular groups of students we find little evidence of efficient procedure. The junior college apparently has yet far to go before it can be said to have solved satisfactorily its own distinctive problems of guidance.

Later data — California and national. A more recent and detailed study of guidance practices was made by Koos and Weersing in their preliminary survey of secondary education in California, in 1928.[2] They secured detailed data from 28 California junior colleges, and for comparison from 24 representative junior colleges outside of the state. A summary of the various methods of imparting educational and vocational guidance in these 52 institutions is found in Table 29, and of the officers by whom it is given in Table 30. This is the best survey of the actual guidance practices in junior colleges yet made. Items "double-checked" in Table 29 refer to those which the administrators particularly emphasize, and "in which they feel they are rendering a more distinctive service than is usual in most junior colleges."

[1] Thomas, *op. cit.*, p. 152.

[2] Reported in part in *California Quarterly of Secondary Education*, vol. 5, pp. 93–104 (October, 1929); more in detail in mimeographed form at California High School Principals Association, at Oakland in 1929. The data are to be presented in a forthcoming book on guidance by Koos and Kefauver. Summarized in article by Kefauver. (See Suggested Readings.)

TABLE 29. NUMBER AND PERCENTAGE OF JUNIOR COLLEGES IMPARTING INFORMATION CONCERNING EDUCATIONAL AND VOCATIONAL OPPORTUNITIES BY VARIOUS METHODS

	Total Reporting			Number from	
	Number (52)	Per cent	Number double-checked	California (28)	Other states (24)
I. *Through publications*					
Printed or mimeographed program of studies	42	81	8	22	20
Booklet describing opportunities	38	73	7	19	19
Literature in library dealing with occupations	36	69	3	23	13
Reading list on occupations not in course work	3	6	0	1	2
Information on college entrance in bulletin	35	67	2	22	13
Special circular on college entrance	7	13	0	5	2
Collection of university catalogues for student reference	42	81	3	25	17
Publication of guidance features in junior college paper	10	19	0	5	5
II. *Through organization of the curriculum*					
Flexible program adapted to needs and interests of students	37	71	11	22	15
Provision of two or more curricula	40	77	5	25	15
Curricula leading to specific occupations or semi-professions	20	38	8	14	6
Part-time coöperative curriculum	5	10	0	5	0
Extension of extra-hour classes	18	35	3	13	5
III. *Through courses*					
Orientation courses	28	54	3	19	9
Vocational information courses	4	8	0	1	3
Community vocational opportunities set forth systematically	13	25	1	8	5
IV. *Through oral presentation*					
Talks explaining courses during last year of high schools, etc.	41	79	7	22	19
Talks by representatives of higher institutions on conditions and opportunities for advanced training	22	42	1	10	12
Talks on occupations by specialists	23	44	1	13	10
Presentation of college and university requirements before assembly	23	44	2	11	12
V. *Through visitation and observation*					
Open-house demonstration for high school seniors	21	40	1	11	10
Visits of junior college students to higher institutions	15	29	1	11	4
Excursions to industrial plants and business enterprises	12	23	1	5	7
VI. *Through interview and conference*					
Personal interviews of pupils with those engaged in specific occupations	27	52	1	15	12
Interviews with students concerning					
(*a*) Quality of work	42	81	0	23	19
(*b*) Educational plans	38	73	0	23	15
(*c*) Vocational plans	41	79	0	24	17

TABLE 30. NUMBER AND PERCENTAGE OF JUNIOR COLLEGES WITH CERTAIN OFFICERS GIVING GUIDANCE AND PERSONNEL SERVICE

	Total Reporting		Number from	
	Number (52)	Per cent	California (28)	Other states (24)
Administrative head				
a. Principal (also of high school)	23	44	13	10
b. Dean (autonomous with respect to high school principal)	12	23	2	10
c. Dean (responsible to high school principal)	20	38	13	7
d. President	9	17	5	4
e. Other title	4	8	2	2
Dean of women	31	60	23	8
Dean of men	12	23	6	6
Large proportion of classroom instructors advise students	22	42	12	10
Have smaller number of advisors, counselors, personnel workers	19	36	11	8
Have guidance committee of junior college faculty	10	19	8	2

FUTURE OF THE GUIDANCE FUNCTION

What is most needed to make the junior college more effective and successful than it has been in a field in which it has a unique opportunity to make such an outstanding contribution? It needs men or women adequately trained to do such work; a recognition of its importance and value in every junior college even the smallest; a definite provision in the budget for adequate financial support; a complete system of records; carefully controlled experiments; and definite follow-up studies over a period of years. Most of the guidance given at the present time is given utterly without knowledge of its real results in later years.

As pointed out in the preceding chapter, it is essential that many students be guided into terminal curricula. A recent study of the lower five per cent of 10,000 students in California junior colleges, as measured by the Thurstone test, showed that over 70 per cent of the men were planning to continue their education beyond the junior college and only 7 per cent were definitely sure they would not do so. Over half planned to pursue professional work. Is this not an excellent example of a group that on the whole needs to have the opportunities of terminal courses definitely set before them? A large percentage are probably doomed to mediocrity if not positive failure if they enter standard universities to prepare for professional life.

There is need for more of the scientific spirit in this most difficult and complex field, the field of personality adjustment to varying social, educational, and vocational situations at the junior college level. There is need for less of the omnibus type of assurance without scientific basis represented by the full, adequate, and accurate information mentioned earlier in the chapter which can be obtained at $2 per head! There is need, too, for a full realization that the guidance function, although it must have a far better basis of scientific fact, should never lose sight of human factors. More careful measurement is desirable and necessary, but it will never be completely sufficient.

QUESTIONS AND PROBLEMS

1. Plan a guidance program for some particular junior college, taking into account type, location, size, and other factors on which you can secure information.
2. List the elements of guidance from the standpoint of private junior colleges discussed by Cox, and show which, if any, apply also with considerable force to public junior colleges.
3. Examine the different types of guidance work described in a group of junior college catalogues, and classify them under a few main types.
4. Are there other ways than those mentioned in the text in which junior colleges have a unique opportunity in the guidance field?
5. Should "moral and ethical" guidance be one of the objectives of public junior colleges? How accomplished?
6. What should be the training required for a junior college counselor?
7. Plan an experiment to determine which of two types of guidance procedure is preferable.

8. Are 200 students, as at Pasadena, too many for one counselor to handle adequately on a one fifth time basis? Would you prefer to have such an assignment, or to teach an additional class?
9. Find the cost, time to give, publishers, and other data that would be of value if you were planning to use the tests used at San José Junior College.
10. What are the limitations of the guidance program as outlined at San Mateo? At La Salle-Peru-Oglesby?
11. From the data collected by Harbeson, write a description of the "typical" junior college orientation course.
12. Should a junior college counselor aim to give vocational *information* or vocational *advice*, or both?
13. Compare the situation with regard to freshmen orientation courses in standard colleges and universities as found by Blackburn, or by Fitts and Swift (see Suggested Readings), with the situation in a group of junior colleges in some state or larger area. Secure information regarding the junior colleges from their catalogues.
14. Make a comparison between the plan for guidance as set forth in the catalogue of some particular junior college, and the effective administration of the plan in that junior college. (The difference between results to be expected under a given plan and the results actually obtained would also make an interesting study.)

SUGGESTED READINGS

Blackburn, G. A. "The Orientation of College Freshmen"; in *Education*, vol. 49, pp. 26-33. (1928.)

A study of the situation in 250 institutions. Valuable for comparisons with the junior college.

Cox, R. G. "Junior College Objectives from the Standpoint of the Private Junior College"; in *Proceedings of the Ninth Annual Meeting of the American Association of Junior Colleges*, pp. 92-96. Fort Worth, Texas, 1928.

Fitts, C. T., and Swift, F. H. *The Construction of Orientation Courses for College Freshmen;* in University of California Publications in Education, vol. 2, no. 3. (1928.)

Based upon questionnaire returns from 270 colleges and universities. Valuable for comparisons with the situation in junior colleges.

"Guidance in Secondary Schools"; in Bulletin no. 19 of the Department of Secondary School Principals of the National Education Association, 94 pp. (January, 1928.)

*Harbeson, J. W. "A Survey of Orientation Courses Given at Public Junior Colleges"; in *Sixth Yearbook of the Department of Secondary School Principals of the National Education Association*, pp. 256-65. (1928.) Also in *High School Teacher*, pp. 203-08. (June, 1929.)

*Harbeson, J. W. "A Suggested Orientation Program for Junior Colleges"; in *Bulletin of the Department of Secondary School Principals of the National Education Association*, pp. 348-59. (March, 1929.)

Jensen, G. C. "The Relation of the Junior Colleges and the High Schools"; in *California Quarterly of Secondary Education*, vol. 4, pp. 129-32. (January, 1929.)

Jones, L. "A Project in Student Personnel Service at the College Level"; in *School and Society*, vol. 28, pp. 765-68. (December 15, 1928.)
Experimental work at Graceland College, Iowa.

*Kefauver, G. N. "The Functions of Guidance at the Junior College Level"; in Gray, W. S. (editor), *The Junior College Curriculum*, pp. 104-19.

*McNutt, L. "Psychiatric Social Work in the La Salle-Peru-Oglesby Junior College"; in *Mental Hygiene*, vol. 12, pp. 271-77. (April, 1929.)

Olson, E. M. *Report of the Director of the Bureau of Educational Counsel.* (1923-26.) La Salle-Peru-Oglesby Junior College, La Salle, Illinois, 52 pp. (February, 1927.)

Plummer, L. E. "The Problem of Scholarship in the Junior College"; in *Proceedings of the American Association of Junior Colleges, Fifth Annual Meeting*, pp. 14-34. Chicago, 1925.
Extensive discussion of use of tests.

Segel, D. "Prediction of Success in Junior Colleges"; in *Junior College Journal.* (May, 1931.)

Smith, L. W. "Counseling and Guidance Problems in the Junior College"; in *California Quarterly of Secondary Education*, vol. 5, pp. 343-48. (June, 1930.)

*Weersing, F. J., and Koos, L. V. "Guidance Practice in Junior Colleges"; in *California Quarterly of Secondary Education*, vol. 5, pp. 93-104. (October, 1929.)

CHAPTER XII
OTHER JUNIOR COLLEGE FUNCTIONS

The public junior college is a new institution, unhampered by traditions. The field is open for experimentation by those in whom sparkles pioneering imagination. — J. E. Gibson.[1]

Contents of this chapter. While the four functions which have been considered in detail in the last four chapters — popularizing, preparatory, terminal, and guidance — are commonly recognized as the outstandingly basic functions of the junior college, there are others which have been less stressed but deserve consideration in any complete discussion of the functions of this institution. Accordingly this chapter is devoted to a discussion of four other functions which may be distinguished: (1) the research function; (2) the instructional function; (3) the cultural function; and (4) the reorganizational function.

THE RESEARCH FUNCTION

Pure research. It is very doubtful whether pure research of the university type should be strongly encouraged on the part of junior college instructors. Such work, if well done, is likely to consume time, thought, and nerve energy which could be better expended in teaching and in student contacts. Occasionally an outstanding man may be able to do both, but the major part of the instructor's time and best intellectual energy should be given to the institution. If he is not satisfied to do this, if he is primarily interested in research, his place is probably in the university, not in the junior college.

At least one junior college — Riverside, California — has

[1] Gibson, J. E. "The Public Junior College in Mississippi"; in *School and Society*, vol. 30, p. 681. (November 16, 1929.)

definitely embarked upon a program of encouragement of research. In 1926, it began the publication of *Occasional Papers*, a series of research monographs, in the first issue of which it was stated:

> The publication of this paper on the *Flora of the Charleston Mountains of Nevada* by Mr. Jaeger, of the Junior College faculty, marks the beginning of an effort on the part of the faculty of the Riverside Junior College to make contributions to the sum of human knowledge in the fields of the natural and social sciences and education. Each volume will consist of four numbers issued during the administrative year.

The first promise of regularity of appearance has not been fulfilled, but a number of issues have appeared. It seems doubtful, however, whether research monographs on the *Birds* or *Flora of the Charleston Mountains*, by a biologist, or on the *Entropy of Physical Growth*, or *Relation Between Chronodynamic Entropy and Time* by a mathematician (four numbers of the Riverside Junior College series), meritorious though they may be in themselves, are essentially a junior college function.[1]

Administrative research. There is, however, another type of research which it is eminently fitting for a junior college to undertake — administrative educational research on the problems directly connected with the junior college. The junior college field is full of problems crying for solution. Many of these can perhaps be best solved from the detached viewpoint of the outside scholar in the university, but many others can best be solved in the junior college itself, an educational laboratory which is too important to be neglected. What are some of these problems? Problems of teaching method at the junior

[1] An apparently good case can perhaps be made out for individual research as a stimulant to teaching growth on the part of the instructor. Such work, well done, however, requires time and nerve force. It is essential to professional growth, in many cases, but can usually be better accomplished during summer vacations, especially through stimulating contacts in university centers.

college level, of curriculum construction, of effective guidance, of test procedure and interpretation, grading systems, relative effectiveness of instruction in different-sized classes, value of sectioning, compilation of records on which to base more intelligent administrative policies, follow-up studies of junior college graduates — there is no end of problems of this type needing solution. The problems at the end of each chapter of this book are of the sort that in many cases can be solved best by men and women actually working in the junior colleges themselves. This phase of the work is admirably illustrated by two other publications of the Riverside *Occasional Papers*, one on modern language texts and the work covered in them in the junior colleges, high schools, and universities of Southern California; another on the separation of the junior college and the high school.

Research at Stephens College. Perhaps the outstanding research department in the country in a junior college is the one at Stephens College, Missouri. Organized in 1920, with Dr. W. W. Charters of the University of Chicago (later of Ohio State University) as part-time director, it has devoted itself with signal success to the problem of organizing the educational curriculum for women so that the subject-matter taught should, as fully as possible, be useful to its students in meeting the problems and carrying on the activities with which women are concerned in the home, among friends, in the community, and in business. The following studies have been completed in sufficient detail to be used as the basis of a revised curriculum:[1]

1. *Women's Education, a Functional Study.* This study is an analysis of the activities and actual needs of over a thousand women, college graduates — both homemakers and professional women.

2. *Sunday School Methods.* Based upon reports from twelve

[1] Condensed from Stephens College Catalogue, November, 1928, pp. 56–60.

hundred of the best Sunday School workers in the country on how they handle typical difficulties faced by Sunday School teachers.

3. *Sunday School Executives.* Based upon analysis similar to that made in the course on Sunday School Methods.

4. *Citizenship.* With the growing importance of social, political, and economic problems in the lives of women a course on social problems has been worked out by the use of technical and scientific methods.

5. *Expressional English.* Many studies have been undertaken looking to the development of ability to write and speak well. The most noteworthy was an extensive analysis of letters written by various groups of men and women.

6. *Service Mathematics.* This course has been developed to assist students of chemistry, clothing, and foods when their knowledge of mathematics proves to be deficient. The amount of arithmetic, geometry, and algebra needed in these fields has been scientifically determined.

7. *Clothing Management.* Twenty-six periodic clothing problems have been collected by the research department from the actual experience of women. Eventually the methods of careful buying in all fields will be covered.

8. *Health.* The physical education department is making a research study of the effect of exercise upon physical and mental health of girls.

9. *Scientific Eating.* Data were collected and presented to the students to teach them how to eat scientifically.

10. *Mental Hygiene.* A wide collection of the personal problems of adolescent girls was made, as the basis for a course in psychology.

11. *The Ten Ideals.* A group of ideals which should become the objectives of the college, were formulated as a result of a number of student and faculty conferences. Methods were worked out for teaching them effectively. These ideals were:

a. Courtesy in speech and action.
b. Forcefulness in accomplishing what one sets out to do.
c. Health in body.
d. Honesty in word and deed.
e. Self-discipline of sufficient power to control thought, speech, and action.
f. Love of scholarship which is careful and exact.

g. Appreciation of the beautiful as an intimate and integral part of one's life.
h. Reverence toward the spiritual.
i. Dedication to service in the interest of one's home, one's friends, and one's community.
j. Maintenance of a cheerfulness of manner and a happy outlook on life.

12. *Survey Units.* Designed to introduce the student to the entire subject in a first course in each department.

13. *Orientation Courses.* The research department has aided in the development of orientation courses in the first two years of the four-year college unit, in humanities, natural sciences, social sciences, and vocations.

Other material will be added from year to year until the entire process of the functional adaptation of the course of study is complete.

Such work has been expensive. The Stephens budget for the research department has been from $10,000 to $15,000 annually, but it has been money well invested. Few other junior colleges will be able to undertake as expensive and ambitious a research program.

Research at San Mateo Junior College. A much less extensive undertaking, however, may also yield rich returns for time and money invested. At San Mateo Junior College, California, the director of research has devoted approximately half of his time to research, endeavoring to secure a factual basis for administrative procedures, and to disseminate research results on local college problems to all members of the faculty in a series of eight or ten research bulletins each year. Some of the topics included in such studies have been:

Distributions of instructors' marks.

Faculty sample file of recommended tests.

Student aptitude for college work (discussion of significance of Thorndike Test results in the college).

Comparative study of records of 100 students at San Mateo Junior College and at Stanford University.

Comparison of faculty training, experience, and salaries with those in other California junior colleges.
Biology test results and their significance.
Comparison of pre-engineering students with regular ones.
Comparison of students according to source of previous work.
Success of San Mateo graduates transferring to universities.
Scholarship and athletic participation.
Standardized examinations for junior college subjects.

Research in other junior colleges. A border line situation is found at Chaffey Junior College, where some non-educational research has been justified. Considerable agricultural research has taken place, but directly related to the peculiar problems of the people in the community in which it is located and from the homes of which most of its students come. Particular problems of citriculture, such as pruning, grafting, and fertilization, have met a real local community need and can be justified on that score.

Several other junior colleges having research departments studied such problems as classification of students, predictive value of test scores, the instructional staff, orientation methods, or organization of a junior college library.

In some cities, such as Pasadena and Long Beach, there is, as a part of the city school system, a well-organized research department under a trained director through which many special studies of junior college problems are carried on.

THE INSTRUCTIONAL FUNCTION

***Instruction* in the university.** As already pointed out in many connections and by various writers, the junior college is primarily an instructional institution. The university exists for research, for specialization, for professional work. The junior college has little or no excuse for existence if it does not place prime emphasis upon superior teaching, superior instructors, and superior methods of instruction. Regarding the fate of the students in these two years in the university, the late Dr. Leonard, of Columbia University says:[1]

These two years are as important, if not more important, than any other two years; what we have to offer them is relatively stupid, lacking in imagination and insight; the young people themselves are reasonably well-prepared; their natural vigor, which is at its height, affords a sound physical basis for creative activity; in short, these young people are ready for something — almost anything; ready to live, to fight, to serve, to create, to destroy. For them, we provide intellectual gloom! We naïvely assume that for their own salvation they must be disciplined intellectually in order that they may be prepared for the freer life of the upper classes, or for the professional school. We offer them the traditional curriculum, with its traditional arrangement, by the traditional modes of college teaching. We assign to their classes inexperienced and underpaid instructors whose futures in the university world rest upon spending as little time and thought as possible in teaching, and as much as possible in research and scholarly production. To those young instructors we add a few older professors whose academic development may have been arrested and who are known as *only teachers*. And thus the creative desires of an eager generation find outlet only in those things for which the college is not primarily responsible: club and fraternity life, athletics, and the whole round of extra-curricular activities. What a blessing that these activities exist, and what a sad commentary upon ourselves!

Improvement of college instruction. It is to be hoped that the situation is not as bad at many universities as it is painted by Dr. Leonard. There is some evidence that it is not. At Stanford University for example, 72 per cent of the lower division instruction is given by men of professorial rank.[2] The fact remains, however, that the emphasis in the university is essentially and rightly upon research rather than upon

[1] Leonard, Robert J. "The Junior College from the Standpoint of the University"; in *Problems in Education*, pp. 49–50. Western Reserve University: Cleveland, Ohio, 1927.

[2] Eells, W. C. "Who Teach Freshmen and Sophomores?" in *School and Society*, vol. 29, p. 258. (February 23, 1929.)

instruction. A noteworthy crusade to improve college teaching, subject to such a storm of vigorous and caustic criticism in the past decade, was instituted by the Association of American Colleges at its meeting at Chattanooga in January, 1929. Its proceedings are rich in suggestiveness for those eager to improve instructional methods in junior colleges.

Reeves has made an extensive study of the efforts to improve instruction in 90 different junior colleges all over the country, and has given us a detailed report of the method undertaken "in a thoroughgoing and scientific manner," in 1928, at Christian College, Missouri. His discussion is full of suggestions for improvement of junior college instruction.

A junior college dean of instruction. So important is this matter in the larger junior colleges that Sears, in his general survey of the Sacramento School System, urged the appointment of a special Dean of Instruction for the junior college, the only major administrative change he felt was needed. The existing and recommended administrative organization for Sacramento is shown in Figure 27 (page 383), in Chapter XIV. Concerning it Sears says: [2]

This chart represents the main features of the organization as it now stands, except for the one office of dean of instruction. This latter office is to provide supervision of instruction, a service now rendered by the president. The purpose here is to bring this function to the front where its importance will be recognized. At present a separate officer may not be urgently needed. At the present rate of growth, however, this need will very soon appear. The service needed is that of classroom supervision, systematic handling of the development of courses, and of advising students. A close contact must be had with the research and guidance machinery at the central office, with the registrar's office, and with such committees as have to do with scholastic matters.

[2] Sears, J. B. *Sacramento School Survey*, pp. 290–92. Sacramento, California, October, 1928.

THE CULTURAL FUNCTION

Palmer's attack. Will the junior college promote or destroy culture? Professor Palmer, in a notable attack on the junior college in the *Atlantic Monthly*, thinks that the junior college "torrent" if unquelled will spell the death-knell of culture. He asserts that it will destroy cultural education, "exterminate our scholarly amateur," and destroy the uniqueness of the system of education in America, the only country which has ventured to interpose four years of cultural study between its day school and its professional training. The unique intermediate cultural college of America will disappear. The junior college, if not checked, "is more likely to bring disaster than anything that has happened in our world of education during the last fifty years." This is a rather severe indictment of the junior college. In the face of it, can it be maintained that the junior college has a "cultural" function?

Is culture vanishing? It may be questioned whether "culture," in the sense that Professor Palmer speaks of it, has not to a large degree vanished from American collegiate education during the past quarter of a century. With university specialization, and in many cases strictly professional or pre-professional training, beginning at the junior year; with university freshmen and sophomores handled in masses in an atmosphere unfortunately not characteristic of the finest traditions of academic culture (see quotation from President Smith, p. 207); and with the rapid increase in enrollment in the "practical" university, one wonders whether as much culture exists west of Harvard as Professor Palmer fondly believes is the case. The scholarly amateur of the type that Professor Palmer justly admires is already rapidly vanishing in the American educational system. It is possible that the junior college can help to save him from complete extermination, rather than hastening the process.

The "New England" college. There is a noteworthy group

of four-year colleges in the New England states, including Amherst and Williams in Massachusetts, Bowdoin, Bates, and Colby, in Maine, Dartmouth in New Hampshire, and Middlebury in Vermont, which represent a type of cultural training that is deserving of the greatest admiration. Modeled on this notable New England group, a remarkable chain of similar institutions has spread over the country, including such institutions as Oberlin, Marietta, Hiram, and Antioch in Ohio; Rollins in Florida; Knox in Illinois; Coe and Grinnell in Iowa; Carleton, Beloit, Ripon, Drury, Washburne, Olivet, and Doane in other Middle Western States; and Whitman, Pacific University, Reed, Willamette, Colorado, Mills, College of the Pacific, and Pomona in the Far West. This selected group of thirty institutions (others could also be named) is suggestive of the finest traditions of the scholarly type of New England culture, "oases of culture in western deserts of agriculture." They have made a notable contribution to American life, and doubtless will continue to do so for many decades.

They can, however, receive only a small fraction of the American youth demanding a college education. The entire group of thirty (four per cent of the colleges of the country) had only 21,000 students in 1928, which was one and one half per cent of the total college enrollment in the country. Only one was founded subsequent to 1885, and half of them were established prior to 1852. Yet today only three have an enrollment in excess of 1000. In the present century they have increased in collegiate enrollment four-fold, it is true, but in the same time the total college population of the country has increased eight-fold. They have also almost reached their limits with present resources. Many of them refuse students every year, and must continue to do so unless wealthy friends contribute extensively to increase endowments. All combined they cannot take care of the college wants of two per cent of the students desiring college education today, and every indication is that this demand for college education will be greatly accentuated in the next decade.[1]

The opportunity of the junior college. Can the junior college preserve, promote, and disseminate something of the fine type of cultural education for which this group of institutions has stood so notably in the last few decades. Cultural education means general education as opposed to specialization; an emphasis on the humanities, classics, history, languages, and literature. Almost every junior college at the present time offers a liberal arts curriculum composed of these subjects. Even in the vocational and semi-professional courses, in many cases, there is an insistence that a liberal amount of these cultural subjects shall be included as well.[2] Cultural education, too, depends not only on a curriculum but on intimate personal contacts with cultured instructors. The junior college, therefore, offers an opportunity to multiply and magnify many fold some of the best elements of cultural education for which institutions of the New England type have so valiantly stood in the past. Instead of a few dozen such centers, the junior college, in its marvelous spread throughout the country as an integral part of the public school system, may offer hundreds, possibly in the future even thousands of such cultural centers, developing not only "scholarly amateurs" among the students, but raising the cultural level of hundreds of communities in which they are located. It is true that the students will not receive a leisurely four years of culture — in the New England type of college — but they would not receive it anyway. Is it not better for thousands to receive at least two years of cultural training, rather than

[1] Of course there are many other colleges in the nation modeled upon the thirty selected for special study, but all together they are taking care of but a small fraction of the total number of students now receiving college education, and are unlikely to expand their resources and equipment to meet the constantly increasing desire for college education on the part of the public.

[2] See question 24, Chapter X.

none? There is no reason why the junior college cannot be an additional torch-bearer of culture, carrying its peculiarly significant light to the great masses of the American people. Certainly culture is the heritage of all and not of a favored few. The junior college proposes to democratize culture by diffusing it among the masses.

Opinions of educators on the cultural function of the junior college. Sarah Lawrence College was founded particularly to develop and preserve this type of culture. Dr. McCracken, president of Vassar College and chairman of the Board of Trustees of Sarah Lawrence College, says:[1]

For the East, the junior college purely of the cultural type, devoted to meeting the needs of those who desire two years of college work and organizing its curriculum along the lines of progressive education, may prove to be the most helpful addition to the institutions of higher learning.

Another writer, Chambers, asserts:[2]

There can scarcely be any doubt that the junior college when it comes into its own, will produce at the end of its two years course a very creditable "scholarly amateur" who will compare very favorably with his prototype of an earlier generation.

President Winfield says:[3]

Not only may the junior college foster the ideals and attitudes which the old college developed in its students, but it may actually teach more than the old curriculum could offer.... It is going to perpetuate, democratize, and disseminate this spirit which we have received from the college of liberal arts.

[1] *Sarah Lawrence College Catalogue*, p. 8.

[2] Chambers, M. M. "The Junior College and the 'Scholarly Amateur'"; in *School and Society*, vol. 28, p. 521. (October 27, 1928.)

[3] Winfield, G. F. "Are the Junior Colleges Tending to Dissipate the Spirit and the Ideals of the American Liberal Arts College?"; in *Proceedings of the Ninth Annual Meeting of the American Association of Junior Colleges*, p. 104. Fort Worth, Texas, 1928.

Finally, the significance of this function is well expressed by Charters:[1]

> The junior college is the terminal for cultural education in school. We agree, of course, that cultural education should continue throughout life but if students go no further than the junior college, their cultural education in school obviously terminates. If, however, they enter a professional school, it is possible that they may continue to carry non-professional courses but the probability is slight. It is well for the junior college to recognize that in the professional school there is ordinarily no time for extra-professional courses and, therefore, students have opportunity to carry cultural courses only in the year before graduating from the junior college. In a very real sense, therefore, the secondary school which includes the junior college is the guardian of culture. It is the people's college where the student acquires the culture of his civilization. Somewhere in this period he must learn how to vote intelligently, to appreciate the beautiful, to acquire good health habits, to understand people, and to perform his duties as a man among men. This is the peculiar responsibility of the junior college which is the inspector of the product and sees that the quality is right. The preparatory function of the junior college will be cared for since both students and professional schools make urgent demands for preparatory courses. The cultural function, however, has no organized advocates. The administration and the faculty of junior colleges must be the guardians.

THE REORGANIZATIONAL FUNCTION

Does the junior college have a distinct function in the reorganization of the American educational system? Koos, in his investigation of expressed objectives of the junior college, found frequent claims for it which he classified under such topics as the following:

> Placing in the secondary school all work appropriate to it.
> Making the secondary school period coincide with adolescence.

[1] Charters, W. W. "Functions of the Junior College"; in *Thirteenth Yearbook of the Department of Secondary School Principals of the National Education Association*, Bulletin no. 25, p. 306. (March, 1929.)

Fostering the evolution of the system of education.
Improving high school instruction.

This function of the junior college will be discussed more fully in Part Three, "The Place of the Junior College in American Education," and especially in Chapters XXV, XXVI, and XXVII, and consequently further consideration of the question will be deferred until Part Three is reached.

QUESTIONS AND PROBLEMS

1. Evaluate the functions in this chapter by the criteria proposed by Thomas, p. 191.
2. Criticize the position taken in this chapter with reference to pure research in the junior college. When, if ever, is it justified?
3. Discuss the research organization and program of Stephens College.
4. Does the public or the private junior college offer the best opportunity for educational research?
5. State in definite language five concrete research projects that a junior college might profitably investigate.
6. Select a single concrete research project for a junior college, and outline the method by which it could be worked out.
7. Should junior colleges endeavor to secure the services of a university professor as part-time director of research?
8. Are there any dangers in organizing a research department in a junior college?
9. Make an investigation, similar to the one reported for Stanford University, of the lower-division instruction in another university.
10. How large should a junior college become before it should have a separate dean of instruction? Would it be better for this service to be performed by the president or administrative dean, rather than by another officer?
11. List a dozen important problems in the field of junior college instruction.
12. Does your experience corroborate Dr. Leonard's description of lower-division instruction and life? How?
13. Look up as many definitions as possible of liberal or cultural education. Do they fit the junior college?
14. Evaluate the six remedies that Professor Palmer suggests for the dangers of the junior college.
15. What is the method by which Sarah Lawrence College proposed to work out terminal cultural education?

16. What further evidence is there to sustain Sadler's contention that professions demand more than technicians? (See *A Study of Engineering Education*, chap. 16. Bulletin no. 11 of Carnegie Foundation for Advancement of Teaching, 1918.)
17. What other institutions might properly be included in the suggested list of 30 cultural colleges of the "New England type"?
18. Compare the possibilities of the public and private junior college as an institution for culture and development of "scholarly amateurs."
19. Is it "mid-Victorian," as Bishop Green suggests, to believe in cultural and liberal education?

SUGGESTED READINGS

Research Function

*Charters, W. W. "Functions of the Junior College"; in *Thirteenth Yearbook of the Department of Secondary School Principals of the National Education Association*, Bulletin no. 25, pp. 300-07. (March, 1929.)

Discusses six functions, including research on curricular and instructional problems.

Charters, Jessie A. "How Two Hundred and Fifty-Eight Junior College Women Study"; in *Journal of Educational Research*, vol. 11, pp. 41-48. (January, 1925.)

A Stephens College research study.

Haggerty, M. E. "Institutional Resources Available for Collegiate Educational Research"; in *School and Society*, vol. 29, pp. 653-64. (May 25, 1929.)

Hardy, E. L. "A Philosophy of Research"; in *California Quarterly of Secondary Education*, vol. 4, pp. 31-32. (October, 1928.)

A pragmatic philosophy should prevail in junior college research.

Hudelson, E. (editor). *Problems of College Education*, 449 pp. University of Minnesota Press, Minneapolis, Minnesota, 1928.

Symposium of 35 addresses and reports of experimental investigations dealing with the administration, curriculum, student personnel, and instructional methods in higher education. Most of the papers deal with the junior college years, and several discuss the junior college as such.

*Leonard, R. J. "The Junior College from the Standpoint of the University"; in *Problems in Education*, pp. 48-58. Western Reserve University. (Cleveland, Ohio, 1927.) Also in *Teachers' College Record*, vol. 28, pp. 543-50. (February, 1927.)

*Report of Research Department"; in *Stephens College Bulletin: The Catalogue*, pp. 55-60. (November, 1928, or later issues.)

Instructional Function

Good, C. V. *Teaching in College and University*. 557 pp. Warwick and York, Baltimore, Maryland, 1929.
Numerous summaries of significant studies and extensive bibliographies in the field of college teaching. Many of them refer explicitly to the junior college field.

Harrison, Mary R. "A Program for the Improvement of Instruction as Initiated at Park College"; in *Education*, vol. 50, pp. 550–53. (May, 1930.)
Contains many suggestions of value to junior colleges from this small Missouri four-year college.

Phelps, S. "One Phase of the Direction of College Instruction, the Visitation of College Teaching"; in *Proceedings of the Ninth Annual Meeting of the American Association of Junior Colleges*, pp. 30–38. Fort Worth, Texas, 1928.
Methods used at Peabody College.

*Reeves, F. W. "Experiments in the Improvement of Instruction in the Junior College"; in *Proceedings of the Ninth Annual Meeting of the American Association of Junior Colleges*, pp. 74–82. (Fort Worth, Texas, 1928.) Also in *Nation's Schools*, vol. 3, pp. 69–75. (April, 1929.)

Sears, J. B. *Sacramento School Survey*, pp. 289–92. Board of Education, Sacramento, California, October, 1928.

"The College Teacher"; in Association of American Colleges Bulletin, vol. 15, no. 1, 220 pp. (March, 1929.)
Addresses and proceedings of the fifteenth annual meeting. Much suggestive pertinent material in subsequent issues of the Bulletin.

Wahlquist, J. T. "The Junior College and Teaching Efficiency"; in *Junior College Journal*, vol. 1, pp. 479–80. (May, 1931.)

Cultural Function

Chambers, M. M. "The Junior College and the 'Scholarly Amateur'"; in *School and Society*, vol. 28, pp. 519–21. (October 27, 1928.)
A reply to Palmer's attack on the junior college.

*Coats, Marion. "A New Type of Junior College"; in *Journal of the National Education Association*, vol. 18, pp. 5–6. (January, 1929.)
Describes work at Sarah Lawrence Junior College.

Coats, Marion. "A New Type of College Work"; in *Proceedings of the Seventh Annual Meeting of the American Association of Junior Colleges*, pp. 7–9. Jackson, Mississippi, 1926.
Describes work at Bradford Academy and Junior College.

Green, W. M. "Sustaining Scholarship Standards"; in *Proceedings of the Seventh Annual Meeting of the American Association of Junior Colleges*, pp. 49–52. Jackson, Mississippi, 1926.

*Palmer, G. H. "The Junior College"; in *Atlantic Monthly*, vol. 139, pp. 497-501. (April, 1927.)

*Palmer, G. H. "The Junior College Again"; in *Atlantic Monthly*, vol. 140, pp. 828-30. (December, 1927.)

Sadler, H. C. "The Junior College Curriculum in Engineering Schools"; in Gray, W. S. (editor), *The Junior College Curriculum*, pp. 93-103.

*Winfield, G. F. "Are the Junior Colleges Tending to Dissipate the Spirit and the Ideals of the American Liberal Arts College?" in *Proceedings of the Ninth Annual Meeting of the American Association of Junior Colleges*, pp. 103-15. Fort Worth, Texas, 1928.

PART TWO

ORGANIZATION AND ADMINISTRATION OF THE JUNIOR COLLEGE

CHAPTER XIII

GENERAL ADMINISTRATIVE CONSIDERATIONS

The junior college movement... seems to me to have more implications for good... than has any other single proposal which is before us for consideration. — G. F. Zook.[1]

Contents of Part Two. The problems of junior college organization and administration are too varied and comprehensive to be treated completely in such a work as this. Many of the methods of organization and administration of junior colleges are common to four-year colleges and universities on the one hand, or to high schools on the other. The junior college administrator should be familiar with the guiding principles as given by recognized authorities in these fields, not only for the light they will throw upon common problems in all educational administration, but also on account of his intimate relationship with the institutions which are immediately above and below him on the educational ladder.[2] All that can be attempted here is to discuss some of the outstanding features and problems which are distinctive of the junior college. Even in the junior college field the problems will vary widely in public and private institutions, in municipal or rural ones, in those connected with high schools and in those operated independently. In succeeding chapters attention will be devoted to the administrative and instructional staff, buildings and equipment, libraries, the curriculum, finance, criteria for the establishment

[1] Zook, G. F. "Is the Junior College a Menace or a Boon?" in *School Review*, vol. 37, p. 425. (June, 1929.)

[2] Such, for example, as Cubberley, E. P., *Public School Administration*, 710 pp., Houghton Mifflin Company, Boston (revised edition, 1929); or Reeves and Russell, *College Organization and Administration*, 324 pp., Board of Education, Disciples of Christ, Indianapolis, Indiana, 1929; or Lindsay and Holland, *College and University Administration*, 666 pp., The Macmillan Company, 1930.

of junior colleges, catalogues and publicity, use of standard tests, and student activities.

Contents of this chapter. This chapter discusses certain general features in the organization and administration of the junior college, including boards of control, independence of the high school, admission and graduation requirements, and the variety of names by which the institution is known.

BOARDS OF CONTROL

Name and function. Practically all public and most private junior colleges, except those classified in Chapter I as "proprietary," are controlled by boards, commonly known as the Board of Education or the Junior College Board in the case of public institutions, and as the Board of Trustees or some similar title in the case of those under private control. In accordance with the best educational theory, the function of the board is to determine policies, both financial and educational, and to select competent administrators, but to leave all details of administration to the executive officers. Just where to draw the line between the duties and responsibilities of the board and of the administrator is not always an easy matter, and at times in other types of institutions has resulted in much friction and misunderstanding. There is nothing distinctive in this for the junior college, however, so the reader interested in this phase may be referred to treatments of the subject in general works on school administration.

Size and term of office. In the public institutions of municipal or local type the junior college is usually placed by law under the control of the board of education of the city in which it is located, and the size varies accordingly, with five or seven as the prevailing number. In the district junior colleges of California the number of members is fixed by law at five, elected for three-year terms. In the state junior colleges, however, very large and unwieldy boards of twenty to thirty members are found in many cases. In the private institutions for which information could be secured from their catalogues, the number of members varied from three to thirty or more, averaging somewhat larger than in public institutions. Terms of office vary from two or three years to indefinite or life terms.

Methods of selection. In the local and district institutions the board is commonly chosen by local election, but in the state type it is more frequently appointed by the governor or the state board of education, or the state board itself is the governing body. Methods of selection vary in private institutions, but in many cases the boards are self-perpetuating.

Jurisdiction. In most of the private institutions the sole responsibility of the board is for the junior college in question, but in the case of many of the institutions under public control the same board directs the elementary schools, the high schools, and special schools of the city, as well as the public junior college. This makes for unity in organization and administration, but is likely to minimize the attention paid to the junior college, which is only a small part of the entire educational system. On the whole it would seem to be preferable that the junior college should have the major attention of a special board, if it is to receive the full recognition of its distinctive place.

Relations of board. The relations of the board to the public supporting constituency on one hand, and to the administrative officers of the junior college on the other, may best be shown graphically as in Figure 25.

In the private junior colleges the board deals directly with the chief administrative officer, usually called the president. This is the best arrangement, making for directness, simplicity, unity, and harmony. In most of the public institutions, however, the situation is different. The board does not see the chief administrative officer, usually called the dean, but deals with the city superintendent or the high school principal (shown in the diagram by the light dotted rectangle). In small cities, or where the city superintendent is *de facto* head of the junior college as well, this is perhaps justifiable and

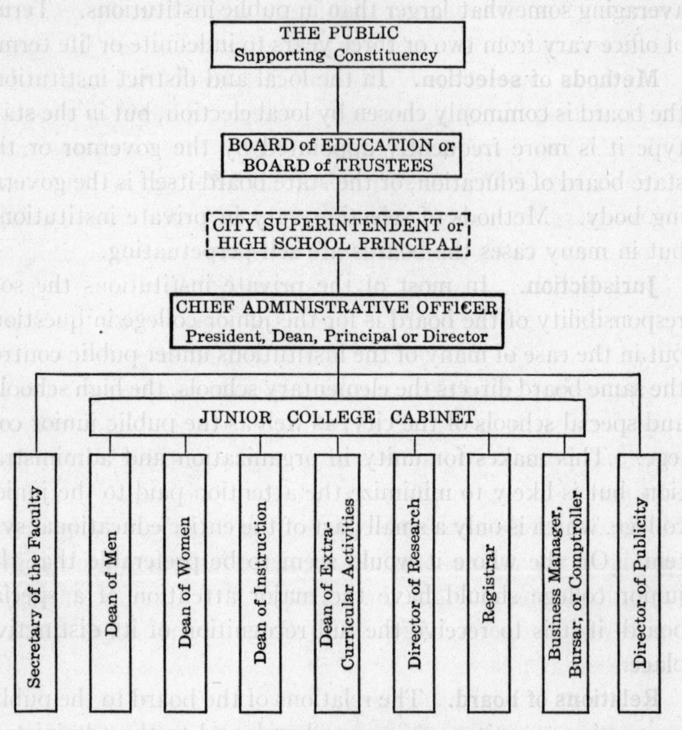

FIG. 25. SUGGESTED ADMINISTRATIVE ORGANIZATION FOR A JUNIOR COLLEGE

desirable, for in such cases the so-called dean of the junior college has little if any independence of action and responsibility. He is a mere assistant to the superintendent.

In California, where in some cases junior colleges exist in connection with union high school districts and are organized independent of the elementary schools, the high school principal is the officer to whom the dean is responsible. However, whenever the junior college administrator is given real executive responsibility and authority, he ought to report directly to the board controlling the institution, not through a third party. This is not impossible, even under existing conditions, as shown in the case of Modesto, California, where the board of education controls not only the elementary schools and the high school, but also the junior college, which is in a separate plant. The dean of the junior college is not responsible to the city superintendent or to the high school principal, but reports directly to the board which determines junior college policies. This seems to be an excellent system, the desirable unity and coherence being given by a common board, the desirable directness and responsibility of the dean, since he reports directly to the board and meets with them. Other junior colleges in California, composed of two or more high school districts, such as San Bernardino or Marin, have separately elected boards whose exclusive responsibility is the junior college.

Actual administrative practice. Brothers has made a recent study of the various ways in which 86 different junior colleges are administered, from the standpoint of executive authority and responsibility. He found wide divergences, which he classified as follows:

Dean of junior college under supervision of high school principal	27
Dean of junior college responsible to city superintendent only	25
Principal of high school — no administrative assistants in junior college	22
City superintendent of schools assumes duties of dean	4
President of junior college responsible to board of education only	3
President of junior college under city superintendent of schools	2
Assistant principal as dean of junior college	2
Dean of men and dean of women responsible to principal of high school	1

He does not report the size of the institutions studied, which evidently has an important bearing on the method of administration.[1] In over fifty cases the junior college is administered directly by the high school principal, or by subordinates immediately responsible to him. That this situation is not considered satisfactory by the administrators, however, is shown by the answers which sixty of them gave to the question "What type of administration of the public junior college do you consider most desirable? Why?" Their answers were:

Separate administrators over high school and junior college	25
Dean of junior college responsible to high school principal	11
One administrator — high school principal over both high school and junior college — no assistants	11
A small junior college under high school principal; large one under separate administrator	5
Varied, or undecided	8

The largest group prefers separate administrators, neither responsible to the other. This is evidently the case when the institution is large enough to justify separate administration.

For junior colleges of less than 100 students, it is very doubtful whether separate administration is desirable or feasible. For institutions of over 200 or 250 students it is probably entirely practicable, and usually desirable.

Reasons for separate administration. The administrators who furnished Brothers his data gave illuminating reasons for preferring separate administration:

The problems of the high school and the junior college are quite distinct.

As the junior college enrollment is smaller than the high school enrollment, the junior college does not receive the recognition nor the interest in its development which its welfare demands if both institutions are under one executive.

The junior college should be free from the influence of the high

[1] He does state that the administrator of the junior college is usually subordinate to the high school principal where the junior college work is conducted in the high school building, which is commonly the case with smaller institutions.

school, and it should be allowed to develop along the lines of a college. Students of junior college age resent paternalistic government and the treatment generally accorded to high school pupils.

High school people, administrators, too often do not understand college work and problems.

Teachers and students both react more favorably, and it affords a better opportunity to introduce college methods and to attain college standards.

A separate administration is desirable as the two schools have divergent aims and interests.

College spirit cannot be developed if the departments are united. A certain amount of freedom must be given junior college students which cannot be extended to high school pupils.

ADMISSION

Accrediting agencies. Requirements for admission of regular students, as set forth by the various accrediting agencies, agree to a considerable extent. Those of the American Council on Education may be quoted as typical:

> The requirements for admission should be the satisfactory completion of a four-year course of study in a secondary school approved by a recognized accrediting agency or the equivalent of such a course of study. The major portion of the secondary school course of study accepted for admission should be definitely correlated with the curriculum to which the student is admitted.

Other agencies give equivalent requirements, with only minor variations, as may be seen by an examination of Figure 17. Several specify fifteen units, and one (Virginia), sixteen units. Several universities require that entrance qualifications shall be the same as for university entrance in the same state, including specified units in certain courses in some cases. In California, however, where entrance to the university has for years been open only to high school graduates who could offer fifteen units of A or B grade, the junior colleges have been open by law to all high school graduates. This is as it should be, if the public junior college is to be a truly democratic institution.

Special students. With reference to the admission of special students, the accrediting agencies are silent, except for the Southern Association, which requires that 75 per cent of the students be taking courses leading to graduation. California requires that special students be eighteen years of age or over, and be recommended by the junior college principal.

Arkansas experiment. The colleges of Arkansas, both standard and junior, have been trying an interesting experiment recently in taking, as the sole criterion for admission to college of a special student, ability to pass the Otis Group Intelligence Scale or the Terman Group Test of Mental Ability with a score of 140 or higher. This seems to have been an entirely satisfactory criterion during the two-year period it has been in operation.

GRADUATION

General requirements. The standard accrediting agencies are a unit in requiring sixty semester units (sometimes exclusive of physical training and military science) for graduation from the junior college. The American Council on Education also recommends that, in addition to this quantitative requirement, each institution should adopt qualitative standards suited to its individual conditions. In accordance with these suggestions some institutions have adopted systems of grade points, honor points, or quality credits, the most common being that in which three grade points are given for each unit of A grade, 2 of B grade, etc., with the requirement of the equivalent of a C average for graduation.

Degrees. While there is almost universal agreement on standards for graduation from the junior college, there is no such unanimity of opinion as to the way such graduation should be symbolized. Shall junior colleges grant degrees? Shall their graduates wear caps and gowns, and otherwise repeat on a smaller scale the academic pageantry of the standard college and university? The baccalaureate degree, marking graduation from a standard four-year college or university, has become so fixed in American educational life that it is probably unwise to attempt to change it. Various proposals looking toward its change or abolition have met with slight enthusiasm. At the beginning of this century, President Butler proposed to cut the college course to two years and award the A.B. degree at its conclusion, but the proposal was never adopted. There is some logic in favor of this traditional degree to mark the completion of the period of general, cultural education, before the specialization commonly characteristic of the junior year begins. On the whole, however, the A.B. degree is too firmly entrenched at the present time to attempt to disturb it and its meaning. One great difficulty in American higher education has been the diversity of terminology and procedure. "College" itself is far from clearly defined. It is certain that the collegiate world will not lightly surrender the right to give the A.B. degree, nor is it desirable that it should do so. Still less is it desirable for the junior college to grant an A.B. degree. This would only add confusion to a situation even now none too clear.[1]

The proposal to grant some sort of degree as a mark of completion of the "junior college" was vigorously debated at the University of Chicago, when President Harper segregated the lower two years there. He felt that a "degree" at the close of the junior college would tend to cheapen the degree, not only at Chicago, but throughout the country. Finally a compromise

[1] Award of the A.B. degree for junior colleges was advocated by President J. M. Wood, at the conference in St. Louis preliminary to the organization of the American Association of Junior Colleges, but met with strong dissent from others present. (See United States Bureau of Education Bulletin no. 19, p. 5, 1922.) More recently he has renewed his advocacy of this plan for Stephens College.

was effected, with an agreement to award not a "degree" of bachelor of arts, but a "title" of Associate in Arts — a happy solution which satisfied all parties. The first such title at Chicago was conferred in 1900. A few private institutions in the South, according to their catalogues, gave an A.B. degree at the close of two years, but the tendency has been away from the practice. More and more junior colleges, especially the private ones, are following the example of the University of Chicago in awarding the title of Associate in Arts.

In California, two types of award have been made to graduates. Those graduating with sufficient credit to enter the state university have been given "Certificates," while the others have been granted "Diplomas." There is a tendency, however, away from this practice as encouraging unnecessary and invidious distinctions, and some institutions favor giving only a single diploma at graduation, thus treating all graduates of the institution exactly alike, while the matter of recommendation to the university is left as a private administrative matter. Many junior colleges probably signalize the completion of the course in some way, and in many graduation is quite an important and imposing occasion.[1]

Academic costume. Some junior colleges have been criticized for donning academic costumes at Commencement exercises. There is much to recommend the use of the traditional cap and gown, however, not only from the standpoint of simplicity and democracy, but of academic interest and symbolism. The best adjustment probably is to reserve the standard black cap and gown as symbolic of the A.B. and

[1] F. L. Whitney found that of 382 institutions, less than a third reported a diploma or title as a mark of graduation, as follows:

	Total	Public	Private
Associate in Arts	19 per cent	16 per cent	21 per cent
Diploma or certificate	9	12	7
None	47	48	47
No report	25	24	25

(*Junior College in America*, p. 153.)

higher degrees, conferred by standard colleges and universities. Junior colleges can, without being accused of trying to ape the university, very properly adopt the traditional gown and mortar-board, but in another color, such as pearl gray or blue.

THE NAME OF THE JUNIOR COLLEGE

Variety of designations found. Even the names by which the institutions described in this book are known show a remarkable variety. Among the public institutions there is reasonable uniformity, since over 85 per cent are known as "junior colleges," but a dozen or more are simply "colleges," and half as many are "schools." Among the private institutions, however, there is a bewildering array of names, less than a quarter of the group being known officially as "junior colleges." Their evolution from other institutions, as already outlined in Chapter III, is reflected in the other titles by which they are known. Over half are "colleges"; there are many "institutes," "halls," "schools," "seminaries," and "academies," and even three "universities."

The term "junior." One other matter may properly be given brief consideration in this chapter — the desirability of the use of the term "junior." By some it is deplored because of an unpleasant suggestion of inferiority in contrast with "standard" colleges, such that the ambitious student will be unwilling to associate himself with it if possible to avoid it. If there is such a feeling, temporarily, it is not general, and can easily be overcome when the true worth of the institution is known, and when dozens of the best graduates of local high schools choose to attend the local junior college rather than the more distant state university. Inferiority is a matter that goes much deeper than the name. If it is essentially an inefficient institution, dropping the name "junior" will be slight if any advantage. If it is efficient and has the respect of the community, "junior" will be only a temporary handicap. Just as junior high school is commonly accepted as the high school for younger pupils, not for inferior ones, so will the term "junior" college mean lower in years and not lower in quality, unless the institution itself deserves such appellation.

There is such confusion of terminology already in the collegiate world, that it is highly desirable that such a distinctive institution as the junior college should have a separate name. As already shown, most of the public junior colleges are known as "junior colleges," but the private institutions, with names inherited from the past century, have a wide variety of designations which serve to conceal their true nature rather than to reveal it. A better name might have been chosen, but the one suggested three decades ago by that educational statesman, President Harper, and popularized in California by President Jordan, has gained such wide currency that it would probably be futile to attempt to change it. The development of the institution itself can give it the honorable standing it deserves, and the broader the use and acceptance of the term the more rapidly will its meaning be understood and appreciated by the general public.

In view of this discussion, it is interesting to note the action of the Board of Regents of the State of New York in refusing to approve the proposed name of Sarah Lawrence Junior College. Instead, they granted a provisional charter to "Sarah Lawrence College" with the explanatory statement:

> By some, the institution has been spoken of as a "junior college," but the Regents eliminated the word "junior" from the title for the reason that it was felt that confusion might arise in the public mind and a conclusion deduced that the college was similar to a type commonly prevailing in the West, where a one- or two-year course is merely superimposed on a high school. The new institution meets all the requirements laid down by the Regents for a full four-year college in the matter of finances, buildings, equipment, and faculty. The only real difference is that it provides a two-year instead of a four-year course.

Is it any wonder that the editors of the *School Review* comment?[1]

Of course that is the essential distinction between the junior college and the four-year college! It is respectfully suggested to the members of that august and ancient body, the Board of Regents of New York State, that they make a trip collectively or singly to Columbia, Missouri, and visit Stephens College, a junior college for women. They will learn something. They will learn how narrow and provincial has been their idea about junior colleges, and how humorous is their present pronouncement.

It is possible that the humor of the situation might be increased if they could be persuaded to continue their visit of inspection as far west as California! This effort to conceal the nature of this interesting experimental junior college at Bronxville would seem to be about as successful as would be one to stem the current of the Hudson at Albany. Unquestionably the term "junior college" is with us, for better or for worse, as the designation of this vigorous member of the educational family. It rests very largely with the administrators to make it an asset, and not a liability.

QUESTIONS AND PROBLEMS

1. What various names are used to designate four-year institutions of higher learning?
2. Does the function of the board of control differ in any essential respects in public and private junior colleges? If so, how?
3. Does the function of the board of control differ in any essential respects in four-year colleges from its function in junior colleges? If so, how?
4. Study size, tenure, and method of selection of boards of trustees in a group of four-year colleges.
5. What is the advantage of a board whose sole responsibility is the junior college? What disadvantages?
6. Make an administrative chart for the college or university in which you are studying. How does it differ from one of those given for junior colleges?

---

[1] "A Junior College in New York State"; in *School Review*, vol. 35, pp. 172–73. (March, 1927.)

7. Are the reasons for separate administration reported by Brothers valid ones?
8. Should high school seniors be eligible to admission into junior college classes before graduation?
9. Should students eliminated from other colleges be accepted into the junior college, either at the time of elimination or at the beginning of the next semester?
10. Should students eliminated for poor scholarship be eligible for re-admittance at the beginning of the next or any subsequent semester?
11. Should foreign students have to pass an examination in spoken English before being admitted to a junior college?
12. Should "recommended" and "non-recommended" students be placed in the same classes? (Of significance only in California.)
13. Should students be compelled to attend study hall or library during free periods?
14. Study the grading systems in junior colleges.
15. Study the matter of graduation honors in junior colleges.
16. Should high schools use the academic cap and gown, or a variation of it, at Commencement?
17. What type of degree, certificate, or title, is given in a selected group of junior colleges — state, regional, denominational, etc.?
18. How much of the N.E.A. discussion of 1903 applies to the junior college situation today?
19. What other institutions or organizations have the word "junior" as a part of their title? Does it imply any inferiority?
20. What administrative elements or topics are omitted in this or following chapters of this division, which should be treated?

SUGGESTED READINGS

Bainter, E. M. *The Administration and Control of Public Junior Colleges.* United States Bureau of Education Bulletin no. 19, pp. 15-18. (1922.)

Based upon experience at Kansas City, Missouri, Junior College.

*Brothers, E. Q. "Present Day Practices and Tendencies in the Administration and Organization of Public Junior Colleges"; in *School Review*, vol. 36, pp. 665-74. (November, 1928.)

Goodspeed, T. W. *A History of the University of Chicago*, pp. 458-59. Chicago, 1916.

Establishment of "Associate" title at University of Chicago.

*Harper, W. R. "A Two-years' College Course"; in *Educational Review*, vol. 19, pp. 411-15. (April, 1900.)

Important early statement regarding junior college at University of Chicago, and the title of "Associate."

Hill, M. E. "Administrative Problems of the Large Rural Junior College"; in Proctor, W. M. (editor), *The Junior College: Its Organization and Administration*, pp. 75-97.
Based upon experience at Chaffey (California) Junior College.

"A Junior College in New York State"; in *School Review*, vol. 35, pp. 172-73. (March, 1927.)
Charter granted to Sarah Lawrence College.

Kefauver, G. N., and Bullard, Catherine. "The Organization of the Junior College as an Agency of Democracy"; in *Bulletin of the Department of Secondary-School Principals of the National Education Association*, no. 35, pp. 182-91. (March, 1931.)

Koos, L. V. *The Junior College*, pp. 638-40.
Discusses granting of degrees and term "junior."

"The Length of the Baccalaureate Course"; in *Proceedings of the National Education Association*, pp. 489-516. Boston, 1903.
A series of addresses by Brown, Eliot, Butler, Harper, and West, with discussion of same.

*Lillard, J. B. "The City Junior College"; in Proctor, W. M. (editor), *The Junior College: Its Organization and Administration*, pp. 110-27. Stanford University, 1927.
Based upon experience at Sacramento (California) Junior College.

MacKenzie, D. *Problems of the Public Junior College.* United States Bureau of Education Bulletin no. 19, pp. 29-37. (1922.)
Based upon experience at Detroit (Michigan) Junior College.

Olney, A. C. "The Administration of the Small Public Junior College"; in Proctor, W. M. (editor), *The Junior College: Its Organization and Administration*, pp. 98-109.
Based upon experience at Marin (California) Junior College.

CHAPTER XIV

THE ADMINISTRATIVE STAFF

The junior college movement cannot be halted or turned aside, but it can be guided and directed. — W. M. PROCTOR.[1]

Contents of this chapter. This chapter contains a study of the qualifications, characteristics, and duties of the chief administrative officers of the junior college. The most complete treatment is given to the administrative head, with briefer consideration of the work of the dean of men, the dean of women, other deans, the registrar, business manager, and other administrative officers.

THE ADMINISTRATIVE HEAD

Public junior colleges. An extensive investigation was made, in 1929, of the administrative dean of the public junior college — his training, experience, duties, salary, and activities. The information given in the next few paragraphs is summarized and adapted from this excellent study.[2] It is based upon replies received from 95 deans in 139 institutions which were asked to furnish information. Seventeen states were represented. The places in which they were located varied in population from 250 to 275,000. More than half of them were in cities of 5000 to 25,000. The institutions themselves varied in enrollment from 25 to 820, with a median of 125. The median number of instructors in these junior colleges (based on full time), was 11, with a range from 3 to 52. All but seven

[1] Proctor, W. M. *The Junior College: Its Organization and Administration*, p. vi. Stanford University, California, 1927.

[2] Green, R. E. "Administrative Dean of the Public Junior College"; in *School Executives' Magazine*, vol. 49, pp. 122–24. (November, 1929.)

of the institutions were established after 1916. All were coeducational.

Title. The title applied to the chief administrative officer varied considerably. Sixty-one per cent employed the title "dean," and 15 per cent "president." In the remaining cases the officials were termed "principal," "director," or "superintendent." All but six of the deans were men: women were found only in the smaller institutions.

Training. Fifty-five per cent of the deans had from five to six years of training above the high school. Twenty per cent had seven years or more. None had had less than four years. The median for the entire group was 5.7 years. All had degrees; 75 per cent had a master's degree; 7 per cent a doctor's degree; 18 per cent the bachelor's degree only.

Professional advancement. Desire for educational advancement is evidenced by the continued professional training of the administrators. Three fourths of them were in attendance at summer sessions of higher institutions during 1927 or 1928, while 90 per cent had attended summer sessions or full academic years since 1922. Two thirds of their degrees had been received since 1920. The typical dean had taken fifteen education courses, representing approximately 45 semester hours of credit. Of the 26 courses listed, 24 were taken by a fourth or more of the deans. The six most frequently taken were: history of education, educational psychology, principles of secondary education, educational measurements, city school administration, and principles of education. An interesting fact revealed was that two specific junior college courses, one dealing with the curriculum and the other with the administration of the junior college, were taken by less than one third of the administrators. Doubtless such courses were not given in many of the institutions attended, and all such courses are of recent development. When asked to state their opinions as to which of the courses seemed to be of most value, the two junior college courses were mentioned most frequently. Courses in educational measurements, psychology, and philosophy were also commonly mentioned.

Educational experience. Only 14 per cent of the deans selected education as their undergraduate major, and 23 per cent selected it as their minor. Of the large group having neither a major nor a minor in education, however, 96 per cent shifted to education in their graduate work. All the deans had had previous teaching experience, the amount ranging from 2 to 35 years. The median for the group was 18 years. Half had had from 13 to 24 years of experience. A wide variety of experience was represented; 43 per cent having taught in graded or rural schools, 18 per cent in junior high schools, 78 per cent in senior high schools, and 72 per cent in college. Half of them had been city superintendents. It has been a common impression that the majority of deans have been men primarily with public school experience, and the fear has been expressed that they would not be men of college caliber, and that they might lack the outlook and training appropriate to administration of true college work. Yet it is seen that almost three fourths of them had had college teaching experience, and slightly over half of them were recruited directly from college teaching positions. Thirty-six per cent came directly from city superintendencies and thirteen per cent from high school principalships.

Tenure. The median length of time in their present positions was 4.5 years, the middle fifty per cent varying from 2.6 years to 8.5 years. These figures indicate a fairly high degree of permanency in the position. Over three quarters stated that they planned to remain in their present work; seven per cent planned to transfer to college work, two per cent to research, and five per cent to public school superintendencies.

Salaries. Salaries of the administrative deans, as far as reported, were found to vary from $1800 to $9000, with a median of $3600. Salary variation with reference to size of institution is shown in Table 31.

TABLE 31. SALARIES OF DEANS OF 72 PUBLIC JUNIOR COLLEGES, ACCORDING TO SIZE OF INSTITUTION

Number of Students Enrolled	Number of Deans	Median Salary	Lower Quartile	Upper Quartile
Total	**72**	**$3600**	**$2830**	**$4372**
0– 50	17	3000	2625	3719
51–100	19	3000	2443	4225
101–200	20	3700	3350	4350
201–500	12	4000	3350	4433
Over 500	4	5550	4500	5850

Duties. Special inquiry was made relative to the proportion of time spent by the dean in administrative, supervisory, and other activities. Forty-nine per cent were teaching from 2 to 23 hours per week, while 51 per cent did no teaching whatever. Two or three hours of classroom teaching per week was

TABLE 32. DUTIES OF DEANS IN PUBLIC JUNIOR COLLEGES

Type of Activity	Per cent of Deans Having: Full Responsibility	Partial Responsibility	No Responsibility
Organizing class schedule	92	3	5
Keeping records and reports	92	2	6
Approving supply lists	88	5	7
Supervising class instruction	88	4	8
Disciplinary control	85	6	9
Holding teachers' meetings	75	15	10
Selecting textbooks	74	16	10
Planning course of study	71	23	6
Selecting equipment	70	21	9
Admitting students	68	26	6
Controlling extra-curricular activities	65	31	4
Directing janitors	60	17	23
Administration of athletics	52	36	12
Expulsion or suspension of pupils	46	25	29
Selecting instructors	31	51	18
Recommending salary promotion	23	45	32
Preparing financial budget	13	35	52

most commonly reported, but 15 per cent were teaching 12 hours or more per week, and four deans had 16 hours or more. The size of the institution bore no marked relation to amount of teaching done. Eight deans of the larger colleges and seven deans of the smaller colleges were not teaching. There was wide variation in the percentage of deans who had full or partial responsibility for the different activities. These are summarized in Table 32.

In general their responsibility tends toward the internal routine of the school, with relatively less emphasis on larger matters of policy and control, such as selection of instructors, salary promotion, and the budget. It is plainly evident that many of the deans were denied, in whole or in part, important administrative functions. This was more markedly true, however, as might be expected, in the smaller institutions operated in close conjunction with the high school.

Green's conclusions. Green's conclusions from his study are well worth quoting:[1]

> The administrative dean is not at present over-burdened with responsibilities. He is apparently endowed with too little initiative in the more critical functions. There is ample evidence that there is too little delegation of responsibility to afford the dean latitude for professionalization. It may be suggested that the dean should first prepare himself through proper training to assume greater responsibilities; he should then be willing to assume these obligations; finally, he should take steps to be assigned such responsibilities. With all of this, the dean must coöperate fully with superior authorities, and seek constantly to secure proper coördination of the several units of the public school system. The present rapidly developing junior college is presenting a new field for educational development, a new challenge to the administrators of this institution. There can be no limit to the high caliber of constructive ability required. The deanship of the public junior college must be placed on a high plane of professionalization.

[1] Green, R. F., *op. cit.*, p. 124.

University of California statement. This statement of the function of the dean may be supplemented by an early one made in the University of California Junior College Bulletin, in 1915:[1]

> The dean of a junior college will act as guide, philosopher, and friend to the students; enter as far as possible into their athletic or social as well as their academic activities; advise them in regard to choice of courses and conduct of life; concern himself with such questions as the housing problem, and with the general policy and special needs of the junior college.... Upon him will depend, in large measure, the success of the junior college.

Private junior colleges. No such complete study of similar character has been made of the administrative heads of the private junior colleges, but a brief summary of information as far as available in catalogues will throw some light upon similar points to those brought out in Green's study.[2] Catalogues of 58 of the 84 institutions listed in the *Directory* of the American Association of Junior Colleges as "private" were studied. Over half the administrators were known as president (31), while other titles were as follows: principal, 11; director, 9; dean, 4; superintendent, 2; and head mistress, 1. The M.A. degree was held by 25 of the 53 for whom information could be secured; 12 had the Ph.D. degree, 9 had the bachelor's degree only, and 5 had honorary doctor's degrees. At least 30 of the administrators were teaching part time, while for several others this information could not be obtained. Tenure of office varied from one to 49 years for a group of 26 for which information could be secured, with a median of 10.5 years, more than twice the length of term of the administrators in the public junior colleges, thus reflecting the greater age and permanence of the private institutions.

[1] *The Junior College in California.* Administrative Bulletin of the University of California, 1915–16, no. 2, p. 25. Berkeley, California, July, 1915.

[2] Made by G. A. Duncan as a term paper at Stanford University.

Freed, in a study of 55 private junior colleges, found that the salary of the president varied from $2000 to $12,500, with a mean of $4261, while that of the "dean" varied from $1400 to $4900, with a mean of $2646.[1] He also found that 16 of 41 presidents were teaching regularly, their teaching load varying from 3 to 15 hours per week, with an average of 9.

Report of the dean. An excellent example of an annual administrative report is that of H. A. Cross, dean of the Phœnix Junior College, Arizona, for 1928–29. In a mimeographed and bound report of 79 pages he gives in considerable detail information on the history of the institution; accreditation; enrollment, classification, age, birthplace, earnings, parentage, scholarship, and other features of the student body; location and occupation of the graduating class; courses offered, with student enrollment in each; staff organization; and preparation, teaching experience, age, salary, and teaching load of members of the instructional staff. If similar reports were made annually by other junior college deans they would form admirable histories of the institutions, and excellent bases for more intelligent determination of policies and action on the part of the controlling board. In addition to the general report, just outlined, special reports were made at Phœnix on finance, instruction, aptitude, new building plans, and recommendations.

DEAN OF WOMEN

Studies available. Next to the administrative head of the junior college, the dean of women is the administrative officer found more frequently than any other, even in the institutions having only very small enrollments. Three rather extensive studies of the work of the dean of women have been made, two

[1] Freed, W. J. *A Study of the Salaries and Teaching Loads in the Denominational Four-year Colleges and Private Junior Colleges in the United States*, 30 pp. Tacoma, Washington, 1929.

of them masters' theses. In an unpublished master's thesis at the University of Nebraska, in 1926, Miss Hilton examined the preparation and experience of deans of women in public junior colleges in the United States, securing her information by means of a questionnaire. She considered their teaching loads, scholarship and disciplinary duties, the housing problem, vocational guidance, employment service, and committee and loan fund work.

Mrs. Tibby's study. Mrs. A. B. Tibby, dean of women at Compton Junior College, in a later thesis (1929) at the University of Southern California, studied the problems of the dean of women by personal interviews with many deans, by questionnaires, and by a survey of the general literature. She found it was desirable that every dean of women should have a specialized knowledge in some field, and should teach at least one class in it. While the subject is not so important, history, social science, and English literature are all good because of their relation to general human problems. She suggests that the teaching of English composition is an especially effective means of learning the intimate thoughts, feelings, and ideals of students, for much of the original narrative in student compositions is a revelation of themselves.

Duties in private junior colleges. Miss Callender made a careful analysis of the duties and qualifications of the dean of women, based upon questionnaires received from 25 private junior colleges in the Eastern and Southern states. She found that 70 per cent of the deans were also teaching, the weekly load varying from 3 to 18 hours. Half of them had some assistance in their work. In reply to the question as to number of hours on duty, daily, replies varied from 5 to 18 hours, while four stated they were on duty "twenty-four hours in the day and seven days in the week." More than half possessed degrees, and a quarter had the M.A. degree. Miss Callender found the desirable qualifications of the dean of women, as

TABLE 33. DUTIES OF DEAN OF WOMEN IN JUNIOR COLLEGES
(Listed in order of frequency)

Administrative	*Advisory*	*Academic*	*Social*	*Miscellaneous*
Select chaperons (23)	Act as adviser for all, or some, of personal problems of students (24)	Teach (17)	Meet parents and visitors (24)	Act as adviser for all, or some of student organizations (17)
Serve on committee (23)	Advise with Health Education department on all matters of health (19)	Share in formulating academic policies (16)	Meet company received by girls (23)	Answer questionnaires (13)
Grant special permissions (22)	Advise with president regarding qualifications of women faculty members with regard to influence on campus (17)		Share in formulating social policies (23)	Write letters of recommendation for teachers (13)
Sponsor girls' problems in faculty meetings (21)	Act as adviser for all, or some, of vocational problems of students (12)		Approve girls' calling and visiting lists (17)	Guard and help build traditions (12)
Assign rooms (20)			Act as hostess at all public functions on campus (14)	Attend to distribution of student and faculty mail (11)
Recommend probation, dismissal, and reinstatement (18)			Speak at meetings in community (13)	
Act as disciplinary officer to girls (17)			Direct social life on the campus (11)	
Assign rooms for meetings (12)			Arrange social calendar (9)	
Classify students (12)			Entertain college guests (6)	
Assist in registration (12)			Represent the college at education convention (6)	
Supervise dormitories (12)			Hold "At Homes" at regular intervals (6)	
Check students for chapel attendance (11)				
Recommend students for loan and scholarship funds (10)				
Chaperon students in a body or in groups to church and other gatherings off campus (7)				
Supervise work of self-supporting students (6)				

judged by the deans themselves, in order of importance, as follows: tact, self-control, patience, sympathy, dignity, firmness, fairness, broad standards in dress and social conduct, good health, sense of humor, resourcefulness, Christian character, good judgment, personality, poise, progressiveness, leadership, ability to speak in public, cheerfulness, at least a Bachelor's degree, refinement, analytical ability, meekness, and unselfishness. Surely she should be almost a paragon of all the virtues! Her duties, arranged in five groups, administrative, advisory, academic, social, and miscellaneous with frequency of mention of each by the coöperating deans, are given in Table 33.[1]

Miss Callender concludes that:[2]

The dean's place in the junior college is not yet fixed. It cannot be. The junior college itself is not yet fully and systematically established; it is still in "swaddling clothes." However, the dean of women, a comparatively new position, in this, a new movement, is less clearly delineated than any other in the institution. The president, the faculty, the students, even the servants have their recognized places. The dean of women finds herself in a position which touches on and is largely shaped by all of them. She has a distinct relationship with each group, closer than the president to the students, students to faculty, or the other way round. Viewed by the members of the faculty the dean stands in varied lights. They expect, and rightly too, that she will coöperate in all problems of discipline and irregularities, and offer impetus and support in both classroom and extra-classroom activities. She must work out the salvation of the maladjusted girl.... They also expect her to be thoroughly familiar with all academic policies, and to be well informed as to the condition of all affairs pertaining to the academic and social interests of the college.... The duties and place must of necessity vary with the type of institution, and with the woman who attempts them. The place of the dean of women is not yet definitely fixed, but while the dean is going through this fixing process,

[1] Callender, Pauline. "The Dean of Women: Her Place in the Junior College"; in *Virginia Teacher*, vol. 8, p. 136. (May, 1927.)

[2] Callender, Pauline, *op. cit.*, pp. 138–39, 142.

if she is a prophet, a dean with vision, she will select the worthwhile and lasting elements, discard the rest, and build for herself a place indispensable in the lives of college girls.

DEAN OF MEN

Many of the larger junior colleges have a separate dean of men having special oversight of the problems of discipline and guidance for men, sometimes also with responsibility for men's extra-curricular activities. His duties are not fully standardized, varying much with the size of the institution, the personality of the man, and his teaching and other duties. In general his duties and responsibilities may be said to be closely analogous to those of the dean of men, or the freshmen dean or deans, in four-year colleges and universities. At Pasadena they are defined as follows:[1]

1. The solution of problems which are of special concern to men of the college, such as disciplinary problems and those involving general morale.
2. The adviser of the Associated Men Students.
3. Supervise social life of the men of the college.
4. The O.K.ing of men candidates for office.
5. Responsibility for maintaining an employment and placement bureau for men.
6. Special responsibilities and duties on assignment by the principal.
7. The maintenance of office hours for special conferences with students, faculty, and patrons, regarding the welfare of men of the college.
8. The maintenance of relationships with community organizations that are interested in young men, and the taking of such steps as are necessary for securing and sustaining public opinion in the community.
9. Chairmanship of the clearing-house committee.
10. Responsible for school supplies.
11. The supervision of the making of requisitions.
12. The O.K.ing of bills and receipts for supplies.
13. The supervision of caretakers.

[1] *Pasadena Junior College Bulletin*, p. 27. (May 1, 1929.)

14. Care of buildings and grounds.
15. Supervision of men's athletics, involving the approval of schedules and special games and checking on athletic eligibility.

Other duties, often falling to the dean of men, are performed at Pasadena by a separate dean — the dean of personnel, whose duties are outlined later. In the smaller institutions, where a separate dean is hardly justified, the duties of the dean of men usually are performed by the administrative head, although specific duties are frequently delegated to other individuals according to their taste and capacity.

OTHER ADMINISTRATIVE OFFICERS

Dean of instruction. This officer, as a separate individual, is found in few institutions, yet in the larger institutions it is quite worth while to have one man who is especially charged with the duties of supervision and improvement of instruction. A man with special interest in this phase of work, with rare skill and tact, and with a rich background of teaching and supervisory experience, can well be made responsible for the improvement of instruction. In many institutions this is tacitly assumed to be the duty of the administrative dean. It is to be feared, however, that all too often it is more nominal than real, and that, in the pressure of his many administrative duties, the supervision of teaching may be slighted if not completely ignored.

There has been little to guide those interested in the supervision of teaching on the college level, yet here is a rich field for study, experimentation, and helpfulness, so far almost untouched. Carefully selected deans of instruction can make an outstanding contribution toward the improvement of instruction and instructional methods, not only in the junior college but in the whole field of higher education.[1] Such men

[1] See Figure 27 and page 341 for Sears's recommendation for such an officer at Sacramento Junior College.

would necessarily have close contact with the research and guidance machinery, and with the registrar's office.

Supervision has been best worked out in the elementary schools. Even in the high school it has been deficient, while in college it has been almost wholly lacking. Doubtless the technique will be quite different in the college, but there is a remarkable opportunity here for the junior college, with its primary emphasis on the teaching function, to make an outstanding contribution to American educational method in the field of higher education.

Dean of personnel. Pasadena Junior College has a dean of personnel, who combines many of the duties of the director of research and the guidance officer. His duties are thus stated:[1]

1. The making of the college schedule of classes.
2. The making and changing of students' programs.
3. Classification of students.
4. Supervision of counseling, involving educational and vocational guidance.
5. Supervision and administration of orientation.
6. Administration of a program of standardized tests.
7. Supervision of special researches and studies.
8. The tabulation of distribution of marks by departments.
9. Official adviser of department heads and instructors on standardized tests.
10. The maintenance of office hours for conferences with students, instructors, and patrons.
11. The supervision of scoring of standardized tests.
12. The enrollment of students.
13. The compiling of a monthly failure list, and assignment to study halls during vacant periods.
14. The maintenance of community contacts for the support of personnel work within the college.
15. The collection of personnel data.
16. The handling of cases of maladjustment, involving delinquency, or pre-delinquency or other serious personal problems of students, in coöperation with the Dean of Men and Dean of Women.

[1] *Pasadena Junior College Bulletin*, p. 28. (May 1, 1929.)

Dean of extra-curricular activities. In most institutions the work suggested by this title is performed by the dean of men, the dean of women, or the administrative head himself. With the growth of the institution to increased proportions, it has seemed best at Sacramento, at least, to unite and coördinate responsibility for supervision of all such athletic, literary, forensic, musical, and dramatic activities in a single administrative officer.

Registrar. This officer, who keeps the records and makes reports on all students in the college, is indispensable. Little need be said, however, regarding his duties, since they are not different, for the most part, from duties of the corresponding officer in the college and university. He is the liaison officer with the high schools on the one hand, whose graduates are received by the junior college, and with the universities on the other, to whose upper divisions so many of his students later transfer. He should be a member of the American Association of Collegiate Registrars, and of its local branch, and should attend all the conventions of the organization possible.

One brief survey of the junior college registrar's activities has been made in a single state, Texas. It includes a study of sixteen institutions, two state, eight church, and six private, varying in size from 64 to 753 students. One only had a full-time registrar. In the others he had, in addition, administrative or instructional duties. Salary and other costs are discussed, but no significant figures can be given due to variety of procedures in the institutions studied. The University of Missouri, in its *Circular of Information to Accredited Junior Colleges*, devotes five pages to suggestions as to records and equipment for the office of the junior college registrar.

Cabinet, or board of deans. In a number of junior colleges the group of deans whose duties have just been considered, varying in number from two or three to six or seven in the different institutions, constitute an administrative cabinet, or board of deans, acting as advisers to the administrative head on many matters of policy and procedure. This cabinet plan of organization, for example, has been very successful at Sacramento, Pasadena, and Chaffey junior colleges. It may be recommended to many others. The general administrative organizations of Pasadena and Sacramento junior colleges are

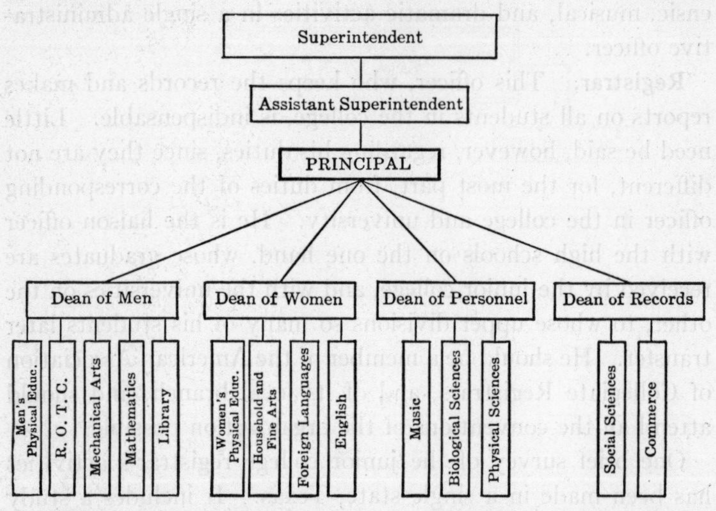

FIG. 26. ADMINISTRATIVE AND SUPERVISORY ORGANIZATION AT PASADENA JUNIOR COLLEGE

shown in Figure 26 and Figure 27. The organization and functions of the administrative cabinet at Pasadena are thus described:[1]

The administration staff consists of the principal, dean of men, dean of women, dean of personnel, and dean of records — the latter four working immediately under the principal and responsible directly to him. Its general duties and responsibilities may be outlined as follows:

1. It is the policy forming body of the college.
2. It receives and considers recommendations from committees and other official groups.

[1] *Pasadena College Bulletin*, p. 33. (May 1, 1929.)

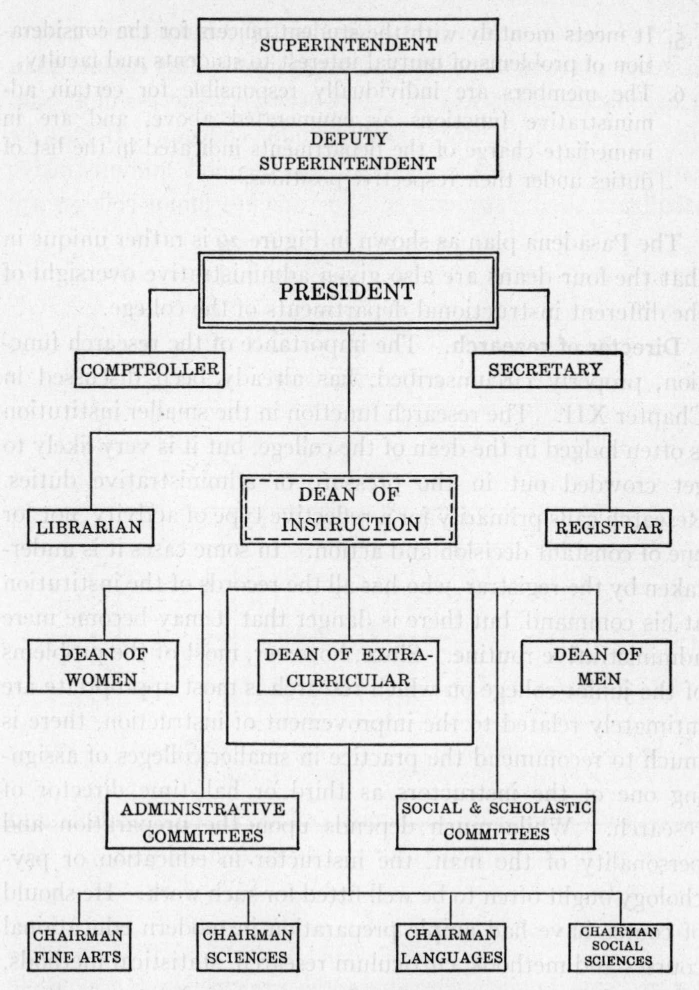

FIG. 27. ADMINISTRATIVE AND SUPERVISORY ORGANIZATION AT SACRAMENTO JUNIOR COLLEGE

3. It meets weekly on Mondays at 1:15 P.M.
4. It meets with the department heads in the principal's council for the consideration of school problems and for the drawing up of recommendations.

5. It meets monthly with the student officers for the consideration of problems of mutual interest to students and faculty.
6. The members are individually responsible for certain administrative functions as enumerated above, and are in immediate charge of the departments indicated in the list of duties under their respective positions.

The Pasadena plan as shown in Figure 26 is rather unique in that the four deans are also given administrative oversight of the different instructional departments of the college.

Director of research. The importance of the research function, properly circumscribed, has already been discussed in Chapter XII. The research function in the smaller institution is often lodged in the dean of the college, but it is very likely to get crowded out in the pressure of administrative duties. Research calls primarily for a reflective type of activity, not for one of constant decision and action. In some cases it is undertaken by the registrar, who has all the records of the institution at his command, but there is danger that it may become mere administrative routine. Since, however, most of the problems of the junior college on which research is most appropriate are intimately related to the improvement of instruction, there is much to recommend the practice in smaller colleges of assigning one of the instructors as third or half-time director of research. While much depends upon the preparation and personality of the man, the instructor in education or psychology ought often to be well fitted for such work. He should of course have had ample preparation in modern educational courses and methods, curriculum research, statistical methods, tests and measurements, etc.

Business manager. The work of the business manager, otherwise known as the bursar, treasurer, comptroller, etc., is indispensable to any educational institution. His duties, however, are not unique so far as the junior college is concerned, and therefore no special discussion will be devoted to them here.

Secretary of the faculty. The secretary of the junior college faculty is another important officer whose duties are in no sense distinctive in the junior college field and to whose work, accordingly, no space need be given.

Director of publicity. Several colleges have a director of publicity.[1] He should be a person of good judgment and keen sense of news values. In many cases he is instructor in journalism. In others he is one of the deans whose work has already been described, or is himself the administrative head. When the head of each junior college in the country was asked to appoint a correspondent for the new *Junior College Journal*, or act himself as such, 53 per cent appointed others, while the remainder preferred to act themselves in this capacity.

Summary. This completes the list of administrative officers, as outlined in Figure 25. The figure is not meant to imply that most junior colleges will have all of these separate full-time *officers*. Pasadena, with almost 3000 students, has only four deans. But the efficiently administered junior college needs to consider all of the *administrative functions* outlined, and to make some provision for carrying them out. In most cases, however, such work will be carried on in connection with other administrative or instructional work. If individuals of proper ability and personality can be secured, it is preferable in many cases that they should also have some teaching responsibility in order to keep them in closer contact with the students and with the fundamental problem of the junior college, that of improving instruction.

QUESTIONS AND PROBLEMS

1. Write a letter to a university appointment secretary outlining the type of individual, as to personality, qualifications, and experience, desired for (1) administrative dean of a junior college; or (2) dean of women; or (3) registrar.

---

[1] The importance of the publicity function, and some of its unique features, will be presented further in Chapter XXI.

2. Take the bulletin of the school of education of some university and list the courses that you think should be taken by a man or woman who is definitely preparing for work in a junior college as: (1) president or dean, or (2) dean of men, or (3) dean of women, or (4) director of research, or (5) registrar, or (6) business manager. What courses not offered should also be taken? Why?
3. You are to be the dean of a public junior college of 300 students. Make a diagram, showing the administrative organization you will set up.
4. In administering your junior college of 300 students, which of the duties in Green's list will you wish to be made fully responsible for?
5. What title is preferable for the chief administrative officer in a public junior college? In a private one? Why?
6. What are the advantages and disadvantages of publishing in the college catalogue detailed lists of the duties of various administrative officers?
7. What ten of the qualifications listed as desirable for a dean of women are most desirable for a dean of instruction? For a dean of men?
8. How large should an institution be before it should have a separate dean of men? Is size a safe criterion? Why?
9. Should administrative deans have oversight of particular departments of instruction, as at Pasadena?
10. Is it better to have a dean of extra-curricular activities, or to divide supervision of such organizations, according to the sex of participants, between the dean of men and the dean of women?
11. Make a study of the duties of the junior college registrar similar to that made by O'Rear for teachers' colleges and normal schools.
12. Should the business manager be a member of the cabinet?

SUGGESTED READINGS

Callender, Pauline. "The Dean of Women: Her Place in the Junior College"; in *Virginia Teacher*, vol. 8, pp. 133-42. (May, 1927.)

Coursault, J. H. *Circular of Information to Accredited Junior Colleges.* University of Missouri Bulletin, vol. 27, pp. 37, pp. 11-16. (October 1, 1926.)

Fitts, C. T. *Pre-Registration Requirements.* Bulletin of Pacific Coast Association of Collegiate Registrars, Fourth Annual Convention, Riverside, California, pp. 92-109. (March, 1929.)

*Green, R. E. "Administrative Dean of the Public Junior College"; in *School Executives' Magazine*, vol. 49, pp. 122-24. (November, 1929.)

Howell, E. J. *The Junior College Registrar.* Bulletin of Association of Texas Colleges, vol. 1, no. 8, pp. 84-88. (June 15, 1928.)

*Lillard, J. B. "Procedure in Organizing the Administration and Supervision of Extra-Curricular Activities"; in *California Quarterly of Secondary Education*, vol. 5, pp. 340–42. (June, 1930.)

O'Rear, F. B. *The Duties of the Registrar*, 173 pp. Springfield, Missouri, 1925.

An analysis of the work of the registrar in teacher training institutions in the United States and a collection of forms for the registrar's office. Although not referring to junior colleges, it has many helpful suggestions for such officers in junior colleges.

**Pasadena Junior College Catalogue*. (May 1, 1929.)

For published lists of duties of all important administrative officers.

CHAPTER XV

THE INSTRUCTIONAL STAFF

The ultimate success or failure of the junior college movement... will be largely determined by the type of men and women who are to serve as the instructors. — C. S. MORRIS.[1]

Contents of this chapter. This chapter first presents standards for junior college faculties as set up by the various accrediting agencies; then certain general qualifications desirable in junior college instructors are discussed. This discussion is followed by a summary of a number of significant studies which have been made, both nation wide and in certain states, dealing with the number, sex, preparation, teaching load, salary, and other features regarding instructors in junior colleges. Finally desirable improvements in standards are suggested.

Importance of the topic. It is a truism to remark that the teacher is the most important element, the "heart and core," in any school. While it is true that the strongest single factor in any educational institution should be its faculty, this is peculiarly and unquestionably so in the case of the junior college. It is a teaching institution *par excellence*. Mark Hopkins and the log still summarize the ideal of college education for many parents who prefer not to have their children begin their college experience by plunging at once into the swirling whirlpool of a great university. Smaller classes, closer personal contacts, and individual instruction are, however, of little value unless the junior college instructor himself is superior in character and quality — unless he is a true *teacher* in the best sense of the word.

The function of the college. One of the best characteriza-

[1] Morris, C. S. "The Faculty of the Junior College"; in *California Quarterly of Secondary Education*, vol. 2, p. 105. (January, 1927.)

tions ever given of the true function of the college was expressed by E. H. Wilkins, in his inaugural address as president of Oberlin College, in 1927. It is quite as true for the junior college as for Oberlin. He said, in part:[1]

The college exists because society desires that youth be taught. Teaching, then, is the thing primarily expected of the college. Teaching is, moreover, precisely what the college itself most desires to do, most delights in doing, is best qualified to do, and does best. The modern college has, to be sure, an extraordinary variety of functions; but teaching is by so far the most important that all the others taken together cannot rival it in significance. Many of the other functions are indeed by-products of the teaching. Teaching is, in the last analysis, *the* function of the college.

The quality of the teaching is the measure of the success of the college. If the teaching is good, the college is a good college, even though its plant be inadequate and its athletic stars be dim. If the teaching is poor, the college is a poor college, even though it has a Freshman Week and a psychiatrist. If the teaching is good, the college justifies its existence and deserves encouragement. If the teaching is and remains poor, the college deserves extinction....

What shall it profit a college to add to its teaching staff a man who has a fine voice, is a natural mixer, plays golf in the eighties, is a tireless and efficient committeeman, a productive scholar, an idealist in life and work — and who cannot teach? Teaching is the soul of the enterprise. Unto the teacher these other qualities may well be added; but teaching ability must be there as the basic quality of all.

True teaching is hard work. Relentless thoroughness in preparation, mastery of all that is new and should be known, long meditation, wherein the significant and the trivial may reach their true proportions and the essential may stand out in focused clarity; then, in class, the utter eagerness to convey all that which you value so to every one of those whom you value so, and the long-drawn-out review of individual reports or experiments. True teaching is hard work — modern teaching, with its individual emphasis, hardest of all.

[1] Wilkins, E. H. "College Teaching"; in *School and Society*, vol. 26, pp. 567–70. (November 5, 1927.)

MINIMUM STANDARDS

As a point of departure, it will be instructive to examine the general standards set up by the various accrediting agencies. As shown in Figure 17, these fall under three heads: minimum number, preparation and qualifications, and teaching load.

Number. While the American Council on Education and the North Central Association are silent on the question of number, a common minimum standard for several agencies is to require at least five full-time instructors. The American Association of Junior Colleges changes "full-time" to "major part of time," while the North Carolina State Department insists only on half-time from each of the five.

Preparation. Every agency states certain minimum standards of preparation and qualifications for junior college instructors. All agree that instructors must have the bachelor's degree, and most of them require a year of graduate work in addition. In a few cases this is "recommended" or required of only a portion of the instructors. Many say the master's degree or its equivalent; in some cases it is required that this degree be taken in the subject taught in the junior college. Several also state a requirement of teaching efficiency or ability, although no way of measuring this is suggested.

Load. The best standard of teaching load prescribed is the statement that it shall not exceed fifteen hours per week, although eighteen and even twenty hours are permitted in some cases. In the phrasing of the American Council, which has been commonly adopted, more than sixteen hours per week "endangers educational efficiency."

Such are the standards set up by the various accrediting agencies. Further details can be found by reference to Figure 17, or to the original standards. It will be significant now to compare them with actual practice in the junior colleges. Before doing this, however, certain desirable general characteristics of junior college instructors, which cannot be expressed in quantitative form, will first be considered.

GENERAL QUALIFICATIONS

Desirable personal traits of character are emphasized by Dean Morris, of Modesto Junior College, who writes, as a part of a very sane and helpful chapter on "The Junior College Faculty": [1]

The nature of the junior college work demands rare qualities of strength of character, inborn capacity, sound understanding, and adequate training. It is because junior college teachers are entering a field of educational pioneering that they need all of the qualities above mentioned, plus the spirit and vision of the pioneer. The pioneer type of service which is necessary is especially evident since junior college training is not to be confused with a simplified collegiate education on the one hand, nor on the other with a sort of glorified high school education. It is a field unique in itself....

The junior college instructor should be especially strong in his intellectual honesty and integrity. He should also be strong in his discernment of what is true and fundamental, rather than merely the reservoir for a vast encyclopedic mass of information.... A profound belief in young men and women, and in the survival of democracy is another essential attribute of the worth while junior college teacher. Of course, character and personality cannot help but be the outstanding characteristics.... This must necessarily be so on account of the close personal touch which the junior college instructor has with his students, which makes it incumbent upon him not only to possess but to radiate character and personality.

"Interest," both in subject matter and in students to be instructed, is placed first, in the opinion of David MacKenzie, dean of the (former) Detroit Junior College. He says: [2]

The foremost problem in all my educational experience has not been to secure money; it is to find real teachers. Our policy has

[1] Morris, C. S. "The Junior Faculty"; in Proctor, W. M. (editor), *The Junior College: Its Organization and Administration*, pp. 41, 43.

[2] MacKenzie, D. *Problems of the Public Junior College.* United States Bureau of Education Bulletin no. 19, pp. 29, 30. Washington, D.C., 1922.

been to obtain teachers who are superior to the instructors generally assigned to underclassmen in the universities.... Underclassmen in the larger colleges rarely meet a great teacher; too often he is only an indifferent drillmaster or at best only an instructor in the literal significance of the word. In the selection of teachers the first qualification is interest in the subject to be taught.... Interest in the student is our second qualification. Too many college instructors seem devoid of any human interest, owing possibly to the great size of their classes.

President Olney, of Marin Junior College, after over twenty years' experience in the junior college field in California, stresses professional preparation in education as essential:[1]

In the candidates recommended by him to his board, he [the principal] should seek to avoid the faults common to college and university instructors. One of the most outstanding of these faults is that of lack of any training in the technique of teaching, fostered by the point of view of the traditional college professor that all one needs to know is subject-matter in order to be able to teach. The junior college executive should look for men and women who have had professional educational training, successful experience in teaching adolescents, and who in addition possess culture and refinement. The junior college teachers should have the social, or humanistic viewpoint, and should be interested in teaching rather than in research.

President Lillard, of Sacramento Junior College, with the largest faculty of any junior college in California, fifty-one members, expresses himself negatively by stating that the junior college should avoid:[2]

The selection of instructors: (*a*) who are interested in research instead of teaching; (*b*) who teach subjects instead of students; (*c*) who rely mainly or exclusively on the lecture method; (*d*) who insist on having readers; (*e*) who depend mainly or exclusively on a

[1] Olney, A. C. "The Administration of the Small Public Junior College"; in Proctor, W. M. (editor), *The Junior College: Its Organization and Administration*, p. 103.

[2] Lillard, J. B. "Pitfalls of the Junior College"; in *Sierra Educational News*, vol. 26, p. 48. (April, 1930.)

textbook; (*f*) who hold that one particular textbook excludes the consideration of any and all others; (*g*) who quit studying after receiving their last degree; (*h*) who have taught too long in some other type of educational institution; (*i*) who oppose all professional training in education; and (*j*) who lack a sense of humor.

PERSONNEL DATA

Personnel data available. Specific information with reference to various features of the instructional staff has been collected by a number of investigators during the past decade. An effort will be made to summarize and compare as far as possible the more important and significant data in several studies which have been made of instructors, in nation-wide and local groups of junior colleges. The dates of publication of these studies (usually representing data of one or two years earlier), groups studied, and source in which the study was published are summarized in Table 34. Subsequently in this chapter these various investigations are referred to in both text and tables by name of author only. None of them consider all of the personnel factors of sex, preparation, load, salary, etc. Nor are the data always in exactly comparable form in the different studies. Definitions differ, units vary, methods of summarization are not the same, and part-time and full-time instructors are often not distinguished. As far as possible, however, significant and comparable data have been selected.

Number of junior college instructors. No complete data are available as to the simplest fact of all that should be known — the total number of junior college instructors in the country.[1] Estimates, indicating at least six thousand instructors,

[1] The American Association of Junior Colleges, in its *Annual Directory*, gives the number of students for each institution, but has never published statistics regarding the faculty. Whitney, in his extensive fact-finding study of the junior college in America, presents a variety of data regarding the students, but gives no information on faculty. Hurt's *College Blue Book* has the most extensive recent data, but it is far from complete. This is also the case with the data published by the United States Office of Education.

TABLE 34. SUMMARY OF INVESTIGATIONS REPORTING PERSONNEL DATA ON JUNIOR COLLEGE INSTRUCTORS

Author	Date Published	Group Studied	Colleges Studied	Instructors Studied	Source
National					
McDowell	1919	Public and Private	66	523	U.S. Bureau of Education Bulletin no. 35. (1919.)
Koos	1924	Public and Private	..	334	*The Junior College*, pp. 189–213.
Whitsitt	1928	Members, American Association of Junior Colleges	111	..	*Proceedings of the Ninth Annual Meeting of the American Association of Junior Colleges*, pp. 89–92.
Vande Bogart	1928	Group of Science Instructors	50	..	*Proceedings of the Ninth Annual Meeting of the American Association of Junior Colleges*, pp. 113–17.
Haggerty	1928	"Half of States"	..	..	*North Central Association Quarterly*, vol. 3, pp. 305–09.
Hurt	1928	Public and Private	295	4660	*College Blue Book.*
Hudelson	1928	Public and Private	70	..	*School and Society*, vol. 30, p. 98.
Freed	1929	Private	55	..	See end of chapter.
Bush	1930	Public	87	..	*Proceedings of Department of Secondary School Principals of N.E.A.* (*Fourteenth Meeting*), pp. 253–62.
Whitney, Miss	1930	Public and Private	201	4020	Unpublished term paper, Stanford University.
North-Central Association					
Reeves-Russell	1929	Public and Private	17	..	*College Organization and Administration*, p. 188.
California					
Proctor	1923	Public	17	277	*School Review*, vol. 31, p. 363.
Morris	1927	Public	..	..	Proctor, W. M. (ed.). *The Junior College: Its Organization and Administration*, pp. 41–59.
Martens	1928	District (11) High School (15)	26	554	*California Quarterly of Secondary Education*, vol. 4, pp. 51–58.
Koos	1929	Public	..	654	*Secondary Education in California* (*Preliminary Survey*), pp. 94–105.
Morgan	1929	District	16	459	Mimeographed Report of State Department of Education.
Texas					
Reid	1929	Municipal	16	195	*Texas Municipal Junior Colleges*, pp. 32–47.

have already been reported in Chapter II (see page 33). In Miss Whitney's study of distribution of Ph.D. degrees in junior colleges (reported later in this chapter), the catalogues of 201 junior colleges available in the library of Stanford University were examined. In them there were listed a total of 4020 faculty members, or an average of 20 per institution. Since there are over 400 junior colleges in the country, the number of instructors must be much larger. It would be unwarranted to assume that it is twice as great, however, for the catalogues available doubtless represented the stronger, larger, and better organized institutions. Thinking of minimum standards for junior colleges, it is certainly very conservative to estimate 5 faculty members for each of the other 200 institutions whose catalogues were not available. It seems more reasonable to estimate 10 instructors for each one. Thus it is practically certain that there are at least 5000 junior college instructors in the country, and it is probable that the number is as high as 6000.

Full-time or part-time. In the case of science teachers in 50 widely scattered junior colleges, Vande Bogart found that 55 per cent were teaching full-time in the junior college. In the Texas municipal colleges, full-time instructors constitute only 48 per cent of the whole. The most striking change is found in a seven-year period in California. In 1921–22, Proctor found, in 8 junior colleges, only 9 per cent of the staff teaching full-time; in the same institutions, in 1928–29, the percentage was 87, and in all the 16 district institutions in the state the percentage of full-time instructors was almost the same, 86 per cent. It is likely that the Texas figure is more nearly typical of the country as a whole, but information is not at hand for other states or groups.

Desirability of part-time instructors. Where institutions are large enough and entirely separated from the high school, with enrollments of several hundred, there seems to be little question that full-time junior college instructors are desirable; there is seldom need for an instructor to teach two or three different subjects. In the case of many smaller junior colleges, however, administered in close connection with the high school, there is strong difference of opinion among many administrators as to the desirability of part-time instructors. Is it better to have a small number of full-time instructors, each teaching two or three different subjects, or a larger number each teaching one subject in both high school and college? Some of the arguments in favor of each plan are summarized below:

For part-time instructors:

1. More expert knowledge utilized in the small college. Better to have high-school instructors in physics, chemistry, and biology each give one or two college courses, than to have a single junior college instructor give all the college courses in science.
2. If close to a university, the junior college can obtain part-time services of university professors.
3. Makes for closer coördination of the curriculum in high schools and college.
4. Junior college instructor understands freshman ability and problems better if he has contact with the high school students.
5. Emphasizes unity of secondary education.
6. Allows greater variety of courses to be given.
7. Often better teachers in high school, although not so highly trained in subject matter. Inspiration, enthusiasm, sympathy more important than advanced knowledge.

For full-time instructors:

1. Difficult for a college teacher to maintain a collegiate point of view and atmosphere in his classes, when time divided with high school.
2. Junior college should not be organized until large enough to require full time of instructors in each of the principal fields.
3. Better teachers can be secured, if given full college positions.
4. Easier to establish a different and higher salary scale when no mixture with high school classes.

5. Difficulty of schedule. Standard high school period is 40 minutes; college, 50 or 55.
6. Insures greater respect of students and of university for the collegiate standard of the institution.
7. Fewer, but better trained teachers required.

One's attitude on this question will be influenced to a considerable extent by his attitude on the more fundamental question of the degree of separation desirable between high school and junior college, a subject to be discussed more in detail in Chapters XXV to XXVII. If an efficient junior college should have at least three hundred students, it will be large enough to justify separate full-time instructors for each of the major lines of work offered. When this is the case, there can be little doubt that full-time status is preferable. For the institutions of one hundred students or less, of which unfortunately there are so many, probably no hard and fast rule can be made. Much will depend upon the personality and qualifications of individual teachers, and upon local conditions. It cannot be too strongly emphasized, however, that the junior college instructor should have sufficient graduate work, personality, and teaching ability to make him really collegiate in character. If there is not sufficient work to keep him busy in the field in the junior college, and if he is not well qualified to teach in two fields, there can be little objection to his using part of his time in high school teaching, provided he can do this and preserve his college attitude and point of view. Many teachers, however, major and minor in two distinct lines in the university, and could therefore give satisfactory freshman or sophomore work in a small junior college in both lines. The overlapping of instructors creates many problems which vanish if this practice can be avoided. The striking change in California district colleges from almost no full-time to almost no part-time instructors, in a short seven-year period, is very significant in this connection. The average number of instructors of each sex in four groups of institutions are shown in Table 35.

TABLE 35. AVERAGE NUMBER OF INSTRUCTORS PER JUNIOR COLLEGE

	TOTAL	MEN	WOMEN	FULL-TIME	PART-TIME
General — Public and private (Miss Whitney)	20	11	9	..	..
North Central — Public and private (Reeves and Russell)	16	..	..	..	..
Texas — Municipal (Reid)	12	6	6	6	6
California — District (Morgan)	29	17	12	25	4

In the California group of district institutions, the smallest school has a faculty of 16; in Texas, the smallest has 6; in the North Central Group of 16 junior colleges, the smallest also has 6. Maximum figures for the three groups are 51, 24, and 51.

Number of students per instructor. In the *Bulletin of the Association of American Colleges* (March, 1917, p. 35), in a study of "The Efficient College," it is stated that one instructor to every ten students, and as many as possible of full professorial rank, is the ideal toward which the efficient college should strive. In *School and Society* for January 23, 1926, statistics were given of enrollment and faculty for 182 principal colleges and universities of the United States. While there are limitations on these figures, since definitions of both students and faculty are not uniform, yet, using them at their face value, interesting comparisons result. For the entire group of institutions the ratio of students to faculty is 9.8 to 1, or practically 10 to 1. For 16 large universities with enrollments of 5000 or over, the ratio varies from 6 to 1 to 23 to 1, with a median of 11 to 1. For 70 institutions with enrollments between 1000 and 5000 it varies from 3 to 1 to 24 to 1, with a median of 12.5 to 1. For 96 institutions with enrollments less than 1000, it varies from

5 to 1 to 26 to 1, with a median again of 12.5 to 1. Thus, regardless of size, the median ratio seems to be fairly constant. A group of 20 of the stronger of the small cultural type of institutions, like Amherst, Beloit, Grinnell, Knox, Pomona, and Whitman, showed an average ratio of 12.4, with only 2 exceeding 15 to 1.[1]

It is exceedingly difficult to make similar computations for the junior colleges of the country, not only because the number of instructors is unknown, but because so many of them are on a part-time basis. The student enrollment, too, in some cases includes a large number of special students taking only partial work. If the estimate of 6000 junior college instructors be taken with the 67,000 students, it makes the ratio 11 to 1, but this is certainly in error on account of the large number of part-time instructors involved. If it be estimated that there is an equivalent of 4000 full-time instructors (only a rough guess), the ratio is about 17 to 1.

An effort was made to determine this ratio a little more carefully, for the California district junior colleges, by making suitable adjustments for the known number of part-time instructors and special students. For 1927–28, the average ratio was 20 to 1. It varied from 28 to 1 (Chaffey and Pasadena), to 11 to 1 (Santa Rosa). For 1928–29, by the same method, for the same institutions the ratio was 21 to 1, due to a greater proportionate increase of students than faculty. The average enrollment in these institutions is over 600, much higher than in the United States as a whole. The ratio is therefore probably much lower in most institutions. In Texas municipal junior colleges, however, the ratio is 20 to 1. Should the collegiate standard of 10 or 12 to 1 be maintained? Probably not, since it also includes provision for upper-division specialization. For true college work, however, it should not

[1] Eells, W. C. "The Standing of the College"; in *Whitman College Quarterly*, vol. 29, no. 3, pp. 11–13.

vary greatly. It may be questioned whether average ratios of 20 to 1 and higher do not also "endanger educational efficiency."

Sex of instructors. The proportion of men and of women in the faculties of the junior colleges is summarized in Table 36.

TABLE 36. SEX OF JUNIOR COLLEGE INSTRUCTORS

	Total Number	Per cent Men	Per cent Women
National			
Public and private (Hurt)	4,660	47	53
Public (Miss Whitney)	2,227	56	44
Private (Miss Whitney)	1,793	53	47
California			
District (Morgan)	459	58	42
Public (Koos)	654	54	46
Texas			
Municipal (Reid)	195	50	50
National groups for comparison *			
High schools	189,683	37	63
Teachers' colleges and normal schools	14,231	41	59
Colleges and universities	43,326	75	25

* United States Bureau of Education, Bulletin no. 25. (1928.)

It is noticeable that the proportion of men is markedly higher than in the high schools of the country, but lower than in the standard colleges and universities — further evidence of the junior college as a transitional institution. The largest proportion of men is found in the California district colleges.

PREPARATION OF INSTRUCTORS

Definite information on the preparation of instructors in the junior colleges can be presented from the standpoint of degrees held, sources of these degrees, length and variety of teaching experience, and type of professional training. These will be discussed in turn.

Degrees held. It was seen that the master's degree or its equivalent was the most common standard set up by the various accrediting agencies for junior college instructors. While the possession of this degree is no criterion of teaching ability or success, it does assure a certain maturity in addition to specialized knowledge of a particular field. It can be easily determined, since catalogues usually publish the names and degrees of the faculty, even if no other information is given concerning them. A number of such studies are summarized in Table 37.

TABLE 37. HIGHEST DEGREE HELD BY JUNIOR COLLEGE INSTRUCTORS

	Total Number	Doctor (per cent)	Master (per cent)	Bachelor (per cent)	None (per cent)
National					
Private (McDowell)	343	8	27	51	14
Public (McDowell)	180	3	39	45	13
Public (Koos)	163	3	47	47	3 [a]
Private (Koos)	129	1	34	60	5 [a]
Science instructors (Vande Bogart)	..	7	70	23 [b]	?
California					
Public and private (Morris)	..	7	40	36	17
Public and private (Martens)	554	7	46	37	10
Public (Koos)	654	4	52 [c]	44	0
District (Morgan)	459	?	63 [d]	29	8
Texas					
Municipal (Reid)	195	2	60	31	7
Groups for comparisons					
Three universities [e] (McDowell)	223	60	26	13	1
Three colleges [f] (McDowell)	58	26	41	26	7
Colleges (Koos)	119	28	49	23	0
Universities (Koos)	121	28	42	30	0
University of Texas [g] (Pittinger)	..	30	52	18	0
Fellows and assistants [h] (Proctor)	..	0	13	83	4
Colleges, freshmen and sophomore instructors only (Koos)	338	32	41	23	4

[a] Not strictly comparable, since Koos omits from his totals special teachers in subjects like home economics, art, music, and physical education.
[b] "With no graduate degrees."
[c] Includes 4 per cent with "other advanced degrees."
[d] "M.A. or higher degree."
[e] Iowa, Illinois, Minnesota.
[f] Coe, Cornell, Grinnell.
[g] *Texas Outlook* (September, 1928).
[h] "In 13 lower-division courses at University of California and Stanford University."

It is evident, as shown by the data in Table 37, that there has been considerable improvement, as far as the proportion of higher degrees is concerned, since McDowell's early study when only about one third of the instructors had a higher degree. Koos showed half of the instructors with such degrees. Later general studies have not been made, but, judging from the science instructors studied by Vande Bogart, or the groups in Texas and California, the proportion is now well over half, although not as great as two thirds. If it is fair to expect a master's degree for junior college teaching positions, and surely no lower standard could be considered as at all satisfactory, there is still room for great improvement. With reference to California, however, the situation is better than the figures would indicate, for credential requirements provide that every junior college instructor shall have had at least one year of graduate work in a recognized university. Many who have had a year of graduate work, roughly equivalent to the M.A. degree, have not taken the degree.

The doctor's degree. A detailed study of the extent to which the doctor's degree is held by different groups of junior college instructors is shown in Table 38[1] based upon an examination of 201 catalogues.

TABLE 38. PROPORTION OF JUNIOR COLLEGE INSTRUCTORS HOLDING THE DOCTOR'S DEGREE

	Colleges	Instructors	Per cent with Ph.D. Degree
Total	**201**	**4020**	**3.4**
Geographical			
Southern	68	1220	1.2
Middle Atlantic	12	211	10.0
New England	3	58	8.6
Middle Western	62	959	3.2
Western	56	1572	4.2
Sex			
Men	..	2201	5.4
Women	..	1819	1.1
Type			
Private	109	1793	3.8
Denominational	91	1438	3.3
Proprietary	18	355	6.2
Public	92	2227	3.1

[1] From an unpublished study by Miss Maxine Whitney, at Stanford University.

It is in the smaller group of Eastern private institutions that the largest proportion of doctors is found, but the proportion for the country as a whole, 3.4 per cent, is so small as to be of little significance. Over 95 per cent of the instruction in the junior colleges of the country is being given by men and women without the doctor's degree.[1] Is this fact to be commended or deplored on the part of the junior colleges?

Should junior college instructors have doctors' degrees? Many junior college administrators feel that the doctor's degree is a doubtful asset. They point out, with much justification, that the Ph.D. degree is essentially a research degree, indicating ability in original investigation, and not ability in teaching, which is the prime requisite in the junior college; that more often than not it tends to make a man a narrow specialist, interested in advancing his field of knowledge, but likely to stifle interest in students and in methods of instruction. The late Dr. Lange, in speaking of qualifications of junior college instructors, said:[2]

> Another *sine qua non* is an ample measure of the liberal culture that embodies the spirit of service, informed by broad scholarship and inclusive appreciations. A mere specialist may do no great harm in a university; in a junior college with its man-centered aims his ways would lead to destruction. Normally a Ph.D. applying for a junior college position should be asked to present a certificate of rebirth.

While there are many cases where the distinguished research scholar is also an inspiring teacher, it must be confessed that in too many instances such is not the case. It is no wonder, then, that the junior college administrator is inclined to discount somewhat heavily possession of the degree of doctor of philoso-

[1] A recent study of Stanford University, however, showed that 72 per cent of all the lower-division instruction at the university was given by men of professorial rank, and 58 per cent by men with doctors' degrees.

[1] Lange, A. F. "The Junior College as an Integral Part of the Public School System"; in *School Review*, vol. 25, p. 475. (September, 1917.)

phy as a marked asset for a junior college instructor. If a man has the degree plus contagious classroom enthusiasm he would be a desirable addition to the junior college faculty. The more desirable doctors, however, can and usually do secure university positions, where the atmosphere is more favorable for the continuation of their research work, leaving the junior college positions to be filled by less able men. A broadly trained master of arts, with a good grasp of his subject matter, even if he has never made any so-called original contribution to it, if he possesses personality, enthusiasm, and real teaching ability, is infinitely to be preferred for a junior college faculty to the most learned doctor who lacks these other qualities so essential to success in a distinctly teaching institution. If the junior colleges should insist to any marked degree upon Ph.D.'s for their faculties it would mean that the universities would be required to turn out a much larger number of men, not primarily interested in or fitted for research, but demanding it simply as a means of securing desirable junior college teaching positions.

Another doctor's degree? There will, however, eventually be need for a higher standard than the master's degree for true college instructors, even in the junior college. Already some states are requiring the master's degree or its equivalent for high school teachers, and others are considering it. This standard is none too high, and is certain to come in many states. In California it is recommended now that junior college instructors should have at least two years of graduate work. To meet the situation created by this demand for better-trained instructors, three leading California universities have established the Doctor of Education (Ed.D.) degree, which requires quite as much work as the doctor of philosophy degree, but represents a broader knowledge and ability than is found in the detailed specialization of the Ph.D., who is sometimes said to learn "more and more about less and less."

At Stanford University and the University of Southern California this degree is of two types, one meant primarily for administrators, the other for teachers. The so-called master-teacher type calls for a knowledge of subject matter in some department other than education, presumably the candidate's prospective teaching field, equivalent to the master's degree, or more; plus a broad training in educational theory and practice, with special emphasis on higher educational problems. The thesis is not necessarily a *contribution* to knowledge, but may be a broad, scholarly *organization* of existing knowledge. Men receiving this type of degree, not easier or cheaper than the classic Ph.D. but different from it, should ultimately form the backbone of our junior college faculties in the same way that the strength of the university faculty is formed largely by the men with the Ph.D. degree. New doctors, turned out by the universities in ever-increasing numbers, are now sometimes forced into the junior college field, although they are neither fitted for teaching nor interested in it. This situation would be relieved if the Ph.D. could be kept as a distinctively research degree.

Sources of degrees. Breadth of training for the faculty of the junior college as a whole is shown not only by the extent of their training, but also by the source of it. To avoid provincialism, the faculty should represent a wide variety and geographical distribution of universities and colleges. Miss Martens found, in her study of over five hundred California instructors with one or more degrees, that they were received from 143 different institutions from the Atlantic to the Pacific, as well as in Australia, Belgium, England, Ireland, and Switzerland. She lists twenty-five distinct institutions represented by five or more degrees each. The first three are California institutions — University of California (211), Stanford (91), and University of Southern California (51) — but the fourth represents the other coast, Columbia University (27). One junior college with forty faculty members lists twenty-eight universities in which they received their training. Koos found that almost half of the California junior college instructors had taken their undergraduate degree outside of the state, although about two thirds had taken graduate work in California, due to the state credential requirements. The undergraduate work of the twenty-seven members of the staff of the Johnstown (Pennsylvania) Junior College has been done in thirty-one colleges and universities, from Massachusetts to Colorado, including the large state university, the municipal university, the privately endowed institution, the land-grant college, men's and women's and coeducational colleges, and denominational and non-denominational types. Only six received their baccalaureate degrees from the University of Pittsburgh. Similar breadth of training is shown by the Erie and Uniontown junior colleges. At Erie no two of the faculty attended the same undergraduate college. All institutions should strive for faculties representing a variety of American and foreign institutions of higher learning, if they are to secure an atmosphere of culture and freedom from provincialism.

TEACHING EXPERIENCE AND PROFESSIONAL TRAINING

Length and variety of teaching experience. Number of years of previous experience is reported by Miss Martens for the group of 554 California instructors, and by McDowell for his earlier study of 523 throughout the country. Their results and those of Koos may be summarized thus:

	Median (years)	Lower Quartile (years)	Upper Quartile (years)
McDowell	8.7	3.9	15.8
Martens	10.8	5.8	16.0
Koos (public)	10.3		
Koos (private)	5.5		
Koos (all) (303)	8.4		
Koos (colleges and universities)	7.3		

The California group studied by Miss Martens, ten years later than McDowell's study, shows a distinctly longer previous experience. She found that teaching experience varied from two to forty years, but that less than 5 per cent had had less than two years experience, while over 5 per cent had more than 25 years experience. "Thus we have the wisdom and judgment of experience coöperating with the freshness and enthusiasm of youth."

Koos says that it is very significant that junior college instructors had, on the average, a year more experience than a group of 237 lower-division college and university instructors used for comparison.

Type of previous experience. As to the type of previous experience, Miss Martens found that the percentage reporting various types of teaching experience was as follows:

College experience	34 per cent
High-school experience	80
Junior high-school experience	4
Elementary school experience	17

Previous experience for the group also included a considerable number who had been elementary and high-school principals (76), school superintendents (18), college presidents (2), and state school officials (3). Fifty-four per cent had had teaching experience outside of the state, in almost every state of the Union, and in thirteen foreign countries — a further evidence of richness and diversity of educational contacts.

With this experience, as actually reported, may be compared the preferences for type of previous experience as expressed by junior college administrators (Vande Bogart). Their preferences were:

College experience	47 per cent
High-school experience	40
Both	13

Thus while only one third of the California group had had previous college experience, almost two thirds of junior college administrators prefer that they should have such experience. After many years experience in administering Chaffey Junior College, one of the oldest California institutions, Hill states it as his opinion that:[1]

> It is of considerable advantage to have instructors who are familiar with high school problems on the one hand and with college and university problems on the other. Where possible, teachers who have had experience in both high school and university are desirable. But in selecting teachers, it is well to have some who have had definite college experience.

Professor Hills, of the University of California, after considerable experience as a junior college inspector, says:[2]

> It is my personal opinion that no high-school teacher should ever be promoted to junior college work without first taking leave of absence for one or two years of additional graduate work in a university.

This is also the opinion of a practical junior college administrator, Morris:[3]

> While many will continue to enter junior college work after having had high school teaching experience, in practically no instance should the high-school teacher step directly into the junior college work without first becoming, for at least a year, a regular registrant in some standard university, having enrolled for research work along

[1] Hill, M. E. "Administrative Problems of the Large Rural Junior College"; in Proctor, W. M. (editor), *The Junior College: Its Organization and Administration*, p. 82.

[2] Hills, E. C. "Relation of the Junior College to the Upper Division of the University"; in *California Quarterly of Secondary Education*, vol. 2, pp. 102. (January, 1927.)

[3] Morris, C. S. "The Junior College Faculty"; in Proctor, W. M. (editor), *The Junior College: Its Organization and Administration*, p. 49.

the lines of the field in which he subsequently expects to instruct in junior college.

Type of professional training. Even more important than the amount of academic preparation is that of its character. In all too many of the smaller junior colleges it is found that instructors are teaching subjects for which they have had little or no preparation in either their undergraduate or their graduate work. Texas has an excellent provision to prevent this, requiring for accreditation that the courses taught by any teacher must be in the field of specialization represented by his graduate work, this being interpreted to mean subjects in which the instructor has taken either a major or a minor in his graduate study. If he has had no graduate work it is similarly interpreted with reference to his undergraduate work. It is highly desirable that such a standard should be adopted in all junior colleges as rapidly as possible as a working principle, although it is easily conceivable that exceptions might be made, under special conditions, where equivalent preparation had been secured by travel or private study or otherwise. Narrowly interpreted, the Texas plan might prevent breadth of the curriculum. Few instructors major in astronomy, yet a man trained in mathematics or physics might profitably give such an introductory course, even if his actual training in it had not been extensive. On the whole, however, the principle is a sound one and should be adhered to if the junior college is to be on a collegiate basis. Koos found that 75 per cent of the public junior college instructors had an undergraduate major or more in the field taught, while in four-year colleges used for comparison the figure was 86 per cent.

Professional courses. Closely related to the above question is the one of professional courses in education. Should they be required of junior college instructors as they are at the present time of prospective elementary and high-school instructors in most parts of the country? Up to the present time the average college instructor has shown a contemptuous disregard of any professional courses in education. As a Canadian educator has aptly expressed it:[1]

> All university teaching has behind it a glorious tradition of amateurishness, with results varying from the highest inspirational teaching to the lowest dry-as-dust.

The opinions gathered by Vande Bogart from a group of junior college administrators is of significance here. In the matter of academic preparation, 77 per cent preferred a major in the subject taught with a minor in education; 5 per cent preferred a major in education with a minor in the subject taught; 16 per cent preferred that the entire time be given to the major field; and 2 per cent favored a few courses in education but not a minor. Unquestionably work in the subject matter to be taught should be stressed, probably even more than it is at present, but this does not imply that professional training should be neglected. It is significant that 84 per cent of administrators want teachers with some such professional training, and 82 per cent feel it should be as much as a minor. It is significant, too, that the Association of American Colleges has recently recommended that some professional courses be required of all college and university graduates who expect to teach in college.

The successful junior college faculty member must be more than a specialist in his own field. He is also a part of a new and significant movement in higher education, perhaps the most significant movement of a century. He must have a broad conception of the entire educational field, and a broad background to evaluate the place of the junior co'lege and to furnish a basis for his philosophy of it. Such a background should require, at the very least, courses in the principles of education, its history, both general and in the United States,

[1] Conacher, W. M. "The Junior College Question"; in *Queen's Quarterly*, vol. 34, pp. 479–80. (April–June, 1927.)

principles of secondary education, college teaching, college administration, statistics and tests, survey methods, and a course, if possible, in junior college organization and administration. While the latter course has been given but occasionally in a few American universities in the past, it is on the increase, and doubtless will increase still more as the junior colleges of the country demand it. The amount and variety of professional preparation of junior college instructors should be studied more carefully than it has been. Certainly no lower standard of professional preparation in education should be tolerated for junior colleges than for secondary schools in general.

Suzzallo's opinion. President Henry Suzzallo, of the Carnegie Foundation for the Advancement of Teaching, in a notable address before the American Association of Junior Colleges, in 1929, said:[1]

In the light of all the previous considerations, what requirements ought to be laid down in the training of teachers for junior colleges? In the first place we ought to require that their collegiate training be broad, that they should acquire mastery of a group of subjects. Only after they are past their own senior college training should they enter upon training that specializes very definitely upon a single course of study. Under the present circumstances, to lay down a requirement for a doctor's degree would be a mistake. We shall be better off if we say two years of sound but broad graduate training than if you say the master's or the doctor's degree.... In addition to scholarship in a broad field of study, we shall require some educational training. Now I know it is going to be difficult to get the academic men of our graduate schools to allow any time for educational training. College departments, covering a major subject, do not like to let go of the student's time so he may take some work in education. It has been a thirty-year battle in the colleges. It will be a worse battle in the graduate school.... What

[1] Suzzallo, H. "The Training of Junior College Teachers"; in *Proceedings of the Tenth Annual Meeting of the American Association of Junior Colleges*, pp. 104–05. Atlantic City, New Jersey, 1929.

are you going to ask graduate schools to do for the training of junior college teachers? If we ask too much, anything similar to what is required in the normal schools and teachers' colleges, we shall not obtain it. I should like to see this association set up some reasonable, initial standards for the training of junior college teachers. If you do not, then one of two things will happen. You will borrow plumage from the professional school of research and insist upon Ph.D.'s who will disappoint you with poor teaching, or you will recruit the teachers from the secondary school — good teachers who are rather late in coming into scholarship. One is as great a danger as the other.

Summary. After various comparisons, a number of investigators have come to the conclusion that the preparation of junior college teachers at present compares very favorably with that of instructors of lower-division courses in colleges and universities, and is perhaps superior in some respects, although still open to much greater improvement. The lower-division instruction in the universities has, however, been an object of such frequent and vigorous criticism that this is not a satisfactory standard for the junior college. It must be content with nothing short of the best. Where the chief emphasis is and should be on instruction, it can and should insist on the highest degree of teaching preparation and efficiency. In order to secure this, however, the faculty must not be overworked and it must not be underpaid. Accordingly matters of teaching load and salary will next be investigated.

TEACHING LOAD

Hours per week. A common standard for teaching load in standard colleges is twelve to eighteen hours per week, the prevailing figure being fifteen or sixteen. While this is only one element of the teaching load, it is the single unit employed by all the accrediting agencies. Eight or ten hours is a more common university load, but there the professor is expected to devote at least half of his time to research.

Number of hours per week is only a crude measure, because it does not take into consideration such important elements as class size, duplicate sections of a class, variations in subject matter, laboratory supervision, method of presentation, conference, paper reading, and administrative and committee work. There is need for a careful study of actual and desirable teaching loads in the junior college, giving proper weight to all of the more important factors involved. In the private junior college the total load of the instructor is not only instructional, but administrative, social, and residential as well. A few studies have covered the matter of teaching load, usually expressed in hours per week. These are summarized in Table 39.

TABLE 39. TEACHING LOAD OF JUNIOR COLLEGE INSTRUCTORS IN HOURS PER WEEK

	MEAN OR MEDIAN	RANGE
National		
Public and private (McDowell)	16	
Public (Koos)	14	
Private (Koos)	15	
Private (Freed)	17	10–25
California		
Public (Morris)	15	12–20
Texas		
Municipal (Reid)	16	12–30
Groups for comparison		
Four-year colleges (Koos)	13	
Universities (Koos)	9	

In Texas, 10 per cent of the instructors had loads in excess of 18 hours. In the private junior colleges, Freed found that more than 25 per cent had loads exceeding 18 hours. Bush made an extensive investigation of teaching load in twelve departments in 87 public junior colleges. In almost every department he found loads as high as 30 hours, although the prevailing load in each department was from 15 to 18 hours. Two thirds of the administrators in these 87 institutions recommended 15 hours as the normal load in most departments, but in one third of the cases their recommendations favored 18 hours.

The question of teaching load is further complicated when teachers are giving part-time instruction in both high school and junior college. In computing the combined load, one and two fifths high school periods are sometimes counted as equivalent to one junior college period. Usually difficulty of the subject as well as length of period in minutes varies in the two schools. Sometimes five high school periods are counted as equivalent to three college periods.

Student hours per week. Student hours per week has also been used to measure teaching load. On this basis, Morris found in the California colleges that the load varied for different instructors from 40 to over 600, with a mean of about 250. At Pasadena, with larger classes than in the smaller institutions, it runs much higher, the mean being 522, the lower quartile 403, and the upper quartile 607. It varied by departments from 360 in journalism to 1153 for physical education. Mathematics, biology, and English were near the median, with 500 to 530 hours each. Quite obviously this, too, is not a satisfactory measure, for few instructors would claim that it is twice as much work to handle a class of forty as it is one of twenty.

Judgments of relative amount of work. The composite judgment of twenty-one members of a liberal arts college faculty was sought on this matter of relative work in handling groups of different sizes. They were asked the question, "Assuming that 100 represents the total amount of work (including time, effort, energy, preparation, paper work, etc.) required to teach a course of twenty-five students in your subject, express your judgment of the relative amount required to handle classes in the same subject of 5, 15, 35, 50, 75, and 100 students." The average of their judgments was as follows:[1]

For class of 5, 79
For class of 15, 88
For class of 25, 100
For class of 35, 115
For class of 50, 144
For class of 75, 171
For class of 100, 197

These are largely subjective judgments, but they represent the composite opinion of an entire faculty on the matter. The opinions showed considerable variation, not only between departments, but also between individuals in the same department. On the whole, however, there was the feeling that little was saved in total load in classes of less than twenty-five students; on the other hand, that in classes of four times that size the work was about doubled, instead of being four times as much, when judged by student hours alone. Junior college administrators would find it illuminating and perhaps helpful to ask a similar question of members of their faculties, and study the results.

Reeves and Russell have used, in college surveys, an interesting method of weighting in which class size counts one half, teaching hours one fourth, and preparation one fourth, in determining the total teaching load of a college instructor.[2] This harmonizes somewhat with the method suggested by composite faculty judgment, in that increase in class size is given but half weight instead of full weight. Undoubtedly the full-weight method, widely used by the United States Bureau of Education in many of its surveys of higher education, is open to very serious criticism, as is any method which

[1] Unpublished study by the author, at Whitman College, Walla Walla, Washington.

[2] Reeves, F. W., and Russell, J. D. *College Organization and Administration*, p. 180. Indianapolis, Indiana, 1929.

judges exclusively by only one of the several important factors which enter into the determination of real working load. There is a field here for a careful study of the whole matter of teaching load in junior colleges. Meanwhile it is interesting to notice the "conscience" method proposed by Morris:[1]

> The determination of the proper teaching load to be assigned to any individual seems to fall right back on the instructor himself, who must conscientiously answer this question, "Granted that I have average health and vitality and the preparation which I should have had for the work I am offering, am I devoting too much of my energy in the educational service which I in good faith have contracted to render?" If the answer is in the affirmative, every effort should be made to enable the instructor concerned to so adjust his burden that maximum results, considering the existing circumstances, may be obtained.

This places the whole matter on a high professional plane. It is feared, however, that such a plan will hardly be satisfactory as a standard method of administration until some means can also be derived for an equalization of the consciences of different instructors!

Morris expresses it as his judgment, however, that:[2]

> As a matter of fact, the schedule of fifteen college units, handled in a genuine college manner, is so taxing upon the individual that but few of the junior college instructors with whom the writer has come in contact are able to finish the year without being in a decidedly rundown condition.

SALARIES

"The laborer is worthy of his hire." If superior instructors — superior in personal qualities, preparation, and ability — are to be secured they must be paid for. Junior college salaries tend to be distinctly higher than high school salaries in the same localities, but lower than those in college and universities.

[1] Morris, C. S. "The Junior College Faculty"; in Proctor, W. M. (editor), *The Junior College: Its Organization and Administration*, p. 56.

[2] Morris, *op. cit.*, p. 51.

The average is higher in public institutions although there is much overlapping, and many of the better private colleges pay much better than the poorer public institutions. Some junior colleges, too, have far higher salary scales than do four-year colleges or universities. Koos found the following median salaries of various comparable groups, as shown in Table 40.

TABLE 40. MEDIAN SALARIES OF INSTRUCTORS IN VARIOUS TYPES OF INSTITUTIONS (1921–1922)

	NUMBER	MEDIAN SALARY
Junior colleges		
Public	202	$2298
Northern private	57	1843
Southern private	37	2175
Groups for comparisons		
Four-year colleges	119	2413
Universities	120	2067
High schools in districts with junior colleges	240	2023
High schools in districts without junior colleges	488	1653

While it is very difficult to be sure that conditions are fairly comparable in salary studies, yet various investigations that have been made show that the salaries have tended to increase in the decade that has passed since Koos's statistics were gathered. Whitsitt, in a study of 94 junior colleges in 1927–28, grouped geographically, found the mean maximum and minimum salaries as follows:

	NUMBER OF COLLEGES	MEAN MAXIMUM	MEAN MINIMUM
Entire group	**91**	**$2650**	**$1625**
West	7	3170	1930
East	5	3160	1640
South	39	2280	1433
North Central	40	2630	1700

For this group as a whole it was found that the median salary of the best paid instructors was about the same as that for an assistant professor in the colleges and universities of the United States, as reported by the United States Bureau of Education; while the median salary for the entire groups was about $2000, slightly better than the median of instructors in colleges and universities. The maximum salary reported was $6600.

Reeves and Russell reported for seventeen junior colleges in the North Central Association a median salary of $2520, with the following distribution:

	Maximum	Average	Minimum
Highest	$9450	$3000	$2200
Median	2520	2050	1700
Lowest	1768	1600	1200

The figures show a very wide variation of salary conditions for junior college instructors, even in this one area. The variation in salary of the administrative head is even greater, with a maximum of $12,500 and a minimum of $1976. The institution which pays its professors $6600 or its president $12,500 is evidently in a position to secure instructors who would be coveted by many universities.

Freed, in his study of private junior colleges, found the mean salary and range as follows, for different grades as far as they were recognized in the 55 junior colleges he studied:

	Typical Salary	Average Range
Professor	$2140	$1210–$6500
Associate Professor	1833	1160– 2500
Assistant Professor	1612	1000– 3000
Instructor	1454	900– 2500

In most of the public institutions these four professorial grades are not distinguished, all members of the instructional staff usually ranking as "instructors," a fact which makes still more difficult a fair comparison between public and private institutions.

Official reports of the public institutions in Texas (for 1929) give a mean salary of $1997. In California the corresponding figures for instructors in the district junior colleges is $2754; for men it is $2810, for women, $2673.

TENURE, SABBATICAL LEAVE, AND RETIREMENT

There has been little study of tenure, sabbatical leave and retirement, and probably little consideration of these features so far on the part of most junior colleges. This new institution has been so busy taking care of present growth that it has had little time to give serious attention to matters of permanent policy dealing with the future. Yet if permanence and stability of faculty are desirable, such features will soon have to be considered. In states such as California, where legally the junior colleges are part of the secondary school system, teachers come under the general provisions covering these matters in the secondary schools.

Tenure. Whitsitt found that in eighty-four junior colleges appointments are made for single-year terms only, with little trend toward permanent tenure. In five colleges reëmployment at the close of the initial contract gives permanent tenure, but this is quite unusual. In one college, the instructors are rated 1, 2, 3, 4. Ratings of 1 or 2 insure permanent tenure. One college grants permanent tenure only to those who have completed twenty years of successful service. In one, the permanent tenure is limited to professors; all other instructors are on annual contracts. If junior college teaching is to be made attractive, unquestionably conditions of tenure must be made comparable with those in four-year colleges and universities. Annual appointments, or a probationary period of two or three years, are satisfactory and desirable for new members of the faculty, but certainly permanence of tenure should be expressed or implied on somewhat the same basis as in other collegiate institutions, after the probationary period is passed. Development of *esprit de corps*, permanence, and professional spirit demand such conditions. Certainly a probationary period of twenty years is indefensible.

Sabbatical leave. It is important that sabbatical leave be granted as in many colleges and universities, on part or full pay, under suitable restrictions. Even before this is accomplished, however, there are variations of the same principle that can be applied. Exchange of instructors with other junior colleges or other institutions for a semester or a year has been practiced in a few cases, with added stimulation for both participating institutions as well as for the instructors involved. Even visiting days, or visiting weeks, are valuable for this purpose.

Retirement. Still less attention has been given to the matter of retirement in this young vigorous movement. Whitsitt found that only nine of the group of colleges studied had seriously considered the problems of age of retirement, relation to the institution after retirement, or retiring allowance. The retirement age in these nine varied from sixty to seventy years. Very few colleges assume any responsibility for instructors after retirement. One executive said his policy was to employ only competent *young* instructors. The limitations of such a policy as a permanent matter are obvious. If retirement allowances are to be a matter of partial coöperation, which seems to be the best accepted policy in the educational world, then the best time to begin is when the contributing instructors are young. One college executive reports that they participate in a teacher's savings up to 5 per cent of his salary, under the plan of the Carnegie Teachers' Insurance and Annuity Association. This is an excellent plan for private colleges. In public colleges, in a number of states and cities, retirement is being reasonably well taken care of under the general provisions of retiring allowances for public school teachers, but in many cases the junior college instructors are not included.

THE FUTURE

The novelty, the pioneer enthusiasm, the missionary spirit, the greater opportunity for advancement which have been more or less potent factors in the field of junior college instruction — all these will lose their force as the institution acquires permanence and stability. If junior colleges are to secure and hold instructors equal to those in the lower divisions of standard colleges and universities, they must do so by making the requirements relatively high and the inducements for permanence more attractive. It is not too much to ask that the standards of preparation should be advanced. It is not too much to expect every permanent, well-qualified instructor to have had at least two years of graduate work, largely in the field in which he expects to teach, or in closely related work; and that he should have had a substantial training in professional courses in education, to prevent him from being a narrow specialist in his own field, and to see his own work in its proper perspective with relation to the rest of the institution. It would be desirable that heads of departments should have had the equivalent of the training and breadth of view represented by the degree of doctor of education. Men and women with such training should be in the best sense instructors of youth, as well as instructors of subjects. Their normal teaching load should not exceed twelve to fifteen hours per week.

Instructors in junior colleges should receive salaries somewhat better than lower-division instructors in the universities. There should be other attractive features of permanence of tenure, professional development, and community standing to place them on a par with university instructors. With such a teaching staff, the possibilities of the junior college for wholesome influence in a widely democratic system of junior colleges is almost limitless. Their potentiality for raising the entire cultural level of American civilization is beyond power of computation. It is true that these suggested standards are higher than those obtaining at the present time, although the facts given in this chapter show that they are not unreasonably higher.[1]

In conclusion, the judgment of President Angell of Yale is worth quoting:[2]

> This independent junior college ought, if possible, to be equipped with even stronger scholars and more commanding personalities than those to whom in the four-year college is often confided the instruction of students in their first two years of college residence. Whatever it is necessary to pay such men should be given. And an institution which cannot see its way clear to the maintenance of such a salary schedule ought to search its heart very thoroughly before it decides to embark permanently on a junior college enterprise. The great bane of American education from the district school up has been the superficiality and crudity of the instruction offered, and it is wholly intolerable that a new educational movement like that of the junior college should be launched without committing itself absolutely to high educational standards.

QUESTIONS AND PROBLEMS

1. Make a study for any state or other group of junior college instructors, similar to Miss Martens's for California.
2. From the academic bibliographies of a university faculty find the degrees, experience, and training of instructors of freshman and sophomore classes, and compare with that of junior college instructors as given in this chapter.
3. What professional courses in education should be taken by a junior college instructor?
4. Prepare a suitable salary schedule for a junior college with twenty-five members of the faculty.
5. Compare salaries of junior college instructors in any state with those

[1] A very extensive study of the social, economic, professional, and legal status of the junior college instructor has been made by J. T. Wahlquist as a doctor's dissertation at the University of Cincinnati. It was based upon returns received from 1236 instructors, in 32 states. The results of this study were made available too late to be included in this chapter. A comprehensive summary of them will be found in two articles by Mr. Wahlquist in the *Junior College Journal* for December, 1930, and January, 1931.

[2] Angell, J. R. "Problems Peculiar to the Junior College"; in *School Review*, vol. 25, p. 391. (June, 1917.)

of high school and college or university instructors in the same state.

6. Would you prefer to teach in a public or a private junior college? Why?
7. Do you agree with President Suzzallo that the American Association of Junior Colleges should set up standards for training junior college instructors?
8. "Is the junior college teacher primarily a scholar or a pedagogue, or must he be both?" (See Stanger, F. M., in Suggested Readings.)
9. Devise a suitable plan for measuring the teaching load of a junior college faculty.
10. Should the number of teaching units vary with the subject taught?
11. Should junior college instructors teach part time in the high school in small institutions where there is not sufficient work in their own field in the junior college to require their full time, or should they attempt work in other junior college departments?
12. What changes should be made in the standards set up by the various accrediting agencies regarding junior college faculties?
13. Which of President Lillard's suggested features to be avoided in choice of junior college instructors would also apply to university instructors?
14. Is it desirable that there should be a larger proportion of men in junior college faculties?
15. When is a Ph.D. desirable for a junior college instructor?
16. Should junior college instructors make use of "readers" for grading written work of their classes?
17. How much research and study should be expected of a junior college teacher?
18. Make a study of teaching load in a group of junior colleges.
19. Make a study of tenure in a group of junior colleges.
20. Make a study of faculty-student ratio in a group of junior colleges.
21. Outline a comprehensive plan for improvement of junior college teachers in service, to be recommended to a Board of Education or a Board of Trustees.
22. Is there any relation between the *age* of junior colleges and the proportion of their faculties holding advanced degrees? Compute the rank correlation coefficient for the two factors in the California district colleges.
23. Is there any relation between the *size* of junior colleges and the proportion of their faculties holding advanced degrees? Compute the rank correlation coefficient for the two factors in the California district colleges.
24. Do you agree with Morris that a high school teacher should spend at least a year in the university before attempting junior college work? Why?

25. Should an applicant with a Ph.D. degree but without teaching experience be given preference over one with only the M.A. but with several years of high school experience, other things being equal?

SUGGESTED READINGS

General

Bush, R. M. "Teacher Load in the Junior College"; in *Bulletin of the Department of Secondary School Principals of the National Education Association*, pp. 253-62. (March, 1930.)
Based upon reports from 87 public junior colleges.

Campbell, L. R. "Teacher Misplacement"; in *School and Society*, vol. 32, pp. 589-90. (November 1, 1930.)

Eells, W. C. "Who Teach Freshmen and Sophomores?"; in *School and Society*, vol. 29, pp. 258. (February 23, 1929.)
Answers the question for Stanford University.

Freed, W. J. *A Study of the Salaries and Teaching Loads in the Denominational Four-Year Colleges and Private Junior Colleges in the United States.* Tacoma, Washington, 1929, 30 pp. (Privately printed.) Summarized in *Journal of Higher Education*, vol. 1, p. 45 (January, 1930), and in *Bulletin of American Association of University Professors*, vol. 25, pp. 520-23 (November, 1920).
A study of conditions in 55 private junior colleges and comparisons with 189 denominational four-year colleges.

*Haggerty, M. E. "Faculty Qualifications for Junior Colleges"; in *North Central Association Quarterly*, vol. 3, pp. 305-09. (December, 1928.)
Detailed tabulation by states as secured from state departments of education.

Koos, L. V. "Junior College Instruction — I. Personnel, Teaching Load, and Remuneration of the Staff"; in *The Junior College*, pp. 189-213, or *The Junior College Movement*, pp. 64-83.

*McKee, W. P. "The Load of the Teacher in the Private School"; in *Proceedings of the American Association of Junior Colleges, Fifth Annual Meeting*, pp. 83-84. Cincinnati, Ohio, 1925.
Considers instructional, administrative, social, and residential duties.

Maxwell, C. R. "Report of Investigation of the Methods by Which Institutions of Higher Learning Adapt Their Work to the Needs of Freshmen"; in *North Central Association Quarterly*, vol. 2, pp. 307-28.
Based on questionnaires to 64 institutions, including some junior colleges.

Pittenger, B. F. "The Need of a Trained Faculty for the Junior College"; in *Texas Outlook*, vol. 12, pp. 15-16, 55, 66. (September, 1928.)
Comparisons of Koos's and Morris's findings with Texas conditions.

Smith, L. W. (chairman). "Current Conditions in Junior College Development"; in *Proceedings of the Tenth Annual Meeting of the American Association of Junior Colleges*, pp. 57-87. Atlantic City, New Jersey, 1929.

Report of research committee, containing considerable data on junior college instructors.

*Stanger, F. M. "Some Questions of Technique in the Work of the Junior College"; in *California Quarterly of Secondary Education*, vol. 5, pp. 171-77. (January, 1930.)

"Is the student to be regarded as an adult or an adolescent? In what sense is his work secondary? Is the junior college teacher primarily a scholar or a pedagogue, or must he be both? Is his technique to be that of the high school or the college, or must he develop a new one?"

*Suzzallo, H. "The Training of Junior College Teachers"; in *Proceedings of the Tenth Annual Meeting of the American Association of Junior Colleges*, pp. 95-105. Atlantic City, New Jersey, 1929.

An excellent general statement of principles by the president of the Carnegie Foundation.

Vande Bogart, G. H. "Professional Preparation of Junior College Teachers"; in *Proceedings of the Ninth Annual Meeting of the American Association of Junior Colleges, Fort Worth, Texas, 1928*, pp. 113-17. Also in *Proceedings of the National Education Association, 1927*, pp. 593-97.

Study of preparation and experience of science teachers in fifty widely scattered institutions.

Whitsitt, E. L. "Salaries and Tenure in Junior Colleges"; in *Proceedings of the Ninth Annual Meeting of the American Association of Junior Colleges, Fort Worth, Texas, 1928*, pp. 89-92.

Based on 111 questionnaires from member colleges of the Association.

Special States

Hughes, R. H. "The Public Junior Colleges in Kansas"; in *School Review*, vol. 38, pp. 450-55. (June, 1930.)

Koos, L. V. *Secondary Education in California: Report of a Preliminary Survey*, pp. 94-105. Sacramento, California, 1929.

Gives considerable recent data on the teaching staff and its preparation.

*Martens, E. H. "Training and Experience of Teachers in the Junior Colleges of California"; in *California Quarterly of Secondary Education*, vol. 4, pp. 51-58. Summarized in *School Review*, vol. 37, pp. 13-14.

A very careful and satisfying statistical study based on questionnaires from 554 instructors in 26 junior colleges.

*Morris, C. S. "The Junior College Faculty"; in Proctor, W. M. (editor), *The Junior College: Its Organization and Administration*, pp. 41-59. Stanford University, 1927. Also in modified form in *California*

Quarterly of Secondary Education, vol. 2, pp. 105-12. (January, 1927.)

An excellent detailed study and discussion of training, qualifications, salary, teaching load, and other features of instructors in California institutions.

Proctor, W. M. "The Junior College in California"; in *School Review*, vol. 31, pp. 363-75. (May, 1923.)

Based on a study of 27 junior colleges in 1921-22.

Reid, J. R. *Texas Municipal Junior Colleges*, pp. 32-47. State Department of Education, Austin, Texas, June, 1929.

Detailed presentation of facts regarding instructors in the public junior colleges of Texas.

CHAPTER XVI

THE PHYSICAL PLANT

> The junior college has grown quite beyond the wildest guesses. It is in its infancy. The future is exceptionally bright. Such an institution is an object of pride for the city. It is an inspiration to every one who sees it.... The college will find it hard to keep its ideals, its program of instruction, its internal scheme of management, and its own social life in line with its growth in numbers. The college should not lay down its brick and mortar too fast. Colleges are not of brick and mortar, but of men and women and ideas. The house is a part of the scheme, however, for it expresses those ideas. — JESSE B. SEARS.[1]

Contents of this chapter. This chapter is devoted to a consideration of grounds, buildings, and equipment for the junior college. Standards advised, extent, and valuation are considered, as far as data permit. While the library might also be included, it is so important that a separate chapter, immediately following, is devoted entirely to it.

Introductory. There have been no comprehensive studies made of the physical plant and equipment of the junior college, nor have any detailed standards been set up except in the case of laboratory equipment. As far as facts are available, they indicate the widest variability from extreme poverty and inadequacy to the most luxurious surroundings and equipment that money can furnish. The latter condition is found in some of the more expensive schools under private management where substantial tuition fees are charged.

In the matter of building and grounds there is little that is different in principle from the needs in the same respect for standard colleges of moderate size. These features will not be discussed here. Reference may be found to them in general treatments of college architecture. In this chapter only

[1] Sears, J. B., *et al.* *Sacramento School Survey*, p. 188.

matters are considered which are unique to the junior college as it exists at the present time.

Existing standards. The accrediting agencies have had very little to say regarding buildings and grounds, and what has been said has been phrased in very general language. Typical of most of them is the statement of the American Council on Education:

> The material equipment and upkeep of a junior college, including its buildings, lands, laboratories, apparatus, and libraries, and their efficient operation in relation to its educational program, should also be considered when judging the institution.

This may mean much, or it may mean little. The University of Illinois in its statement of standards goes a little further, however, and says:

> The segregation of the junior college students is desirable. Separate quarters should be set aside on a distinct floor or in a distinct wing or in a separate building, in which should be housed the study rooms for junior college students, a separate junior college library, and separate junior college laboratories.

Similar recommendations have been made by the University of California.

We shall try, in this chapter, to set up the best existing standards as to plant, based on what has been worked out so far.

GROUNDS

Extent of campus. The grounds of junior colleges vary widely in extent, according to type of college and other considerations. In fourteen municipal junior colleges in Texas, the grounds are reported as varying from 0.5 acre to 17 acres, with an average of 8.5 acres. In many cases they run from 15 to 60 acres; some of the state agricultural and mechanical junior colleges have grounds which exceed 500 acres, if the experimental farm area is included.

Desirable size. It is unfortunate for the efficient junior college to have a campus smaller than twenty acres, and one of forty or fifty acres is preferable to allow for necessary buildings, artistic landscaping, athletic fields, and future growth.[1]

In a crowded city, grounds of this size may be impracticable, but in selecting a new site it will often be preferable to sacrifice proximity of population for adequate space, and choose a location on the outskirts rather than concentrating in a single city block where college life and institutional consciousness will be much harder to develop. A college campus should be a thing of beauty as well as utility. Perhaps nothing is so conducive to the development of a fine college spirit as a beautiful campus and buildings.

Valuation. The American Association of Junior Colleges, in its 1929 *Directory*, gave a property valuation of $132,000,000 for the 285 junior colleges which reported, while in 1930 the corresponding figure for the 323 institutions reporting was $149,000,000. This means little, however, for in many cases the valuation given represents the combined high school and junior college plant. Nor is it possible in many cases to segregate the two.[2] Twenty-seven institutions reported property valuations of $1,000,000 or over, ten of which exceeded $2,000,000

[1] The Division of Schoolhouse Planning of the California State Department of Education says that 30 acres is an absolute minimum for any genuine college, and that 100 to 125 acres is desirable. The minimum area suggested includes:

Stadium	4½ acres
Parking	1½
Two practice fields	6
Auxiliary games	1
Two women's fields	4
Roads and gardens	3
Buildings	10
Total	30

No allowance is made in these estimates for residences, agricultural work, botanical gardens, Greek theater, etc.

[2] In cases in California where the junior college pays rent to the high school district for its portion of the plant, the determination of the proper rent to be charged is a difficult problem, and there is no uniformity in method of determining it.

and two of which exceeded $4,000,000. One of the latter is private and one public. The plant of Crane Junior College in Chicago is valued at $5,000,000, while the highest valuation of all, $6,000,000, is given to the magnificent buildings and grounds of National Park Seminary, Maryland, in the suburbs of the national capital. According to the catalogue: "The estate on which the Seminary is located comprises 300 acres of pleasant slopes and wild ravines, noble forest land and winding paths, running brooks and flowering meadows, combined by nature to make the scenery varied and enchanting. Beautiful, picturesque Rock Creek is the most famous stream near Washington, save the Potomac. Almost a mile of the creek runs through the Seminary grounds, and is being prepared as a delightful canoeing course. Miles of bridle paths are being laid out through the forests on the estate." It has twelve school buildings, including four dormitories, chapel, auditorium, gymnasium, recitation building, science building, and library; eight social club houses; and numerous service buildings, making a total of thirty-two in all. There is doubtless no other school in the country of like valuation devoted largely to the private education of girls on the junior college level. While not exclusively a junior college, over three fourths of its students are reported in the junior college division. Other junior colleges for women with unusually extensive and well-equipped plants are Stephens College, Missouri, and Sarah Lawrence College, New York.

BUILDINGS

Dormitories. Eighteen state and 123 private junior colleges report dormitories for students. Total accommodations for each sex are summarized in Table 41.[1]

Since the total enrollment in private junior colleges is approximately 30,000, it is seen that dormitory facilities are

[1] Data summarized from Hurt's *College Blue Book.*

TABLE 41. DORMITORY ACCOMMODATIONS IN STATE AND PRIVATE JUNIOR COLLEGES

	Number of Colleges Having Dormitories	Total Dormitory Accommodations	Average per College	Maximum
State				
Men	16	1,796	112	225
Women	14	1,272	91	200
Private				
Men	64	5,360	84	350
Women	114	12,336	108	560

provided for considerably more than one half of the students. The public junior college (with the exception of the state type), is essentially a local institution, with the majority of the students living at home; but this is by no means the case for the private junior colleges. The California legislature in 1929 passed a law authorizing district junior colleges to build dormitories, but no institutions have yet done so. In some of the institutions, however, where half or more of the students are from homes out of the district, dormitory facilities would be a valuable addition. Two California junior colleges of the high school type, Kern County and Antelope Valley, share dormitories with high school students. In each case about half the residents are junior college students.

Junior colleges with separate plants. There are no complete data available as to the number of public junior colleges which have plants entirely distinct from other institutions. In California such complete separation exists for six of the sixteen district junior colleges, or seven if Pasadena is included; in Texas for five of the sixteen municipal ones. Certain significant data regarding these two groups are given in Table 42.

A study of this table shows not only wide differences between the two states, but even greater variability between the relatively homogeneous institutions in a single state. The Texas

Table 42. Data on Public Junior Colleges in Texas and California Occupying Plants Entirely Separate from the High School

	California	Texas
Number of institutions	6	5
Number of separate main buildings	4–7	1–2
Number of classrooms per college in use	14–39	......
Average value of grounds	$46,500	$21,500
Range in value of grounds	$19,000–$75,000	$10,000–$34,000
Average value of buildings	$300,000	$192,000
Range in value of buildings	$60,000–$494,000	$10,000–$425,000
Average value of buildings and grounds per student enrolled	$504 *	$1058
Range in value of buildings and grounds per student enrolled	$253–$1442	$338–$5247

* California enrollment estimated by multiplying average daily attendance by 1.37. (See page 508.)

college with the highest per capita valuation is Clarendon, which with only 81 students occupies a plant valued at $425,000. This was not built for its own use, however, but was taken over from a previously existing senior college, so that it is not typical. The next highest Texas figure is $207,000, with a per student valuation of $2435.

Wide variation is shown in the valuations per student in California. The minimum, $253, is found at Marin, a new institution, opened in 1926, and far from adequately supplied, as it is using temporary buildings, in part, until funds will permit of more adequate building without a bond issue. At the other extreme, San Bernardino has bonded itself for a $500,000 plant, somewhat in excess of the needs of the present student body, but with the expectation that it will require additional facilities in a few years. This makes the present per student valuation, the maximum in the state, $1442. Sacramento, with the largest enrollment, which taxes its plant to capacity and demands new buildings in the immediate future, has a per capita valuation of only $335.[1] The Sacramento

[1] The Sears Survey recommended an expenditure of $475,000 (practically the cost of the present buildings) for library and art building, auditorium, and music and drama building. (See Sears, J. B., *et al.*, *Sacramento School Survey*, 577 pp. Sacramento, California, October, 1928.)

plant, with its splendid group of buildings of brick and tile in Florentine Renaissance architecture on a campus of 65 acres, is one of the outstanding junior colleges in California. Its most distinctive feature is the restrained but monumental entrance arch. The complete plan calls for a group of buildings about a great quadrangle.

Pasadena is not included in the summary of California colleges in Table 42, because it is operating on the 6–4–4 basis, and thus is not entirely comparable. It has a site of 40 acres, valued at approximately $1,000,000, and 17 buildings which, with furniture and equipment, are valued at another million, giving the entire plant a valuation of practically $2,000,000. With 2500 students in the upper and lower division of the institution, this makes a per capita valuation of about $800 per student.

In the proposed junior college for Siskiyou County, California, a plant for 250 students was estimated to cost $148,500 exclusive of dormitories. This would be approximately $600 per student. This provided only for minimum essentials — a building with ten classrooms, a library, three laboratories, and a combined gymnasium and auditorium.

Per capita costs would be somewhat decreased with increase in size of school. It is probable, however, that an adequate separate plant cannot be provided for less than $500 per student for grounds, plant, and equipment, and $1000 per student can be spent without extravagance if desirable facilities and equipment are provided for the most efficient type of work. In the Massachusetts survey, Zook estimated a low building cost per student as $500; medium, $750; high, $1000.

Should there be separate plants? Most of the junior colleges in existence at the present time share their buildings and grounds to a greater or less extent with the high school, or an equivalent institution. This is markedly true of the younger and newer public junior colleges, but it is characteristic also of many of the private colleges. In some cases separate floors or wings are assigned to the junior college; in others separate buildings for academic work are provided, but library, laboratory, or athletic facilities are shared with the high school. The varying relationship makes any facts that are secured difficult to interpret fairly in terms of the junior college. In large cities, having more than one high school, the ideal plan would seem to be to have a separate building under an administration of its own. This plan is successfully practiced at Crane (Chicago), Kansas City (Missouri), and several California cities. Even in cities where there is a single high school, the junior college plant is often separate, either on an adjacent campus or on one entirely removed from the high school location, as found in several Texas and California colleges. Many problems of discipline are simplified when separate buildings and grounds are available, and a separate college spirit, traditions, and atmosphere develop more rapidly and substantially. In its inceptive stages, especially where the attendance is small, it may be necessary or expedient to house the junior college in the high-school building, but the tendency is away from this as the institution gathers size and strength of its own. When the number of junior college students exceeds 200 or 300, separate buildings and equipment may well be given serious consideration. With 500 or more it is highly desirable and administratively practical, unless local financial conditions forbid an immediate realization of such an educationally beneficial condition.

An adequate site and buildings. What are the different elements that should be taken into consideration in the selection of a site and the erection of buildings for a junior college with an enrollment of approximately 500 students? At Columbia University a detailed score card for college buildings has been developed through the composite judgment of two hundred college teachers and administrators. This score card,

SCORE CARD FOR COLLEGE BUILDINGS

	Points	Sub-Totals	Totals
I. Site			140
A. *Location*		65	
1. Accessibility	35		
2. Environment	30		
B. *Size and form*		55	
C. *Nature and condition*		20	
1. Landscaping and upkeep	15		
2. Elevation and drainage	5		
II. Buildings			160
A. *Campus plan*		25	
B. *Gross structure*		65	
1. Type and architectural consistency	15		
2. Material	10		
3. Foundations and supporting walls	10		
4. Window placement	10		
5. Condition of upkeep	10		
6. Entrances	5		
7. Roofs	5		
C. *Internal structure*		45	
1. Stairways and stairwells	10		
2. Corridors	5		
3. Modifiability	10		
4. Economy of space	5		
5. Basements	5		
6. Doors	5		
7. Attics	5		
D. *Interior finish and decoration*		25	
1. Floors	5		
2. Walls and ceilings	5		
3. Woodwork	5		
4. Color schemes	5		
5. Condition of upkeep	5		
III. Service Systems			185
A. *Heating and ventilation*		50	
1. Effectiveness	20		
2. Kind and installation	15		
3. Special provisions	15		
B. *Fire protection*		35	
1. Fireproofness	20		
2. Exits and fire escapes	10		
3. Apparatus and special provisions	5		
C. *Water supply system*		25	
1. Adequacy of supply	5		
2. Washing and bathing	10		
3. Drinking facilities	5		
4. Hot water supply	5		
D. *Toilet system*		25	
1. Adequacy	10		
2. Distribution and seclusion	5		
3. Fixtures	5		
4. Sanitation	5		
E. *Artificial lighting*		20	
1. Fixtures and illumination	10		
2. Installation and outlets	5		
3. Kind — gas and electricity	5		
F. *Other service systems*		30	
1. Cleaning	5		
2. Clocks, bells and telephones	5		
3. Locker systems	5		
4. Laundry system	5		
5. Elevators and lifts	5		
6. Sewer and garbage disposal	5		

Score Card (*continued*)

	Points	Sub-Totals	Totals
IV. Instruction Rooms (class and laboratory)			280
A. *Number* (adequacy)		60	
B. *Availability* (accessibility)		30	
C. *Size and shape*		40	
D. *Natural light* (amount and control)		50	
E. *Equipment*		55	
1. Seats, desks, and chairs	20		
2. Instructional — amount and quality	15		
3. Demonstrational — amount and quality	10		
4. Special provisions	10		
F. *Blackboards and other special features*		25	
G. *Teachers' offices and studies*		20	
V. General Units			235
A. *Administration*		45	
1. Adequacy (number and size)	10		
2. Office equipment	10		
3. Special provisions	5		
4. Accessibility	5		
5. Arrangement of rooms	5		
6. Other furnishings	5		
7. Faculty and other rest rooms	5		
B. *Library*		60	
1. Books, references and magazines	25		
2. Reading rooms and seminars	10		
3. Catalogue	10		
4. Stocks	5		
5. Offices	5		
6. Work rooms and equipment	5		
C. *Auditorium and chapel*		25	
1. Adequacy (size)	5		
2. Seating	5		
3. Stage and dressing rooms	5		
4. Attractiveness	5		
5. Special equipment	5		
D. *Health, recreation, and athletics*		55	
1. Gymnasiums	25		
2. Medical offices	10		
3. Game courts and athletic fields	10		
4. Infirmary and isolation unit	5		
5. Swimming pool	5		
E. *Dormitories and social rooms*		50	
1. Adequacy	10		
2. Social and recreational rooms	10		
3. Dining rooms (cafeteria, commons)	10		
4. Kitchens and storerooms	5		
5. Arrangement of rooms	5		
6. Furnishings	5		
7. Offices and special provisions	5		

reproduced on pages 435, 436, was used in the survey of higher education for the United Lutheran Church to score sixteen colleges, including two junior colleges, which ranked eleventh and twelfth in the group.[1]

[1] Leonard, R. J., Evenden, E. S., and O'Rear, F. B. *Survey of Higher Education for the United Lutheran Church in America*, vol. 1, pp. 183–85. Teachers College, New York City, 1929.

LABORATORY EQUIPMENT

Standards. The standardizing agencies have little to say on equipment in general, except that it should be "adequate," nor is it possible, probably, to be more specific under the variety of conditions found in different parts of the country and in all classes of institutions. On the matter of laboratory equipment, however, more definite statements are common. While reference to Figure 17, page 180, will show that some are expressed only in terms of "adequate," "subject to inspection," or "provision for annual income for upkeep," others endeavor to be more specific. The American Association of Junior Colleges specifies a minimum evaluation of $2000 each for physics, chemistry, and biology; other limits suggested vary from $1500 to $3000 per science. These are definite, objective standards, but it may be questioned whether they are satisfactory in form or correct in amount. A physics laboratory can easily have equipment valued at $3000 — largely invested in a few expensive instruments or pieces of apparatus, and not be at all adequate for the course offered. It may, for example, be largely invested in electrical apparatus, with inadequate provision for the study of heat or light. Detailed check lists of the apparatus and materials are needed, with quantities and prices necessary for giving desired college courses in various subjects. There have been a few approximations toward this, but none that are adequate. Adequacy depends upon enrollment, interest in science, number of courses offered, rotation of experiments, and similar factors.

Present conditions. Little information is available as to the actual adequacy of junior college laboratories. The catalogue statements are usually vague or, too often, omitted entirely. Seldom can one secure from the catalogue any knowledge as to the laboratory equipment — in far too many cases it is impossible to discover whether any laboratories are provided — although pages may be spent in detailed accounts of student activities and pictures of athletic teams.

A detailed tabulation has been furnished for the Texas municipal colleges showing value of the science equipment and the number of semester hours offered for each institution in physics, chemistry, biology, zoölogy, botany, and home economics. Maximum, minimum, and average figures are as follows:

	Number of Colleges	Average	Maximum	Minimum
Chemistry	15	$3,647	$10,000	$ 486
Physics	9	4,104	8,297	2,000
Biology	7	3,317	8,360	125
Home Economics	6	2,638	7,000	225
Zoölogy	5	2,990	5,000	1,000
Botany	2	1,500	2,000	1,000

Miss Workman has studied the replacement value of the science equipment in 33 junior colleges of the North Central Association, in comparison with 147 colleges and universities and 49 teachers' colleges. Results are expressed in terms of value per regular student enrolled in the different types of colleges (omitting special, summer, and evening students), as follows:

	Junior Colleges	Colleges and Universities	Teachers' Colleges
Chemistry	$28.03	$25.71	$8.98
Physics	33.35	18.95	7.83
Biology	21.04	21.38	7.70

This table makes an exceedingly favorable showing for the junior colleges, but it may be questioned whether value per enrolled student is an entirely fair unit to use in this case. The large values given for the junior colleges may be due, for the most part, to small enrollments in comparison with the larger colleges with which comparison is made. Much of the equipment will cost the same, whether the enrollment be 200 or 400. Enrollment figures are not given for any of the institutions. A similar computation for the Texas junior colleges gives the following results:

	Number of Colleges	Average Enrollment in Subject	Average Regular Enrollment	Average Value per Regular Student
Chemistry	15	31	157	$23.23
Physics	9	24	173	23.72
Biology	7	39	129	25.71

In a study of thirty junior colleges in the Middle West, Johnson found that:[1]

One junior college was offering chemistry and physics in a $800 laboratory, while another had $14,500 invested in chemistry equipment alone. The median chemistry laboratory layout was appraised at $3400. In physics the range was from $800 to $15,000.

The California district junior colleges reported an average annual expenditure for laboratory supplies for 1928–29, of $4049 per institution, which amounted to a little more than $4 per student enrolled.[2] This annual expenditure was 3.7 per cent of the total current expense budget, as compared with 4.1 per cent for libraries.

Suggestions as to laboratories and equipment. Detailed suggestions as to location, arrangement, use, and upkeep of laboratories are furnished by the University of Missouri in its circular to accredited junior colleges in the state.[3] It includes more or less complete lists of general and individual equipment for courses in art, botany, chemistry, home economics, physical education, physiology, and zoölogy. Although far from

[1] Johnson, E. A. "Some Financial Phases of the Establishment and Support of Thirty Representative Public Junior Colleges in Six Central States of the United States"; in *Bulletin of the School of Education of Indiana University*, vol. 5, pp. 7–13. (July, 1929.)

[2] Enrollment being estimated as 1.37 times the average daily attendance. (See page 508.)

[3] Coursault, J. H. (editor). *Circular of Information to Accredited Junior Colleges.* University of Missouri Bulletin, pp. 46–69. (October 1, 1926.)

complete and satisfactory, it is the most extensive list available, and is suggestive and helpful in many respects.

Costs for chemistry. One of the author's students [1] made a detailed analysis of cost of essential equipment for a junior college chemistry laboratory, including all necessary equipment for the proper teaching of general chemistry, qualitative analysis, and elementary organic chemistry. It was assumed that a main laboratory, at least 23 by 28 feet in size, could be equipped for 24 students working simultaneously. Estimates, based in many cases upon practice at Stanford University for similar courses, were as follows:

Permanent equipment and furniture (includes $1500–$1800 for tables and plumbing)	$6500
Annual expense for chemicals	$500–$800
Costs for individual equipment:	
General chemistry, 24 at $17	408
Qualitative analysis, 24 at $17	408
Organic chemistry, 24 at $40	960
Replacements	450
	$9526

Thus it may be estimated that from $8000 to $9500 would be required to completely furnish and maintain a chemistry laboratory in a junior college for 24 students in each of the three courses mentioned.[2] If quantitative analysis were offered also, approximately $1000 would need to be added for additional balances and weights.

Future needs. There is need for a better determination of minimum essentials in laboratory standards than that furnished by the generalizations of the accrediting agencies. Probably it will have to be secured by careful analysis of actual equipment in junior colleges where efficient work is being done, and by a study of equipment for similar courses in standard colleges and universities, determined by experienced instructors

[1] Wirt, S. K., in an unpublished term paper at Stanford University.

[2] The lower figure would apply if tables and plumbing were not included.

in each science. It will require, also, a differentiation between built-in furniture, plumbing, shelving, etc., as a part of the laboratory, and movable equipment purchased subsequent to building.

QUESTIONS AND PROBLEMS

1. Use the Columbia University score card as given in the text to score the buildings and grounds of a junior college you are familiar with or can visit. (See Leonard, Evenden, O'Rear, in Suggested Readings.)
2. Compare the score card for junior college buildings and grounds, devised by M. E. Hill (given in Proctor, W. M. (editor), *The Junior College: Its Organization and Administration*, pp. 80–81), with the one given in the text.
3. Make a list of the advantages of having junior college buildings and campus entirely separate from the local high school.
4. In what respects would an ideal set of buildings for a junior college differ from those for a four-year college?
5. From a group of junior college catalogues, make a study of the campus and grounds, tabulating as many features as possible.
6. Under what circumstances should dormitories be provided for public junior colleges?
7. In what ways should the standards of accrediting agencies be changed with reference to laboratories? Outline a plan for a more scientific determination of standards.
8. Make a list of equipment for any laboratory science course in a junior college. Assume a definite number of students.
9. Find the per capita cost of laboratory equipment in certain four-year colleges.
10. Compute costs of laboratory equipment per student enrolled, in the Texas municipal junior colleges.
11. How should junior college laboratory facilities differ from those of the high school? From those of the university?
12. Is per capita cost a suitable unit for measuring laboratory equipment?

SUGGESTED READINGS

Coursault, J. H. *Circular of Information to Accredited Junior Colleges.* University of Missouri Bulletin, vol. 27, no. 37. (October 1, 1926.)
Contains suggested lists of apparatus and equipment and suggestions for outfitting laboratories in different sciences.

Kelly, R. L. "Questions and Answers on Practical Problems of College

Architecture"; in *Association of American Colleges Bulletin*, vol. 11, pp. 269-300. (November, 1925.)

Contains thirty answers to practical problems as given by the American Institute of Architects. Suggestions for junior colleges.

Klauder, C. Z., and Wise, H. C. *College Architecture in America*, 301 pp. Charles Scribner's Sons, New York, 1929.

*Leonard, R. J., Evenden, E. S., and O'Rear, F. B. *Survey of Higher Education for the United Lutheran Church in America*, vol. 1, pp. 177-262. Bureau of Publications, Columbia University, New York City, 1929.

Contains score card and detailed survey of buildings and equipment of Lutheran colleges in the country, including junior colleges.

A School for Girls (Catalogue, 1929-30), 133 pp. National Park Seminary, Forest Glen, Maryland.

"Sacramento Junior College, California"; in *Sierra Educational News*, vol. 22, pp. 512-13. (October, 1926.)

Smith, L. W. "Current Conditions in Junior College Developments — Laboratories"; in *Proceedings of the Tenth Annual Meeting of the American Association of Junior Colleges*, pp. 81-82. Atlantic City, 1929.

View Book, 88 pp. National Park Seminary, Forest Glen, Maryland.

View Book of Stephens College, Missouri. Stephens College Bulletin. (September, 1929.)

*Workman, V. O. "Replacement Value of Science Equipment"; in *North Central Association Quarterly*, vol. 4, pp. 349-51. (December, 1929.)

Comparisons of junior colleges, teachers' colleges, and universities and colleges.

CHAPTER XVII
THE LIBRARY

> It is not too much to say that at present the junior college libraries as a group fall far short of efficiency, either in service or in books. This deficiency is one of the most serious counts against the junior college as it now exists. If junior colleges are to be admitted to full academic fellowship, they must look to their libraries at once. — *College and Reference Yearbook*, no. 1.[1]

Contents of this chapter. This chapter discusses the importance of the junior college library; summarizes present standards, as established by the principal accrediting agencies; presents actual practice and conditions in the country, as far as incomplete and inadequate data permit; proposes desirable improvements in standards; and suggests methods for improving the library, particularly in describing book lists that have only recently become available.

Importance of the library. The junior college library has not received the recognition and emphasis that it merits in most of the institutions of the country. Standards have been low, actuality has been lower, facilities have been inadequate, administrators have slighted it when budgets were made, and investigators have usually ignored it in published studies. In the university, with its emphasis on upper-division and graduate specialization, the library is commonly recognized as the "throbbing heart" of the institution, indispensable to intellectual life and growth. In the junior college, in far too many cases, the pulsations have been weaker and the intellectual life has suffered accordingly. It is not necessary to have extensive specialized collections of books in the junior college, which is working essentially in the field of general education, but it is indispensable that an adequate library be available,

[1] Quoted in resolutions of the Junior College Section of American Library Association, 1930; in *Junior College Journal*, vol. 1, p. 47. (October, 1930.)

not only for collateral reading in connection with the courses offered in the institution, but also as a training school for the student who later enters the university.

Transitional function. As a transitional institution from the high school, with its emphasis on textbook treatment, to the university, with its emphasis on library treatment, the junior college needs to give the student the experience gained by thorough familiarity with a library which though small in extent, is organized and administered in accordance with the best-recognized library standards. The importance of the junior college library from this standpoint is well expressed by the librarian of one of them:[1]

I mean no disparagement of the work done in the high school library, but the average student goes from a high school where he studied his texts, took notes from books named and paged by his teachers, both being limited by the time and nature of the school work. In the university he is expected to "develop" a subject from many books, and there he is lost! The junior college library fills the gap between the two: the high school work of gaining facts and the university research which must coördinate facts by an application of the student's own reasoning faculty. In the junior college library, he is inducted gradually into this mental process — the child must walk before he can run. There is, also, a closer relation with the individual in our smaller libraries, by reason of which the librarian can teach him where to look for information; where he can familiarize himself with the standard source and reference books, learning to follow up cross-references; where he can begin research work in a small way.

That this need has not always been successfully met under present conditions is the feeling of a member of the library staff of Mills College, who says:[2]

[1] McClanahan, Mrs. B. B. "What are the Greatest Needs and the Greatest Handicaps to the Average Junior College Library?" in *Libraries*, vol. 31, p. 201. (April, 1926.)

[2] Ludington, F. B. "Standards Reached by the Smaller College Libraries of the Pacific Coast"; in *News Notes of California Libraries*, vol. 23, p. 5. (January, 1928.)

My experience in a California college for six years has been that the junior college student entering into the academic work of the college proper in her junior year works in the library at a decided disadvantage. She is not only handicapped by the fact that she has a strange library to use, but her professors expect her to use reference tools that she has never seen before.

Instructional function. It is not only, or chiefly, in its transitional function, however, that the junior college library is important. Perhaps the greatest reason for the existence of the junior college, as already insisted upon in various connections, is as a *teaching* institution. To do real college teaching, according to present methods, a well-stocked library, closely related to the subjects of instruction, is indispensable. It should be the throbbing heart of the junior college, as well as of the university. The mental and moral vigor of the institution rises or falls with the efficiency of the library. It should contain not only the standard reference books and bibliographical aids, but a careful selection of the most appropriate books to supplement the work of each course offered. Every facility should be offered, in the way of cataloguing, accessibility, a trained and helpful staff, attractive and adequate quarters, and proper instruction and guidance, to make the library constantly and completely useful.

While the library should be the heart of the institution, an examination of the catalogues of junior colleges leaves one in considerable doubt whether it is considered much more than a secondary appendage by a majority of the administrators. For example, a study of the catalogues of forty California junior colleges reveals the fact that only a dozen indicated the existence of a library, and only seven thought it worth while to mention the number of volumes contained therein. One institution states that:

Exceptionally fine library facilities are at the disposal of students in the college. A large number of up-to-date books on all subjects taught, with ample general reference works and periodical literature, may be found.

This is typical of many such statements in other catalogues. One may be pardoned for accepting with some reservations such vague generalities, which may mean much or little — with the probabilities somewhat in favor of the latter alternative.

PRESENT STANDARDS

Standards of the American Council on Education. What are the present minimum standards, as defined by the principal national and local accrediting agencies, for the junior college library? These have been summarized briefly in Figure 17, page 180. As already indicated, the statement of standards of the American Council on Education has been used as the model for many of the other accrediting agencies. In their definition of standard four-year colleges, they state:[1]

> A college should have a live, well-distributed, professionally administered library of at least 8000 volumes, exclusive of public documents, bearing specifically upon the subjects taught and with a definite annual appropriation for the purchase of new books.

This standard is certainly none too high for a junior college library, unless it be in the number of volumes required. Hence it is disappointing to find the American Council, when it establishes junior college standards, dismissing the subject in part of a sentence with the vague phrase:[2]

> ... libraries, and their efficient operation in relation to its educational program, should also be considered when judging the institution.

Other standards. Fortunately, however, many of the regional and state agencies have followed the model indicated

[1] Ratcliffe, E. B. *Accredited Higher Institutions.* United States Bureau of Education, Bulletin no. 10, p. 6. Washington, D.C., 1926.

[2] Ratcliffe, E. B., *loc. cit.*, p. 7.

by the American Council's definition of the four-year college library, rather than their indefinite one for the junior college. Thus the North Central Association says:[1]

> The junior college shall have a live, well distributed and efficiently administered library of at least 3000 volumes, exclusive of public documents, selected with special reference to college work and with a definite annual appropriation for the purchase of current books and periodicals. It is urged that such an appropriation be at least $800.

As indicated in Figure 17 on page 180, other agencies give similar standards involving number of volumes, administration, and annual support, but with varying specific amounts, where given in more than general terms. Thus, the minimum number of books (sometimes "bound volumes") specified varies from 2000 to 5000, and annual appropriations for new purchases from $200 to $800. There is almost complete agreement in emphasizing the fact that the junior college library must be chosen with reference to college work and be adequate for it. This ought to mean that there must be furnished a good supply of books, in addition to the regular high school library.

Improvement in standards. To show the advance in thought regarding standards, during a seven-year period, it is enlightening and encouraging to compare the standards adopted by the American Association of Junior Colleges in March, 1922, with those in its revised statement of standards adopted at Atlantic City in November, 1929. The first statement reads[2]

> There should be at least 2000 volumes selected with special reference to college work. There should be an annual appropriation for each subject taught, and there should be provided a reasonable supply of carefully selected periodicals.

[1] Ratcliffe, E. B., *op. cit.*, p. 25. [2] *Ibid.*, p. 29.

Whereas their revised statement reads: [1]

A working library, adequately catalogued, modern and well distributed, of not fewer than 3500 volumes, exclusive of public documents, with appropriate current periodicals, shall be maintained and there shall be a reading room in connection with the library which is open to the students throughout the day. A trained librarian shall be in charge of the library. A definite annual appropriation for the support of the library shall be provided. It is recommended that this be not less than $500.

This is the most comprehensive statement of any accrediting agency up to 1930, and represents the highest general standard, although the minimum number of volumes specified, 3500, is less than the number prescribed by Utah State Department, or by the Universities of Illinois and Indiana, where 4800 or 5000 are required. [2] It is in marked contrast with the standards adopted by the University of Missouri, where the subject is briefly disposed of in seven words, "There must be an adequate library equipment." [3]

Legal standards. One state, Mississippi, includes library standards as an integral part of the junior college law, which reads: [4]

The library in a junior college attempting to do freshman work shall have not less than one thousand well selected volumes, not including pamphlets or government publications, and if attempting both freshman and sophomore work it shall not have less than one thousand and five hundred volumes.

[1] *Proceedings of the Tenth Annual Meeting of the American Association of Junior Colleges*, p. 156. Atlantic City, New Jersey, 1929.

[2] At the meeting of the American Association of Junior Colleges at Berkeley, California, in November, 1930, the library standards were still further modified, including a provision that "for the smallest junior college there should be a carefully chosen library, adequately catalogued, modern and well distributed with moderate duplication, of not less than 4000 volumes as an initial collection." See *Junior College Journal*, vol. 1, p. 334. (February, 1931.)

[3] Ratcliffe, *op. cit.*, p. 71.

[4] Section 309, paragraph 5.

PRESENT CONDITIONS

Inadequate information available. The status of the junior college library has been all but neglected in the national investigations of the movement. McDowell asked for no data whatever in his various questionnaires. Koos, in his seven-hundred-page Commonwealth Fund investigation, devotes a bare half-page to a report, in general terms, regarding library facilities in thirty-seven junior colleges which he had visited. In comparison with the standards suggested by the accrediting agencies, he reports that: [1]

For 26 public junior colleges visited whose work is accepted by standard higher institutions he [Koos] has notes on 21 which indicate that the library facilities of 8 were only "fair," of 7 were "good," and of 6 were "very good" or "excellent." All but 2 were equipped with card catalogues, and most of them had trained librarians. More commonly the libraries were those maintained also for the high school with which the junior college was associated, although there were several exceptions. Of the libraries of 11 accredited private junior colleges visited, 5 were noted as "poor," one as "fair," and 5 as "good." Nine had card catalogues, although one did not follow a standard classification, while 6 did not have trained librarians.

Whitney, in his later survey of 1929, gives no facts regarding junior college libraries, but contents himself with an analysis of the library standards of the accrediting agencies.

Although no national data have been gathered as to number of volumes, annual purchases, budget, staff, and relationship to high school libraries, some information is available on these points for the junior college libraries in Texas, California, and certain other selected groups of institutions. Unfortunately this is not always in comparable form, but a summary of it will be of value since more comprehensive information is lacking.

Texas. In the sixteen municipal junior colleges of Texas, in 1928–29, trained librarians were employed in all but three of

[1] Koos, L. V. *The Junior College*, pp. 635–36.

the institutions. In only six of them was the junior college library distinct from the high school library. One had a separate library building, valued at $30,000. In most instances, in Texas and elsewhere, the public junior college library has been built upon the high school library with some saving in costs, especially in the use of reference works, biography, and classics. The danger in such a method, however, is in relying too much on books suitable for distinctly high school instruction.

The amount actually spent for the purchase of books during the year, as reported by fourteen of the colleges, varied from $250 to $5152, the latter being for an initial purchase for the new institution at San Angelo. The median figure, which in this case is probably most representative, was $500. Ten of the institutions fell below the $800 recommended by the American Association of Junior Colleges.[1] The size of the Texas junior college libraries varied from 1113 to 4205 volumes, only two falling below the very low standard set by the Association of Texas colleges (2000), but none reaching the more desirable standard of 5000. The average size was 2873 volumes.

Mere number of volumes, of course, is no guarantee that they are up-to-date and well-balanced. No standards for desirable distribution of books by departments have been made, although the studies of Hilton and Miss Stone, to be reported later, are approaches to the problem. The actual distribution of 45,966 books by subject matter, for the sixteen Texas institutions, was as follows:[2]

English	38.9 %	Home Economics	3.0%
History and Social Science	23.8	Art	0.6
Education and Psychology	12.9	Music	0.6
Mathematics	2.0	Commercial	1.2
Natural Science	6.4	Reference	3.5
Latin	0.5	Miscellaneous	1.7
Modern Language	4.9		100.0

[1] *Texas Municipal Junior Colleges.* Bulletin no. 255, pp. 79, 83, State Department of Education, Austin, Texas, June, 1929.

[2] Summarized from Table 2, in *Texas Municipal Junior Colleges*, p. 81.

This seems to be unusually heavily weighted with English and the social sciences.

Private junior colleges for women. In comparison with the relatively new municipal junior colleges of Texas, with average enrollment of 206 and average existence of three and a half years (in 1928–29), may be contrasted the situation in eleven private junior colleges for women, whose library conditions were studied by Miss Stone in 1929.[1] These eleven colleges, widely distributed over the country,[2] had an average existence of over thirty-four years (not necessarily as junior colleges, in the present meaning of the term, but since their organization as institutions), and an average enrollment of 293 students. Thus they have had a much longer time in which to accumulate a stock of books than the younger public institutions. While the number of volumes is much larger, some of them are probably obsolete or are becoming so.

Miss Stone found that the libraries of these institutions varied in size from 3566 volumes at Averett to 11,181 in the oldest one, Bradford. The average number of volumes per student enrolled varied from 13 to 65. For the entire group of colleges it was 23 per student.[3] The average annual budget for books and periodicals varied from $200 to $2000, with an average of $923, somewhat above the highest minimum recommended by the accrediting agencies, $800. Only five of the eleven, however, exceeded this figure. When reduced to

[1] Stone, Ermine. *A Book Collection in the 300's for a Junior College Library.* Unpublished master's thesis at Columbia University, 1929. 131 + 47 pp.

[2] Averett College, Danville, Virginia; Bradford Academy and Junior College, Bradford, Massachusetts; Frances Shimer School, Mt. Carroll, Illinois; Howe-Marot School, Thompson, Connecticut; Mt. Vernon Seminary, Washington, D.C.; St. Mary's College, Dallas, Texas; Sarah Lawrence College, Bronxville, New York; Stephens College, Columbia, Missouri; Sullins College, Bristol, Virginia; Ward-Belmont School, Nashville, Tennessee; and Westmoorland College, San Antonio, Texas.

[3] Stone, Ermine, *op. cit.*, p. xxxvi.

terms of book budget per student, the amount varied from \$1.25 to \$12.50, with a median of \$2.66. Only three had budgets in excess of \$5 per student.[1]

Miss Stone made no classification by subject matter of the total books in the libraries, but she did classify those in the "300" group. She found that the 300's constituted 4.7 per cent of the total number of volumes in all eleven libraries, varying from 2.4 per cent to 8.8 per cent in the different institutions. In each case the proportion was far less than in the Texas libraries reported above. The number found, including duplicates, in the different groups, was as follows:

Group	Subject	Number of Volumes
300–309	Sociology	344
310–329	Political Science, Statistics	345
330–339	Political Economy	695
340–359	Law, Administration	338
360–369	Associations, Institutions	115
370–379	Education	1227
380–389	Commerce	41
390–399	Customs, Popular Life	280
Total		3385

A total of 566 titles were duplicated in two or more libraries, leaving 2318 different titles found in the fields studied. Only 60 titles were common to five or more of the libraries. Not a single volume was found in all of the eleven, the best record being made by Bryce's *American Commonwealth*, which was common to ten.[2]

After a consideration of various elements of the problem, Miss Stone suggests the following tentative distribution for a working junior college library of 8000 volumes (the minimum number recommended by the American Council on Education for a four-year college library):[3]

[1] Stone, Ermine, *op. cit.*, p. xxxviii.

[2] *Ibid.*, pp. xl–xliii.

[3] *Ibid.*, p. xliv.

	Class	Number	Per cent
General works	000	800	10
Philosophy	100	600	7½
Religion	200	200	2½
Sociology	300	800	10
Philology	400	160	2
Science	500	800	10
Useful Arts	600	320	4
Fine Arts	700	480	6
Literature	800	2240	28
History	900	1600	20
		8000	100

California. Miss Ludington, of the Mills College library, in 1927 studied the libraries in twenty-two California junior colleges (names not given). Seven were found that operated their libraries exclusively for their own students; twelve operated with the high school library, only one of which made special provision for junior college students; one operated with a public library. The junior colleges with separate libraries reported an initial stock of ten books per student, and accessions of 2.6 books per student during the previous year. This data is directly comparable with similar facts which Miss Ludington secured from twenty-three small college libraries in the Western States, in institutions having less than 2000 students. These reported average accessions of 3.2 volumes per student. The ten institutions with less than 500 students reported 3.4 per student. With the much newer junior colleges it is evident that the rate of accession should be more rapid until an adequate library can be built up.

In the group of junior colleges the annual book budget was $8.96 per student or $145 per instructor. In ten standard colleges with less than 500 students it varied from $1 to $16.03 per student, averaging $6.66 per student, and $69.99 per instructor. For a group of fourteen New England college libraries the corresponding figure per student was $9.39.[1]

[1] Ludington, Flora B. "Standards Reached by the Smaller College Libraries

Certain facts have been gleaned from the reports of the California State Library Department regarding the libraries in the seven district junior colleges in the state which are operated independently of high school connections. They are summarized in Table 43.

TABLE 43. LIBRARY STATISTICS FOR SEVEN DISTRICT JUNIOR COLLEGES IN CALIFORNIA NOT CONNECTED WITH HIGH SCHOOLS (1928-29)[1]

Name	Number of Volumes	Magazines Regularly Received	News-papers Regularly Received	Staff
Marin	1,681	9	..	1
Modesto	3,700	52	..	1
Pasadena (6-4-4)	21,517	144	4	4
Riverside	4,050	100	5	2
Sacramento	8,800	54	1	3
San Bernardino	4,375	84	4	2
San Mateo	4,994	67	11	3

Unit costs. According to unpublished data from the California State Department of Education, the average value of library books in sixteen California district junior colleges,[2] in 1928-29, was $9363, ranging from $940 in the newly organized Yuba County Junior College, to $25,000 in the largest of the group, Sacramento Junior College. In these institutions there was reported for the same year an enrollment of regular and special part-time students of 11,716, and an average daily attendance of 7218. It may be estimated for computational purposes that this is equivalent to an enrollment of 9889 regular full-time students.[3] Using this figure as a divisor, the

of the Pacific Coast"; in *News Notes of California Libraries*, vol. 23, pp. 4-6 (January, 1928). Reference for New England data to information by Lewis in *Library Journal*, vol. 51, p. 576. (June 15, 1926.)

[1] Compiled from "California Libraries — Annual Statistics"; in *News Notes of California Libraries*, vol. 24, pp. 302-475. (October, 1929.)

[2] Probably some overlapping with high school libraries is involved in some of the institutions.

[3] See Chapter XIX, page 508, for B. M. Woods's multiplier of 1.37 to justify this equivalence.

average value of books per student is $15.15. Total library expenditures in the sixteen colleges were $72,342, or $7.32 per student. Henry finds that thirty-one college and university libraries varied in annual budget from $69 per student at Princeton to $8.20 at Purdue. The mean for the entire group was $24.90.[1] Of course it is not to be expected that junior college library expense need be nearly as great as in the university, but it is doubtful whether $7.32 per student is sufficient, especially when in most of the institutions the library must be built up almost from the beginning. Four Southern California colleges, Occidental, Pomona, Redlands, and Whittier, in 1925–26 showed an average expenditure per student of $6.75 for books and $11.60 for administration.[2] Comparison may also be made with Jacobsen's finding of $12 per capita as the average for 35 small Mid-Western colleges, and $18.44 for twenty listed in the library survey,[3] with Lewis's of $23.69 per student as the average in fourteen New England colleges in 1926,[4] and with Patton's ideal figure of $25 per student for total library expense.[5]

Percentage of total college budget. The group of California district junior colleges, in 1928–29, devoted 4.1 per cent of their current expense budget to the library. There was a range from 2.2 per cent at Pasadena to 8.1 per cent at San Bernardino. San Bernardino had extra expense due to the fact that in 1928 they had just opened their new library built at a cost of over $50,000 — one of the outstanding junior college library build-

[1] Henry, E. A. "College Library Expenditures"; in *School and Society*, vol. 29, pp. 746–47. (June 8, 1929.)

[2] "College Library Expenditures"; in *Libraries*, vol. 33, p. 156. (March, 1928.)

[3] Jacobsen, K. T. "Mid-West College Library Budgets"; in *Library Journal*, vol. 53, p. 263. (March 15, 1928.)

[4] "New England College Libraries"; in *Library Journal*, vol. 51, p. 576. (June 15, 1926.)

[5] Patton, W. M. "The College Library Budget"; in *Libraries*, vol. 31, pp. 151–55. (March, 1926.)

ings of the country. In the group of Mid-Western standard colleges the library expense varied from 1.2 per cent to 8.2 per cent of the entire budget.[1] Four per cent was tentatively recommended as a minimum for this purpose. In a paper before the American Association of Junior Colleges, in 1929, Miss Lucy Fay, associate professor in the library school of Columbia University, recommended the following minimum annual budget for the library of a junior college with annual income of $125,000:

	Amount	Per cent of Total
Librarian (A.B. and one year technical training in accredited library school)	$2000	40
Junior assistant (Summer course at library school, 9 months)	900	18
One student assistant selected by librarian	100	2
Books	1250	25
Periodicals	250	5
Binding	250	5
Supplies and printing	150	3
New equipment and emergency fund	100	2
	$5000	100

Comparisons of holdings and budgets. The most significant comparative facts regarding both junior college libraries and those of standard colleges are summarized in Table 44. The averages there given are taken, for the most part, from data given in the preceding paragraphs, or from computations based upon them. Since these represent many different investigators and methods, it is certain that they are not strictly comparable. The definitions of "student" and of "volume" are varied; methods of accounting are far from uniform. An effort has been made to make such selections that results may be fairly comparable. They are only offered because better data, uniformly gathered and treated, are not available.

[1] Jacobsen, K. T., *loc. cit.*

TABLE 44. COMPARISONS OF AVERAGES OF VARIOUS LIBRARY DATA FOR SELECTED GROUPS OF JUNIOR COLLEGES AND OF STANDARD COLLEGES

	Number of Colleges	Total Volumes	Volumes per Student	Accessions per Student	Annual Book Budget	Book Budget per Student	Total Library Budget per Student	Per cent of Total College Budget
Junior colleges								
Texas public (State report)	16	2,873	13.9	..	$500 *	$2.42	..	..
Women's private (Stone)	11	6,653	23	..	923	2.66	..	..
California, varied (Ludington)	22	..	12.6	2.6	..	..	..	..
California, district (State report)	16	..	..	..	..	..	$7.32	4.1
California, independent of high school library (State library and state department)	7	7,017	9.3	..	..	..	9.08	5.1
Phœnix, Arizona (Annual report)	1	..	..	..	..	7.71	13.71	7.3
Recommended, 300 students (West)	..	18,000	60	..	..	10.00	..	..
Standard colleges								
Small Western (Ludington)	23	..	..	3.2	..	8.96	..	..
Small Western, under 500 (Ludington)	10	..	..	3.4	..	6.66	..	..
Southern California (*Libraries*, vol. 33, p. 156)	4	..	..	..	..	6.75	18.35	..
New England (Lewis)	14	..	..	..	..	9.39	23.69	..
Small Mid-Western (Jacobsen)	35	..	..	..	..	12.00	26.34	4.0
Large colleges and universities (Henry)	31	..	..	..	..	..	24.90	..
Minnesota colleges	6	..	115	..	..	..	..	..
Recommended (Patton)	..	..	..	..	..	..	25.00	..

* Median

Outstanding junior college libraries. While many junior college catalogues ignore their libraries entirely, or mention them in the most casual or indefinite manner, a few have such outstanding collections or unique features that they are given considerable prominence. Two of these, of special interest, may be mentioned.

National Park Seminary (Maryland) has, in addition to a well-selected general library, a special library of 20,000 volumes, most of which are either first or autographed editions, editions *de luxe*, antiques, finely bound or literary curiosities. A separate building houses this special collection. It is rare that any school has such an opportunity to create in its students a love for books, apart from their literary content, an appreciation of the beautiful and artistic in bookmaking, an interest in book lore, and a habit of fellowship with genuine literary treasures.

Chaffey Junior College (California) has a library of 23,000 volumes, which includes a special collection of 7000 volumes on agriculture, a field in which the institution specializes. This library has a special income from the Chaffey Endowment Fund, established through the generosity of two public-spirited men of the community, an unusual feature for a public junior college library. It has assets, including endowment, of $140,000, and is thus assured of constant growth.

Duplicate volumes for class use. Only two of the junior college libraries studied by Miss Ludington kept open in the evening, and one of these was open only one evening a week.[1] She suggests that this fact will necessitate a relatively larger number of duplicates for circulation and reserve than would be the case in institutions where the libraries are open in the

[1] Even this is a marked advance over the conditions in standard colleges in the middle of the last century. Thus the Williams College Catalogue of 1849–50 states that "The college library is open to the senior and junior classes the first Friday of the term and every Wednesday, to the sophomore and freshman classes every Saturday."

evenings.[1] A common university standard for books frequently used for supplementary work is one copy for each ten members of a class.

Whether a large number of different books is needed, or many duplicates of a smaller number, is a question discussed by President Evans of Ripon College, who says:[2]

> In my own classes of undergraduates, in the interests of efficiency which my experience has very well proven, I do not wish my students grazing in wide pastures of the vast library. I prefer to put on the reserve shelf ten or fifteen books, with duplicates, which are very expressly the effective library for the purpose of my class at that time. I can do little with pupils in the stupor of bibliographical dyspepsia.... The professor must often create the thirst and lead the student to the book trough.

This condition may be true to a limited extent in some cases, but it causes at least one experienced librarian to wonder whether it is not better for the student to be subjected to a slight attack of bibliographical indigestion in his junior college years, in order to establish an immunity against death by bibliographical asphyxiation in his later university career when he is required to do really independent library work.[3] There is little or no danger, however, of bibliographical dyspepsia for the average junior college student in most of the libraries found at present. While many of them may be technically up to the standards set forth in the first of this chapter, many others are not, and, even where they are, there can be little doubt that these standards as established by the accrediting organizations are far lower than they should be.[4] We turn, then, to a consideration of desirable standards.

[1] Ludington, F. B., *op. cit.*, pp. 5–6.

[2] Evans, S. *The Contribution of the Library to Effective Teaching.* Association of American Colleges Bulletin, vol. 13, pp. 110–11. (April, 1927.)

[3] Ludington, F. B., *op. cit.*, p. 6.

[4] One librarian, after a study of conditions in fifty-three junior colleges, reached the conclusion that "junior college library conditions, on the whole,

DESIRABLE STANDARDS

Need for adequate standards. Standards should be made with great care, and after considerable research by those who are experts in the field. Such studies have not yet been more than begun in the junior college field. The best that has been done, at the present time, has been an effort to adapt standards that have been accepted as moderately satisfactory as the result of the experience of librarians in other fields. Standards should not represent such a high ideal that few if any institutions can reach it, nor so low an ideal that an institution is likely to be lulled into a sense of unjustified satisfaction with low hurdles too easily cleared. The latter is unquestionably the case with most of the standards now in existence, as reported in the earlier part of this chapter. Even if they be retained as *minimum* standards, it cannot be too strongly emphasized that they are not at all *satisfactory* standards for a progressive junior college, but only represent the barest essentials.

Especially in the case of new libraries — and most of those, particularly in the public junior colleges are very new — there are many qualifications which need to be kept in mind to avoid a sense of false security. These are well stated by Miss Ludington, who says:[1]

The measuring stick must not be an arbitrary thing but should provide for the "ifs": if the library is well established, if the books are plentiful, up-to-date, well-selected, if the building permits economical supervision, if the catalogue is well made and not in need of revision, if the student enrollment and faculty members are fairly uniform from year to year, if the curriculum is not subject to radical changes, if you do not have to provide research materials in

do not compare favorably with the standards recommended by the American Library Association for high schools." (Memmler, Gertrude. "Junior College Library Service"; in *California Quarterly of Secondary Education*, vol. 5, p. 361, June, 1930.)

[1] Ludington, F. B., *op. cit.*, p. 6.

new fields, then and only then are standards justly applicable and truly measuring sticks. In practical library administration, as in most fields, standards set are guide posts, not paths to be literally followed.

American Library Association standards. A special round table conference of junior and senior college librarians at the annual meeting of the American Library Association in Los Angeles, in June, 1930, devoted most of their time to a long and thoughtful discussion of standards. They finally agreed that in establishing standards for junior college libraries the following minimum requirements should be recommended:

Be it resolved that it is the consensus of the Junior College Round Table of the American Library Association in conference assembled, June, 1930, that, in establishing standards for junior college libraries, the following minimum requirements be recommended:

I. Book stock:

1. For libraries of 500 students or less, it is recommended that the initial book stock for any junior college, no matter how small, be not less than 5000 well-selected volumes, with moderate duplication, these to be acquired before opening if possible, or certainly within three years. It is recommended that the basic book collection for this group be at least 10,000 volumes to be acquired as quickly as possible.

2. For libraries of 500 to 1000 students, it is recommended that the initial book stock be 6000 well-selected volumes, with moderate duplication, these to be acquired before opening if possible, or within two years. The basic book collection for this group should not be less than 15,000 volumes.

3. For libraries of more than 1000 students, it is recommended that the initial book stock be 7000 well-selected volumes with moderate duplication, these to be acquired before opening if possible, or within one year. The basic book collection for this group should not be less than 20,000 volumes.

II. Book budgets:

1. For the library of 500 students or less, there should be at the disposal of the librarian for the first three years while the initial book

stock is being purchased (over and above maintenance) $6500 per year for books and periodicals. After the initial stock is obtained, the budget for books and periodicals should not be less than $1500 per year.

2. For the library of 500 to 1000 students, there should be at the disposal of the librarian for the first two years while the initial book stock is being purchased (over and above maintenance) not less than $10,000 per year for books and periodicals. After this is obtained, the annual appropriation for books and periodicals should not be less than $2500.

3. For the library of more than 1000 students, there should be at the disposal of the librarian for the first year while the initial book stock is being purchased (over and above maintenance) not less than $25,000. The annual appropriation for books and periodicals, thereafter, should not be less than $5 per pupil.

III. Personnel:

1. For the library of 500 students or less, it is recommended that there should be two professional librarians, supplemented by student help and clerical assistance.

2. For the library of 500 to 1000 students, it is recommended that there should be a librarian and three professional assistants (a cataloguer, a reference librarian, and a loan desk assistant), to be supplemented by student help and clerical assistance.

3. For the library of more than 1000 students, it is recommended that there should be the same staff as for group 2, with an additional professional librarian for each additional 500 students.

In every case the person designated as head librarian shall be equal in rank with the full professor and department head; the professional staff with the grade just below the department head, or at least with the grade of instructor.

Miss West's proposals. Since the library needs of the junior college may be considered, in a general way, somewhat comparable with those of two-year normal schools, standards worked out for such institutions by W. H. Kerr, and adopted by the American Library Association and the National Education Association, were taken as the starting-point by Miss West, of Texas, in formulating a set of desirable standards.

Suggestions made by Miss Skinner of Pasadena, California, have been incorporated in them. Miss West's standards are not meant as minimum essentials, but as fair working standards for a moderately adequate library for a junior college enrolling three hundred students. They were published prior to the meeting of the American Library Association just mentioned. They are more comprehensive, covering rooms, equipment, and salaries, as well as book stock, funds, and personnel. For example, her standards for rooms and book stock are as follows: [1]

Rooms. Five rooms are desirable for a college enrolling 300 students: Reading and periodical, 1875 square feet capable of seating 75 persons; a reference room, 500 square feet, to seat 20 persons; library classroom, 600 square feet, 50 seats; cataloguing and workroom, 225 square feet; librarian's office, 180 square feet. For each additional 300 students there should be added 1250 square feet of reading room space, 500 square feet of reference room space, and 200 square feet of workroom space. There should be storage space, preferably in a closet opening out of the workroom, large enough to store a year's stock of stationery and supplies. The workroom should be planned as carefully and equipped as efficiently as the means at hand will allow, so that the work of preparing material for the shelves may progress in an orderly and expeditious fashion. A small kitchen sink, with running water — if there is a hot water supply, so much the better — is an essential part of the workroom equipment; electric service outlets are also needed. If it is at all possible, the work will be greatly helped by having a staff room with lockers and toilet, easy of access to the desk, office and workroom. In a really live institution there is no harder working group than the library staff; none who find it more advantageous to have facilities for health and comfort close at hand.

Book stock. Eighteen thousand volumes, distributed thus: For general circulation and required reading, 15,000; for special reference, 3000, including bound periodicals; for each additional 300 students, 5000 volumes in the general group and 1000 reference books should be added.

[1] West, Elizabeth H. "Suggestions for Texas Junior College Libraries"; in *Texas Outlook*, vol. 13, p. 38. (June, 1929.)

If these standards are at all valid, then a large majority of the junior college libraries are not really adequate to real college needs at the present time. Many four-year colleges could not measure up to them either, but that does not excuse the junior college. As to book stock, so much depends upon the courses offered that one cannot lay down hard and fast rules regarding number of volumes per student. Intrinsic value and suitability to courses are most important, with ample reference material for broad, vital, and thorough work. The number suggested is not likely to be over-large. Miss Stone, after experience in the Bradford Junior College library, says:[1]

Speaking from my own experience in the largest collection of the eleven, I will say that we found 11,000 entirely inadequate for our purposes. This library was fortunately located so that extensive loan collections were available. Of the student body of 175 only 100 were in the junior college. I have the gravest doubts of doing effective work with any less. In fact, I rather approve of the 18,000 advocated by Miss West as her minimum for a junior college library of 300 students.

The American Library Association Committee on Library Revenue, in its *Report* for 1923, stipulated a minimum book expenditure of $5 per student for the small college of 500–1500 students, with the added statement that "no college should be considered worthy of the name that expends less than $2000 per year for . . . reading matter . . . regardless of the number of students." The American Library Association standard adopted in 1928 stipulates $10 per student for reading matter, and $15 per student to make it available, as a reasonable yearly expenditure for a four-year college.

Nor are the personnel standards too high for real college work. High demands should be made of the librarian in re-

[1] Stone, *op. cit.*, p. xliv.

spect to personality and academic and professional training. Miss West characterizes him thus:[1]

The librarian ought to be certainly no less scholarly, no less alert than the most scholarly, the most alert, the most serviceable of the teaching faculty. He should be alive to the finger tips, perennially young in mind and spirit, forever growing; catholic in tastes and interests; full of the spirit of service; a tireless worker; an executive; a diplomat; endowed with a feeling for the ordered beauty of life. He should not be so tied down by routine duties that he is unable to work at the larger aspects of his task — such, for instance, as conferring with faculty members in regard to their work and the best schemes of library coöperation; studying out ways and means for building up the collections, enriching the college life through the library.... If the librarian does for a college what a good librarian is capable of doing, he will be at least as useful to the college as any other faculty member; his rank, his salary, his opportunity for growth, should be in proportion.

METHODS OF IMPROVEMENT — BOOK LISTS

Financial. The most important method of improvement, in most junior colleges, is to secure additional revenue to bring the library approximately up to the standards outlined in the last section. Few boards, trustees, legislators, or even presidents or deans are fully conscious of the importance of the library as the "central dynamo" of the junior college. From five to ten per cent of the annual budget is none too much to put into the junior college library, especially when it is in the formative stage and needs to be rapidly built up to full working efficiency. E. C. Hills of the University of California, when university examiner for junior colleges in the state, said:[2]

I might say, as I moved about the state, I received the impression that some junior colleges were neglecting their libraries while doing

[1] West, E. H. "Suggestions for Texas Junior College Libraries, II"; in *Texas Outlook*, vol. 13, p. 51. (July, 1929.)

[2] Hills, E. C. "Relation of the Junior College to the Upper Division of the University"; in *California Quarterly of Secondary Education*, vol. 2, pp. 101–05. (January, 1927.)

full justice to their scientific laboratories. In such subjects as English, history, foreign languages, etc., the library occupies virtually the position that the laboratories hold in chemistry and physics. And we should all bravely face the fact that in the long run a satisfactory library will cost as much as do the scientific laboratories.

Book lists. Even with funds provided, however, the problem of desirable books to order is a critical one, especially when many of the libraries are administered by librarians not fully trained and with little or no experience in ordering. There has been nothing reliable and comprehensive in the junior college field to guide new institutions in their initial library set-up. Nor are the instructors always well prepared to suggest the most valuable books when only a limited appropriation is available. It is questionable whether all can come up to the standard reported by the president of Sullins College (Virginia):[1]

> This is our record thus far: every book that every teacher has ever requested, she has always gotten, and in some way we have been able to pay for them.

It may be doubted whether such a bibliographical millennium would be either feasible or desirable in many institutions.

Standard lists of books and other aids, specifically suggested to fit junior college courses and conditions, similar to those now used in other fields, are urgently needed. A few such lists, not scientifically selected, however, have been available in the past. Much better ones have been made in the past year or two. These are briefly characterized in the paragraphs that follow:

The Missouri list. In its *Circular of Information to Accredited Junior Colleges*, published in 1926, the University of Missouri gives a list of over two thousand titles, for twenty-three subjects for which curricula outlines are given in the

[1] Martin, W. E. *Proceedings of the Fifth Annual Meeting of the American Association of Junior Colleges*, p. 20. Cincinnati, Ohio, 1925.

same bulletin. The circular states, however, that these are not intended to indicate a well-proportioned library, but are reference lists for the courses outlined in the bulletin.

The list was first published in the 1918 *Bulletin*, and was not adequately revised in the 1926 edition, therefore it is not of great value at the present time. At the time the library was being ordered for the new Sarah Lawrence College, this list was considered so inadequate that no use was made of it.[1]

Gibson, in an unpublished master's thesis at the University of Iowa (1928), furnished a list of fifty books in each of ten courses usually taught in first-year public junior colleges, as selected by professors teaching the branches covered in 77 colleges and 45 junior colleges in the middle west.[2] The books are given in order of desirability for each course. The courses covered are American history, chemistry, economics, English, European history, French, mathematics, psychology, and speech.

Hilton's extensive list. The most extensive and scientific list yet made is one prepared by Hilton, as his doctor's dissertation at the University of California in 1929. His study developed lists of books for supplementary work in thirty-two basic junior college courses. It contains a total of 4676 titles, which are ranked according to subjects by the pooled judgments of 1193 instructors in twelve universities and fifty junior colleges, each judging in his own teaching field. The number of judgments obtained for each course ranged from sixteen to

[1] Stone, Ermine, *op. cit.*, p. xxii. Early mimeographed lists issued by the University of California are not mentioned or described in this book, since they are no longer obtainable and have not been revised. They have been superseded, essentially, by Hilton's study.

[2] Gibson's reasons for limiting his lists to 50 books are interesting but hardly conclusive: "The reason for limiting the lists recommended to 50 each is that very few of the public junior colleges... could possibly afford to purchase more than this number. Second, it is doubtful whether for the first few years the average junior college would have occasion to need more than this number in any one subject." (Gibson, W. W. *Selection of Basic Library Books for Certain Courses in Junior Colleges*, p. 19. Iowa City, Iowa, 1928.)

seventy-seven, with an average of thirty-seven per course. The combined bibliographies for each course represent from four to seven reliable sources, including two leading American universities and eighty-six American publishers. The relative value of each book for use in a particular course is indicated and a statistically calculated numerical value is determined. Author, title, date, price, and publisher are given. This list has been published in abbreviated form (upper 50 per cent of the titles in each list only) by the University of California.

American Library Association list. Another important and comprehensive list has been prepared under the direction of Miss Hester, librarian of Pomona Junior College (California), which will be given prestige and a semi-official standing when published by the American Library Association. It contains approximately 3000 titles, carefully proportioned to cover the entire field. Selection of titles has been made largely through the coöperation of different colleges and universities. Books are listed as "indispensables," "second purchases," and "books of especial value to teachers and advanced students." This and Hilton's study should make two very excellent basic lists for junior college libraries, for use in the next few years.

Other lists. Two other lists, covering limited portions of the field, should also be mentioned. A group of professors at the University of California, representing the library committee of the Mathematical Association of America, published, in 1925, a list of 149 mathematical books recommended for junior college libraries.

Miss Stone, in her master's thesis at Columbia University, 1929, prepared a carefully annotated list, with bibliographical details, of books for the "300's" of the Dewey Decimal Classification, covering the fields of social science, economics, and education. Her selection was based upon the actual holdings of the eleven private junior colleges for women, already mentioned, but is not limited to these. It contains 800 numbered titles, with supplementary titles in the notes bringing the total up to almost 1200. No books are included which are out of print. It is not available in published form, but both it and the Gibson thesis can be secured through inter-library loans.

QUESTIONS AND PROBLEMS

1. What are some of the reasons why number of volumes is not a fair basis for judging the efficiency of a library?
2. How many duplicates of a book are needed for constant reference in a course of 20, 50, 100 students? (*a*) If the library is open evenings? (*b*) If the library is not open evenings? (See Hicks, F. C. "Library Problems in American Universities"; in *Educational Record*, vol. 49, pp. 331-32; 1915.)
3. Are there any general methods for determining the desirable ratio in size between a junior college library and one for a four-year college? Consider number of students, number of courses offered, types of courses offered, number of years, and other factors.
4. Compute and study the variation of per capita costs for libraries in a group of junior colleges in any state, or other group for which data are available. Compare with costs in four-year colleges and universities.
5. List, and arrange in order of merit, methods of compiling book lists for junior college libraries mentioned in this chapter, and others that you can devise.
6. Measure the library of any selected junior college by the standards suggested by the American Library Association in this chapter.
7. Investigate relation of age of institutions, junior college or other, to size of library.
8. A new junior college is to be started with prospects for 150 students the first year, and 250 the second. What initial library appropriation will you recommend?
9. Frequent statements in standards are requirements that the books shall be "live," "well-distributed," and must "bear specifically on the subjects taught." As a junior college inspector, devise some means of judging how successfully these standards are met.
10. Should junior college students be assigned to the library during free periods?
11. Make a list of periodicals, 25 "indispensable" and 25 "desirable," for a junior college library.
12. What should be the relation of the periodical budget to the book budget?
13. What is the average number of periodicals per student in a selected group of libraries? Consult library reports.

14. What proportion does and should the seating capacity of a library bear to entire student body in colleges?
15. What are the signs of an efficient library in a junior college? (See Robertson, D. A. "The College Library"; in *Educational Record*, vol. 10, pp. 3-28; January, 1929.)
16. A library authority states: "Some librarians who have given much thought to this problem have as a result of years of observation reached the decision that a relatively small number of books will meet practically all the needs of an undergraduate college. They place the number at 75,000 to 100,000 for a student body of not more than 2500." (Dr. G. A. Works, in *College and University Library Problems*, p. 12; 1927.) Discuss the relation of this standard to that for a *two-year* junior college of 300 or 500 students.
17. Prepare a list of thirty to fifty desirable books for a special junior college course such as aviation, civil engineering, nursing, etc.
18. What constitutes a well-balanced college library? Look up recommended proportions of books in each of the Decimal Classifications, and see how well these are fitted to junior college purposes.
19. Devise a questionnaire suitable for making a national or regional survey of junior college libraries and library conditions.
20. Should a separate junior college library fee be charged?
21. The North Central Association recommends that colleges make a "definite annual appropriation for new books and current periodicals, of at least $5 per student." Is the same standard applicable to junior colleges? Is amount per student a proper criterion for comparison of junior college libraries in book and salary budgets? If not, what is, and why?
22. How much overlapping of high school and junior college libraries is possible? How much is desirable?
23. Investigate the ratio of library valuation and annual expenditures to similar figures for science laboratories in a group of junior colleges; in a group of four-year colleges.
24. Check the actual holdings in some junior college library with the Hilton list or the American Library Association (Hester) list.
25. Compare the Hilton and American Library Association lists.
26. Exhibit in tabular form the recommendations of the Junior College Section of the American Library Association.
27. President Wilbur, of Stanford University, says: "The facilities required for the junior college are practically those of a good high school, with some extension of libraries and laboratory equipment, and with a better trained teaching staff." (Proctor, W. M. *The Junior College: Its Organization and Administration*, p. x.) A librarian comments on this statement: "I am not ready to admit that the first two college years demand only a slight expansion of

library equipment. In these two years the student learns how to study and how to use the library; he should have a generous book supply, ample reference books, and an extensive periodical collection to experiment with." (Ludington; see Suggested Readings.) Which is right? Why?

SUGGESTED READINGS

General

*Coulter, Edith M. "The Functions of the Junior College Library"; in *Junior College Journal*, vol. 1, pp. 481-86. (May, 1931.)

*Fay, L. E. "The Library in the Junior College"; in *Proceedings of the Tenth Annual Meeting of the American Association of Junior Colleges*, pp. 118-24. Atlantic City, 1929.
Excellent discussion of functions of the library, book collections, library staff, budget, buildings, and equipment.

Henry, E. A. "College Library Expenditures"; in *School and Society*, vol. 29, pp. 746-47. (June 8, 1929.)
In 31 large college and university libraries.

*Hilton, E. "Book Selection in Junior Colleges"; in *California Quarterly of Secondary Education*, vol. 5, pp. 178-81. (January, 1930.)
Contains brief account of the method used in working up the book lists in his dissertation.

"Junior College Section of American Library Association"; in *Junior College Journal*, vol. 1, pp. 47-48. (October, 1930.)

Ludington, F. B. "Standards Reached by the Smaller College Libraries of the Pacific Coast"; in *News Notes of California Libraries*, vol. 23, pp. 4-6. (January, 1928.)
Reports results of survey of 22 junior college and of 32 four-year college libraries.

*McClanahan, Mrs. B. B. "What are the Greatest Needs and the Greatest Handicaps to the Average Junior College Library?" in *Libraries*, vol. 31, pp. 201-03. (April, 1926.)

Memmler, Gertrude. "Junior College Library Service"; in *California Quarterly of Secondary Education*, vol. 5, pp. 360-63. (June, 1930.)
Based upon questionnaires from 53 junior colleges in 19 states reporting conditions in 1927-28.

*Robertson, D. A. "The College Library"; in *Educational Record*, vol. 10, pp. 3-28. (January 1, 1929.)
Excellent general discussion, with many applications possible to junior college libraries.

Skinner, Winifred. "The Junior College Library"; in *Junior College Journal*, vol. I, pp. 269-73. (February, 1931.)

*Stone, Ermine. "Book Collections in Junior College Libraries"; in *Junior College Journal*, vol. 1, pp. 28-33. (October, 1930.)
A summary of her master's thesis at Columbia University.

Van Patten, N. "Book Collections in Junior College Libraries"; in *Junior College Journal*, vol. 1, pp. 104-05. (November, 1930.)

Works, G. A. *College and University Library Problems.* 142 pp. American Library Association, Chicago, Illinois, 1927.
A detailed study, financed by Carnegie Corporation, of 18 larger university libraries. Interesting comparisons possible with junior colleges.

Book lists

Bernstein B. A., *et al.* "A Suggested List of Mathematical Books for Junior College Libraries"; in *American Mathematical Monthly*, vol. 32, pp. 462-68. (November, 1925.)

Coursault, J. H. (editor). *Circular of Information to Accredited Junior Colleges.* University of Missouri Bulletin, vol. 27, no. 37 (Education Series, 1926, no. 21). (October 1, 1926.)

Gibson, W. W. *Selection of Basic Library Books for Certain Courses in Junior Colleges.* Unpublished master's thesis at University of Iowa, 142 pp. 1928.

Hilton, E. *Junior College Booklist.* 1930. 84 pp. (University of California Publications in Education, vol. 6, no. 1.)

Stone, Ermine. *A Book Collection in the 300's for a Junior College Library.* Unpublished master's thesis at Columbia University, 178 pp. 1929.

Thompson, M. Florence. *A Book Collection in American History for a Junior College Library in California.* Unpublished master's thesis at Columbia University, 67 pp. 1930.

West, Elizabeth H. "Suggestions for Texas Junior College Libraries"; three articles in *Texas Outlook*, vol. 13. (June, July, and August, 1929.)

CHAPTER XVIII
THE CURRICULUM

> Not only may the junior college foster the ideals and attitudes which the old colleges developed in their students, but it may actually teach more than the old curriculum could offer.... It is going to perpetuate, democratize, and disseminate this spirit which we have received from the college of liberal arts. — G. F. Winfield.[1]

Contents of this chapter. This chapter reviews some of the more significant recent literature on the junior college curriculum, and mentions several outstanding comprehensive studies of it. The bulk of the chapter, however, is devoted to a presentation and discussion, from several points of view, of an extensive original study of curricular offerings as actually found in 1930 in almost three hundred junior colleges in the United States. This study, and another one based on an analysis of nineteen public institutions, are used to summarize general tendencies in junior college curriculum development during the past decade. Finally, the questions of the extent to which courses offered are actually given, and the extent to which they are taken by students, are considered.

PREVIOUS STUDIES OF THE CURRICULUM

The literature of the field. The literature of junior college curriculum construction and analysis — aims, methods, criteria, objectives, tendencies, and results — is very extensive. It covers hundreds of pages, and is far too vast to be summarized in a single brief chapter of a general work. References to some fifty of the more important books and articles, most of them written during the past decade, will be found at the

[1] Winfield, G. F. "Are the Junior Colleges Tending to Dissipate the Spirit and the Ideals of the American Liberal Arts College?" in *Proceedings of the Ninth Annual Meeting of the American Association of Junior Colleges*, pp. 104, 105. Fort Worth, Texas, 1928.

close of the chapter. This array of material can only be touched upon briefly, the major portion of the chapter being devoted to a presentation of original material which should give a truer and more complete picture of the actual junior college curriculum in 1929–30 than has been available before, and which should correct some misapprehensions which have been disseminated in recent years.

Bobbitt's opinion. With reference to the general field, Bobbitt says:[1]

During recent years an enormous amount of work has been expended in attempts to improve and even to reformulate the curriculum of general education. National committees, one after the other, have deliberated and reported. The Department of Superintendence of the National Education Association recently devoted five years of research to the curriculum. The North Central Association has long been at work upon the problem. Hundreds of city school systems are literally expending millions of dollars upon labor in reformulating their curriculums. National foundations have been generously supporting phases of curriculum research.

The junior college has come in for a generous share of this general study and change. It is to be hoped that the results have been somewhat more satisfactory than Bobbitt pictures them for the general field when he says, continuing the above quotation:[2]

And yet the results of this gigantic labor have been disappointing. Here and there, they have made some advance, and have improved details. They aid in formulating syllabi that are vastly more voluminous than those of former days and look very impressive. But after all, it is little more than a dressing up of old things in new styles. Of fundamental changes, there are few. Of fundamental improvement, there is little.

[1] Bobbitt, F. "Are There General Principles that Govern the Junior College Curriculum?" in Gray, William S. (editor), *The Junior College Curriculum*, p. 14. University of Chicago Press, Chicago, 1929.

[2] Bobbitt, F., *loc. cit.*

The University of Chicago Institute. The most important publication on the junior college is the volume of 261 pages edited by W. S. Gray, *The Junior College Curriculum.* This volume consists of nineteen papers on various phases of the subject, presented at the Institute for Administrative Officers of Higher Institutions held at the University of Chicago in the summer of 1929. It contains two articles on foundational principles by Dr. Judd and Dr. Charters; four general surveys of the junior college curriculum in colleges and universities, in engineering schools, in California, and with special reference to guidance, by Reeves, Sadler, Koos, and Kefauver; four reports on the Stephens College curriculum work by President Wood and three of his associates; a report on a survey course in contemporary civilization at Columbia University; and similar reports on survey courses at the junior college level at the University of Chicago, by eight members of the faculty, covering the fields of orientation, modern foreign languages, economics, geology, history, art, sociology, and anthropology. The volume closes with a valuable and carefully annotated bibliography of one hundred and seven titles. The contents of this volume should be familiar to every student of the junior college curriculum.

The general aims of the junior college are well expressed by two of the leaders at the Chicago Institute. Judd says:

> The junior college is the institution which should mark the transition from emphasis on content to emphasis on organization. The junior college has a double function. It is the final institution to deal with general education, and it is also under obligation to use the last stages of general education in preparing the student to undertake critical, independent thinking. The student should pass out of the junior college matured by his training to the point where he is ready to enter the field of constructive thinking.

Bobbitt says:

> We believe that it is the culminating level of general education,

namely, the junior college, that should provide leadership in this matter for all of general education. We believe that if the junior college can achieve its intellectual freedom here and formulate the general principles, then the lower levels of general education in high schools, junior high schools, and elementary schools will have their proper leadership and guidance for their portion of this same general education.

These are two admirable general statements, but the difficulty comes in trying to translate them into concrete terms of subjects, credits, and classroom methods. They may, however, be accepted as excellent guiding principles.

The four generally accepted functions of the junior college — popularizing, preparatory, terminal, and guidance — have already been discussed and considerable evidence as to the success of curricula designed to carry out these functions has been given in the four chapters, VIII to XI. In this chapter, information is presented regarding the quantity and nature of the different subjects, with special emphasis on the development of so-called terminal or culminal courses as compared with the academic or college-preparatory type.

History of junior college curriculum studies. At least seven rather extensive curriculum studies made during the past decade are deserving of brief mention.

1. *Bolton*, in 1918, at the University of Washington, secured by questionnaires the judgments of 200 public school administrators as to what subjects should be offered in the junior college. Of those answering, 117 would give English, 146 foreign languages, 144 mathematics, and 130 social sciences. The whole number of votes for academic subjects was 663 as contrasted with 93 for various vocational subjects; i.e., only 12 per cent were for vocational subjects.

2. *McDowell*, in his 1919 doctor's dissertation, studied the actual offerings of nineteen public and twenty-eight private junior colleges. He found that 18 per cent of the total offerings

was vocational in public junior colleges, but only 9 per cent in the private institutions.

3. *Koos*, in 1921, in his Commonwealth Study investigation, analyzed in detail the curricular offerings of 23 public and 35 private junior colleges. His findings will be summarized later in this chapter, in comparison with two later studies.

4. *Walker*, in a master's dissertation at Kansas State Agricultural College, in 1926, reported the opinions of a considerable group of educators with respect to junior college curricula, classifying them as conservative, radical, and progressive. He studied in detail the offerings in 35 public junior college catalogues, and made comparisons with Koos's earlier work. He found that only 14 per cent of the curricular offerings could be classified as vocational.

5. *Whitney*, in 1928, made an extensive analysis of curricular offerings in both public and private junior colleges in the United States, following very closely the pattern of Koos's work, so that results might be comparable. This was presented in his book *The Junior College in America*, and also printed in various other forms. His results will be discussed later.

6. *Vandervort*, in 1929, found that in the average California junior college a little over half of the work offered was distinctly preparatory for upper-division work in the university; that the total amount of preparatory work offered was about half of that in the lower division of the three California universities, but that in the best of the junior colleges it was virtually equivalent.[1]

7. Subsequent to the completion of the Hollingsworth-Eells study, reported later in this chapter, Campbell published a brief summary of the types of curricula offered in 343 junior colleges whose catalogues he examined. These are sum-

[1] For bibliographical references to these six studies, see Suggested Readings at the end of the chapter.

marized for four types of colleges in Table 45.[1] For many purposes his first two groups might be considered preparatory, the last two terminal.

TABLE 45. TYPES OF CURRICULA OFFERED IN 343 JUNIOR COLLEGES IN THE UNITED STATES

TYPE	TOTAL	PUBLIC	STATE	DENOMINATIONAL	OTHER PRIVATE
Totals	**343**	**116**	**22**	**140**	**65**
College preparatory	312	115	21	132	44
Pre-professional	111 *	56	10	29	15
Vocational	216	72	20	94	30
Terminal	75	26	6	23	20

* Evidently an error exists in his table, since the four groups add to make 110, not 111.

Curriculum revision at Stephens College. Much publicity has been given to the extensive work of curriculum revision and reconstruction in progress at Stephens College, Missouri, a four-year junior college for women. The work has been based primarily on the activity-analysis method under the direction of Dr. W. W. Charters. For example, a list of 7493 distinct problems of women were collected from several hundred women who kept, for many occupations, detailed lists covering every month of the year. These were classified into twenty-five groups which, in the words of President Wood of Stephens, "represent the problems of women, irrespective of their vocations in life, and constitute the irreducible minimum in a comprehensive curriculum. Unless some other social agency has already supplied the experience needed for meeting these problems, clearly it is the duty of the school to do so."

The chief work at Stephens has been devoted to the development of general survey courses in social sciences, humanities, æsthetics, and vocations. All of these, however, are designed especially for the first year of the four-year junior college,

[1] Campbell, D. S. *A Critical Study of the Stated Purposes of the Junior College.* George Peabody College Contribution to Education, no. 170, 126 pp. Nashville, Tennessee, 1930.

which is equivalent to the third year of high school, and so do not cover at all the subject matter of the junior college curriculum as ordinarily understood, that is, the freshman and sophomore years of college grade. Accordingly they will receive no further consideration in this chapter, since they are not applicable to the level here discussed.[1]

RECOMMENDED PREPARATORY CURRICULA

Koos's recommendations. It will be interesting and valuable for later comparisons to present here two important recommendations or suggestions for desirable minimum preparatory curricula for a junior college. Similar suggestions have not been made for vocational curricula. Koos, in 1921, suggested a minimum preparatory curriculum for "a group of students representing a legitimate range of liberal arts needs and interests," based largely upon the actual offerings in over a hundred liberal arts colleges, especially in the Middle West.[2] His total suggested offering totals 225 hours, exclusive of physical education.

Woods's recommendations. On quite a different basis, Woods, in 1928, suggested a curriculum totaling 265 hours, inclusive of physical training. He assumed a junior college of 300 students, with a faculty of 24, of which each member was to teach an average of 12½ units per semester, and 16 were to teach academic subjects. The list of courses to be offered was based, not on catalogue offerings, as Koos's and others have been, but on the actual preferences of students at the University of California and on lower division prerequisites for majors, both of which are essentially practical rather than

[1] An effort was made to try out some of these courses in 1930 in the freshman year of certain California junior colleges, both public and private, which are discussed in an article by J. M. Wood in the *Junior College Journal*, February, 1931. For further discussion of the Stephens College experiment, see Chapter XXVII. For reports, see four articles in Gray, W. S. (editor), *The Junior College Curriculum.*

[2] Koos, L. V. *The Junior College*, pp. 61–63.

theoretical bases. Woods finds that the curriculum as proposed would have actually satisfied the major choice of 78 per cent of the students at the university.[1] He comments: [2]

The list provides the minimum requirements for the majors listed and in addition a slight amount of selection. In constructing the list the method of satisfying demand has been followed. However, it is the duty of the junior college, not merely to satisfy a demand, but also to create a demand for idealistic studies. Classical languages could well be represented. Additional courses in the social sciences, anthropology, history, etc., are worthy of consideration. The extent to which a junior college can undertake such extensions depends upon its financial strength and the needs it endeavors to meet. Clientèle, locality, and resources should suggest the character of desirable modifications.

Recommended curricula compared. These two suggested university preparatory or academic curricula are given in Table 46.

TABLE 46. ACADEMIC PREPARATORY JUNIOR COLLEGE CURRICULA AS SUGGESTED BY KOOS AND WOODS

Subject	Koos		Woods	
	Semester hours	Per cent of total	Semester hours	Per cent of total
English	24	10	18	7
Public Speaking	4	2	12	5
Languages, Modern	46	20	84	32
Social Sciences	54	23	32	12
Natural Sciences	63	28	56	21
Mathematics	21	9	38	14
Philosophy	9	4	15	6
Psychology	4	2	6	2
Physical Education	(4) *	2	4	1
	229	100	265	100

* "The usual offering in physical training should be added." Estimated as same as suggested in Woods's curriculum.

[1] Tweedy found in a similar study of Idaho conditions, that a junior college curriculum of 163 semester hours would have been sufficient to meet the needs of 70 per cent of the upper division students of the University of Idaho. Unpublished master's thesis at Stanford University, *Can Idaho Establish More Junior Colleges?* pp. 50–54. (1930.)

[2] Woods, B. M. "Junior College Preparation for University Work"; in *Bulletin of the Pacific Coast Association of Collegiate Registrars*, p. 34. (March, 1929.)

There are rather striking differences between the two recommendations. Ancient languages are omitted from both, but Woods's places much greater emphasis on modern languages. Koos recommends that a fifth of the curricular offerings be in this field, but California practice requires approximately a third of the work here, which seems rather out of proportion. On the other hand, Woods would place only half as much emphasis on social studies as Koos, somewhat less on natural sciences, and considerably more on mathematics. On the whole, Koos's plan seems to be the better balanced. The one suggested by Woods, however, is based upon "takings," instead of on offerings.

PRESENT STATUS OF THE CURRICULUM

Occasion for the study. Mention has been made previously of Whitney's detailed analysis of the junior college curriculum. It was based upon an analysis of the catalogue offerings for 1927–28 of "thirty representative junior colleges, located in eighteen different states," from which he made extensive and detailed comparisons with Koos's earlier study to show major changes and tendencies in the seven-year interval. The details of his findings will be presented in Table 47 on page 485, but the two major conclusions may be stated here:[1]

> As to changes in total offerings, it is seen that there is an increase from 215 to 253 hours and that this increase occurs in the private schools, while in public junior colleges there has been a decrease from 255 to 214 hours. Evidently, the public junior colleges are concentrating on more specific objectives while the private schools are exhibiting more and, no doubt they hope, more attractive offerings for prospective matriculates.

According to his Table 88, there was an increase from 191 to 289 hours for the private colleges.

These are such startling generalizations and explanations

[1] Whitney, F. L. *The Junior College in America*, pp. 121–23.

regarding tendencies that one may be pardoned if he pauses to examine whether they are entirely justified by the data. There is no question of the approximate *accuracy* of the data secured from the catalogues analyzed.[1] The real question, however, is whether the author is justified in his assumption that they are "representative" of the entire group, as he tacitly assumes in the quotation given above, and more explicitly at the close of his curriculum chapter, when he says: [2]

> This chapter has given rather a complete account of the present status of the junior college curriculum offerings of the 146 public and 236 private junior colleges now in operation and has traced lines of development observed over a period of seven years.

Doubt as to whether they were really representative [3] led the author of this volume to encourage one of his graduate students to undertake a much more extensive catalogue study of the same type, but based upon many more than thirty junior college catalogues. All catalogues were used that could be secured by writing directly to all of the 405 junior colleges

[1] The author properly calls attention to the difficulty of exact classification of the variety of offerings found in various terminology and units in a group of junior college catalogues, a difficulty which any one who has attempted similar analysis will readily appreciate and agree with.

[2] Whitney, F. L., *op. cit.*, p. 152.

[3] Whitney names the thirty junior colleges studied, 15 public and 15 private. Doubt as to their adequacy as a sample, and their comparability with Koos's study, is based upon four considerations: (1) The small proportion of the total number used as a sample, less than one twelfth of the total. (2) Unrepresentative geographical distribution. Although California had only 31 of the 146 public junior colleges studied, 7 of the 15 catalogues of public junior colleges studied were in California; Iowa with 19 was represented by one; Texas, with 17 was not represented at all. Neither were any of Texas's 25 private junior colleges represented in the 15 private ones chosen for study. (3) The size of institutions in the sample. Only one of the seven used in California had an enrollment as large as the average of the 31 public junior colleges in the state. Two were new ones, with only small freshman classes and no sophomore curriculum, one dying after a year's experimental existence before the study was published. (4) All classes not represented. Koos's study included public, "state," and private institutions. Whitney's, which was intended to be comparable, eliminated all state institutions from consideration.

listed in the Directory of the American Association of Junior Colleges. A few had to be rejected because the information was not given in comparable form, but a total of 279 different catalogues were examined by J. E. Hollingsworth. Since the results of such an extensive investigation have not been made available, they are reported in summary form for various groups of schools in this chapter.

The present study is based upon an analysis of over two thirds of the existing institutions (nine tenths of the public colleges), while Koos's was based upon one third and Whitney's upon less than one twelfth of the total group.[1]

Total offerings by institutions. The total number of semester hours offered by institutions is summarized in Figure 28, based on 284 colleges.[2] It will be noted that the most frequent number of hours offered is by the group of 63 institutions with 150 to 199 hours each. These are all less than the minimum efficient offering as recommended by either Koos or Woods in Table 46. In fact it may be estimated from Figure

[1] The number and proportion of catalogues out of the total number of institutions existing at the time of the three respective studies are shown below:

	Total	Public	Private
Koos — 1921			
Number existing	175	51	124
Number examined	58	23	35
Per cent examined	**33**	**45**	**28**
Whitney — 1928			
Number existing	382	146	231
Number examined	30	15	15
Per cent examined	**8**	**10**	**6**
Hollingsworth-Eells — 1930			
Number existing	405	147	258
Number examined	279	129	150
Per cent examined	**69**	**90**	**58**

All of the detailed examination, analysis, and classification of the catalogues was made by Mr. Hollingsworth, thus insuring a uniformity of method and judgment which is difficult to secure when a group of students work on such an extensive project. All essential computations were checked independently by Mrs. Hollingsworth.

[2] Five colleges are included here in total offerings which proved unsuitable for classification in later groups.

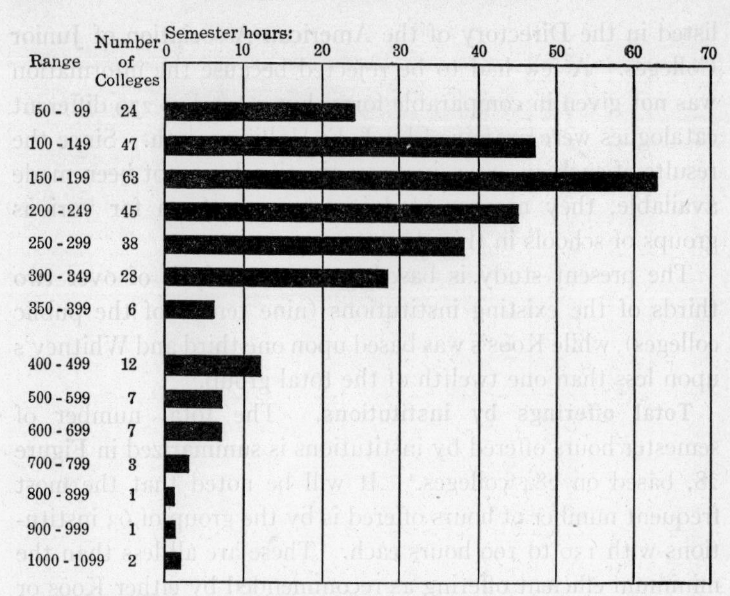

FIG. 28. TOTAL CURRICULAR OFFERINGS, IN SEMESTER HOURS, IN 284 JUNIOR COLLEGES

28 that only 45 per cent of the colleges have more extensive curricula than the minimum one suggested by Koos, and only 32 per cent exceed the standard suggested by Woods. There are, however, twenty-one colleges which have offerings in excess of 500 hours each, and two that pass the thousand mark. The four with the largest offerings are North Texas Agricultural (1035); John Tarleton Agricultural, Texas (1001); Pasadena, California (973); and Modesto, California (817).[1]

Comparison of offerings by subjects in three studies. In Table 47 and Figure 29 are summaries of the offerings in the

[1] The others with curricular offerings in excess of 500 hours, by states, were: Colorado: Colorado Women's College (695). California: Glendale (769), Sacramento (764), San José (698), Riverside (697), Los Angeles (668), Long Beach (635), Compton (601), Santa Ana (571), Fullerton (518). Maryland: National Park Seminary (544). Idaho: Southern Branch (772). Illinois: Crane (656). Iowa: Graceland (504). Michigan: Grand Rapids (587). Missouri: Kansas City (574). West Virginia: New River (591).

TABLE 47. COMPARISON OF AVERAGE OFFERING IN SEMESTER HOURS IN THREE STUDIES OF THE JUNIOR COLLEGE CURRICULUM

	Public			Private		
	1921 Koos (23)	1928 Whitney (15)	1930 Hollingsworth-Eells (129)	1921 Koos (35)	1928 Whitney (15)	1930 Hollingsworth-Eells (150)
Total	**255.0**	**214.1**	**285.9**	**191.1**	**289.0**	**223.5**
Academic	**175.1**	**148.9**	**191.1**	**143.1**	**181.4**	**157.7**
English	17.7	14.6	20.9	16.0	17.3	14.8
Public Sp aking	3.0	5.9	6.8	2.8	16.3	5.7
Languages, Ancient	12.8	9.2	4.9	19.5	15.2	16.0
Languages, Modern	42.1	32.0	38.3	38.6	36.9	31.1
Social Science	27.5	22.1	35.1	18.9	26.4	23.8
Natural Science	44.5	32.9	49.1	22.6	26.3	25.0
Mathematics	19.3	17.4	21.4	13.6	13.2	13.1
Philosophy	2.4	3.9	2.4	1.9	6.2	2.1
Psychology	3.1	5.8	6.2	2.9	6.2	5.7
Bible and Religious Education	0.0	1.6	0.3	3.9	8.1	11.0
Physical Education	2.7	3.5	5.7	2.4	9.3	4.4
Non-Academic	**79.9**	**65.2**	**94.8**	**48.0**	**107.6**	**65.8**
Agriculture	5.8	0.0	6.8	1.1	1.2	1.3
Art	3.1	9.5	6.6	4.9	18.5	6.5
Commercial	26.7	21.2	18.2	0.5	30.0	11.4
Education	5.3	10.1	8.7	9.7	17.7	12.1
Engineering	16.6	10.2	16.9	10.7	0.0	1.1
Home Economics	7.8	7.0	8.7	16.0	15.1	10.7
Music	8.8	5.6	17.7	4.4	25.1	17.9
Extension	0.0	1.6	8.5	0.0	0.0	3.5
Others	3.8	0.0	2.7	0.7	0.0	1.3

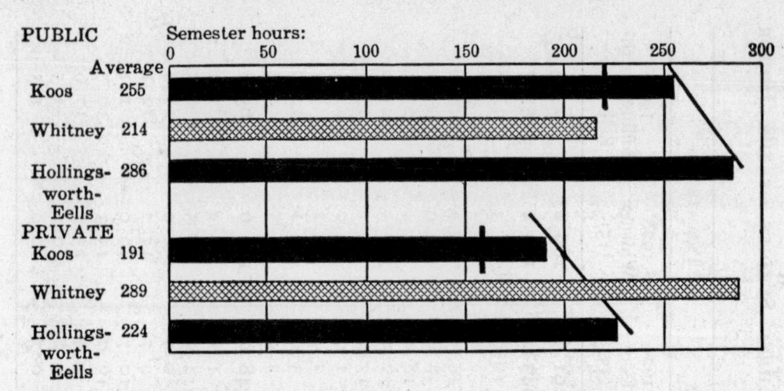

FIG. 29. COMPARISON OF AVERAGE OFFERINGS, IN SEMESTER HOURS, IN THREE STUDIES OF THE JUNIOR COLLEGE CURRICULUM

twenty fields of the curriculum, as reported in the three studies, for both public and private junior colleges.[1] From them it is seen that there has been an increase almost equal in amount for both public and private colleges in the nine-year interval.[2] Whitney's results, on the other hand, showed marked variations, as is indicated by the central cross-hatched bars. Instead of the marked shrinkage for public junior colleges and the pheonomenal increase for private junior colleges, which he was led to assume from the inadequate nature of the catalogues selected, and the reasons vouchsafed for these phenomena, it is found as a matter of fact that there has been a sane, healthy growth in the curricula in both types of institutions, and in almost equal amounts, as shown by the approximate parallelism of the sloping lines at the extremities of the black bars of Figure 29. The increase for public junior colleges amounted to 31 hours, or 12 per cent; for the private institutions, to 32

[1] Koos and Whitney do not classify them as academic and non-academic, but report the twenty in a single alphabetical group. It is felt that the distinction is fairly easy to make, on broad general lines, and that it will be useful to reveal tendencies in the two groups. While there may be some overlapping, as between mathematics and engineering, or education and psychology, the main lines of demarcation are clear.

[2] Koos's study was based largely upon 1920–21 catalogues; the Hollingsworth-Eells study largely on those for 1929–30.

hours, or 17 per cent. In 1920 the average public junior college offering, as shown by this data, was 64 hours greater than the offering of the private college. In 1929 the corresponding difference was 62 hours! There seems to be no valid evidence of concentration on more specific objectives for the public colleges nor of undue experimental expansion for the private institutions.

Seven of Koos's group of 23 public junior colleges were state institutions. Had they been omitted from his totals, the length of the upper bar in Figure 29 would have extended only to the vertical line (219) on it. Also in the private group he included three institutions which were doing senior college work, but claiming still to be performing junior college functions. If these had been omitted the total for the private junior colleges would have been reduced to 160, as shown by the vertical bar in the private group of Figure 29.

Change by departments offered. The most striking changes in individual departments of study between 1921 and 1930 for the public junior colleges are found in the marked reduction in foreign language offerings, and in the increase in music. For the private institutions the greatest decrease was in engineering courses, and the greatest increase in music.

Trends of academic and non-academic groups. The relative amounts of the curriculum devoted to academic and non-academic offerings, as exhibited in Table 47, are shown in Figure 30. It is evident that the non-academic group (which may perhaps be thought of as a combination of terminal, semi-professional, and pre-professional offerings) have shown a small increase for both types of institutions over the nine-year period. Approximately one third of the offerings in both types of institutions are of the non-academic type. It is interesting to compare this with Woods's proposed faculty of 24 for a junior college of 300 students, of which one third was to teach non-academic subjects. This is distinctly greater than the pro-

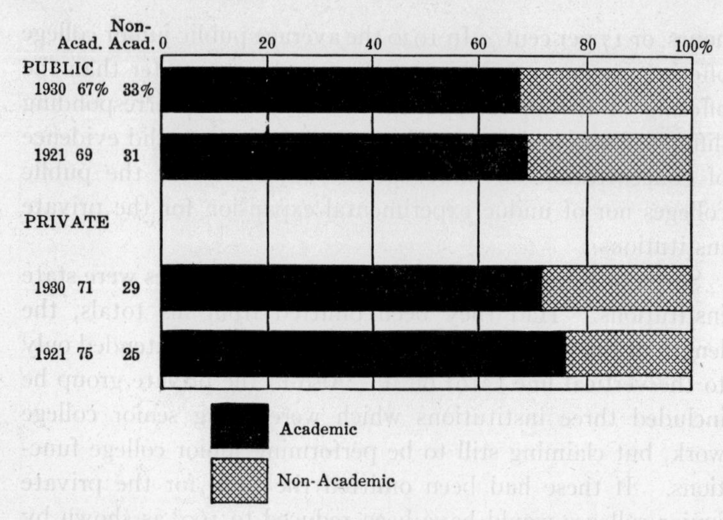

FIG. 30. CHANGE IN AVERAGE OFFERINGS, ACADEMIC AND NON-ACADEMIC, 1921–30

portions of vocational work found for the small groups studied in 1921 by Koos.

Summary of curriculum in 1930. A summary of several significant features for the entire group of 279 colleges is exhibited in Table 48. This shows the number and the percentage of the entire group offering courses in each department; the average for the 279 colleges, the percentage that each subject is of the total offering; and the average for the colleges actually offering any courses in the department. Thus for public

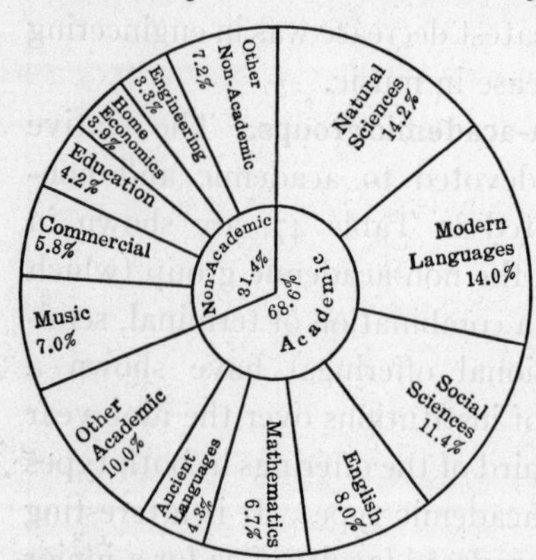

FIG. 31. AVERAGE CURRICULAR OFFERINGS, BY DEPARTMENTS, IN 279 JUNIOR COLLEGES, 1930

TABLE 48. SUMMARY OF CURRICULAR OFFERINGS, IN SEMESTER HOURS, BY DEPARTMENTS, IN 279 JUNIOR COLLEGES (1930)

	Number of Colleges Offering (1)	Per cent of Colleges Offering (2)	Average for 279 Colleges (3)	Average for Colleges Offering Any (4)	Per cent Each Subject is of Column (3) (5)
Total	**279**	**100**	**253.5**	...	**100.0**
Academic	...	...	**174.1**	...	**68.6**
English	279	100	20.3	20.3	8.0
Public Speaking	205	73	6.2	8.5	2.4
Languages, Ancient	154	55	10.9	19.7	4.3
Languages, Modern	274	98	35.5	36.1	14.0
Social Sciences	278	99	29.0	29.1	11.4
Natural Sciences	272	97	36.1	37.1	14.2
Mathematics	270	97	17.0	17.5	6.7
Philosophy	100	36	2.2	6.2	0.9
Psychology	250	90	5.9	6.5	2.3
Bible and Religious Education	125	45	6.0	13.4	2.4
Physical Education	170	61	5.0	8.2	2.0
Non-Academic			**79.4**		**31.4**
Agriculture	46	16	3.8	22.9	1.5
Art	124	44	6.6	14.8	2.6
Commercial	134	48	6.6	14.8	2.6
Education	180	65	10.6	16.4	4.2
Engineering	109	39	8.4	21.4	3.3
Home Economics	131	47	9.8	20.8	3.9
Music	160	57	17.8	31.1	7.0
Extension	36	13	5.8	44.9	23.0
Other	48	17	2.0	...	0.8

speaking, the table shows that the subject is offered in 205 colleges, which is 73 per cent of the total of 279 colleges; the average offering in public speaking in the entire group of 279 is 6.2 semester hours, but in the 205 institutions actually giving any such courses the average is 8.5 hours. The offering of 6.2 hours is 2.4 per cent of the entire average curricular offering of 253.5 in all subjects combined. Similar information for other subjects is given in Table 48. The data in Column Five of Table 48 for the more important departments are shown graphically in Figure 31 (p. 488).

Summary by types of junior colleges. As shown by Figure 32, there is considerable agreement between the four types of

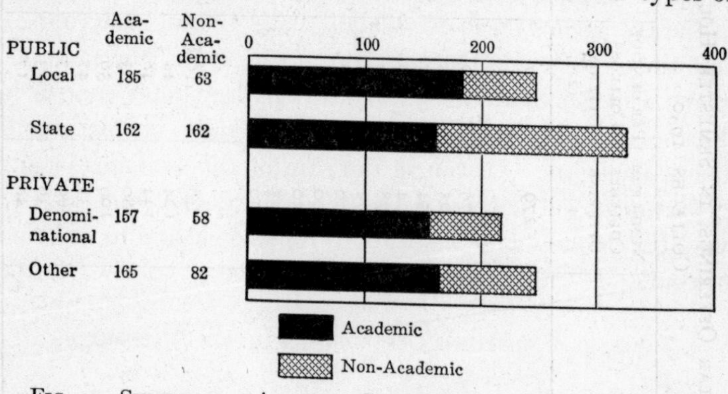

FIG. 32. SUMMARY OF AVERAGE CURRICULAR OFFERINGS IN FOUR TYPES OF JUNIOR COLLEGES, 1930

junior college in the amount of academic work offered, but a wide variation in non-academic work, both in amount and proportion. The proportion of the total offering given to non-academic work in the four types is as follows:

State	50 per cent
Other private	33
Denominational	27
Local and district	26

It is hardly creditable to the local and district junior colleges, which are supposed in general to be the newer and more progressive institutions, that they rank lowest in proportion of non-academic work. Possibly their very newness accounts for this, since, as will be shown later, there is a strong tendency for the longer established institutions to add non-academic courses after the academic courses have been in existence for some time.

Data on separate courses by departments. Finally, there is given for each department, for the entire group of 279 colleges, a summary of the principal courses offered by departments. For each department, and for each of the more important courses which are given in it, the number of colleges offering the course indicated and the average offering in each will be found in Table 49. In this case, however, the average shown is the average for the institutions actually offering such courses, not the average for the entire group of 279. For example, under English there are 52 institutions that offer courses in Business English, the average offering in these 52 institutions being 4.3 hours. Of course the sum of the averages in any department will not equal the departmental average, due to variation in number of institutions considered, and to omission of courses given by only one or two colleges.

TABLE 49. CURRICULAR OFFERINGS OF JUNIOR COLLEGES, BY DEPARTMENTS

Academic	NUMBER OF COLLEGES OFFERING	AVERAGE HOURS FOR COLLEGES GIVING COURSE
English	**279**	**20.3**
Literature	273	10.9
Composition	270	7.4
Journalism	69	6.1
Business	52	4.3
Grammar	15	3.5
Public Speaking	**205**	**8.5**
Argumentation	177	3.9
Debating	59	2.9
Extemporaneous	35	2.8
Oratory	23	2.3

TABLE 49 (*continued*)

Academic	Number of Colleges Offering	Average Hours for Colleges Giving Course
Languages, Ancient	**154**	**19.7**
Latin	154	15.5
Greek	50 *	12.8
Languages, Modern	**274**	**33.9**
French	241	18.5
Spanish	176	16.2
German	137	17.0
Other	21 †	11.6
Social Sciences	**278**	**29.1**
History	275	15.5
Economics	203	7.4
Political Science	172	6.2
Sociology	147	5.9
Orientation	44	2.6
Citizenship	11	5.1
Natural Sciences	**272**	**37.1**
Chemistry	252	16.6
Botany	161	6.5
Physics	152	11.8
Zoölogy	149	7.7
Biology	129	6.2
Physiology	78	5.0
Geology	62	6.8
Bacteriology	43	4.3
Mathematics	**270**	**17.5**
Trigonometry	258	3.4
Algebra	255	4.4
Analytics	209	4.4
Calculus	152	6.8
Geometry	113	3.2
Philosophy	**100**	**6.2**
Ethics	56	3.1
General	46	4.6
Logic	42	3.1
Traditional and Historical	18	5.2

* Includes three colleges offering Hebrew.
† Includes Scandinavian, 5 colleges; Italian, 3; Slavic, 3; and Esperanto, 1.

TABLE 49 (*continued*)

	Number of Colleges Offering	Average Hours for Colleges Giving Course
Academic		
Psychology	**250**	**6.5**
General	218	4.3
Educational	143	4.2
Social	29	3.0
Experimental	7	2.9
Bible and Religious Education	**125**	**13.4**
History and Literature	120	9.7
Character Education	38	5.0
Philosophy	25	5.1
Physical Education	**170**	**8.2**
Gymnastics	138	3.4
Hygiene	91	3.0
Sports	60	3.3
Methods of Training and Directing	44	4.6
Dancing	39	2.4
Athletics	36	2.3
Individual Exercise	20	2.0
First Aid	15	1.7
Administration and Organization	3	2.7
Non-Academic		
Agriculture	**46**	**22.9**
Animal Husbandry	35	9.1
Crops and Soils	31	9.0
Horticulture	28	6.7
Poultry Production	17	3.6
Engineering	15	6.1
Business Management	9	6.6
Art	**124**	**14.8**
Drawing and Painting	80	5.8
History and Appreciation	70	5.6
Design	64	5.4
Crafts	57	5.1
Lettering and Sketching	26	4.7
Interior Decoration	25	4.5
Costume	22	3.8
Modelling and Sculpture	7	3.0

TABLE 49 (*continued*)

Non-Academic	Number of Colleges Offering	Average Hours for Colleges Giving Course
Commerce	**134**	**30.4**
Accounting	102	8.9
Shorthand	92	9.7
Typing	86	8.7
Law	79	4.4
Business Organization and Management	66	6.7
Bookkeeping	58	7.0
Salesmanship	36	5.1
Education	**180**	**16.4**
History and Principles	132	5.0
Methods	124	7.5
Elementary	80	5.3
Teacher Training	72	6.1
Supervision and Administration	47	3.0
Primary and Kindergarten	19	6.9
Secondary	17	4.6
Engineering	**109**	**21.4**
Mechanical	90	13.2
Civil	64	7.0
Electrical	52	5.9
Military	15	9.1
Aviation	9	9.9
Mining and Metallurgy	7	5.0
Home Economics	**131**	**20.8**
Foods	122	8.8
Clothing	116	8.2
Art	65	4.4
Home Management	58	4.5
Nursing	32	2.2
Child Care	14	4.1
Music	**160**	**31.1**
Voice	123	8.0
Harmony	122	13.5
History	119	5.6
Instrumental	99	9.1
Piano	76	8.6
Pipe Organ	22	8.6
Extension	**36**	**44.9**

A decade's change in the same colleges. L. R. Hiatt has made a significant comparison of the changes in curricula of a group of junior colleges after a ten-year interval. He took all institutions listed in Koos's *Junior College* as existing in 1920 for which catalogues were available for that date, and compared their offerings in 1920 with the offerings in the same colleges ten years later. There were nineteen junior colleges for which this comparison was possible. His chief results are summarized in Table 50.[1]

TABLE 50. COMPARISON OF OFFERINGS IN NINETEEN PUBLIC JUNIOR COLLEGES (ABOUT 1920 AND 1930)

	AVERAGE HOURS 1920	AVERAGE HOURS 1930	PER CENT OF INCREASE
Total	**180.4**	**316.0**	**75**
Academic	**149.3**	**236.1**	**58**
English and Public Speaking	19.4	28.9	49
Languages, Ancient	9.1	7.5	−18 *
Languages, Modern	30.9	49.5	61
Social Sciences	31.1	49.6	59
Physical Sciences	23.5	43.1	83
Biological Sciences	11.2	21.5	93
Mathematics	20.0	26.9	34
Physical Education	4.2	9.1	119
Non-Academic	**31.1**	**79.9**	**157**
Agriculture	0.8	1.6	100
Art	2.6	10.0	295
Commercial	14.3	20.7	46
Drawing	2.5	8.6	242
Engineering	3.6	12.5	230
Home Economics	2.5	8.7	243
Music	4.5	17.0	280
Other	0.4	0.8	100

* Decrease.

This comparison shows emphatically that in older established institutions the change has been much more marked than

[1] Hiatt, L. R. "Curricular Changes in Junior Colleges"; in *Junior College Journal*, vol. 1, pp. 6–11. (October, 1930.)

in the larger group studied in Table 47. There has been an increase of 75 per cent in total offerings as compared with only 14 per cent in the larger group. The great youth of most of the public institutions, as compared with Hiatt's group of 19, suggests that as soon as an institution begins to arrive at moderate stability it tends to increase its offerings materially. This tendency is particularly strong in the non-academic subjects. While the offerings in the academic group increased 58 per cent, in the non-academic group they increased almost three times as fast, or 157 per cent. While in 1920 the non-academic subjects constituted only 17 per cent of the offerings, ten years later they had increased to over 25 per cent, but still are not as great, relatively or absolutely, as in the entire group of public junior colleges studied by Hollingsworth where it was 94.8 hours, or 33 per cent of the total offering.

"Offerings" *vs*. "Givings." All data reported so far in this chapter have referred to "offerings" of courses, as indicated by catalogue statements. To what extent have they actually been given? Is there any padding for effect, as is sometimes found in the catalogues of overambitious four-year colleges and would-be universities? [1] The chief evidence known to the writer on this subject is that found by Koos ten years ago. On his visits to fourteen institutions, nine of them public, he checked courses actually given with those offered in catalogues. He found that the average reduction from courses offered in catalogues to those actually given in public junior colleges was 9.5 per cent, in private colleges 5.4 per cent. Probably many four-year institutions would not make any better showing than this. After a detailed analysis he concluded that neither the average amount of reduction nor the extent of disappearance of particular courses was large enough to discredit the

[1] Nor is this necessarily derogatory to the institution. In the cases of elective courses, while offered in good faith, it is frequently found that there is not sufficient demand to justify giving them.

results of subsequent studies based on catalogue announcements. Probably the situation is better, rather than worse, at the present time. In Texas, in 1929, in sixteen municipal junior colleges, 273 different courses were offered in the catalogues and 239 actually given — a shrinkage of 12 per cent. For a group of twenty private junior colleges in the same state, the shrinkage in 297 courses offered was also 12 per cent.

"Offerings" *vs.* "Takings." Finally we are interested not only in the extent of "offerings" and "givings," but also of "takings." To what extent do students actually take the different courses offered? Data are available for 1929 for 43,761 registrations in 19 California junior colleges, and for 11,279 registrations in 16 Texas municipal colleges, which are summarized in Tables 51 and 52.[1] In these two leading junior college states, the actual student enrollment in non-academic courses was approximately one fifth of the entire enrollment.

TABLE 51. PROPORTIONAL STUDENT ENROLLMENT BY SUBJECTS IN NINETEEN CALIFORNIA PUBLIC JUNIOR COLLEGES (1929)

	PER CENT OF TOTAL
Total	**100**
Academic	**80**
English	15
Language, Foreign	10
Social Sciences	15
Physical Sciences	10
Biological Sciences	5
Mathematics	3
Philosophy and Psychology	11
Physical Education	11
Non-Academic	**20**
Fine Arts	9
Practical and Industrial Arts	11

[1] Table 51 is based on Koos and Weersing's *Secondary Education in California: A Preliminary Survey,* p. 91; Table 52 upon Reid's *Texas Municipal Junior Colleges,* pp. 71–72.

TABLE 52. PROPORTIONAL STUDENT ENROLLMENT BY SUBJECTS IN SIXTEEN TEXAS MUNICIPAL JUNIOR COLLEGES (1929)

	PER CENT OF TOTAL
Total	100
Academic	77
English	21
Public Speaking	2
Languages, Ancient	1
Languages, Modern	11
Social Sciences	16
Natural Sciences	12
Mathematics	11
Philosophy and Psychology	1
Physical Education	2
Non-Academic	23
Commercial	5
Education	13
Engineering	2
Home Economics	2
Music	1

It cannot be assumed from these figures, however, that only one fifth of the students are taking terminal or vocational courses. These are only the student enrollments in the different subjects. Many well-organized terminal courses require a considerable amount of work in English, the social sciences, and sometimes other subjects. Yet on the whole the data seem to indicate that the proportion enrolled in the non-academic courses is too small, if the institution is to function as it should as a terminal institution for a large proportion of the student population.

Conclusions. This chapter has tried to give an adequate presentation of the present status of the junior college curriculum, and of the trends in its development during the past decade. Little has been said regarding the ideal curriculum, nor how it should ultimately be secured. It is necessary to have a definite basis of fact as to past tendencies and present conditions before planning for the future. Although much has been done, perhaps even more remains for curriculum experts to do in developing satisfactory techniques in curriculum construction. Even Dean Oppenheimer, of Stephens College, feels that only the first step is satisfactory. He says: [1]

Curriculum workers, I believe, are painfully aware of the needs for further steps to complete the process. The two major difficulties are time and adequate techniques. At present we have fairly adequate techniques to determine objectives of subjects, but beyond that stage little has been done. Methods of selecting materials, types of optimum organization, style of writing, grade placement, methods of teaching, and adequate tests of informational and behavior achievements are serious problems that require long periods of time and expenditure of a great deal of effort.

Bobbitt is doubtful whether even this much progress has been made. He says: [2]

With a few exceptions curriculum research has not yet recognized its problems. It has not found them, much less solved them. It has not yet even acceptably defined the term *curriculum.* It has not yet made clear the substance of the educative process that is to be programmed in the curriculum. It has not formulated the general principles of educational science which should guide judgment in arranging the details. And what is more, for the most part, it is not yet willing even to consider most of the problems in a dispassionate and genuinely scientific way. Its thought is conditioned by practices, inherited assumptions, and the demands of a mechanical type of administration. Its science is mainly a rationalizing of the existing system. It uses certain elements of scientific method, it is true. But it assumes the general substance of the curriculum prior to organizing its scientific procedures. The latter are then merely for working out details in harmony with *a priori* assumptions.

[1] Oppenheimer, J. J. "Particularized Techniques in Curriculum Construction in a Junior College"; in Gray, W. S. (editor), *Junior College Curriculum*, p. 59.

[2] Bobbitt, F., *op. cit.*, p. 15.

When experts are so far from being able to designate adequate techniques for curriculum construction in the junior college field, it would evidently be fruitless to attempt to make this chapter an outline of the ideal junior college curriculum of the future. It has been limited to finding and presenting facts regarding the junior college curriculum as it actually is today and as it has developed during the past decade. This is essential information as a point of departure for any further revision. Furthermore, in spite of Bobbitt's pessimistic strictures just quoted, it is probable that most reform of the curriculum will be evolutionary rather than revolutionary. We will build upon what we have, not junk it completely and start afresh. It is important, then, to know what we have and how we got it, before making changes. It is possible, too, that the accumulated experience of successive academic generations may have some value and validity, even though it may not be "genuinely scientific" and free from "inherited assumptions." Constructive experimentation in improvement, however, should be eagerly welcomed and encouraged.

QUESTIONS AND PROBLEMS

1. Make a detailed comparison of McDowell's findings on the curriculum of the junior college, as given in the United States Bureau of Education, Bulletin no. 35 (1919), with the Hollingsworth-Eells report in this chapter.
2. Compare the junior college curriculum in any state with that of the state university, or other standard collegiate institutions.
3. How do you account for the major differences in the curricula suggested by Koos and Woods?
4. Make a study, similar to that of Woods at the University of California, to suggest a curriculum based upon the actual courses taken by students in some other university.
5. Can an adequate academic curriculum be less extensive than that recommended by Koos? Are the curricula in over half of the junior colleges in the country "inadequate"?
6. Bobbitt was quoted on page 474, regarding the general curriculum field, as saying: "Of fundamental changes there are few. Of fundamental improvement, there is little." Is this true, in your

opinion, for the junior college field? Give reasons and specific examples to justify your answer.

7. What significance has the Stephens College curriculum experiment for junior college education of freshmen and sophomore level?
8. How would you select a group of thirty junior colleges in the United States to be most representative for a curriculum study?
9. Sadler says, in discussing "The Junior College Curriculum in Engineering Schools" (Gray, *Junior College Curriculum*, p. 93): "At the risk of bringing down upon my unguarded head the wrath of many of my esteemed colleagues on the numerous faculties of our institutions of learning, I venture to suggest that their most popular indoor sport, if faculty meetings could be described in this somewhat flippant way, is that of arranging curriculums." Do junior college faculties spend too much time on curriculum work? Can it be done most effectively by the faculty? What other methods are possible? desirable? preferable?
10. In the ideal junior college, what proportion of the curriculum should be non-academic?
11. Make a detailed analysis, in a group of junior colleges, of commercial, engineering, agricultural, home economics, art, or music curricula.
12. What place should and do modern languages have in the junior college curriculum? See Koos's and Woods's recommendations.
13. How much English, if any, should be required of all junior college students?
14. What other subjects, if any, should be required of all junior college students?
15. What academic subjects, if any, should be required of all students taking terminal or semi-professional courses?
16. In his article on "The Junior College Curriculum in California," in Gray's *Junior College Curriculum*, Koos says: "In pointing out what seem to be the limitations of the offering in the junior colleges of California, he [the author] hopes to stimulate further inquiry and greater constructive effort in this most important phase of junior college organization. It must be admitted that development in the curriculum on the junior college level in that state is more advanced than in any other state or section of the country" (page 73). List the different limitations he points out, and suggest the ways they may be removed. What evidence is there to substantiate his last sentence?
17. What, if any, differentiation of curricula should there be in California for "recommended" and "unrecommended" students?
18. Exhibit the data of Tables 45, 46, and 49, by circle diagrams.
19. Make a study similar to Hiatt's for private junior colleges; or for state junior colleges.

20. Compare "offerings" and "givings" in selected four-year institutions for comparison with the conditions in junior colleges.
21. Summarize enrollment by courses in the lower division of some college or university or group of them, and compare with Figure 31. (Data for student enrollment by classes are given regularly in the *Register* of Stanford University.)

SUGGESTED READINGS

General

Bobbitt, F. *How to Make a Curriculum.* Houghton Mifflin Company, Boston, Massachusetts, 1924. 292 pp.

Chapter 5 contains statement of fifty principles for "all levels of education from kindergarten to junior college."

Bolton, F. E. "What Should Constitute the Curriculum of the Junior College or Extended High School?" in *School and Society*, vol. 8, pp. 726–30. (December 21, 1918.)

Booth, C. J. "Articulation of Junior College and University Curricula"; in *Bulletin of the Pacific Coast Association of Collegiate Registrars*, pp. 70–75. (March, 1929.)

Boucher, C. S. "Curriculum and Methods of Instruction in the Junior College of a University"; in *Proceedings of the Eighth Annual Meeting of the American Association of Junior Colleges*, pp. 24–34. Chicago, Illinois, 1928.

Bush, R. "Curricular Problems in the Junior College"; in *California Quarterly of Secondary Education*, vol. 5, pp. 87–92. (October, 1929.)

California, University of. *The Junior College Bulletin.* Administrative Bulletins of the University of California, no. 11, 39 pp. (August, 1926.)

Contains detailed suggestions for curricula, by departments.

Clement, J. A. *Curriculum Making in The Secondary Schools*, 534 pp. Henry Holt and Company, New York, 1923.

Chapter XI, "The Junior College Idea of the Twentieth Century and Curricula in the Making" (pp. 222–39).

Coursault, J. H. (editor). *Circular of Information to Accredited Junior Colleges.* University of Missouri Bulletin, vol. 27, no. 37, 134 pp. Columbia, Missouri, October 1, 1926.

Contains detailed suggestions for curricula, by departments.

Crawford, C. C. "Principles Affecting the Junior College Curriculum"; in *California Quarterly of Secondary Education*, vol. 4, pp. 70–72. (October, 1928.)

Cross, H. A. "What are the Predominate Objectives of Junior Colleges as They are Reflected in Junior College Curricula?"; in *Proceedings of the Ninth Annual Meeting, American Association of Junior Colleges*, pp. 132–34. Fort Worth, Texas, 1928.

Based upon study of fifteen public junior colleges in North Central Association.

*Douglass, A. A. "Curriculum Determinants in the Junior College"; in *California Quarterly of Secondary Education*, vol. 4, pp. 37–44. (October, 1928.)

Why terminal courses have not lived up to their promise and possibilities.

Eells, W. C. "The Present Status of the Junior College"; in *School Review*, vol. 27, pp. 388–89. (May, 1929.)

Review of Whitney's *The Junior College in America*.

Gray, W. S. "Educational Readjustment at the Junior College Level"; in *Proceedings of the Ninth Annual Meeting of the American Association of Junior Colleges*, pp. 39–46. Fort Worth, Texas, 1928. Also in *School and Society*, vol. 30, pp. 135–43. (August 3, 1929.)

*Gray, W. S. (editor). *The Junior College Curriculum. Proceedings of the Institute for Administrative Officers at the University of Chicago*, vol. 1. University of Chicago Press, Chicago, Illinois, 1929.

Summarized in first part of this chapter.

*Hiatt, L. R. "Curricular Changes in Junior Colleges"; in *Junior College Journal*, vol. 1, pp. 6–11. (October, 1930.)

Kemp, W. W. "Junior College Curriculum"; in *Sixth Yearbook of Department of Superintendence of National Education Association*, pp. 245–49. (1928.)

Koos, L. V. "The Junior College and the First Two Years of College Work"; in *The Junior College*, pp. 27–64; also essentially the same in *School Review*, vol. 29, pp. 586–92, 668–78. (October, November, 1921.)

Koos, L. V. *The Junior College Movement*, pp. 29–63.

Koos, L. V. "The Junior College Curriculum"; in *School Review*, vol. 35, pp. 657–72. (November, 1927.)

Koos, L. V., and Weersing, F. J. *Secondary Education in California: Report of a Preliminary Survey*, pp. 83–93. Sacramento, California, 1929.

McDowell, F. M. *The Curriculum of the Junior College*. United States Bureau of Education, Bulletin no. 19, pp. 37–42. (1922.)

Newlon, J. H. "Integration in High School and Junior College Curriculum"; in *Fourteenth Yearbook of the Department of Secondary School Principals*, Bulletin no. 30, pp. 185–95. (March, 1930.)

Prescott, H. W. "The Junior College from the Standpoint of the University"; in *Proceedings of the Sixth Annual Meeting of the American Association of Junior Colleges*, pp. 69–75. Chicago,

Illinois, 1926. Also in *Western Reserve University Centennial Conference*, pp. 7-13. Columbus, Ohio, 1926.
Based on study by special commission at University of Chicago.

Proctor, W. M. "The Curriculum of the Sacramento Junior College"; in *Sacramento School Survey*, pp. 33-35, 364-73. Sacramento, California. (October, 1928.)

Reid, J. R. *Texas Municipal Junior Colleges.* Bulletin no. 255 of the State Department of Education. Austin, Texas. (June, 1929.)
Course of study, pp. 59-77.

Stowe, A. M. *Modernizing the College.* 119 pp. A. A. Knopf, New York, 1926.
Description of three-year experiment in introducing a humanized junior college curriculum at University of Toledo.

*Thomas, F. W. "The Junior College Curriculum"; in Proctor, W. M. (editor), *The Junior College: Its Organization and Administration*, pp. 60-74.

Vandervort, C. T. "The Preparatory Curriculum of California Junior Colleges"; in *Public School Journal of California*, vol. 4, pp. 2-4, 16. (April 1, 1929.)

*Voegelein, L. B. "An Annotated and Selected Bibliography on the Junior College Curriculum"; in Gray, W. S. (editor), *The Junior College Curriculum*, pp. 244-58.
Contains 107 titles.

Walker, L. E. *The Curriculum of the Public Junior College — A Survey.* Kansas State Agricultural College Bulletin, vol. 10, no. 3, 40 pp. (November 1, 1926.) Bibliography, 61 titles, briefly annotated.
Symposium of views, historical résumé, and analysis of catalogues of 35 public junior colleges.

*Whitney, F. L. *The Junior College in America*, 258 pp. Greeley, Colorado, 1928.
Chapter VI deals with the curriculum of the junior college (pp. 92-153). Discussed in this chapter.

Wood, J. M. "A College Curriculum for Women"; in Hudelson, E. (editor), *Problems of College Education*, pp. 369-82. Minneapolis, Minnesota, 1928.

*Woods, B. M. "Junior College Preparation for University Work"; in *Bulletin of the Pacific Coast Association of Collegiate Registrars*, pp. 31-41. (March, 1929.)

Special Subjects

Barnhart, E. W. "Making Commercial Curriculums for Junior Colleges"; in *Yearbook of the Eastern Commercial Teachers' Association.* New York, 1929.

Burlingame, L. G., and Martin, E. G. "General Biology and the Junior College"; in *Science*, n.s., vol. 51, pp. 452-55. (May 7, 1920.)

Chappell, H. F. "Shall the Junior College Offer Agriculture?" in *Vocational Education News Notes*, vol. 5, pp. 40–41. (May, 1929.)

Clark, A. B. "Art in the High School and Junior College Curriculum"; in *Proceedings of the Pacific Art Association*, pp. 37–43. Stanford University, California, 1927.

Dadisman, H. S. "Agriculture in the Junior College"; in *Sierra Educational News*, vol. 14, pp. 575–77. (December, 1918.)

Hoy, E. A. "Junior College Mathematics in California"; in *School Review*, vol. 36, pp. 370–73. (May, 1928.)

Johnson, R. E. *English Expression, a Study in Curriculum Building*, 106 pp. Public School Publishing Company, Bloomington, Illinois, 1926.

Kemp, W. W. "The Junior College Movement in California"; in *Eighth Yearbook of National Association of Secondary School Principals*, pp. 82–94. (1924.)
Detailed consideration of curriculum in physics.

La Dow, R. *A Survey of Commercial Education in the Junior College.* University of Iowa Monograph in Education. Iowa City, Iowa, April, 1929.

Lange, A. F. "A Junior College Department of Civic Education"; in *School and Society*, vol. 2, pp. 442–48. (September 25, 1915.)

Marshall, L. C. "Junior College Curriculum Building in Economics and Business"; in *Proceedings of the Eighth Annual Meeting of the American Association of Junior Colleges*, pp. 1–21. Chicago, Illinois, 1928.

O'Neill, K. N. "French, German, and Spanish Texts"; in *Occasional Papers of Riverside Junior College*, 86 pp. Riverside, California. June 1, 1927.
Curricula in Southern California institutions.

Shields, H. G. "Junior College Business Education"; in *Proceedings of National Education Association*, pp. 319–22. (1929.)

Shields, H. G. "Economics and Business Education on the Junior College Level"; in *Proceedings of the Tenth Annual Meeting of the American Association of Junior Colleges*, pp. 16–24. Atlantic City, 1929.

Shields, H. G. "Objectives in Junior College Economics"; in *Historical Outlook*, vol. 20, pp. 113–14. (March, 1929.)

Thompson, R. H. "English Courses in California Junior Colleges"; in *English Journal* (college edition), vol. 19, pp. 156–63. (February, 1930.)

Ward, H. M. "Junior College Art"; in *Sierra Educational News*, vol. 22, p. 264. (April, 1926.)

CHAPTER XIX

PROBLEMS OF FINANCE

Adequate figures in regard to costs in junior colleges are not at present available. — H. F. CLARK.[1]

Contents of this chapter. This chapter considers various problems of finance, for the most part relating especially to public junior colleges, but with some reference to private institutions as well. Significant studies of unit costs are first presented, and their limitations pointed out. Sources of income for both public and private institutions are classified, and their relative importance considered. Finally, the questions of tuition and state support for junior colleges are discussed.

COSTS IN JUNIOR COLLEGES

Importance and difficulty. The first question to come to the administrator in taking charge of a new junior college, to the citizens considering the establishment of a junior college in the community, or to the law-maker when junior college legislation is proposed, is: "What will it cost?" There is no question more difficult to answer definitely and without numerous qualifications to insure against danger of misinterpretation. Data are available in state reports — some on a moderately scientific basis, and some useless because misleading. Involved techniques lie behind cost studies that have any reliability.

Most of the studies that have been made have been in terms of "cost per student." What is a student? Does this mean student enrolled, or student in average daily attendance? How are part-time and extension students counted? What

[1] Clark, H. F. *Junior College Costs.* Bulletin of the School of Education of Indiana University, vol. 4, pp. 68–78. (September, 1927.)

elements are considered in "cost"? In some studies it is salary cost, in some instructional cost, in some total current cost, and in some capital outlay, depreciation, and replacement are considered. Careful definition is necessary if the results are to be properly interpreted. The difficulty is greater than definition, however — it is a matter of accounting in the institutions themselves. The majority of the junior colleges are operated in more or less close relationship with high schools, and the finances of the two institutions are inextricably interwoven. The allocation of salaries for instructors teaching in both institutions, of administrative expense, of heat, light, and janitor service, library and laboratories, and rental of building are problems that are handled differently in different parts of the country, and with institutions of different size and condition. The only statement that can be made with confidence regarding "cost" data collected from such institutions is that they are sure to be not strictly comparable.

Probably the only results which can be accepted, with even a moderate degree of confidence, are those based on the findings of an investigator who has visited a group of institutions in person and endeavored to secure the desired data in comparable form. A few investigations of this type will be summarized briefly, although it is noteworthy that their makers are most careful to hedge their findings about with numerous restrictions, qualifications, and cautions. Two states, California and Texas, have also published official reports which have some value for a study of unit costs.

Koos's two studies of costs. Koos, in his Commonwealth Fund investigation, studied costs in fifteen public junior colleges whose enrollments varied, in 1921–22, from 27 to 657. He found "teaching cost per student" varying from $83 to $224, with a median of $117. He discussed in detail "other costs" and estimates the total annual cost per student as follows:

Teaching	$125
Other instructional	21
Plant replacement	25
Other non-instructional	17
	$188

He concludes:[1]

It does not appear to be especially hazardous to assume that a reasonable approximate average cost over all per student in cities of the size represented is $185, with a division of something like $125 for teaching-items and the remaining $60 for non-teaching items. It is easy to conceive of situations in which this average cost will and should rise to $200, or beyond, with $135 for teaching-items and $65 for non-teaching items. A safe range of cost where conditions are satisfactory is probably somewhere between $175 and a little more than $200.

The investigation just mentioned was made ten years ago and many conditions and cost elements, especially instructional salaries, have increased since that time. The investigation is valuable, however, for the technique of segregation of high school and junior college costs which was developed, and which was used by the same author in a study of costs of ten California junior colleges in 1928. This showed an average cost of $331 per student in average daily attendance. It is to be noted, however, that average daily attendance is an entirely different unit from enrollment. Dr. B. M. Woods, as a result of a careful analysis of the factors of absence, drop-outs, part-time, and extension students in California, has shown that an average daily attendance of 100 may be taken as equivalent to a full-time enrollment of 137.[2] This coefficient of 1.37 has already been used several times in this volume to change California average daily attendance to enrollment. On this basis, an average cost of $331 per student in average daily

[1] Koos, L. V. *The Junior College Movement*, p. 401. Ginn and Company.

[2] Woods, B. M. "Economic Analysis of an Effective Junior College"; in *California Quarterly of Secondary Education*, vol. 4, pp. 20–24. (October, 1928.)

attendance would be equivalent to one of $242 per student enrolled. Replacement charges, which account for $25 in the first study, were not included in the California analysis, however, so that the comparison between the two periods is better represented by the difference between $163 and $242, about a 50 per cent increase. This difference is partially accounted for by increased costs in the intervening decade, and partially by higher costs in California. In the earlier study three out of four California institutions which were included showed lower costs than the median of the entire group. This suggests that the principal change was due to the temporal element rather than to the geographical one.

The results of Koos's 1928 California study, for ten different junior colleges of three types, are summarized in Table

TABLE 53. COSTS PER STUDENT IN TEN CALIFORNIA JUNIOR COLLEGES OF THREE TYPES (1927–1928) [1]

	ENROLLMENT	TEACHING COSTS	OTHER COSTS	TOTAL COSTS
Separate junior colleges				
A	825	$133	$70	$203
B	216	203	163	366
C	162	212	159	371
Mean		**183**	**130**	**313**
District junior colleges in connection with high school plant				
D	211	135	66	201
E	273	205	106	311
F	562	222	78	300
Mean		**188**	**83**	**271**
Junior college departments of high schools				
G	76	137	117	254
H	156	186	138	324
I	58	213	72	285
J	45	476	222	698
Mean		**253**	**137**	**390**

[1] Koos, L. V., and Weersing, F. J. *Secondary Education in California: Report of a Preliminary Survey*, pp. 116–17. Sacramento, California, 1929.

53. Concerning these results, however, Koos is careful to say:[1]

More pains were taken in gathering and handling the data in this field than in perhaps any other, and with less reliable results.... Although the data may prove interesting to the reader, because of the difficulty of securing comparable data, the reader is once more admonished *not to rely heavily* on comparisons for individual institutions.

In the same California study Koos also secured data on "teaching costs per student in average daily attendance" for thirty different institutions, showing variations for this element alone from $102 to $751. If "teaching costs" are about two thirds of total cost, as indicated by Table 53, the corresponding variation in total costs in the California group of thirty institutions runs from about $150 to over $1100. The danger of placing much confidence in averages or medians, when the individual colleges show such a wide variation, is evident.

Reeves's study. Dr. F. W. Reeves, formerly of the University of Kentucky, has participated in a large number of surveys of higher educational institutions. In 1926, he reported at the meeting of the American Association of Junior Colleges on a comparison of costs in five liberal arts colleges of the Middle West, having enrollments from 290 to over 700, and in two private junior colleges for young women, both with enrollments under 250. "No two of the seven colleges had similar accounting systems!" Extensive reclassification of expenditures was necessary. In the four-year colleges represented, current expenditures per student enrolled varied from $174 to $447, with an average of $308. For the two junior colleges it was $234 and $300, an average of $268. Reeves's general discussion of junior college costs is excellent, due to his

[1] Koos, L. V., and Weersing, F. J. *Secondary Education in California: Report of a Preliminary Survey*, pp. 114, 117. Sacramento, California, 1929.

background of survey experience and analysis, but the two institutions represented are too few to be more than suggestive, even of the private type for women.

Johnson's study. E. A. Johnson, in his doctor's dissertation at Indiana University, studied costs in a group of thirty junior colleges in the Middle West to which personal visits were made to secure data. He found that the mean current expenditure per student enrolled was $200; per student in average daily attendance $232.

Clark's study. H. F. Clark, in 1927, reports junior college costs for 38 junior colleges (type or location not stated) as varying from $94 to $472, with a median of $208. He is careful to state, however, that:[1]

> The figures are not "cost" figures in any sense of the word. One might be grossly misled if he should so consider them. Unfortunately many people are likely to take them as such, and attempt to establish institutions on this basis.... The low figures represent junior colleges that are in high schools and the "cost" is not a real cost figure, but only an allocation of high school expenditures. The institutions reporting "costs" under $300 [31 of the 38] per student are in many cases not reporting "costs" at all but certain disbursement figures divided by total enrollment. In some cases the low cost has been obtained at a sacrifice of satisfactory libraries, equipment, laboratories, buildings, and teachers. There is nothing in these figures to suggest that a junior college of the highest grade can be run on less than $300 per student.

Stronger disclaimer of reliability of such data could scarcely be made. These figures would hardly be worthy of mention had they not been republished widely in recent publications, without Clark's qualifications upon them, and unjustified conclusions drawn from them.[2]

[1] Clark, H. F. *Junior College Costs*. Bulletin of the School of Education of Indiana University, vol. 4, p. 70. (September, 1927.)

[2] For example, Whitney, in his *Junior College in America* (pp. 161–63), prints the entire table of thirty-eight institutions, without qualification except to report them as "actual total and student unit costs in thirty-eight junior colleges,"

Costs in Kansas and Missouri. Obrien, in his *Atchison Survey* (p. 28), reports cost per student in average daily attendance in four Kansas junior colleges as varying from $205 to $230, and in two in Missouri as $212 and $213.

California costs. Data on costs in the district junior colleges of California are published annually by the California State Department of Education. These are not strictly comparable since several of the institutions are in separate plants, while others share the high school plant with varying methods of charging rent, proportionate operating cost, and administrative expense. The 1929 legislature passed a bill authorizing the State Board of Education to prescribe a uniform accounting system for all junior colleges, but no data on such a basis are yet available. Average daily attendance, total enrollment, tax levied per $100 of assessed valuation, and total current expenditure for California district junior colleges in 1928–29 are given in Table 54.[1]

Here an average cost per student in average daily attendance of $285 is found. If adjusted to the equivalent full-time enrollment (Woods's factor of 1.37) it is found to be $208; if adjusted to the actual enrollment figure it is only $172. The latter figure would be quite misleading, as is evident at a glance, for Sacramento or Chaffey. If it were used, the Sacramento cost would drop to half the figure given in the table, while Chaffey would be only one fourth. Such facts simply illustrate still further the difficulty of securing fair and comparable cost

and uses them as the basis of an involved correlational analysis of causation to determine that 75 per cent of the factors determining total cost are due to size of student body! In another publication, designed especially for popular use in Colorado, the same table is repeated with the assurance that the data in it "are very useful, if any taxpayer wants to know exactly what this proposed junior college really costs in other states." (Whitney, F. L., and Shaw, J. H. *The Junior College Movement*, pp. 36–37. Greeley, Colorado, 1928.)

[1] Three newly organized institutions, Compton, San José, and Yuba County are omitted, since, due to the method of financing new institutions in California the first year of their existence without state aid, the average based upon them and resulting averages for the entire group would be misleading.

TABLE 54. COST AND ENROLLMENT DATA FOR THIRTEEN CALIFORNIA DISTRICT JUNIOR COLLEGES (1928-29)

	Current Expenditure per Student in Average Daily Attendance	Tax Rate	Average Daily Attendance	Enrollment
Averages	**$285**	**.25**	**478**	**801**
*Riverside	$452	.39	251	371
*San Bernardino	369	.38	285	478
Fullerton	335	.16	383	494
Chaffey	329	.41	390	1676
Glendale	295	.14	290	326
Pasadena	278	.08	832	1045
Santa Ana	272	.22	362	608
*Marin	261	.48	228	414
Santa Rosa	242	.15	213	302
*San Mateo	238	.40	596	979
*Modesto	237	.30	477	713
Long Beach	224	.07	729	794
*Sacramento	174	.12	1175	2211

* Plants and administration independent of high school.

figures. The danger of trusting the average is shown, also, when the extremes are compared. The cost at Riverside is two and a half times that at Sacramento. There is some relationship between size and enrollment, but the relation is not marked. The correlation is only .50. There is considerable tendency for small junior colleges to have higher per capita costs than large ones when the enrollment is very small — less than 100 — as is shown in Table 53, but Reeves has found that this tendency is slight when the enrollment exceeds 250. In colleges of 250 or more, other factors are more important, as for example, more expensive terminal courses. It is interesting that the six institutions occupying independent plants are scattered over the entire range from highest to lowest unit cost.

Average per capita costs over a series of years for the California district junior colleges are shown in Table 55.

With large increases in enrollment during the past four or five

Table 55. Per Capita Cost per Student in Average Daily Attendance in California District Junior Colleges (1922–23 to 1928–29)

	Number of Colleges	Cost per Student in Average Daily Attendance
1922–23	7	$251
1923–24	7	342
1924–25	8	321
1925–26	8	321
1926–27	10	314
1927–28	13	284
1928–29	13	285

years the per capita cost has shown a tendency to decline, but it is doubtful whether it will fall much lower.

Costs of Texas municipal colleges. Costs as reported for the Texas junior colleges are much lower than for the California group, although the enrollments are much smaller. They are

Table 56. Cost per Student Enrolled in Municipal Junior Colleges of Texas (1928–29)

	Cost per Student	Enrollment
Average — 5 in separate buildings	**$161**	**199**
Average — 10 with high schools	**116**	**196**
*San Angelo	238	91
*Texarkana	196	167
Wichita Falls	190	273
Edinburg	187	242
*San Antonio	148	296
Victoria	121	69
*Clarendon	116	81
Brownsville	114	138
*Paris	110	360
Gainesville	108	93
Hillsboro	100	175
Tyler	98	163
Ranger	93	53
Temple	81	122
Houston	69	635

* Housed in separate plants.

figured on the basis of cost per student enrolled, students taking one course and those taking six courses being all counted equally, and high school segregations not being made in many cases, as is pointed out in the bulletin from which the data of Table 56 are taken.[1] They do not include complete costs.

The average enrollment varies but slightly in the Texas institutions in the groups housed with high schools and those housed independently. With this factor thus held constant, it is noticeable that the per capita costs are reported as almost 40 per cent higher in the latter group.

Summary of cost studies. With the most reliable data available, but with the limitations already noted, the best evidence seems to be that in the larger district type of California junior college, with attendance of 500 students or more, the cost per student in average daily attendance is almost $300, or something over $200 for each student in full-time enrollment. In the smaller high school type, with prevailing enrollments of 100 or less, the corresponding figures seem to be about $100 higher. The data are meager and inaccurate, and not entirely comparable. Further there is such great variation between institutions, costs being from three to six or seven times as much in one institution as in another, that too much reliance cannot be placed upon averages as a guide to action. In Texas, costs average $160 per student enrolled in institutions occupying separate buildings, $116 per student in those administered in the high school plant. The latter figure is probably nearer instructional cost than total cost.

Costs advised. In the light of the facts so far given, it is instructive to notice the recommendations of some investigators in the field. Koos's recommendation of approximately

[1] Reid, J. R. *Texas Municipal Junior Colleges.* Bulletin, State Department of Education, vol. 5, no. 5. Austin, Texas, June, 1929.

$200 has already been mentioned. Reeves concludes, after numerous extensive studies:[1]

> An effective junior college of 250 or more students should expect to have a cost per student of approximately $340, which figure represents the approximate cost per student at the junior college level of an effective four-year college of 500 students. An effective junior college of 200 students should expect to have a cost per student of at least $375, while an effective junior college of only 150 students will cost at least $400. In interpreting these cost figures it should be kept in mind that we are speaking of *thoroughly effective* colleges — institutions superior, and therefore more expensive than the typical institution accredited by regional accrediting associations.

These figures are considerably higher than those found in any junior colleges except a very few of those in California.

Clark, after a detailed study of the junior college situation and conditions in Indiana, estimates the costs of four types of tax-supported junior colleges, if established in Indiana, as follows:[2]

	Enrollment	Per Capita Cost
Unsatisfactory junior college	60	$135
Poor junior college	200	200
Good standard junior college	250	300
Good small junior college	100	500

The figure of $135 is the average cost of instruction for high school students in Indiana.

Kibby, after a detailed analysis of the probable cost of a junior college for Siskiyou County, California, arrived at a figure which was approximately $300 per student enrolled, when an enrollment of 250 was assumed.[3]

[1] Reeves, F. W. "The Cost of Education in an Effective Junior College"; in *Proceedings of the Seventh Annual Meeting of the American Association of Junior Colleges*, p. 58. Jackson, Mississippi, 1926.

[2] Clark, H. F., *op. cit.*, p. 73.

[3] Kibby, I. W. "Can Siskiyou County Afford a Junior College?" in *Junior College Survey of Siskiyou County, California*, p. 51. Yreka, California, July, 1928.

Woods estimates a desirable cost, allowing a 10 per cent increase over present average salary scale in the California district colleges, of $370 per student in average daily attendance; or $345, if there were no increase in salary scale such as he recommends as a basis in computing the larger figure.[1]

Distribution of actual expenses in California. Figure 33 shows the actual distribution of expenses in sixteen California district junior colleges in 1928–29. It will be noted that instructional salaries account for approximately two thirds of the total expense, while library, laboratories, and other items bring up the total instructional expense to approximately four fifths of the total.

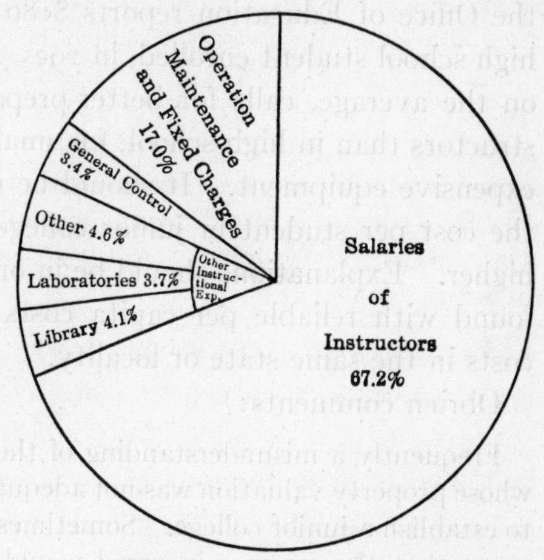

FIG. 33. DISTRIBUTION OF EXPENDITURES IN SIXTEEN CALIFORNIA DISTRICT JUNIOR COLLEGES, 1928–29

Reeves and Russell, in a detailed study of ten liberal-arts denominational colleges, found that costs were distributed as follows:

Instruction	67 per cent
Administration	20 per cent
Operation and maintenance	13 per cent

Data which they collected from over forty colleges in the North Central Association showed about 65 per cent for instruction, but 70 per cent in the better colleges.[2]

Comparison with high school costs. Average current ex-

[1] Woods, *op. cit.*, p. 23.
[2] Reeves, J. F. *College Organization and Administration*, pp. 221, 222.

penditure per high school student in average daily attendance in California, in 1927–28, was $189; in elementary schools, $99. In Indiana, the cost per high school student enrolled was found to be $135; in Arizona, $194. In the United States as a whole the Office of Education reports $186 as the average cost per high school student enrolled, in 1925–26. College instruction, on the average, calls for better-prepared and better-paid instructors than in high school, for smaller classes, and for more expensive equipment. It should be expected, therefore, that the cost per student in junior college should be considerably higher. Explanations should be in order if junior colleges are found with reliable per capita costs lower than high school costs in the same state or locality.

Obrien comments: [1]

Frequently a misunderstanding of the cost has led communities whose property valuation was not adequate for such an undertaking to establish a junior college. Sometimes actual assurance has been given that the expense incurred would be equivalent only to an extension of the high school enrollment. Such misinformation distributed in a community may not indicate intentional misrepresentation, but it certainly indicates lack of definite information.

Dr. Eby, of Texas, says: [2]

There is a widely spread misconception in regard to the cost of a junior college. Many think the junior college years can be added to the high school with little or no additional expense. It is a somewhat general belief, and some high educational authorities have unfortunately lent credence to the error, that such institutions can actually be made self-supporting by charging a tuition fee. Now nothing is farther from the truth, unless the tuition is made extremely high, in which case the institution will probably lose its character as a democratic public institution.

[1] Obrien, F. P. "Conditions Which Justify Establishing a Junior College"; in *Proceedings of the American Association of Junior Colleges, Eighth Annual Meeting, Chicago, Illinois, 1928*, pp. 76–77.

[2] Eby, F. "Shall We Have a System of Public Junior Colleges in Texas?" in *Texas Outlook*, vol. 11, p. 23. (January, 1927.)

Comparisons with costs in higher institutions. Comparisons have sometimes been made with costs in universities, to show that the junior college can give education much more economically. Such comparisons are full of difficulties and pitfalls. It is doubtful whether a fair technique can be worked out for comparing the two. Certainly it has not yet been done. Part-time and summer-school students confuse the problem from one standpoint; segregation of upper-division, lower-division, graduate, and pure research costs complicate it still more. Proctor has estimated the cost per student in the University of California at from $350 to $450. The United States Office of Education reports cost per student for 1927–28 in all public universities and colleges as $592; in private institutions as $508. It cannot be assumed, however, that any such figures represent at all the cost of a student *in the lower division*. Upper-division work, with smaller classes, higher salaried professors, and more expensive equipment, cannot fail to be more expensive than in the lower division, and graduate work is yet more expensive.

The best study of unit costs in various departments, schools, and levels of higher education has been made by the Educational Finance Inquiry Commission. The most significant facts for the purpose of the present discussion are summarized in Table 57, which is based upon a detailed analysis by departments, of costs for over two and a half million student-clock-hours at the University of Washington.

From this table it is seen that lower-division instructional costs were less than two thirds of upper-division costs; and approximately one fifth of graduate study costs. It is quite evident that any cost data for universities, especially where graduate work is an important element, derived by dividing total cost by total enrollment, is quite misleading and fallacious for determining true costs in the lower division. The ratio of the three groups at the University of Washington was 20 : 34 : 100.

TABLE 57. STUDENT-CLOCK-HOUR COSTS AT UNIVERSITY OF WASHINGTON FOR LOWER DIVISION, UPPER DIVISION, AND GRADUATE WORK (1921–22) *

	Cost per Student-Clock-Hour			Ratio of Lower Division to Upper Division	Ratio of Lower Division to Graduate Division
	Lower division	Upper division	Graduate division		
All	**$0.25**	**$0.41**	**$1.22**	**.63**	**.21**
Liberal Arts	.21	.30	1.10	.70	.19
Science	.26	.42	1.08	.63	.24
Engineering	.39	.58	1.28	.67	.30
Education	.16	.28	1.28	.57	.12

* Condensed from Table 74, in Stevens, E. B., and Elliott, E. C., *Unit Costs of Higher Education* (Educational Finance Inquiry Commission, The Macmillan Company, New York, 1925). The last two columns are computed by the author from the data given by Stevens and Elliott.

For example, an approximate computation for Stanford University, for 1928–29, is illuminating on the basis of the University of Washington figures. The total academic expense for the year at Stanford was $2,328,080. Reducing summer-session students to equivalent three-quarter students, it may be estimated that there were the equivalent of 3737 full-time students — 1015 in the graduate division, 1483 in the upper division, and 1239 in the lower division. If total expense is divided by total number of students, the average cost per student is $623; but if the ratio 20:34:100 is used, the average cost per lower-division student is only $239. This is only illustrative, since conditions at Stanford and Washington can easily be shown not to be comparable in various respects, but it is suggestive of the great differences found when an effort is made to segregate lower-division costs in a university, especially in one which places emphasis on graduate work.

Comparisons with four-year liberal arts colleges which give little or no graduate work should be somewhat more valid. The most reliable data of this type are those obtained by Reeves and Russell by personal visits to 32 liberal arts colleges of the North Central and Southern Associations, in 1925–26. Their results may be summarized thus:

	Number of Colleges	Average Enrollment	Educational Expenditure per Student
Entire group	32	639	$266
Small colleges	8	279	369
Medium colleges	16	473	258
Large colleges	8	1329	249

When allowance is made for variations in methods and units used, it is seen that these are well within the range of many junior college costs.

The economy of the junior college. A strong reason for the establishment of junior colleges is the economic one — it is frequently pointed out that junior college education can be given at a great saving in the local junior college, rather than in the university. There are two aspects to this question — the cost to the individual student in attendance, and the cost to the taxpayer. From the standpoint of the individual student the argument is perfectly sound, and is a very potent one. Saving in travel expense, in extra cost of board and room, and in other expenses incurred when living away from home amounts to a substantial sum, and means college attendance for many who would otherwise find it financially impossible.

When the total cost to the taxpayer is considered, however, the argument is open to question. In the first place, cost to the taxpayers of the state as a whole is undoubtedly increased by the establishment of junior colleges. When the total freshman and sophomore population is increased from 50 to 150 per cent, it cannot fail to increase the *total cost* of education. When educational opportunity is brought closer to the people, more of them take advantage of it, the total amount of education secured is increased, and the total cost is increased correspondingly. Even on a unit basis, however, it may be questioned whether the argument is sound. Until reliable data are furnished giving actual costs per student *in the lower division* of the university, the real difference in cost cannot be stated.

Even without such data actually at hand, if costs are adequately determined on a comparable basis, there is no reason to suppose that cost per student will be less in the local junior college than in the university. If it is, something is seriously the matter with the education given in the local junior college. The general economic law of economy of mass production is as valid in education as it is in industry. Ten thousand freshman and sophomore students herded together in one university, in large classes, with poorly paid instructors, with greater common use of the same library and laboratory equipment, and with one set of administrative machinery, can surely be given a certain kind of education at less net cost than the same students can be given the same amount of education in a hundred scattered units, with smaller classes, duplication of plant and equipment, and separate administration.

The justification of the junior college. The justification is to be found not in terms of reduced cost per student, but in larger educational opportunity to a larger number of students, in better instructional methods, and in adaptation to local community needs. Mass production unquestionably is more economical in education, as well as in industry, but it does not follow, at least in education, that mass production is more efficient and of a higher quality. It would be well to admit frankly that real junior college education is more expensive to society as a whole, both in total cost and in cost per student, but to justify it on the basis of the increased quantity and improved quality of instruction resulting. If junior college costs per student are in reality markedly lower, it is probably secured at the cost of underpaid or overworked instructors who cannot maintain a real college standard, or of inadequate library or laboratories, or similar deficiencies. The costs may *seem* to be lower because of inadequate accounting methods, particularly in incomplete segregation of high school expenses; but if they are really lower it should be a cause, not for congratulation, but for grave concern and prompt investigation.

INCOME OF JUNIOR COLLEGES

The main sources of income for both public and private junior colleges may be classified as follows:

PUBLIC JUNIOR COLLEGES	PRIVATE JUNIOR COLLEGES
1. Local taxation	1. Endowment
2. Tuition paid by county or district	2. State or local aid
3. Tuition paid by student	3. Tuition
4. State aid	4. Assessments
5. Gifts	5. Gifts
6. Sale of bonds	

PUBLIC JUNIOR COLLEGES

Local taxation. In most states where public junior colleges have been established, they are operated in connection with the high school, and expressly or by implication the local tax is the same for the junior college as for the support of the high school. In a few states, however, a special junior college tax is authorized, as in California and Arizona. In California, high school departmental junior colleges are supported as part of the high school, by local taxation, plus state and county aid of $30 and $60 per student in average daily attendance, as in high school (local district taxation is limited to 75 cents on $100); but in the district type there is no limit on local taxation. In practice, as shown in Table 54, the tax rate varied, in 1928–29, from 7 cents to 48 cents on the $100, with an average of 15 cents.

Tuition paid by county or district. In California, when non-resident students attend a junior college from outside the district of residence, the county of residence has to provide by local tax for the entire cost or "tuition" of the student at the junior college, such cost being determined as total current expense, less state aid received, plus $65 per student to defray estimated cost of interest on plant investment and depreciation. This is a substantial amount in the case of some three or four junior colleges, where almost half of the students come from outside the district. Modesto received $50,000 from this source in a single year.

Tuition paid by students. In most states where public junior colleges have been established, the students are charged a tuition, in some cases rather nominal, but in many cases a fairly large amount. The highest one noted is $200, while in forty-six institutions it is $100 or more. The only states where tuition is not charged in any of the public junior colleges in the

TABLE 58. ANNUAL TUITION AND FEES FOR RESIDENT STUDENTS IN PUBLIC JUNIOR COLLEGES, BY STATES *

	NUMBER OF COLLEGES		TUITION AND FEES REPORTED			STUDENTS IN REPORTING COLLEGES	
	Charging tuition	Not charging tuition	Average	Maximum	Minimum	Charging tuition	Not charging tuition
Total	**72**	**61**	..	..	..	**8,906**	**21,907**
Massachusetts	1	0	$180	..	..	35	..
Arkansas	3	0	127	$150	$100	197	..
Texas	17	0	112	155	60	3,461	..
Nebraska	2	0	104	108	100	159	..
Washington	2	0	103	105	100	205	..
Florida	1	0	100	..	..	150	..
Iowa	21	0	98	120	50	1,177	..
Colorado	2	0	75	75	75	134	..
Georgia	2	0	75	100	50	212	..
Oklahoma	3	2	70	125	0	67	269
Illinois	3	2	56	200	0	397	4,281†
Missouri	4	2	56	108	0	272	460
Minnesota	3	4	49	200	0	454	762
Michigan	6	1	46	75	0	1,746	203
Mississippi	2	4	17	54	0	240	323
California	0	33	0	..	..	..	13,103
Kansas	0	10	0	..	..	..	1,778
North Carolina	0	2	0	..	..	..	306
Arizona	0	1	0	..	..	..	422

* *Directory of the American Association of Junior Colleges*, and Hurt's *College Blue Book*.
† Crane — 4000 students.

state are California, Kansas, North Carolina, and Arizona. Pertinent facts regarding tuition are given in Table 58.

Approximately one half of the junior college students in public junior colleges in the country are in states where a tuition is charged. In six of these states (Oklahoma to Mississippi, inclusive, in Table 58) not all of the colleges charge tuition, but of the 36 colleges reported for those states 21 of them do. Of the 133 public junior colleges for which information is available, 72, or 54 per cent, charge their students tuition. In some of these it is rather nominal, but in many it is a substantial sum. Tuition is charged by institutions in fifteen of the nineteen states. It is charged in over half of the junior colleges. The enrollment in the colleges charging tuition, however, is only 29 per cent of the total enrollment. The average enrollment in the institutions charging tuition is 122; while in those not charging tuition it is 359 — almost three times as great. It may be estimated that the 9000 students in institutions which charge tuition are paying close to $1,000,000 annually for education similar to that furnished an equal-sized group in California and Kansas without any tuition charge to the individual student.

Two conflicting views. Regarding the payment of tuition, Koos says:[1]

> To aid in the support of junior colleges in the proportion only that lower schools are being aided could not be regarded as a generous policy of encouragement, especially if it is borne in mind that the state is now paying most of the cost of providing education on this level to students fortunate enough to be able to attend the state university. Logic seems to point toward providing junior college education, which is essentially secondary in character, free of tuition to the student.

Brothers, on the other hand, favors an annual tuition fee of $50, with provisions for free scholarships and loan funds for worthy

[1] Koos, L. V. *Junior College*, p. 624.

students who are financially unable to meet the charge. He says:[1]

> Many people, including those who are careful students of educational finance, share the opinion that where the student has monetary investment he is going to attack the problem of education more seriously than he does when it is handed to him for the asking.

If this is a valid argument, however, why does it not apply equally well in the university, the teachers' college, the high school, and the elementary school? If it proves anything, it proves too much.

State aid. In the so-called "state" type of junior colleges, usually the support is largely or entirely from appropriations by the state legislature, supplemented by special or permanent funds, and in some cases, although rarely, by student tuition fees. In the district and municipal junior colleges, however, California is the only state providing regular substantial state aid.[2] The high school departmental junior colleges receive, like all high schools, $30 per student in average daily attendance; the district institutions are supposed to receive $2000 per year plus $100 per student in average daily attendance. This amount is derived from federal oil and mineral land leases, which was ample to meet the demand upon it up to 1928. With increased junior college attendance and decreasing federal income, this fund was insufficient, and a special act of the legislature in 1929 provided for making up the balance, up to $30 per student, from the state treasury. Even this amount proved insufficient, however, in 1930, and the junior colleges

[1] Brothers, E. Q. "A Plan for State Support for Public Junior Colleges"; in *Proceedings of the Ninth Annual Meeting of the American Association of Junior Colleges*, p. 123. Fort Worth, Texas, 1928.

[2] Perhaps an exception should be made in the case of Mississippi, where special biennial appropriations are made. In 1930 the legislature made a blanket appropriation of $170,000, to be divided as the Board of Education saw fit on a per capita basis among the public junior colleges of the state. This was double the appropriation made two years earlier.

were likely to receive less than $60 per student unless the legislature of 1931 afforded further relief. A deficit of $500,000 in the state junior college fund was anticipated for 1930–31. The only satisfactory solution will be to separate state support entirely from the fluctuating, uncertain, and inadequate federal mineral fund, and make it a general charge on the state treasury.

No other state has gone as far as Texas, in its new 1929 law, in its antipathy to state aid. That law provides (Section 14):

> No funds received for school purposes from the state available school fund... shall be used for the establishment, support, and maintenance of the junior college, and provided further that the legislature shall not make an appropriation out of the General Fund of the state for the establishment, support, or maintenance of any junior college established or that may be established under the provisions of this Act.

It also provides for a fine up to $1000 or imprisonment up to six months, or both, for any presumptuous official who dares think of violating this section. The contrast between this attitude and Zook's recommendations for state support in Massachusetts, or California practice, is as great as between daylight and darkness. It is interesting to compare the Texas legislation with the recommendation of the Texas Educational Survey Commission (p. 29), that the cost of junior colleges should be borne in part by the community and in part by the state!

Gifts. Gifts form a relatively small source of income for most public junior colleges. The notable bequest of $2,000,000 to the public junior college of Little Rock, Arkansas, has already been mentioned; similar gifts will doubtless be made in the future as the junior colleges become more firmly established. Until the passage of the law of 1929, Texas municipal junior colleges could not be supported by taxes, but depended largely on tuition. They could accept "donations," however, from the public school funds in the local school districts, and such donations comprised an important element of support in several cases. At Centralia, Washington, in a state where there is no legal warrant for junior colleges and they have to exist largely on a tuition basis in the high school plant, over a hundred business men have signed a guarantee to make up any deficit that may occur in operating expense for the year. A similar situation has been found in at least one Texas community.

Sale of bonds. Since most of the junior colleges are housed in the high school plants, they have not had to consider bond issues. The laws of California, Texas, Mississippi, and Arizona, and possibly other states, provide for the issuance of bonds, under certain legal restrictions, for securing buildings and grounds. The following bonded indebtednesses are reported for California and Arizona junior colleges.

Phœnix, Arizona	$175,000
Riverside, California	300,000
Sacramento, California	534,000
San Bernardino, California	485,000
San Mateo, California	255,000

Most of the institutions with separate plants have bonded themselves for their establishment. Modesto and Marin, however, are proceeding on a pay-as-you-go policy, endeavoring to add a building every two or three years out of current taxation.

PRIVATE JUNIOR COLLEGES

Endowment. About one third of the private junior colleges, according to Hurt's *College Blue Book*, report endowments varying from $1000 to $1,250,000; the latter amount being credited to Sarah Lawrence College. Only thirty-three of the group have endowments of $100,000 or over. The North Central Association standard requires a junior college to have an income of $20,000, of which $6000 must be from "stable sources other than students." If this stable source is endowment, not over thirty-three private junior colleges in the country can qualify. The American Council on Education and some other agencies specify $10,000 instead of $6000, which would require an endowment of $200,000 if 5 per cent interest be assumed, a standard reached by only seventeen of the group. Distribution is shown as follows:

Range of Endowment	Number of Colleges
$ 0–$ 24,000	27
25,000– 49,000	14
50,000– 74,000	11
75,000– 99,000	4
100,000– 199,000	16
200,000– 299,000	6
300,000– 399,000	5
400,000– 499,000	3
500,000	1
600,000	1
1,250,000	1
	89

State or local aid. In a few cases state or local aid is given to private junior colleges. Thus, in Maine, as indicated on page 136, there is a graduated scale of assistance to local junior colleges meeting such conditions, varying from $8 to $20 per student, according to enrollment. Another example is afforded by Pennsylvania, where at Erie, Johnstown, and Uniontown the local school boards are authorized to rent and furnish buildings and equipment for the local private junior colleges administered by the University of Pittsburgh.

Tuition. Practically all the private junior colleges charge tuition, varying from amounts that are merely nominal, in institutions which are predominantly missionary in character, to very substantial charges in some of the more exclusive women's institutions, with numerous "extras" for special subjects. Fees and tuition as reported often include board and room as well as academic tuition, so that summaries and comparisons are difficult. As reported in the American Association of Junior Colleges *Directory*, however, conditions in 229 colleges may be summarized in Table 59.

TABLE 59. TUITION CHARGES IN VARIOUS TYPES OF PRIVATE JUNIOR COLLEGES

	Number of Colleges	Average Tuition	Maximum	Minimum	Number with Tuition under $100
Denominational	**168**	**$111**	**$400**	**$0**	**76**
Coeducational	97	97	400	0	56
Men	16	131	350	0	2
Women	55	130	400	25	18
Non-Denominational Board of Trustees	**25**	**274**	**600**	**81**	**3**
Coeducational	9	209	360	81	2
Men	6	300	450	85	1
Women	10	318	600	150	0
Proprietary	**14**	**305**	**700**	**75**	**2**
Coeducational	5	299	700	75	2
Women	9	309	450	150	0
Board, room, and tuition combined	**22**	**1038**	**1800**	**400**	**0**
Men	7	686	1400	400	0
Women	15	1177	1800	600	0

A few private colleges for men or women include board, room, and tuition in a single charge, which runs as high as $1800 in the case of the Porter School, Connecticut, and almost as high in the case of several others. The tuition in the denominational type averages less than half that in other types of junior colleges listed in the table. In almost half of the denominational colleges (45 per cent) the tuition is less than $100. In the non-boarding groups there is no significant difference in trend between the colleges for men and those for women, but both tend to be much higher (from a third to a half) than in the coeducational colleges, when both denominational and non-proprietary colleges are considered. In the boarding institutions, however, the expense for women is very much higher than for men.

Assessments, appropriations, and gifts. In some of the denominational junior colleges there are definite assessments on the churches or membership of the supporting constituency. In others the national or local regional church board makes regular annual appropriations for the maintenance of the college. In addition, gifts for endowment, for buildings, or for current expenses are made by friends of the institution. It is noteworthy that in many cases where a weak four-year college has reduced itself to junior-college status, with consequent improvement in courses and accreditation by the state university, gifts from friends have in many cases increased markedly.

Relative amount of income from different sources. The relative amount of income received from various sources may be shown in the case of two groups of public junior colleges, those in California and Texas. The relative amounts received from the three principal sources of revenue are shown in Figure 34.[1] California has been credited with a strong attitude of state support. It was originally intended that the state support should be approximately 40 per cent of the total cost, which in 1921 was estimated at $250 per student. It was on this assumption that the state appropriation was made $100 per student, in addition to $2000 per institution, amounting, on the basis of the 1928 enrollment, to approximately $105 per student in average daily attendance.

[1] Green reported source of revenue for thirty public junior colleges in various states:

Source	Per cent
Tuition	49 per cent
Tax levies	46
State aid	3
Other	2

These figures represent a situation between the extremes shown by California and Texas. (Green, Rhue E. "Where to Locate Junior Colleges"; in *School Executives' Magazine*, vol. 49, p. 180. December, 1929.)

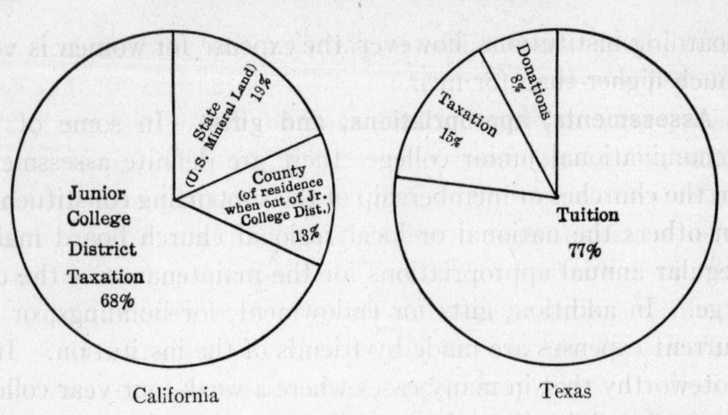

FIG. 34. SOURCES OF INCOME OF JUNIOR COLLEGES IN TWO STATES

Why then does the California portion of Figure 34 show only 19 per cent of the cost furnished by the state? There are two reasons: first, total cost is closer to $300 per student than to $250; second, and more important, the payment is made for the current year on the basis of the average daily attendance of the preceding year. For several years the attendance each year has shown an average increase of 36 per cent over the attendance of the previous year. These two factors make the proportion of the current cost furnished by the state for the current year less than one fifth of the total.[1] Direct district taxation is required to care for two thirds of the total current cost.

The corresponding distribution for the sixteen Texas municipal colleges in 1927–28, as shown in Figure 34, is very different. One district, Edinburg, was permitted by a special act of the legislature to levy a tax which yielded $45,000, 70 per cent of its entire income, but this was permitted no other. City districts, however, could make "donations" to their local junior college, and this was done to a limited extent in a half dozen

[1] Judd falls into the error of stating, in the Texas Survey Commission Report, that: "In California... half of the support and maintenance of the institutions [junior colleges] is derived from state sources."

cases. In the cases of nine institutions, the entire support was reported as coming from student tuition and fees. The fact that 77 per cent of the income was from tuition and fees in the entire group, and 100 per cent in the case of over half of the institutions composing it, is in marked contrast with the California situation where none came from student tuition. Probably the situation for Iowa, Washington, and other states would be similar to that for Texas, if data were available for analysis. A word of caution should again be given, however; namely, that this probably is not entire cost, but largely instructional cost. Even if it were assumed that costs reported in Texas were only 70 per cent of true costs, as discussed earlier in this chapter, it would mean that students were still paying in tuition over fifty per cent of the total true junior college costs.

Such was the situation before the passage of the 1929 junior college law in Texas. This law provides for no state support, but specifically authorizes collection of student fees "for matriculation, laboratories, library, gymnasium, and tuition." It also authorizes a local district tax for maintenance and buildings. It is uncertain how many of the existing junior colleges will choose to reorganize under the district plan authorized in the new junior college law.

Two conceptions of junior college support contrasted. The two parts of Figure 34 will serve to illustrate admirably two entirely different conceptions of the support of public junior colleges. Shall the student be expected to pay the major part of the cost of his college education, or shall he be expected to pay little or none of it? Before discussing this question, it will be enlightening to consider the major divisions of income for the 226 public and 850 private colleges and universities in the United States, as given by the United States Office of Education for 1927–28.[1] This is shown in Figure 35. While it is

[1] Bulletin no. 38, pp. 34, 40. (1929.)

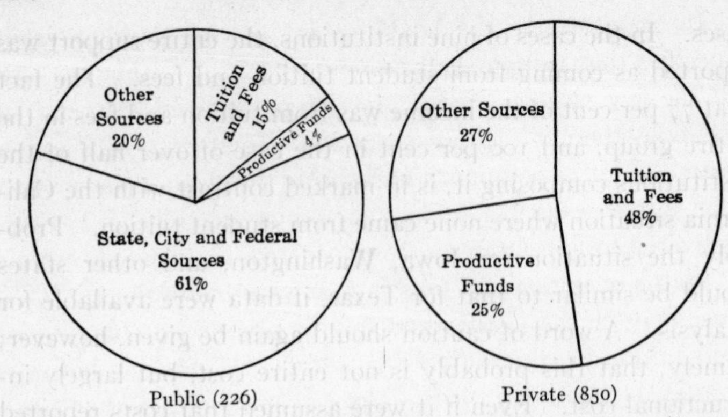

FIG. 35. SOURCES OF INCOME OF PUBLIC AND PRIVATE FOUR-YEAR COLLEGES AND UNIVERSITIES IN THE UNITED STATES

our general theory that public education should be free from tuition charges, this unfortunately is not always the case in the field of higher education. With the marked increase in college and university attendance, many of the state universities have added tuition, or fees, or both. Regarding this, Cubberley says:[1]

> With the expansion of the universities, the increasing costs for all forms of instruction, the development of junior colleges that provide instruction analogous to and better than provided by the universities a generation ago, the change of the university from an arts college to a group of professional schools, and the growth of the idea that there comes a time in higher education when the gains to the individual as contrasted with those to the state are such that he may properly be called upon to contribute something to the cost of his training — we may expect to see both fees on the one hand and scholarships on the other become more and more common in our institutions of higher learning. It must be acknowledged, however, that such theory as to student fees for university instruction is as yet based rather on the need of the institution for additional funds than on any sound social reasoning or facts as to relative costs and values, and that an equally good argument can be advanced for the assumption of such costs by society.

[1] Cubberley, E. P. *State School Administration*, pp. 344–45. Houghton Mifflin Company, Boston, Massachusetts. (1927.)

In many states the enabling act of the state university specifies that tuition shall be free. To keep within the letter of the law various "fees" are charged instead. In one, for example, there is a janitor fee of $50. In another each student pays a fee of $5 per month for heating the classrooms. Education is free — but the student should pay roundly for having it delivered to him properly swept, dusted, and heated.

Status of tuition and fees in four-year institutions. Whatever may be the justification for the practice of charging fees and tuition in state universities, and, as Cubberley indicates, it may be defended on the basis of need rather than sound reasoning if there is any justification for it at all, it is far more defensible in the upper-division and graduate fields of specialization and professional preparation than in the freshman and sophomore field of general education. A recent check of the state universities in forty-two states, listed in Hurt's *College Blue Book*, shows that in eighteen states tuition varying from $10 to $125 was charged to residents of the state. In the twenty-four others no such tuition was charged, but various fees were found, varying in the non-tuition institutions from $2 to $100. If tuition and fees are taken together, however, they are found to average only $59 per institution, and in only six cases do they exceed $100. They are thus only a small part of the total income — about one seventh. In contrast, as already shown, over half of the public junior colleges charge their students tuition, and in the case of over a third of them this is in excess of $100. In many cases the students in the local *public* junior colleges are paying a far larger proportion of the entire costs of instruction than is the case even in the private institutions of the country, as shown by Figure 35.

Tuition indefensible on either of two theories. There are two theories of the junior college years to be discussed later. These two years are *collegiate*, or they are *secondary*. The above facts have shown the injustice and lack of logic in such heavy junior college tuition, on the tacit assumption that it is collegiate work, i.e., the same grade of education as furnished by universities. Suppose, however, that it is secondary. Even more firmly established in almost every state is the theory and practice that secondary education should be free to all the youth of the land. If this theory of the place of the junior college in the American educational system is accepted, the tuition charge is still less defensible. It sounds like a return to the old public school rate bills which were eliminated after a hard fight in the middle of the last century.

Another Kalamazoo case needed. In the famous Kalamazoo case, in 1872, it was decided that a city had a right to establish a high school as a part of the authorized public school system, and to levy taxes to support it. Perhaps the junior college will need to have the stimulation of another Kalamazoo decision before it is entirely freed from the shackles of excessive individual tuition. Yet no more striking evidence could be produced of the essential virility and vigor of the junior college than the fact that it has prospered and developed in so many states in spite of this heavy tuition handicap. Dr. Eby, of the University of Texas, well expresses the situation in that state:[1]

> Who should bear the cost of instruction of the junior college child? Everyone must agree that this is a practical question. If the student is sent away from home to any one of our twelve state colleges all instruction is free. If he is sent to the public school in his home district, provided he is not yet twenty-one years of age, all instruction is free. But if he happens to be a smart and promising child, and he is sent to a public junior college in his home town, except in South Park and Wichita Falls, he is fined for his ability and in all places must pay a heavy tuition. Now just why this discrimination? There does not seem to be any way for honest folks to get rid of the application of logic in our affairs. Why should a child under twenty-one receive free schooling in the home high school, but not in the home college; why if he goes away from home, but not at home?

[1] Eby, F. "The Junior College Movement in Texas"; in *Texas Outlook*, vol. 11, p. 10. (February, 1927.)

Are students in Texas, in Iowa, in Washington attending public junior colleges, or are they really attending private institutions supported by their own contributions, but maintained in public buildings? There can be but one logical outcome to the questions thus raised. Abolish tuition in the junior college, or at least reduce it in any state to an amount no greater than that charged students in the state university. The only procedure logically possible in a country which has adopted the general principle of free public education, at least through the period of general education prior to specialization, is to make junior college education completely free, as in California.[1] Cubberley[2] has outlined seven great battles which have been fought for free public schools in the last century. Are we to be faced today with an eighth battle before true freedom is won?

Can society afford junior college education? The answer of the taxpayer to the suggestion of abolition of tuition is that the state cannot afford such educational expense, even if it is logical. He says it is a condition and not a theory with which we are confronted. It is admitted that California spends more money per capita and more as a total sum on junior college education than any other state. Let us see, then, just how great a proportion of the total education burden in California is furnished by the junior college. California is spending over $160,000,000 a year on education, and on the whole considers it an excellent investment, paying the richest dividends, economically and socially. Already the thirty-five public junior colleges are doing much to popularize higher education and to raise the cultural level in the state.

[1] "We ought to commit ourselves definitely in practice, as well as in theory, to the principle of free education and equality of educational opportunity.... If education at public expense is a sound principle of government, it ought then to be put into practice whenever and wherever possible." (Holst, J. H. "The Imposition of Fees in State Supported Institutions"; in *Educational Review*, vol. 65, p. 39. (January, 1923.)

[2] Cubberley, E. P. *Public Education in the United States*, 517 pp. Houghton Mifflin Company, Boston. (1919.)

The distribution of this educational expenditure among the various units of the system is shown in Figure 36. The narrow wedge representing the expense of over $2,000,000 for junior college education in 1927–28 is only one and one third per cent of the entire circle. Two and a half times as much was spent in the state for kindergartens. Society can well afford to expand the narrow black sector of Figure 36 considerably before claiming inability to support junior college education. Society should support the public junior college in large part, if not exclusively. But how? Shall this support be state, or county, or local? It remains then, to discuss the important question of state aid.

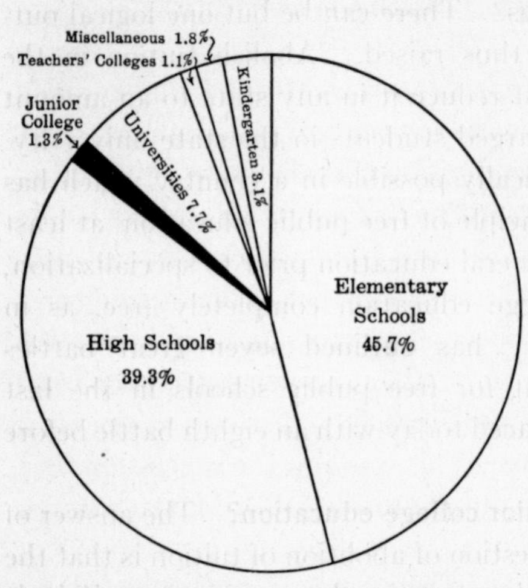

Fig. 36. Distribution of Total Expenditures for Public Education in California, 1927–28

STATE AID FOR JUNIOR COLLEGES

Proportion of state support. Even if it be admitted that society as a whole ought to support the junior college, the question remains: should it be done by the state, or purely as a local matter. Theory and practice vary widely in this respect. Various proposals and practices are found regarding the proportion of the cost which should be borne by the state treasury. The following are typical and illustrative:

100 per cent state support — state junior colleges
75 per cent state support — Zook's suggestion

50 per cent state support — suggested by various writers
40 per cent state support — California theory
33 per cent state support — Eby's suggestion
20 per cent state support — California practice
0 per cent state support — practice in most states

One hundred per cent state support. Most of the so-called "state" junior colleges provide 100 per cent state support. This is also the case in the lower division of many state universities.

Seventy-five per cent state support. Zook, in an address before the National Association of State Universities, in 1922, proposed that the state should pay 90 per cent of the expenditures for salaries of all junior college instructors and administrative officers. Assuming these to be about 80 per cent of the total cost, this would lead to approximately 75 per cent of the total cost being met by the state. This was also the suggestion that he made for a state system of junior colleges for Massachusetts, although it was never adopted.

Fifty per cent state support. This plan is discussed more fully below.

Forty per cent state support. As already stated, forty per cent state support was the theory behind the California law of 1921 providing for state support of $100 per student in average daily attendance, when total cost was estimated at $250.

Thirty-three per cent state support. Eby suggests $150 as normal cost of junior college education in Texas, which should be divided equally between the state, the local district and tuition paid by the student or his parents. This is only one half the amount provided by the state of California. Texas, however, as already seen, has adopted the strongest possible non-state-support attitude.

Twenty per cent state support. A state support of twenty per cent has been shown to be the California practice, under conditions of the past four or five years (see Figure 34), i.e., one half of the expected proportion. For Kansas, Mort advocates an equalization plan whereby the wealthiest districts in the state would receive $30 per junior college student, out of an estimated total cost of $150 per student. He says:[1]

In their present stage, the state is justified in rendering financial assistance to junior colleges organized within local school systems, either as state supervised and controlled experimentation, or in recognition of the loss of high-school attendance resulting from the establishment of junior colleges.

No state support. Unfortunately and indefensibly, no state support is the practice in every state where local public junior colleges have been established, except in California and Mississippi.

In some states junior college students are treated in the same category as high school students, and state aid is given in the same amount as to high school students, but this is usually only nominal.[2] In many cases, however, even this slight acknowledgment of the place of the junior college is refused. Legal decisions in North Carolina and Indiana, for example, have said that the poor junior college student is literally a homeless waif, financially speaking; he is neither entitled to the support accorded high school students, nor to that given to college students.[3] Possibly he may be graciously and generously permitted to make use of public school buildings, if space can be found, and if he will agree to pay sufficient tuition to meet the entire costs of instruction! That the public junior college has made its way under such formidable financial disability and handicap is nothing short of remarkable.

[1] Mort, P. R. "State Participation in the Financing of Junior Colleges"; in *Teachers' College Record*, vol. 30, pp. 751. (May, 1929.)

[2] Thus Missouri gives $100 per teacher for each teacher with a salary in excess of $1000. This amounts to approximately $1 per junior college student annually.

[3] For the ruling of the attorney-general in North Carolina, see page 144. His opinion, however, was overruled in an important court decision rendered August 30, 1930. See *School Review*, vol. 38, pp. 723–26, or *Junior College Journal*, vol. 1, 214–15.

Proposals for state aid. As early as 1921, the Ohio Joint Commission on Administrative Reorganization recommended state aid to junior colleges.[1] Bills similar to that of California, providing for state aid to the extent of $100 per student, were introduced in Kansas in 1925, in Colorado in 1927, and in Nebraska and Utah in 1929, but in each case failed of passage. Again in Kansas in 1929, a plan was proposed that would provide from state sources approximately $800 for each junior college instructor, but this also failed of passage. In states where a strong attitude of state aid has not already been taken for the support of local elementary and high schools the fight is harder, and it will require longer to educate the people and their legislative representatives, but it is bound to come in time. In such states it may be wiser to stress the similarity to the state university, already state supported, to which it will afford a relief, at much less cost to the state treasury, if something following the California plan is provided.

Why state support instead of local maintenance? The principle of equalization of school costs over a larger area has been discussed and accepted in theory, if not in practice, as a sound principle of educational finance. It is peculiarly applicable in the junior college field,[2] as a few concrete illustrations from California and Texas will show. Some districts are much richer than others, but the local district educates people from

[1] "The state should consider helping cities bear the expense of junior colleges on the double ground that it wishes to place the advantages of higher education as equally as possible, and that the home town or home county junior college will relieve the state of still greater expense at Columbus than would be involved in state aid for cities or counties that decide to maintain junior colleges." (*Report of Joint Committee on Administrative Reorganization*, p. 390. Columbus, Ohio, 1921.)

[2] "The state should be chiefly responsible for the current expenses of junior college work. The justification for this statement arises out of the accepted policy of every state in the Union that higher education, including the field of junior colleges, *is a state obligation*." (Zook, G. F. "Model Junior College Legislation"; in *Proceedings Tenth Annual Meeting, American Association of Junior Colleges*, pp. 43–44. Atlantic City, 1929.)

many parts of the state, and those it educates go to all parts of the state. Thus at Chaffey Junior College it was found that three fourths of the graduates were living outside of the district. Because of the differences in ability to pay, and the fact that any junior college is serving a much wider territory than its local community, ultimately if not immediately, the state should bear a liberal share in support. The assessed valuation, in 1928–29, was $13,000,000 in the Yuba county (California) junior college district, but it was more than sixteen times as much in the Long Beach district. The assessed valuation per student was $37,000 at San Mateo, while at Long Beach it was eight times as much, or $300,000. The local district tax rate was only seven cents at Long Beach and eight cents at Pasadena, while the taxpayers of the Marin junior college district were laboring under a burden of forty-eight cents — six or seven times as heavy, and getting an institution with inferior equipment for their money. Similarly, in Texas, assessed valuation varied, in 1927–28, from $4,000,000 at Clarendon to $300,000,000 at Houston. Assessed valuation per junior college student varied from $33,000 at Paris to $471,000 at Houston — fourteen times as great. Similar examples could be given from other states.

What should be the proper amount of support for the junior college? There is much logic in favor of 100 per cent state support. If furnished to a high school graduate in the university, in the state college, in the state teachers' college, and in the state normal school, why should it be denied to the same individual if he chooses instead to enroll in a local junior college? No state has gone this far in its educational practice — or thought. It would be folly to advocate complete support at this time. It is a condition and not a theory which confronts us. Moreover, the junior college has resulted in popularizing education to such an extent that at least one half of the students attending it would probably never have gone to college at all, at state expense. Further, the individual community receives great value, directly and indirectly, from the presence of the local junior college in the community. Complete state support, too, would presumably imply complete state control, with some loss of local interest, pride, and responsibility.

From many standpoints of local interest, control, and responsibility, it would seem that the state and the local district might fairly meet each other halfway. Let each furnish 50 per cent of the cost. It is worth noting in this connection that a plan has been proposed in California to raise state aid from \$100 to \$150, which would approximate 50 per cent of the cost if conditions should become static. With continued growth at the present rate, this figure would need to be raised to almost \$200, so long as it is based on the previous year's attendance, if it were designed to furnish 50 per cent support for the current year.

Opinions on proportion of state support. Brothers, in 1928, secured the opinion of two leaders in the junior college field, Koos and Proctor, on this question.[1] He quotes Koos as saying:

> I have not yet come to the stage in my own thinking with reference to the financial problems of the junior college that warrants me in recommending any single desirable plan of state aid for junior college units. As a matter of fact this problem will need to be worked out after extended investigation in each state, and in relationships to the program of aid for schools on other levels.

Proctor suggests that when the local junior college district matches the state aid fifty-fifty, it tends to stimulate economy in expenditures for the maintenance of this institution.

Zook, in 1930, was inclined to favor a fee for all junior college

[1] Brothers, E. Q. "A Plan for State Support for Public Junior Colleges"; in *Proceedings of the Ninth Annual Meeting of the American Association of Junior Colleges*, pp. 122. Fort Worth, Texas, 1928.

students, but did not recommend more than $50 per year. If total costs amount to $300 per student, he recommends that $150 be furnished by the state, $100 by the district, and $50 by the individual student. He says:[1]

> There is the strongest argument, both from logic and precedent, for state subsidies to local junior colleges. At the time I carried on the survey of higher education in Massachusetts it seemed to me that it ought not to be less than 90 per cent of the current cost. *Certainly it should be as much as one half the current cost or not less than $150 per student.*

It is significant to consider the opinion of two nationally recognized leaders in the general field of educational administration and finance. Cubberley says:[2]

> Just how large a proportion of the total cost for education the state should provide is as yet an unsettled question, and one capable of different answers in different states. That it should be large, in view of the growing needs for education and the marked inequalities of resources of the different counties, there can be little question. Theoretically, it would be more equitable if the entire support, up to a certain fixed standard, came from the state.... That from 40 to 60 per cent of the annual maintenance cost for elementary and secondary education ought to come from state sources, under modern conditions of wealth distribution, probably would be approved by most students of educational finance.

Swift feels that 65 to 75 per cent of the cost of education, under modern conditions in the distribution of wealth, ought to come from state sources.

If Cubberley and Swift are right as applied to elementary and high school education, there is all the more reason why at least 50 per cent of the support of the local junior colleges should also come from the state, when practically all of the

[1] Zook, G. F. "Junior College in the State's Program of Education"; *Fourteenth Yearbook of the Department of Secondary School Principals*, Bulletin no. 30, pp. 81–82. (March, 1930.) (Italics are not in the original.)

[2] Cubberley, E. P. *State School Administration*, pp. 436–37. Houghton Mifflin Company, Boston, 1927.

support for state universities and teachers' colleges come from it.

A battle cry. The eighth battle for free public schools is at hand. What shall be its battle cry? *Elimination of tuition: fifty per cent state support!* The foes are firmly entrenched behind defenses of conservatism and tradition. Let the friends of the junior college rally to the standard and win another battle for free public schools in America.

QUESTIONS AND PROBLEMS

1. What dangers are there in averaging data which show such wide variations as many of those in the tables of this chapter?
2. Which is the better unit for studies of junior college costs, average daily attendance or enrollment? Why?
3. List as many elements as possible that make fair comparisons difficult between junior college costs and costs of the lower division in the state university.
4. Compute unit cost of lower-division education in your university on the assumption made for the University of Washington data, giving the ratio 20:34:100. Compare with junior college costs.
5. Estimate, as closely as possible, how much the junior college saves the parents of students who live 300 miles from the state university.
6. Compare unit costs in California junior colleges operating in high school plants, with those in separate plants, as given in Table 53.
7. Using the method worked out by B. M. Woods, modify the multiplier for ratio of average daily attendance to equivalent full time enrollment in accordance with latest available California data.
8. For Table 53 compute cost per student enrolled, and compare with cost per student in average daily attendance. Why is enrollment a dangerous unit to use in California? Is it equally objectionable in other states?
9. How do you account for the fact that cost per student enrolled seems to be so much lower in Texas than in California?
10. How do you account for the fact that costs per student enrolled in both California and Texas seem to be much less than those recommended by Clark, Reeves, and Koos?
11. From Table 55, compute correlation between size of college and cost per student in the fifteen California junior colleges.
12. Should a student in a public junior college pay tuition? If so, how much?
13. Make a circle diagram showing the distribution of income for the

twenty-three public junior colleges given in Table 18 and Table 19, pp. 83–84, of the *Proceedings of the Tenth Annual Meeting of the American Association of Junior Colleges*, at Atlantic City, 1929.

14. Do the same for the forty-one private junior colleges, Tables 20 and 21, pages 85–86, *ibid.*
15. Analyse and evaluate the Mort plan for financing junior colleges.
16. Should income from permanent endowment be required for recognition of junior colleges by regional accrediting associations? (See Suggested Readings, Berry, and Lee.)
17. In what ways will a budget for a junior college differ from one for a standard four-year college? (See Friley, and Hill.)
18. Explain the wide variation in methods of financing public junior colleges found in the different states.
19. How is the question of the desirability of modification of the general property tax as a principal source of taxation related to the question of junior college finance?
20. Make a figure similar to Figure 36, showing the proportional expense for different educational units for any state having a group of public junior colleges. Could it afford more for junior college education?
21. "Three-fourths of the income of the four-year college from tuition is received from freshmen and sophomores, and three-fourths of the expense is upon the junior and senior year's work." (G. F. Winfield, *Journal of Education*, vol. 94, p. 228; September 15, 1921.) Verify or disprove this statement for selected four-year colleges.
22. Proctor states that in California junior college education "was secured in local communities at just about one-fourth what it would have cost the state treasury if given in the state university." (Proctor, W. M. (editor), *The Junior College: Its Organization and Administration*, p. 10.) Discuss this statement. Is it true? Is it likely to be misunderstood?
23. Should state aid be granted to a junior college on the basis of students enrolled, students in average daily attendance, number of instructors, the existence of the institution, or some other method?
24. Trace the history and use of the state junior college fund in California, as derived from leases on federal oil and mineral lands.
25. Answer the question asked by Eby of Texas, page 536.

SUGGESTED READINGS

Arnett, T. *College and University Finance*, 212 pp. General Education Board, New York, 1922.

Berry, M. P. L. "Junior College Endowments"; in *Proceedings of the Fifth Annual Meeting of the American Association of Junior Colleges*, pp. 88–93. Cincinnati, 1925.

*Brothers, E. Q. "A Plan for State Support for Public Junior Colleges"; in *Proceedings of the Ninth Annual Meeting of the American Association of Junior Colleges*, pp. 119-23. Fort Worth, Texas, 1928.

Clark, H. F. *Junior College Costs.* Bulletin of School of Education of Indiana University, vol. 4, no. 1, pp. 68-78. (September, 1927.)

*Frazier, A. M. "The Taxpayer and the Junior College"; in *American Educational Digest*, vol. 47, pp. 291-93, 332. (March, 1928.)
Based on Texas data.

Friley, C. E. "The Junior College Budget"; in *Proceedings of the Ninth Annual Meeting of the American Association of Junior Colleges*, pp. 57-63. Fort Worth, Texas, 1928.

Greenleaf, W. J. "Financial Support of Colleges"; in *Journal of Higher Education*, vol. 1, pp. 254-60. (May, 1930.)
Includes data on 114 public and 134 private junior colleges.

Hill, M. E. "Administrative Problems of the Large Rural Junior College"; in Proctor, W. M. (editor), *The Junior College: Its Organization and Administration*, pp. 75-97. Stanford University, California, 1927.
Outline of budget for Chaffey junior college (75-79).

Johnson, E. A. *Some Financial Phases on the Establishment and Support of Thirty Representative Public Junior Colleges in Six Central States of the United States.* Bulletin of the School of Education of Indiana University, vol. 5, no. 6, pp. 7-13. (July, 1929.)
Summary of portion of his doctor's dissertation.

*Kibby, I. W. "Can Siskiyou County Afford a Junior College?" in *Junior College Survey of Siskiyou County, California*, pp. 46-67. Yreka, California. (July, 1928.)

Kolbe, P. R. "Junior Colleges"; in *School and Society*, vol. 14, pp. 463-64. (November 19, 1921.)
Adequate state support essential to junior colleges.

*Koos, L. V. "The Financial Problem"; in *The Junior College*, pp. 591-624.

Koos, L. V. "The Financial Problem"; in *The Junior College Movement*, pp. 392-420.

*Koos, L. V., and Weersing, F. J. "Financial Problems"; in *Secondary Education in California: Report of a Preliminary Survey*, pp. 106-24. Sacramento, California, 1929.

*Lawson, F. "State Aid for Public Junior Colleges," in *Junior College Journal*, vol. 1, pp. 487-93. (May, 1931.)

Lee, E. D. "The Basis of Determining the Amount of Endowment for a Junior College"; in *Proceedings of the Sixth Annual Meeting of the American Association of Junior Colleges*, pp. 38-45. Chicago, 1926.

Mort, P. R. "State Participation in the Financing of Junior Colleges"; in *Teachers' College Record*, vol. 30, pp. 745–51. (May, 1929.)

*Reeves, F. W., and Russell, J. D. "Computation of Unit Costs in Higher Education"; in *Nation's Schools*, vol. 4, pp. 29–36. (October, 1929.)

Reeves, F. W., and Russell, J. D. *College Organization and Administration*, 316 pp. Board of Education of Disciples of Christ, Indianapolis, Indiana, 1929.

Smith, L. W. "Current Conditions in Junior College Development"; in *Proceedings of the Tenth Annual Meeting of the American Association of Junior Colleges*, pp. 57–87. Atlantic City, New Jersey, 1929.

*Stevens, E. B., and Elliott, E. C. *Unit Costs of Higher Education.* Report of the Educational Finance Inquiry Commission, vol. 13; 212 pp. The Macmillan Company, New York, 1925.

*Whitney, F. L. "The Cost of the Public Junior College"; in *The Junior College in America*, pp. 154–72. Greeley, Colorado, 1928.

Woods, B. M. "Economic Analysis of an Effective Junior College"; in *California Quarterly of Secondary Education*, vol. 4, pp. 20–24. (October, 1928.)

Zook, George F. "The Financial Support of Municipal Universities"; in *School and Society*, vol. 31, pp. 74–80. (January 18, 1930.)
Considers state support of junior colleges in seven states and state aid in others.

CHAPTER XX

CRITERIA FOR ESTABLISHING JUNIOR COLLEGES

The only fundamental justification for the junior college being democracy . . . the question is never how few junior colleges can the state get along with, but always how many can be produced that will live, grow, and flourish. — A. F. LANGE.[1]

Contents of this chapter. What are the conditions under which junior colleges may be expected to "live, grow, and flourish"? This chapter summarizes criteria that have been set up in the legislation of states that have passed laws regulating their organization, as well as criteria suggested by students of the movement. These are discussed, compared, and evaluated. Recommended procedures to follow in investigations of the desirability of the establishment of junior colleges are presented. Finally criteria for an effective junior college, rather than a minimum junior college, are briefly considered.

Importance of the subject. It is important to know, if possible, under what conditions a junior college is likely to be successful. Friends of the junior college who believe in its future are quite as much interested in seeing that new institutions are not established where conditions do not warrant them, as in having them established where they are needed. In a number of cases junior colleges have been started with more enthusiasm than judgment, due to local pride, community rivalry, or inability to count the cost. Some such institutions have perished from malnutrition when the first enthusiasm has waned, or are struggling along at a standard of inefficiency that would justify their early demise. Such con-

[1] Lange, A. F. "The Junior College"; in *Sierra Educational News*, vol. 16, p. 485. (October, 1920.)

TABLE 60. MINIMA CRITERIA FOR ESTABLISHING JUNIOR COLLEGES — LEGAL STATE REQUIREMENTS

State	Date of Law	Type of District	Population	Assessed Valuation	H.S. Average Daily Attendance	Junior College Enrollment	Petition of Voters	Approval of State Authority Necessary	Election Necessary	Designation
Arizona	1927	High school or union high school		$5,000,000	100		no	no	no — board only	"Junior college"
California	1917	(*H.S. Department*) high school district		$3,000,000			no	no	no — board only	"Junior college course"
	1929	(*J.C. District*) one or more high school districts, or counties		$25,000,000	1,000 (county — 500)	200 *	yes — 500	State Board of Educ. — State Dept. of Finance	yes	"District junior college"
Iowa	1927	Any "Board"					no	State Superintendent	yes	"Public junior college"
Kansas	1917	City of first or second class or county high school					no	no	yes	"High school extension"
Louisiana	1928	Parish † (except Orleans)					no	no	no — board only	"Junior colleges"
Michigan	1929	Any district with required population	18,000 ‡				no	no	no — board only	"Junior collegiate department"

* After second year of existence.
† Limit of one junior college to each parish.
‡ Formerly 25,000.

TABLE 60 (*continued*)

State	Date of Law	Type of District	Population	Assessed Valuation	H.S. Average Daily Attendance	Junior College Enrollment	Petition of Voters	Approval of State Authority Necessary	Election Necessary	Designation
Minnesota	1925	Independent or special					no	no	yes — ¾ vote	"Dep't of jr. coll. work"
	1927	Any district with required population	50,000				no	no	no — but may have one	"Junior college"
Mississippi	1928	Municipal, county or joint county with approved high school	10,000 *			1 yr. jr. coll. — 20; 2 yr. jr. coll. — 35	Municipal, no; Joint, yes — 10%	yes	Municipal — no Joint — yes	"Junior college"
Missouri	1927	Any district with fully accredited high school					no	State Superintendent	no — board only	"Two-year college courses in high school"
Montana	1921	Any accredited high school					no	Chancellor of state univ.	no — board only	"Junior college courses"
Texas	1929	(Single) independent district or city unit		$12,000,000	400		yes — 5%	State Board of Education	yes	"Junior college"
	1929	(Union) two or more districts or counties		$12,000,000	500		yes — 10%	State Board of Education	yes	"Union county or joint county junior college"
Wisconsin	1919	Any city					no	no	yes	"College"

* Does not apply to county agricultural college which must be twenty miles or more from any state college.

ditions tend to bring the entire movement into disrepute. Some parts of the country have suffered from a superabundance of weak four-year colleges, founded in the last century in an excess of denominational enthusiasm in communities where the need for them was not evident. If possible, the mistake should not be repeated by the junior college.

Under what conditions should new public junior colleges be encouraged? Unfortunately there is no simple formula that will answer this question. Numerous criteria have been suggested and many have been enacted into law, some perhaps wisely, some without doubt unwisely. It will be desirable to examine first some of the legal standards that have been set up as necessary prerequisites for the organization of public junior colleges, and then those that have been recommended by various students of the junior college movement.

STATEMENTS OF CRITERIA

Legal standards for junior colleges. At least a dozen states have set up legislative standards for the establishment of junior colleges. These vary all the way from the detailed standards in California and Texas, covering many different features, to the extreme simplicity of those in Louisiana, where a parish board may establish a junior college without an election, or approval of state officials, or any fixed assessed valuation.

The principal features of the requirements in the different states are summarized compactly in Table 60. In only three states — Arizona, California, and Texas — is there any minimum assessed valuation required, the limits varying from three to twenty-five million dollars. In practice in Mississippi, where approval of the State Commission is required, the Commission has established an assessed valuation of $20,000,000 as a condition precedent to approval. The same three states are the only ones which specify a certain average daily attendance in the high schools of the proposed district. Two require a certain enrollment or average daily attendance in the junior college for its continuance. The approval of some state authority is required in five states. An election is required, under certain conditions, in five states. In eight, a junior college may, under certain conditions, be established by vote of the local board only.

The Mississippi plan. The grouping of all the counties in the State of Mississippi, not already supplied with higher education facilities, into thirteen zones, comprising from one to four counties each, was accomplished by the recent junior college commission of that state. It was based upon a careful survey, which included such items as length of term and rating of the elementary schools, number and standards of high schools, number of high school graduates, percentage of high school graduates attending college, rating of the high school in connection with which the junior college was proposed, potential resources of the proposed zone, a minimum of $20,000,000 assessed valuation, possibility of an ultimate minimum enrollment of 150 junior college students, and proximity to other colleges and transportation facilities.

Recommended standards for junior colleges. There have been half a dozen or more rather careful studies made of the conditions under which junior colleges should be encouraged. Several of these are based upon detailed reports of conditions existing at the time of the investigation in some section of the country. In some the basis upon which a particular recommendation was made is open to question; reëvaluation in the light of changed conditions, either in time or location, may be desirable. The outstanding recommendations of this type are given in Table 61.

Zook's early recommendations were made in connection with his survey of higher education in Massachusetts, and were based largely upon existing practice in Michigan and Cali-

TABLE 61. MINIMA CRITERIA FOR ESTABLISHING JUNIOR COLLEGES — VARIOUS RECOMMENDATIONS

Author	Date	Population	Assessed Valuation	High School Enrollment	Junior College Enrollment	Proportion in Soph. Year	Miscellaneous
Zook	1923		$10,000,000	500 — average daily attendance			Require approval of State Board of Education and vote of district.
Koos	1924	25,000—40,000		1200	200		
Obrien	1928		$15,000,000	600	150	⅓	Serve area of radius, 20–25 miles.
Colorado Committee (Whitney)	1928	10,000	$10,000,000	800	150	⅓	Not over 25% of enrollment *may* be "specials"; 200 high school graduates; require ⅔ vote, after petition of 500 electors.
Clark	1928		$10,000,000	600–1,000	60 for poor, 200 for good junior college		
Holy-Green	1929	17,000	$15,000,000 or $30,000,000*	900	150	⅓	
Gattis	1929	12,000	$1,500,000	600	100 †		100 graduates annually from high school; willingness of community to increase tax rate 10 to 20 cents per $100.

* Recommends $15,000,000 if local district furnishes half of total support, $30,000,000 if all of it.
† "Eligible individuals desiring college opportunities within a radius of 100 miles."

fornia. Koos's recommendations resulted from extensive objective studies of conditions, especially in the Middle West, usually for the year 1920 or thereabouts. The methods which he used at that time are excellent, but the conclusions need reëvaluation on account of numerous changes in conditions which have occurred since that time. Obrien's studies are the outgrowth of a number of surveys to determine the feasibility of the establishment of junior colleges in various Kansas cities. Whitney's study and the recommendation of the Colorado committee follow many of Koos's techniques, but are somewhat limited in their application since they are largely expressed in terms of Colorado conditions. Criteria are considered under community status, feasibility, financial data, and public school background.[1] Clark's conclusions are intended especially for Indiana conditions, and the basis of them is not always clear in his published statements. Gattis's recommendations are definite and detailed, covering fourteen general points under need, cost, ability of the community, and willingness of the community, but the basis for them is not stated. The recommendations which seem to be based upon the most extensive and scientific analysis of recent data, covering a considerable scope of the country, are those worked out at Ohio State University by Holy and Green. Data upon which the recommendations were based were confined largely to the states included in the North Central Association.

None of the investigations summarized in Table 61 seem to have considered in detail high school enrollment, population, and valuation data for California or for the Southern states. Conditions vary so much in different sections that it is doubtful whether satisfactory standards can be set up to cover the entire country. Perhaps detailed regional standards will be

[1] Whitney and Shaw state that "the people of any community will not wisely extend high school education to include the junior college" unless no less than thirteen distinct conditions (one of them with fourteen subdivisions) are found to hold in the community.

more representative and useful than national ones. This is what has been accomplished, to a considerable extent, in the criteria set up in the legislation of the different states. In too many cases, however, the laws as passed represent the results of compromise, political manipulation, and guesswork rather than careful scientific educational investigation and statesmanship. They represent what is, not necessarily what should be.

EVALUATION OF CRITERIA

MOST VALUABLE CRITERIA

Of the various criteria suggested or legalized, as summarized in Tables 60 and 61 and elsewhere, some are of considerable value, while others are of doubtful utility. The following criteria are those which seem to be of the greatest worth. Some could be expressed in legislative terms; others would be difficult to express thus definitely.

District election. As noted, in over half the states that provide for establishment of junior colleges, a decision by the local board is all that is necessary. This means that a single man may make the decision (if the vote is three to two in a board of five). Unquestionably this is too great power to give any man or small group of men. The theory has been, in many cases, that the junior college is just another high school department, like domestic science, or auto mechanics, and so can be added by the local board; but, fully understood, it is much more. It is not simply a broadening of function on the high school level, but an additional two years of work on a higher level — a distinct change of policy. It needs the backing of the community to be successful.

There is an excellent chance to compare both methods in California, for in the high school departmental type only a resolution of the board is necessary, while for the district type an election is required. It is significant that of twenty-two California institutions which have given up the struggle for existence after a few years, every one had been established by vote of the local board. The average length of life of those institutions was less than five years. The infant mortality rate has been high — much higher than necessary. Birth has been too easy, and without due consideration of the factors involved. On the other hand, a healthy birth control has been exercised by the requirement of an election to establish a district junior college. None of the sixteen district junior colleges, so established, has ever been abandoned. All have thrived, expanded, and developed a vigorous childhood and youth. There is no prospect that any will die. There are some of the other type, however, that should be eliminated.

One of the few requisites that can be stated with assurance as necessary for the establishment of a public junior college is this one of *at least a majority vote of the electors voting on the question of establishment at a regular or special election.*

Approval by state board of education, state department of education, or a special commission. An excellent general provision, although it has its dangers, is the approval by the state board of education, the state department of education, or a special commission. A state board may be dominated by political or financial considerations, and not by educational motives. It depends somewhat upon the make up of the approving body, its method of selection, possible responsiveness to public opinion, and possibility of change if it becomes a political body instead of an educational one. If the state department or state board is exercising real constructive educational leadership, its approval of the plan to establish a junior college in any locality may well be made a necessary condition, preliminary to the vote of the people of the district.

Such approval, however, should be by a body primarily educational in its function. Nothing could be more vicious in its possibilities than the provision inserted in the California law in 1929 that a petition for a new junior college must be approved by the State Department of Finance. To allow a single watchdog of the treasury, whose interests are not primarily educational, to control the entire higher educational destiny of any community cannot be justified on any rational grounds.

Assessed valuation. Although it has some disadvantages, assessed valuation may also be favored as a criterion for the establishment of a junior college. It may be objected that assessed valuation does not bear any constant ratio to true valuation, and that true valuation is not necessarily a good index of ability to support education. Income, rather than wealth, is the real factor. Conditions are essentially different where the bulk of the tax burden is on personal property than where part of it is on other bases. Furthermore, the method of support adopted is fundamental. Is the junior college to be supported one third by tuition, one third by the state, and one third by local taxation, as suggested by Eby of Texas; one half by local tuition and one half by local taxation, as suggested by Holy and Green; prevailingly by individual tuition, as in Iowa and Texas; half by state aid and half by local taxation, as recommended in the last chapter; or 68 per cent by local taxation, as is the practice in California; or by other methods? It is obvious that such questions must be decided for any state before a proper limit of assessed valuation can even be considered.

Many writers have advised a $10,000,000 valuation; some proposed bills have copied this amount from California without full consideration of the different conditions of support holding in other parts of the country. If such an underlying philosophy can be adopted, then the criteria of assessed valuation forms a valuable means of suppressing unhealthy junior college ambitions on the part of communities obviously unable to support adequately a junior college program. Holy's suggested valuation of $15,000,000 is based upon an assumed cost of $400 per student and a maximum tax rate of 20 cents per $100, with half local support, or $30,000,000 for full local support. His cost per student may be seriously questioned, as the evidence of the last chapter shows. Also many communities can afford more than a 20-cent tax rate. Half the district junior colleges in California levy a tax rate greater than 20 cents, and in three of them it is at least double that figure. Is there any good reason why a prosperous community, or one less prosperous but isolated, shall not be permitted to levy a higher rate if the voters of the district so desire?

California's experience with valuation. California, in 1907, placed no minimum of assessed valuation — and "junior college departments" of two or three to half a dozen students sprang into existence. Then $3,000,000 was set as a limit, in 1917, for high school departments. This still remains, although probably it is much too low. The district law of 1921 established $10,000,000 as a minimum limit, and all sixteen of the district colleges in the state were organized under this provision. It seems to have worked well in practice, although the institution with the smallest valuation, thirteen million, has had a hard struggle to maintain satisfactory college standards, and has recently enlarged the district. Several have been organized and done excellent work over a period of years with valuations under $20,000,000. Unfortunately the 1929 legislature, without educational leadership in the matter, arbitrarily raised the limit to $25,000,000 and no new institutions have been organized on that basis, although several had been planning on it prior to the enactment of the 1929 law. As stated in Chapter IV, seven of the outstanding district junior colleges in California had assessed valuations varying from thirteen to twenty-two million dollars, averaging nineteen million when this law was passed.[1] The average enrollment

[1] Names and enrollments are: Chaffey, 1185 (second largest in state); San Mateo, 829; Modesto, 826; Riverside, 330; Marin, 328; Santa Rosa, 260; Yuba County, 96 (newly established, all freshmen).

in the six existing in 1927–28 was 626; average number of graduates, 64. Both figures were larger than the corresponding averages for all the district junior colleges in the state. None of these institutions could have been organized under the new law. No stronger evidence is needed that a valuation of $25,000,000 is too high for California conditions.

There should be a minimum valuation, to prevent clearly unworthy districts. Some California districts, however, draw approximately one half their students from outside the district, with an obviously lower burden of support from taxation. California experience has shown that $10,000,000 has been a very satisfactory minimum standard. Probably a change to $15,000,000 would not prevent any really meritorious district from establishing a junior college, but a figure higher than that is of very doubtful wisdom. Other conditions, geographical, educational, and so on, are important factors, the influence of which should not be made inoperative by unnecessarily and arbitrarily high minimum assessed valuation limits. One isolated county in the extreme northern portion of the state, 250 miles from another district junior college and 300 miles from the state university, had an assessed valuation of $22,000,000, ample need for a junior college, and ability to support it on an estimated tax levy of 37 cents or less. Yet the new law made it impossible for them even to vote on the question.

Assessed valuation is a valuable criterion if it is placed low enough not to exclude any really meritorious district, and with due regard to proportion of total support to be borne by local taxation.

High school population, enrollment, or graduates. A very valuable index of potential junior college attendance is the high school population. Proportion of students completing the high school and proportion continuing their education have changed so much in the last decade, however, and vary so much in different parts of the country, that little dependence can be placed upon standards derived from them a decade ago. If a junior college enrollment of 200 is desired, the various studies seem to show that a local high school attendance of close to 1000 will be required. This depends, however, upon the number of students who can be expected to attend from outside the immediate local district, upon the character and variety of courses offered, and upon proximity of other higher educational institutions.

There are many conditions, also, which will justify a junior college of less than 200 students. A smaller one may grow to that figure in four or five years, although not reaching it at first. Geographical isolation may justify an institution with no prospects of over 100 or 150 students for many years to come.

A high school average daily attendance of 100 is required in Arizona, a figure so low as certainly to be harmless. Recommendations of various writers suggest from 500 to 1000. Texas requires 400 average daily attendance (500 in county type), and this was also the California figure until the 1929 law, when it was changed to 1000. This figure is too high, as a minimum requirement. There was, in 1929, one California locality where a junior college was amply justified, having an assessed valuation of $65,000,000, but with a high school average daily attendance of about 900, which could not organize under the new law. The attendance figure should be kept low if it is not to bar cases of real merit.

A requirement for a high school average daily attendance of four hundred, or an enrollment of five hundred, would probably be reasonable. Any higher one is of very doubtful wisdom.

Other opportunities for higher education. The consideration of other opportunities for higher education is also an important factor, but one that it is unwise to try to put into legislative terms. The need for a junior college may be greatly modified by the presence in or near it of a state college or university, teachers' college, normal school, or private college or university. That there should be no junior college organized if there is any other college work, public or private, within twenty-five to one hundred miles, as proposed by some as a fair criterion, would automatically eliminate Pasadena, Glendale, Los Angeles, Santa Monica, Compton, and several other of the strongest and most useful junior colleges in southern California. Criteria in terms of distance are dangerous. Conditions in the deserts of Utah and the concentration of population around Chicago or Los Angeles make any fixed criteria on a distance basis untenable.

Efficiency of elementary and secondary education. The first obligation of any community is to give reasonably adequate elementary and secondary education to its youth. A community that is distinctly below the average for the state in measurable factors, such as teachers' salaries, length of term, and educational achievement, should usually bring these foundational elements up to par or better before taking on the additional burden and responsibility of higher education. This is a sound principle to apply within any state. It is more doubtful whether it should be applied between states. To demand that any state come up to the educational standards of the average state in educational matters before establishing junior colleges would result in denying the obvious advantages of junior college education to whole states for many years or decades to come. A moderate amount of higher educational facilities will operate to raise the whole educational level, elementary and secondary, as well as collegiate. To demand (as is done by Whitney and Shaw in Colorado) that no junior college be established until local educational needs are adequately met for pre-school and kindergarten education, elementary schools, high schools, adult education, and continuation and part-time education, seems rather a rigid standard.[1] It is

[1] The comment of Dr. Zook on this point is worth quoting: "Some of our friends in the field of elementary and secondary education are a bit alarmed at

quite probable that adult and part-time education may be better taken care of through junior colleges than otherwise. The form of statement used by Holy is to be preferred as one of the determining factors:

The ability and effort to support schools should at least approximate and preferably be higher than that found to exist in comparable districts.

Community attitude. The community attitude toward education, as reflected in its support of the high school, libraries, newspapers, and other factors, is another valuable criterion. The mere commercial-club "booster" spirit and small-town rivalry is not sufficient. Rather it should be a deterrent. It is doubtful whether this can be placed in legislative form, however, except in the way of a requirement of a petition signed by a certain number of voters, as required in Texas and California. This is a distinct measure of community attitude, but may quite as well be a measure of small-town rivalry and ambition as of true educational outlook.

Which criteria are of greatest value? Of the criteria for establishing junior colleges suggested above, the only ones, in the opinion of the author, which are of real value to enact into legislation are the first four: *approval by state authority*, *local election*, *moderate assessed valuation*, and *moderate high school attendance or enrollment*. This, however, distinctly does not mean that every community which can meet these very moderate requirements should be encouraged to establish a junior

the establishment of junior colleges in local centers for fear that it may have an adverse effect on the amount of money available for elementary and secondary education. I presume there are possible examples of this situation. I don't believe I have ever seen any of them. I think that I would be entirely willing to agree, however, that a local school system should not establish a junior college until its system of elementary and high-school education was fully standard in all respects." (Zook, G. F. "Junior College in the State's Program of Education"; in *Fourteenth Yearbook of Department of Secondary School Principals of the National Education Association*, Bulletin no. 30, p. 78. March, 1930.)

college. Further desirable considerations will be presented a little later; but first a few less desirable criteria will be considered, all of which have been suggested or advised by various investigators, or are found somewhere in legal form.

CRITERIA OF DOUBTFUL VALUE

To the author, the following criteria seem to be of very doubtful value as necessarily prerequisite to the establishment of a junior college:

Population of a community. The population of a community has little necessary relationship to probable junior college attendance. The presence of a large foreign element, industrial element, or Negro element may make the high school attendance in one community double that in another. It is of value only as it is closely related to high school attendance, and that factor is more accurately secured directly and at more frequent intervals than population, which can only be found exactly only at intervals of a decade.

Percentage of high school graduates now in college. Percentage of high school graduates attending college is likely to be largely conditioned by geographical and economic conditions. The fact that few high school graduates from a given community attend a college may be the strongest reason in favor of a junior college, not against it.

Minimum junior college enrollment. Minimum junior college enrollment is not, strictly speaking, a condition prior to establishment, but a condition for continuance. Yet if it exists in law, it must be seriously considered before organization occurs. Two states have such a requirement. Mississippi requires that an enrollment of 20 be maintained in a one-year, or 35 in a two-year junior college. The various standardizing agencies that mention this factor require from 30 to 60 students. California formerly required an average daily attendance of 75 after the second year of existence in a district junior college, but in 1929 this was changed to 200 — probably the equivalent of requiring an enrollment of 250 or more.

It is very doubtful whether any such arbitrary limits should be set. A variety of conditions, local or national, might change it. Thus another great war might temporarily deplete the enrollment of many colleges by half or more. Under the California law, unless emergency legislation were enacted, a junior college organized under it, with a capital investment of perhaps a half million dollars would have no option but to close its doors and sell its plant and equipment if, for any one of many good but unforeseen reasons, its average daily attendance chanced to drop below the arbitrary limit of 200. Due care may be taken to see that as high standards as feasible are set for organization of a junior college, but it is doubtful wisdom to provide by legislation for unforeseen future conditions. Educational statesmanship of the future might well be assumed to be willing and competent to meet its own problems when they arrive.

Proportion of students in the sophomore year, or proportion taking courses leading to graduation. The Southern Association requires that 75 per cent of the students in a junior college shall be taking courses leading to graduation. This of course ignores the possibilities of the popularizing function, as exemplified in extension, extra-hour, and adult courses for special students. Chaffey junior college, in California, with an enrollment of 1676 in 1928–29 and an average daily attendance of 390, could not meet the standards of the Southern Association. For similar reasons the suggestion of several men, given in Table 61, that one third of the enrollment should be in the sophomore year is an unwise standard. It also partakes of the nature of legislating for future unknown conditions. It is undoubtedly desirable that a large proportion of regular freshmen should continue as sophomores, but it is not a suitable criteria to set for organization of a new institution.

Territory to be served. That the prospective student body sufficient to meet the proposed enrollment should be drawn from a range of fifteen to twenty-five miles is suggested by some. Again geographical conditions, proximity of other institutions, and other factors operate to make this factor too variable to be of value as a criterion, suggestive and important as it may be in a special case.

Details of organization. The Mississippi law prescribes in detail minimum standards for number of instructors, number of volumes in library, value of laboratory equipment, and similar features. Such factors seem much too detailed to solidify in fixed law as precedent to the organization of any junior college, desirable as they usually are in most cases.

CRITERIA ADVISED

How shall the question of establishment be determined? Are the few minimum standards outlined on pages 556–563 sufficient for the establishment of a junior college? By no means. If they were, a multitude of small, weak, struggling junior colleges might spring into existence all over the country. They seem to be about all, however, that can safely and fairly be put into legal requirements without working unnecessary hardships and imposing unnecessary restrictions on communities really needing colleges and able to support them. Conditions vary so greatly in the South, in the East, in the Middle West, and in the Far West; in agricultural, industrial, and residential communities; according to educational background, and theories and practice of school support; and in wealth, interest, and traditions that it is not only impossible but unwise and dangerous to set up more than the most general minimum standards for the organization of an institution which may show such varied forms of development and local usefulness as the junior college.

It would be very convenient if a series of ten or twenty

definite standards could be set up, which could be mechanically applied to any given situation. This is entirely possible, but would be educationally disastrous. Conditions differ so widely, and the various factors are not independent but so closely interrelated that the whole problem must be considered in the light of all these varying factors. It is not meant to disparage such investigations as have been reported in Table 61. These are exceedingly valuable, and more of them are needed. Any one considering the establishment of a junior college needs to be familiar with all of them. It is the attempt to apply them slavishly and mechanically to any situation that is undesirable. The educational quack doctor with a single ready-made formula could settle the question quickly and positively for any community. What is needed is the skilled educational diagnostician, or even a group of such diagnosticians, who shall take account of all the pertinent symptoms, not only individually but collectively and in their interrelations, and base decisions upon them.

A preliminary survey. Already the reaction against the unreasonably high qualifications set for California in the 1929 law has set in. Two different conferences of junior college leaders in the state have recommended that the entire present procedure be modified, as follows:

> *Resolved*, that the present procedure for the establishment of junior college districts be revised to provide for a petition from the high-school boards of the proposed area, requesting the state department to survey the situation and recommend to the state board, the latter to have power to approve or reject the petition, on recommendation of the department, an election to be held in the proposed district if approval is given by the state board.

The essence of this recommendation is local election, conditioned upon approval by the state board, conditioned in turn upon an impartial expert survey by outside authorities. It proposes to abandon the effort to establish numerical restrictions, unless of the most elementary and general type, and instead to base action in each case upon an expert educational diagnosis of local conditions. This is the logic of the psychology of individual differences applied to communities, instead of to individuals. Whether the proposal is adopted by the legislature or not, the principle is a sound one for securing the healthiest junior college development; for advising against their establishment even though minimum requirements may in some cases be met; and for advising in favor of them in other cases, regardless of artificial standards which may not be fulfilled.

This procedure of a survey preliminary to the establishment of a junior college has been followed in the case of a number of communities in Kansas, where the assistance of the state university was secured in making the necessary survey. As a result, in at least four cases, communities decided against junior colleges. An even more advanced position has been taken in Mississippi, where a special junior college commission was set up by state law, which has districted the entire state into zones, as mentioned in Chapter V. It is still left to local initiative to decide whether a junior college will be established in any given zone. The most satisfactory method for deciding whether or not to establish a junior college is undoubtedly the slower individual method of the local expert survey. The expense is only nominal compared with the financial and educational investment involved. Such a survey should furnish the body of pertinent facts in each case upon which a decision can be made intelligently.

Published surveys. Several such surveys have been made, but unfortunately only a few of them have been published. Two have been published covering entire states, and therefore these have not been able to deal intensively with the situation in any one locality, although they have offered many valuable suggestions. These are Zook's survey of Massachusetts, and

Judd's of Texas. Of published surveys dealing with local communities may be mentioned those of Obrien at Chanute and Atchison, Kansas; of Morris at Mount Pleasant and surrounding country in Pennsylvania; and the one of Siskiyou County, California, made by two members of the State Department of Education with the coöperation of two members of the faculty of the School of Education of Stanford University.

THE SISKIYOU COUNTY SURVEY

Because the Siskiyou County survey is the latest and the most detailed study made of a local situation it will be described a little more fully. The questions that it tried to answer are those that would have to be considered, with only minor modifications, in the survey of any local community with reference to the establishment of a junior college. It endeavored to answer five main questions:

1. Does the county need a junior college?
2. What kind of a junior college would meet the needs of the county?
3. Can the county afford a junior college?
4. Where should a junior college be located?
5. When could a junior college be established?

The question of need. To answer the question of need, investigations were made of geographical conditions and relations, community attitudes, general population trends, high school enrollment and attendance, high school graduates and college attendance, and probable junior college attendance. For the latter question, while some dependence could be placed upon statistical studies of existing data, much importance was attached to a questionnaire given to every high school junior and senior in the county, and a similar one mailed to the parents of all such students. The questionnaire to parents was accompanied by a brief explanation of the nature of the junior college. Essentially the same questionnaire has

FORM I

QUESTIONNAIRE TO HIGH SCHOOL JUNIORS AND SENIORS

SISKIYOU COUNTY JUNIOR COLLEGE SURVEY

Name of High School..

Name of student...

Name of parent or guardian...

(On remainder of this page, answer whenever possible by checking in front of the item, the answer which best fits your case.)

1. CLASS: ....Senior   2. SEX: ....Boy
   ....Junior   ....Girl

3. How many years have you been in this high school?

  1 2 3 4

4. After graduation from high school what is your present intention regarding further education, in college, university, normal school, or junior college? (Answer without reference to a possible junior college in Siskiyou county.)

   ....a. I fully expect to continue my education.

   ....b. I shall probably continue my education.

   ....c. I am uncertain as to whether I will continue.

   ....d. I have no expectation of going beyond high school.

5. If you have checked (a) or (b) above, please write below the name of the institution which you are most likely to enter after graduation from the high school.

   Probable institution..

6. If there were a good junior college in the county, with free bus transportation daily, for a distance of not over 25 or 30 miles, would you probably attend it?

   ....YES   ....UNCERTAIN   ....NO

7. If there were a good junior college in the county, but over 30 miles distant, would you probably attend it, if adequate dormitories were provided?

   ....YES   ....UNCERTAIN   ....NO

8. If you should attend a Siskiyou County Junior College, which of the following courses would you be interested in and most likely to take?

   ....Academic or college-preparatory.

   ....Agricultural course.

   ....Elementary engineering course.

   ....Forestry and lumbering course.

   ....Business and commercial course.

   ....Home economics course.

   ....Mining course.

   ....Other course (name it)...

FORM 2

INFORMATION TO PARENTS

May 1, 1929

WHAT IS A JUNIOR COLLEGE?

The Junior College is a comparatively new institution which aims to offer two years of education in advance of the regular high school course. It has developed almost entirely in the present century and largely during the past ten years. Today there are over 400 junior colleges in the country with over 50,000 students. California has taken the leading place in this development and now has 33 public junior colleges with approximately 12,000 students.

Many parents have hesitated to send their immature children, upon graduation from high school, away from home to distant colleges or universities especially when the student body and sometimes the freshman class alone of such institutions was numbered in the thousands. The junior college has enabled students to secure two years of college education at or near their homes and has made the transition easier from the high school to the university. In the smaller junior college they come into closer contact with instructors, do their work in smaller classes, and have a chance for all round development with better co-operation between home and school authorities. At the same time this is done at a considerable saving in cost.

The fully organized junior college aims to meet the higher education needs of the community in which it is located, including preparation for the university, general education for those not going to the university, specialized preparation for particular occupations, and special courses of college grade for adults in the community.

In preparation for advanced work in the University the junior college offers work that is the equivalent of that given in the freshman and sophomore years of our standard colleges and universities. Careful studies made recently have shown that junior college graduates in California who enter leading universities do work equal to or better than students who enter as freshmen directly from high school.

But the junior college is not exclusively an institution to prepare students for advanced work in the university. It offers a chance for two years of general college education at home to many who otherwise would go no further than high school. By state law it is open to all high school graduates, regardless of grade of work done in the high school. Thus it offers an opportunity for public education of college grade to approximately one-half of each high school graduating class, which could not, under present conditions, enter the state university. Many of these, after making good in the junior college, enter the university who could not otherwise have done so. Then there are a number of occupations, often called semi-professions, for which it has been shown that two years of college work furnish adequate preparation. These include such courses as agriculture, engineering, forestry, business and commercial, mining, home economics, etc. Not all of these are given by any one junior college but two or three of them are found in a number of the best colleges in the state and are working very successfully. Many junior colleges are also giving special courses for adults, who wish to take additional work in music, art, literature, and other subjects of college grade. Last year over 2600 students, mostly adults, took such special courses in California junior colleges.

been since used in more extensive surveys of junior college prospects in Oakland, Berkeley, and San Francisco. The explanatory statement to parents, with slight modification, has been used in an extensive investigation involving high school students all over the State of Utah. For those reasons it may be worth while to reproduce both of these forms (pp. 570–71).[1]

The question of type. This survey showed what the junior college was doing in various kinds of work, preparatory, terminal, and popularizing, for other communities in California where it was operating; the type of courses needed in the county and desired by the students (as shown by the questionnaire); and an outline of teaching staff, buildings, and equipment necessary to carry out the suggested educational program.

The question of cost. Detailed estimates of cost were made, on the basis of the type and size of institution assumed, including current costs, bond redemption, and capital outlay. Whether and how the county could meet such a cost was presented with care from the standpoint of comparative assessed valuation, true valuation, bonded indebtedness, tax rate, annual income, and other factors.

The question of location. All feasible locations were considered in detail, with relative transportation and other costs, road conditions, and community sentiment. This question would be a minor one in many cases, but would be important if two or more towns or cities were involved, or various sites in a single city were under consideration.

The question of organizational details. Finally, various conditions dealing with possible time and method of organization, largely local in character, were taken up.

[1] Both forms were prepared by the author of this volume. The questionnaire to parents was essentially the same as the one to students, except for obvious changes of pronouns. Both are reproduced in the Siskiyou Survey. The statement to parents was necessarily brief, because it was desired to keep it within the limits of one typewritten page.

The whole procedure, facts gathered, and conclusions arrived at were embodied in a printed report of eighty-seven pages, and published by the County Supervisors for the information and guidance of the people of the county.

Procedure advocated. It is this sort of procedure with reference to the establishment of any new junior college that is recommended, rather than any arbitrary set of formulated standards. If it had been followed, undoubtedly some institutions now existing, which are bringing discredit rather than credit to the movement, would never have been established. Such a procedure in competent hands, subject to review by the State Department of Education, and to final approval by the electors of the proposed district, should provide ample safeguards against hasty and ill-considered establishment of institutions likely to be an educational liability, and would not shut out any proposals of real merit. It is strongly to be recommended as a desirable procedure, whether required by law or not, precedent to the establishing of any junior college, public or private, in any part of the country. No community would think of establishing a system of waterworks without a preliminary survey and competent engineering advice. The need for educational engineering at the junior college level is more important and more complicated, and calls for even greater technical skill and judgment. Ready-made formulas, quack doctoring, and amateur decisions will not permanently suffice.

THE EFFECTIVE JUNIOR COLLEGE

This chapter has dealt for the most part with the *minimum* junior college. An equally important question is that of the *effective* junior college. With reference to the standard college, President Cowling, of Carleton College, says: [1]

[1] Cowling, D. J. "The Future of the Liberal Arts College"; in Hudelson, E. (editor), *Problems of College Education*, pp. 401–02. University of Minnesota Press, Minneapolis, Minnesota, 1928.

I think it fair to say that an institution with less than five hundred students may be regarded as incomplete.... In order to present to its students a situation sufficiently complex to be fairly representative of the important interests of life, without loading them with individual programs too complex for their good, a college needs about five hundred students.

Is this true for the four-year college? If true, how does it need modification, if at all, in considering the effective junior college? Some of the studies reported deal with this question slightly, but none deals with it comprehensively. It is worthy of a major investigation. Are there limits of junior college effectiveness? Are institutions of 1000 or 2000 students, such as Crane, Kansas City, or Sacramento, too large to be really effective? Do many of the advantages claimed for a junior college lose their force for a larger institution? Does it begin to fall heir to the faults, without the compensating virtues, of the large university? Can a range of maximum and minimum standards for a truly effective junior college be set up in terms of size, equipment, personnel, service, curriculum, faculty-student relationships, instruction, finance? These are questions which no one yet has answered satisfactorily. Valuable suggestions may be found in the volume on the *Effective College*, by a group of American students of Higher Education, published by the Association of American Colleges. What constitutes an effective junior college has not yet become a vital question, but with almost five hundred junior colleges in the country it is worthy of careful study.

QUESTIONS AND PROBLEMS

1. For any state, make a list of cities in which junior colleges might be established in accordance with one of the standards set up in this chapter, or in Table 61.
2. District a state into "zones," as in Mississippi, for possible establishment of junior colleges in accordance with reasonable standards.
3. Study a group of junior colleges that have been discontinued to find the reasons for their discontinuance.

4. What colleges in a given area should be continued? Why?
5. Using the techniques developed by Koos, or Holy and Green, verify or modify one or more of the criteria objectively developed on the basis of data from some other state, preferably not included in their studies; for example, California, or one or more states in the territory of the Southern Association.
6. Study critically the original statements of criteria of any of the authors listed in Table 61. Which seem to be the most valuable? Which the least valuable?
7. Apply the Holy-Green criteria, or some other recent ones, to a group of junior colleges now existing in some state. Which of them could not have been organized under the proposed limitations?
8. Formulate a set of criteria for junior colleges to be incorporated in the school code of the Utopian state of Osceola. Include also provisions for support, based on discussion of previous chapter.
9. The Holy-Green standards are based on an assumed cost of $400 per student. Is this too high? How would they be modified if based on an assumed cost of $300? If on a tax levy of thirty cents or forty cents, instead of twenty?
10. A committee of the Alabama Teachers' Association recommended against junior colleges. Why? Do you approve?
11. Find the ratio of junior college students (including freshmen and sophomores in four-year institutions) to total high school enrollment in a selected state. What are the junior college implications?
12. Investigate the relation of high school enrollment to community population, and of each to junior college enrollment for a selected area.
13. What are the objections to making a detailed survey the principal criterion for establishment of a junior college?
14. Compare the Siskiyou county junior college survey with one of those made by Obrien, to see which topics are common to the two and which are unique in either.
15. What additional information would it be desirable to secure from high school students beside that called for in the questionnaire, page 571?
16 Outline a plan for investigating the factors comprised in an analysis of an "effective junior college."

SUGGESTED READINGS

General

Broom, K. M. *Public Junior College Bulletin*, 43 pp. State Department of Education, Jackson, Mississippi, 1929.

*Carr, W. G. "The Junior College in State School Surveys"; in

Junior College Journal, vol. 1, pp. 357-62. (March, 1931.)
A comparison of various features in surveys of California, Massachusetts, Mississippi, New Jersey, Texas, Utah, and West Virginia.

Clark, H. F. *Junior College Costs*. Bulletin of School of Education of Indiana University, vol. 4, no. 1, pp. 68-78. (September, 1927.)

Cockrell, E. R. "Under What Circumstances Should a Junior College be Established?" in *Proceedings of the Ninth Annual Meeting of the American Association of Junior Colleges*, pp. 123-26. Fort Worth, Texas, 1928.

Eells, W. C. "The New California Junior College Law"; in *School and Society*, vol. 30, pp. 65-68. (July 13, 1929.)

Ford, W. S. "The Social-Economic Background Essential for an Effective Junior College"; in *California Quarterly of Secondary Education*, vol. 4, pp. 32-34. (October, 1928.)

Gattis, W. E. "Certain Conditions which Justify the Establishment of Public Junior Colleges"; in *Texas Outlook*, vol. 13, p. 37. (May, 1929.)

*Green, R. E. "Where to Locate Junior Colleges"; in *School Executives Magazine*, vol. 49, pp. 178-80. (December, 1929.)

*Holy, T. C. "Criteria for the Establishment of Public Junior Colleges"; in *Thirteenth Yearbook of the Department of Secondary School Principals of the National Education Association*, Bulletin no. 25, pp. 308-18 (March, 1929); also in *High School Teacher*, vol. 5, pp. 118-20, 133-34. (April, 1929.)

*Kelly, R. L. (editor). *The Effective College*, 302 pp. Association of American Colleges, New York, 1928.

Koos, L. V. "The Residential Distribution of College Students and its Meaning for the Junior College Problem"; in *School and Society*, vol. 13, pp 557-62. (May 7, 1921.)

Koos, L. V. "Where to Establish Junior Colleges"; in *School Review*, vol. 29, pp. 404-33. (June, 1921.)

*Koos, L. V. "The Source of the Student Body"; in *The Junior College*, pp. 573-90. (1924.)

Koos, L. V. "The Problems of Location and Maintenance"; in *The Junior College Movement*, pp. 374-92.

*Obrien, F. P. "Conditions Which Justify Establishing a Junior College"; in *Proceedings of the Eighth Annual Meeting of the American Association of Junior Colleges*, pp. 73-81. Chicago, 1928. Also similar but not identical in *School Review*, vol. 36, pp. 128-37. (February, 1928.)

Proctor, W. M. "Student Interest in Junior Colleges"; in *Junior College Journal*, vol. 1, pp. 84-88. (November, 1930.)

Samuelson, A. *Public Junior Colleges: Preliminary Bulletin*, 13 pp. State Department of Education, Des Moines, Iowa, 1928.

*Whitney, F. L. "Criteria for the Organization of a Public Junior College"; in *Junior College in America*, pp. 173-205.

Whitney, F. L., and Shaw, J. H. *The Junior College Movement with Special Reference to Educational and Economic Conditions in Colorado.* Colorado State Teachers' College Bulletin, series 28, no. 7. 42 pp. Greeley, Colorado, October, 1928.

Zook, G. F. "Junior College in the State's Program of Education"; in *Fourteenth Yearbook of Department of Secondary School Principals*, Bulletin no. 30, pp. 74-83. (March, 1930.)

Surveys

*Judd, C. H. *Texas Educational Survey Report*, vol. 3, *Secondary Education*, 103 pp. Austin, Texas, 1924.

Chapter III (pp. 25-80) deals with many features of 18 private and 15 public junior colleges in the state.

Morris, J. T *Considerations in Establishing a Junior College.* Teachers' College Contributions to Education, no. 343, 63 pp. New York, 1929.

Ph.D. thesis, dealing with junior college needs of southwestern Pennsylvania.

Obrien, F. P. *Report of a Survey in Atchison Dealing with the Establishment of a Junior College.* Kansas Studies in Education, vol. 1, no. 2. 32 pp. Lawrence, Kansas, October 1, 1923.

Obrien, F. P. *Survey Report of the Chanute, Kansas School System*, 134 pp. Lawrence, Kansas, 1924.

Chapter IV deals with the problem of a junior college.

*Obrien, F. P. *College Standards and a Public Junior College.* Kansas Studies in Education, vol. 1, no. 4. Lawrence, Kansas, March 1, 1926. Also in essentially same form in *American Educational Digest*, vol. 45, pp. 58-61, 99-102, 132-35. (October and November, 1925.)

Survey of conditions at Hutchinson, Kansas.

*Ricciardi, N., Kibby, I., Proctor, W. M., and Eells, W. C. *Junior College Survey of Siskiyou County, California*, 87 pp. Board of Supervisors, Yreka, California, July, 1929.

Zook, G. F. *Report of a Fact-Finding Survey of Technical and Higher Education in Massachusetts.* House Document no. 1700, General Court of Massachusetts, 358 pp. (December 26, 1923.)

Chapter XVII, pp. 253-64, deals with a system of junior colleges for the state.

CHAPTER XXI

PUBLICITY AND CATALOGUES

> Because of its immense experimental possibilities, it is safe to say that, dollar for dollar, money put into junior colleges of flexible progressive type will do more for the cause and progress of education just at this moment than money spent for any other educational purpose. For if these junior colleges succeed in making education fascinating, as the progressive schools are doing in the lower levels, then college education would indeed become "a new and entrancing adventure." — STANWOOD COBB.[1]

Contents of this chapter. This chapter contains a brief discussion of the significance of publicity in the junior college program; national and local methods of securing it; agents for furnishing it; and costs of publicity. This is followed by a more extensive consideration of one important medium of publicity, the junior college catalogue. An objective score card for measuring the presence of desirable qualities in it is presented, its validity and reliability discussed, and the results of the evaluation of the catalogues of over ninety junior colleges are presented.

PUBLICITY IN THE JUNIOR COLLEGE

Significance of publicity for the junior college. In all educational work, either public or private, it is essential to keep the public informed as to purposes, progress, and prospects. This is even more important, however, for a new form of educational development, such as the junior high school or the junior college, whose distinctive functions and methods are only very gradually recognized and finally understood by the general public. In the case of the public junior college, supported in large part by taxation, the taxpaying constituency must know its plans, work, and success if adequate funds are

[1] Cobb, S. *The New Leaven*, p. 263. John Day Company, New York, 1928.

to be voted for maintenance. In the case of private institutions, supported by denominational groups or private tuition or both, it is even more essential that the supporting constituency, both givers and students, should be equally well informed.

It is not for financial reasons alone, or chiefly, that such publicity is desirable, however. The educational nature of the publicity should have a more far-reaching social and cultural effect than can be measured in financial terms alone. The junior college represents a new educational philosophy — the conception of college education of a general type, whether for preparatory or terminal purposes, for a vastly greater collegiate population than ever before dreamed of "going to college." It is important that its value and also its limitations should be thoroughly understood by parents and students alike, if severe scholastic disillusionment and educational disappointment are not to result. Contented students are essential, and this means complete understanding of purpose, methods, courses, and results. The junior college has a deep obligation, not only to furnish college education to the masses, but to furnish the masses reliable information concerning itself as an institution.

The amount of misinformation that has been spread concerning the junior college is astonishing; the amount of misunderstanding that is rife is appalling. Great sections of the country are largely ignorant concerning this latest member of the educational family, and even in states where it has been most extensively developed many people have only a hazy idea of what it is really trying to do. To many it is "just some more high school," a place for students who haven't the brains for real college, a weak imitation of the real thing. Even the educational world itself is not fully educated regarding the junior college, nor is this surprising since even the leaders in the junior college movement are not entirely agreed on its functions. Why, how, whither the junior college? — are questions that are not yet answered with unanimity. Yet there is much reliable information to be disseminated that would help to give professional educators a truer conception of it. Publicity is an essential matter for the junior college, and, as already suggested in Chapter XIV, it should be considered an administrative function and definitely provided for in the administrative organization of the institution.[1]

National methods of publicity. Three methods of publicity, national in scope, that have been used or proposed may be mentioned: (1) coöperative advertising, (2) a code of ethics, and (3) national journals.

Coöperative advertising. In 1926, at the meeting of the American Association of Junior Colleges, an address by a professional advertising man pointed out the possibilities of coöperative commercial advertising of the junior college movement in national magazines in order to explain and popularize the type of education it offers. A committee was appointed to work on this, but, after two years of study and effort to secure the desired coöperation and financial support, the plan was dropped. The reasons for doing so are well summarized in the final report of the committee:[2]

There are members of this association and prominent junior colleges that do not advertise at all. They perhaps have field representation as a substitute for advertising. There are others that cannot afford it; still others that are full to overflowing and feel no need of advertising or extra pressure of any sort; still others who

[1] Unfortunately the word "publicity," although expressing an excellent idea, has fallen somewhat into disrepute because of its association with paid publicity agents and insidious propaganda. It might be better to use the word "interpretation." What the junior college needs is sane, intelligent, constructive interpretation to its constituency, to its students, and to the general public. It is in this entirely respectable and praiseworthy sense that the word publicity will be used in this chapter.

[2] Cox, R. G. (chairman). "Report of Committee on Coöperative Advertising"; in *Proceedings of the Ninth Annual Meeting of the American Association of Junior Colleges*, p. 131. Fort Worth, Texas, 1928.

feel that such an advertising campaign might result in unfavorable influence upon the junior college movement. Still others, and perhaps this is almost universal, feel that the junior college is growing fast enough, quite as fast as is safe, and that no such advertising is necessary.... We recommend that no further active effort shall be made at this time to advertise the junior college movement.

A code of ethics. Miss Templin, in 1926, at the meeting of the American Association of Junior Colleges, presented a paper calling attention to some notably unethical and deceptive practices made use of by some junior colleges or their agents in competition for students, of false claims of accreditation and recognition by outside universities or other agencies, and of misleading claims in their advertising. She emphasized the importance of a high standard of professional ethics in the administration of the junior college, and proposed a tentative code of ethics of nine features.[1] While they were not formally adopted by the Association, nevertheless they had their effect and probably have had a substantial influence in eliminating undesirable and unprofessional actions on the part of some over-zealous junior college administrators.[2]

National journals. Much valuable and discriminating publicity regarding the junior college movement as a whole, as

[1] These nine features may be summarized thus: competition should be placed on a more legitimate basis; no attempt should be made to influence a student to change her decision with reference to entrance to a college; a contract to attend a particular college should be regarded as permanent; all publicity material should be confined to statements regarding the advantages of a particular college with no insinuations regarding other institutions; extravagant statements should be carefully eliminated from all published material; where two colleges are located in the same town no attempt should be made to induce students to change institutions; the only legitimate financial reductions should be in the form of honor scholarships; all statements printed in the catalogue should be strictly enforced; no financial inducements should be offered to students prominent in athletics, music, etc.

[2] As a result of Miss Templin's address, a committee was appointed to prepare a code of ethics for junior colleges, and to report at the next annual meeting. Such a report, however, seems never to have been made.

well as special phases of it, has been found in the national educational journals during the past fifteen years. The bibliography mentioned in Appendix I is a striking evidence of the extent and variety of this type of publicity. There has been some in the daily press, also, but this is mostly local in nature. Only a few articles are found in the non-professional journals, such as the *Atlantic Monthly*, *Scribners*, *Harpers*, and the *Forum*. There is need for more authoritative articles which will reach the intelligent lay reader. One of the earliest, if not the earliest, interpretative article of this type was one by Marion Coats, which appeared in the *Red Book Magazine* in 1923. The inauguration of the *Junior College Journal* in 1930, under the joint auspices of the American Association of Junior Colleges and the School of Education of Stanford University, already mentioned, should be a powerful factor in unifying the junior college movement and in interpreting it more fully to the educational world, but such a periodical will have little influence on the general public.

Local methods and media. There are two general types of educational publicity: continuous and special. The former is the more important, for rightly understood and used it will gradually build up good will, loyalty, and coöperation on the part of the constituency when by a long process of continuous interpretation its purposes and needs are fully understood. Special publicity campaigns, for buildings, endowment, removal of indebtedness, and other purposes are also essential at times, and are more likely to be successful if built upon a foundation of continuous publicity.

There is scarcely any limit to the variety of methods of publicity or interpretation open to the junior college, either public or private. Every student, and every member of the faculty, is a more or less conscious publicity agent for the institution. Among the more important special methods in common use, however, are college catalogues, view books, newspaper reports, radio programs, personal visitations, advertising in church and secular journals, periodicals, and student publications. No effort will be made to discuss all of these in detail. Most of them are methods common to all educational publicity, and ample information regarding them may be found in general treatments.[1] More detailed treatment will be given to the matter of junior college catalogues later in this chapter.

The agents of publicity. Carpenter and Carter, in a study of the duties of forty-six junior college deans, found 85 per cent of them reporting that they furnished publicity for school activities or policies. The local newspaper, supported by various other methods, seemed to be almost universally used. A large percentage of the deans made talks before local civic organizations. One used the open-house program method of interesting the public in his junior college; another radio broadcasting; another posters, parades, and theater slides. In some institutions, however, this duty is assigned specifically to some member of the faculty, more often the head of the journalism department, or the registrar. It has already been suggested in Chapter XIV that some one in the institution should be made responsible for coördinating the publicity work of the junior college.

The costs of publicity. Two brief studies of publicity costs have been reported. Koos, in 1922, found that many private junior colleges seemed to have rather excessive publicity costs, amounting in nine institutions studied to an average of $24 per student, and in some running up to $40. In eight public ones, on the other hand, he found an average of only 70 cents per student, largely for modest bulletins or catalogues. He sug-

[1] As particularly valuable first sources of information for junior college administrators and publicity directors may be mentioned: Quiett and Casey, *Principles of Publicity* (D. Appleton and Company, New York, 1929), especially Chapter XIV, "University and College Publicity," pp. 234–69; Moehlman, A. B., *Public School Relations* (Rand McNally, 1927); Stevenson, *Campaign Publicity for Schools* (Ohio State University Press, 1926); and the issue of the *Journal of the National Education Association* for March, 1930.

gested the desirability of efforts on the part of private junior colleges toward a reduction of publicity costs in order to secure a reduction of student tuition, or a diversion of a larger proportion of the school's funds to educational functions.[1]

Craft, in 1925, in a questionnaire study of seventy junior colleges, fifty-eight of them private institutions, found costs of publicity ranging from nothing to $120 per student, with an average for a majority of them of over $30. More such studies should be made, including costs of the same function in four-year colleges, with careful definition of terms, and detailed segregation of various items of the publicity budget. What part do printing, postage, salary, traveling expense, commissions, stenographic help, direct advertising, and other features make up in the complete publicity cost? What part of the total current expense should be devoted to publicity? Can separate norms be set up for various types of public and private institutions? There is need for an investigation along these lines, which will be of real value.

THE CATALOGUE

Variety of catalogues. One of the most common and important means of publicity is the college catalogue. Some, especially those issued by private institutions for women and by military colleges, are very expensive productions, the finest examples of the master printer's art, profusely illustrated, duotone printing, handsomely bound in cloth or imitation leather, and resembling a handsome college annual more than a matter-of-fact college catalogue. At the other extreme are found ungrammatical and misspelled booklets, slovenly printed on the cheapest of stock, that would reflect only discredit on a second-rate country printer.

Catalogue reflects the college. The character of an educational institution is closely reflected in the catalogue which

[1] Koos, *Junior College*, p. 562.

it publishes. To those not in immediate contact with it, the catalogue often is the most important means of judging the institution. It is thus exceedingly important that the catalogue should be complete, accurate,[1] clear, and honest. There have been a few general discussions of desirable and undesirable features of college catalogues, but little if any effort to evaluate them by any objective means. The junior college, in particular, just making its place in higher education in America, often suffers from inadequate and mediocre catalogues. Four quotations from different junior college catalogues will be enlightening.[2]

Why attend college? The human heart yearns for companionship and a college education introduces one to a world of wonders, surpassing in awe-inspiring fascination the magical creations of the Arabian Nights. The mind of the artist transforms a lurid blotch on the evening sky into a glorified sunset tinged with the sublime. To him who understands physical geography, the dewdrop speaks a various language; the chemist, learned in the astronomy of the atom, knows a universe never dreamed of by the unenlightened; the botanist communes with the lily and the rose whose whispers keep him company of a rare and spiritual nature that the unlettered can never know. Also the astronomer, viewing the sweep of the sidereal universe, attains a fellowship with Mother Nature's heavenly creatures — a companionship transcending any that earth can

[1] Two examples of inaccuracy in junior college catalogues may be mentioned: The catalogue of McCook Nebraska Junior College, for 1929–30, enthusiastically states, in a full page display:

"Junior colleges are here to stay. Total public and private junior colleges in 53 states and territories of the United States, 780. California has 77; Iowa has 53; Kansas has 37; Texas has 76. In 1927–28 the public junior colleges in Iowa doubled in number."

This is worthy of the best traditions of the most enthusiastic California real estate promoter, but hardly to be expected of a presumably accurate and reliable college catalogue. None of the statements quoted even approximate the truth.

The catalogue of Jackson Junior College (Michigan), for 1930–31, contains the information that California had ten junior colleges in 1910 — actually there was one!

[2] The four quotations that follow represent both public and private junior colleges. All are taken from catalogues dated 1929–30.

give. The foregoing are but a hint of the mysteries, hidden from him who cannot speak their tongue. Now a college course is a harp of a thousand strings and one of these may tune in with your greater self and arouse your dormant possibilities and start you on the road to fame and achievement. Uneducated, you run the race of life with a ball and chain to your foot; but learned you hop off on the wings of wisdom to soar above the sordid difficulties that otherwise would impede your progress and form stumbling blocks for your feet.

Girls will dress in suits which have ample skirts, and shirt-waists, not transparent, with not less than three-quarter length sleeves and collars of proper height. Skirts must, under no conditions, be more than twelve inches from the floor. The use of lipsticks, rouge, and all like cosmetics is strictly forbidden. Girls over fourteen years of age are not permitted to bob or shingle the hair. Those whose hair has already been cut may enter the school on the condition only that it be allowed to grow. This rule will be strictly enforced.

Since the printed page is one of the mightiest forces for good or ill in the life of the reader, students are asked to read only that which ennobles and uplifts, and to abstain from reading "frivolous, exciting tales," "story magazines," and other forms of questionable literature.

We do not enroll or retain students who visit the motion picture theaters. The reason for this is very clear. The training that we desire to give is the direct opposite of that which the theaters give. There are amusements — such as dancing, card-playing, chess, checkers, etc. — which we cannot approve because Heaven condemns them.

The reader is left to judge the extent to which such selections indicate the nature of the junior colleges which they represent, and their suitability for insertion in the catalogue.

Characteristics of a good catalogue. In form, in style, and in content the college catalogue should be above reproach. It should be attractive, orderly, dignified, sincere, dependable. That it does not always meet these specifications in the general college field is unfortunately too often true. In the junior college field, so new in the realm of higher education, the catalogue often lacks much of perfection. Sometimes, of necessity, it is hastily edited by a man crowded with other duties, who has little or no knowledge of printing and the printer's art, and with slight conception of what its contents should be, or of the needs of those who will later consult it. It seems desirable that there should be a list of minimum essentials for a junior college catalogue, and a method of objective measurement to find how successfully the catalogue is reaching such standards.

Construction of a score card. In this chapter a report will be made of the work of three different classes of graduate students, in a course in Junior College Administration at Stanford University, in determining such minimum essentials, and in constructing and using a score card to evaluate catalogues. The score-card method, originating in the agricultural field, has been most widely used in education in scoring school buildings. It has also been used for judging textbooks, and for evaluating standard tests, but no application of it has been made to the evaluation of college catalogues.[1]

The catalogue of a junior college should furnish reliable information to six groups: (1) to students, both present and prospective; (2) to parents of prospective students; (3) to the faculty of the college; (4) to high schools, preparing students to enter the college; (5) to colleges and universities to which the junior college student may transfer, especially to the administrative officers of such institutions; (6) to research workers, investigators, and students of the junior college movement. Bearing in mind these different expressed objectives, each member of the class in Junior College Administration in the spring of 1928, after a considerable use of such catalogues in other assignments, was asked to submit a list of desirable characteristics and contents for a junior college catalogue. These were discussed, revised, classified, and arranged in eight groups. Each member of the class was then asked to express his best

[1] For examples of building score card, see pages 435–36.

SCORE CARD FOR JUNIOR COLLEGE CATALOGUE

(Total points possible, 100)
(Half points, but not smaller fractions, may be used in scoring)

......(15) I INTRODUCTORY AND GENERAL
- ......(2) Cover. (Appearance, color, style, weight)
- ......(1) Binding. (Opens flat. Saddle-stitch or sewed)
- ......(1) Quality of paper
- ......(2) Type, make-up, general appearance. Dignity, restraint
- ......(1) Page size. (Between 5 × 7 and 6 × 9)
- ......(1) Pages numbered
- ......(2) Title page. (Appearance, name, date, location)
- ......(2) Calendar. (Form, completeness)
- ......(2) Table of contents. (Adequate)
- ......(1) Index

......(10) II. OFFICERS AND FACULTY
- ......(2) Board of Education, or Trustees. (Names)
- ......(1) Officers of Administration. (Names, degrees)
- ......(7) Faculty
  - ......(2) Names
  - ......(1) Subjects taught
  - ......(1) Degrees held
  - ......(1) Sources of degrees
  - ......(1) Experience. Academic biography
  - ......(1) Part time or full time

......(15) III. GENERAL INFORMATION
- ......(3) History. (Brief, but comprehensive and exact)
- ......(3) Reasons for a Junior College. Aims and functions
- ......(2) Location and campus
- ......(3) Buildings. (Descriptions simple, compact, complete)
- ......(2) Financial statement. (Resources, income, expenditure)
- ......(2) Organization. (Relation to high school, etc.)

......(10) IV. EQUIPMENT
- ......(4) Library. (No. volumes, periodicals, care, growth)
- ......(3) Laboratories. (Subjects, adequacy, value)
- ......(2) Other equipment. (Museums, shops, athletic, art, music, domestic science, etc.)
- ......(1) Extent to which equipment is shared with other institutions, e.g., high school

......(20) V. ACADEMIC INFORMATION
- ......(3) Admission conditions and requirements. (In detail)
- ......(3) Departments and curricula. (For whom, advantages, etc.)
- ......(4) Graduation requirements. (Courses, units, certificates)
- ......(1) Limitations on number of units permitted
- ......(1) Relationship to Universities or accrediting agencies

SCORE CARD (*continued*)

......(1) System of grades or marks used
......(2) Expenses and fees. (Scholarship aid)
......(2) Health and recreation
......(2) Student activities. (Brief, dignified)
......(1) Honors, prizes, honor society

......(20) VI. COURSES OF STUDY
......(3) Arranged by departments
......(1) General limitations or conditions under which given
......(2) Number of students enrolled previous year, in each
......(14) Description in detail of each course
......(2) Title of course
......(4) Content. (Brief but significant)
......(2) Instructor by whom offered
......(2) Length of course
......(2) Units of credit
......(1) Prerequisites and limitations on enrollment
......(1) Special fees. (Laboratory, etc.)

......(10) VII. STUDENTS
......(6) List of students enrolled previous year
......(2) Names of students
......(2) Classification as freshmen, sophomores, special, etc.
......(2) Residence given
......(2) List of graduates of previous year
......(1) Names of graduates
......(1) Department or course from which graduated
......(2) Summaries of Enrollment

......(− 25) VIII. NEGATIVE CHARACTERISTICS
(Deduct from total positive score)
......(− 2) Pictures, except buildings
......(− 2) Elaborate descriptions of student activities, etc.
......(− 2) Names of athletes, debaters, etc. Lists of victories
......(− 2) Paid advertising matter
......(− 2) Minor rules and regulations, inappropriate rules of conduct, trivial advice, etc.
......(− 1) Excessive academic biographies of faculty
......(− 1) Lengthy descriptions of courses
......(− 3) Self-laudatory and boastful tone. Flamboyant
......(− 2) Clear-cut, logical arrangement lacking
......(− 2) Inaccuracy, inconsistency, misrepresentation, dishonesty
......(− 2) Poor literary form
......(− 2) Spelling, grammar, punctuation, careless proofreading
......(− 2) Other extraneous and irrelevant matter

judgment as to the relative weight that ought to be given to each of the eight divisions. The sum of the scores was to be 100. The weightings thus suggested were averaged, and slight adjustments made to secure round numbers. The weights for each main topic were then subdivided among its component parts by majority opinion of the class, subject to the restriction that no fractional points should be used. In this way a tentative score card for junior college catalogues was built up by a class of twenty students, and a number of catalogues were scored by it.

In the spring of 1929, when the course was given again to a class of twenty-five, the entire process was repeated with this group of students. While there were a few changes, the significant feature was the close agreement of the two classes, not only on topics to be included, but on relative weights to be assigned to them. Some revisions were made, and some ambiguities that had developed were clarified. The final form of the score card thus developed, which has not been previously published, is reproduced on pages 588–89.

This score card consists of fifty-four positive items, in seven groups, and a final group of thirteen negative items in which conspicuous defects are penalized by subtracting points from the total positive score as found from the first seven groups. The items on the card as printed are largely self-explanatory.

Each student in the class in the spring quarter and summer quarter of 1929 was asked to use the score card in carefully evaluating three or four catalogues of different junior colleges of various types. Before reporting the results, and making some significant comparisons, it will be instructive to consider the validity and reliability of the score card.

Validity. The validity, as just explained, is based essentially upon the composite judgment of competent judges. The members of the classes were all graduate students in education, many of them with considerable administrative or teaching experience. It is not claimed that the score card includes all desirable contents for a junior college catalogue. In many cases local conditions or other considerations will require the inclusion of additional matter. It is believed, however, that it represents fairly adequately a body of material, in acceptable form, which may reasonably be expected in a junior college catalogue. The relative weight to be given to each item represents the consensus of judgment of some forty-five graduate students. The score card, then, measures something worth while to measure, but how accurately does it measure it?

Reliability. There seems to have been no systematic study of the reliability of other score cards used in the educational field, yet it is highly important to know how accurately any such device measures whatever it does measure. How nearly will two equally competent judges agree in their scores of the same catalogue? Following are the actual scores given by different students to the same catalogue in each of four different colleges:

College A	79, 78, 77, 77, 77, 74, 74, 73, 70, 69	Mean 75
College B	51, 46, 45, 43	Mean 46
College C	89, 84, 76, 71, 71	Mean 78
College D	75, 74, 69, 67, 67	Mean 70

These scores were given by students the first time they attempted to use the score card. Further practice doubtless would reduce their variability considerably. However, the data as given will be used to secure a measure of reliability. There were ten college catalogues, similar to the four given above, for which four or more scores by different students were available — a total of fifty-two different scores. If it be assumed that the mean represents the true score in each case, differences from it may be computed. In twenty-four of the fifty-two cases the deviation of any score from the assumed true score was two points or less. Thus it may be estimated that the probable error of a single scoring of a catalogue is about 2.3 points. There is about one chance in five or six that the true score on a catalogue varies from the one obtained by a single scoring of it by more than five points. This seems to be a fairly satisfactory degree of reliability for a measuring device of this type. The probable error of some of our longer and better intelligence tests, involving hundreds of items, is proportionately larger. If one uses this score card with care and judgment he may be reasonably sure that another equally competent user is not likely to differ with him by more than four or five points. An average of scores by two or three individuals would reduce the probable error a third or more.

The reliability may be further illustrated by reporting, for two colleges, the scores given by different scorers on the eight different parts of the score card. This is done in Table 62.

TABLE 62. SCORES OF TWO JUNIOR COLLEGE CATALOGUES FOR EACH MAIN SUBDIVISION OF THE SCORE CARD

	Total	I	II	III	IV	V	VI	VII	VIII
College A....	79	13	10	10	9	19	18	0	0
	78	13	9	10	9	19	18	0	0
	77	14	10	10	9	18	16	0	0
	77	13	10	10	9	18	18	0	−1
	77	13	9	10	8	20	8	0	−1
	74	13	10	9	8	16	18	0	0
	74	13	8	10	9	16	18	0	0
	73	13	10	8	8	17	18	0	−1
	70	12	10	7	7	18	16	0	0
	69	12	9	8	9	15	16	0	0
College B....	51	12	5	2	0	16	16	0	0
	46	12	3	0	0	15	16	0	0
	45	12	3	0	0	16	14	0	0
	43	11	3	0	0	13	16	0	0

It will be seen from the above figures that the discrepancies in the separate parts are comparatively slight.

Results of the use of the score card. The members of the spring and summer classes of 1929, making use of the score card as given herewith, scored the catalogues of ninety-two different junior colleges, located in all parts of the country.

The number of scores on any one catalogue varied from one to ten. These are summarized, for five groups of colleges, in Table 63. To fully understand this table it should be recalled that there are two distinct types of public junior colleges in California, the district type and the high school departmental type. The catalogues of these two types of colleges are reported separately in Table 63. The non-California colleges reported were found in eighteen different states.[1]

TABLE 63. MAXIMUM, MINIMUM, AND MEAN SCORES ON JUNIOR COLLEGE CATALOGUES, BY GROUPS OF COLLEGES

	Number of Colleges	Number of Scorings	Maximum	Minimum	Mean Score
Entire Group	**92**	**165**	**94**	**15**	**61.1**
California					
District type, public	15	55	79	47	64.5
High school type, public	14	32	63	20	47.7
Private	7	15	68	52	58.3
Non-California					
Public	27	31	88	28	59.7
Private	29	32	94	15	67.7

The best as well as the poorest catalogue was found in the group of non-California private junior colleges. This group also shows the highest mean score, 67.7, followed closely by the California district type.

Improvement of catalogues. If the score card is at all a valid measuring instrument, there are very few junior college catalogues that could not be greatly improved, both in style and in content. To show the features in which they are weakest, Table 64 exhibits, for the three California groups, the maximum, minimum, and mean scores for each of the eight parts.

[1] Arizona, Arkansas, Colorado, Idaho, Illinois, Indiana, Iowa, Kansas, Kentucky, Massachusetts, Michigan, Mississippi, Missouri, Oklahoma, Pennsylvania, Texas, Utah, and Washington.

TABLE 64. MAXIMUM, MINIMUM, AND MEAN SCORES ON EACH OF THE EIGHT PARTS OF THE SCORE CARD, FOR CALIFORNIA JUNIOR COLLEGES

	TOTAL	I	II	III	IV	V	VI	VII	VIII
Possible score....	**100**	**15**	**10**	**15**	**10**	**20**	**20**	**10**	**− 25**
District type									
Maximum.....	79	15	9.5	15	9	18	17	8	0
Minimum.....	47	8	3	1	0	12	13	0	− 3
Mean.........	**64.5**	**12**	**8**	**9**	**4**	**16**	**16**	**1**	**− 1**
High school type									
Maximum.....	63	14	9	11	5	19	15	16	0
Minimum.....	20	2	3	0	0	5	6	0	− 3
Mean.........	**47.7**	**10**	**6**	**5**	**1**	**12.5**	**13.5**	**.5**	**− 1**
Private colleges									
Maximum.....	68	14	9	14	5	17	16	4	0
Minimum.....	52	8	6	8	0	6	9	0	− 5
Mean.........	**58.3**	**11**	**7**	**10**	**3**	**13**	**14**	**1**	**− 1**

The strongest features are seen to be: I, Introductory and General; II, Officers and Faculty; V, Academic Information; and VI, Courses of Study; but even in these the scores only average about three fourths of what they might be. The weakest features are III, General Information, averaging about half of the possible score; IV, Equipment, averaging only one fourth of the possible score; and, poorest of all, VII, information regarding students and graduates, in which the average score is only one tenth of what it might be.

How can the junior college catalogue be improved? The method followed at Drexel Institute is worthy of thoughtful consideration. Over four hundred catalogues were carefully analyzed. Eighteen different type pages were set up as samples and submitted to printing experts, to oculists, and to illuminating engineers. The writing of the catalogue was considered as carefully as the mechanics. Each year it is written by one man, whose work is then criticized by three trained writers and editorially amended and checked. To obtain directness and honesty all essential facts are submitted both to the faculty and to upper classmen. Students and faculty meet in conference, and criticize any word or phrase which in any way is untrue or misrepresentative. When junior college executives exercise a fraction of this care in the construction of their catalogues, marked improvement may be expected. Here is an excellent suggestion for student coöperation.

A number of California institutions have used this score card as a guide for the modification of their catalogues. One institution, whose catalogue scored 75 on it in 1929, raised its score to 94 on its 1930 catalogue.

QUESTIONS AND PROBLEMS

1. Criticize the code of ethics suggested by Miss Templin.
2. List the advantages and disadvantages of a coöperative advertising plan for junior colleges.
3. Outline a form for a publicity budget.
4. Who can best furnish publicity for a junior college? Should the responsibility be concentrated or divided?
5. List as many articles as possible on the junior college that have been printed in non-professional journals of national circulation. Is there a larger number in more recent years?
6. Would it be desirable to abolish the word "publicity" from the educational vocabulary?
7. You have been appointed publicity officer for a particular junior college. Outline a publicity policy for the institution.
8. Make an analysis of the contents of a group of junior college catalogues, similar to that made of university catalogues in the *Eighth Annual Report of the Carnegie Foundation* (1913), p. 114.
9. The catalogue of one junior college was mailed with the following inserted note: "The printer has changed the capitalization to suit himself. It is too late now to reprint, so we send it out with this explanation." Does such an explanation absolve the junior college from responsibility? How could the necessity for such an explanation have been avoided?
10. Who should be the editor of the junior college catalogue?
11. Select from junior college catalogues examples of the various "demerits" listed in Section VIII of the catalogue score card.
12. For any junior college, score two catalogues separated by an interval of three or four years. What improvement is noted?
13. Test your reliability with the score card by scoring a catalogue, and rescoring it after an interval of a month or more.

14. Criticize the weights assigned to the various elements that make up the proposed catalogue score card.
15. What features, if any, should be added to the proposed catalogue score card?
16. What features, if any, should be removed from the proposed catalogue score card?
17. How much change would be necessary to adapt the catalogue score card to use for catalogues of four-year colleges?

SUGGESTED READINGS

Publicity

*Applegate, J. S. "The Possibilities of Co-operative Advertising of Junior Colleges"; in *Proceedings of the Seventh Annual Meeting of the American Association of Junior Colleges*, pp. 19–21. Jackson, Mississippi, 1926.

Address by a professional advertising man. For results, see *Proceedings of the Eighth Annual Meeting of the American Association of Junior Colleges*, pp. 61–63 (Chicago, 1928); and *Proceedings of the Ninth Annual Meeting of the American Association of Junior Colleges*, pp. 130–31 (Fort Worth, Texas, 1928).

Benner, T. E. "College and University Publicity"; in *Teachers' College Record*, vol. 31, pp. 422–29. (February, 1930.)

Based on questionnaires answered by 48 public and 71 private colleges and universities — some suggestions for junior colleges.

Carpenter, W. W. "Means for School Publicity Utilized by Public Junior Colleges"; in *Peabody Journal of Education*, vol. 8, pp. 165–71. (November, 1930.)

Coats, Marion. "The Junior College in the Education of Girls"; in *Red Book Magazine*, February, 1923.

Craft, J. P. "Report on Enrollment: Method of Securing Students"; in *Proceedings of the Fifth Annual Meeting of the American Association of Junior Colleges*, pp. 79–83, 85–88. Cincinnati, Ohio, 1925.

*Templin, Lucinda de L. "The Need of a Higher Code of Ethics in Administering Junior Colleges"; in *Proceedings of the Seventh Annual Meeting of the American Association of Junior Colleges*, pp. 21–26 (Jackson, Mississippi, 1926); also in slightly different form in *Educational Review*, vol. 74, pp. 94–98 (September, 1927).

View Books of National Park Seminary, Forest Glen, Maryland; and of Stephens College, Columbia, Missouri.

For bibliographies on educational publicity in general, see Alexander, Carter: *School Statistics and Publicity*, 332 pp. (Boston, 1919, Silver, Burdett); Alexander, Carter: "Research in Educational Publicity; Outstanding Achievements and Needed Studies"; in *Teachers'*

College Record, vol. 29, pp. 479–85 (March, 1928); Voegelein, L. Belle: "Selected Bibliography on School Publicity"; in *Educational Research Bulletin of Ohio State University*, vol. 3, pp. 162–65, no. 8 (April 16, 1924).

Catalogues

(There is no literature of value regarding the junior college catalogue, and only a little dealing with college catalogues in general. The five given below are most helpful.)

Pritchett, H. S. "College Catalogues"; in *Eighth Annual Report of the Carnegie Foundation for the Advancement of Teaching*, pp. 111–24. New York, 1913.

An illuminating and helpful study, criticizing many catalogues and suggesting desirable improvements.

Ward. H. P. *The American College Catalogue*, 298 pp. Columbus, Ohio, 1917.

A finely printed, comprehensive volume. Particularly strong from standpoint of style and form, but with some consideration of content, as well. Unfortunately printed in a limited edition of 300 copies. Available in larger libraries.

Jarvis, J. D. *The College Catalogue*. United States Bureau of Education, Higher Education Circular no. 13. (January, 1919.)

Result of analysis of catalogues of land-grant colleges, but has many helpful suggestions for other colleges.

Godfrey, H. *University Training for Public Service*, in United States Bureau of Education, Bulletin no. 30, pp. 35–36. (1916.)

President of Drexel Institute describes careful methods of catalogue construction at that institution.

Bright, A. *A Study of the College Catalogue*. Bulletin of the American Association of Collegiate Registrars, vol. 3, no. 1, pp. 75–84. (July, 1927.)

Registrar of Carnegie Institute of Technology presents desirable contents of college catalogue as agreed to by various authorities. Discussion by members of the Association.

CHAPTER XXII

STANDARD TESTS IN JUNIOR COLLEGES

It can no longer be doubted that the recent development and wide-spread adoption of standard tests for measuring pupil ability and pupil achievement marks the beginning of a new epoch in the history of educational practice. Youthful as the movement is, we have already passed well beyond the stage of question and debate as to the usefulness of mental and achievement tests when they are employed with a due regard for their acknowledged limitations. — L. M. Terman.[1]

Contents of this chapter. Youthfulness is a characteristic of both the standard test movement and the junior college movement. Each has developed almost entirely within the past two decades. Each has great potentiality for educational progress in America. It is fitting, therefore, that one chapter should be devoted to a brief survey of the results of applying the scientific test procedure to obtain a clearer and more reliable measure of the ability and accomplishment of students who are being educated in the junior college. In Chapter XI, in discussing the guidance function, the use of standard tests in individual guidance problems in different institutions was reported, and additional references suggested. This chapter is restricted to a brief résumé of the important general surveys that have been made covering groups of institutions, including studies by Reeves, Koos, and Stoddard, and a more detailed report of the most extensive one yet undertaken, made by the author in the autumn of 1929, involving over 11,000 students in California junior colleges.

VALUE AND LITERATURE OF TESTS

The value of standard tests in colleges. It is doubtless quite unnecessary to urge the value of standardized tests for college

[1] From the Editor's Introduction to *Interpretation of Educational Measurements*, by T. L. Kelley. Copyright, 1927, by World Book Company, Yonkers-on-Hudson, New York.

administrative purposes. Such value may be assumed. Yet college administrators are often somewhat conservative, and there is a feeling in some quarters that while such quantitative measuring devices may be useful and desirable in the more formalized curricula of the elementary school, and even of the high school, the splendid independence of *college* education cannot be circumscribed by such devices. In this connection it may be still of value to quote a few sentences, written in 1923 by Lewis M. Terman, one of the pioneers in test development:[1]

From the language of statistics there is no escape if we wish to go beyond the limits of personal opinion and individual bias. Worth-while evaluations in higher education will continue to be as rare as they now unhappily are until the rank and file of college and university teachers become able to think in more exact quantitive terms than they are yet accustomed to.... There is no intention to suggest that only the most brilliant young men and women should attend college. There are colleges and colleges, also departments and departments within the same college. If we had an intelligence index representing the average mental ability in each college, the indices for a hundred representative colleges would be found to cover such an enormous range that the average as well as the brilliant youth could readily select a college that would correspond to his own grade of ability. The purpose of intelligence tests is not to deprive any one of any educational opportunity from which he is fitted by ability to derive normal profit, but rather to enable us to select the type of curriculum from which a given individual can profit, whether he be bright or dull.... Comparatively speaking, some student bodies are made up largely of intellectual cream while others have been drawn almost entirely from the lower levels. Such differences may have been suspected in some quarters, but only recently has it been possible to measure them.... For lack of the kind of facts which tests give us regarding the raw material in our institutions of higher education it has been impossible to evaluate the institutions themselves, their departments, their professors, their curricula, or their

[1] From Introduction to *Measurement in Higher Education*, by B. D. Wood. Copyright, 1923, by World Book Company, Publishers, Yonkers-on-Hudson, New York.

methods.... There are but two essential factors going to make a university, or for that matter any other kind of school; namely, raw material and educational processes. Each of these factors enters into every sample of the school's product. As long as the raw material is an unknown quantity the merits of the processes also remain unknown and unknowable. Wherever schools are conducted without the use of modern methods of testing the quantity of their material, their work is done largely in the dark.

Although these statements were made regarding the entire field of higher education, they become even more significant when read with the junior college especially in mind. Their junior college implications are so obvious that they will not be pointed out in detail. Much evidence of their truth will be found in the concrete data presented in the latter part of this chapter.

The literature of standard tests. There is an extensive literature covering the entire field of intelligence and achievement testing in general but very little applying expressly to the collegiate field. Wood's *Measurement in Higher Education*, published in 1923, deals in detail with the experience at Columbia University in the use of the Thorndike Intelligence Test, and with the development of achievement tests in some of the college subjects. The 1930 *Yearbook* of the National Society of College Teachers of Education, of 253 pages, is devoted exclusively to a study of "Quantitative Measurement in Institutions of Higher Learning." Perhaps the feature in it of greatest permanent value and direct usefulness is the annotated list of two hundred and thirty-four different standard tests suitable for use in institutions of higher learning, compiled by Dr. Woody, of the University of Michigan. This has been reprinted as a seventy-two-page monograph by the American Council on Education. It should prove an invaluable guide to administrators, guidance directors, and research directors in the junior college field.

Many helpful suggestions will be found in books covering the field of tests in general, especially in the two books by Symonds, and by Ruch and Stoddard, dealing with tests for secondary schools.[1]

SPECIAL TEST STUDIES

Status of tests as found by Reeves. At the 1928 meeting of the American Association of Junior Colleges, Reeves reported the results of a questionnaire survey of the administration and use of tests in seventy-nine junior colleges in all parts of the country. One question asked was "Have intelligence tests been administered in your institution during the past five years?" Forty-two institutions, constituting 60 per cent of the number replying to this question, reported that such tests had been administered. This is almost the same percentage found by Jones in an investigation, in 1926, of the use of intelligence tests in three hundred and thirty standard four-year colleges. Not all of the institutions which reported giving tests had made direct use of the results obtained, but twenty-eight stated definite ways in which they had been used in administering the work of the institution. A summary of these uses will be found in Table 74 (page 613), where they are compared with uses reported for the California study.

Koos's Army Alpha study. Koos, in 1922, reported an extensive analysis of scores on the Army Alpha test, given to eight hundred and fifty-four students in ten northern junior colleges, both public and private, and on the Thurstone Cycle Omnibus Intelligence Test, given to two hundred and six freshmen in five public junior colleges. Army Alpha is not as suitable for the measurement of ability of college students as are the Thorndike or American Council tests, which have since been developed, but it was chosen primarily because extensive

[1] Symonds, P. M. *Measurement in Secondary Education*, 588 pp. The Macmillan Company, New York, 1927.

Ruch, G. M., and Stoddard, G. D. *Tests and Measurements in High School Instruction*, 381 pp. World Book Company, Yonkers, New York, 1927.

results from its use in the army and in many standard colleges and universities were available for comparison. It is not possible to summarize here all of the various comparisons made by Koos. In general, the percentage distributions of scores resembled very closely those for freshmen in large Middle Western state universities, such as Ohio and Minnesota. When compared with such institutions as Yale and Oberlin, however, there was a remarkable difference in higher scores for the latter type of institution. This was quite to be expected in view of the highly selective admission requirements of these private institutions, as compared with the state universities which usually are open with slight restriction to any high school graduate. Koos comments:[1]

> Our interest is chiefly in the large proportion of less capable students admitted to the state universities and the serious problem of adapting the curriculum to the abilities and needs of these students. If the question is raised as to whether such students should have open to them the opportunities of education on this level, it may be pointed out that, as compared with the general populace, even these less capable junior college freshmen represent a somewhat select group.

Koos's California study. In his preliminary survey of secondary education in California, in 1929, Koos made a comparison of scores on the Thorndike College Aptitude Test by freshmen in six public junior colleges, with those made by freshmen in "three other higher institutions... among the most estimable in the state, which admit only on a highly selective basis" — presumably private institutions. Comparisons were made between 1172 junior college students and 1710 in the other type of institutions. Comparisons were not made with the University of California because such tests had not been regularly administered at Berkeley. Koos feels that it might

[1] Koos, L. V. "Junior College Curricula in California"; in Gray, W. S. (editor), *The Junior College Curriculum*, p. 64. Chicago, 1929.

be safely assumed that the distribution of scores for freshmen at the University of California would not be widely at variance with that for the three other higher institutions represented, because requirements for admission there are also intentionally selective in character.

The median score for the junior college freshmen was found to be 61.2, for freshmen in the other institutions it was 75.8, a difference of practically one standard deviation. This indicates a marked difference in average ability of the two groups. Although there were junior college freshmen with scores almost as high as the highest in the other group, the proportion of high scores was much smaller. Only about 17 per cent of the junior college group exceeded the median of the other group. This is striking evidence, of course, of the democratizing function of the junior college in California, as far as collegiate education is concerned; a particularly important fact in a state where college education is not open to all high school graduates on the more democratic basis characteristic of most of the Middle Western state universities. Koos says:[1]

This comparison is not presented in order to disparage the junior college or to discredit it for admitting high school graduates of less ability than those entering the other higher institutions represented. The junior college was long since advocated as a development aiming in part to popularize this level of education, and popularization can hardly be achieved without relinquishing in some measure the other selective standards of the four-year college and university. On the other hand, it should be apparent without argument that standards of admission as much less selective as those of the junior colleges are shown to be, call for efforts toward the adaptation of the work offered to the ability of students on a scale much more vigorous than are necessary to the traditional and more highly selective standard higher institution. It will not suffice to reproduce without modification for such students the courses offered in the standard four-year colleges. At the same time, the junior college has the

[1] Koos, L. V., and Weersing, F. J. *Secondary Education in California: Report of a Preliminary Survey*, pp. 69–70. Sacramento, California, 1929.

task of maintaining high standards for the large proportions of its students who are on a par in ability with those admitted to the other higher institutions.

The way in which this desirable result is being carried out in practice is shown by the increasing amount of non-academic courses, as indicated in Chapters X and XVIII.

The Iowa Survey. Quite different results were found in the Mental-Educational Survey of Iowa junior college students, conducted by Stoddard and Chandler in 1927. To understand their significance it should be kept in mind that admission to the University of Iowa is not on the selective basis, but open to all qualified high school graduates. In the Iowa Survey, four different tests, covering both ability and achievement, were used, as named in Table 65. All of these tests were taken by 373 freshmen in 11 junior colleges, and also by 1016 freshmen at the University of Iowa. A weighted composite score was computed, secured by combining scores on the individual tests approximately inversely proportional to their standard deviations. A summary of the results is found in Table 65.

TABLE 65. COMPARISON OF MEAN TEST SCORES ON FOUR TESTS FOR FRESHMEN IN IOWA JUNIOR COLLEGES AND STATE UNIVERSITY OF IOWA, 1927

	Junior College Students (373)	University of Iowa Students (1016)
Iowa Comprehension Test, D-1	23	22
English Training, A	90	88
Mathematical Aptitude, A	22	20
Iowa High School Content, A-1	116	113
Composite	366	347

While the differences between the groups is slight in each of the four tests, it is quite significant that in every case it is in favor of the junior college group, instead of against them, as in the California situation. Further, when the composite score is statistically derived and evaluated, the difference of nineteen points in favor of the junior college group turns out to be highly significant, since it is approximately five times the probable error of the difference. Where entrance to junior college and university are on a comparable basis, the junior college has nothing to fear from a comparison of ability or achievement, as far as the Iowa data may be representative and significant.

THE CALIFORNIA MENTAL-EDUCATIONAL SURVEY

Extent and method of the survey. Much the most extensive mental-educational survey of junior college students yet made is the one initiated by the author in California, in the autumn of 1929, in which the ability and achievement of over eleven thousand students in forty-seven junior colleges were measured by means of two nationally known standard tests.[1] More than seven thousand junior college freshmen, and over twenty-four hundred sophomores were tested; special students and lower-division students in one four-year junior college brought up the grand total to over 11,000. The tests were given to approximately two thirds of all the junior college students in the state; to over two thirds of the freshmen, and to over one half of the sophomores.

Data are available from which it is possible to make com-

[1] The two tests selected for the survey were the *Psychological Examination for High School Graduates and College Freshmen, 1928 edition* (referred to hereafter more briefly as the "Thurstone test"), prepared by L. L. Thurstone and Thelma Gwinn Thurstone, and published by the American Council on Education, which has been widely used in four-year colleges and universities throughout the country; and the *Iowa High School Content Examination, form B* (referred to hereafter as the "Iowa test"), by G. M. Ruch, G. D. Stoddard, Lonzo Jones, and Nell Maupin, which covers, by four hundred multiple-choice questions, the general fields of English language and literature, mathematics, science, history, and social science. The Thurstone test requires sixty minutes of working time, the Iowa test eighty minutes. As far as possible the colleges were asked to give both tests on the same half-day, within two weeks of the opening of college; the Thurstone test first, with a ten-minute intermission before giving the Iowa test.

parisons of the scores of California junior college students on both the Thurstone and the Iowa tests, with those made by students in four-year colleges and universities in the United States as a whole, and with those of students in a few other junior colleges as well.

Thurstone test: freshmen. The American Council on Education reports briefly the results of giving the 1928 edition of the Thurstone test to 30,653 freshmen in 112 colleges in the United States.[1] Median and quartile scores, and comparisons with similar data for the California groups, are summarized in Table 66.

TABLE 66. COMPARISON OF MEDIAN AND QUARTILE SCORES OF FRESHMEN IN CALIFORNIA JUNIOR COLLEGES AND IN NATIONAL COLLEGES AND UNIVERSITIES ON THE THURSTONE TEST

Group	Number of Colleges	Number of Students	Lower Quartile	Median	Upper Quartile	Inter-Quartile Range
National Four-Year Colleges	**112**	**30,653**	**99**	**138**	**179**	**80**
Public	32	13,409	96	129	170	74
Private	80	17,244	105	145	186	81
California Junior Colleges	**45**	**6,279**	**101**	**135**	**171**	**70**
District	15	3,653	103	137	174	71
High School	16	2,021	97	129	165	68
Private	9	208	107	136	164	57
Special	5	397	104	143	182	78

The California group as a whole scores slightly lower on the Thurstone test than the entire national group of colleges, but, since 96 per cent of the California group are in public junior colleges, it may be more significant to compare them with the 13,000 freshmen in thirty-two public colleges and universities. When this is done, it is seen that the California junior college group shows considerable superiority to the public colleges, and

[1] Thurstone, L. L., and Thurstone, T. G. "Psychological Examination for 1928"; in *Educational Record*, vol. 10, pp. 105–15. (April, 1929.)

corresponding inferiority to the private colleges. These differences are at least in part explained by factors affecting the enrollment in the several types of institutions. The junior colleges and most of the public institutions are open to all who may come. On the other hand there is a considerable degree of selection due to limitation of enrollment in many of the private institutions in the country. The California students form a more homogeneous group, as is shown by the smaller spread of the middle 50 per cent (interquartile range), than is the case of students enrolled in the four-year colleges.

While the differences between groups are noticeable, as judged by the median scores, it is impossible to judge the true significance of the differences due to the absence of probable errors. Table 67, therefore, exhibits mean scores, with their probable errors, for the national and the California groups.

TABLE 67. COMPARISON OF MEAN SCORES FOR FRESHMEN IN CALIFORNIA JUNIOR COLLEGES AND IN NATIONAL COLLEGES AND UNIVERSITIES ON THE THURSTONE TEST

Group	Number of Students	Mean Score	P.E. of Mean
National Colleges	**30,653**	**140.65**	**0.20***
Public	13,409	132.62	0.30*
Private	17,244	146.88	0.26*
California Junior Colleges	**6,279**	**137.47**	**0.43**
District	3,653	139.66	0.58
High School	2,021	132.18	0.73
Private	208	138.27	2.20
Special	397	143.87	1.78

* Thurstone does not give these values. They have been computed by the author on the assumption that the standard derivative (sigma) is the same for the national group as for the California group, 50.74.

Here again the mean score of the entire California group is seen to be significantly lower than that of the entire national group (seven times the probable error of the difference), but even more significantly superior to the national public group (nine times the probable error of the difference). Each of the

California groups is superior to the national public group, except the high school type of junior college which differs from it but slightly.

Iowa test: freshmen. Extensive data are not available for similar national comparisons on the Iowa test, but comparisons may be made with freshmen at the University of Iowa. This is done in Table 68.

TABLE 68. COMPARISON OF MEAN SCORES FOR LOW FRESHMEN IN CALIFORNIA JUNIOR COLLEGES AND IN THE UNIVERSITY OF IOWA ON THE IOWA TEST

Group	Number of Students	Mean Score	Sigma	P.E. of Mean
University of Iowa	**1,134**	**181.2**	**50.***	**1.0**
California Junior Colleges	**5,918**	**178.5**	**49.4**	**0.4**
District	3,228	180.0	50.3	0.6
High School	2,084	173.3	47.0	0.7
Private	208	186.6	47.9	2.2
Special	398	189.4	52.2	1.8

* Approximate.

The entire group of low freshmen of California junior college students stands slightly lower on the Iowa test than the University of Iowa freshmen, but the difference is not significant (two and a half times the probable error of the difference). The California high school type of junior college, however, is distinctly lower.

Tests of sophomores. The number of low sophomores tested was sufficiently large to make similar comparisons between the different groups fairly significant. These are shown in Table 69.

Table 69 shows test results which are markedly different from those which were shown in Tables 67 and 68. In both tests the low sophomores of the high school type of junior college made higher mean scores than did the district type of junior college students. The difference in mean score is too slight to be significant in the case of the Thurstone test, but is

TABLE 69. COMPARISON OF MEAN SCORES FOR LOW SOPHOMORES ON THURSTONE AND IOWA TESTS

Group	Number	Mean	Sigma	P.E. of Mean
Thurstone Test—All	**2,043**	**158.4**	**51.9**	**0.8**
District	1,572	157.8	51.4	0.9
High School	196	158.6	52.5	2.5
Private	98	150.5	56.3	3.8
Special	177	168.3	51.8	2.6
Iowa Test—All	**2,045**	**196.4**	**49.6**	**0.7**
District	1,568	194.7	48.8	0.8
High School	204	201.1	50.5	2.4
Private	97	193.0	52.8	3.6
Special	176	207.6	52.0	2.6

distinctly significant in the case of the Iowa test. Is the freshman instruction superior in the smaller high school type of junior college, or is the elimination of the poorer students more rapid, so that only the better students survived to take the tests as sophomores? Either hypothesis would serve to explain the striking difference between the freshman and sophomore results, but unfortunately the tests do not furnish an answer to either question; they only raise the question. That the elimination of students is an important factor, however, is shown by the fact that the sophomore enrollment of October 1, 1929, in the high school type of junior colleges was only 45 per cent of the freshman enrollment in the same institutions at the same time during the preceding year, while in the district type of junior colleges the corresponding figure was 65 per cent. The district type institutions held two thirds of their freshmen; the high school type less than one half. These facts suggest that the superiority of score shown by the high school type of junior college sophomores may be due to more rapid elimination of the inferior students during or at the end of the freshman year.

Comparisons by classes. At Pasadena, where the 6–4–4 plan of organization is in effect, the tests were given to 1218 "lower division," or 11th and 12th grade students, as well as to the freshmen and sophomores in junior college classes. Comparative scores can thus be given by half-year intervals from the low eleventh grade to the junior college high sophomores. This is done in Table 70.

TABLE 70. COMPARISON OF MEAN SCORES BY CLASSES, THURSTONE AND IOWA TESTS

Class	Number	Mean	Sigma	P.E. of Mean
Thurstone Test—				
Low Eleventh	473	106.2	47.7	1.5
High Eleventh	165	115.7	47.2	2.5
Low Twelfth	375	126.6	48.0	1.7
High Twelfth	131	127.7	54.7	3.2
Low Freshmen	6,279	137.5	50.7	0.4
High Freshmen	832	144.2	52.9	1.2
Low Sophomores	2,043	158.4	51.9	0.8
High Sophomores	395	159.0	51.2	1.7
Specials	270	131.6	52.9	2.2
Iowa Test—				
Low Eleventh	473	144.6	45.6	1.4
High Eleventh	165	157.9	45.5	2.4
Low Twelfth	375	168.3	50.0	1.7
High Twelfth	131	175.8	58.0	3.4
Low Freshmen	5,918	178.5	49.4	0.4
High Freshmen	835	184.6	51.0	1.2
Low Sophomores	2,045	196.4	49.6	0.7
High Sophomores	397	201.5	46.8	1.6
Specials	261	167.0	56.1	2.3

There seems to be a constant though somewhat irregular increase in score from class to class. The mean scores of the two freshman groups are but slightly different in either test, and this is also true of the scores made by the two sophomore groups. On both tests, however, the mean scores of the sophomore groups are considerably higher than those of the freshmen. The inferior freshmen apparently tend to be eliminated to a considerable extent before the sophomore year. If the differences shown in Table 70 were due entirely or even largely to added maturity, the differences between the mean scores of successive classes should be approximately equal. The differences between high freshman and low sophomore scores are two or three times as great as those between other groups separated by half-year intervals. This fact supports the elimination hypothesis, previously stated.

Comparisons by sex. Separate studies by sex were made for the largest and most significant group, the low freshmen. These are summarized for the Thurstone test in Table 71.

TABLE 71. COMPARISON OF SCORES OF LOW FRESHMEN ON THE THURSTONE TEST, BY SEXES

Group	Men			Women		
	Number	Mean score	P.E. of mean	Number	Mean score	P.E. of mean
All	**3,444**	**138.0**	**0.6**	**2,835**	**136.8**	**0.6**
District	1,964	139.9	0.8	1,689	139.3	0.8
High School	1,115	133.0	1.0	906	131.2	1.1
Private	123	145.2	2.8	85	128.3	3.5
Special	242	141.6	5.4	155	147.4	2.7

The chief fact of interest shown by Table 71 is that, as a whole, the Thurstone test does not reveal significant sex differences. The situation is strikingly different in the case of the Iowa test, as shown in Table 72.

A glance at the last column of Table 72 shows that there are

TABLE 72. COMPARISON OF SCORES OF LOW FRESHMEN ON THE IOWA TEST, BY SEXES

Group	Men			Women			Difference	
	Number	Mean	P.E of mean	Number	Mean	P.E. of mean	Amount	P.E.
All	**3,243**	**188.4**	**0.6**	**2,675**	**166.5**	**0.6**	**21.9**	**0.8**
District	1,745	189.2	0.8	1,483	169.1	0.8	20.1	1.1
High School	1,132	184.4	0.9	952	160.1	1.0	24.3	1.3
Private	123	200.9	2.6	85	165.8	3.4	35.1	4.3
Special	243	194.8	2.4	155	180.9	2.5	13.9	3.3

large and significant differences in mean scores in favor of the men, in every group tested. This superiority of the men in the Iowa test scores is found in all but four of the individual institutions involved. In only one of these four does the number of women tested exceed five. The implication of Table 72 is clear. The Iowa test cannot be used safely for individual diagnosis and guidance without taking into account sex differences on the test. As far as is known, norms for the two sexes have never been published.[1]

Part scores. Since the Iowa test shows such striking sex differences, it will be instructive to consider the sex differences on the four component parts of the test. Do the men make superior scores in all four fields? The answer to this question will be found in Table 73. An analysis on the basis of sex has also been made for two of the parts of the Thurstone test, namely, those testing knowledge of arithmetic and linguistic ability as shown by the "artificial language" test.

TABLE 73. COMPARISON OF SCORES OF LOW FRESHMEN ON THE FOUR PARTS OF THE IOWA TEST AND ON TWO OF THE PARTS OF THE THURSTONE TEST, BY SEXES

Tests	Men			Women			Difference in Favor of
	Number	Mean	P.E. of mean	Number	Mean	P.E. of mean	
Iowa Test—							
English	3,453	49.9	0.2	2,880	55.3	0.2	Women
Mathematics	3,453	34.7	0.2	2,880	25.2	0.2	Men
Science	3,453	47.7	0.2	2,880	35.6	0.1	Men
History	3,243	57.7	0.2	2,675	52.2	0.2	Men
Thurstone Test—							
Arithmetic	3,236	29.6	0.2	2,632	21.9	0.2	Men
Artificial Language	3,236	22.8	0.1	2,632	29.5	0.2	Women

[1] Detailed percentage sex norms based on the California junior college score will be found for the entire test and the four parts of it in Bulletin J-3, *California Junior College Mental-Educational Survey*. Sacramento, California, 1930. This bulletin contains twenty-seven detailed tables of norms for various classes and groups, and comparisons of the participating institutions.

It will be noted that in every one of the six part-tests tabulated, marked and highly significant differences exist between the scores of men and of women. The women excel in English and artificial language, the men in the other fields measured by these particular tests. The differences revealed appear to be sufficiently significant to render the use of the part-scores of value in programs of guidance. These differences should also be taken into consideration in comparisons of student achievement in coeducational institutions, or in those in which enrollment is limited either to men or to women.

Usefulness of the survey. Summaries of scores were sent to each of the participating institutions prior to their more detailed presentation and analysis in the Bulletin published by the State Department of Education. Of course much greater use of the scores could be made after the publication of the

TABLE 74. STATEMENT OF USES MADE OF TEST SCORES BY TWENTY-TWO CALIFORNIA JUNIOR COLLEGES, AND BY TWENTY-EIGHT JUNIOR COLLEGES STUDIED BY REEVES

Reason	California Colleges	Reeves' Group
1. In determining amount of school work students may carry	19	24
2. In encouraging bright students to undertake senior college or university work	22	23
3. In advising students in the selection of their academic work	21	20
4. In dealing with disciplinary cases	4	17
5. For aid in vocational guidance	14	15
6. In determining probation for low scholarship	11	14
7. In determining dismissal for low scholarship	10	12
8. In determining amount of work for self-support	11	11
9. In hiring student clerical help	7	11
10. In making recommendations for scholarships	6	10
11. In sectioning students according to capacity for progress	9	10
12. In making recommendations for positions	12	
13. In making recommendations for entrance to senior colleges or universities	16	2
14. As a basis for guiding students into positions of leadership	8	1
15. As general faculty and institutional stimulus	18	*
16. Other uses	10	*

* Not included by Reeves.

Bulletin, but at the time preliminary results were sent out they were accompanied by a one-page questionnaire asking the junior college executives which of fifteen suggested possible uses of the data had actually been already developed, and which it was expected would be developed in the future.[1] Replies were received from twenty-five institutions, which are summarized in Table 74. In this table will also be found a summary of the answers received by Reeves from twenty-eight junior colleges on a similar questionnaire.

The following "other uses" were specified by various institutions: Principal use — as a basis for intelligent guidance and counseling; in establishing departmental norms; basis for interviews; study of groups, by source; for encouragement in special cases; as a check on our grading system; for study of entrance requirements in "diploma" course; checks findings of our first time students' examinations; by showing weak spots in students' equipment, it aids in curriculum building; reflexively on student, increasing his respect for knowledge and his desire to utilize the mental ability he has.

Further possible studies. In addition to securing test scores, considerable personnel data were secured from each of the eleven thousand junior college students tested: — class, high school previously attended, course of study, whether living at home, hours of outside work per week, nationality and occupation of father and mother, student's nationality, his intended occupation, when his occupational choice was made, amount of occupational preparation expected in junior college, expectation of further education, name of institution in prospect after completion of junior college, certificate or diploma status, number of recommending units at entrance, academic record for each semester at junior college, and number of en-

[1] Adapted from a list used by F. W. Reeves in a study of twenty-eight junior colleges, reported in *Proceedings of the Ninth Annual Meeting of the American Association of Junior Colleges*, p. 76. Fort Worth, Texas, December, 1928.

trance units in different subjects. This mass of information has been made the basis of several special studies of junior college students, and more are planned. In a few years, especially valuable follow-up studies can be made of the group.

QUESTIONS AND PROBLEMS

1. In the quotation which introduced this chapter, Terman speaks of the "acknowledged limitations" of standard tests. What are such limitations for the junior college field?
2. Which were earlier in developing — standard tests or the junior college?
3. Select a list of approximately a dozen standard aptitude and achievement tests which you would recommend as most desirable for use in a junior college. Justify your choice.
4. To what extent may tests designed especially for high school be useful in the junior college?
5. As director of research and guidance, outline a preliminary bulletin to be distributed to a junior college faculty to present the general usefulness and importance of standard tests as an aid to better administration and instruction.
6. What are the practical junior college implications of the fact found by Koos that the median Thorndike score for junior college freshmen in California was 61.2; in other higher institutions, 75.8?
7. Stoddard concludes his study (*School Review*), "Are the junior colleges of Iowa securing the cream of the Iowa high school graduates? They are not. Are they getting chiefly those who ought never to be registered in the four-year colleges and universities? Decidedly they are not. Whether this is a blessing or a calamity must be decided independently." Is it a blessing or a calamity? Why?
8. What tests, besides the two used in the California Junior College Survey, would be suitable for a state-wide junior college testing program?
9. Why should the Iowa test show such marked differences in junior college students when only insignificant differences are shown by the Thurstone test?
10. Account for some of the marked differences in relative importance of the uses made of tests, as reported in the California and Reeves's studies. (Table 74.)
11. Outline in some detail one or more significant studies that could be made on the basis of the California test and personnel data.
12. Which is the better general aptitude test for junior college use, the Thorndike or the Thurstone? Consider cost, time, ease of administration, ease of scoring, validity, reliability, norms, and similar points.

SUGGESTED READINGS

*Eells, W. C. *California Junior College Mental-Educational Survey.* Bulletin no. J–3, 61 pp. California State Department of Education, Sacramento, California, 1930, also in abbreviated form in *Educational Record*, vol. 11, pp. 281–91. (October, 1930.)

Eells, W. C., and Jones, H. F. "Higher Educational Aspirations of California Junior College Students"; in *California Quarterly of Secondary Education*, vol. 6, pp. 239–44. (April, 1931.)

Kilby, C. S. "Intelligence Tests for Adult Admission"; in *Junior College Journal*, vol. 1, pp. 135–39. (December, 1930.)

Kinder, J. S., and Odell, C. W. *Educational Tests for Use in Institutions of Higher Learning.* University of Illinois Bulletin, vol. 27, no. 49. (August 5, 1930.) 96 pp. 321 titles.

Koos, L. V. "The Junior College and Mental Democratization of Higher Education"; in *The Junior College*, pp. 87–122.

Koos, L. V. "The Junior College in its Democratizing Function"; in *The Junior College Movement*, pp. 100–20.

Koos, L. V., and Weersing, F. J. *Secondary Education in California: Report of a Preliminary Survey*, pp. 63–82. Sacramento, California, 1929.

*National Society of College Teachers of Education. "Quantitative Measurement in Institutions of Higher Learning"; *Eighteenth Yearbook of the Society*, 253 pp. University of Chicago Press, 1930.

*Reeves, F. W. "Experiments in the Improvement of Instruction in the Junior College"; in the *Proceedings of the Ninth Annual Meeting of the American Association of Junior Colleges*, pp. 74–82. Fort Worth, Texas, 1928.

Stoddard, G. D. "A Mental-Educational Survey of Iowa Junior Colleges"; in *School Review*, vol. 36, pp. 346–49. (May, 1928.)

Wood, B. D. *Measurement in Higher Education*, 337 pp. World Book Co., Yonkers, New York, 1923.

Dr. Terman's Introduction (pp. 1–11) is particularly stimulating and suggestive.

Woody, C. *Standardized Tests Designed for Use in Institutions of Higher Learning*, 72 pp. American Council on Education, 26 Jackson Place, Washington, D.C., 1930.

Annotated list of 234 tests, reprinted from the *Eighteenth Yearbook* of the National Society of College Teachers of Education.

CHAPTER XXIII
STUDENT ACTIVITIES

> Student activities have an important place in the program of the junior college. The opportunity for true socialization and the development of abilities and attitudes which lead to successful and happy participation in the activities of the community, the development of specialized interests which lead to effective use of leisure time, and the enrichment of the curriculum extending it beyond the more formal curriculum, especially important for the brighter students, and other outcomes that may be possible, urge their serious promotion by administrators of junior colleges. — G. N. KEFAUVER.[1]

Contents of this chapter. This chapter discusses the significance of student activities[2] in the junior college, their extent and variety, and the amount of student participation in them. Special attention is given to eligibility conditions attending the transfer of athletes from junior colleges to universities, and their opportunities for university athletic participation and success; also to a study of the relative participation of junior college students in various student activities before and after transfer to the university. Finally, the development of honor societies in the junior colleges is sketched.

Significance of student activities; training for leadership. That a well-developed program of student activities, under suitable supervision, is an important feature of a complete education in the junior college is the opinion of all thoughtful

[1] Kefauver, G. N. "Student Activities in Junior Colleges"; in *Proceedings of the Tenth Annual Meeting of the American Association of Junior Colleges*, p. 34. Atlantic City, New Jersey, 1929.

[2] In this chapter the term "student activities," instead of "extra-curricular activities," is used advisedly. The latter term makes unnecessary and undesirable distinctions, and is a relic of the period when such activities were thought of as apart from if not indeed inimical to the serious business of education — scholastic work in the classroom. A broader and more modern conception is to think of classroom activities and other student activities as supplemental phases of the curriculum in its broadest and best sense. If they are really an essential and integral part of the educative process, the designation "*extra*" is unfortunate and misleading.

educators who have studied the subject. It is especially in the potentialities for the development of leadership that the program of student activities has a unique place to fill in the well-rounded junior college plan. There are two reasons why such opportunities are more likely to be found with greater frequency in the junior college than in the university.

In a small college of a few hundred students, or less, a student is much more likely to make a place on a team, or to participate in an activity, than in an institution of thousands of students where the competition is much keener. The athlete may not be on as fine a team in the junior college, but it may be much better for him to be an active participant in athletics, dramatics, or debate in a small institution than to be the most enthusiastic sideline participant in a university. Is the chief emphasis on the student or on the activity — "student-centered" or "activity-centered," to paraphrase a distinction recently brought into prominence by the so-called "progressive education" movement? "Activity-centered" makes a greater appeal to the metropolitan press; possibly "student-centered" has far more individual value, even if not as potent as an advertising feature.

Mere membership in teams, societies, or other activities may bring out certain qualities, but not necessarily those of leadership. Offices such as captains, presidents, and managers develop initiative and leadership. Quite properly, in the four-year college or university these positions of responsibility are necessarily given to upper classmen. A student has to wait two or three years to have such an opportunity. In the two-year junior college, with its full quota of student activities, the positions of leadership and responsibility are necessarily filled by sophomores, and in some cases by freshmen. One year instead of three is the normal time to wait for selection to a college position of leadership. In this connection it is interesting to observe that the chapter of Koos's monograph dealing with junior college student activities is not entitled "student activities" nor "extra-curricular activities," but "The Junior College and Training in Leadership."

What are the aims of student activities? Kefauver reports the replies of sixty-eight public junior college deans who were asked to state, in their own words, the values they were attempting to realize through their program of student activities. The outstanding objective, stated by twenty-four, was training for leadership. The social-civic-moral objectives also received large emphasis. The most frequently mentioned of this group were the development of school spirit, socialization, citizenship, character, and coöperation. The opportunity provided for individual development was also stressed. Initiative, responsibility, self-reliance, and self-confidence represent the type of qualities resulting from participation in such activities.

STUDENT ACTIVITIES IN GENERAL

What student activities are found in junior colleges? Practically all activities that are found in any college or university are also found in junior colleges, the greater variety of course being found in colleges with large enrollments. Kefauver, in 1929, reported one hundred and seventy-nine student activities in a study of over a hundred junior colleges. Pasadena junior college catalogue lists seventy clubs and similar organizations, not including various types of athletic teams and activities. A half-hour during the middle of the morning session is allowed daily for the meeting of these organizations, thus emphasizing still more the conception of them as an integral part of the total curriculum. No effort is made to list the extensive array of activities found in the junior colleges — athletic, musical, literary, linguistic, dramatic, scientific, religious, journalistic, or social. For the most part they are analogous to similar organizations in standard colleges. In this chapter the effort will be made to report certain features regarding activities that are somewhat distinctive of the junior college, as well as to make comparisons of opportunities for and participation in them by junior college students before and after transfer to a university.

Control of student activities. In high schools, student activities to be successful are usually rather closely supervised by faculty sponsors; in the university there is frequently a large measure of independence, with little or no faculty connection — financial, administrative, supervisory, or even advisory. The most successful junior college administration of student activities seems to have struck a golden mean between these two attitudes. With a large degree of student initiative and leadership, but with definite faculty oversight and friendly guidance, the junior college is acting in this field also as a valuable transitional institution between necessary high school restrictions and the more complete freedom and responsibility of the university student. It offers guided transition from youthful irresponsibility to adult responsibility. The faculty relationship varies in different colleges, and with different activities and periods in the same college, but this is the ideal which most of the successful institutions seem to have in mind. As a result of his experience with student activities at one junior college, Fuller says: [1]

> Junior college students are easy to lead; they are not spoiled nor hampered by traditions. They welcome leadership but not domination. The work is somewhere between that of the high school and the university in the matter of direction. Space does not permit a discussion of the influence of the outside activities entered into by the faculty members themselves in developing a genuine college atmosphere. Another factor in the development of activities is the harmonious and coöperative spirit of the faculty itself, working under a dean who is always conscious of the educational value of the activities and ready to listen to the desires of the students.

[1] Fuller, W. D. "Extra-Curricular Activities in a Junior College"; in Proctor, W. M. (editor), *The Junior College: Its Organization and Administration*, p. 138.

Student activities in 1921. Koos, in 1921, studied the student activities in a group of twenty-six public and sixteen private junior colleges. He classified almost fifty varieties into four main groups. Basketball was the only activity he found represented in all of the private institutions. This activity also ranked highest in the public junior colleges, where it was found in 85 per cent of the institutions. Other activities found in half or more of the private junior colleges were tennis, literary societies, dramatics, language clubs, annuals, women's glee clubs, orchestra, and Y.W.C.A.; in the public institutions, football, baseball, track, dramatics, language clubs, annuals, men's glee clubs, women's glee club, and orchestra.[1] He found an average of eleven activities in each of the public, and twelve in the private institutions. Two thirds of the public institutions had less than 150 students.

Koos secured facts as to student membership and office holding in some of the junior colleges, and also, for comparison, in three four-year colleges and one state university. In the latter, two groups of sophomores only were taken, while in the junior colleges both freshmen and sophomores, thus making the comparison somewhat unfavorable to the junior college. He found the average memberships in different activities per student as follows:

For 995 students in 15 public junior colleges	2.2
For 680 students in 7 private junior colleges	3.4
For 227 sophomores in 3 four-year colleges	3.2
For 116 sophomores in one state university	2.0

The private junior colleges, although averaging only ninety-seven students each, showed a greater participation than the

[1] Koos (*Junior College*, p. 183), indicates sixteen "public" and twenty-six "private," but these are inconsistent with the figures for the same two groups on pages 184 and 185. There is evidently an error in table 68, p. 183, due to an accidental interchange by compiler or printer of the column headings "public junior colleges" and "private junior colleges." The statement above is based upon a correction of this interchange, not upon the table as printed.

sophomores in the colleges or universities, while the public institutions, with average enrollment of only sixty-six, exceeded the university sophomores. It is also interesting to compare the percentage in each group who participated in no activities. These were:

For the public junior colleges	22 per cent
For the private junior colleges	8 per cent
For the four-year colleges	7 per cent
For the state university	31 per cent

Because training in leadership is afforded by directing activities, rather than by membership in them, a more significant comparison is one which can be derived from data which Koos gathered on responsible offices, such as presidencies, secretaryships, chairmanships, and managerships, held by the different groups. It is here that the opportunity for this sort of development in the junior college is most strikingly shown: The number of office holders for each one hundred students was:

In public junior colleges	21
In private junior colleges	41
In four-year colleges	15
In state university	9

As a result of his study, Koos reached the conclusion:[1]

As these activities come in all types of institutions to be administered with a view to their educational possibilities, the junior college will not lag behind its elder sisters in the family of educational institutions. In fact, the larger proportionate extent of office-holding in junior colleges owing to the absence of upper classmen assures us that, as we attain the desired level of efficiency, students enrolled in them will have much more satisfactory conditions for laboratory work in leadership than will freshmen and sophomores in institutions in which upper classmen naturally fall heir to the positions of responsibility.

This conclusion was reached ten years ago, since which time the junior college has developed into a much stronger and a

[1] Koos, L. V. *Junior College*, p. 188.

more vigorous institution, while during the same time there has been a striking development of the value and significance of student activities in the educational process. We turn, then, to summarize some of the more significant facts brought out in a study of student activities reported in 1929.[1]

Conditions in 1929. This survey, made in 1929, gives the most recent and most comprehensive data available, covering the entire country. It included forty-eight public and fifty-six private institutions,[2] with enrollments varying from 8 to 2883. As to general attitude of administrators toward student activities, the following percentage distribution was found:

	Public (per cent)	Private (per cent)
Definite encouragement and direction	87	84
Encouragement, but left to student direction	9	10
No encouragement, but supervision given	2	6
Discouragement	2	0

In only one institution was there definitely found an attitude of discouragement of student activities. There was one exception to the generally favorable attitude, however, in the case of secret societies or fraternities, about which special inquiry was made. Seventy per cent of the public, and 66 per cent of the private junior colleges prohibited secret societies, and even where permitted they were not always looked upon favorably. In this respect the junior college attitude more nearly resembles the high school than the college. In some states, for example Kansas and California, fraternities are prohibited by law in the secondary schools, and the junior colleges have been classified, at least legally, in this category. In spite of this fact, however, it is known that they exist *sub rosa* in some institutions.

In number and type of activities Kefauver reports a striking variation among the different junior colleges.

[1] A study by G. N. Kefauver and Miss Catherine Bullard, reported by Dr. Kefauver at the meeting of the American Association of Junior Colleges at Atlantic City, November, 1929. (See *Proceedings*, pp. 24–34.)

[2] Kefauver also states that the investigation covered a total of 110 institutions.

Number and type of activities. The range in number of activities for the public junior college was from 2 to 86, and for the private institutions from 2 to 44. As would be expected, the larger institutions had the larger number of activities. The median number of activities for public junior colleges with enrollments under 100 was 9.5, in contrast with 15 for those with enrollments from 100 to 199, and 19 for those with enrollments of 200 and over. The situation for the private junior colleges was practically the same; the median number of activities for the three groups of schools being 16, 22.5, and 20. Three fourths of the public junior colleges had more than eleven activities, and three fourths of the private institutions had more than fourteen.

Larger contrasts were noted between public and private institutions in the type of activity considered. In both instances, the athletic activities dominated. There were 252 such activities in the public, and 310 in the private institutions. Included among these activities were athletic associations, letter clubs, athletic council, football, basketball, soccer, baseball, track, hockey, volley-ball, tennis, swimming, wrestling, boxing, archery, hiking, dancing, folk dancing, military drill, rifle practice, canoeing, golf, horseback riding, handball, gymnastic club, fencing club, and horseshoe club.

The second position in number of clubs is held by the literary group. They rank equally high in the public and private schools, with a frequency of 170 for the public and 185 for the private institutions. This group includes literary society, English club, booklovers club, reading club, poetry club, library club, French club, Spanish club, German club, dramatic club, school paper, school magazine, humor magazine, annual, forensic club, oratory, intercollegiate forensics, creative writing, and dramatic workshop. The most frequent of this group were school paper, dramatic club, annual, and literary society.

The social-civic group of activities also received approximately equal emphasis in the public and private institutions, with a frequency of 112 for public and 129 for private institutions. The activities included in this group were the all-school organization, student council, civics club, leaders club, fraternities, sororities, men's welfare club, women's welfare club, history club, international relations club, junior league of women, government club, social service club, dormitory club and council, men's club, booster club, inter-fraternity and Pan-Hellenic council, men's union, and women's union.

The musical activities were emphasized more in the private institutions, with a frequency of 148 for the private and 98 for the public institutions. The activities included choruses, men's glee clubs, women's glee club, orchestra, band, music club, music appreciation, operetta, cantata, quartette, trio, opera, choir, college players, and violin club.

The religious and moral organizations were also given much larger emphasis in the private institutions, 31 for the public and 63 for the private institutions. Included in this group are the Bible study club, Young Men's Christian Association, Young Women's Christian Association, Sunday school, student volunteers, missionary club, Christian association, Gospel team, and the Christian union. The Y.M.C.A. and Y.W.C.A. are the only organizations of this group that appeared in the public institutions.

The science organizations were more common in the public institutions, the frequency being twenty-eight for the public and twelve for the private type. In this group were the science club, nature-study club, radio club, biology club, aeroplane club, hygiene club, chemistry club, pre-medic club, first-aid club, and others.

In addition to the above groups there were a number of activities that did not lend themselves to grouping. Typical of this group were the honor club, camera club, pep club, chess club, bridge club, travel club, excursion club, and study club.

In all, one hundred and seventy-five different named activities were reported.[1]

Problems connected with student activities. In another phase of Kefauver's investigation he asked the administrators to state the problems and difficulties connected with their program. Sixty-seven replied. The most frequently mentioned problems were: (1) the financial problem (mentioned by 11 institutions); especially, how to obtain adequate funds. Two institutions indicated that students objected to paying fees.[2] (2) Obtaining capable and willing sponsors was a concern in nine schools. (3) The difficulty of scheduling activities for the

TABLE 75. PERCENTAGE OF JUNIOR COLLEGE STUDENTS IN CALIFORNIA WHO PARTICIPATED IN VARIOUS STUDENT ACTIVITIES

ACTIVITY	Total Number of Students (2,924)*	Students in District Type of Junior College (2,026)	Students in High-School Type of Junior College (744)	Freshmen (1,781)	Sophomores (989)	Men (1,443)	Women (1,327)
Football	13.2	10.3	18.0	11.3	14.6	23.9	......
Basketball	17.8	15.7	24.5	16.6	21.3	20.7	15.6
Baseball	11.1	10.3	12.0	9.4	13.2	14.3	6.9
Track	11.3	11.6	9.1	10.8	11.0	19.6	1.3
Minor sports	24.4	24.0	25.5	23.7	25.7	23.0	26.0
Dramatics	13.9	13.8	16.8	12.3	18.8	13.5	16.0
School clubs	34.9	39.0	26.0	27.6	49.1	27.6	43.8
Glee club	13.5	14.5	12.2	11.3	20.3	12.5	15.3
Band or orchestra	6.2	5.5	7.5	5.3	7.3	8.2	3.7
Honorary societies	9.1	10.1	7.9	4.7	17.9	7.4	11.7
Forensics	3.7	3.4	5.4	3.1	5.6	5.8	2.0
Publications	11.8	11.8	12.4	8.0	19.0	13.0	10.7
Student offices **	3.0	3.1	2.6	1.9	4.8	3.9	1.9

* Replies from the small number of students in the state and private institutions are included in the total but not in the groups classified by type of junior college, class, and sex.

** "Student offices" was not included in the check list submitted to the students, but was written in by so many of them that it was added in the tabulations. On this account, the report is doubtless much too small for this particular item.

[1] Kefauver promises a much more extensive report on student activities in the junior colleges in the near future.

[2] For a valuable study of methods of financing junior college athletics, see Chadwick, R. D., "The Financing of Inter-Junior College Athletics"; in *School Executives' Magazine*, vol. 50, pp. 15–17, 42. (September, 1930.)

satisfaction of all was mentioned by seven institutions. A similar frequency of mention occurred for (4), lack of feeling of responsibility of students. This problem was also presented in other forms, as (5) immaturity of students, (6) lack of participation, (7) too much responsibility on a few students, and (8) the lack of coöperation among students. (9) The prevalence of outside interests was indicated for six institutions. The amount of participation appears as a problem in two forms. Five institutions report lack of participation as a problem, and three reported over-participation.

Student activities in California. Brand, in 1929, secured data from over three thousand students in twenty-eight California junior colleges regarding their participation in student activities. Table 75 shows the percentage of students in the entire group and in various subdivisions of it who participated in the various types of activities.

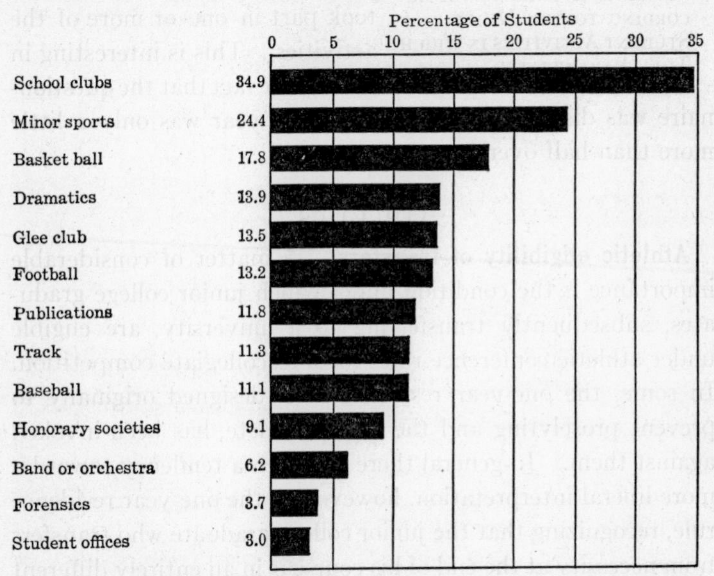

FIG. 37. PERCENTAGE OF JUNIOR COLLEGE STUDENTS IN CALIFORNIA WHO PARTICIPATE IN EACH OF THIRTEEN TYPES OF STUDENT ACTIVITIES

The most significant facts in the first column of Table 75 are shown graphically in Figure 37.

In Figure 38, constructed from Brand's data, is shown the percentage distribution of the California group, according to the number of student activities in which they participated. It is seen that approximately one fourth of the students (26.4 per cent) did not participate in any of the activities listed. Nearly one fourth (23.7 per cent) participated in a single activity, while 14.1 per cent took part in four or more activities. Sixty-eight per cent of the freshmen took part in one or more of the activities. This is interesting in view of the fact that the questionnaire was distributed when the school year was only a little more than half over.

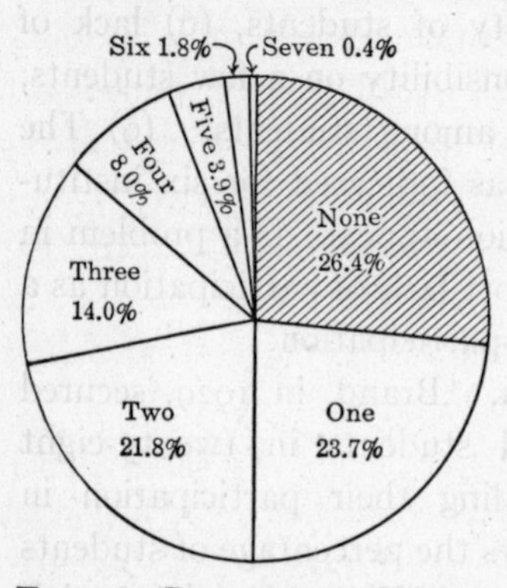

FIG. 38. PERCENTAGE DISTRIBUTION OF JUNIOR COLLEGE STUDENTS IN CALIFORNIA ACCORDING TO THE NUMBER OF STUDENT ACTIVITIES IN WHICH THEY PARTICIPATED

ATHLETICS

Athletic eligibility of transfers. A matter of considerable importance is the condition under which junior college graduates, subsequently transferring to a university, are eligible under athletic conference rules for intercollegiate competition. In some, the one-year residence rule, designed originally to prevent proselyting and the tramp athlete, has been invoked against them. In general there has been a tendency toward a more liberal interpretation, however, of the one-year residence rule, recognizing that the junior college graduate who transfers from necessity at the end of his course is in an entirely different category from the tramp athlete who transfers from choice, or from "inducements." A very valuable study of the status of this entire matter, in forty-five different college athletic conferences comprising 425 colleges and universities, was published by Vande Bogart in December, 1928. The results he found are compactly summarized in Table 76, by which a student can tell at a glance his athletic status upon transfer to any of the principal institutions of higher learning in the country.[1]

Vande Bogart, as a result of his extensive study, feels that one of the best suggestions for an eligibility rule was the one proposed by the president of one of the largest and best known athletic conferences in the country:[2]

> Graduates of accredited junior colleges shall be eligible to participate in intercollegiate athletics on conference teams their first year, but the time of their participation shall be limited to two years over a period of two college years counting from the time of first matriculation. Non-graduates of accredited junior colleges shall not be eligible until they have been in college one full year and the time of participation shall be limited to two years over a period of three years, counting from the time of first matriculation.

Participation in university athletics. The foregoing section has dealt with the possibility of athletic competition of the junior college student after his transfer to the university. To what extent does he actually participate? Chapter IX showed that the transfer holds his own or better scholastically in the university. How does he fare athletically? Is he handicapped in his effort to take part in intercollegiate sports? Is he a grind and not an athlete? Davis, in a master's thesis at Stanford University, tried to answer these questions for three leading California universities.[3] For the five-year period,

[1] Vande Bogart, G. H. "Eligibility for Conference Competition of Students who Enter Higher Institutions from Junior Colleges"; in *Athletic Journal*, vol. 9, p. 15. (December, 1928.)

[2] Quoted by Vande Bogart, *op. cit.*, p. 16.

[3] Condensed from article by W. C. Eells and H. M. Davis, "The Junior College Transfer in University Athletics"; in *School Review*, vol. 37, pp. 371–76. (May, 1929.)

Table 76. Eligibility for Intercollegiate Competition, in Athletic Conferences of the United States, of Students who have Previously Competed in Junior Colleges

	Full competition, no deduction	Deduct one year for all junior college competition	Deduct number of years of junior college competition from four years	Deduct number of years of junior college competition from three years
Any junior college transfer eligible immediately	Missouri Intercollegiate Athletic Association (5) Northwestern Ohio Conference (5) Pacific Northwest Intercollegiate Conference (6) Texas Collegiate Athletic Conference (6)	Far Western Conference (6)	Central Intercollegiate Conference (Kansas) (7) Inter-state Athletic Conference (9) Iowa Intercollegiate Athletic Conference (15) Missouri College Athletic Union (10) Texas Intercollegiate Athletic Association (9) Smoky Mountain Conference (7)	Wisconsin Inter-Normal School Athletic Conference (10)
Any junior college transfer matriculating with sophomore, or higher, classification eligible immediately			The Pacific Coast Intercollegiate Athletic Conference (9) Southern California Intercollegiate Conference (7)	
Any junior college transfer matriculating with junior classification eligible immediately	Minnesota Intercollegiate Conference (9) West Virginia Athletic Conference (15)		Illinois Intercollegiate Athletic Conference (22) Oklahoma Collegiate Athletic Conference (10) South Dakota Intercollegiate Athletic Conference (12) Southern Intercollegiate Athletic Association (26) Nebraska College Athletic Conference (8)	

TABLE 76 (*continued*)

	Full competition, no deduction	Deduct one year for all junior college competition	Deduct number of years of junior college competition from four years	Deduct number of years of junior college competition from three years
One semester or term of residence required prior to intercollegiate competition			National Collegiate Athletic Association	
One year of residence required prior to intercollegiate competition	North Carolina Intercollegiate Athletic Conference (10) Southwest Athletic Conference (7) Virginia Intercollegiate Athletic Conference (9)	Rocky Mountain Faculty Athletic Conference (12)	Green Mountain College Conference (4) Indiana Intercollegiate Conference (20) Kansas Intercollegiate Athletic Conference (10) Michigan Intercollegiate Conference (4) *Middle Atlantic States Collegiate Athletic Conference (19) Mid-West Conference (9) Intercollegiate Athletic Association of Nebraska (6) Ohio Athletic Conference (23) Southern Conference (22)	Athletic Association of Arkansas Colleges (5) Intercollegiate Conference of Faculty Representatives (Big Ten) (10) Michigan Intercollegiate Athletic Association (6) Missouri Valley Conference of Faculty Representatives (4) North Central Intercollegiate Conference (6) Southeastern Intercollegiate Conference (colored) (12) Wisconsin Intercollegiate Athletic Conference (4)

Note: Figures in parenthesis indicate number of members of each conference; this table includes data for 452 universities and colleges.

The following conferences have not decided the question of period of participation or eligibility, for students transferring from junior colleges:

Central Intercollegiate Conference (4).
Missouri Valley Intercollegiate Athletic Association (Big Six) (6).
New England College Conference on Intercollegiate Athletics (5).
Association of New England Colleges for Conference on Athletics (28).

* Competition in basketball and tennis only.

1923–24 to 1927–28 inclusive, he secured data from the eligibility lists of the Pacific Coast Intercollegiate Athletic Conference. The fact that a man had his name on an eligibility list did not necessarily mean that he had participated in an intercollegiate contest. It was a list of men, however, whose interest and ability in the particular sport was such as to meet the requirements of the coaches, marking them as likely varsity material. From such lists the actual participants in any contest had to be chosen. In general, these lists may conveniently be thought of as lists of members of the squads in the different branches of sport — potential participants. These eligibility lists are carefully prepared, checked, and officially certified. They furnish the most reliable, extensive, and complete data available on a comparable basis concerning the composition of the athletic squads in the different sports in the three different institutions each year. Since, under the conference rules, freshmen, special students, and graduate students are not eligible for intercollegiate athletics, these types of students were omitted from the comparisons which involved the proportion of the student body participating in athletics.

During the five-year period, as nearly as could be determined, the junior college transfers in Stanford University, the University of California, and the University of Southern California averaged 6.3 per cent, 3.1 per cent, and 2.6 per cent, respectively, of the entire non-freshman undergraduate student bodies. It might normally be expected, therefore, that they would have composed about the same percentages of the various athletic squads in their respective institutions. The extent to which this expectation was realized in the three institutions, during the five years studied, is shown in Table 77. The normal expectation was exceeded in most sports at the University of California and the University of Southern California, but not at Stanford University.

A summary from a different standpoint for all sports com-

Table 77. Summary of Participation of Junior College Transfers in University Athletics by Sports for the Five-Year Period 1923–24 to 1927–28, Inclusive

Sport	Stanford University		University of California		University of Southern California	
	Total Number on Squad	Percentage of Squad from Junior Colleges	Total Number on Squad	Percentage of Squad from Junior Colleges	Total Number on Squad	Percentage of Squad from Junior Colleges
Football......	189	5.8	220	3.2	253	8.7
Basketball....	102	4.9	80	2.5	95	9.5
Baseball......	151	4.0	224	6.7	123	11.4
Track.........	319	2.8	437	7.3	204	10.9
Tennis........	64	0.0	53	0.0	42	4.8
Golf..........	32	0.0	24	0.0	35	2.9
Boxing........	84	3.6	115	4.3	....	....
Swimming....	152	1.3	149	0.7	56	0.0
Soccer.......	109	2.8	133	4.5	....	....
Fencing......	....	....	....	....	15	20.0

bined is shown in Table 78. The last two columns in this table indicate that, in the three institutions combined, the junior college transfer had almost twice the probability of participating in university athletics that the student entering the university as a freshman had. At Stanford University his chances

Table 78. General Summary of Participation of Junior College Transfers in University Athletics for the Five-Year Period 1923–24 to 1927–28, Inclusive

Institution	Total Non-Freshman Registration		Number of Registrants Participating in Athletics		Percentage of Registrants Participating in Athletics	
	Non-Junior College	Junior College	Non-Junior College	Junior College	Non-Junior College	Junior College
Stanford University.....	13,676	912	1,086	39	7.9	4.3
University of California..	42,336	1,354	1,263	68	3.0	5.0
University of Southern California...........	14,962	406	722	80	4.8	19.7
Total...........	70,974	2,672	3,071	187	4.3	7.0

have been about one half as great, at the University of California almost twice as great, and at the University of Southern California about four times as great.

Trends in junior college participation. The junior colleges are themselves rapidly evolving, and in most cases developing systematic athletic programs and policies under well-organized departments of physical education. As a result, it is reasonable to expect that the students transferring from them will take their places in university athletics in increasingly larger proportions.

The extent to which this expectation was realized in the three institutions under consideration is shown in Table 79.

TABLE 79. PARTICIPATION OF JUNIOR COLLEGE TRANSFERS IN UNIVERSITY ATHLETICS BY YEARS

Year	Stanford University		University of California		University of Southern California	
	Percentage of Student Body	Percentage of Athletic Squads	Percentage of Student Body	Percentage of Athletic Squads	Percentage of Student Body	Percentage of Athletic Squads
1923–24...	2.4	1.2	2.8	3.2	....	11.4
1924–25...	5.2	1.5	3.0	3.4	1.3	9.0
1925–26...	6.5	3.3	5.4	5.7	2.9	6.0
1926–27...	7.8	2.8	5.8	4.8	2.6	9.0
1927–28...	9.1	7.0	6.9	7.5	4.2	8.8

This table shows, for each institution, the percentage of junior college transfers in the entire non-freshmen undergraduate student body for each year, and the percentage of junior college transfers on athletic squads.

It will be observed that the actual percentage of junior college transfers on athletic squads increased markedly at Stanford University and at the University of California, and remained consistently high at the University of Southern California. An analysis of the different sports for 1927–28 is shown in Table 80.

In interpreting Table 80, the reader should keep in mind the

TABLE 80. PARTICIPATION OF JUNIOR COLLEGE TRANSFERS IN UNIVERSITY ATHLETICS IN 1927–28 BY SPORTS

Sport	Stanford University		University of California		University of Southern California	
	Total Number on Squad	Percentage of Squad from Junior Colleges	Total Number on Squad	Percentage of Squad from Junior Colleges	Total Number on Squad	Percentage of Squad from Junior Colleges
Football	58	6.9	59	6.8	56	5.4
Basketball	16	18.8	22	4.5	25	4.0
Baseball	37	13.5	47	4.3	27	14.8
Track	59	5.1	77	10.4	47	14.9
Minor sports	128	4.7	110	5.5	39	7.7

fact that the junior college transfers composed the following percentages of the non-freshman undergraduate student bodies in the three institutions, for the year 1927–28: Stanford University, 9.1; University of California, 6.9; University of Southern California, 4.2.

From Table 80 it is seen that, for the last year for which data were available, the percentage of junior college transfers at the University of Southern California on the squad was much higher than the expectancy (4.2 per cent) in baseball, track, and minor sports; slightly higher in football; and slightly lower in basketball. At the University of California the percentage of junior college transfers was much higher than the expectancy (6.9 per cent) in track, but slightly lower in the other sports. At Stanford University the percentage of junior college transfers on the squad was markedly higher than the expectancy (9.1 per cent) in basketball and baseball, slightly lower in football, and much lower in track.

With reference to Stanford University, it is significant to note the marked change in the case of football for the year 1928–29. The Stanford University eligibility list under which games were being played that season contained ninety names. Thirteen, or 14.4 per cent of the men were from junior colleges.

This percentage was much higher than any corresponding percentage for an earlier year, and much higher than the percentage of junior college transfers in the student body.

These facts indicate that the junior college student was more than holding his own from the standpoint of athletics in the three largest universities in California, the state in which the public junior college has, up to the present time, had its fullest development.

While it is not the primary function of the junior college to develop athletes for the university, the junior college is fulfilling to a greater degree its obligation to its students if, in addition to giving them an excellent academic preparation, it offers them more athletic activity, a well-rounded program of physical education, and sends them to the university able to compete on an equal basis with students who have had their whole collegiate course under university coaches.

THE TRANSFER IN THE UNIVERSITY

Participation in student activities of junior college transfers to the university. Does the junior college graduate who transfers to the university hold his own in student activities? Does he find a better or a poorer opportunity in the larger institution for the experiences that constitute laboratory work in leadership? To what extent does he avail himself of his opportunity? How does he compare with the student who has entered directly from high school? A very interesting attempt to answer these questions for the University of California has been made by L. C. Gilbert.[1] Extensive questionnaires dealing in detail with participation in various activities each semester, with reasons for changes, were given to 278 juniors and seniors in certain classes in education at the university. One hundred and eleven of these were junior college graduates. No men-

[1] Gilbert, L. C. "Activities of Junior College Transfers"; in *Junior College Journal*, vol. 1, pp. 418–26. (April, 1931.)

tion of junior college connections was made, but the study was announced as one of student activities. The least satisfactory feature of the study is that only thirty of the junior college transfers (27 per cent) were men, and 27 of the non-transfers (16 per cent) were men. These numbers are much too small to give reliable conclusions, but they are suggestive of tendencies. Very largely, then, Gilbert's study is a comparison of two groups of women.

His most significant findings are summarized in Figure 39, showing the average number of activities engaged in by each

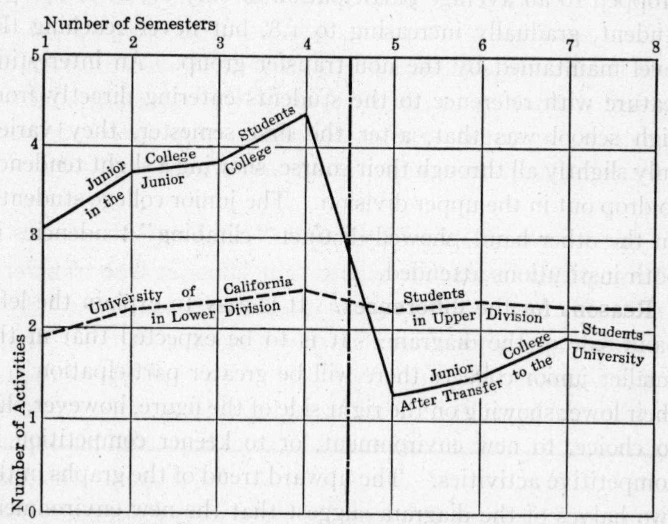

FIG. 39. PARTICIPATION IN STUDENT ACTIVITIES BY JUNIOR COLLEGE TRANSFERS AND NATIVE STUDENTS AT THE UNIVERSITY OF CALIFORNIA

group of students for each of the eight (or six in the case of juniors[1]) semesters of their academic history. The left half of the figure shows a comparison of the two groups when the

[1] There were forty-two junior college seniors, and sixty-five non-junior college seniors.

junior college graduates were still in the junior college, and the others were freshmen and sophomores in the university. During this period the junior college students showed a markedly greater participation, and a decided increase in the fourth semester (4.35) over the first one (3.1) in average number of activities in which they participated. In the university, on the other hand, the participation was much less, and it increased but slightly, from 1.9 to 2.4, in the first two years. When both groups were together in the junior and senior years, however, the situation was different. Junior college transfers dropped to an average participation of only 1.3 activities per student, gradually increasing to 1.8, but never reaching the level maintained by the non-transfer group. An interesting feature with reference to the students entering directly from high school was that, after the first semester, they varied only slightly all through their course, showing a slight tendency to drop out in the upper division. The junior college students, on the other hand, showed distinct "climbing" tendencies in both institutions attended.

Reasons for the differences. It is easy to explain the left-hand side of the diagram. It is to be expected that in the smaller junior colleges there will be greater participation. Is their lower showing on the right side of the figure, however, due to choice, to new environment, or to keener competition in competitive activities? The upward trend of the graphs in the two halves of the diagram suggest that the new environment is a factor. Do they feel they have gotten the greatest profit that can be secured from student activities in the junior college, and decide to emphasize more in the university the serious pursuits of the classroom? Or are they compelled to do so by the more rigorous standards maintained? Positive answers cannot be given to these questions, in general, nor even for this particular group of students studied, although an effort was made to secure their reasons for changed attitudes.

Why activities were dropped. The three most important reasons given by both groups for dropping activities in the upper division were the increasing demands of classroom work, the increasing demands of part-time work, and the desire to devote more time to other activities. The last is a matter of choice, but the first two more or less a matter of necessity. Similarly, for both groups, the reasons in order of importance for never engaging in various activities were given as lack of interest, lack of ability, and lack of time. When asked to state the reasons for general decrease of activity after the sophomore year, eighty-nine gave answers as follows, expressed in percentage of the entire group.

1. Disadvantages due to transfer................ 81 per cent
2. More time required for classroom work........ 68 per cent
3. More time required for part-time work........ 38 per cent
4. Too many participants now.................... 35 per cent
5. Less encouragement to participate........... 28 per cent
6. Loss of interest in activities................ 27 per cent
7. Lack of friends among participants.......... 16 per cent

The junior college students who did go out for added activities in the university gave as their major reason the desire to make new friends.

What proportion engaged in no activities? In the first semester of their freshman year, 12 per cent of the junior college graduates participated in no activities whatever, in the last semester of their sophomore year there were less than 3 per cent who were non-participants. For the university the corresponding figures were 19 per cent and 13 per cent. In the upper division, non-participants amounted to 31 per cent of the junior college group in their first semester in the university (fifth), but this figure dropped to 18½ per cent for the last semester. For the university group it was 16 per cent for the fifth semester, and increased to 19 per cent for the last — practically the same as the junior college transfers.

Athletics. Further analysis showed that athletic participation was over twice as frequent for the junior college student during his first two years; this dropped materially upon his transfer to the university, but was still greater than for the university group. Similar results were found in musical activities. In the group of literary, social, and religious activities the frequency of participation for the junior college group was only about half as great as for the university group in the upper division.

HONOR SOCIETIES

Phi Theta Kappa. From 1926 to 1929 the question of recognition of an honor scholarship society analogous to Phi Beta Kappa was under consideration by the American Association of Junior Colleges, and various committee reports were made and discussed at its annual meetings. Finally, at the 1929 meeting, Phi Theta Kappa was in effect given the official endorsement of the Association, and it was recommended that all honor scholarship societies in junior colleges apply for a charter in the national organization, provided certain conditions should be met later. In 1929 it was also voted to approve any other honor scholarship societies, provided their standards were found to be "on a level equivalent to those of Phi Theta Kappa." This latter provision was especially designed to take care of the situation in certain states, such as Kansas, which do not permit in their high schools any fraternity or sorority which has Greek letters in the designation of its name. Such, in the minds of some legislators, is the sinister power of the Greek alphabet!

In Missouri, about 1910 or 1912, an honor scholarship society grew up at Hardin Junior College, and similar organizations were established in other junior colleges for women in the state. About 1917–18, the presidents and deans of these junior colleges met in Columbia, Missouri, and worked out an organization for an honor scholarship society for women, to be known as Phi Theta Kappa, and a charter was given it by the state legislature. By 1923 petitions began to come to it for charters from coeducational junior colleges. Two such were granted to Missouri institutions in 1926, St. Joseph and Flat River. The matter of giving the growing society national recognition through the American Association of Junior Colleges was presented at the annual meeting of the Association in 1926. A general motion favoring the organization of local honor societies was passed, with the understanding that they would probably affiliate with Phi Theta Kappa. By 1928 the organization had twelve chapters, including institutions in Oklahoma, Virginia, West Virginia, and Minnesota. At this time they formally petitioned the American Association of Junior Colleges "to recognize our organization as the national honor scholarship society of junior colleges."

Meanwhile, however, other similar organizations had been started in Arizona, California, and other states, with somewhat different objectives or requirements for membership. In particular the question was raised whether it should be more nearly akin to Phi Beta Kappa, with its major emphasis on scholarship, or to the national honor societies in high schools, with their four requirements of scholarship, leadership, character, and service. The whole matter was finally referred to a committee, which reported provisionally in 1928 as indicated above, but with the condition attached that "Phi Theta Kappa agrees to a modification of its constitution acceptable to the Honor Scholarship Committee" of the Association.

Before the 1929 meeting the committee gathered information from 78 different junior colleges, showing the existence of honor societies in 19 of them, with 50 favoring their organization and ten unfavorable to them. Seven of those reporting had chapters of Phi Theta Kappa, 5 were organizations of the California Honor Scholarship Society, while 5 others (three of them with the fatal Greek symbols) were reported from Kentucky, Georgia, Texas, Arizona, and Mississippi. The constitutions of all of these were secured and studied. A revised proposed constitution was formulated and sent to all junior colleges listed by the Association. In the light of replies received a second revision was made which provided for a society acceptable to the largest number of institutions from which the committee had secured opinions, and which was presented at the Atlantic City meeting of the Association in November, 1929. This was approved, with a statement to the effect that:

> Provided Phi Theta Kappa accepts this constitution, acceptable to the Honor Scholarship Society of the American Association of Junior Colleges, the Association will recommend that all honor scholarship societies now forming or already formed in junior colleges, which are members of the American Association of Junior Colleges, apply for a charter in Phi Theta Kappa.

No action on the part of this organization had been reported at the time of writing, but it was expected that the proposed constitution would be approved.[1] Requirements for membership were made analogous to Phi Beta Kappa, the requirements for membership being based upon scholarship and good moral character. The scholarship requirement was made the equivalent of at least a B average, with the provision that the total active membership of the local chapter should not exceed ten per cent of the total regular enrollment.

Phi Rho Pi. A national honorary forensic society for junior colleges, Phi Rho Pi, was organized in 1928 at Grand Rapids Junior College, Michigan. Its object is to promote interest in debate, oratory, extemporaneous speaking, and other forms of public address. When it held its first national convention at

[1] Since this was written, new chapters of Phi Theta Kappa have been reported, at Gulf Park College, Mississippi, Highland Manor Junior College, New York, Tyler Junior College, Texas, Junior College of Connecticut, Compton Junior College, California, and at other institutions.

Grand Rapids, in 1929, there were chapters in nine junior colleges in Michigan, Illinois, Kansas, Minnesota, West Virginia, Texas, and California.

QUESTIONS AND PROBLEMS

1. Kefauver lists four different procedures used in junior colleges for selecting sponsors for student activities. Which of these is the best? Which the poorest? Why?
2. Of the problems and difficulties connected with student activities, as given in Kefauver's study, which are unique or peculiar to the junior college, which common to all institutions having such activities? Suggest solutions to some of them.
3. Make a study similar to Davis's for junior college athletes who have transferred to other universities.
4. Make a study similar to Davis's for junior college transfers in other student activities, for example, literary, social, journalistic, or dramatic.
5. Should a junior college scholarship society be modeled more on Phi Beta Kappa, or on the high school honor society?
6. If a junior college administrator, would you favor petitioning for a charter in Phi Theta Kappa?
7. Should Greek letter fraternities of the American college type, social not honorary, be permitted in junior colleges?
8. Are high school fraternities permitted in the United States? In what states? What are the arguments for and against? To what extent do they apply to junior colleges?
9. Should a junior college have a "Dean of Extra-Curricular Activities"? If so, under what circumstances? (See *Sacramento School Survey*, pp. 396–400.)
10. Can continuity in student activities be maintained when two thirds of the students are new each year? (See *Sacramento School Survey*, p. 397.)
11. What dangers are there in the abolition of the one-year residence rule for junior college athletes transferring to the universities? What restrictions or safeguards are desirable?
12. Report on the student activity program and its management in any selected junior college.
13. State what you feel are the three most important objectives for junior college student activities.
14. What student activities are better fitted for the junior college than for the university? Than for the high school?
15. Secure the opinions of a group of junior college transfers as to the

degree of handicap they felt, if any, in regard to student activities in universities.

16. Make an investigation similar to Gilbert's at some other university.
17. Is it desirable or undesirable for students to participate as extensively in student activities in the upper division as in the junior college?
18. Should there be compulsory student-body fees in the junior college? If so, how large?
19. How may desirable college traditions be developed in a two-year institution?
20. Should junior college teams play against high schools? Normal schools? University freshmen teams?
21. How should student activities be financed?
22. Investigate the status of student journalism in the junior college.

SUGGESTED READINGS

*Chadwick, R. D. "The Financing of Inter-Junior College Athletics"; in *School Executives' Magazine*, vol. 50, pp. 15–17, 42. (September, 1930.)

Cross, H. A. "Report on Honor Scholarship Societies for the Year 1929"; in *Proceedings of the Tenth Annual Meeting of the American Association of Junior Colleges*, pp. 163–71. Atlantic City, New Jersey, 1929.

Davis, C. W., and McDonald, H. C. "Intercollegiate and Intramural Athletics in the Junior Colleges of California"; in *California Quarterly of Secondary Education*, vol. 6, pp. 85–90. (October, 1930.)

*Eells, W. C., and Davis, H. M. "The Junior College Transfer in University Athletics"; in *School Review*, vol. 37, pp. 371–76. (May, 1929.)

Eells, W. C., and Brand, R. R. "Extra-Curricular Activities in California Junior Colleges"; in *School Review*, vol. 38, pp. 276–79. (April, 1930.)

*Gilbert, L. C. "Activities of Junior College Transfers"; in *Junior College Journal*, vol. 1, pp. 418–26. (April, 1931.)

Harnish, W. E. "Junior College Athletes and Athletics"; in *Proceedings of the Sixth Annual Meeting of the American Association of Junior Colleges*, pp. 33–39. Chicago, Illinois, 1926.

*Kefauver, G. N. "Student Activities in Junior Colleges"; in *Proceedings of the Tenth Annual Meeting of the American Association of Junior Colleges*, pp. 24–36. Atlantic City, New Jersey, 1929.

*Koos, L. V. "The Junior College and Training in Leadership"; in *The Junior College*, pp. 182–88.

*Lillard, J. B. "Procedure in Organizing the Administration and Supervision of Extra-Curricular Activities"; in *California Quarterly of Secondary Education*, vol. 5, pp. 340–42. (June, 1930.)

O'Mara, J. P. "Extra-curricular Activities of the Four-Year Junior College"; in Superintendent's Bulletin, Pasadena City Schools, no. 3, Pasadena, California, 1929.

Vande Bogart, G. H. "Eligibility for Conference Competition of Students who Enter Higher Institutions from Junior Colleges"; in *Athletic Journal*, vol. 9, pp. 14–16. (December, 1928.)

"Discussion of Athletic Eligibility, Especially the One-Year Residence Rule"; in *Proceedings of the Sixth Annual Meeting of the American Association of Junior Colleges*, pp. 80–82. (Chicago, Illinois, 1926); *Proceedings of the Ninth Annual Meeting of the American Association of Junior Colleges*, pp. 127–43 (Fort Worth, Texas, 1928).

Reports and Discussions on Honor Scholarship Society; in *Proceedings* of the Annual Meetings of the American Association of Junior Colleges, *Sixth* (Chicago, 1926), pp. 59–60; *Eighth* (Chicago, 1928), pp. 64–67; *Ninth* (Fort Worth, Texas, 1928), pp. 135–39; *Tenth* (Atlantic City, 1929), pp. 163–71. (Proposed constitution printed in Atlantic City report.)

Hilliard, J. H., "Procedure in Organizing the Administration and Supervision of Extra-Curricular Activities," in *California Quarterly of Secondary Education*, vol. 5, pp. [illegible] (June, 1930).

O'Mara, J. P., "Extracurricular Activities of the Four-Year Junior College," in *Superintendent's Bulletin*, Pasadena City Schools, no. [illegible] Pasadena, California, 1930).

Young, Robert [illegible], "Eligibility for Conference Competition of Students who Enter Higher Institutions from Junior Colleges," in *[illegible] Journal*, vol. 9, pp. 14–[illegible] (December, 1928).

Discussion of Athletic Eligibility, especially the One-Year Residence Rule," in *Proceedings of the Sixth Annual Meeting of the American Association of Junior Colleges*, pp. 80–[illegible] (Chicago, Illinois, 1926); *Proceedings of the Ninth Annual Meeting of the American Association of Junior Colleges*, pp. [illegible] (Fort Worth, Texas, 1928).

Reports and Discussions on Honor Scholarship Society, in *Proceedings of the Annual Meetings of the American Association of Junior Colleges*, Sixth (Chicago, 1926), pp. 55–62; Eighth (Chicago, 1928), pp. [illegible]; Ninth (Fort Worth, Texas, 1928), pp. [illegible]; Tenth (Atlantic City, 1930), pp. 105, [illegible]. (Proposed constitution printed in March, 1929, report.)

PART THREE

PLACE OF THE JUNIOR COLLEGE IN AMERICAN EDUCATION

CHAPTER XXIV

THE REORGANIZATION OF AMERICAN EDUCATION

> The great value of the junior college at present comes from its freedom from the compulsion and the rigidity of a system.... The glory of the junior college is that it offers boundless opportunity for exploration, both in the variety of institutions embraced by it, and in the latitude given in each. — MARION COATS.[1]

Contents of this chapter. This chapter sketches briefly the general reorganization of American education, especially in the secondary field, and various plans for its modification, particularly as they affect the junior college, are described or illustrated. The present relation of the public junior colleges of the country to these various plans of reorganization is presented, and consideration is given to the statement that the junior college is "essentially secondary." The relation of the junior college to reorganization in the field of higher education is reserved for treatment in Chapter XXVIII.

THE TREND IN REORGANIZATION

Many writers have pointed out the fact that our traditional school system of eight elementary grades, four high school years, and four college years, represents a somewhat accidental growth, and one not best adapted to actual student needs at the different levels. For over fifty years there has been more or less agitation for reorganization, which has resulted in many fundamental changes, especially since 1910. In the late eighties of the past century, President Eliot of Harvard, in addresses before the National Education Association and elsewhere, urged that the high school should dip down to in-

[1] Coats, Marion. "The Junior College"; in *Forum*, vol. 80, p. 90. (July, 1928.)

clude two years of work in the elementary school. Proposals of President Harper of the University of Chicago, in 1902, for the organization of six-year high schools to extend upward into two years of the college field have already been reviewed in an earlier chapter.

Various committees of the National Education Association, especially the "Committee of Ten" in 1892 and the "Committee on the Reorganization of Secondary Education," whose first report appeared in 1913, followed by others at intervals for a decade or more, have given careful consideration to the many problems of interrelation and articulation involved and have been powerful influences in hastening experiments in readjustment and reorganization.

The factors in reorganization. What are some of the factors which have been controlling elements in the proposed reorganization? They are numerous, including such matters as articulation, exploratory courses, survey or orientation courses, departmentalized instruction, guidance needs, economy of time, transitional adjustments, specialized physical and psychological needs, and many others. There is no space in this work, nor is it the appropriate place, to discuss this matter of reorganization in general. It is only the special junior college implications that need to be considered here. It is not easy to draw the line, however, since the junior college cannot be detached entirely and considered as a distinct feature, but has many interrelations with all proposed plans of reorganization at various levels.

Beginnings in California. The features of greatest interest, from the junior college point of view, date from 1910. In that one year, it is interesting to observe, the first public junior college in the state and the first three-year junior high school in the country were both organized in California. The junior college work initiated at Fresno, in 1910, has already been described in Chapter IV. In the same year the first junior high school was organized at Berkeley, under Superintendent F. F. Bunker. Thus in the same year, but quite independently, in widely separated parts, there were initiated in California two experimental schools whose influence was destined to be of vast importance in the educational development of the nation. The two schools were similar in one fundamental respect — each contemplated an extension of what has been somewhat loosely spoken of as the period of "secondary" education — one upward two years, and one downward two years.

Development since 1910. In the two decades since these feeble beginnings in California, both types of schools have experienced an unprecedented development. The public junior college, while not indigenous to the California soil, has had its best development there. Its remarkable and significant growth has already been presented in sufficient detail in earlier chapters. The development of the junior high school has been, if possible, even more remarkable in many ways. The latest statistics of the United States Office of Education show that in 1928 there were 4326 reorganized high schools of various types, including 1403 that were classified as distinctly junior high schools. In the six-year period since 1922 the number of junior high schools, of junior high school teachers, and of junior high school students each increased approximately fourfold.[1] The growth has been particularly significant in the larger cities of the country. In 1929 it was reported that 72 per cent of the 68 cities of over 100,000 population, and 61 per cent of the 180 cities with population from 30,000 to 100,000 had already established separate junior high schools.

Opinions of two leaders. A. A. Douglass, a recognized authority in the junior high school field, states that "It is not an exaggeration to say that the nation is committed to the policy of reorganizing its schools upon a broad and compre-

[1] Phillips, F. M. *Statistics of Public High Schools*, 1927–28. United States Office of Education, Bulletin no. 35, pp. 3–6. (1929.)

hensive junior high school basis."[1] Koos, in the junior college field, speaks with equal conviction when he says, "The upward extension of the American high school to include junior college years is logical and inevitable. The question is not whether, but how."[2] It is the very important question of *how* that will concern us in the remainder of this and the two following chapters.

PLANS OF REORGANIZATION

Numerous plans recognized. The Office of Education lists no less than forty-three different types of public high school organizations. Some of these are only slight modifications of others, but at least eight distinct types may be distinguished which are of interest for students of the junior college. These are summarized in Figure 40.

Eight-four-two plan. The eight-four-two plan represents the traditional or "regular" type — eight years of elementary school, four years of "standard" high school, and two years of junior college. In spite of two decades and more of vigorous efforts at reorganization, over three quarters of the high schools of the country are still on the four-year basis. It will be many years before complete reorganization is achieved, if indeed it is ever accomplished. Consequently any practical junior college program, for a long time to come, must be prepared to articulate with the widespread "standard" four-year high school represented in this type of organization.

Eight-six type. The eight-six type was proposed by President Harper in the early years of the century, and flourished for a time in a few localities as the six-year high school, the two additional years being taken from the freshman and sophomore years of college. Few, if any, of this type of organization

[1] Douglass, A. A. *Secondary Education*, p. 138. Houghton Mifflin Company, Boston, 1927.

[2] Koos, L. V. "The Junior College Movement"; in *New Republic*, vol. 36, p. 22. (November 7, 1923.)

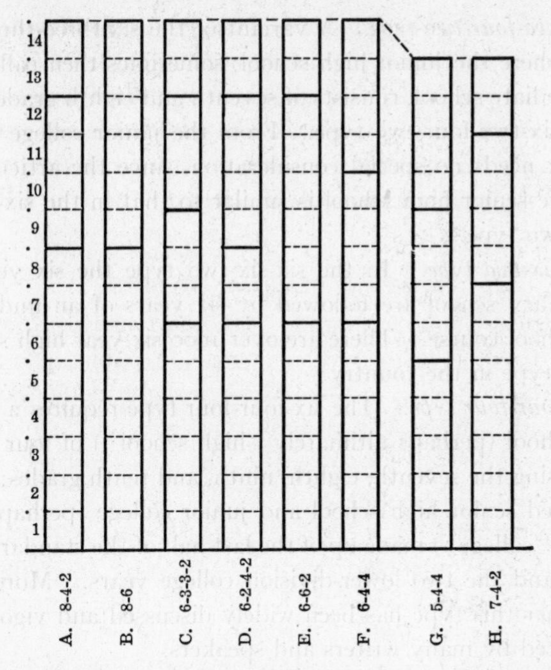

FIG. 40. PRINCIPAL TYPES OF SECONDARY SCHOOL ORGANIZATION IN THE UNITED STATES

are found to-day. None are reported by the federal office.[1] In effect, however, it is approximately the situation in some small junior colleges connected with public high schools, with administration, teaching staff, and buildings common to the two institutions.

Six-three-three-two type. The most common reorganized type in existence at the present time is the six-three-three-two plan: six years of elementary school, a three-year junior high school, a three-year senior school, and a two-year junior college. Its advantages will be discussed more fully in Chapter XXVII.

[1] Brothers, Table 81, page 655, shows one.

Six-two-four-two type. A variant of the six-three-three-two type, where the junior high school, sometimes then called the intermediate school, consists of seventh and eighth grades only is the six-two-four-two type. From the junior college standpoint it needs no special consideration, since the articulation with the senior high school is similar to that in the six-three-three-two type.

Six-six-two type. In the six-six-two type the six years of elementary school are followed by six years of an undivided high school course. There are over 1000 six-year high schools of this type in the country.

Six-four-four type. The six-four-four type requires a junior high school (perhaps ultimately "high school") of four years, comprising the seventh, eighth, ninth, and tenth grades; and a combined senior high school and junior college (perhaps ultimately "college") made up of the last half of the standard high school and the two lower-division college years. More than any other this type has been widely discussed and vigorously advocated by many writers and speakers.

Five-four-four type. The southern variant of the six-four-four type is the five-four-four type. As is well known, in many parts of the South the elementary school period is only seven years in length instead of eight. For junior college purposes, this type may be regarded as equivalent to the six-four-four type.

Seven-four-two type. The seven-four-two type is the southern variant of the eight-four-two type, shown first in Figure 40.

Junior college implications. In spite of the numerous variations as indicated in Figure 40, and many minor modifications of them reported by the federal office, it is noticeable from the junior college standpoint that, with the exception of the defunct eight-six type, there are just two main types — the *two-year junior college*, and the *four-year junior college.* The former fits in with all of the proposed or existing plans with the exception of the six-four-four plan and its southern variant — the five-four-four type. These two types, therefore, will be discussed in much greater detail in the three chapters which follow. Before doing this, however, it is desirable to give some idea of the number of junior colleges in the country operating under these different plans.

PRESENT CONDITIONS

Brothers's study. Unfortunately such information is not available for all junior colleges. Brothers, however, has made an effort to collect figures for public junior colleges for 1927–28. His data are incomplete, but they probably represent the proportionate distribution of the various types fairly satisfactorily. At any rate no better data are available. Based upon ques-

TABLE 81. DISTRIBUTION OF EIGHTY-THREE PUBLIC SCHOOL SYSTEMS HAVING JUNIOR COLLEGES, ACCORDING TO PLAN OF ORGANIZATION IN 1928 AND ACCORDING TO PLAN OF ORGANIZATION PREFERRED BY ADMINISTRATORS

TYPE OF ORGANIZATION	NUMBER OF SYSTEMS OPERATING IN 1928	NUMBER OF ADMINISTRATORS PREFERRING
8–4–2	21	5
6–3–3–2 †	31	25
6–2–4–2	13	5
7–2–3–2	1	1
6–3–5	1	0
8–6	1	0
6–4–2–2	1	1
7–3–4	0	1
6–2–3–2 *	2	0
5–3–3–2 *	2	2
7–4–2 *	5	1
5–2–4–2 *	1	0
6–2–4–1 *	2	0
5–4–4 *	2	2
6–4–4 †	0	31

* Only seven years in the elementary school.
† The two main type plans.

tionnaire returns from 88 junior colleges in fifteen states,[1] he reports the existence of types as given in Table 81.[2]

It is noticeable that the six-three-three-two type comprises the largest group of any, and that there are only four institutions that are not some type of two-year junior college. Two of the institutions had one year of junior college work above the regular high school. Two Southern junior colleges of the five-four-four type were found, and none of the six-four-four type, although over a third of the executives expressed a preference for it.

THE JUNIOR COLLEGE "ESSENTIALLY SECONDARY"

Meaning of the term. Many educational leaders, beginning perhaps with President Folwell at the University of Minnesota, in 1869, have expressed the conviction in varying forms that the freshman and sophomore years did not properly belong in the university, but were essentially secondary in nature. Many of these men have been quoted on this phase in earlier chapters, and further quotation of such opinion is unnecessary at this time. Unfortunately, however, there has been some confusion as to the meaning and implications of this term *secondary*. In its broadest sense, secondary education has been taken to mean *general education*, preliminary to university specialization and professional study. Taken in this sense, there can be no objection to designating the ordinary freshman and sophomore college years as secondary. They may be taken as marking the completion of broad cultural education — of general courses in language, literature, history, and science, as a foundation to later university specialization. In this

[1] California, 25; Texas, 12; Iowa, 10; Kansas, 9; Minnesota, 7; Michigan, 6; Missouri, 5; Illinois, 4; Oklahoma, 3; Washington, 2; Arizona, 1; Georgia, 1; Louisiana, 1; Massachusetts, 1; and Nebraska, 1. Five institutions did not answer the question tabulated in Table 81.

[2] Brothers, E. Q. "Present Day Practices and Tendencies in the Administration and Organization of Public Junior Colleges"; in *School Review*, vol. 36, p. 671. (November, 1928.)

sense, the educational field may be thought of as consisting of elementary education, secondary education, and higher education. This is the sense in which it was spoken of by President Jesse of the University of Missouri in 1896, when he said:[1]

The first two years in college are really secondary in character. I always think of the high school and academy as covering the lower secondary period, and the freshman and sophomore years at college as covering the upper secondary period. Until so much, at least, of academic training has been received, higher education, in my opinion, does not really begin. In the secondary period... the chief function of the instructor is to teach well what has been discovered and arranged, and thereby to form mind and character.

"Secondary" education misunderstood. Unfortunately, however, the term *secondary* has been misunderstood by many people who have rather carelessly assumed that high school and secondary were synonymous. That *secondary education* and *the secondary school* have had somewhat different meanings has been well expressed by Pittenger, who has shown how, historically, secondary education should be conceived in terms broader than and different from the content of the accepted secondary or high school. He says:[2]

Starting with the conception that secondary education was identical in nature and limits with the work of a so-called secondary school, we reached the point of rather generally differentiating between them. Secondary education became larger in its circumference than the secondary school.

Some writers properly speak of the junior colleges as the *completion unit* of secondary education. The entire expanded secondary period, eight years from grade seven to grade fourteen inclusive, is thought of (as pictured in most of the diagrams of Figure 40) as comprising three distinct but closely related educational units — the junior high school, the senior

[1] Quoted in *School Review*, vol. 23, p. 197. (March, 1915.)

[2] Pittenger, B. F. "Use of the Term 'Secondary' in American Education"; in *School Review*, vol. 24, p. 141. (February, 1916.)

high school, and the junior college. Many people, however, assume that secondary is used in a restricted sense as identical in meaning with high school, and obtain an entirely erroneous concept in thinking of the junior college and the junior college years as "merely some more high school."

"Collegiate" preferred. The writer prefers to use the terms *secondary*, *collegiate*, and *university* or *higher* education, in speaking of the different educational levels. He feels that the junior college is not to be merely an appendix to the high school, nor merely a prefix to the university, but that it can and should have an individuality and personality of its own. Most of the previous chapters of this book have been devoted to developing and discussing various aspects of that educational personality. He feels that there is ample place in the American educational order for the junior college to live a life of its own, under its own management, and that by so doing it can make its most valuable and most needed permanent contribution to the welfare of society. Further reasons for this conviction will be presented in Chapter XXVII. He is not disposed to press the matter of terminology unduly, however. If the majority prefer to think of the junior college as upper secondary, and will thus differentiate between different levels of secondary education, he has no objection to their so doing. Since there seems to be so much confusion of thinking, from lack of a clearly differentiated conception, he feels that it would make for clarity of thought and unity of understanding if the section of the educational process covered in this volume were generally designated as *collegiate*.

Conclusion. Although there are many ramifications of the matter of educational reorganization to which whole volumes have been devoted, as far as the junior college aspect is concerned it resolves itself very largely into a question of the relative desirability of two main types of organization. An examination of Figure 40, as already stated, shows that all of the junior college units there indicated were either two-year or four-year units. There is room for much difference of opinion between educators as to the relative merits of these two types of organization. There has been much vigorous discussion, particularly in advocacy of the six-four-four plan, which is hailed as progressive and inevitable. It seems desirable, therefore, to examine somewhat more in detail the facts regarding these two types of junior college organization, and some of the reasons urged in favor of and against them.

QUESTIONS AND PROBLEMS

1. Collect all possible statements from various prominent educators tending to show the essentially secondary nature of the junior college years. Classify and discuss them.
2. Collect all possible definitions of "secondary education." Classify them and discuss their junior college implications.
3. Collect information, similar to that secured by Brothers, regarding the form of organization of the private junior colleges in the country.
4. S. P. Capen says, "The junior college is the product of a variety of local ferments and hence is different both in form and purpose in the various areas in which it has sprung up." (See Suggested Readings.) Select junior colleges to illustrate his meaning. Is it likely that there will ultimately be one type of junior college the country over? Why?
5. Compare the suggested forms of organization of the whole field of secondary education in the broadest sense, as outlined in this chapter, with that found in England, France, Germany, Denmark, or Japan.
6. Pittenger considers various definitions of "secondary" from the chronological, institutional, curricular, methodological, psychological, social, and age points of view. (See Suggested Readings.) Examine them for their junior college bearings.
7. Examine the report of the Committee on the Reorganization of Secondary Education, *Cardinal Principles of Secondary Education* (United States Bureau of Education, Bulletin no. 35, 1918), for material bearing on the place of the junior college in educational reorganization.
8. Why did the eight-four plan of elementary and secondary education develop? Has it any right to be considered "standard"?
9. Report on the junior high school status in any single state. How is it related to the junior college situation in the same state?
10. Classify the forty-three types of organization recognized by the United

States Office of Education as to their suitability for a two-year or four-year junior college organization.

11. Are there objections to designating junior college work as "collegiate"?
12. Why did the six-year high school, the "high school of the future" according to President Harper, fail to win a permanent place in American education? Does its failure suggest anything for or against the two-year junior college?
13. What was the conception of secondary education held by Dr. A. F. Lange?
14. Compare the distribution of various types of organization as reported by Engelhardt in 1930 with that found by Brothers. (See Suggested Readings.)

SUGGESTED READINGS

*Brothers, E. Q. "Present-Day Practices and Tendencies in the Administration and Organization of Public Junior Colleges"; in *School Review*, vol. 36, pp. 665–74. (November, 1928.)

Capen, S. P. (chairman). "The Reorganization of the American Educational System"; in *School and Society*, vol. 27, pp. 509–15. (April 28, 1928.)

Capen, S. P. (chairman). "Articulation at the Professional and Higher Educational Level"; in Part 4 of *Seventh Yearbook of the Department of Superintendence of the National Education Association*, pp. 287–392. Washington, D.C., February, 1929.

Carman, G. N. "Articulating Elementary School, High School, and College"; in *School Review*, vol. 23, pp. 197–98. (March, 1915.)

Cooper, W. J. "Some Observations and Comments on the Present Status of Secondary and Higher Education"; in *North Central Association Quarterly*, vol. 4, pp. 366–70. (December, 1929.)

Engelhardt, F. "Determining the Plan of Organization for a Local School System"; in *School Executives' Magazine*, vol. 50, pp. 75–77. (October, 1930.)

Francis, J. H. "Reorganization of our School System"; in *Proceedings of National Education Association*, pp. 368–76. Washington, D.C., 1912.

*Gray, W. S. "Educational Readjustments at the Junior College Level"; in *School and Society*, vol. 30, pp. 135–43. (August 3, 1929.)

Harper, W. R. "The High School of the Future"; in *School Review*, vol. 11, pp. 1–3. (January, 1903.)

Judd, C. H. "The Meaning of Secondary Education"; in *School Review*, vol. 21, pp. 11–25. (January, 1913.)

*Koos, L. V. "The Trend of Reorganization in Higher Education"; in *School Review*, vol. 32, pp. 575–86, 656–66. (October, 1924, and November, 1924.)

Koos, L. V. *The Junior College Movement.* 436 pp.

Ladd, G. T. "The Development of the American University"; in *Scribner's Magazine*, vol. 2, pp. 346–60. (September, 1887.)

*Lange, A. F. "The Junior College as an Integral Part of the Public School System"; in *School Review*, vol. 25, pp. 465–79. (September, 1917.)

Learned, W. S. "The Junior College"; in *Twenty-first Annual Report of Carnegie Foundation for Advancement of Teaching*, pp. 128–29, 134–36. New York, 1926.

Melcher, G. B. "The 7–4–2 School System of Kansas City, Missouri"; in *Seventh Yearbook of the Department of Superintendence of the National Education Association*, pp. 222–25. Washington, D.C., February, 1929.

Moore, E. C. "Fundamental Concepts Underlying Junior College Education"; *California Quarterly of Secondary Education*, vol. 4, pp. 9–14. (October, 1928.)

Newlon, J. H. "Shall the Junior College be Externally Controlled?"; in *School Executives' Magazine*, vol. 49, pp. 332–33. (March, 1930.)

*Newlon, J. H. (chairman). "Articulation at the Secondary School Level: Junior High School through Junior College"; in Part 3 of *Seventh Yearbook of the Department of Superintendence of the National Education Association*, pp. 114–286. Washington, D.C., February, 1929.

*Pittenger, B. F. "Use of the Term 'Secondary' in American Education"; in *School Review*, vol. 24, pp. 130–41. (February, 1916.)

Proctor, W. M. "The Place of the Junior College in Educational Reorganization"; in Proctor, W. M. (editor), *The Junior College: Its Organization and Administration*, pp. 188–202.

School Review. "Proceedings of the Seventeenth Educational Conference of the Academies and High Schools Affiliating or Coöperating with the University of Chicago — The General Conference"; in *School Review*, vol. 12, pp. 15–28. (January, 1904.)

Smith, L. W. "The Junior College — a Two, Four, or Six Year Institution"; in *Proceedings of the Sixth Annual Meeting of the American Association of Junior Colleges*, pp. 1–5. Chicago, Illinois, 1926.

CHAPTER XXV

THE FOUR-YEAR JUNIOR COLLEGE

I summarize by stating it as my belief that for most American cities and for thickly settled rural areas the four-four type of secondary school organization promises to meet satisfactorily the new demands made by American society and that, as a scheme of administration, it possesses advantages which far outweigh the disadvantages so far urged against it. — W. J. COOPER.[1]

Contents of this chapter. This chapter outlines the origin of the so-called six-four-four plan, and gives a brief sketch of its developments in the few institutions which have so far adopted this form of organization. The greater part of the chapter, however, is devoted to a presentation of the reasons urged in favor of this plan as the ultimate form of desirable reorganization of the American educational system.

HISTORY OF SIX-FOUR-FOUR PLAN

Origin of the plan. As far as the writer has been able to discover, there has been no published study or even summary of the beginnings and development of the six-four-four plan, a plan of public school reorganization in favor of which so many articles have been written and so many addresses made in the past decade. Koos advocated it in an address at Harvard University, in 1922. President E. L. Hardy, of San Diego State Teachers' College, claims in a personal letter that his article in *School and Society*, in 1917, "contained one of the earlier proposals of the six-four-four plan." As a matter of fact, however, the essential features of this plan, in surprising detail, were published both locally and nationally almost a decade earlier than that date.

[1] Cooper, W. J. "Some Advantages Expected to Result from Administering Secondary Education in Two Units of Four Years Each"; in *School Review*, vol. 37, pp. 346. (May, 1929.)

The first clear statement of such a plan in published form seems to have been contained in the report of George A. Merrill, Director of the Wilmerding School of Industrial Arts of San Francisco, to the President of the University of California under date of July 1, 1908.[1] In it he says:

> The elementary school should end with the sixth grade. Grades seven to ten (the last two of the present grammar grades and the first two of the present high school) should be made to constitute a new intermediate or secondary school.... The last two grades of the present high school should be grouped with the two lowest grades (the freshman and sophomore years) of the present college course, to form a new high school or college. The actual teaching of trades, if that ever becomes a recognized function of the public schools, must fall within the province of this new high school, in which pupils would range from sixteen or seventeen years of age to twenty or twenty-one. The intermediate school that I have suggested (grades seven to ten, ages twelve or thirteen to sixteen or seventeen) cannot be relied upon to give anything more than a preliminary industrial training of a very general sort, valuable indeed, but not specifically vocational. Differentiation would most likely begin with the higher school or college, of which there would be several kinds — some trade schools, some classical schools, some pre-medical, some technical high schools leading to engineering, some commercial, etc.

A more nearly complete proposal of the six-four-four plan could scarcely be asked for. The germ of the idea in Mr. Merrill's mind may be found far earlier, however, for in 1894 he recommended that students should be admitted to his school at the average age of thirteen or fourteen "before the end of the grammar school course." [2] Eighteen years experience with this requirement thus led to the complete development of the

[1] Published in *Biennial Report of the President of the University*, 1906–08, University of California Bulletin, third series, vol. 2, no. 3, pp. 69–72.

[2] Cooke, R. L. "Some Contributions of the Lick and Wilmerding Schools of San Francisco to the Administration of Vocational and Secondary Education." Unpublished master's thesis at University of California, p. 23. 1930.

idea in the form quoted above. It may be felt, however, that its publication in a university presidential report was scarcely likely to give such a proposal due publicity.

The idea was foreshadowed, however, in an address by Mr. Merrill before the National Education Association at Los Angeles in 1907,[1] and was stated completely in the "Report of the Subcommittee on Industrial and Technical Education in the Secondary Schools" of the National Education Association, of which Mr. Merrill was a member, at its Boston meeting in 1910. Quoting from Mr. Merrill, this report says:[2]

> The elementary school should end with the sixth grade. The present high school should be cut exactly in two. Grades 7, 8, 9, 10 should constitute an intermediate or secondary school by itself. Grades 11, 12, 13, and 14 should be grouped together as a higher school or college. If the tendency throughout the nation is the same as it is in California, it is in the direction of some sort of an arrangement such as I have outlined.... The importance of subdividing grades 7 to 14 into two stages of four years each is what I want to emphasize, though speaking only from the industrial point of view for the time being.

A complete statement of the plan was also made at the meeting of the California High School Teachers' Association at San Jose in 1908, and again before the same Association in 1914.[3] It was discussed in the Missouri Junior College Union, and recommended by this organization, prior to 1915.[4] Thus there is ample proof that the six-four-four plan was completely worked out in all of its essential features and proposed, not only locally in California but nationally as well, years before its actual adoption anywhere in the country.

[1] Merrill, G. A. "Trade Schools and Trade Unions"; in *Proceedings of the National Education Association*, p. 1054. Los Angeles, 1907.

[2] *Proceedings of National Education Association*, p. 756. Boston, 1910.

[3] Cooke, R. L., *op. cit.*, pp. 24, 26.

[4] Coursault, J. H. "Standardizing the Junior College"; in *Educational Review*, vol. 49, p. 61. (January, 1915.)

Further advocacy of the plan. The six-four-four plan was also outlined in detail and proposed in a committee report which was adopted by the North Central Association, in 1915.[1] It was advocated by E. L. Hardy, of San Diego, in 1917, as already mentioned; by President James J. M. Wood, of Stephens College, Missouri, as chairman of a North Central Association Committee, in 1919, and at the first National Junior College Conference at St. Louis in 1920; by H. L. Miller, of the University of Wisconsin, in the *Wisconsin Journal of Education* in 1922, and by William M. Proctor, of Stanford University, in the *Educational Review* in 1923. In addition it has been advocated by George F. Zook, of the University of Akron; by Frederick Eby, of the University of Texas; by W. W. Kemp, of the University of California; by L. W. Smith, formerly of Joliet Junior College, Illinois; by W. F. Ewing, formerly of Pasadena; by J. A. Sexson, and J. W. Harbeson, of Pasadena; and by others.[2]

Six-four-four colleges organized. It is difficult to obtain an authentic list of systems organized under the proposed plan, or to know just where to draw the line in defining them. The best example of the complete six-four-four plan in operation at the present time is to be found at Pasadena, California. In this chapter, however, we shall also consider the four-year junior college, whether or not it exists directly in connection with a lower four-year unit. In other words, this chapter is concerned with the four-year junior college as an institution, regardless of whether it is found as a part of the widely known six-four-four plan. As far as the writer has been able to discover, the following may properly be considered under such a classification:

[1] See Koos, L. V. *The Junior College*, p. 565, for report of this committee.

[2] Reference to some of the more important articles by most of these men will be found in the Suggested Readings at the close of the chapter. Others may be found by consulting the Eells bibliography. (United States Office of Education, Bulletin no. 2. 1930.)

Public junior colleges.

Hillsboro, Texas	(5–4–4)
Edinburg, Texas	(5–4–4)
Pasadena, California	(6–4–4)
Ventura, California	(6–4–4)
Moberly, Missouri	(6–4–4)
John Tarleton Agricultural, Texas	(4 only)
North Texas Agricultural, Texas	(4 only)

Private junior colleges.

Stephens College, Missouri	(4 only)
Menlo School and Junior College, California	(4–4)

A paragraph may well be devoted to each of these institutions.

Hillsboro, Texas. It is claimed by Professor Eby, of the University of Texas, that Hillsboro not only is the earliest institution of the four-year type now existing in the country, but that it "has gone further than any other public junior college" in this form of organization.[1] Due to the seven-year elementary school common in the Southern states, it is an example of the five-four-four type of organization rather than six-four-four, but this does not have any essential bearing from the junior college standpoint. Hillsboro junior college was organized in 1923 as a two-year junior college. Reorganization as a four-year institution was effected in the summer of 1925 under the leadership of W. F. Doughty, former state superintendent in Texas, who became president of the Hillsboro institution in July, 1924. According to its catalogue the enrollment in the upper division for the first year was 87; for the session of 1926–27, 167; for the session of 1927–28, 176; and for 1928–29, 176. In 1928–29 there were also 289 first and second-year students. The population of Hillsboro in 1930 was 7823.

Edinburg, Texas. With the benefit of two years of experi-

[1] Eby, F. "The Four-Year Junior College and the Advent of the 6–4–4 Plan"; in *Educational Administration and Supervision*, vol. 14, p. 536. (November, 1928.)

ence of Hillsboro to guide it, Edinburg junior college opened in 1927 with the five-four-four plan from the first. Bonds of $3,000,000 were voted to finance a complete scholastic reorganization and extensive buildings were constructed. The plan was abandoned, however, after two-years' trial, the two lower years being moved to the high school building. Beginning in 1929, it has since operated as a two-year junior college.

Pasadena, California. A complete plan of six-four-four organization was presented to the Pasadena board of education by the principal of the high school, W. F. Ewing, in the fall of 1924, and was endorsed by the board and by the superintendent of schools. After a vigorous campaign of six months or more, the city voted, in March, 1924, to establish a district junior college. This was done in the autumn of the same year, and it was operated as a two-year unit in the same building as the high school. The junior college enrollment the first year was 267. By the autumn of 1925, all ninth-grade pupils were eliminated. Elimination of the tenth grade, and complete reorganization on a unitary four-year basis, did not occur until the autumn of 1928, under the principalship of J. W. Harbeson. For some administrative and curricular purposes a distinction is made between "upper-division" and "lower-division" students in the Pasadena junior college. The population of Pasadena in 1930 was 76,000. The enrollment for the two years since establishment has been as follows:

	Total	Upper Division	Lower Division
1928–29	2890	1045	1845
1929–30	2636	1195	1441

Pasadena also maintains a separate four-year high school of standard type. The Pasadena experiment with the six-four-four plan may be considered the most significant and interesting of any in the country. Here the six-four-four plan seems to have an ideal opportunity, under the most favorable conditions, to demonstrate its worth. Of course two years is much too short a time to evaluate such a far-reaching and fundamental reorganizational experiment, but the eyes of the junior college world can well afford to keep close watch on developments at Pasadena. Much information regarding the philosophy of the plan and its success in the first two years will be found in the writings of Superintendent J. A. Sexson and Principal J. W. Harbeson, references to some of which will be found in the Suggested Readings at the close of the chapter.

Ventura, California. In the autumn of 1929, Ventura (1930 population, 11,603) followed the example of Pasadena in inaugurating the six-four-four plan with an enrollment the first year of 48. Organization was effected under the superintendency of Melrowe Martin, who, however, resigned at the end of the year. There were, in 1930, one or two other California junior colleges which were looking in the direction of the six-four-four plan, but no one of these had been fully organized on this basis. Among them may be mentioned Compton and Salinas.

Moberly, Missouri. In 1929 Dean M. G. Neale, of the University of Missouri, in a building survey of Moberly, Missouri, a town with a population of 13,722, recommended the adoption of the six-four-four plan. His recommendation was approved by the board, and in 1930 the erection of a special building to house the upper four-year unit was undertaken.[1]

Texas agricultural colleges. John Tarleton Agricultural College at Stephensville, and North Texas Agricultural College at Arlington (formerly Grubbs Vocational College) are technically branches of the Agricultural and Mechanical College of Texas. Since their establishment, in 1917, they have given two years' work of high school grade followed by two years of

[1] For further details see article by W. W. Carpenter, "Junior College Building at Moberly, Missouri"; in *Junior College Journal*, vol. 1, pp. 119–24. (December, 1930.)

college grade. The organization, however, at least in the former, seems to make rather marked distinctions between the two groups. Thus the John Tarleton catalogue says:

> The instructional services of John Tarleton State Junior Agricultural College fall into two rather distinct divisions; the preparatory and vocational division, and the college division. The preparatory and vocational division comprises the tenth and eleventh grades as ordinarily presented by the standard high schools of the state.... It is intended by this division of the college to meet the needs especially of the students coming from the rural schools and small villages who for worthy reasons have been denied the advantages of advanced high-school training. The college division largely duplicates the first two years of the college work of the standard senior colleges of Texas, but especially emphasizes the first two years of the course of study as presented at the Agricultural and Mechanical College of Texas.

Stephens College, Missouri. With the possible exception of Pasadena, Stephens College at Columbia, Missouri, a junior college for women, is better known than any other in the country as an institution experimenting with the four-year type of junior college. As already stated, President J. M. Wood, who in 1912 became president of this Baptist institution (chartered in 1856), has been an enthusiastic advocate of the four-year junior college for over a decade. Stephens was one of the first junior colleges in the state to accept the standardization of the state university, as described in Chapter III. This was done in 1914.

One reason sometimes stated for the slow development of four-year junior colleges is the attitude of the standardizing agencies, which have rather consistently demanded a certain degree of separation of college and high school sections. In March, 1926, however, the North Central Association agreed to modify these standards as far as they might apply to Stephens College, in order to give it the fullest freedom to experiment with a four-year junior college organization. It was designated as an experimental four-year junior college, its experimental work for a five-year period to be carried on under the supervision of an advisory committee composed of C. H. Judd, University of Chicago; L. V. Koos, University of Chicago, formerly of University of Minnesota; and G. F. Zook, president of University of Akron and formerly specialist in higher education in the Federal Bureau of Education.[1] In September, 1927, Stephens College actually reorganized its last two years of high school work into the freshman and sophomore classes of a four-year college unit. Enrollment since that date and its significance will be presented in Chapter XXVII. Much information regarding the "Stephens plan" will be found in the published addresses of President J. M. Wood, Dean J. J. Oppenheimer, and members of the staff.

In the same way that Pasadena may be considered the outstanding experimental four-year institution in the public junior college field, Stephens is unquestionably the outstanding institution in the private field. Its work is given an official status and national recognition on account of the advisory committee of the North Central Association under which it is working. In 1930, G. F. Zook, secretary of the Commission on Higher Education of the North Central Association, announced that permission had been extended to the public junior colleges at Joliet, Illinois, and Kansas City, Missouri, to carry on experi-

[1] The exact wording of this permission may be of sufficient historical interest and importance to warrant its inclusion here: "Voted that Stephens College be permitted to carry on an educational experiment for a period of five years involving the downward extension of the junior college into the fields of junior and senior high school education and contemplating the obliteration of the lines of demarcation now existing between the last year of the usual four-year high school and the first year of the junior college; provided that in order to assure the maintenance of proper junior college standards the President of Stephens College be required to report annually on the progress of the experiment to a committee of three persons appointed by the chairman of the commission." (Wood, J. M. "The Four-Year Junior College"; in Hudelson, E., editor, *Problems of College Education*, p. 156. Minneapolis, Minnesota, 1928.)

mental work contemplating the elimination in some form of the present line between high school and junior college.[1]

Menlo junior college, California. The work of this institution, a four-year junior college for men, has been outlined in a previous chapter.[2] It has been conducted in a scientific experimental manner since its organization on the present basis, in 1927. A large amount of reliable data covering educational, social, financial, and other aspects of the experiment have been assembled by the Director, Lowry S. Howard, but this is not yet ready for publication. For 1928–29 there were 83 students; for 1929–30, 147.[3]

Hibbing, Minnesota. It has been stated that Hibbing, Minnesota, in 1916, was the first city school system in the country to organize on the six-four-four basis[4] but this seems to be in error. Two members of the Hibbing staff in 1920 described in detail the junior college at Hibbing as a two-year institution and made no mention of the six-four-four plan.[5] G. H. Vande Bogart, who was in charge of the institution from 1925 to 1929, could find no evidence that it had ever been operated on the six-four-four plan, although he found that there had been some discussion of it.[6]

[1] Zook, G. F. "Junior College in the State's Program of Education"; in Bulletin of Department of Secondary School Principals, no. 30 (*Fourteenth Yearbook*), p. 75. (March, 1930.)

[2] See page 106.

[3] The latest official published statement regarding the work and plans at Menlo may be found in the address made by W. M. Proctor, chairman of the executive committee of the board of trustees, at Fort Worth, Texas, in 1928. See reference at end of chapter.

[4] Koos, L. V. *The Junior College*, p. 566.

[5] Alexander, C. C., and Willett, G. W. "Some Aspects of a Junior College"; in *School Review*, vol. 28, pp. 15–25. (January, 1920.)

[6] In a letter of August 27, 1930, Mr. Vande Bogart, then president of the Northern Montana School (Junior College) of Havre, Montana, says: "Although I was engaged in junior college administration in Minnesota for several years before going to Hibbing to take charge of the college there, I had not heard of the Hibbing 6–4–4 plan until I received an inquiry some three or four years ago at the time that I was at Hibbing. I investigated and found that although an organi-

REASONS FOR THE SIX-FOUR-FOUR PLAN

Introductory. The principal facts regarding the actual development of the four-year junior college and of the six-four-four plan in American education have been presented. It must be admitted that they are somewhat meagre in comparison with the extensive development of other types of junior colleges throughout the country. More important than these facts, however, is a presentation of the reasons favoring the development of such institutions. Is there "good reason to believe that when this type of institution is fully developed it will become the modern substitute for the standard four-year American cultural college — the ideal training institution for later adolescence," as W. F. Ewing believes? [1]

It is desirable that the reader should have the strongest possible presentation in favor of the six-four-four type of organization. The writer, after several years of study, has quite strong convictions in favor of the two-year type of institution. Therefore he feels unable to write a sincere and convincing argument in favor of the six-four-four plan. Yet it is desirable that both sides of the question should be presented as vigorously and fairly as the facts warrant. Accordingly it has been decided to present the controversial part of this chapter very largely in the words of some of its strongest advocates.

Commissioner Cooper's statement. The strongest, clearest, most concise, most recent, and most authoritative article which was found, after a careful perusal of all the literature of the subject, is that written by the United States Commissioner of

zation of this type was contemplated it was apparently not completed nor put into effect. The only records available in the college office show no indication of any regular organization that would justify classifying it as an early type of the 6–4–4 plan. The junior college at Hibbing was organized as a two-year institution in 1916."

[1] Ewing, W. F. "The 6–4–4 Plan of Educational Reorganization"; in Proctor, W. M., editor, *The Junior College: Its Organization and Administration*, p. 168.

Education, William John Cooper, and published in the *School Review*,[1] in 1929.[2]

If it is assumed that the American secondary school needs further reorganization, the question arises: What administrative organization is likely to prove most successful? Students of education who have given the secondary field the most consideration are almost unanimous in recommending for American public schools two secondary school units of four years each, preceded by a six-year elementary school.... May I suggest some advantages I believe inhere in this plan.

1. For the *average* child the secondary-school field is organized under the four-four plan in a way that allots the first unit to the period of early adolescence and the second unit to the period of later (perhaps more exactly, "middle") adolescence.

"Middle adolescence," says Frederick Eby, "is the age of great decisions. The deepest decisions of life are confronted at this era, and permanent choices are made which determine the future and affect every feature of the rapidly congealing personality. Nine-tenths of our youth settle at this stage their life-attitude in regard to religious beliefs and practices. Ideals are never so pure, lofty, uncompromised, and imperative. The most enduring as well as the deepest friendships are formed; intelligence reaches its climax; and for all normal individuals the mating instinct with its secondary and associated phenomena begins to dominate the mind and will. It is, above all others, the era when the main feature of personality, the lifelong habits of thought and action are determined. Along with these other decisions a final choice of vocation is made, and the life-career motive becomes the impelling force."[3] If a single school unit

[1] Cooper, W. J. "Some Advantages Expected to Result from Administering Secondary Education in Two Units of Four Years Each"; in *School Review*, vol. 37, pp. 335–46. (May, 1929.) Reprinted with permission of the author and the publishers. A slight rearrangement has been made in one section for greater clarity, since the entire article is not reproduced here.

[2] Another outstanding presentation of the advantages and implications of the six-four-four plan, with special reference to Pasadena, was made by Superintendent J. A. Sexson, of Pasadena, at the 1930 meeting of the Department of Superintendence of the National Education Association in Atlantic City. It is too long for quotation, but several features of it will be discussed in the next two chapters.

[3] Eby, Frederick. "Should the Junior College Unite with the Senior High School?" in *Nation's Schools*, vol. 3, p. 36. (February, 1929.)

with a trained staff could deal with this period of life, most beneficial results might be expected.

2. The problems of articulation now causing great concern among American educators should be lessened through the consolidation of the three units involved in the three-three-two plan now quite common into the two units of the four-four plan.

One of the serious problems of articulation between college and high school today is found in the duplication of courses. This overlapping can be eliminated more readily in a four-year upper secondary unit than in the two-year junior college or in the four-year arts college. College men have been working on this problem ever since 1913, when President James R. Angell, of Yale University, justified the college in offering certain work of secondary grade in order that a student who had not obtained it in high school might take it in college but questioned the policy whereby the student, "when once he is safely inside the college walls, finds himself set to doing right over again much which he has already done in school.[1] Professor Koos, for instance, studied the problem in 1922 from several points of view. First, he examined certain subject offerings in 86 colleges and 250 high schools. The courses were classified as secondary, partly secondary, and collegiate. His findings were that, on the average, the freshman and sophomore offerings of the eighty-six colleges were to be classified as follows: secondary, 20 per cent; partly secondary, 25 per cent; and collegiate, 55 per cent.[2] Again, two hundred Freshmen and Sophomores in the University of Minnesota enrolled in the College of Science, Literature, and Arts were asked to estimate the duplication of their high-school work in the various college subjects. The overlapping was found to vary from less than 1 per cent in occupational subjects, ancient languages, and mathematics to 36 per cent in English. An estimated average duplication of 15 per cent for all subjects was found to exist in the experiences of these two hundred students.[3]

3. The four-four plan should effect economies in administration. In general, only two administrative staffs would be required to do

[1] Angell, James Rowland. "The Duplication of School Work by the College"; in *School Review*, vol. 21, p. 2. (January, 1913.)

[2] Koos, Leonard Vincent. *The Junior College*, p. 395. Research Publications of the University of Minnesota, Education Series, no. 5. Minneapolis, Minnesota, University of Minnesota, 1924.

[3] *Ibid.*, p. 399.

the work of the three engaged in a three-three-two organization. The cost of housing also, especially with respect to maintenance and operation, should be considerably lessened. Moreover, the curriculums of the lower unit would be so different from those of the upper unit that highly specialized workrooms and laboratories would be required in the higher unit only. Likewise, the libraries of the lower unit would be less expensive to purchase, to maintain, and to operate than would be those of the upper unit. The three-three-two organization makes necessary two library organizations of the expensive type, while the four-four organization necessitates but one. School auditoriums, stadiums, cafeterias, and other service features are expensive. Any scheme affording opportunity to reduce these from three units to two must be considered.

4. The time of the student should be conserved in the four-four organization for several reasons. It is a well-established fact that two-year units afford almost no opportunity for the bright student to make rapid progress. The three-year unit has not proved satisfactory in accelerating pupils because it is difficult for even a bright pupil to do three years of work in two years and the peculiar prejudices of the high school age work against graduating a pupil from a three-year unit in two and one-half years. One of the major administrative advantages of the old four-year high school is that many pupils can be graduated in three years.

5. The four-four organization would enable the upper unit to render a distinctive educational service not now satisfactorily performed in the public schools. I refer to education for the so-called "semi-professions." Four years ago R. J. Leonard, of Teachers College, Columbia University, called attention to the fact that studies of occupations indicate that training for them belongs on different educational levels. Professor Leonard suggested a permanent field for our proposed upper secondary unit. He said in part: "In so far as universities concern themselves with professional education, their efforts will be confined to the higher and highest levels. Those are the permanent university fields. No other institutions can perform these services satisfactorily. And, in so far as junior colleges concern themselves with occupational education, their efforts will be confined to the middle level, and, in like manner, this will be their permanent field." [1]

[1] Leonard, Robert Josselyn. "Professional Education in Junior Colleges"; in *Teachers College Record*, vol. 26, p. 729. (May, 1925.)

Studies by Koos[1] in the fields of engineering, commerce, and agriculture and by Thomas, who carried Koos's engineering studies farther, indicate that an upper secondary unit of the type proposed can make a real contribution. Koos listed 104 so-called "engineering occupations" and asked one hundred deans of schools of engineering to designate which occupations are professional in character, requiring four years of college work; which are semi-professional, requiring probably only two years of college work; and which are on a trade level, requiring no college work. In spite of much variation in opinion, approximately 50 per cent of the deans agreed that 43 of the 104 occupations are on the semi-professional level and 32 on the professional level.[2]

Thomas explains his investigations as follows: "In order to determine how the workers in engineering occupations were distributed among these groups, the writer undertook in 1926 an inquiry among the larger corporations in California which employed trained engineers. The two groups of occupations, segregated in accordance with the findings of Koos, were listed but with no suggestion that the first forty-three of these were classified as semi-professional and the remaining thirty-two as professional. These lists were sent to the employment managers of the twelve corporations carrying on the most extensive engineering projects in the state. Each was requested to indicate the number of men employed by his organization in each occupation listed. The replies in every case were prompt and carefully prepared. These showed 755 men employed in semi-professional work and 289 employed in fully professional engineering work."[3]

Moreover, to the man in the street even the existence of numerous schools and colleges of business, commerce, engineering, etc., operated for private gain is sufficient evidence that a large field of education is inadequately served by the present public-school system.

[1] Koos, Leonard Vincent. *The Junior College*, pp. 145–52. Research Publications of the University of Minnesota, Education Series, no. 5. Minneapolis, Minnesota, University of Minnesota, 1924.

[2] *Ibid.*, pp. 152–60.

[3] Thomas, Frank Waters. "The Functions of the Junior College"; in *The Junior College: Its Organization and Administration*, p. 21. Edited by William Martin Proctor. Stanford University, California, Stanford University Press, 1927.

6. The combining of the two upper high school years with the two lower college years should afford a large enough body of students to justify colleges in centers of population insufficient in size to maintain four-year colleges of liberal arts or even two-year junior colleges. Of course, we are still in the midst of a controversy between the college administrators regarding how many persons should go to college. Only two years ago Chancellor Ernest H. Lindley, of the University of Kansas, was applauded when he insisted that "in a democracy the chief duty of the college is to train for useful and intelligent citizenship the largest possible number of young men and women."[1] If we approve this stand, we should note that college surveys — especially surveys of publicly supported colleges and universities — which have given any consideration to the location of the students' homes are in agreement that a high correlation exists between attendance at college and nearness of residence to college. In the Texas study, for example, where the survey staff divided the state into five groups of counties, the first fifth having the fewest college students per thousand population and the last fifth having the most college students per thousand population, it was concluded that, "on the whole, it is the counties which have the least access to the state schools... which... have the lowest percentage of college students per unit of population."[2]

Studying the student population in twenty-one land-grant colleges scattered all over the United States from Rhode Island to Oregon and from Michigan to Florida, Arthur J. Klein, of the United States Bureau of Education, finds that, of a grand total of 63,177 students... 27 per cent of the students enrolled in these colleges live within 25 miles of college; 36 per cent, within 50 miles; 55 per cent, within 100 miles; 38 per cent, from 101 to 500 miles; and 6 per cent, more than 500 miles.[3]

Additional reasons for the plan. An examination of the voluminous literature on the six-four-four plan shows a re-

[1] Reported in *The Articulation of the Units of American Education*, p. 292. *Seventh Yearbook of the Department of Superintendence.* Washington, Department of Superintendence of the National Education Association, 1929.

[2] Coffman, L. D., Hill, Clyde M., Kelly, F. J., Zook, George F., and Works, George A., *Higher Education*, p. 175. *Texas Educational Survey Report*, vol. 6. Austin, Texas, Texas Educational Survey Commission, 1925.

[3] Unpublished data in the United States Bureau of Education.

currence time after time of many of the arguments so admirably stated by Dr. Cooper. In addition, certain other reasons have been advanced by other writers which should be indicated here for the sake of making the strongest and most complete presentation of the advantages of the six-four-four plan. Accordingly, five more are briefly outlined below in the words of some other leading advocates of this plan.

7. *Better guidance possibilities.* (Koos.) [1]

Another consideration supporting organizational integration of junior college with high school years is associated with the need of an adequate program of guidance. The full period of secondary education from the seventh grade through the second year is that in which the population is being distributed to occupational life. It is the feeling of the writer that one significant explanation of our failure to discharge more efficiently this important obligation is the fact that this period has been divided among three different types of institutions, the elementary school, the four-year high school and the college.

8. *Increased flexibility of the curriculum.* (Sexson.) [2]

The six-four-four plan implies that the thirteenth and fourteenth year student must be permitted to take a reasonable percentage of his work from the twelfth grade. This would make it unnecessary to duplicate beginning courses of the twelfth grade with similar beginning courses in the thirteenth or fourteenth.... For the same reason, twelfth-grade students who have met the subject-matter requirements for the completion of that grade must be permitted to take thirteenth year work for credit, up to a reasonable percentage of the student load.

9. *Analogy with German education.* (Eby.) [3]

An examination of the studies taken by many students during the

[1] Koos, L. V. "Progress and Problems of the Junior College"; in *Problems in Education*, pp. 14–15. Western Reserve University Press, Cleveland, Ohio, 1927.

[2] Sexson, J. A. "The Organization and Administration of the Four-Year Junior College"; in Bulletin of the Department of Secondary School Principals, no. 30 (*Fourteenth Yearbook*), 226 pp. (March, 1930.)

[3] Eby, F. "The Four-year Public Junior College"; in *Proceedings of the Ninth Annual Meeting of the American Association of Junior Colleges*, pp. 69–70. Fort Worth, Texas, 1928.

last two years of the high school and the first two years of college resembles futuristic landscape paintings. Placed along side the orderly program of the four upper years of the German gymnasium, one wonders whether American educators are actually sane. Just at the age when the student should be held to study, persistent effort, and consecutive thinking, we impose upon him an organization which encourages him to flounder from course to course, from subject to subject, and from one school to another. He comes out with a hodge-podge.

10. Relation to compulsory school laws. (Proctor.) [1]

The legal school-leaving age in many of the states is now sixteen, and the age for beginning the apprenticeship to an industrial vocation is also quite generally placed at age sixteen by the trades concerned. Thus the tenth school grade marks a more natural terminal point for thousands of pupils whose formal schooling must end at age sixteen than does the eighth or the ninth school year.

11. Attracts superior teachers. (Harbeson.) [2]

The four-year college is educationally the most efficient form of organization for the upper secondary school system. It provides an organization of such dignity and scope as to attract the best trained and most experienced staff of teachers and administrators. It is supported by a taxable valuation of sufficient magnitude to provide adequate resources in buildings, grounds and equipment, and a faculty of outstanding size to provide an adequate enrollment for the best classification of its students.

Such are the principal arguments which have been advanced by various writers in behalf of the six-four-four plan of organization. Their significance and validity will be discussed in the next chapter.

[1] Proctor, W. M. (editor). *The Junior College: Its Organization and Administration*, p. 199.

[2] Harbeson, J. W. "The 6-4-4 Plan of School Organization, with Special Reference to its Application in the City of Pasadena"; in *California Quarterly of Secondary Education*, vol. 4, p. 47. (October, 1928.)

QUESTIONS AND PROBLEMS

1. Look up concrete data tending to substantiate or to extend any one of the six points in favor of the six-four-four plan made by Dr. Cooper.
2. Do the same for any of the points made by any of the other five men quoted.
3. From your reading, select a group of brief quotations from as many authors as possible, favoring the six-four-four plan.
4. Compare the reasons for the six-four-four plan, as given by some of the earlier authors mentioned, with the reasons as given by Dr. Cooper and others in this chapter.
5. Why did so long a time elapse between the first proposal of the six-four-four plan, and the organization of the first institution under it?
6. Arrange the eleven arguments in favor of the six-four-four plan, as given in this chapter, in order of importance. State briefly reason for first and last positions.
7. Secure the name of any junior college organized on the six-four-four basis, not listed in this chapter, and find out everything possible regarding it.
8. Where has the six-four-four plan the greatest probability of success — in the public junior college, or the private one?
9. Report more in detail regarding the adoption and development of the six-four-four plan in any of the institutions mentioned in this chapter.
10. List possible objections to the six-four-four plan.
11. In what size or type of cities is the six-four-four plan most likely to be successful?
12. Should there be an enabling act authorizing the establishment of junior colleges on the six-four-four plan? If so, draft one for a particular state.

SUGGESTED READINGS

Carpenter, W. W. "New Building for Moberly Junior College"; in *Junior College Journal*, vol. 1, pp. 119-24. (December, 1930.)

Committee. "A Plea for the 6-4-4 Plan in San Francisco"; in *California Quarterly of Secondary Education*, vol. 4, p. 50. (October, 1928.)

Cooke, R. L. "The Origin of the Six-Four-Four Plan"; in *Junior College Journal*, vol. 1, pp. 370-73. (March, 1931.)

Cooper, W. J. "Trends in Reorganizing California's Secondary School System"; in *Bulletin of American Association of Collegiate Registrars*, vol. 4, pp. 83-92. (April, 1929.)

*Cooper, W. J. "Some Advantages Expected to Result from Administering Secondary Education in Two Units of Four Years Each"; in *School Review*, vol. 37, pp. 335-46. (May, 1929.)

Davis, J. T. "Adolescence and the Junior College"; in *Proceedings of the Seventh Annual Meeting of the American Association of Junior Colleges*, pp. 63–67. Jackson, Mississippi, 1926.

Eby, F. "The Four-Year Junior College and the Advent of the Six-Four-Four Plan"; in *Educational Administration and Supervision*, vol. 14, pp. 536–42. (November, 1928.)

*Eby, F. "The Four-Year Public Junior College"; in *Proceedings of the Ninth Annual Meeting of the American Association of Junior Colleges*, pp. 63–73, 96 (Fort Worth, Texas, 1928); also in *Nation's Schools*, vol. 3, pp. 33–38. (February, 1929.)

*Ewing, W. F. "The 6–4–4 Plan of Educational Reorganization"; in Proctor, W. M. (editor), *The Junior College: Its Organization and Administration*, pp. 155–69.

Frazier, A. M. "The Taxpayer and the Junior College"; in *American Educational Digest*, vol. 47, pp. 291–93, 332. (March, 1928.)
Based upon experience at Hillsboro Junior College.

French, J. W. "The Junior College and 6–4–4 Organization"; in *American Educational Digest*, vol. 45, pp. 365–66. (April, 1926.)

*Harbeson, J. W. "The 6–4–4 Plan of School Organization, with Special Reference to its Application in the City of Pasadena"; in *California Quarterly of Secondary Education*, vol. 4, pp. 45–50. (October, 1928.)

Hardy, E. L. "The Reorganization of our Education System"; in *School and Society*, vol. 5, pp. 728–32. (June 23, 1917.)

Kemp, W. W. "The Junior College in California"; in *California Quarterly of Secondary Education*, vol. 5, pp. 188–94. (January, 1930.)

Koos, L. V. "The Junior College Movement"; in *The New Republic*, vol. 36, pp. 22–24. (November 7, 1923.)

Koos, L. V. "The Logical Organization of Secondary Education"; in *Junior College*, pp. 564–68.

*Koos, L. V. "Progress and Problems of the Junior College"; in *Proceedings of the Eighth Annual Meeting of the American Association of Junior Colleges*, pp. 68–73. Chicago, Illinois, 1928.

*Proctor, W. M. "The Junior College and Educational Reorganization"; in *Educational Review*, vol. 65, pp. 275–80. (May, 1923.)

Proctor, W. M. "Possibilities of the Double Four Organization in Private Secondary Schools"; in *Proceedings of the Ninth Annual Meeting of the American Association of Junior Colleges*, pp. 22–26, 111–12. Fort Worth, Texas, 1928.

Sexson, J. A. "Six-Four-Four Plan of School Organization"; in

American Educational Digest, vol. 48, pp. 56–59, 79. (October, 1928.)

*Sexson, J. A. "The Organization and Administration of the Four-Year Junior College"; in Bulletin of the Department of Secondary School Principals, no. 30 (*Fourteenth Yearbook*), pp. 210–28. (March, 1930.)

Slawson, S. J. "The 6–4–4 Plan in Johnstown, Pennsylvania"; in *Seventh Yearbook of the Department of Superintendence of the National Education Association*, pp. 233–34. Washington, D.C. (February, 1929.)

Wood, J. M. *The Function of the Junior College.* United States Bureau of Education, Bulletin no. 19, pp. 2–6. (1922.)

Wood, J. M. "The Four-Year Junior College"; in Hudelson, E. (editor), *Problems of College Education*, pp. 153–63. Minneapolis, Minnesota, 1928.

*Wood, J. M. "Future of the Whole Junior College Movement in its Relation to Secondary Schools"; in Bulletin of the Department of Secondary School Principals of the National Education Association (*Thirteenth Yearbook*), no. 25, pp. 376–84. (March, 1929.)

Zook, G. F. "Junior College in the State's Program of Education"; in Bulletin of Department of Secondary School Principals of the National Education Association (*Fourteenth Yearbook*), no. 30, pp. 74–83. (March, 1930.)

CHAPTER XXVI

DISADVANTAGES OF THE FOUR-YEAR PLAN

We are about ready in America to stop that fetish worship of the numeral four — four years of school, four years of college, and so on.
— RAY LYMAN WILBUR.[1]

Contents of this chapter. This chapter and the one which follows it are frankly argumentative. After mentioning a few misconceptions and misunderstandings, we will first consider, in some detail, the eleven arguments for the six-four-four plan advanced in the preceding chapter, and then point out some of the disadvantages of the four-year junior college.

Introductory. In reviewing the literature on the six-four-four plan, one is reminded of the classic remark of Mark Twain with reference to the weather, that a great deal has been said about it, but very little seems to have been done about it! Much has been said and written about the six-four-four plan, as the last chapter and the suggested readings at its close abundantly testify, but only a few such institutions have been established. Little has been written about the two-year junior college *per se*, as the scanty readings at the close of chapter XXVII also testify, but much has been done about it, as indicated in the bulk of the entire volume that has preceded the previous chapter, and by the number of institutions following the plan (see Table 81, page 655). There is danger that practical school administrators, hearing so much of the advantage of the progressive six-four-four plan, will come to believe, on account of the frequent repetition of the same statements, that there is only one side to the question, and that they are distinctly unprogressive if they do not work toward it. There is no diffi-

[1] Wilbur, R. L. "The Junior College: A Message"; in *Sierra Educational News*, vol. 22, p. 147. (March, 1926.)

culty in finding numerous presentations and re-presentations of the advantages of the four-year junior college. Search as one may, however, he will not find a single systematic presentation of the other side of the question, except for J. B. Lillard's brief article in *School and Society*.[1] It seems, therefore, that there is a distinct occasion for a further discussion of the disadvantages of the six-four-four plan, and of the points in favor of the prevailing type of institution. The writer may be entirely wrong in his opinions and conclusions. He is sure, however, that there is a place for a comprehensive and systematic statement of the side of the question which seems to have been so largely neglected in the literature, in order that the intelligent reader and the careful student of the problems of the junior college may weigh the arguments, both pro and con, and draw his own conclusions.

MISCONCEPTIONS AND MISUNDERSTANDINGS

Types of arguments found. In reviewing the extensive six-four-four literature, the writer has been impressed with the number of arguments stated by many writers which are excellent reasons for the existence of junior colleges (as outlined in Chapter VII), but are not at all distinctive of the six-four-four plan. In many cases, however, they are *assumed to be* unique in their application to the six-four-four situation. There is another group of arguments which if valid and logical are even stronger arguments for a single unified six- or eight-year secondary school, rather than for one broken into two four-year units. A few examples of the first type may well be presented here.

"Basic concept of six-four-four." On several occasions, Principal J. W. Harbeson of Pasadena has made the following

[1] Lillard, J. B. "The 6–3–3–2 *versus* the 6–4–4 Plan of Organization for the Public Junior College"; in *School and Society*, vol. 32, pp. 262–64. (August 23, 1930.)

statement, which has also been made by Superintendent J. A. Sexson:[1]

> The most basic concept of the six-four-four plan is a recognition of the fact that the thirteenth and fourteenth years, the years now embraced in the junior college, are, in reality, secondary in character and are, in fact, a part of a well-rounded system of secondary education. If they are a part of the secondary school system they should be attached to the public schools, as it is a recognized fact that universal public education stops with the completion of the secondary education.

Although the writer has studied this statement carefully, since it is said to be "most basic," yet it seems to him to be an example of a *non sequitur* argument as far as it applies to the *four-year* junior college. It is just as basic to the two-year or to the six-year junior college. There seems also to be a hiatus between the first and second sentences. Why does it follow, even if these two years are "secondary" (whatever that may mean), that they should be "attached" to the public schools in a peculiar administrative relationship which means splitting the prevailing high school squarely in two and welding its upper half into an integral whole with the two junior college years? It may be frankly admitted that the junior college is a part of the public school system, as is the case in practically every state where it is found (except for the small number of state junior colleges), without any necessary implication whatever that it must be administratively united with two and only two years of secondary education immediately adjacent to it. If this is a true "basic concept," it is basic to all junior college education and not to a particular type of administrative plan.

Misconception of *secondary*. A misconception of the meaning of the term *secondary* has already been mentioned in

[1] Harbeson, J. W. "The Six-Four-Four Plan of School Organization, with Special Reference to its Application in the City of Pasadena"; in *California Quarterly of Secondary Education*, vol. 4, p. 45. (October, 1928.)

Chapter XXIV. To some people secondary seems to be synonymous with *high school*, instead of *general* as distinguished from *special* education.

Twelfth-grade graduation. Another statement, made by Superintendent Sexson in his Atlantic City address, will bear examination:[1]

> Twelfth-grade graduation must ultimately disappear. Under the six-four-four plan, the twelfth grade cannot be recognized as a legitimate stopping place. In other words, to use the language of Woodrow Wilson, while President of Princeton, "Nobody ever heard of graduating a sophomore."

It is hard to see the application of this statement. Why must high school graduation ultimately disappear? Just whom did President Wilson mean by a "sophomore"? Wasn't he, as a matter of fact, the individual that finishes the Pasadena junior college at the end of the upper four-year level, and is ready to transfer, perhaps, to the junior year at Princeton?

If President Wilson's opinion were valid and applicable at all, it would seem to operate to prevent any graduation from the Pasadena institution. He was referring to Princeton sophomores, not to high school seniors, who are known as "sophomores" at Pasadena. Furthermore, if President Wilson were living today, even conservative Princeton might have heard of graduating many people of sophomore grade in hundreds of junior colleges throughout the country. President Harper was graduating sophomores with the title of Associate in Arts at the University of Chicago thirty years ago.

San Francisco committee. A committee of twenty-five members of the faculty of the Polytechnic High School of San Francisco, in a preliminary report, advocated the six-four-four plan on twelve grounds. This report is cited by J. W. Harbe-

[1] Sexson, J. A. "The Organization and Administration of the Four-Year Junior College"; in Bulletin of the Department of Secondary School Principals of the National Education Association, no. 30 (*Fourteenth Yearbook*), p. 227. (March, 1930.)

son in his discussion of the six-four-four plan.[1] It is also quoted approvingly by Dean W. W. Kemp, of the University of California, as "one of the best briefs for the six-four-four plan."[2] Several of the reasons given in this brief, duplicate the arguments presented in the last chapter, but at least four of the twelve do not. These four are as follows:

(6) The educational progress of the pupil through the adolescent period is less strenuous.

(9) The administration can bring cultural, vocational, and pre-professional training nearer to the people and thus encourage adult education.

(10) It offers larger opportunities for extension courses.

(11) It gives the opportunity of having better trained instructors for the adolescent periods and for the corresponding courses of the universities, and at the same time eliminates the large classes so prevalent in the freshman and sophomore years in the university.

The writer fails to see how any of these arguments apply to the four-year junior college with any more force than to the two-year college. They may be valid arguments for junior colleges in general, although the validity of "less strenuous progress" might be questioned, but in what respect are they unique to the six-four-four plan?

Pasadena reasons. Principal Harbeson, of Pasadena, has furnished the writer with answers to questionnaires filled out by administration staff officers, heads of departments, and student body officers at Pasadena, after the complete adoption of the six-four-four plan there. The following question was asked of them: "State the main advantages of the four-year junior college over other forms of organization, placing them in

[1] Harbeson, J. W. "The Six-Four-Four Plan of School Organization, with Special Reference to its Application in the City of Pasadena"; in *California Quarterly of Secondary Education*, vol. 4, p. 50. (October, 1928.)

[2] Kemp, W. W. "The Junior College in California"; in *California Quarterly of Secondary Education*, vol. 5, p. 194. (January, 1930.) Dr. Kemp, however, gives only eleven points instead of twelve. It is of passing interest that a university administrator omits number 11, as printed on this page.

the order of their importance." Twenty-six reasons were given. Some of them are valid and duplicate the reasons presented in the last chapter. To the writer, however, over half of them seem to be just as applicable to the two-year junior college, or to be statements of fact rather than of advantage. His judgment may be wrong; therefore, his selection of those of doubtful validity are given below, in order of importance:

Financial saving to the student.
Offers vocational course for unrecommended students.
Small classes and personal contact with teacher.
Reduces lower-division registration in universities.
Keeps students under home influence longer time.
Possibility of improving standard of scholarship.
Opportunity for leadership.
Greater development and more thorough training of student.
Greater freedom.
Thirteenth and fourteenth years made part of a four-year unit.
Higher professional standard for faculty.
Coördination with the university, which wants upper-division students.
Elimination through diploma course of unfit college material.
Increased opportunity for student self-government.

Were the writers of these statements really thinking in terms of the *four-year unit in particular*, or of the *junior college in general*?

MAIN ARGUMENTS FOR SIX-FOUR-FOUR PLAN

Introductory. With these words of caution regarding the nature and applicability of some of the arguments which have been advanced for the six-four-four plan, let us turn now to a consideration of the main arguments for it, as set forth in the preceding chapter by Commissioner Cooper and others. For convenience they may be summarized briefly as follows:

1. *The psychological argument.* The four-year junior college is peculiarly fitted to the needs of the periods of adolescence.
2. *The articulation argument.* The four-year junior college would

eliminate undesirable overlapping of courses (amounting to an average of at least 15 per cent) between high school and college.

3. *The economy-of-cost argument.* The four-year plan will make notable savings in housing, maintenance, and operation.
4. *The economy-of-time argument.* The superior student can finish the course in three years instead of four.
5. *The argument of vocational preparation.* The four-year junior college can do a distinctive and unique work in training students for semi-professional occupations.
6. *The argument from size.* The four-year junior college permits college opportunity in places too small to justify a two-year college.
7. *The guidance argument.* More effective, organized guidance is possible in the four-year institution than in the two-year one.
8. *The argument of flexibility of the curriculum.* A more varied curriculum is open to election by a wider range of students.
9. *The argument of analogy with German education.*
10. *The compulsory school law argument.* The legal school-leaving age in most states is sixteen, coinciding with the beginning of the four-year junior college.
11. *The argument of superior teachers.* The four-year college attracts better teachers and administrators.

Let us examine each of these arguments in turn. The reader would do well to re-read the argument in favor of each of these in the preceding chapter, in connection with the following discussion.

The psychological argument. There are two main theories of psychological development, the saltatory theory and the gradual theory. The former, holding that there are certain periods when sudden and pronounced mental, physical, and social changes occur, has been popularized by G. Stanley Hall and his followers, and has had a profound influence on educational thought and administrative practice. The theory of gradual development, resulting from thousands of careful scientific measurements by Thorndike and his followers, seems, however, to be far better established at the present time and destined to modify practical school procedure still more.[1] It is the former theory, however, that is represented by the picturesquely rhetorical statement of Professor Eby, quoted with approval by Dr. Cooper in presenting this argument in the preceding chapter. Is it a question of rhetoric *versus* facts? To the writer, after some study of the literature of adolescence, it seems that the saltatory theory has little to support it. However, there are many who still hold to the older theory, and it will be worth while to examine the psychological argument from the point of view of each theory, in turn.

The saltatory theory. Let it be assumed, for the sake of argument, that the saltatory theory is true. There are well-marked stages of adolescence — early, middle, and late. Students can be divided into well-marked groups — pre-pubescent, pubescent, and post-pubescent. Pubescence occurs about the age of fourteen. The lower four-year unit (average age twelve to sixteen) covers the period of pubescence, and the upper four-year unit (average age sixteen to twenty) covers post-pubescence. The two units are especially adapted to the peculiar needs of these two periods. So runs the argument.

The best evidence shows that there are no such sudden changes at these periods as has been supposed in the past. Even if this feature be admitted, however, the matter of *age* will bear investigation. The ages given are *average* ages.

[1] E. P. Cubberley thus summarizes the situation, in his Editor's Introduction to a recent textbook on *The Psychology of Adolescence* (Brooks, F. D., Houghton Mifflin Company, 1929), which is an admirable summary of the whole field of experimental studies: "We now know that the adolescent period, while marked by certain distinct and pronounced physical changes, from the mental and personal points of view is very largely only a maturing of individual traits and habits of thinking and acting that have been developing since childhood. Even in the matter of the emotional and volitional changes and the development of personality traits which take place with adolescence, there now seems to be little reason for believing that what a youth becomes is to any degree independent of his own past environment and training. While these changes are marked and important, they are in the nature of a continuous development of what has gone before, rather than an abrupt transition to some new and different type of living."

There is nothing so comforting as an average — and nothing so dangerous to rely upon at times. How wide is the distribution that leads to the average? The average difference in age of maturity between boys and girls is about a year. Furthermore, the extensive researches of Crampton and of Baldwin, based on over six thousand cases, show that maturity in girls varies all the way from ten to seventeen years of age, and in boys from twelve to eighteen years.[1] At age fourteen, for example, only 28 per cent of the 4800 boys studied by Crampton were pubescent, while 26 per cent were still pre-pubescent. At sixteen, the assumed average age of entrance to an upper four-year unit, some 10 per cent of each sex are still pubescent or pre-pubescent. Even among a reasonable proportion of children, the range of variation is at least three years. Consequently it is impossible to fix the time of the secondary school entrance to fit such a variable factor.

The varying age of pubescence is not the only factor, however, which makes it difficult to organize a rigid school system so as to fit such a widely varying function as pubescence. If fourteen-year-old children were all in the same grade, it might be possible to have some slight degree of uniformity in relation to pubescence. Every school survey, however, has found a wide age-grade distribution. For example, at Sacramento Sears found fourteen-year-old children in every grade from the first through the ninth, with no data from the senior high school. In the eighth grade, students varied from ten to nineteen years of age. Only 43 per cent, somewhat less than half, were normal for their grade.[2] Or take the situation with 546 members of the entering class of the Pasadena four-year junior college, in the autumn of 1929. Since they were in the eleventh grade it might be expected that they would average *sixteen*

[1] See tables in Douglass, A. A. *Secondary Education*, p. 173. Houghton Mifflin Company, Boston, Massachusetts, 1927.

[2] Sears, J. B. *Sacramento School Survey*, p. 486. Sacramento, California, 1928.

years of age, and such was the case, but only 45 per cent of the boys and 44 per cent of the girls were of that age. Twenty-four per cent of the boys and 31 per cent of the girls were 14 or 15 years of age, while other members of the class varied from 17 to 25.[1]

With such wide variability in chronological age in any grade, and with such equally wide variability in development of pubescence, the futility of adjusting a curriculum or a system of school organization to the supposed peculiar psychological characteristics of a population is evident. Such adjustment might conceivably be made to the average, but how closely would it fit the needs of a large proportion of the individuals whose most striking characteristic is marked variability, both chronologically and psychologically, from the average?

The gradual theory. There is not space, nor is this the appropriate place, to review the extensive experimental literature of the past two or three decades showing the gradual as contrasted with the saltatory development of the chief features, physical, mental, and social, with which the schools have to deal. The consensus of opinion at the present time seems to be that the differences between childhood and adolescence, or between the different stages of adolescence, are by no means so profound or sudden as many school men have been taught to believe.[2] If this is true, then most assuredly the psychological foundation for a four-year junior college rests upon unstable and shifting sands.

Campbell's study. Doak S. Campbell, secretary of the American Association of Junior Colleges, in his doctor's dis-

[1] Inglis, the well-known authority on secondary education, has shown that the grade distribution of sixteen-year-old students in school is as follows: Grades 1–5, 2.7 per cent; grade 6, 1.9 per cent; grade 7, 5.8 per cent; grade 8, 12.6 per cent; grade 9, 20.7 per cent; grade 10, 31.0 per cent; grade 11, 19.4 per cent; grade 12, 5.9 per cent. (*School Review*, vol. 23, p. 316. May, 1915.)

[2] See Brooks, F. D., *The Psychology of Adolescence* (Houghton Mifflin Company, 1929), for summaries of a wealth of material to support this statement.

sertation, made an attempt to evaluate the whole psychological argument especially from the junior college point of view. He attempted to answer the question, "Does the junior college logically attempt its adaptation to the period of later adolescence?" He examined all available literature dealing with the psychology of adolescence, particularly stressing experimental, quantitative studies. His conclusions, therefore, are worth quoting:[1]

1. That, so far as the literature discloses, there has been no experimentation in this field which bears directly upon the problem of fitting the junior college unit to the period of later adolescence.
2. That there has been considerable study of the physical, physiological, and anatomical aspects of adolescence to the extent that the upper and lower boundaries have been defined, but with considerable variation. It is significant that there is such a wide range with respect to the age at which the period begins that it is hardly possible to state a definite age limit with the rigidity necessary for the administration of a separate educational unit. It is even more difficult to establish the upper limits of the period than it is the lower.
3. That the assumption, though not supported with experimental evidence, is quite general that periods of mental growth and maturity are consistently parallel with physical growth, and upon this assumption is based justification of the statement that given administrative units in education are fitted to the period of adolescence.
4. That such experimentation as has been reported in this field shows that these periods are not radically different and distinctly separable from those immediately preceding or immediately following, and that the consideration of them in this light is responsible for certain erroneous conceptions concerning them.
5. That the conception of the junior college as a completion unit of secondary education, designed to fit the period of later

[1] Campbell, D. S. "A Critical Study of the Stated Purposes of the Junior College"; in *George Peabody College Contributions to Education*, no. 70, pp. 73–74. Nashville, Tennessee, 1930.

adolescence, involves more than the mere mechanical readjustment of administrative machinery.

6. If we are to define education in terms of maturity, it remains for these maturities to be discovered and defined and a means devised for adjusting the educational unit to them.

The psychological argument, then, may be dismissed from consideration at the present time as having little if any bearing on the question of the relative merits of the two-year or four-year junior college.

The articulation argument. (Fifteen per cent or more overlapping.) A certain amount of overlapping is not only permissible, but desirable. The writer, in teaching freshman mathematics in college, found it highly profitable to spend fully 15 per cent of the time in reviewing high school mathematics, even though it would be classed as duplication by the criteria employed by Koos. Furthermore, even though the same subject matter is treated, it may be dealt with from different points of view in different schools. Take, for example, the subject in which Koos found the greatest overlapping, English literature. He found that *The Cotter's Saturday Night* was specified in twenty-one high school and twenty-two college courses of study; that Shakespeare's *Sonnets* were read in fifteen high schools and twenty-two colleges. It is possible that if a student took a course in Shakespeare in the upper division, he might read the *Sonnets* again, and study them still again in his graduate work.

It is quite possible, though, that he would study the *Sonnets* from different standpoints each time — historical, vocabulary, appreciation, and critical. Possibly when he teaches English literature in the junior college he may overlap even more and read them again — and not without profit. The writer feels by no means sure that the "bootless repetition that has been incontrovertibly demonstrated" by Koos is entirely censurable. Koos's conclusion that "the actual repetition of materials can hardly be less than a full fifth of all the work taken in the high school" has been widely quoted. Mere duplication of material, however, is not necessarily to be condemned. It may be handled by different methods and with different objectives at different levels.

It may be frankly admitted, however, that there is some undesirable overlapping. It by no means follows that such overlapping and duplication of material will be eliminated because courses are given in one institution. The writer has heard occasional complaints of overlapping between departments in the same institution. He has an impression that overlapping of courses has also been found to exist even in a single department — the department of education, for example. Overlapping, then, is not a matter that is necessarily related to the question of a two- or a four-year institution. The elimination of undesirable duplication and closer articulation is a matter essentially of curriculum revision and organization. Let Superintendent Sexson characterize the unique opportunity of the four-year junior college at Pasadena in this respect: [1]

> When the eleventh and twelfth grades are organized as one institution and the thirteenth and fourteenth grades as another, duplication [of curriculum] cannot be controlled. If, however, these four years are united as a single institution with one student body and one faculty and administration, the possibilities of curriculum revision know no limitations.

Unfortunately curriculum revision is not accomplished when a four-year administrative organization is set up. Mr. Sexson, in the same address, tells what else is necessary at Pasadena. He says [2] that

> curriculum revision is a long and tedious process. In the Pasadena Junior College, this is being accomplished by curriculum committees

[1] Sexson. "The Organization and Administration of the Four-Year Junior College"; in Bulletin of the Department of Secondary School Principals (*Fourteenth Yearbook*), no. 30, pp. 223–24. (March, 1930.)

[2] Sexson, *op. cit.*, p. 219. Italics not in the original.

working under the direction of the assistant Superintendent of Schools. There is a committee for each major subject of the curriculum, and each committee is endeavoring to reorganize the curriculum *throughout the entire system* in such a way as to remove duplication and overlapping.... A syllabus is finally worked out and printed for each subject covering all the grades in which it forms a part of the curriculum.

This statement forms an excellent description of the technique of curriculum revision that has been carried out at Sacramento during the past two years under the able leadership of Dr. W. M. Proctor. There is this difference, however — Sacramento has an independent *two-year college.* Subject-matter committees have studied each subject throughout the entire system, from the kindergarten through the junior college; they have eliminated duplication, coördinated the whole, and published tentative syllabi, almost exactly as described at Pasadena. The writer is willing to guarantee that Dr. Proctor and his committees have evolved a curriculum at Sacramento which shows no more duplication, from the grades through the junior college, than is found at Pasadena. "In Sacramento all units have coöperated splendidly," reports Dr. Proctor. Curriculum revision and the elimination of undesirable duplication and overlapping thus is independent of the existence of a two-year or a four-year junior college. At least it has so worked out at Sacramento.

Another phase of overlapping has been mentioned by some writers — the giving of identical courses in college and high school. The statement of President Angell quoted by Dr. Cooper in the last chapter may be questioned, when he speaks of the college freshman being set to do right over again what he has already done in school. In the same paper from which Dr. Cooper quotes, President Angell says: "The mere fact that the two institutions offer the same work is not in itself conclusive evidence of waste." French I, for example, will be given in both college and high school, or in both junior college and senior high school, but it will not ordinarily be taken by the *same student* in both institutions.

The economy of cost argument. Unquestionably one institution can be operated at less expense than two, and in so far as this is true it constitutes an argument for a four-year institution which is particularly potent with the taxpayer. The saving may be somewhat overestimated, however, and there may be other factors that more than offset any financial gain. It is easy to make general statements of economy. What facts can be found with regard to this feature? There are two aspects to be considered: (1) saving in capital outlay, buildings, and grounds; and (2) saving in maintenance and operating costs. These will be considered separately.

Saving in capital outlay. Regarding saving in capital outlay, Harbeson says:[1]

> The cost of a junior college housed in a separate plant in the local community as a two-year institution is far in excess of what it need be if housed in the high school plant. Three secondary schools, the junior high school, the senior high school, and the junior college, all housed in separate plants constitute not only poor educational organization but an intolerable waste of public funds as well.

It must be remembered that the same total school population must be provided for under either form of organizations, with sufficient classrooms in either case. There should be some saving in construction of auditorium, laboratories, and other special features. It should be remembered, however, that the majority of two-year junior colleges are and for some time to come can be housed with the high school, using one wing or one floor of the existing high school building, with common use of auditorium, cafeteria, gymnasium, athletic fields, and other relatively expensive special features and equipment.

[1] In *California Quarterly of Secondary Education*, vol. 4, pp. 45–50. (October, 1928.)

Even in the most expensive case, however, where three complete plants are built instead of two, the savings for two plants only would be much less than 33 per cent, since the same school population must be accommodated in either case. Let us make a liberal estimate, and assume a net saving of 15 to 20 per cent of capital outlay in favor of the six-four-four plan. With the life of a building estimated at twenty to thirty years, this would mean a net annual saving of ½ to 1 per cent of the total building cost. On a half-million-dollar plant, the annual saving on capital outlay would amount to $2500 to $5000 per year — worth saving, of course, but scarcely an "intolerable waste," especially if any educational advantage can be shown as a compensating feature.

Saving in maintenance. The division of current expense among the different items of the budget was exhibited in Figure 33 (page 517). From this it is seen that instructional salaries constitute 67 per cent of the total cost, while all instructional costs are 80 per cent of the total. There can be little, if any, saving in instructional salaries. The same number of classes, with minor exceptions, will have to be maintained in the four-year unit as in the two separate ones. In fact the proponents of the six-four-four plan state that it makes possible better instructors. If this is the case, will not better instructors expect and receive better salaries, thus costing the taxpayer more? There will be some saving in library and laboratory costs, although maintenance costs in them have been seen to vary to a considerable extent on a per capita basis — and the same number of students must be provided for in either case.

The chief saving should be found in the general items of operation, maintenance, and fixed charges. Heat, light, and janitor service will be less, but in two institutions it will be more than two thirds of what it would be in three, because they will be more than two thirds as large since they must accommodate the same total population. If we estimate a saving in each of the items of library, laboratory, and other instructional costs, and in operation, maintenance, and fixed charges of approximately one half (surely a liberal estimate), the maximum saving would amount to approximately fifteen per cent. There would be a saving in the salary of one administrator, but the larger four-year institution would probably require a vice-principal or similar officer whose salary would largely offset this saving.

This is only a rough estimate assuming entirely separate plants. Where the senior high school and junior college are operated in the same plant, as is the case in most institutions, the saving in the adoption of the six-four-four plan would be much less. Pasadena furnishes an excellent example where definite facts can take the place of the type of estimates made in the preceding paragraph. Before the organization of the four-year institution in Pasadena, the two-year junior college and the three-year senior high school were operating independently, but in the same plant. Superintendent Sexson in discussing the economies effected through the administrative organization of the Pasadena Junior College, stated that:[1]

> Inasmuch as the organizations were regarded as separate and distinct institutions, it was necessary to set up separate administrative machinery for the high school and for the junior college.

Under the new form, however, he states that the result was:[2]

> That large savings were effected in administrative offices and in the reduced secretarial staff necessary to handle the unit organization. It is difficult to estimate accurately, how much of a saving was effected by reason of the new organization, but a conservative figure would be twenty per cent of the total overhead.

Assuming the total overhead as 20 per cent of the budget, this means that the net saving was 20 per cent of 20 per cent, or 4 per cent of the entire budget. The budget for 1928–29

[1] Sexson, *op. cit.*, p. 215. [2] Sexson, *loc. cit.*

amounted to $233,000. Truly a saving of $9000 in a budget of a quarter of a million is not to be despised — if it is not obtained at too great a cost of other features. It is somewhat less than might have been anticipated, however, in view of the sweeping claims for economy made for this type of organization. It may be noted that Pasadena ranked sixth in cost per student in average daily attendance among the thirteen California district junior colleges, tabulated in Table 53, p. 509.

Extensive as the junior college plants are in California, and expensive as the institutions housed in them seem to be in operating costs, yet it has already been shown (Figure 36, p. 538) that they constitute only one and one third per cent of the total educational cost in the state. A saving of four per cent, or even 15 per cent of this amount, therefore, is not going to reduce the educational burden in the state enough to cause an immediate thrill on the part of the taxpayers.

With the financial saving thus demonstrated to be such a minor feature, the ultimate criterion must be in terms of educational desirability, not of minor economy.

Economy-of-time argument. That the plan under discussion does save time is undoubtedly true, and forms a valid argument for the four-year junior college — at least in theory. It would be interesting to have data from Pasadena showing what percentage of the students actually graduate in three years instead of four, but sufficient time has not yet elapsed to secure such information. It will probably be only a small proportion. The two-year junior college is not a strait-jacket, however, for the same brilliant student who can finish the four-year course in three years has the opportunity to finish the four-semester course in three semesters.

There are two educational philosophies. One holds that *material* is the basic unit, the other that *time* is the basic unit. Should the student scurry through the curriculum as fast as possible, or should he remain in school the normal amount of time, and if he is especially gifted spend his time in getting just that much more out of a so-called "enriched curriculum," rather than hurrying on to join an advanced group to which he may not be socially adjusted? The writer strongly favors the theory that *time* is the basic unit. He would urge that every student entering junior college should remain for the entire two years, taking only the normal number of units, but being encouraged to do *superior work* in those units, and to benefit by supplementary collateral work, if his ability permits. The economy-of-time argument seems partially true, but not highly important. Should the junior college encourage speed or enrichment?

There are those, too, who point out the fact that college freshmen a century ago were on the average two years younger than they are today. They claim that the graduate of the upper four-year secondary unit can and should be as adequately prepared as his grandfather when he graduated from the four-year college. They overlook the fact, however, that conditions have changed vitally since their grandfathers were educated. We are living in a different age, with different conditions. We cannot go back to the "good old days," and we would not if we could. President Wilbur, of Stanford University, has admirably summarized the new conditions in the following statement:[1]

> The increasing wealth and free time of the American people have prolonged the period of training for our American youth. The growing complexity of a human society which is being remodelled by scientific discovery of all sorts has in itself compelled more understanding on the part of men and women of their environment, and the need of democracy for a better contributing citizenship has become of paramount significance.

The argument of vocational preparation. Dr. Cooper's argument for vocational preparation is difficult to understand

[1] Wilbur, R. L., in *Junior College Journal*, vol. 1, page 3. (October, 1930.)

or to accept. It seems to rest upon a misconception of Dr. Leonard's meaning in the quotation which he uses to prove his case. Dr. Cooper says: "Professor Leonard suggested a permanent field for our proposed upper secondary unit." A careful reading of Dr. Leonard's entire article, however, originally an address before the American Association of Junior Colleges, shows that he was not thinking at all of the four-year, but of the two-year college. A few quotations from his article, of many that might be selected, will clearly establish this point:[1]

> It requires no unusual prophetic vision to see that junior colleges will be transitory institutions unless they find distinctive fields of service.... Are there distinctive fields for the junior college so that it may have a permanent place in the educational scheme? Personally I am convinced that there are distinctive fields which schools of the junior college type, alone, can serve successfully.... Let us examine a few occupations within the middle level, choosing from among those adapted to *full-time* junior college instruction. Pharmacy clearly falls within this level.... The typical course for pharmicists covers two years of study.... Optometry... nursing... commerce... public service... engineering... the great majority of agricultural pursuits, in which our agricultural colleges are interested, are really of the middle level, and require only *two* years of training instead of four or five.... To make a very long story short, the middle level occupations are all potentially open to junior colleges. They represent permanent and distinctive fields for which junior colleges alone can best train prospective workers.... Although there are instances where universities are offering courses of training for middle-level occupations, to encourage this practice is harmful. *Two-year* courses in pharmacy, optometry, secretarial work, salesmanship, etc. — ... state institutions have been forced into these fields. One state institution which I know well used to receive urgent requests for *two-year courses*.... As long as the junior college fails to enter such fields, universities will be pressed to do so.

[1] Leonard, R. J. "The Contributions of a Study of Occupational Levels to Junior College Policy"; in *Proceedings of the Fifth Annual Meeting of the American Association of Junior Colleges*, pp. 94–101. Cincinnati, Ohio, 1925. Italics are not in the original.

Nothing could be clearer from the entire address than that Dr. Leonard was not suggesting a "permanent field for our proposed upper secondary unit." A stronger argument could scarcely be made for the *two-year junior college*, from the vocational or semi-professional point of view, than is found in his address.

In the studies by Koos and Thomas, to which Dr. Cooper also refers, the two-year unit of preparation was the very definition of the occupations suitable for junior college courses in the fields of commerce, agriculture, and engineering. The same definition, essentially, was used by Bennett in his elaborate selection of occupations of junior college grade. These studies have all been summarized in Chapter X. The fact is that the possibility for short, intensive training of two-year duration in various semi-professions is one of the strongest arguments for the two-year junior college. Occupational intentions at the middle of the high-school period are often not formed, or if formed are none too stable.[1] It would be a mistake to start on definite semi-professional training at the beginning of the eleventh grade and continue it over four years. Two years is sufficient, and the later it comes the better. It is hard to see how this argument can be twisted into one supporting the four-year junior college. Even Professor Eby, of Texas, a strong advocate of the six-four-four plan, says that the highly specialized vocational junior college might well continue on its present two-year basis. The numerous private schools of business, commerce, and engineering, to which

[1] Concerning vocational education, Dr. George F. Zook says: "Progress has been discouragingly slow, chiefly, it seems to me, because many if not most boys and girls of high-school age do not begin to think vocationally until about the time they graduate from high school." ("The Junior College Movement"; in *School and Society*, vol. 23, p. 603. May 15, 1926.) Marion Coats, former president of Sarah Lawrence College, says: "Not knowing surely what they want to do, boys and girls are reluctant to commit themselves, and the education which forces them into early decisions is likely to be mistaken." ("The Junior College"; in *Forum*, vol. 80, p. 90. July, 1928.)

Dr. Cooper refers have, for the most part, curricula whose duration is two years or less.

The argument from size. It is not easy to see the significance of the argument from size. If one hundred students is too small a number for a separate two-year unit, how will two hundred be much better for a four-year unit? Athletically it may be a little better off, but scholastically what is the difference? There will be no reduction in the number of small upper-division classes. The additional eleventh- and twelfth-grade students are not going to increase the *size* of the thirteenth- and fourteenth-grade classes. The tendency will be to multiply small local junior colleges unduly, whereas the trend in California, and the best educational opinion everywhere, seems to be distinctly in favor of larger units and the combination of smaller high-school districts, or even entire counties, to form more efficient district junior colleges. This will be made much more difficult, if not impossible, if there is extensive adoption of the four-year unit. In California today the small high school type of junior college, operated administratively in connection with the local high school, is much more nearly like the four-year unit proposed by Dr. Cooper. It requires no argument to show that the institutions of the high school type in the state have been far less successful and far less satisfactory than those of the independent two-year district type.

There would be some advantage in size, since it would reduce the number of teachers giving instruction in more than one subject. In the two-year junior college of two or three hundred students, however, this situation is seldom found.

Superintendent Sexson brings out another phase of the size argument, when he says: [1]

> Almost any city of reasonable size can develop a four-year junior college with a student body of sufficient size to make possible a satisfactory classification of students into homogeneous groups.

[1] Sexson, J. A., *op. cit.*, p. 221.

Homogeneous grouping, however, is very largely a matter of grades. There will be eleventh-, twelfth-, thirteenth-, and fourteenth-grade English classes, whether in two institutions or in one. Homogeneous grouping according to ability into fast, average, and slow sections in the fourteenth grade, is dependent almost entirely upon the number of students *in that grade*, and the situation is not affected by the presence in the same school of any number of eleventh- and twelfth-grade students. In subjects where there is some overlapping of upper- and lower-division students in the same class, the statement might apply to a limited extent, but such cases form the exception rather than the rule. As regards the courses which make up the bulk of the curriculum the situation is not affected, either favorably or adversely, by adding any number of lower-grade students in different classes.

The guidance argument. There is some strength to the guidance argument, but even, as Koos implies in his statement of it, its logic really leads to a single eight-year unit, with a unified guidance policy covering the entire period. As has been pointed out in Chapter XI, junior college guidance is not a matter so much of advice as information, and there is no reason why this cannot be given in different units, and with some benefit through contacts with new personalities and different points of view. In a well-organized guidance program a student's test records, personality ratings, and all other pertinent personnel data in a constantly increasing amount accompany him in every transition from the kindergarten through the university. The work that is already being done in the guidance field at the junior college level, as reported in Chapter XI, is by no means a failure. The whole guidance field at all levels needs much work done upon it before it is perfected, but there seems hardly enough to this argument from the junior college standpoint to make it a very weighty one for the four-year institution.

The argument of flexibility of the curriculum. Mr. Sexson's statements in regard to the flexibility of the curriculum should be admitted. It is a question how many students are affected by such an arrangement — a question that can only be answered by a study of the records of a large group of students. This seems to presuppose, however, an organization of the college by year-strata as in the elementary grades with grade promotion, rather than organization primarily by subject-matter, with subject promotion and credit.

The argument of analogy with German education. The German *gymnasium* is a single unit, not two four-year separate institutions. Furthermore, the conditions of the German two-class educational system are so very different from the American single educational ladder for all classes, that analogy with German education is remote. It is worthy of note also that the German educator, Friedrich Paulsen, twenty-five years ago, expressed dissatisfaction with the unreasonably long period of secondary education in Germany, and looked admiringly at the American college method as a possible relief, "with more freedom than the secondary school, more direction than required by professional study." [1]

A more convincing answer, however, is found in the experience of the American Lutheran Church. To train educated leaders, Americanized *gymnasia* were established in the United States as early as 1839, with the curricula of the German humanistic *gymnasia*. The intellectual advancement of the young men was equal to that obtained in a high school and the two years of junior college. After extensive study, the general convention of the Church, in 1920, decided to change all the schools of this type, nine in number, into four-year high schools, and two-year classical junior colleges.[2]

[1] *Monatschrift für Höhere Schulen*, vol. 4, p. 65 ff. (1905.)

[2] Buenger, T. *A Change of Gymnasia to Junior Colleges.* United States Bureau of Education, Bulletin no. 19, pp. 51–52. (1922.)

The compulsory school law argument. It is true that in thirty-one states sixteen years is the compulsory school age, but there are ten states in which it is seventeen or eighteen years, and the tendency seems to be to raise it rather than to lower it.[1] Further, we have seen in discussing the psychological argument that less than half the students at Pasadena in a single grade were actually sixteen years of age where theoretically they should all be. This argument, therefore, seems to have a maximum efficiency of less than half the students in less than two thirds of the states, with the probability of a further shrinkage as more states advance their age limits.

The inquiry may also be made whether it is an unmixed blessing to have the school unit coincide with the compulsory age limit. At the present time there is a strong tendency for a boy who arrives at the age of sixteen at the middle of his high school course to go on and finish it, possibly taking special trade or commercial work in the last two years, thus securing two years of education beyond the legal requirement, which is of great value in making him more than a common laborer. The same boy is much less likely to secure any further education if he "finishes" the lower four-year unit at sixteen. It is much harder to enter a new and strange institution than to continue in the old one. It is not contemplated, as the writer understands it, that the lower unit should offer actual trade and commercial courses. The compulsory-age argument applies to but a fraction of the school population, and it is doubtful how beneficial it is even to those to whom it does apply. It is logical, but of doubtful desirability.

The argument of superior teachers. We have no desire to argue the question as to whether Pasadena has superior

[1] In twenty-eight states the compulsory-attendance age has been increased since 1914. In all but one of the ten having a limit of seventeen or eighteen years, the change has occurred since 1914. (Information furnished by W. W. Keesecker, of United States Office of Education.)

teachers. We are sure that it has. We inquire, however, whether it is the four-year junior college with its accompanying "dignity and scope," or the superior salary, enticing climate, and excellent administrative control of the schools of Pasadena that are chiefly determinative. The average salary of junior college principals in California, in 1928–29, according to official state reports, was $5613; at Pasadena it was $237 higher. The average salary of instructors was $2754; at Pasadena it was $2780. Has Hillsboro attracted markedly superior teachers? There is little evidence of it. The instructors have the heaviest teaching load of any of the municipal junior colleges in Texas. The average Texas salary is $1997; at Hillsboro it is $1933.[1] From all reports, very superior teaching is found at Stephens College. Is this due to "dignity and scope"? Possibly so. It is worth noticing, however, that the typical salary of a professor at Stephens is $6500, of an instructor in the state,[2] $2175. Given similar resources, one might be able to secure a moderately high grade of administrators and instructors even in a two-year college.

If salaries and living conditions are similar, it is by no means certain that the four-year junior college would attract the superior teachers. In the universities, the better professors find it much more interesting and stimulating to teach upper-division classes. Does not the same principle hold at a lower level? Would not many instructors prefer to teach students of collegiate grade and maturity, than those of high school rank? In the two-year institution they are assured of all collegiate-grade classes.

[1] Reid, J. R. *Texas Municipal Junior Colleges.* Bulletin of the State Department of Education, vol. 5, no. 5, p. 42. Austin, Texas, 1929.

[2] Freed, W. J. *A Study of the Salaries and Teaching Loads in the Denominational Four-year Colleges and Private Junior Colleges in the United States*, p. 17. Tacoma, Washington, 1929.

DISADVANTAGES OF SIX-FOUR-FOUR PLAN

The educational millennium that is within our grasp if we will but adopt the six-four-four plan is thus portrayed by Principal Harbeson, of Pasadena:[1]

> What a wonderful opportunity looms before the high schools and junior colleges in the six-four-four plan of school organization!... in the formation of a great upper secondary school — an institution open to the masses and providing educational guidance and educational opportunities for all the young people of America. From the union of the upper high school years with those of the junior college there will emerge the great American secondary school of tomorrow, strong in spirit, large in numbers, and powerful in influence.

Before accepting this enthusiastic appraisal completely it may be well to consider some possible objections to the plan. At least half a dozen distinct and important disadvantages, difficulties, and dangers, may be pointed out:

1. Difficulty of intercollegiate competition.
2. Difficulty of adjustment to existing administrative practice.
3. Difficulty of adjustment to varying geographical conditions.
4. Difficulty of too great variety in age of students.
5. Difficulty of adjustment of instruction to different levels.
6. Danger of stopping school at compulsory age limit.

We will consider each of these difficulties, in order.

Difficulty of intercollegiate competition. Chapter XXIII has shown the essential place that student activities play in the complete program of the effective junior college. While interschool competition may not be essential, in theory, to the success of such activities, yet it cannot be denied that great zest and stimulus to such activities, especially in athletic and forensic lines, is given by such contests between different schools. With what schools can the four-year junior college have such athletic contests — with two-year junior colleges, or with four-year high schools? Neither type of school, quite properly, feels that competition with the four-year junior college is fair.

[1] Harbeson, J. W., *op. cit.*, p. 50.

The only alternative is for the four-year institution to maintain "upper division" teams, who play with other junior colleges, and "lower division" teams who play with high schools. This is exactly what is done at Pasadena, but this does not make for unity of spirit and student relations within the institution. The four-year institution is not a unit, from the point of view of student activities, but an awkward hybrid.

The ready answer of the six-four-four advocates, of course, is that this condition is but temporary, a mere transitional annoyance which is only incidental, and that it will disappear as soon as sufficient four-year junior colleges are established to organize separate athletic conferences of their own. This is perfectly true, if and when a majority or a large number of schools adopt this form of organization. The practical administrator, however, facing facts and not theories, may well pause to wonder just how long it is likely to take to achieve such a result, when over twenty years of argument and effort have resulted in the organization of less than a dozen such institutions in widely scattered parts of the country. With hundreds of two-year junior colleges and thousands of senior high schools more or less definitely committed to their type of organization, the transition is not likely to be rapid.

It may be freely admitted that this objection to the six-four-four plan has no force whatever, if all schools are organized on such a basis. Until such a condition holds, however, and it may be seriously doubted whether such a consummation is in immediate prospect, the practical man must consider this situation as a very real and immediate difficulty in his own junior college if he contemplates a change to the six-four-four basis.

Difficulty of adjustment to existing administrative practice. Like the preceding objection, the difficulty of adjustment to administrative practice would also vanish if the six-four-four plan could be adopted *in toto* in all parts of the country by a single administrative decree. This would be possible in a strongly centralized government with all educational organization under the control of a single cabinet officer, as in France, but it is impossible in a nation such as the United States, so strongly committed throughout its whole existence to local independence, initiative, and self-determination in educational matters. As already pointed out, there is not one system of secondary school organization in the United States, but no less than forty-three, according to the classification of the Federal Office of Education. By reference to Figure 40, page 653, which illustrates the principal types of these organizations, it will be seen that the two-year junior college articulates with all but three of these main types. The only exceptions are the eight-six (practically obsolete), six-four-four, and five-four-four types, of which all told there seem at the present time to be less than a dozen examples in the country. On the other hand, there are over eighteen thousand units of the other types, with any of which the two-year junior college articulates without bisection and disruption of the secondary school unit below it. In spite of all that has been said and done toward reorganization on the junior high school basis in this century, the four-year high school is still the prevailing type, there being over twelve thousand such institutions in the country. Are students in all of these institutions to be denied the opportunity of the junior college, unless and until such time as the four-year high schools which they are attending are willing to cut themselves in two in the middle, in order to achieve the six-four-four type of organization? With transfer of students, mobility of population, necessity for articulation with the high school units as actually found — it is quite evident as a practical matter that the two-year institution is the one that will best fit the great variety of educational conditions actually existing in the country.

Difficulty of adjustment to varying geographical conditions. The six-four-four plan may be feasible in cities, but is it equally adaptable to rural conditions? The tendency in different parts of the country, notably in California and Mississippi, is toward the development of regional or county junior colleges. One of the greatest faults of the junior college as it has developed to date is the large number of institutions with very small enrollments, as shown in detail in Chapter II. The six-four-four advocates say that the quickest, surest, and best way to cure this situation is to include the eleventh and twelfth grades, thereby doubling or tripling the enrollment. They overlook the fact, however, that the chief objection to the small junior college scholastically is not that it has too few individuals in the institution, but too few in individual classes. As already shown in an earlier section, in discussing the argument of size, increasing the number of twelfth-grade students is going to have little effect on the scholastic situation of those two years in advance of them. The most successful practical method for increasing the size of the institution is by combination of two or more existing high school districts to form a single junior college district. Formation of such union districts, in some cases to cover the entire county, is definitely encouraged in the legislation in force in Texas, in Mississippi, and in California. County-unit organization, too, will be the natural unit of organization in the so-called "county-unit states," of which there is an increasing number.

The tendency toward larger unit organization in California has been marked during the past two years. Until 1926 there were no union junior college districts in the state. Since that time, however, both San Bernardino and Marin have been formed by the combination of two high school districts. Santa Rosa, after several years of struggle to maintain itself, in 1930 annexed an adjacent high school district to form a union junior college district, with distinct advantage to the various high schools concerned. Modesto and other institutions are contemplating similar annexation of territory to enlarge their districts. While it is not impossible to form union four-year junior colleges, it is so difficult as an administrative matter as to be practically out of the question. To persuade a group of high school districts to unite in the formation of a *two-year* junior college as a culmination of secondary education is not an easy matter, although it does not disrupt their own institutions; to urge successfully that in addition such union must mean *sacrificing the last two years* of each of their local high schools in order to make a central *four-year* junior college, is a task before which even the most ardent six-four-four crusader might well pause and consider.

An analogous situation is found in California in the effort to promote the junior high school. It has had a remarkable adoption in the cities of the state, where segregation of grades has been easy, but the difficulties of securing the coöperation of a group of local districts for a single junior high school in a rural section has proved all but insurmountable.[1] Even such a vigorous advocate of the six-four-four plan as Dean W. W. Kemp, of the University of California, admits that the plan is not applicable under the variety of geographical conditions found in California. He says: [2]

> It is recognized, of course, that there will be need of other programs than the six-four-four in a great many districts. The six-three-three-two plan will best fit certain sections. Take the situation surrounding the Marin Junior College for example. It will probably be a great many years before a six-four-four program would be advisable for that region.

[1] For discussion of this phase of the situation, see the recent book edited by W. M. Proctor and Nicholas Ricciardi, *The Junior High School; Its Organization and Administration.* (Stanford University Press, Stanford University, California, 1930.) Chapter 15 (pp. 272–94) tells how such unionization was accomplished after much trouble, tribulation, and ingenuity in two districts of the state under peculiar local conditions.

[2] Kemp, W. W. "The Junior College in California"; in *California Quarterly of Secondary Education*, vol. 5, pp. 193–94. (January, 1930.)

It is perfectly possible, of course, to have quite distinct types of organization in the city and in the country. It may be seriously questioned, however, whether even in America, with its astonishing variety of educational types, it is wise to work toward such a definite differentiation of educational organization, as a permanent policy, for urban and rural communities.

Another phase of the geographical question is of interest. In the larger cities, is it proposed to establish a series of junior colleges; that is, to make every high school into a junior college? Los Angeles has at least thirty-two senior high schools. Would the adoption of the six-four-four plan mean thirty-two four-year junior colleges? San Francisco has the six-four-four plan under consideration, but they are faced by the practical difficulty of six or seven junior colleges in the different high schools of the city if they adopt the plan.

Difficulty of too great variety in age and interests of students. Is there too wide a spread in age, experience, and background of students in the four-year junior college unit for the best educational results? Are high school juniors and college sophomores sufficiently alike in physical, mental, social, and personal characteristics that they can be best handled in a single institution, as a single administrative unit, with a single set of regulations? There is not only theory, but some evidence beginning to accumulate, where the plan has been tried, that the affirmative answer to this question is open to doubt. The college sophomore is much more mature, can be given greater independence, does not require such rigid restrictions, is on a different social plane, and constitutes a very different disciplinary problem from the high school junior.

Even at Pasadena there are evidences that there is not the homogeneity that is desirable if an institution is to be administered as an integral unit. Take the single matter of use of spare time outside of scheduled classes. In college and university, a student is supposed to be mature enough not to be compelled to observe stated study hours. In high school, on the other hand, almost universal experience indicates that the average student has not developed sufficient sense of responsibility to be given such freedom. Definite assignment to specific rooms every hour of the school day, whether in classes or not, has been found commonly desirable for high school students. At Pasadena, lower-division students are assigned to study hall in all vacant periods; upper-division students are free from such restrictions and may go and come as they please, unless their work is below passing, in which case they are required to observe study hours, also. Is such a situation in keeping with "college" atmosphere, and conducive to unity and harmony of feeling in the student body?

Superintendent Sexson stated, at Atlantic City in 1930, that Pasadena Junior College had about seventy clubs, "all of which are open to students in the entire four years." A check of the Pasadena catalogue, however, shows seventy such clubs and organizations listed, but with the definite statement in the announcement of them that only *forty-five* are open to all students. The remaining twenty-five, over a third of the entire number, are definitely restricted to upper-division or to lower-division students. This is further evidence of lack of homogeneity in social and student relations on the more informal basis of student clubs. There is no evidence in the catalogue, of course, of the extent to which the forty-five organizations technically open to upper- and lower-division students are actually dominated by the upper-division students.

One of the most thoughtful of the author's students made the following statement: [1]

I have had the opportunity of watching a combination of the last two years of high school and the first two years of college fail quite miserably. The buildings, equipment, faculty, situation, and other conditions usually making for success were possessed in their finest

[1] Louise Artz, in a term paper at Stanford University.

and most modern forms, but the spirit of the high school college was deadening. The high school students disliked being with older students, and the dignity of the college students was decidedly offended by the combination.

This may be called unreasoning prejudice, but it is an attitude that must be recognized, and it is probably indicative of more than prejudice — of rather wide differences in many ways between students who differ in age and maturity at this period of life by as much as four years.

In an address at Fort Worth, Texas, in 1928, Dr. W. M. Proctor, of Stanford University, chairman of the executive committee of Menlo Junior College, said, in speaking of the "double-four plan": [1]

> The handling of social privileges also demands attention. Are high school seniors and juniors ready for the larger freedom now accorded two-year junior college students? We have been studying this problem carefully, and have reached the decision that our high school seniors are now ready for the transition, but that the high school juniors are not.... Since it will be two or three years before we can make the transfer to the Stanford campus site, we will have time to determine whether eleventh-grade students can be socially assimilated into the four-year junior college organization.

A statement of this character, from an institution that is doing such outstanding experimental work with the four-year unit, indicates that it is only an assumption as yet that the high school junior is readily assimilable into the student body — that possibly a little hesitation is permissible before accepting the four-year junior college as the "great American secondary school of tomorrow!"

An even more significant piece of evidence in this connection is the action of Edinburg Junior College, Texas, which, after experimenting for two years with the four-year plan gave it up,

[1] Proctor, W. M. "Possibilities of the Double-Four Organization in Private Secondary Schools"; in *Proceedings of the Ninth Annual Meeting of the American Association of Junior Colleges*, p. 24. Fort Worth, Texas, 1928.

and in the fall of 1929 moved the high school students into a separate building, primarily because "senior high and college students do not mix well."[1] Edinburg furnishes, not theory, but experience and fact. It may be that an ounce of Edinburg fact is worth a pound or more of educational theory.

Difficulty of adjustment of instruction to different levels. A corollary to the difficulty just discussed is the difficulty of adjusting instruction to different levels. Many instructors, teaching both high school and junior college courses, have stated that they have difficulty in preserving collegiate standards, atmosphere, methods, and point of view in their college classes, while at the same time giving instruction in high school classes. The teaching on the college level should be somewhat different in type, tone, and method if it is to recognize advancing maturity and is to be a suitable transition to the still more complete freedom and responsibility characteristic of the university classroom. It seems to be difficult for many teachers to maintain such a standard and also do work of high school grade at the same time. Dr. Eby, of the University of Texas, says:[2]

> The instructor who teaches both high school and junior college classes will be tempted to use the same method with both groups, and in this way do less effective work. The method of instruction ought to be more advanced for the junior college group.

Of course this applies to the junior college and the high school as separate institutions, but the subject matter taught and the instructional methods should not differ materially, if at all, where the four years of work are combined in a single institution. The skillful teacher can undoubtedly adapt his work to levels of ability and development differing by a four-year

[1] Statement in a letter of August 15, 1930, from H. U. Miles, dean of the junior college and acting superintendent of schools at Edinburg.

[2] Eby, F. "The Junior College Movement in Texas"; in *Texas Outlook*, vol. 11, p. 11. (February, 1928.)

interval, but it will not be easy in many cases. As a rule a more uniform method of instruction adapted to work of collegiate students can be developed in the two-year institution, where it does not require a constant effort to make the adjustment between different levels.

Danger of stopping school at compulsory age limit. The danger of stopping school at compulsory age has already been pointed out in a previous paragraph, in discussing the implications of the compulsory attendance laws. If a student is required to attend school until age sixteen, but finds himself in the middle of the high school course at that time, he is more likely to go on for two years more than he is to enter a new institution, as would be required when the sixteen-year point falls between the two units of the four-four plan. Thus the four-year junior college tends to discourage voluntary attendance of students beyond the compulsory attendance age limit, rather than to encourage it. It has already been pointed out, of course, that this applies only to a portion of the students and in a portion of the states. As far as it does apply, however, it may be considered another disadvantage of the six-four-four plan.

QUESTIONS AND PROBLEMS

1. Examine the eleven arguments in Chapter XXV in favor of the six-four-four plan, and see how many of them are as valid for a single six-year or eight-year secondary unit as for two distinct units.
2. Examine the eleven arguments in Chapter XXV in favor of the six-four-four plan, and see how many of them are arguments for the junior college in general, but not uniquely for the six-four-four plan.
3. Look up and evaluate from the psychological point of view all the arguments for various types of junior college organization.
4. Examine Koos's determination of overlapping in high school and college. Do you feel that the various processes by which he measured it are valid? Why?
5. Should there be uniformity of type of educational organization throughout the country? Throughout one state? Why?

6. How has the average age of college freshmen changed during the past century? What significance has it for the discussion of this chapter?
7. Look up data on change of occupational intention, especially during the high school period. What implications does it have for the discussion of this chapter?
8. Should a student hurry through college as rapidly as possible, or remain the standard length of time and get everything possible during the time? Why?
9. How extensive should be the development of the institutions on the six-four-four basis to make athletic relations satisfactory?
10. Should junior college students be assigned to study hall or library during free periods?
11. Can college standards be satisfactorily developed and maintained in a junior college housed in a high school plant? How?

SUGGESTED READINGS

See list at the end of Chapter XXVII.

CHAPTER XXVII

THE TWO-YEAR JUNIOR COLLEGE

There should be a college course two years in length, carefully constructed as a thing in itself. — NICHOLAS MURRAY BUTLER.[1]

Contents of this chapter. This chapter, in a certain sense, is a continuation of the argument of the preceding chapter. It presents the advantages of the two-year type of junior college, considers the judgment and the experience of history regarding both the two-year and the four-year types, considers certain objections that have been advanced to the two-year junior college, and in conclusion suggests the need for further experimentation.

ADVANTAGES OF THE TWO-YEAR UNIT

There will next be considered eight advantages which are characteristic of two-year types of organization for the junior college years.

1. Ease of adjustment to existing administrative and geographical conditions.
2. Advantages of new contacts.
3. Development of leadership.
4. Transitional advantages.
5. Advantages for vocational preparation.
6. Advantages of homogeneity of age.
7. Distinctive collegiate atmosphere.
8. Psychology of the American people.

Ease of adjustment to existing administrative and geographical conditions. This very real practical advantage of the two-year junior college need be only touched upon briefly at this point. It has already been discussed in pointing out the

[1] Butler, N. M. "The Length of the Baccalaureate Course"; in *Proceedings of National Education Association*, p. 503. (1903.)

practical difficulties of the four-year unit from the administrative and geographical points of view. The flexibility of the two-year institution, its possibility of adjustment to all prevailing types of secondary school organization with a minimum of administrative friction and realignment, forms one of the strongest practical arguments in favor of the two-year institution. An Ohio educator says that there are those who feel that the six-four-four plan may become the typical city secondary school system of a half-century hence. Most practical educators, however, especially in the junior college field, are far more interested in developments in the next decade than in those of a half-century hence. If we are to wait a half-century for the justification and fruition of the six-four-four plan, then there is all the more reason to consider the present very practical and definite administrative advantages of the two-year unit for purposes of the next decade or two. The flexibility and adaptability of the two-year junior college is one of its very significant present advantages.

Advantages of new contacts. The advantage of new contacts on the part of the student is worth considering. There is a general feeling in European education that students gain considerably by attending a variety of institutions. There is considerable migration of students, especially at the university level. In America there has been more of a tendency for a student to remain in the same institution for a long period of time. There are some advantages in this, from the standpoint of long-standing friendships, interests, and loyalties. On the other hand there is a tendency toward restricted points of view and continuation in a rut. There is value in change, as well as in continuity. There has been a marked increase in college migration and flexibility in the United States in the past few years, as witness the "floating university," the junior year abroad, the transfer from college to university at the end of the junior year, and increasing individual transfer. The student undoubtedly gains much in educational outlook and breadth of vision by contact with a variety of instructors and with a different student body. The wealth of new and stimulating contacts in another institution are a very valuable experience for the average student. To have three such experiences, instead of two, in the entire range of his "secondary educational" experience, is often highly profitable and stimulating.

Development of leadership. Development of leadership is an exceedingly important function of college education. In the long run, it is the college men and women of today who are to be the country's leaders of tomorrow. One of the most important agencies for the development of leadership is that of student activities. It is quite obvious, however, that mere membership in student clubs, societies, teams, or other organizations does not in itself develop leadership to any marked extent. Voting for leaders in an organization is not productive of leadership and initiative on the part of the rank and file. Vicarious training for leadership is not likely to be highly successful. It is the holding of responsible offices that is most potent. One learns to do by doing. It is the president, the manager, the captain, and the committee chairman who develop real leadership in the group. It is perfectly natural in the four-year institutions that the majority of such positions go to the upper classmen. In fact it is inevitable and right. This fact is recognized but rather unsatisfactorily excused by Superintendent Sexson of Pasadena, when he says:[1]

> It is true, however, as would be expected, that the outstanding positions of leadership are occupied by the thirteenth and fourteenth grades. This condition, however, merely recognizes the fact that the whole four years are operating as a single institution, and the students in the eleventh and twelfth grades will be given the oppor-

[1] Sexson, J. A. "The Organization and Administration of the Four-Year Junior College"; in *Fourteenth Yearbook*, Department of Secondary School Principals, p. 221. (March, 1930.)

tunity of increased training in leadership *when they arrive in the upper division.*

With the high school and junior college as separate units, the same student has two opportunities for such training in leadership. In the two-year junior college he waits but one year, instead of three, for election to the most responsible offices in student organizations. It may not be as important an office, but the potentialities of it for training in leadership do not depend upon the size of the office but on the way in which the individual fills it when given the opportunity. Opportunity comes far more quickly in the two-year institution.

Transitional advantages. Much was written and said in the earlier years of the century regarding the "classic gap" between the elementary school and the high school. The transition was too sudden and abrupt from one institution to the other. As a result the junior high school was developed, which among other valuable contributions acted as a transitional institution and has succeeded very largely in closing the gap formerly so noticeable.

Similarly there has been an equally bad gap, in most cases, between high school and university. The tragic freshman mortality in many universities has been pointed out in a previous chapter. The junior college, like the junior high school, has operated to close this unfortunate gap and make the transition easier from high school restrictions to university independence. The development of these two transitional institutions has broken up what were formerly two hazardous and often disastrous steps of unnecessary difficulty, into four much shorter and easier ones. The situation may be illustrated graphically by Figure 41. The "risers" of the educational stairway have been shortened and the upward progress of the student made "safe and sane."

Experience has shown that the jumps from the grade school to the four-year high school, and again from the four-year high school to the four-year college, were often too long for safety and happiness. Have we any reason to suppose that transitions from one unit to the other of the six-four-four plan will not be equally difficult and unhappy in many cases? The

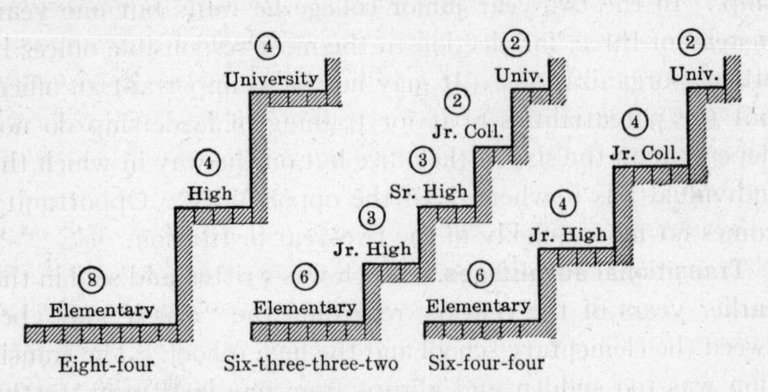

FIG. 41. COMPARISON OF THREE METHODS OF TRANSITION FROM ELEMENTARY SCHOOL TO UNIVERSITY LEVEL

length of the units has not been changed — they have only been shifted two years. Is it not likely that transition from the upper four-year unit to the university may still be fraught with difficulty and peril? The tendency of a quarter century of American education has been toward breaking up educational progress into a larger number of easier steps with shorter transitions. A study of most of the reorganizational plans proposed will amply substantiate this statement. The retention and solidification of the four-year unit, or rather of two of them in the six-four-four plan, is not in line with this apparently desirable educational tendency.

The transitional function is actually accomplished in a multiplicity of ways. It is found in increased freedom and responsibility, in modified classroom methods and requirements, in independence in the use of the library, in freedom from study hall requirements and other necessary high school restrictions, and in more mature disciplinary methods.

Advantages for vocational preparation. The unique opportunity of the two-year junior college to furnish intensive semi-professional courses two years in length has already been stressed sufficiently, in the refutation of the argument which claimed this as a special advantage of the four-year institution. It is here only desired to mention it as one of the very important positive factors which should be included in a list of the outstanding advantages of the two-year institution. Numerous examples of its effectiveness have been presented in Chapter X.

Advantage of homogeneity of age. Much stress has been placed on the advantage of the four-year institution from the point of view of adjustment to ages of psychological maturity. This feature has already been discussed. Here it is only desired to point out an entirely non-controversial feature — that the age-group and its accompanying physical, social, educational, and psychological characteristics, whatever they may be, is certainly much more nearly homogeneous in this respect in the two-year institution. Even if as many as ninety per cent of the students in the upper four-year unit were physiologically mature, one hundred per cent of those in the upper two-year period would be, with whatever psychological advantage may come from this greater homogeneity.

Distinctive collegiate atmosphere. College atmosphere is elusive and intangible when a definition is attempted, but it is very real and important to achieve, and not difficult to recognize. It probably can be maintained in either a four-year or a two-year junior college, but the effort is less likely to be successful in the former case. It is doubtful whether calling high-school juniors and seniors "college" students ("lower-division college students," at Pasadena) is going to make them real college students in the eyes of high school graduates, upper-division students, their parents, or the public. The great danger is that the four-year junior college in which normally a considerable preponderance of the students will be found in the two high school years, will tend to be more "high-schoolish" in atmosphere than collegiate. When the student has graduated from high school — a well-established educational landmark in parent and pupil consciousness — and then goes to college, even if only to "junior college," he feels the distinct break in atmosphere, spirit, and traditions.[1] He is much less likely to have this feeling in an institution which begins at the middle of the high school period.

There is enough difficulty in developing a college atmosphere where the junior college and the high school are administratively separate, as many junior college administrators can testify. Thus Dean R. W. Goddard, of the Rochester, Minnesota, Junior College says:[2]

> My experience in seven years' work in the field has brought me to the realization of the difficulty of creating a college atmosphere. It is exceedingly difficult for the students and some of the faculty members to get away from high school methods and customs.

This difficulty is only accentuated in a four-year junior college. Although separate buildings are not essential to the development of real college life and atmosphere, undoubtedly they are very helpful and desirable when an institution is of sufficient size to warrant them.

Psychology of the American people. For generations it has been the deepest desire of thousands of American parents to give their sons and daughters the benefits of a "college" education. Going to college has been the great American ambition, and it is rapidly becoming the great American habit. America may not know exactly what the college stands for, and it may not recognize the technical distinctions between "secondary"

[1] For an expression of the viewpoint of students, see resolutions of the California Junior College Student Presidents Association, in *Junior College Journal*, vol. 1, p. 486. (May, 1931.)

[2] In a letter to the author, February 6, 1928.

and higher education, but it is very sure that college means something distinctive and worthwhile. America has a fairly definite concept, too, of the high school and of a definite point in educational progress marked by high school graduation. In the popular mind college means an institution in advance of high school graduation, not merely a glorified and amplified high school. It is difficult enough to get the notion into the public consciousness that the two-year junior college is real college; it will be far more difficult for it to feel that "college" is a centaur-like hybrid, half high school and half college. It is not only a matter of the psychology of the public, but of that of the students as well. Thus Dr. Obrien, of the University of Kansas, says:[1]

> The criticism has been seriously offered by university professors to the effect that students coming from junior colleges still have the high school viewpoint as juniors in the university. They say virtually what some speakers on this program have stated — perhaps inadvertently, perhaps all too truly — that we have actually brought the college *down* to the student.

If there is a danger that the present existing junior college will be brought *down* to the student, and it must be recognized that there is such a danger, there is still greater danger that it will be brought *down* to him in the four-year unit which in the lower half has more than half of the students of high school grade.

The friends of the four-year institutions do not consider this matter important. They dismiss it all as mere "tradition" and "prejudice." Thus Koos says:[2]

> One may summarize all these arguments for separation by saying that they are prompted by the mere tradition of separation of col-

[1] Obrien, F. P. "Conditions which Justify Establishing a Junior College"; in *Proceedings of the Eighth Annual Meeting of the American Association of Junior Colleges*, p. 79. Chicago, Illinois, 1928.

[2] Koos, L. V. "Progress and Problems of the Junior College"; in *Proceedings of the Eighth Annual Meeting of the American Association of Junior Colleges*, p. 71. Chicago, Illinois, 1928.

lege from high school, and are not of the more fundamental character of the considerations supporting integration of junior college with high school work now to be reviewed. They have at most a temporary significance only.

Whether we call it "psychology" or "tradition," it is certain that this feeling regarding college education is deeply imbedded in the fundamental consciousness of the American people, and that it is a powerful factor that must be considered. Even traditions in a country of one hundred and twenty million people are not to be lightly cast aside as having "at most a temporary significance only." It is more than likely that after even a half-century of six-four-four promotion the college "tradition" will remain quite fundamentally fixed in the psychology of the American people.

Koos recognizes the expediency of temporary separation, but feels that a few years will be sufficient to modify it. He says:[1]

> There is the feeling on the part of parents of some prospective students where the work is provided in connection with the high school that it can be "only more high school work anyway" and that, therefore, it is not worth their children's time to attend, especially if they can afford to send them to "college." While the best view that can be taken of the work of the first two college years is that it is secondary and not higher, it may be expedient, in order to secure all desirable encouragement of the new unit in some localities, to effect at least partial separation until the tradition of attending the local junior college has been established.

Then quietly annex the upper two years of high school and the unsuspecting public will be none the wiser! It will all be "college"!

Of course the six-four-four advocates have a quite simple solution for the situation. Just drop "junior" from the vocabulary entirely. Call the lower four-year unit "high

[1] Koos, L. V., *op. cit.*, p. 70.

school," and the upper one "college." Then America can go to college — only beginning two years earlier. There is already a bewildering array of institutions that call themselves "colleges," from barber colleges up. Surely it would do no harm to drop the "junior" and have still another variety of college. It should be remembered, however, that there are some hundreds of standard four-year colleges in this country, almost all of them definitely built upon a foundation of a four-year high school course, and that these are not going to perish over-night, nor for a long time to come. Reasons have already been presented in a previous chapter why it is desirable and seems likely that the term "junior college" will be a permanent addition to our educational vocabulary, and these need not be repeated here.[1] If all high schools and colleges in the country could be abolished by legislative fiat, the long historical development blotted from the memory of the people, and the six-four-four plan be organized *de novo*, it would be possible to call its upper two units merely high school and college. At the rate of progress shown by the six-four-four plan during the present century, however, it is likely to be many decades before it will be the *prevailing* type of institution, sufficient to arrogate to itself the proprietary rights in commonly accepted terms, and insist that other uses of the terms are but temporary and unwarranted usurpations on the part of other institutions. If, on the other hand, it insists that it is high school and college, when thousands of other well established institutions already bear such names but with a different meaning, it will only make the existing confusion worse confounded. It is feared that the fundamental psychology, or "tradition" if you will, of the American people will not be seriously affected by the use of any such naïvely assumptive nomenclature. It is rather significant that President W. F. Doughty of Hillsboro Junior College, the earliest five-four-four institution in the country, quite frankly

[1] See page 363.

prefers the name "senior school" to "junior college" for the upper four-year unit. He says:[1]

> The third grouping includes grades ten and eleven of the traditional high school [in Texas] together with the freshman and sophomore years of college, ordinarily mis-named the junior college, and is designated the senior school, being adapted to later adolescence.

Is this not a sincere recognition of the fact that the upper four-year unit after all is not "college"?

THE ARGUMENT FROM HISTORY AND EXPERIENCE

Introductory. An argument from history and experience is never conclusive. There is no assurance that what is, or what has been, necessarily should be. Yet the argument from history is often enlightening, and, combined with other facts and arguments, it often forms valuable corroborative material. It is of especial significance in the present instance, because the two-year junior college, the three-year junior high school, and the six-four-four plan are so nearly of common age and geographical propinquity in origin and early development.

Origin of the three movements. It has been pointed out, in the previous chapter, that the six-four-four plan was first proposed in California in 1908, while the junior high school movement was launched at Berkeley, in the same state, in 1910, and the first two-year junior college in the state was established at Fresno in the same year, in accordance with the enabling legislation of 1907.[2] Consider now the following facts:

Since the first three-year junior high school was established, in Berkeley in 1910, it has spread until in 1928 there were at least 1818

[1] Doughty, W. F. "The Five-four-four Plan of Coördinating the Junior College"; in *Texas Outlook*, vol. 11, p. 17. (October, 1927.)

[2] We do not forget that the first public junior college now existing is found in Joliet, dating from 1902. Its general influence on the growth of the public junior college movement has not been marked, however, in the way that the California development has. Nor do we forget the few earlier private junior colleges in Texas. The present section is concerned essentially with the public junior college movement.

such institutions. While these constitute but 10 per cent of the high schools of the country, they are the largest group of "reorganized" schools of the various types under trial, and 24 per cent of the ninth-grade enrollment of the country is found in them. In twenty years the junior high school has certainly made a place for itself.

Since the first public two-year junior college in California (and second in the country) was established, in Fresno in 1910 (or authorized in 1907), it has spread until in 1930 there were at least 171 public junior colleges in the country with an enrollment of over 39,000 students. In twenty years the two-year junior college has certainly made a place for itself.

Since the six-four-four plan was first proposed, in California in 1908, almost two decades passed before the first institution of this type was organized, and by 1930, the number, even including the private institutions, could be counted on the fingers of the two hands. Why has not the six-four-four plan in the same twenty years, with the many advantages claimed for it, kept pace with the other two in this race in which all three had so nearly an even running start?

It surely has not been for lack of advocacy on the part of an imposing array of vigorous and powerful friends. It may be entirely right, and the other two plans entirely wrong, but it seems a little strange that, with such a long time to prove itself, actual results of the six-four-four plan are as yet so very meager.

Why change again? Even though the three-year junior high school has shown such growth, as an institution it is far from universally accepted. Does it not seem a little unfortunate, to say the least, after two decades of effort to get the junior high school idea into the consciousness of the country, to turn now and say, "after all, the six-three-three plan is entirely wrong. Don't adopt it. Or, if you have adopted it, junk it. It is the six-four-four plan that represents the ultimate, the *summum bonum* of educational reorganization."

When Koos advocated the six-four-four plan in his Harvard University address in 1922, it was Professor Inglis who urged that it should not be proposed in the East, since they were only beginning to adjust themselves to the underlying philosophy and practical application of the six-three-three plan, and that it would confuse and not clarify the situation to propose a six-four-four plan at such a time. In the same vein, in 1930, E. E. Cortright, of Bridgeport, Connecticut, in discussing the six-four-four plan, wrote:[1]

> Our American public school systems have been under reorganization administratively for more than thirty years.... The situation is peculiarly delicate in this matter of the junior high school. The movement has only recently become rooted, and it would be extremely embarrassing for superintendents of schools to be forced at an early date to go back to their communities and plead for additional or enlarged buildings to accommodate the new plan of reorganization. The communities might very easily raise the question as to why this change of policy followed so rapidly upon the heels of the recent plea for a three-year junior high school.

It requires some time to work out such a fundamental educational experiment as the junior high school or the junior college. Why uproot it when it is just getting a start, until there is time to let it come to maturity and show the type of fruit it may produce?[2] Even if the six-four-four plan were theoretically desirable, which is not admitted in this chapter, it might still be gravely questioned whether advocacy of it should not

[1] Cortright, E. E. "How Shall We Interpret the Junior High School and the Junior College Movement?" in *School and Society*, vol. 31, pp. 27–374. (March 1, 1930.)

[2] J. B. Lillard, president of the American Association of Junior Colleges, says: "Only a few years ago, the taxpayers were presented by the educational leaders of America with a new discovery in Education — the junior high school. The taxpayers were told that instead of the obsolete eight-four, we should have a six-three-three set-up. They accordingly invested, and are still investing millions of dollars in the junior high school; and we believe these millions will have been wisely invested. But now many of these educational leaders are saying: 'We were a bit premature; we should have said six-four-four.' Those who are directly charged with the administration of schools know that taxpayers are growing more and more reluctant to make considerable expenditures of money for repeated changes in educational procedure." (In *School and Society*, vol. 32, pp. 262–64. August 23, 1930.)

be deferred for a decade or two until present experiments had been proved inadequate.

The argument from history: a six-four-four point of view. History has also been appealed to by the advocates of the six-four-four plan. Thus Principal Harbeson, of Pasadena, says:[1]

> The typical junior college with its two-year course labors under many and serious handicaps. If we judge from history such an institution cannot survive. The experience of the University of California at Los Angeles, Stephens College, and many others has demonstrated that an isolated two-year institution is not a feasible proposition.

One is tempted to inquire as to the number of individual cases required to "demonstrate" the infeasibility of a two-year isolated institution, or the reason for limiting the institutions named to the very exceptional University of California at Los Angeles, which began as a two-year institution only as a step in securing a branch of the state university in the southern part of the state, and to Stephens College. The sufficiency of Stephens as an example of the principle stated will be discussed on a later page.[2] As a principle of logic, a general proposition of the type enunciated can only be proved by a consideration of all cases; it can be disproved by citing a single exception. Riverside and Modesto have managed to survive as two-year institutions since 1921; Fullerton, Santa Ana, Chaffey, and San Mateo date from 1922; and there are dozens of others in all parts of the country. We await proof that none of these are "feasible propositions" under present conditions.

Dr. Lange's judgment. From the standpoint of early history, some California writers have made an effort to identify Dr. A. F. Lange, "beloved prophet of the earlier junior college movement," as he has been characterized by his successor as

[1] Harbeson, J. W., *op. cit.*, p. 47.

[2] See page 736.

dean of the school of education at the University of California, with the six-four-four plan, stating that it was quite in accord with his educational philosophy, the implication being that it had not yet been proposed in his day, else he would have espoused it. The historical facts presented in the last chapter, however, show that a detailed outline of the plan was printed in 1908, in the *Annual Report* of the President of the University of California, in which institution Dr. Lange had been a member of the faculty since 1890, and in which he was professor of education from 1907 until his death in 1924. It was also proposed and discussed at the meetings of various educational associations between 1910 and 1920, and it could thus have hardly failed to come to his attention. Is it not strange, then, that there is no advocacy of it in any of his published writings?

Perhaps the clearest statement of his philosophy of the junior college is to be found in his address before the California Teachers' Association, in 1917, on "The Junior College — What Manner of Child Shall This Be?"[1]

> The junior college is by descent and nature a secondary school. Its legal existence as far as California is concerned was ushered in by the law of 1907 as an extension of the high school.... This [the junior high school], the high school and the junior college occupy the domain of secondary education.... The junior college must never be thought of in terms of the old obsolescent order. In the new order, its place is at the top. It is the culmination and fulfillment of the educational design incorporated in the intermediate [junior high] and the high school.

It is difficult to see how Dr. Lange can be claimed as a supporter of the six-four-four plan. The above quotation reads as though he had a six-three-three-two plan in mind. This address was delivered almost ten years after the six-four-four plan was printed in detail in the *President's Report* of his own

[1] In *School and Society*, vol. 7, pp. 211–16. (February 23, 1918.)

university. Again, at a University of Chicago Conference earlier in the same year, he had said:[1]

Here and there it may be found most practicable to assign the tenth as well as the ninth grade to the intermediate school, and then to make the eleventh and twelfth grades constitute parts of the junior college. Plans of this sort are actually under serious consideration in Los Angeles and Sacramento. The typical junior college, however, will doubtless consist of a two-year addition to the existing high school.

Are present experiments representative? Much has been written recently regarding the experiments with the four-year unit, especially at Hillsboro, Stephens, and Pasadena. It will be worth while to consider certain features regarding these institutions to see whether they are really representative, and whether their experience with the six-four-four plan can be accepted without qualification.

Hillsboro. This Texas public junior college is on the five-four-four basis, but this should probably not seriously affect the experiment from the junior college point of view. Hillsboro is a city of 7,823 inhabitants, with a total assessed valuation in 1928–29 of only nine million dollars. It had 175 junior college students, and six instructors, only three of whom were on full time. Their average teaching load was nineteen hours per week, the highest for any municipal junior college in Texas. Three of the instructors were teaching more than one college subject. There was laboratory work in two subjects only — biology and chemistry. No semi-professional or pre-professional courses were given.[2] Thus from numerous points of view Hillsboro can hardly be considered representative.

A report in 1926 is entitled "Hillsboro Junior College Reveals High Standards of Efficiency Through Grades of Former

[1] Lange, A. F. "The Junior College as an Integral Part of the Public School System"; in *School Review*, vol. 25, p. 474. (September, 1917.)

[2] Reid, J. R. *Texas Municipal Junior Colleges*. Bulletin of the State Department of Education, no. 255, pp. 10, 36, 42, 74. Austin, Texas, June, 1929.

Students."[1] This report was based upon the records of twenty-seven Hillsboro students who transferred to nine different Texas senior colleges and universities, and shows that they obtained higher average grades than a group of students used for comparison in the University of Texas. It is assumed, however, that grading standards in the other eight institutions were identical with those in the state university — an assumption that may be open to question.

Athletics properly play a prominent part in most junior colleges. They are a powerful means of developing student morale and spirit. What is the situation at Hillsboro? Mr. Reid, chairman of the state board of examiners, in his detailed study of Texas municipal junior colleges, tabulates twenty-eight student activities in the different institutions, in order of importance. As might be expected, athletics is most important in the largest number of institutions. At Hillsboro, however, athletics is not mentioned at all. Orchestra and glee clubs are placed first. Mr. Reid comments:[2]

Possibly more notable than any other fact from this table is that Hillsboro does not rank athletics as one of their activities, thus indicating that they are not interested in athletics in any form.

Stephens College. Much publicity has been given to the four-year junior college experiment under way at this institution under the auspices of the North Central Association, as already mentioned in Chapter XXV. Whatever the experiment proves in the five-year period given it for trial, it should be borne in mind that Stephens is a private junior college for girls, under Baptist auspices. Thus both from the point of view of sex of students and of denominational control it is not at all typical of the public junior colleges of the country. The experiment, important as it is, is being watched with great

[1] Helm, Willie, in *Texas Outlook*, pp. 30, 35. (September, 1926.)

[2] Reid, J. R., *op. cit.*, p. 91.

interest, but it cannot be considered representative from the public junior college point of view.

There is a most interesting feature of the Stephens College enrollment which is not without significance, however. The enrollment data by classes for four years under the four-year plan has been as follows: [1]

	Seniors	Juniors	Sophomores	Freshmen	Specials	Per cent Freshmen and Sophomores
1927–28 . . .	215	329	18	10	9	4.8
1928–29 . . .	224	350	15	14	6	4.8
1929–30 . . .	227	375	20	16	6	5.6
1930–31 . . .	213	375	22	6	3	4.5

The distribution of students by classes at Stephens, for 1929–30, is shown graphically in Figure 42. Nothing could show so eloquently as these figures that Stephens College is a four-year institution in name, but not in fact. *Essentially it is a two-year junior college*, not a four-year one. To be strictly accurate this statement should be amended to say it is 95 per cent a two-year institution! This student distribution is a most important fact to keep in mind in evaluating all reports of the success of the Stephens College experiment. From all that the writer has been able to learn Stephens is doing a very superior piece of junior college in-

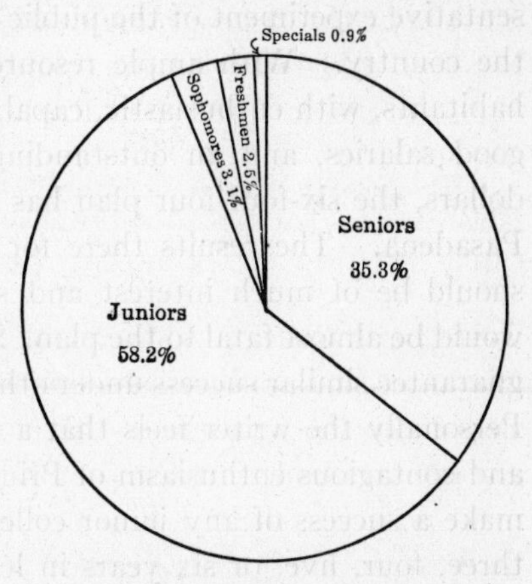

Fig. 42. Enrollment by Classes in Stephens College, a Four-Year Junior College, 1929–30

[1] Taken from annual catalogues of Stephens College.

struction, but as already suggested this can be accounted for by superior salaries and inspirational instruction rather than type of organization. Whatever success is achieved by Stephens College should be credited, at least 95 per cent of it, to a two-year junior college! This situation is even more significant when it is recalled that its president has been perhaps the most outstanding apostle of the six-four-four plan. For over a decade he has most eloquently preached the doctrine of six-four-four the country over, both by word and by pen. The net result of four years organization on this basis in his own institution is indicated by the slender sectors representing freshmen and sophomores in Figure 42.

Pasadena junior college. We have yet to consider the experiment with the six-four-four plan at Pasadena. In the opinion of the writer this is in every respect the most representative experiment of the public junior college movement in the country. With ample resources, in a city of 76,000 inhabitants, with enthusiastic, capable administrators and staff, good salaries, and an outstanding plant worth two million dollars, the six-four-four plan has every chance to succeed at Pasadena. The results there for the next five or ten years should be of much interest and significance. Failure there would be almost fatal to the plan. Success, however, would not guarantee similar success under other less favorable conditions. Personally the writer feels that a man of the dynamic power and contagious enthusiasm of Principal J. W. Harbeson could make a success of any junior college, whether it be one, two, three, four, five, or six years in length. Personality is more important than type. "Institutions are often but the lengthened shadow of a man." Even Pasadena is not irrevocably committed to the six-four-four plan, however. The statement by Superintendent Sexson at Atlantic City shows a commendable attitude of scientific caution. He said:[1]

[1] Sexson, J. A., *op. cit.*, pp. 212–13.

Statements to the effect that we have abolished the high school as it has heretofore been known in American education, or that we are committed to the conclusion that the total period of the public school offering should be fourteen years rather than thirteen years or twelve years or any other specified period are premature at this time. We are not committed to any form of organization as a finality. We can only express our opinion that the six-four-four plan is both theoretically and practically feasible, and that a four-year junior college of the kind and type we are now conducting is worthy of the thorough consideration and careful study of all those leaders in education, both professional and lay, who are interested in experimentation with a view to determining the best possible type of integrated school organization.

OBJECTIONS TO THE TWO-YEAR INSTITUTION

There remain to consider certain objections that have been raised to the two-year unit, and that have not been sufficiently considered in other connections already. Three such may be mentioned:

1. A two-year institution is too short for development of traditions and college spirit.
2. The two-year institution will develop ambitions to become a four-year, degree-granting college.
3. The two-year institution is only a segment of true education.

Let us next consider each of these objections.

Development of traditions and college spirit. Various writers have expressed the belief that two years is too short a time to instill the traditions, sense of atmosphere, ideals, habits, attitudes, or whatever else may be essential to the formation of "college spirit." As President Wood, of Stephens College, has so aptly expressed it, "The minority is continually striving to absorb the majority." Superintendent Sexson would leave no room for doubt in his categorical statement: "It is impossible to develop a very dynamic school spirit in a two-year institution.... The ideal situation is to have a school organization of four years in length."[1] Yet both of

[1] Sexson, J. A., *op. cit.*, p. 224.

Mr. Sexson's statements may be questioned. Even if it is impossible to develop a dynamic school spirit in two-year institutions, why does it follow that a four-year college is ideal for the purpose?

Is it true, however, that a two-year institution cannot develop a dynamic school spirit? One essential for school spirit is a feeling of freedom and independence on the part of the students, and a consciousness of unity in a common purpose. This is more likely to be found in a two-year institution with a separate plant and school consciousness, than in one where lower-division students with separate clubs, study-hall regulations, and other necessary disciplinary restrictions tend to break up the unity of feeling and experience. Fortunately, however, it is not necessary to depend upon theory, for the experience of many two-year junior colleges is available for study. It is doubtful whether a finer school spirit and loyalty can be found anywhere than at Sarah Lawrence College. The same may be said for Stephens College. The writer has visited the former, but has never had the privilege of visiting Stephens. From all reports received from others, however, from conversations with some of its graduates, from reading the *Stephens Standard* and other student publications, and from a contemplation of the unity and spirit which resulted in the Stephens Ten Ideals, quoted in an earlier chapter, he would judge that Stephens has had little difficulty in developing an admirable college spirit. At Stephens the minority does not seem to have been entirely unsuccessful in its efforts to absorb the majority, and to instill in them the Stephens spirit. It should be remembered, of course, that Stephens is 95 per cent a two-year junior college.

At Sacramento there is an interesting system, where the mid-year entering class has averaged over 150 students during three years since 1927–28. The school is divided into four classes instead of two — high and low freshmen, and high and low sophomores, with semi-annual class elections. Thus there is never a majority of "new" students. Something like the advantages claimed for the four-class system of the standard college are found here, only in accelerated form. After a careful study of the situation, Proctor wrote, regarding the Sacramento Junior College:[1]

While the intervals are shorter and the total time is only half that for the standard college, the fact that more than three fourths of the college population is acclimated to customs and traditions which have been established in the institution, makes it possible to develop a real student "morale" or "spirit," and helps to give the student a feeling of loyalty which promotes contentment.

A similar system is found at the new Los Angeles Junior College, another two-year institution. Here the four classes are designated, Alpha, Beta, Gamma, Delta.

The Sacramento four-class system is not at all necessary, however. From visits to over thirty California junior colleges, and from conversations with students, graduates, and faculty, the writer cannot see but there is quite as fine an institutional loyalty, college spirit, and atmosphere at Sacramento, Modesto, Chaffey, or San Bernardino — all two-year colleges — as there is at Pasadena.[2] Even Principal Harbeson, of Pasadena, recognizes the actual facts of the case, as contrasted with *a priori* theory, when he says:[3]

The writer wishes to make due recognition of the wonderful contribution that has been made by the two-year junior colleges....

[1] Proctor, W. M. "Extra-Curricular Activities in the Secondary Schools"; in *Sacramento School Survey*, p. 397.

[2] President J. B. Lillard, of Sacramento Junior College, writes: "Cliques and political manipulators do not seem to gain a foothold in the two-year, as they do in the four-year institution. According to the junior college graduates who are now attending higher institutions of learning, the two-year junior colleges have as fine a morale as exists in any other kind of collegiate institution; there is more actual participation in extra-curricular activities; and there is a relatively larger attendance at student assemblies than in the four-year colleges and universities." (In *School and Society*, vol. 32, p. 262. August 23, 1930.)

[3] Harbeson, J. W., *op. cit.*, pp. 46–47.

They have developed a school spirit of greater dynamic quality than, *a priori*, would have seemed possible in a two-year organization.

Another aspect of the situation is thus stated by Proctor:[1]

The four-year junior college would have a chance to develop institutional *esprit de corps* because ninety to ninety-five per cent of its students would be physiologically mature. This would permit a larger measure of social and disciplinary freedom than appears to be feasible in the four-year high school, with its incongruous mixture of near infants and near adults.

Is institutional spirit dependent chiefly upon physiological maturity? If so, the advantage would seem to be with the upper two-year unit where one hundred per cent physiological maturity is assured. One also wonders why the four-year high school can cover such a wide range from near infants to near adults, while, if the division line is moved only two years, the resulting four-year institution is then transformed into a group of homogeneous students.

The president of a leading two-year junior college in the Middle West which was formerly organized on the four-year basis (including the two upper high school years), says that ninety per cent of his disciplinary problems have vanished since the two lower years were discontinued. His two-year student body is far more satisfactory from the point of view of homogeneity, discipline, and spirit.

Perhaps the gloomiest picture of all is given by Dr. Eby, of Texas. He says:[2]

Some private junior colleges have fair college spirit; few public junior colleges have it.... As a two-year institution, the college can never be anything but a connecting link, a bleak and infertile isthmus, joining the high school and the regular arts college. It can-

[1] Proctor, W. M. "The Junior College and Educational Reorganization"; in *Educational Review*, vol. 65, p. 277. (May, 1923.)

[2] Eby, F. "The Four-Year Public Junior College"; in *Proceedings of the Ninth Annual Meeting of the American Association of Junior Colleges*, p. 67. Fort Worth, Texas, 1928.

> not feel the verve of independent being, and develop conscious self-respect. It will remain a poor, dependent, imitative, servile thing, trotting obediently at the heels of the higher institutions, and pecked at from from behind by the high schools.

Rhetorical statements such as this lose their force in the face of the actual experience of successful junior colleges in all parts of the country.

Ambitions to become four-year, degree-granting colleges. This danger in the two-year junior college is thus stated by Commissioner Cooper:[1]

> The local college may develop ambitions to do senior college work. This is a serious danger which should be carefully guarded against. I believe, however, that it is more likely to occur where the two-year college exists. Koos discovered enough evidence of this tendency in California to lead him to sound a note of warning.

There is some danger here, but to recognize it is to guard against it. This has been done by law in many states where extension upward is forbidden. Unquestionably such development is justified in some cases, however, as in the development of the College of the City of Detroit, in America's fourth city, from the former Detroit Junior College. Is it necessary, in order to prevent such development, to weight down the two-year institution with an additional two years below, because a few institutions, whether under justifiable conditions or not, may develop ambitions to add two years above?

How great is this danger? Dr. Campbell, secretary of the American Association of Junior Colleges, has tried to trace the fate of all junior colleges in the country which have died, merged with other schools, or expanded into four-year senior colleges. He was able to discover exactly eleven, since the beginning of the movement, which had expanded into four-year

[1] Cooper, W. J. "Some Advantages Expected to Result from Administering Secondary Education in Two Units of Four Years Each"; in *School Review*, vol. 37, p. 305. (May, 1929.)

institutions — considerably less than one a year.[1] In the same period several times this number of four-year colleges have decapitated themselves and have become junior colleges. The balance is decidedly on the credit side of the junior college ledger!

Junior college as a segment of true education. Various authors call attention to the two-year junior college as a "mere segment" of true education, and stress the extra "breaks" in the educational program introduced by the two-year institutions.[2] This seems to be merely a matter of words. Using the term "breaks" suggests discontinuity and disorganization, whereas if the term "transition" or "step" is used for identically the same organization the implication is quite different. The advantages of the two-year institution from the transitional point of view of simpler easier steps has already been pointed out, and shown graphically in Figure 41, page 724.

As to "segment," Webster defines it primarily as "one of the parts into which any body naturally separates or is divided," a definition which has nothing to express unpleasant connotations for the two-year junior college. Two-, four-, or six-year institutions are all segments of the complete educational ladder, and there is no reason to single out a two-year segment,

[1] Campbell, D. S. "A Brief Study of the Development of the Junior College Movement"; in *Proceedings of the Tenth Annual Meeting of the American Association of Junior Colleges*, pp. 11–15. Atlantic City, New Jersey, 1929.

Dr. Campbell has kindly furnished the author a list of these eleven, as follows: Public: Detroit Junior College, Detroit, Michigan; Tennessee Polytechnic Institute, Cookeville, Tennessee; New River State School, Montgomery, West Virginia; Southeastern Louisiana College, Hammond, Louisiana; Private: Bethany-Peniel College, Bethany, Oklahoma; Mt. St. Scholastica College, Atchison, Kentucky; Chicago College of Osteopathy, Chicago, Illinois; Youngstown College, Youngstown, Ohio; Bowling Green Business University, Bowling Green, Kentucky; Subiaco College, Subiaco, Arkansas; Villa Madonna College, Covington, Kentucky.

[2] For example, Proctor says: "The proposed [four-year] type of junior college would be more attractive to students and teachers as well, because it would no longer be a mere segment but a full-fledged, going institution, with separate buildings and equipment of its own and capable of maintaining interscholastic relations with other schools of like nature." (Proctor, W. M., *loc. cit.*, p. 277.)

merely because it is a "segment," as particularly obnoxious. Why is a two-year institution a "mere segment," while a four-year school is a "full-fledged going institution"? Are there not many two-year institutions with "separate buildings and equipment," and "capable of maintaining interscholastic relations with other schools of like nature"? Can there not be many more such?

Superintendent Sexson says:[1]

The difficulty with a two-year junior college up to the present time has been that the advocates and administrators have regarded it not as an educational entity in itself, with character and individuality of its own, but rather as a fractional part of some other institution of larger length; to be specific, a fractional part of the college of liberal arts. The junior college, however, cannot justify itself on such grounds. It cannot continue to live on borrowed light.

This is surprising information. The writer had been of the opinion that the junior college has developed a very striking individuality of its own. This entire volume has been an effort to picture that individuality. The chapters on the popularizing and terminal functions, in particular, contain ample evidence that the junior college is not a mere fractional part of a liberal arts college and is not living entirely on borrowed light. Mr. Sexson continues:

The solution of the problem must inevitably be that if the junior college is to enjoy any degree of permanency, it must develop as a unique institution with character, individuality, and intrinsic merit of its own (—)

This is quite true, but a doubting Thomas may question why the conclusion, as stated in the latter half of his sentence, *necessarily* follows:

and this can best be accomplished by the joining of the freshman and sophomore college years with the upper years of the secondary school as the topmost unit of the public secondary school system.

[1] Sexson, *op. cit.*, p. 225.

General considerations. Many of the objections urged against the two-year junior college turn out to be, upon examination, what the attorney designates as "irrelevant and immaterial." Many are based upon *a priori* grounds, and vanish when submitted to the acid test of experience. That examples of many objections can be found in numerous specific junior colleges would not for a moment be denied. The only claim made here is that they are incidental, not essential to the two-year junior college *as such*.

CONCLUSION

President Ray Lyman Wilbur was quoted at the beginning of the preceding chapter as saying that we are about ready to stop the "fetish worship" of the numeral four in American education. The next chapter will show on what a tenuous and illogical basis the present standard *four-year* college exists. In contrast with the tendency to abandon this fetish worship of the numeral four, the Pasadena plan, in its entirety, proposes instead to double and intensify it. In its full development the Pasadena plan carries down into the kindergarten and preschool age, and in its complete form contemplates an organization which shall be four-four-four-four. This is beautifully symmetrical and mathematically perfect. Is it educationally desirable? This chapter has tried to present the reasons why an affirmative answer is questionable.

It is fortunate that we do not all agree on educational policies. Educational progress results from difference of opinion — from clash of points of view. It would be a drab, monotonous, uninteresting world if we all saw alike. There seems to be no immediate danger that the junior college world will be drab, monotonous, or uninteresting! Many writers have set forth the advantages as they see them in favor of the six-four-four type of organization. The writer has tried to present clearly and forcefully the situation from the point of view of the two-year junior college. It cannot be denied that the latter is the prevailing type of organization at the present time. Therefore the burden of proof rests upon the four-year advocates to justify a change. After a careful study of all the arguments, on both sides of the question, the writer feels that that burden is a considerable one.

Educational progress results from difference of opinion — if that difference of opinion is followed by constructive experimentation. Nothing said in this chapter should be construed to discourage further experimentation along the line of the six-four-four organization. If the six-four-four plan is best, it will win out. It will demonstrate its worth, in spite of all arguments to the contrary. Several more Pasadenas are needed in the next decade. The writer feels, however, that junior college educators should not hurry to adopt this plan in their institutions, without a full consideration of the arguments on both sides.

It has been necessary to examine critically some of the arguments of many leaders who stand high in the educational world. It is unnecessary to state that the effort has been to do this from a thoroughly impersonal point of view. In spite of the criticism which he has made of Mr. Sexson's 1930 address at Atlantic City, the writer is greatly impressed with a portion of the final sentence of that address:

> Pasadena is committed to nothing but a sincere search for the truth, and in case the experiment does not develop satisfactorily she will be the first to recognize the fact and profit by the experience.

The writer is also quite as strongly committed to a sincere search for the truth in the junior college field. It is desirable that the strongest possible presentations should be made of the advantages and disadvantages of both types of organization in such a sincere search for the truth.

It is even more important that such discussion should be

followed by extensive experimentation, and a dispassionate scientific evaluation of the results from various points of view. In such a worthy objective all friends of the junior college movement, regardless of whether they see through two-year spectacles, four-year spectacles, or tinted glasses of other hues, may enthusiastically unite — the "sincere search for truth" — which may well be the closing word in these two chapters of controversy.

QUESTIONS AND PROBLEMS

1. A junior college president writes: "In my judgment the first distinctive problem of the junior college is to define the amount of self-determination advisable for its students." How can he do this? Does the problem differ in the private and public institutions?
2. Give examples of existence of distinctive college spirit and atmosphere, or lack of it, in some junior college with which you are familiar.
3. Find, if possible, the reason for the change, in the case of each of the eleven junior colleges named that have become four-year degree-granting institutions. Can the reasons be generalized?
4. Examine the reports of the Texas Educational Survey (vol. 3) on Hillsboro, Wichita Falls, and El Paso junior colleges. What significance do they have for the discussion of this chapter?
5. Are there special local conditions to which the six-four-four plan might be particularly well adapted? What are they?
6. What are some of the particular administrative difficulties for a special junior college which is contemplating a change to the six-four-four type of organization? Are they important, or not?
7. To what extent do students leave four-year colleges at the close of the sophomore year to take up work at some university?
8. In a selected four-year institution of any type, find what proportion of the positions of student leadership is filled by students of the two lower years.
9. What reasons are there for stating that the six-three-three plan should be given a longer trial period? How long is needed?
10. Why has the enrollment of freshmen and sophomores at Stephens College been so small?
11. What means are there of measuring whether college spirit is satisfactory in a two-year institution? Is there any published evidence regarding it?
12. State and consider any objections to the two-year junior college which have not been mentioned in this or the preceding chapter.

SUGGESTED READINGS

Buenger, T. *A Change of Gymnasia to Junior Colleges.* United States Bureau of Education, Bulletin no. 19, pp. 51–52. (1922.)

Bunker, F. F. *Reorganization of the Public School System.* United States Bureau of Education, Bulletin no. 8. 186 pp. (1916.)

*Campbell, W. W. "The Junior Colleges in their Relations to the University"; in *California Quarterly of Secondary Education*, vol. 2, pp. 97–101. (January, 1927.)

*Cortright, E. E. "How Shall We Interpret the Junior High School and the Junior College Movement?" in *School and Society*, vol. 31, pp. 273–76. (March 1, 1930.)

Harper, W. R. "A Two-Years' College Course"; in *Educational Review*, vol. 19, pp. 411–15. (April, 1900.)

*Leonard, R. J. "Professional Education in Junior Colleges"; in *Teachers' College Record*, vol. 26, pp. 724–33. (May, 1925.)

*Lillard, J. B. "The 6–3–3–2 Versus the 6–4–4 Plan of Organization for the Public Junior College"; in *School and Society*, vol. 32, pp. 262–64. (August 23, 1930.)

Marot, M. L. "The Junior College, A Link Between Secondary and Higher Education"; in *Proceedings of the Sixth Annual Meeting of the American Association of Junior Colleges*, pp. 8–15. Chicago, Illinois, 1926.

"A Six-Four-Four Plan of School Organization"; in *School Review*, vol. 36, pp. 485–86. (September, 1928.)

CHAPTER XXVIII

EFFECT ON OTHER HIGHER EDUCATIONAL INSTITUTIONS

Without additional expense, the effectiveness of our higher institutions might be increased at least one fourth. — P. P. CLAXTON.[1]

Contents of this chapter. Various attitudes of the university toward the junior college, and several effects of the junior college on university organization are considered first in this chapter; next the advantages and disadvantages of a coalition of junior colleges with normal schools and teachers' colleges are briefly treated; finally the relations of the four-year colleges to the junior colleges, and the possible effects of the junior college on future four-year college organization, are discussed.

RELATION OF THE JUNIOR COLLEGE TO THE UNIVERSITIES

The attitudes of the university to the junior college. Four distinct attitudes on the part of the universities toward the junior colleges may be distinguished: (1) legal control, (2) contractual affiliation, (3) domination, through requirements, and (4) recognition and coöperation.

Legal control. Legal control is found in the case of junior colleges which have been established as branches of universities, especially in the case of some state junior colleges. Thus the branch junior colleges in Idaho and Tennessee are as much a part of the state universities there as if they were administered on the same campus. In the private field, Seth Low Junior College of Columbia University furnishes a similar example. In western Pennsylvania the three local junior colleges at Uniontown, Erie, and Johnstown are interesting examples of

[1] Claxton, P. P. "The Junior College's Opportunity"; in *School Life*, vol. 5, p. 1. (July 15, 1920.)

complete administrative control by the University of Pittsburgh, as already pointed out. (See page 13.) In Texas, the two state junior colleges legally are branches of the State Agricultural and Mechanical Colleges, although permitted a certain degree of local autonomy. This group furnishes examples of the centralized control theory of education — a theory which, on the whole, has not found great favor in America.

Affiliation and inspection. Definite contractual affiliation agreements with local junior colleges were proposed by President Harper between the University of Chicago and junior colleges in the Middle West, early in this century, but the junior colleges feared that these agreements would mean virtual if not legal surrender of their independence, and very few of them ever became effective. In the public junior college field, the California law of 1921 provided for voluntary affiliation agreements between junior colleges and the state university, under which all collegiate courses and the qualifications and appointment of faculty members were subject to the approval of the university and of inspectors sent out by it.[1] Seven or eight junior colleges took advantage of this plan, and for a year or two the state university maintained a special junior college coördinator, in addition to sending out many faculty members as inspectors. The arrangement, however, was more productive of friction than of helpfulness, and was soon dropped by common consent, although the law still remains on the statute books.

[1] The text of the law (Section 18, Act 1477, Deering) is as follows: "The governing board of any junior college or of the junior college department of any high school or of any teachers' college, may enter into an agreement of affiliation with the University of California to provide that the courses in such junior college whose purpose is to prepare for advanced university standing shall be visited, inspected, and accredited by said university, and that the qualifications of teachers in such courses shall be as recommended by said university. Such arrangement of affiliation may include such other matters as may be mutually advantageous and as may be approved by the state board of education." See Chapter IV for further details of "affiliation" in California.

Domination through accrediting and requirements. Most state universities maintain more or less domination and control over the junior colleges by accreditation and entrance requirements. The junior college, if it is to be successful, must arrange to have its graduates eligible to enter the state university. This leads to control of a major portion of the curriculum through entrance requirements, and of other features as indicated in Figure 17 of Chapter VI. Such requirements have usually not been burdensome, and often they have been helpful to the young junior college, just learning to toddle in the educational field. On the whole, however, it is probably better that the matter of accrediting should be left to the regional agencies, rather than have a varying standard from state to state.

The private universities have adopted varying attitudes, some welcoming junior college graduates without annoying technicalities if they have done two full years of college work, others insisting that all requirements for their own freshman and sophomore years shall have been met to the letter. On the whole the junior college is in a position similar to that of the high schools a quarter of a century ago, in the way of domination by college entrance requirements. To a considerable extent the high schools have won their fight for local self-determination, although even yet there are many exceptions. The junior college probably has much the same fight ahead of it in the next quarter century to establish its right to educational self-determination.

Recognition and coöperation. Finally there is the attitude of recognition, friendly advice, and cordial coöperation toward a common goal, manifested by a few universities, especially the private institutions, which see in the junior college a welcome relief from the freshman and sophomore problems which have been troubling them for a decade or more. They welcome the junior college as a younger brother in the field, peculiarly fitted to handle freshmen and sophomores, and do all they can to encourage and assist it. Ultimately this is the state which all universities should reach, but most of them are as yet only in the third stage — if they have progressed even that far.[1]

Effect of the junior college on university organization. There are three ways in which the university has met the new conditions to which the junior college has given rise: (1) by announced abolition of junior college work in the university, (2) by segregation of it, and (3) by a continuance of the old organization without change.

Abolition of the lower division. The announced intention to abolish freshman and sophomore work at Johns Hopkins and Stanford Universities has already been outlined. Dr. Jordan began urging such a move at Stanford University at least as early as 1907,[2] but actually it was not feasible to begin it until the state was fairly adequately supplied with junior colleges. In neither university has the lower division abolition been completed as yet, although the freshman and sophomore enrollment is being decreased in both institutions.[3]

[1] It is significant of this spirit of coöperation that the American Association of University Professors, which has never recognized the junior college nor admitted junior college professors to membership, appointed, late in 1930, a special committee to study and report on the relation of the junior college to higher education and to the association, the report to be made at the annual meeting in December, 1931.

[2] In his *Fourth Annual Report* to the Trustees Dr. Jordan said: "To make a university, in the world sense, of Stanford University the following elements seem to me essential: the elimination as soon as possible, let us say in the course of five years, of the junior college [first two years] by the addition of two years to the entrance requirements. I ask your board to consider the project of the immediate separation of the junior college from the university or the university college, and to consider the possibility of requiring the work of the junior college as a requisite for admission to the university on and after the year 1913, or as soon as a number of the best-equipped high schools of the state are prepared to undertake this work." (Stanford University, Trustees Series, no. 15, p. 4. 1907.)

[3] President Goodnow, of Johns Hopkins, in his *Presidential Report* for 1928–29, noted that the enrollment in the undergraduate department continued to decrease, the figure for 1927–28 being 805, and for 1928–29, 705. The old state

The serious situation facing the universities is thus strikingly expressed by Dean Haggerty, of the University of Minnesota:[1]

Certain figures compiled by Dean Johnston show that a very large percentage of the budget of the Arts College is going into the instruction of the freshman and sophomore groups. As a matter of fact, it appears as if the effort made in teaching students in elementary science will be so great as to prevent work in advanced fields and in research. The very growth of interest in science in an institution like this almost imperils the growth of science itself. When you are spending from 80 to 85 per cent of your budget for junior college instruction, there is not much left for what a good many people think is the real work of a university.

After discussing the Stanford and Hopkins plans, Dr. Walker, President of the Association of Colleges and Secondary Schools of the Southern States, remarked, in 1926:[2]

We may look for similar announcements from many other institutions within the next few years. I for one shall not be surprised to see many of the state universities within the next decade advance their admission requirements by two full years, and require for admission the completion of the junior college course.... The possibilities of a more natural and a more effective reorganization of higher education in America and the emergence of influences already at work in the direction indicated are sufficient evidence of the tremendous significance of the junior college movement.

This matter is definitely under consideration at the University of Georgia, which is also proposing to abolish its lower division.

Segregation. Many other universities, not yet committed

law which compelled the university to accept for admission graduates of all public high schools in the state, was changed in 1927 to permit restriction. He says: "When the time comes for dropping the first two years of college, which was an important part of the new plan, we shall find it much easier to confine the work of the philosophical faculty to strictly advanced work, which was our purpose in the adoption of the plan." (*Report of the President*, pp. 4–5.)

[1] Haggerty, M. E. "Educational Research in the University of Minnesota"; in Hudelson, E. (editor), *Problems of College Education*, pp. 18–19.

[2] Walker, N. W. "The Significance of the Junior College Movement"; in *Proceedings of the Seventh Annual Meeting of the American Association of Junior Colleges*, p. 30. Jackson, Mississippi, 1926.

to the policy of abolition, have within the past ten or fifteen years introduced separate administrative organization and supervision for the freshman and sophomore years. Among these are California, Chicago, Washington, Minnesota, Nebraska, Oregon, Michigan, and George Washington, in the order named. Chicago has just announced a policy of further segregation which will make of its junior college almost an independent institution, maintained on the same campus, as an experimental college for experiments in the improvement of collegiate instruction.

As to desirable administrative organization in a segregated junior college or lower division, President Wilkins, of Oberlin College, says: [1]

> If a junior college is retained, its separate administration will involve at least the appointment of a special dean or equivalent officer, with such assistants as may be necessary, and the existence of a faculty organized as an independent body. It should also involve the existence of a faculty actually distinct, in large part or wholly, from the rest of the university faculty; and, as corollary thereto, the use of a separate budget for junior college instruction. Preferably, the separation should further involve the physical removal of the junior college from the main campus of the university.

On the other hand, Dr. Ernest C. Moore, Director of the University of California at Los Angeles, feels that such segregation of divisions is undesirable. He says: [2]

> One consequence of the movement to organize junior colleges outside the university seems to me to be unqualifiedly bad, i.e., the movement to organize them inside the university. There, at least, it seems to fracture the continuity which should obtain. Just so soon as you create a lower division and an upper division, instructors

[1] Wilkins, E. H. "The Relation of the Senior College and the Graduate School"; in *Journal of the Proceedings and Addresses of the Twenty-Eighth Annual Conference of the Association of American Universities*, p. 68. Chicago, 1927.

[2] Moore, E. C. "Fundamental Concepts Underlying Junior College Education"; in *California Quarterly of Secondary Education*, vol. 4, p. 13. (October, 1928.)

with one accord, almost, begin to look upon the work of the lower division as beneath them in dignity. It has come to pass, therefore, that there are two distinct American ways of regarding and treating freshmen — the Yale way, which is to think of them as the most important students in the university and to give them the best instructors the university has, and its opposite, which for lack of a better designation, I shall call the California method of putting them off by themselves on the theory that if any one is to be sacrificed, the newcomer must be that one.

No change in organization. The conclusion of Koos in regard to changes in organization may be quoted:[1]

Some of our higher institutions, among them both colleges and universities, on account of the grip of tradition and a selected persisting clientèle, will doubtless be able to withstand for a long period the forces of reorganization.... It is likely, moreover, that there may be a place in the American system for a small proportion of institutions of the type that assumes the longer period of unapplied training before entering upon the work of the professional school. In the face of the apparently inevitable tendencies of reorganization shown, however, they may come to be regarded as atypical, the prevailing type conforming to the trend of reorganization as disclosed.

RELATION OF THE JUNIOR COLLEGE TO NORMAL SCHOOL AND TEACHERS' COLLEGE

Experience in Wisconsin and California. Quite a different problem is presented by the question of the relation of the junior colleges to teacher training institutions. In Wisconsin, for a time subsequent to 1911, the normal schools began functioning as junior colleges, offering two-year liberal arts courses as part of their curricula. The situation did not work out entirely happily, however, perhaps in part because of unsympathetic administration.[2] In California, six of the seven state

[1] Koos, L. V. *Junior College*, p. 381.

[2] The State Superintendent of Schools, John Callahan, explains the situation thus: "In 1911 we passed a law in the state of Wisconsin making junior colleges out of our nine normal schools and during the years that followed, up to about 1923, the thing they were advising most was free medical courses, free law

teachers' colleges established junior college departments under the contract provisions of the law of 1921. With the development of the teachers' college curricula and the organization of upper and lower divisions in these institutions, junior college segregation and financing has been dropped in all but two of them — Fresno and San José. In the others, however, the lower divisions continue to function to a considerable extent as junior colleges for the local communities.

Conflicting opinions. Maxwell, in 1921, argued that a junior college program in the teachers' college would provide a broader scholastic opportunity for prospective teachers, would lead naturally into the four-year professional curriculum, would increase the number of men, and would stimulate faculty growth. The argument against such a combination has perhaps best been stated by President Pritchett of the Carnegie Foundation, as follows: [1]

Another movement has shown signs of extension that are disquieting. This is the attempt to combine with teacher training institutions the first two years of a college of liberal arts — the so-called "junior college" curriculum.... Evidence is lacking as to the comparative performance of teachers trained in such double-headed institutions and of those who attended schools in which a single professional motive prevailed. It is possible to offer only the judgment of careful observers and the inference from common experience. These are against the plan. The fundamental objection is the

courses, free engineering courses. That was what was getting their attention until the state superintendent and county superintendents in the state of Wisconsin rose up and made an awful fuss about it. Now they are preparing people who enter them to teach school. We have no objection if they go into these normal schools and take what they can get in an academic line out of the course, making preparation for teachers actively, and get what credit they can for the university and the colleges. That is all right, but make the backbone of it the course of study such as is recognized in normal schools. That is the conclusion we came to, and cut them out about five or six years ago. We had some job cutting them out, too." (*Proceedings of the Association of Governing Boards of State Universities and Allied Institutions*, p. 70. Ames and Iowa City, November 15–17, 1928.)

[1] Pritchett, H. S. *Sixteenth Annual Report of Carnegie Foundation for Advancement of Teaching*, pp. 83–84. New York, 1921.

perverted psychology of the proposed arrangement. The driving spirit of any successful professional institution lies in its unity of aim and purpose; it owes its students the inspiration and self-confidence that comes from the determination to do one thing supremely well. Now the makers of curricula for elementary teachers find it impossible to bring what they consider indispensable requirements for such training within the limits of the customary two years of collegiate work; every subject presented within this brief period is selected, organized, and conducted with the requirements of a teacher of a particular sort solely in view.... In Wisconsin, where several schools admit college students, the resultant combination appears to depend on the sympathies of the principal. In one, the collegiate courses are magnified, and the students intending to teach find their interests overshadowed by a more distinguished group bound for the university; in another, the academic students are tolerated only, and furnish a subject for invidious comparison with the future teachers. Cross purposes such as these react inevitably on the instructors. Instead of focusing every effort on giving students the best possible preparation for teaching, the object of the staff is to discover, in the interest of economy, how many courses can be given that will carry credit with both types of student. Substantive courses in language, science, mathematics, and so forth, are therefore neutralized and stripped of material highly characteristic of good teachers' courses, while the work in education is reduced to minimum essentials. It is useless to look for single-minded and progressive professional activity under such conditions; the main stream is divided; and the impact upon each student is hopelessly weakened; the plan is as preposterous in some respects as it would be to combine curricula in law with curricula in theology.... Experience has made clear beyond question that a sound school for teachers must have its own exclusive curricula and student body, its own staff of teachers, its own buildings and equipment, and its own independent budget and administration for the reasons that hold good of every other form of advanced professional training.

Advocating quite the opposite point of view, Almack thus states the special function that the junior college may play in an ideal teacher training program:[1]

[1] Almack, J. C. "The Issue in Teacher Training"; in *Educational Administration and Supervision*, vol. 11, p. 275. (April, 1925.)

The normal schools were "put over" on the American people in the first place by a little group of educational theorists and propagandists who had had no real contact and no real experience with them. There was no real demand for them from the American people, and they were not an outgrowth of American needs and conditions. At the same time, their introduction resulted in putting into disrepute a distinctly native idea, which, in spite of the weight of authority against it has persisted and demonstrated its usefulness. One of the main sources of strength of the normal school idea has been the approval of Horace Mann. An examination of his reasons for its support, however, shows that most of them were wrong in the first place, and that the few which were not do not apply today. In the meantime, there has developed a junior college idea, with the teacher-training department. It appears to have the merit of the original New York idea, and, in addition, many others, and lacks the disadvantages of the conventional normal school. Its general adoption seems to be a logical step in the gradual development of an efficient public school system.

More specifically he states the advantages of the teacher-training idea in junior colleges as follows:[1]

There are certain advantages in the junior college teacher-training idea.

1. The idea is a natural outgrowth of American needs and ideals.
2. There is abundant precedent for it, not only in teacher-training, but in training for other professions.
3. It offers an opportunity for a well-organized student social life.
4. It brings opportunities to students who would otherwise be denied them. This applies to those who wish to become teachers, as well as to others. Therefore, the number of candidates for the profession is increased. As Koos has shown, around three-fourths of the enrollment of a junior college is drawn from an area of 100 mile radius. It is observed that many, rather than few schools are needed. It is reported that normal schools as a rule draw three-fourths of their students from an area of 75 miles radius.
5. When a student in the teacher-training department has shown his inability for the profession, he may be transferred to an-

[1] Almack, J. C., *op. cit.*, pp. 273–74.

other department with a minimum of loss. This is considerably better than advising him to leave the institution, and much better than what usually happens — leaving him to pursue his course undisturbed.

6. Many promising young people may be attracted into the teaching profession who would otherwise have gone into some other vocation. Experience shows that from 10 to 20 per cent of the enrollment may be expected to transfer to the teacher-training department, either before or after graduating from the junior college.
7. It is reasonable to suppose that instruction in the academic subjects is better under the junior college plan. The teachers have their fields sufficiently narrowed to permit genuine specialization.
8. It is possible to insist upon adequate grounding in subject matter before entering upon professional training.
9. It actually makes possible the preparation of high school teachers in teachers' colleges.
10. Teacher-training may be carried on more economically than at present.
11. The normal school department is made an integral part of the public school system.

The fears expressed by Dr. Pritchett do not agree with the observations of Koos, who says:[1]

> Although the writer spent a number of days visiting five normal schools and teachers' colleges in which junior college units are maintained, endeavoring to discover both in class and out evidences of untoward influences on the teacher-training function, he became aware of few, if any.... Instead of its being detrimental, the visitor felt that the junior college was as a whole positive in its effect upon the primary function of the institutions visited.

As already shown in previous chapters, the junior colleges at the present time are in many cases acting as teacher-training institutions. In many states their graduates, if they have the requisite number of units in educational courses, are given state teaching credentials. This is markedly true in Texas.

[1] Koos. *Junior College*, pp. 559–60.

Hollingsworth's curriculum study showed sixteen states in which an average of ten hours or more of professional courses were given in the junior colleges.

Success at San Jose. The place where the teachers' college-junior college combination has been worked out most successfully seems to be at the San Jose State Teachers College, at San Jose, California. In particular the advantages found for the combination there are the ones indicated in Almack's summary in points 3, 4, and 5. It seems to be especially desirable for the prospective teachers unsuited to the profession, who can be shunted into other courses. There is no perceptible feeling of inferiority of either group. In fact, as far as possible, the entire student body is a unit with little segregation except for administrative and accounting purposes. That such an arrangement is possible, and that it works out so satisfactorily from both the teachers' college and junior college points of view, is suggestive of a similar possibility of success in other states, when sympathetically administered by competent men. The dangers of incompetent or biased administration have already been indicated by Pritchett. There seem to be much greater possibilities in a closer coördination of junior college and teacher-training programs than have yet been worked out.

RELATION OF THE JUNIOR COLLEGE TO FOUR-YEAR COLLEGES

The attitude of the four-year colleges to the junior college. The attitude of standard four-year colleges to the junior college is even more varied than that of the universities. If freshman and sophomore work should ultimately be taken over entirely by junior colleges, there would still be ample scope for the universities in specialization, graduate work, pure research, and professional schools. Would such a change, however, threaten the very existence of the four-year colleges?

For them the situation is fraught with greater possibilities of violent readjustment, if not extinction. Three distinct attitudes on the part of the four-year colleges toward the junior colleges may be distinguished: (1) hostility, (2) indifference, and (3) encouragement.

Fear and hostility. Hostility may be born of fear that the junior college is going to usurp the field of the four-year college, or of honest doubt whether the junior college can really furnish the education it claims to offer, or of a combination of the two motives.

As an example of the first type we have the fear expressed by President Penrose, of Whitman College, that the "American college will find its life ground out" through the development of junior colleges.[1] The latter type is best expressed by the late President Main, of Grinnell College, who said, before the North Central Association in 1916:[2]

> Strictly speaking there is no such thing as a junior college... limiting itself... to two years of work. If such an institution were theoretically possible... it would be regarded as an educational malformation. Such an institution would not be a college. It would not even be a junior college.... A normal quick-witted boy or girl would not care to enter there.... The youth that wants to go to college should not be deceived by names and false promises. He asks for bread; he should not be given a stone. The junior college... does not have a living chance in our education system.

This represented President Main's sentiments fifteen years ago, before the junior college had reached its present state of development. That he had not changed his opinion in the in-

[1] Penrose, S. B. L. "The Relation of the College Association to the Existing Association"; in *Association of American Colleges Bulletin*, vol. 1, p. 54. (January, 1915.)

[2] Main, J. H. T. "No Institution of College Grade, Which Offers Few Advanced Courses, Should be Classified as a Senior College"; in *Proceedings of North Central Association of Colleges and Secondary Schools*, vol. 21, pp. 152–58. Chicago, 1916.

terval is shown by his Report to the Board of Trustees of Grinnell, in 1927, in which he said:[1]

> The so-called "junior college" is attacking, whether consciously or unconsciously, the regular liberal arts college. The stock argument is: it is college at home; it is cheaper than college away from home; it gives two years of work at home like that given in any regular college at a minimum cost. The fact is it is two years' additional work in high school; two years in the same atmosphere, under the same teachers (with perhaps the addition of one or two others); two years more under the conditions of stimulus and environment already exhausted. It is two years of additional high school, at the great price of time and energy and opportunity that should have been capitalized by the boy or girl in some other way or in some other place. The so-called junior college is extraordinarily expensive (when we stop to consider what expense means) as compared with the expense at a regular liberal arts college, which among other things means release from the worn-out conditions of the high school and introduction into an entirely new environment of persons, conditions and obligations. College education in the real sense means a journey out into the world. The "junior college" does not afford any such opportunity — this is especially true of the junior colleges in the smaller towns. But it is equally true of those in the larger towns unless there are separate buildings, different teachers and an entirely distinctive and a more inclusive educational purpose. But in any case the junior college is not inexpensive. It is on the contrary very costly in all that means life. It is cheap — just a cheap imitation of the real thing!

On the other hand, Klein, specialist on higher education in the United States Office of Education, says:[2]

> Four-year colleges may be tempted to jump to the conclusion that they will be squeezed out between the junior college and the university. In view of the diversity of American educational tastes and ambitions and the ever-growing demand for education, this would be an inference founded upon insufficient considerations.

[1] Main, J. H. T., in *The Grinnell Herald*, June 4, 1927.

[2] Klein, A. J. *Higher Education*. United States Bureau of Education Bulletin, 1928, no. 25, p. 5. Washington, D.C., 1928.

Indifference. Many of the four-year colleges, especially of the more conservative type, have maintained an attitude of indifference to the junior college. They continue on the even tenor of their way without a realization that a major movement in the reorganization of higher education is going on which must eventually affect their status and function profoundly. They need to be awakened to a realization of the changes that are taking place — to be ready to adopt a constructive attitude, either of hostility or of encouragement to the new junior college. Anything is better than indifference, if an institution is to be a positive educational force.

Encouragement. Some college and university administrators, however, look with favor on the advent of the junior college. Thus President Zook, of the University of Akron, says:[1]

> The junior college movement is in no wise a fundamental attack on the existence of the liberal arts college.... It is rather a supplement.

And President Lowell of Harvard, says:[2]

> They [junior colleges] do not seem to me a menace to the good American college, but on the contrary a benefit.

A few far-sighted colleges, in various parts of the country, are taking a position of constructive leadership and encouragement of the junior college movement; unquestionably others, but not all, will follow. Sensing the transformation in progress, they will realize that the junior college should not be considered an enemy of the type of education they are trying to give, but a supplement to it. They will change the emphasis on the work they are doing, perhaps change their organization as indicated later, and instead of combating the inevitable spread of the junior college they will recognize it as a powerful agency

[1] Zook, G. F. "Is the Junior College a Menace or a Boon?" in *School Review*, vol. 37, p. 425. (June, 1929.)

[2] Lowell, A. L. "The Outlook for the American College"; in Kelly, R. L. (editor), *The Effective College*, p. 283.

for the popularization with the masses of the type of cultural education for which they have stood so notably, with much smaller groups, for a century or more. They will welcome this evidence that cultural education is finally coming to be recognized as the heritage of all the people, and will readjust their own work accordingly. They will build a new and better type of cultural college education than was possible when no such foundations existed upon which to build. The way in which this may be accomplished will be brought out later in this chapter. It is here only meant to suggest that a few of our outstanding four-year colleges of the better type, on a firm financial basis, under the guidance of far-sighted men of courage, judgment, and vision, will not hesitate to seize the banner of leadership and make a step forward into fields impossible before. They will recognize the junior colleges as their best allies; will encourage, stimulate, and lead them; and will themselves do a distinctive service that the junior colleges cannot do.

Will there not be a distinctive and unique field remaining for the four-year colleges of the so-called New England type, whose contributions to American life have been of inestimable value in the past? The spirit which they have shown in the development of leaders of culture and distinction is far too fine and precious a contribution to be lost. They must not, however, be content to rest on their laurels. New conditions demand new service. With unique opportunities ahead, it will be nothing short of tragedy if they spend their energy in futile rivalry with the spreading junior college, rather than in a big brother attitude of leadership, and in constructive educational statesmanship in a higher field.

Effect of the junior college on the four-year college. What, then, may the four-year college do? What will be the effect of the junior college movement on it? Four different results may be suggested, all of which will doubtless be exemplified in the case of different four-year colleges in different parts of the nation: (1) extinction, (2) reduction, (3) continuation, or (4) advancement.

Why the four-year college? Before discussing these various possibilities, however, it will be worth while to stop for a moment to consider why we have four-year colleges at all, and how they have developed. The reason for the four-year college is thus tersely summarized by President Wilkins, of Oberlin College:[1]

> The reason why we have a four-year college in America to-day is that the first American institution of higher learning, Harvard, took form in the seventeenth century as a four-year college.
>
> The reason why Harvard in the seventeenth century took form as a four-year college is presumably that the University of Cambridge in the seventeenth century required a four-year course for the bachelor's degree....
>
> The reason why the University of Cambridge originally required a four-year course for the bachelor's degree is presumably that the University of Oxford required a four-year course for the bachelor's degree.
>
> The reason why the University of Oxford originally required a four-year course for the bachelor's degree is presumably that the students of the English nation at the University of Paris followed such a course. A statute of that nation, adopted in February, 1252, specifies that the candidate for the bachelor's degree "fidem faciet... quod audierit in artibus per quinque annos vel quatuor ad minus."
>
> The ultimate reason why we have a four-year college in America to-day is then presumably that the students of the English nation at the University of Paris in the thirteenth century followed a course of four years as a minimum for the bachelor's degree.
>
> Naturally, the content of the course has changed completely.... Yet with all the changes wrought in the curriculum, the four-year mould has been kept as sacrosanct. It would seem to be unworthy of the spirit of modern America longer to be bound by an educational form devised to meet conditions which obtained in Europe in the thirteenth century.

It is, of course, perfectly true that an ancient form might by a

[1] Wilkins, E. H. "The Relation of the Senior College and the Graduate School"; in *Journal of the Proceedings and Addresses of the Twenty-Eighth Annual Conference of the Association of American Universities*, pp. 59–60. Chicago, 1926.

combination of chances remain appropriate under changed conditions. If the four-year college is thus appropriate, well and good. If not, it should be recognized as vestigial, and should in general make way for a more modern type of educational organization.

In point of fact the four-year college reveals no peculiar adaptation to our present needs. On the contrary, it is betraying more and more clearly the truth that it no longer constitutes a normal educational unit. [1]

Let us now consider the four possible results indicated on the preceding page.

Extinction. While the small college has been typical of higher education in the United States, the work done in these institutions has by no means been of uniform standard, either in quality or quantity. A Carnegie Foundation study indicated approximately a thousand so-called colleges or universities, offering work of a great variety from that of a first-class standard four-year course to that of a very poor high school. With increasing standardization, even independent of the junior college, many of these colleges-in-name, with little or no financial backing,[2] or educational standing, have been forced to give up the struggle for existence or to re-define their purpose. The mortality of insufficiently supported "colleges," whether founded in an excess of denominational enthusiasm or as a result of community pride and rivalry, has been heavy in the past. It may be even heavier in the future with the development of the public junior college.

In the last century denominational and other private acad-

[1] With this statement may be compared one by President Nicholas Murray Butler, of Columbia:

"Dr. Wayland said, over sixty years ago, 'there is nothing magical or imperative in the term of four years, nor has it any natural relation to a course of study. It was adopted as a matter of accident, and can have, by itself, no important bearing on the matter in hand.' To suppose that a four-year baccalaureate course is necessary, *semper, ubique, ab omnibus*, is to elevate an accident to the plane of a principle." (Butler, N. M. "Length of the Baccalaureate Course"; in *Proceedings of National Education Association*, p. 501. Boston, 1903.)

[2] Cubberley, in his *State School Administration* (p. 738), gives a chart that shows that 266 out of 778 colleges in the United States had no endowment whatever.

emies flourished throughout the land. Most of these have vanished completely from the educational landscape, supplanted by the public high school, more adequately financed and adapted to a wider range of educational needs. Unquestionably the same fate awaits some of the weaker four-year colleges, as they come into competition with more adequately supported public junior colleges offering a richer and more varied educational program. The small, struggling, four-year colleges are facing a crisis in their existence. Their future is very uncertain. Several have recently closed their doors. They will be compelled to give up the struggle for existence, become junior colleges, or secure more adequate support to become really efficient four-year colleges. No ready-made formula can be produced to indicate what should be the fate of each institution, but certain generalizations may be made, as is done by former Commissioner of Education Claxton, in the next section.

Reduction. It will be recalled from Chapter III that President Harper suggested that a quarter of the small colleges then existing would probably give up the struggle for existence, and that half of them might well become junior colleges. More recently, Dr. Claxton, of the Federal Bureau of Education, compiled figures on the income of 507 colleges existing in 1915–16, which may be summarized as follows:[1]

Range of Income	Number	Approximate Average per Student
$2,000,000–$4,000,000	8	$500
1,000,000– 2,000,000	14	450
500,000– 1,000,000	30	375
250,000– 50,0000	56	335
100,000– 250,000	92	250
50,000– 100,000	102	185
25,000– 50,000	122	145
15,000– 25,000	54	120
3,000– 15,000	29	75

[1] Claxton, P. P. *The Better Organization of Higher Education in the United States.* United States Bureau of Education, Bulletin (1922.) no. 19, pp. 22–23.

He comments:[1]

In many of the poorer and smaller schools the numbers in the two higher classes are so small as practically to prohibit options and specialization, and to make the sections in some subjects, even without division, so small as to destroy the interest both of the students and of teachers, and at the same time make the cost of instruction per pupil comparatively very large. In many of these colleges nearly half the class sections have less than five students, and a large number of the class sections have only one, two, or three students. ... Here is the opportunity for the junior college and for a very important economy in college organization. Practically all the 307 colleges having incomes of less than $50,000 to $100,000 should cease to try to do more than two or three years of work — preferably only two years — and should concentrate all their means of money and men on doing well the work of these two years, employing as teachers men and women of the best native ability, the finest culture, and the largest skill that educational and professional training can give; men and women having the power to inspire and direct as well as to instruct.... Should these poorer and smaller colleges thus limit their field and change the character of their work, most of them would soon find themselves with two or three times their present number of students and with incomes three or four times as large as they now have. In addition they would have the consciousness of serving their country and the world more effectively than they now do or can.... Thus, with the same amount of money, the effectiveness of our schools of higher learning might be increased from 20 to 30 per cent. In the discussion of the work, organization, and courses of study of the junior colleges, these schools should not be thought of as in any way inferior to schools doing the full four-years' work. No school should lose any of its dignity or worthiness of support by confining its work to the first two college years. On the other hand both dignity and worthiness will be increased if they do the work of these two years in a better and a larger way, such as this change should make possible.

In an effort to see how the situation has changed in the fifteen years since the period represented by Dr. Claxton's figures, a study has been made on the same basis to-day, based

[1] Claxton, P. P., *op. cit.*, pp. 23–24.

on the latest reports of the United States Office of Education and on Hurt's *College Blue Book*. While definitions may vary somewhat,[1] it is evident that there has been a marked change. Many of the colleges existing in 1915–16 have either ceased to exist, or have become junior colleges as he advised, or have materially increased their resources. The study of 1928 data shows 77 four-year colleges with incomes reported under $50,000, and 141 more between $50,000 and $100,000. They are found in all but a half dozen of the smaller or less populous states, as indicated on the map of Figure 43. These then, constitute the borderline cases in the four-year college field. For some there is no adequate field, and they should be given decent burial as quickly as possible. Others can well exist as vigorous junior colleges, with improved financial and educational status. Some of the others, with strong friends and adequate fields, will doubtless develop into permanent four-year institutions. If it be assumed that half of those in the $50,000–$100,000 class and all of those with incomes below $50,000 need attention, there are approximately 150 four-year colleges in the country at the present time which should seriously consider changing to junior college status, if they are to remain in existence at all. Dr. Claxton said, in another connection, that two hundred or more of the smaller colleges should become junior colleges, centering all of their energies and all of their equipment on teaching.

Another point of view; are some four-year colleges virtually junior colleges? Another interesting criteria of the real efficiency of the four-year college is offered by President Cowling of Carleton College, who says:[2]

If I were asked to assist a prospective student in selecting a col-

[1] It is not clear whether theological seminaries, law schools, and similar professional schools are included in Dr. Claxton's tabulation. They have been excluded from the study made by the author, as summarized in Figure 43.

[2] Cowling, D. J. "The Future of the Liberal Arts Colleges"; in Hudelson, E. (editor), *Problems of College Education*, p. 389.

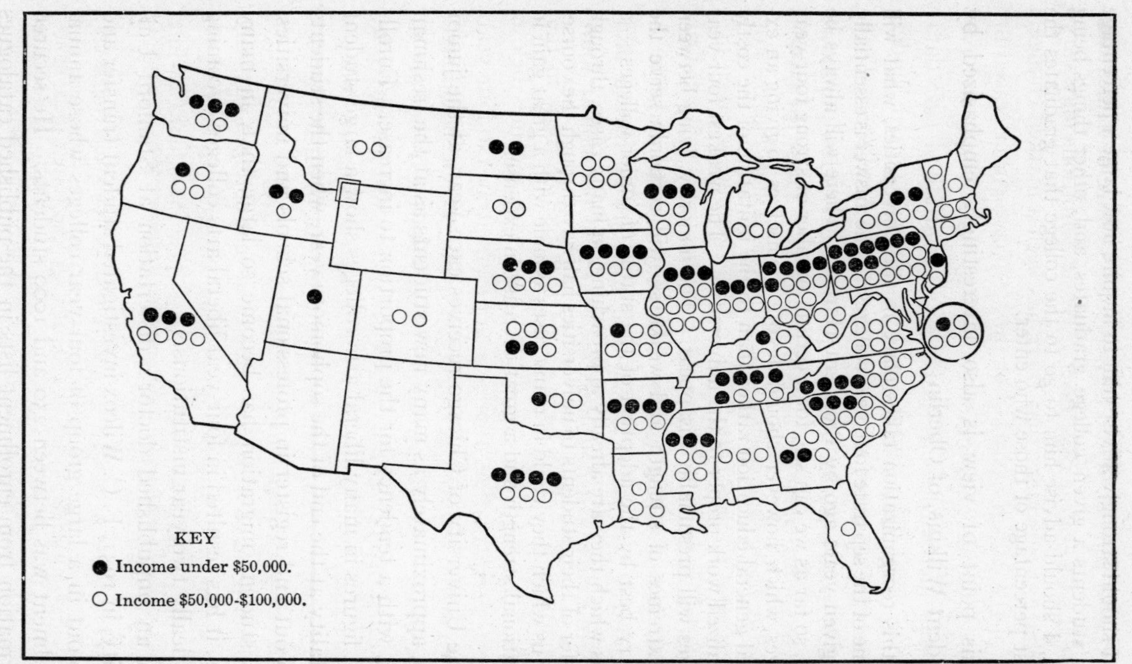

FIG. 43. FOUR-YEAR SENIOR COLLEGES, POTENTIAL JUNIOR COLLEGES, 1928
(According to criteria suggested by Commissioner Claxton)

lege, I should strongly advise him to inquire how large a percentage of its students a given college graduates, and, other things being equal, I should advise him to go to the college that graduates the largest percentage of those who enter.

This point of view is also interestingly emphasized by President Wilkins, of Oberlin:[1]

If this reorganization takes place in the universities, what will become of the separate four-year colleges? The answer is essentially that given years ago by President Harper. There will always be room, so far as we can see, for a certain number of strong four-year colleges, which, however, should devote themselves to giving an extended general education rather than to the imitation of the costly specialized work proper to the universities. The weakest four-year colleges will presumably disappear. The majority, lying between the extremes of strength and weakness, will certainly serve the country best by the adoption of the status of junior colleges — a status which they are already approaching, in many cases, through transfer of their students to universities halfway through the course, a status which they could in many cases assume with a great gain in educational strength and a great decrease in expense.

The University of Chicago receives each year, at the junior level, approximately as many new students as at the freshman level, with a tendency for the proportion to increase. Enrollment figures in many liberal arts colleges show a large student mortality at the end of the sophomore year, when the students drop out and register in professional schools and universities. This student migration has become so large that, in many cases, it has resulted in four-year liberal arts colleges becoming practically two-year institutions.

In an unpublished doctor's dissertation at Stanford University, in 1931, F. C. Wilcox investigated student transfer and drop-out in a large group of four-year colleges whose annual enrollment was between 250 and 1000 students. He secured information from enrollment lists in the published catalogues

[1] Wilkins, E. H., *op. cit.*, p. 70.

and from the registrars of the institutions concerned. A portion of his study, dealing with forty typical colleges, is summarized in Table 82.

TABLE 82. PERCENTAGE OF STUDENTS IN FOUR-YEAR COLLEGES WHO REMAINED UNTIL GRADUATION, TRANSFERRED TO OTHER INSTITUTIONS, OR DROPPED OUT OF COLLEGE

College	Remaining until Graduation	Transferring to Other Institutions	Dropping out of College
Hamline	13.1	0.02	86.88
Washburn	13.7	29.4	56.9
Franklin	15.3	12.3	72.4
Lawrence	15.6	22.2	62.2
Illinois Wesleyan	16.3	19.1	64.6
Kansas Wesleyan	16.9	11.5	71.6
Milwaukee-Downer	18.6	46.6	34.8
Western College for Women	23.3	39.1	37.6
Ripon	23.9	18.7	57.4
Morningside	24.3	11.3	64.4
Rockford	24.7	11.5	63.8
Iowa Wesleyan	25.7	0.1	74.2
Alma	26.0	27.1	46.9
Ottawa	26.3	15.1	58.6
Kenyon	27.5	14.7	57.8
Wheaton	28.5	14.4	57.1
Monmouth	28.7	17.1	54.2
Hillsdale	30.4	25.4	44.2
Hiram	30.8	23.2	46.0
Albion	31.3	15.0	53.7
Franklin and Marshall	31.3	23.4	45.3
Kalamazoo	32.1	17.1	50.8
Grinnell	33.9	35.1	31.0
Earlham	35.4	22.0	42.6
Carleton	35.9	34.7	29.4
Wooster	36.0	24.1	39.9
Hobart	36.6	0.1	63.3
Mount Union	38.8	14.1	47.1
Heidelberg	38.9	0.1	61.0
Washington and Jefferson	39.2	17.8	43.0
Hamilton	41.8	12.7	45.5
Union	42.7	19.7	37.6
Alfred	43.6	20.1	36.3
Gettysburg	49.3	0.03	50.67
Colby	51.2	0.05	48.75
Middlebury	53.4	0.06	46.54
Bates	54.3	0.05	45.65
Bowdoin	58.1	0.03	41.87
Haverford	63.3	0.06	36.64
Williams	74.9	0.03	25.07

In over half of the colleges listed in Table 82, less than one third of the original enrollment remained for graduation. In only a half-dozen institutions, located in the New England states and New York and Pennsylvania, did over half of the students complete their courses. In three quarters of the colleges there was considerable transfer to other institutions, principally to large universities. This transfer was as high as 47 per cent from Milwaukee-Downer College, where less than one fifth of the students remained for graduation. It was over 20 per cent in one third of the colleges named. It averaged 15 per cent in the entire group of colleges. Drop-out of students varied from 25 per cent at Williams to 87 per cent at Hamline, and averaged 51 per cent for the group. Thus, an average of 66 per cent of the students enrolled in this representative group of smaller four-year colleges either dropped out of college entirely or transferred to other institutions. A study of the time of transfer showed that the greatest number occurred at the end of the sophomore year. The number at other times was almost negligible. These typical colleges are furnishing two years of education, either terminal in nature or preparatory to higher institutions (two well-recognized junior college functions), to two thirds of their students, while only one third of them remain for graduation. Already many four-year colleges, to a surprising degree, are operating as predominantly junior colleges.

As long ago as 1901, a Southern educator urged that "C" class colleges in the Southern states adopt the junior college program.[1] In 1917 a Catholic leader urged the desirability of weak Catholic colleges dropping their senior and junior years.[2] Similar recommendations were made by Dr. Zook, in his survey

[1] Babbitt, E. H. "The Problems of the Small College in the Southern States"; in *Proceedings of the Association of Colleges and Preparatory Schools of the Southern States*, pp. 56–70. (1901.)

[2] Burns, J. A. *Catholic Education: A Study of Conditions*, pp. 136–41. Longmans, Green & Co., New York, 1917.

of higher education in Arkansas, with reference to the weaker four-year denominational institutions in that state. Noffsinger, in 1925, after a detailed survey of the colleges of the Church of the Brethren in the United States, recommended that half of them become junior colleges — a recommendation which has in part been carried out. Unquestionably the junior college is the ultimate solution for many of the smaller four-year colleges of the country which cannot, in justice to their constituency or to true educational ideals, continue indefinitely on their present basis.

Continuation in present status. Educational changes take place slowly in a democracy. Educational leaders have been urging reorganization in higher education for a third of a century, and yet actual modifications have been slow to come. Many of the weaker institutions have vanished, or have become junior colleges, or should do so. On the other hand, there is another considerable group of vigorous four-year colleges which have made most notable contributions to the higher educational life of the nation, and undoubtedly will continue to do so. Will they remain unchanged, or will they also reorganize on a different basis: There are some leaders who feel that they should remain essentially as they are, four-year bulwarks of culture whose unique mission is to withstand the trend toward reorganization.

Thus President Cowling, of Carleton College, says: [1]

> The four-year liberal arts college is America's unique contribution to the educational organization of the world. Its ideals were never more needed than now.... A college cannot accomplish its full purpose with the average student in less than four years.

Douglass, of Pomona College, says: [2]

> The liberal arts college of the future will, perhaps, occupy a posi-

[1] Cowling, D. J., *op. cit.*, pp. 389, 402.

[2] Douglass, A. A. "The Junior College and the Liberal Arts"; in *Pomona College Magazine*, vol. 18, p. 103. (January, 1930.)

tion analogous to that now held by the private secondary school. Patronage will come from those who prefer the training it can give to that offered by the public secondary schools, including the junior college and the universities. Campus life, and all it stands for, is a not unimportant consideration. Added time for the pursuit of intellectual interests will be desired by many.... The greatest contribution of the liberal arts college is the continuous interpretation of the intellectual, moral, and æsthetic contributions of the race in the terms of life in the present and future. The movement now in progress in many colleges to re-interpret culture should be given every encouragement.

Dean McConn, of Lehigh University, says: [1]

I look upon the junior college movement as the thing which will eventually give the four-year colleges both the opportunity and the necessary stimulus to confine themselves to their own proper work. A widespread system of junior colleges will cut heavily into present enrollments, to the good of all concerned. Some of the weaker colleges will go to the wall or be reduced to the status of junior colleges, which again will be all to the good. And the four-year colleges which survive will be forced to differentiate themselves from the competing junior colleges by offering superior training to the superior few.

President Wilbur, of Stanford University, says: [2]

For a long time to come the four-year college course will find some place in American education. No doubt some institutions, with the usual reluctance for change, which in many ways is salutary, will continue to insist upon it as the basis of all culture and education. It is difficult even for those who are in the midst of the strong tides of education which are flowing to sense the shifting of basic standards which has come into American life with the wide distribution of wealth and of educational opportunity.

[1] McConn, M. "College or Kindergarten"; in *The New Republic*, p. 1274. New York, 1928.

[2] Wilbur, R. L. "Trend of the University"; in *Annual Report of the President of Stanford University*, p. 2. Stanford University Bulletin, fifth series, no. 81. (November, 1929.)

Advancement. The point of view presented in the last section suggests that there may always be an adequate field for the superior four-year colleges of the country. While without doubt there will be always a rich *need* for such work, it may be questioned whether it necessarily must be done or can best be done in our present four-year educational unit. The ancient origin of the four-year tradition from the University of Paris, as traced by President Wilkins, has already been quoted. President Wilkins further says that the four-year college reveals no peculiar adaptation to our present needs, but that, on the contrary, it is betraying more and more clearly the truth that it no longer constitutes a normal educational unit. President Wilbur, of Stanford, was quoted in Chapter XXVI as stating that we are about ready to abandon the "fetish worship of the numeral four" in American education.

The fundamental changes that have been going on for some time suggest that in all probability the next quarter-century will see the present freshman and sophomore field almost completely preëmpted by the junior college, either public or private. It looks as if there were about to be repeated, at a higher level, the experience of the last half-century. Even less than fifty years ago most of the four-year colleges had academies or preparatory schools operated in connection with them. In many cases the academy enrollment was far greater than that of the "college." Thus of the thirty institutions mentioned on page 343, all but the seven New England colleges had substantial enrollments in the academy in 1900. In fact, the total enrollment in the college departments of these twenty-three colleges was 2860, and in the academies 2849 — practically the same for each.[1] In the thirty years since that time, with the development of the public high school, these acad-

[1] In 1900, the college enrollments in Mills College, Rollins College, Drury College, and Whitman College were 32, 40, 88, and 48, respectively, while in the same institutions the academy enrollments were 185, 140, 214, and 138.

emies have all been eliminated and the colleges have been greatly strengthened as a result.

A possible new position. With the newer conception of freshman and sophomore work as secondary or general in character, the question comes up whether, in time, the New England type of cultural college may not again profitably "raise its sights" and aim at a higher target. As two years of college education becomes fairly general in public junior colleges all over the country, will not the cultural colleges come to accept students on this level, rather than at high school graduation as at present? Unquestionably they can give a very fine type of education for a selected group of students, but they can never meet the needs of the great mass.[1] Their resources are limited. Many if not most of them find it necessary to limit their enrollments. In some cases less than half of the qualified applicants are actually admitted. In such a situation the question may properly be raised whether they can best serve the cause of higher education by duplicating the work done more extensively in junior colleges, or whether they have a more distinctive mission to fulfill.

Why should not their peculiar advantages be open to a larger number of students on a higher level? Why fill them with freshmen and sophomores, especially when the facts show that even now increasing numbers of these students are transferring to universities at the end of the sophomore year? Let these colleges make a distinct selection of superior students at the junior level, and then give them the benefit of the finest liberal arts training possible, for two or three years, and in accordance with the best New England cultural tradition. Even President Cowling, a vigorous advocate of the present four-year college, admits that the first two years are of little importance

[1] The thirty mentioned had approximately three per cent of the college enrollment of the country in 1900, but only one and a half per cent of it in 1928.

for giving the student the ideals for which the cultural college stands:[1]

> It may justly be maintained that it is in the last two years, and not in the first two, that a college accomplishes its purpose with a student, and creates within him its distinctive ideal. It is not in connection with freshman mathematics, or the beginning languages, or elementary sciences that a college finds its real opportunity. The work of these first years is largely a preparation for what the college has to offer in the years that follow. It is only when the student begins to delve into philosophy and economics and the social sciences, and when he begins to understand the natural sciences in their implications, and has developed a real taste for literature and something of perspective in history — it is only then that his personal philosophy of life begins intelligently to take on final form.

President Wilkins, of Oberlin College, goes even further in pointing out the advantages of separation of the junior and senior colleges, as follows:[2]

> But the fundamental advantage common to the junior and senior colleges which will result from their dissociation is, I think, the termination of a type of community life in which men and women of senior college age, powers, and influence live in constant association with boys and girls of freshman-sophomore age, in a social atmosphere which is essentially freshman-sophomore rather than upperclass in character. Entrance into the third year is not now marked by any such change in environment or in occupation as would suggest a change in attitude toward life. Consequently upperclassmen are inclined to spend their mental and physical energies on interests and indulgences which are essentially juvenile, and thus to develop a false sense of values — a sense which is likely to abide with them permanently. Furthermore, since these same upperclassmen are in constant association with, and are very influential upon freshmen and sophomores, they tend authoritatively to impart to them this same false sense of values. If, on the other hand, students of freshman-sophomore status are separated from those of upperclass status, the former will constitute a homogeneous and a

[1] Cowling, D. J., *op. cit.*, pp. 389–90.

[2] Wilkins, E. H., *op. cit.*, pp. 64–65.

frankly and rightly boyish and girlish body; and the latter, brought into conditions and relations worthy of their maturity and associated rather with their intellectual elders than with their intellectual juniors, will be inclined to spend their energies on interests more proper to the life of manhood and womanhood.

Extension upward. Do such suggestions imply that the present liberal arts college should limit itself to a two-year course? By no means! Why should not the ultimate objective for the majority of students in these colleges be the master's degree instead of the bachelor's degree? Why should they not continue their general policies of cultural training, eventuating in a year of graduate work? There is an increasing cultural need for this amount of training; there is also an increasing practical or vocational need. Almost universally the standards set up for junior college instructors require the master's degree. In California, a year of graduate study is a prerequisite even for teaching in any high school in the state. The state of Washington has adopted the same plan, to become fully effective in 1933. In time other states are sure to adopt the same standard. More and more the possession of a master's degree will come to be looked upon as a highly desirable criterion for advancement in many occupations, if not a prerequisite for entrance to them. In many subjects work for the master's degree can be given satisfactorily in the standard college.

Is it a radical suggestion that two years of work below be dropped, and one added above? Such a proposal is far less radical than would have been the suggestion, in 1900, that Mills, or Rollins, or Drury, or Whitman should drop their academies, then containing over three fourths of their total enrollment. Yet as their field has been adequately covered by the public secondary schools, these institutions have not suffered but profited by the upward movement of their work. Similarly, is there any logical reason to suppose that, in the next quarter-century, as the freshman and sophomore field is largely taken care of by the public junior college, the present college cannot gladly and happily surrender any distinctive claim to proprietary rights in this field of instruction and build upon it as a firmer foundation instead? Unless this is done, there is reason to fear that some institutions may tend to be squeezed out of existence.

Not in five or ten years, or even much longer is the well-established, adequately endowed, private college in danger of extinction. Educational needs and tastes in a country the size of America are highly varied. For many years to come it can continue to exist on exactly the present basis, but it is to be feared that, if it does continue on the present basis, content to rest on its achievements of the past, it may ultimately cease to command the respect and admiration which has rightfully belonged to it for so many years. It will gradually become reactionary and conservative, when it might be culturally progressive. It is to be hoped that a number of our stronger liberal arts colleges, in parts of the country where the junior college movement is firmly established, will move forward as prophets and leaders of a new educational epoch; that they will severely restrict and gradually eliminate their freshman and sophomore years; and then devote three years of intensive effort toward the development of the ideas and ideals of a new era of culture. Thus they will not be in unfriendly rivalry with the increasingly popular and spreading junior college. They will instead take the junior college product, and endeavor to build upon it in three years a finer civilization than any they have yet had a part in developing. Their graduates will be "masters" in truth as well as in name. This is the position of constructive leadership which many of our better four-year colleges can well afford to consider during the next decade.[1]

[1] Koos's general conclusions on the future of the college are worth quoting here: "It is doubtless too early to essay prophecy concerning them that will ap-

Trial of the plan. Such a plan has been under consideration at Westmoorland College, Texas, but lack of adequate means has prevented its definite inauguration. Perhaps destined to be of very great significance, however, is the action of George Washington University, in the autumn of 1930, in adopting a threefold divisional organization.[1]

1. The establishment of a junior college to care for the first two college years, underlying the senior college and all the professional schools;
2. The reorganization of Columbian University, the college of letters and sciences of George Washington University, as a senior college, embracing the junior year, the senior year, and one year of graduate study, leading to the baccalaureate and master's degrees;
3. Organization of a Council for Graduate Study which conceives the work of the Ph.D. purely as professional research training, separate and distinct from that for the master's degree. *The master's degree is transferred to the senior college.*

It will require time to determine the value of this plan, but it

proach realization in any significant degree, but at least some conjecture can be ventured. As admitted, a small proportion of the separate colleges, especially those with a ballast of endowment and a host of well-to-do and tradition-loving alumni, may be able to withstand the inevitable trend and remain institutions affording unspecialized training throughout a four-year period. Most of them, however, must make further accommodations to the trend, serving their generation in the way in which it insists upon being served. For the weaker units this will be as junior colleges which will draw their students from secondary schools in communities too small to warrant offering the work on the junior college level. In time, however, these junior colleges must go the way of the private academy in territory where the public high schools have seen a vigorous development. The remainder, for the most part in a better state of development than those just referred to, can serve in the dual capacity of (1) junior colleges and (2) senior colleges in which certain types of liberalized occupationalization and specialization are featured. Few such institutions will be able to afford the variety of opportunities for specialization of universities, but they can devote their energies and resources to one or a few, e.g. teaching, commerce, home economics, etc. In the remote future the junior college division for the reason given will atrophy, and these colleges will then devote themselves exclusively to the senior college task." (Koos, L. V. *Junior College*, p. 382.)

[1] "George Washington University Restores Educational Democracy"; in *School*, August 7, 1930.

may well be watched with unusual interest by the four-year colleges of the country.

For many of the strong four-year colleges added strength and vigor and a unique contribution to the higher cultural life of America in the next half-century is possible if they abandon unnecessary and unhealthy rivalry with educational institutions of junior college grade and endeavor instead to supplement and extend their work to higher levels than they have yet found possible.

QUESTIONS AND PROBLEMS

1. What are the advantages and disadvantages of control of junior college curricula through prescription of entrance requirements on the part of the state university?
2. Investigate the degree of independence enjoyed by any junior college which is a branch of a university.
3. What should be the relationship of the junior college to engineering schools? (See Clark, Faig, Spahr, and Zook, in Suggested Readings.)
4. List all universities which have separated their lower divisions. Classify them according to degree and character of separation.
5. What progress toward elimination of the Lower Division has been made by Stanford and Johns Hopkins since this chapter was written?
6. What other universities are planning on similar action, and how far have they gone with their plans?
7. Is a university justified in spending 80 to 85 per cent of its budget for junior college instruction? If not, what percentage is justified?
8. What are the essential features of the University of Chicago plan for dealing with the junior college years, as announced by President Hutchins in 1930? How does it differ from President Harper's plan?
9. Is it desirable for all the junior colleges in a state to adopt for the courses which they offer the designations and numbers of similar courses given in the state university?
10. A junior college dean writes, as follows: "Can anything be done to get senior colleges and universities, at least in California, to adopt uniform requirements for upper-division standing? The junior college is confronted with a most difficult and perplexing task when it undertakes to prepare students for junior standing in some ten to twenty institutions. The differences in requirements do not seem to me to be of fundamental importance. Were it possible for all four-year colleges to agree on a uniform lower-division requirement the gain in clarity and definiteness would be so great that all parties concerned

would be benefited." Discuss the solution of the problem which he raises.

11. Criticize the reasons for a junior college as a teacher training institution, as stated by Almack. Are all valid?
12. Look up all reasons possible for the discontinuance of the normal-school-junior-college relationship in Wisconsin. Do the same for the four California normal schools which have dropped their junior college departments.
13. From the catalogue, or otherwise, report in detail on the junior-college-teachers'-college relationship in effect at San Jose State Teachers' College, or at Fresno State Teachers' College.
14. The public high schools have very largely superseded the academies and private secondary schools, but the public colleges and universities have by no means superseded the private institutions of the same grade. Is there any reason to suppose that the junior college will be more like the former than the latter?
15. How many four-year colleges in the country have more than 500 students, the figure suggested as desirable by President Cowling?
16. What proportion of new undergraduate students in one or more universities enter with advanced standing at the junior level?
17. Take a sample of ten or more graduates from each of five or more different departments, and study their programs of studies during college. What proportion of "general studies" is there in the first two years? Of specialization? Of general studies and of specialization in the last two years?
18. In a given state or locality, make a study of existing four-year colleges to determine which could well become junior colleges. Consider history, attendance, field, control, resources, relation to other institutions, and similar ascertainable factors.
19. Make an intensive study of a single small four-year college, to determine the advisability of its changing to a junior college.
20. Make a study similar to Noffsinger's for colleges of some other denomination.
21. In 1915, Miss E. A. Colton wrote: "There are in the South 380 institutions claiming to be colleges or universities, only 30 of which are recognized by the Association of Colleges and Secondary Schools.... The South offers a flourishing field for the junior college. No other section of the country would be more benefited than the South by such a reorganization of its higher institutions of learning." What has happened in the South since 1915? How many of the 380 colleges have become junior colleges? How many more should?
22. Of the four-year colleges existing in President Harper's time, how many survived and how many have vanished today?
23. What has happened to the denominational colleges of Arkansas since

Zook's recommendations concerning them, in 1922? (See United States Bureau of Education, Bulletin no. 7. 1922.)

24. Of the colleges with incomes of less than $100,000, in 1915–16, as discussed by Commissioner Claxton, how many survive at the present time?
25. Make a map, similar to Figure 43, but using as a criterion enrollment instead of income.
26. "The traditional liberal arts college has its back to the wall," says J. T. Wahlquist (*Journal of Education*, vol. 110, pp. 433–37, November 18, 1929), and lists seven forces tending to limit its influence and growth. Arrange these seven forces in order of importance and justify your judgment.
27. What do you feel is the place of the four-year cultural college in the educational scheme of the future?

SUGGESTED READINGS

*Almack, J. C. "The Issue in Teacher Training"; in *Educational Administration and Supervision*, vol. 11, pp. 267–75. (April, 1925.)

Brown, J. S. *Normal Schools and Junior Colleges.* United States Bureau of Education, Bulletin no. 19, pp. 56–60. (1922.)

Campbell, W. W. "The Junior Colleges in Their Relation to the University"; in *California Quarterly of Secondary Education*, vol. 2, pp. 97–101. (January, 1927.)

Capen, S. P. (chairman). "Articulation at the Professional and Higher Education Level"; in *Seventh Yearbook of the Department of Superintendence of the National Education Association*, pp. 295, 302–05, 315. (February, 1929.)

Clark, L. W. "Junior Colleges"; in *Journal of Engineering Education*, vol. 16, pp. 337–46. (December, 1925.)

Claxton, P. P. "The Junior College"; in *Association of American Colleges Bulletin*, vol. 2, pp. 104–12. (April, 1916.)

*Claxton, P. P. *The Better Organization of Higher Education in the United States.* United States Bureau of Education, Bulletin no. 19, pp. 21–27 (1922); also in *School Life*, vol. 5, pp. 1, 10–11. (July 15, 1920.)

Colton, E. A. "Southern Colleges for Women"; in *Proceedings of the Association of Colleges and Preparatory Schools of the Southern States.* (1911.)

Deutsch, M. E. "The University and the Junior College"; *California Quarterly of Secondary Education*, vol. 6, pp. 133–42. (January, 1931.)

*Douglass, A. A. "The Junior College and the College of Liberal Arts"; in *School Life*, vol. 15, pp. 172–74. (May, 1930.)

Faig, J. T. "Junior Colleges and Technical Institutes"; in *Journal of Engineering Education*, vol. 16, pp. 450–52. (January, 1926.)

Goddard, C. B. *The Articulation of Junior College and Teacher College Curricula.* Bulletin of the Pacific Coast Association of Collegiate Registrars, Riverside, and Claremont, California, pp. 85–91. (March, 1929.)

*Haggerty, M. E. "Current Educational Readjustments in Liberal Arts Colleges"; in *Seventh Yearbook of the National Society of College Teachers of Education*, pp. 27–28. Chicago, 1929.

Harper, W. R. "A Two-Years' College Course"; in *Educational Review*, vol. 19, pp. 411–15. (April, 1900.)

*Harper, W. R. "The Small College — Its Prospects"; in *Proceedings of the National Education Association*, pp. 67–87 (Charleston, South Carolina, 1900); also in *The Trend in Higher Education*, pp. 375–90. Chicago, 1905.

James, H. G. "The Doom of the Arts College"; in *New Republic*, vol. 51, pp. 96–99. (June 15, 1927.)

Koos, L. V. *The Junior College*, pp. 241–386, 550–66.

Lowell, A. L. "The Outlook for the American College"; in Kelly, R. L. (editor), *The Effective College*, pp. 281–88. Association of American Colleges, New York, 1927.

Lyon, J. A. "Study of the Curricula of Junior Colleges as Affecting Their Graduates Entering Four-Year Colleges"; in *Proceedings of the Sixth Annual Meeting of the American Association of Junior Colleges*, pp. 27–33. Chicago, Illinois, 1926.

McConn, M. "Is it Practicable"; in *College or Kindergarten*, pp. 269–75. New Republic, New York, 1928.

Maxwell, G. E. "The Junior College Question — the Other Side"; in *National School Digest*, vol. 40, pp. 600–02. (June, 1921.)

Newlon, J. H. "Shall the Junior College be Externally Controlled"; in *School Executives' Magazine*, vol. 49, pp. 332–33. (March, 1930.)

Noffsinger, J. S. *A Program for Higher Education in the Church of the Brethren.* Teachers' College Contribution to Education, no. 172, 80 pp. New York, 1925.

Pearse, C. G. "The Junior College and the Normal School"; in *American Educational Digest*, vol. 42, pp. 417–18. (May, 1923.)

Spahr, R. H. "Engineering Education on the Junior College Level"; in *Proceedings of the American Association of Junior Colleges, Tenth Annual Meeting*, pp. 106–18. Atlantic City, New Jersey, 1929.

Stevens, E. B. "The Relation of Junior Colleges to the Four-Year Colleges and Universities"; in *Bulletin of American Association of Collegiate Registrars*, vol. 4, pp. 65–76. (April, 1929.)

*Wahlquist, J. T. "The Traditional Liberal Arts College"; in *Journal of Education*, vol. 110, pp. 433–37. (November 18, 1929.)

Way, W. W. "The Objectives of the Church Junior College"; in *Proceedings of the Ninth Annual Meeting of the American Association of Junior Colleges*, pp. 97–100. Fort Worth, Texas, 1928.

*Wilkins, E. H. "The Relation of the Senior College and the Graduate School"; in *Twenty-Eighth Annual Conference of the Association of American Universities* (1926), pp. 59–70; also in *Bulletin of the American Association of University Professors*, vol. 13, pp. 107–21. (February, 1927.)

Winfield, G. F. "Are the Junior Colleges Tending to Dissipate the Spirit and Ideals of the American Liberal Arts College?" in *Proceedings of the Ninth Annual Meeting of the American Association of Junior Colleges*, pp. 103–05. Fort Worth, Texas, 1928.

Zook, G. F. "Junior Colleges"; in *Journal of Engineering Education*, vol. 16, pp. 333–37. (December, 1925.)

CHAPTER XXIX

THE FUTURE OF THE JUNIOR COLLEGE

This new type of higher education, the junior college, is now on its way. I think there can be no reasonable doubt that within the next half-century it will sweep the country as irresistibly as the public high school swept it during the second half of the last century. — MAX McCONN.[1]

Contents of this chapter. He would be rash indeed who would attempt to prophesy with any assurance the future of the junior college movement, yet a few significant trends may be seen. This final chapter considers first some of the dangers and objections that may condition progress; then some of the problems facing the movement; next the opportunity of the junior college in the future development of American education; and finally the permanency of the movement.

Dangers and objections. Every step in the evolution of public education in the United States, from the kindergarten through the university, has met with criticism and opposition. Eternal struggle seems to be the price of educational progress. Progress under opposition and criticism may not be so rapid, but it is likely to be safer and more enduring than that which is made in haste and without true perspective and sound reasoning. The junior college movement cannot be checked; it must, therefore, be guided, and sometimes this is best accomplished by the chastening of its foes. Many of the dangers mentioned by some of the outstanding critics of the junior college movement have been considered in previous chapters, including the danger to culture and the scholarly amateur as seen by Professor Palmer of Harvard,[2] the dangers of unprepared

[1] McConn, M. *College or Kindergarten*, pp. 271–72. New Republic, New York, 1928.

[2] See Chapter XII, page 342.

instructors, of inadequate standards, of insufficient financial support, of high school contamination, of university domination, and others. These have been presented and discussed in their appropriate places. Attacks on the movement by Sachs, Burnham, and Holliday, and dangers to avoid as seen by Campbell, Lillard, and Brand will not be taken up in detail, but are referred to in the Suggested Readings at the close of the chapter.

Nature of the junior college movement. The junior college movement is a youthful movement. It is full of vitality. It is a vigorous movement. In three short decades it has shown a growth which compares favorably with three centuries of development in the senior college and university world. Its rapid growth has not been equal in all directions. It has had many growing pains, with difficulties of adjustment and articulation. Like a wedge it is gradually separating secondary from higher education, but at the same time, paradoxically enough, it is uniting them instead of separating them. D. S. Campbell, Secretary of the American Association of Junior Colleges, says:[1]

> Our information leads us to believe that the junior college, having to meet both the secondary standards below and the higher standards above, has found it hard to serve two masters. There are, even now, indications that this difficult amphibian existence will not always be demanded of the junior college.... Except in occasional instances where there may be local irritation, the junior college of the future will not be a source of discord and of enmity between itself and the schools below or above it. The opposition to the movement is serving to purge it of undesirable qualities and to force it to show fruits which justify its existence. In the main, even now, the relations between the junior colleges and the other institutions are cordial. This prophecy indicates that the tendency will grow.

A heterogeneous movement. The junior college movement, so-called, is a heterogeneous movement. It has many

[1] Campbell, D. S. "The Future of the Junior College"; in *Association of Texas Colleges Bulletin*, vol. 1, pp. 31–32. (May, 1929.)

aspects in different parts of the country and in different types of institutions. It is found in all but five states of the union. Recognized by law in over a third of the states, it exists as a public institution, in spite of legal handicap, in twice that number. There are public junior colleges, there are private junior colleges; there are coeducational colleges, and those for men and those for women; there are junior colleges with enrollments of only a dozen students, and there are those with enrollments in the thousands; there are those that are adequately supported, and those that are too poverty-stricken to do real college work; there are many that fill a real need, and there are some that have no excuse for existence.

An experimental movement. The junior college movement is an experimental movement. The field is full of problems of many kinds. There are problems of organization — Shall the junior college be a two-year, or a four-year institution? There are problems of articulation — with the high school below and with the university above. There are problems of the curriculum — Shall greater emphasis be placed upon vocational and extension courses? There are problems of faculty, of buildings, of library, and of equipment. There are critical problems of finance — What proportion of the support of the public institution shall come from the state; from the local community; from the student? There are problems of minimum criteria for establishment of junior colleges, and of desirable standards for their efficient administration. There are many problems peculiar to the private junior colleges. This volume is full of problems. It is hoped that it has suggested far more problems in the junior college field than it has solved. A dozen or more have been proposed in connection with the subject matter of each chapter. Some can be decided by logic or by research, but many will require careful experiments. A few general problems whose solution lies in the future, may, however, still receive brief consideration.

The problem of number of institutions. Is the rapid increase in the number of junior colleges — an average of thirty a year for the decade from 1920 to 1930 — likely to continue indefinitely? Probably not. Yet it is likely to increase materially for some time to come. Dr. Campbell, who has been closest in touch with the development of the movement during the decade, through his secretaryship of the junior college association, believes that the number in the country will continue to increase materially from year to year for at least a decade.[1]

California has fifty junior colleges, public and private, or one for each 113,000 population. If the entire country were similarly supplied, there would be well over a thousand, instead of four hundred and fifty. The question of number of junior colleges, however, cannot be considered independently of existing four-year colleges and universities. Some other states do not have as great needs, due to the existence of a relatively larger number of four-year colleges and universities within their borders. These are insufficient in number in many cases, however, and usually are not fulfilling some of the unique functions of the well-developed junior college, especially in the way of semi-professional courses.

Let us consider, then, the way in which the higher educational needs in California are met by junior and senior colleges combined. There are eighteen senior colleges and universities in the state, according to Hurt's *College Blue Book*. There is thus one college, senior or junior, for each 72,000 people. If the entire country were similarly supplied there would be 1660 colleges in the country. Hurt lists almost 800 four-year colleges and universities. This would leave 860 junior colleges needed to furnish higher educational facilities equivalent to those now found in California, as far as such facilities can be judged by number of institutions alone.

[1] See quotation, page 794.

Even California, however, with its fifty junior colleges, is far from adequately supplied. A general survey of the state would probably show at least twenty-five additional localities with junior college needs not at present met. State Superintendent Kersey, in 1930, named ten localities contemplating immediate organization of new junior college districts. It is not at all unreasonable to suggest that California may, within a decade, have approximately one hundred colleges and universities, public and private, senior and junior, to meet fairly adequately her higher educational needs, or one for each 56,000 of her 1930 population. A similar development in the entire country would mean approximately 2150 collegiate institutions, where there are now 1250 — 800 senior and 450 junior.

None of the facts given in this section should be interpreted as definite predictions. Many factors enter into the situation, such as character of population, wealth, educational traditions, and size of existing institutions. They are, however, suggestive of possibilities, and point toward the probability of considerable further increase in total number of higher educational institutions. Nor is there much probability of any marked increase in the number of four-year colleges and universities, judging by the experience of the first third of this century.[1] In fact, many existing four-year colleges are likely to become junior colleges, as already indicated in Chapter XXVIII. This will not change the total number, but will serve still further to augment the number of junior colleges. Thus every indication points to a substantial increase in the number of junior colleges in the country during the next decade or two. If the number should go on increasing at the rate of thirty a year, there would be 750 institutions by 1940. It is not unreasonable to estimate

[1] "Not many four-year colleges have been chartered since 1900, due to the growing tendency of extending the financial support and increasing available facilities of institutions already established." (Greenleaf, W. J. "Financial Support of Colleges"; in *Journal of Higher Education*, vol. 1, p. 254. May, 1930.)

that by 1940 or a little later there are likely to be as many junior colleges in the country as there are four-year colleges. Ultimately there may be two or three times as many.

The problem of enrollment. It is much more difficult to estimate enrollment in the junior colleges of the future than it is to estimate their number. Enrollment is sure to show great strides in the next decade. In 1928, the writer published a detailed study of enrollment trends in California junior colleges, taking into consideration population, elementary school enrollment, high school enrollment and graduation, and other factors. With the assumption that trends of the previous decade might be expected to continue, he ventured to predict a probable junior college enrollment in the state of at least 20,000, and perhaps 30,000 by 1934–35; and of at least 35,000, and possibly 50,000 by 1939–40. Actual enrollment figures for the three years since these estimates were made have been decidedly in excess of those estimated.[1] The average annual rate of increase in the average daily attendance in the district junior colleges of California, since 1923, has been no less than 40 per cent. During the two latest years it has been 52 per cent and 64 per cent. The State Department expects similar increases during the next few years. President Wilbur, of Stanford University, in 1929 stated that careful estimates indicated that within ten years the number of students doing work in junior colleges or in the lower division of state universities in California would be in the neighborhood of 50,000.[2]

A recent critic of the junior college states that "It is a ques-

[1] The following comparisons may be made of enrollments estimated with enrollments actually reported by the State Department:

Year	Estimated	Reported
1927–28	6,284	10,787
1928–29	8,868	13,492
1929–30	11,682	20,561

[2] Wilbur, R. L. "The Organization of Stanford University"; in *School and Society*, vol. 29, pp. 286–87. (March 2, 1929.)

tion whether the junior college movement has not reached its peak."[1] What is the evidence in the case? California has about one twenty-second of the population of the country; in 1929–30 it had one fifth of the junior college enrollment. May we expect a four- or five-fold increase in the rest of the country? There are over four million high-school students in America today. All are possible junior college material. If all went to junior college the attendance at any one time would be upward of two million. Of course not all will go, soon or ever, but may not many more be expected to do so as the junior college movement spreads and gains age and prestige?

A study was recently made of eight district junior colleges in California. For each thousand students enrolled in the high schools of the districts it was found there was a junior college enrollment of 282. If the same ratio held throughout the nation, there would be an enrollment in excess of 1,128,000. Conditions are not the same in California as in the rest of the country. Take only one fourth or one fifth of this suggested enrollment, if desired, and still the present enrollment of approximately 70,000 looks like only a beginning. Has the junior college movement reached its peak? A conservative view of the facts and the tendencies suggests that it has scarcely yet reached the foothills!

The problem of type. There is probably rapid and continued growth ahead of the junior college movement as a whole for many years to come, but will all types of institutions share equally in this growth? Dr. Campbell thinks not. He says:[2]

As to numbers, it would seem fairly safe to believe that the total number of junior colleges will be materially increased year by year for a number of years to come, perhaps a decade. Of this total the private schools will probably discontinue nearly as many as will be

[1] Holliday, C. "This Junior College Movement"; in *School and Society*, vol. 30, p. 888. (December 28, 1929.)

[2] Campbell, D. S., *op. cit.*, pp. 30–31.

established, the net number probably increasing slightly. The public junior colleges, however, will increase very rapidly, especially during the next five years. This is based not merely upon the immediate past history, but also upon the unmistakable evidences of pressure in many states for a public junior college program.

It is becoming clearer day by day that the public demand for college education cannot be met by the private institutions alone, of either the four-year or junior college type. As the public high school gradually displaced most of the private academies of the last century, it is logical to suppose that the public junior colleges may gradually supplant many of the private institutions. At any rate, there is likely to be a much more rapid growth of the public institution, both in number and in size. American educational democracy will eventually insist upon college opportunities for all at public expense. It is by no means likely, though, that the private junior college, now in the majority in number although not in enrollment, will not also have a permanent place in American education, as its elder sister, the private four-year college, has had. The denominational junior college fills a genuine need, is in many cases economically, educationally, and patriotically sound, and when such is the case may be expected to endure for many years to come. With such diversity of character and belief in our population, there are bound to be many people who prefer the private to the public institution.

The problem of organization. Whether the desirable form of organization of the junior college shall be the two-year or the four-year type has already been adequately discussed. There is a possibility, however, that an alternative in the way of a three-year college might have many of the virtues of both and few of the faults of either. It is strange that, with the amount of experimentation which has gone on for so many years in almost every conceivable form of reorganization in the secondary field, that a three-year junior college unit has not been tried more seriously and extensively. While it would not fit well with the six-three-three plan, or any other plan which proposes to make use of one or more of the lower years of the four-year high school, it would fit perfectly with the prevailing types. A reference to plans A, D, and H in Figure 40, page 653, will show that in these types of organization the upper year of the high school could easily be spared, and still leave a three-year unit for a senior high school. There are over five hundred "reorganized" schools in the country on a six-two-four basis, and some twelve thousand on the eight-four basis. In many of these such an experiment could be tried with interest and profit.[1]

There is room, then, for a variety of types of public institutions. There should be freedom to experiment with two-, three-, or four-year junior colleges, under a variety of circumstances and conditions. Junior colleges should not yet be all poured into the same mould. They should have the right to experiment irrespective of established forms. "In any new investigation, it is the period preceding crystallization which is the most promising." It would be unfortunate now, if ever, to restrict them too rigidly by legislation. It is desirable, however, that legislation should be so framed as to prevent the organization of too many weak, struggling, inefficient units, with insufficient attendance and inadequate support.[2] The

[1] The brief quotation on page 716, with reference to the experience of Menlo Junior College suggests that the students in the *senior* year of high school may integrate well with the two junior college years, while those in the junior high school year may not. Even Koos is by no means sure that the four-year unit is the ultimate form for he says that the "junior college years should be worked out in integration with *one or more* high school years below." (*Junior College*, p. 73.) The small junior college at Salinas, California, has had a three-three form of organization, covering the four-year high school and the junior college years. This arrangement has been only tentative and transitional, looking in the direction of ultimate six-four-four organization, but it seems to have given general satisfaction during the brief period it has been in operation.

[2] "Unfortunately, there will be many tragic attempts to establish junior colleges where they are to serve scarcely any purpose other than to give the local

existence of many of this type of institution is likely to cast discredit upon the entire movement.

The problem of size; the opportunity of the junior college. One of the important problems of the junior college is the problem of size. The junior college is typically a small institution, in many cases far too small for efficiency and success. The junior college of the future will undoubtedly be a larger institution with more diversified offerings. Some of the small ones now existing will disappear from the landscape; others will grow to more satisfactory proportions. It is to be hoped, however, they will not be afflicted with the malady of "gigantitis" which has plagued too many universities. There is a vital distinction in the field of college education between bigness and greatness. The junior college of the future must be a bigger institution than the junior college of the present, but it must not be too big. On the other hand it can be and must be a great institution in the true sense of the word. It will be truly great, great in its unique educational contribution, if it recognizes fully the limitations and boundaries of its own field, deliberately delimits its functions, and represses any ambitious university aspirations; if it finds supreme satisfaction and contentment in doing thoroughly the work of the freshman and sophomore years better than they have ever been done before; if it has the courage to experiment with the expansion of these two years laterally to include new fields and unexplored opportunities at the same level, but does not try to usurp the field of the university above or of the high school below. Herein lies the opportunity of the junior college in the next decade to be a really great institution, regardless of size of enrollment, and to make a really distinctive contribution to the democratization of collegiate education.

Chamber of Commerce one more reason for advertising the virtues of the city. Their funerals will be expensive but necessary incidents. States will gradually take a hand in the movement, and will, doubtless, make such tragedies the exception." (Campbell, D. S. "The Future of the Junior College"; in *Association of Texas Colleges Bulletin*, vol. 1, p. 32. May, 1929.)

The problem of permanence. A recent critic of the junior college says that "whether this is a mushroom growth, destined to flourish for a brief time as an educational fad and then speedily wither, is a question not yet answered in school circles."[1] It would seem, however, that a movement whose roots go back into the nineteenth century, which has developed in the present century from almost nothing to one numbering institutions by the hundred, students by tens of thousands, and property valued at over a hundred million dollars — to one that is sending thousands of its graduates into advanced work in the universities which they are completing with success and distinction, or into life better prepared for their vocations — to one formally authorized in the fundamental law of over one third of our states, and recognized in many others — in some way it becomes just a trifle difficult to characterize such a movement as a temporary fad which is destined speedily to wither. This is not the way, according to the biologist, that the mushroom ordinarily develops!

In the minds of many of our best educational leaders the junior college is fully accepted as a permanent feature, an established fact, a lasting contribution, destined to develop rapidly and vigorously. True it has its imperfections and limitations. Some junior colleges have been formed with more enthusiasm than judgment. Four-year colleges have not been entirely free from the same fault. The movement, however, cannot be judged a failure because some of its units were ill-advised and are destined to perish. The law of the survival of the fittest will assure larger and better junior colleges if not more of them. There are many questions unsettled in the junior college field, but the question of existence and permanence is not one that longer concerns most educators. As Koos has so aptly phrased it, "It is not a question of whether, but how."

[1] Holliday, C., *op. cit.*, p. 598.

Fad or fixture? With reference to this question of permanence, the author wrote an editorial for the educational section of the *Red Book Magazine* in 1929,[1] in which he tried to express his generalized philosophy of the junior college movement. With slight modifications, this may not inappropriately be used as the closing words of this final chapter:

Education ever has been a subject close to the heart of America. Only sixteen years after the Pilgrims landed on the "bleak New England Coast," they founded Harvard College — the beginning of higher education in the United States. For over a century the education it furnished was for the professional classes. Education for the masses was peculiarly the contribution of the nineteenth century. That century witnessed the widespread development of the grammar school and of the high school. Secondary education was popularized and universalized.

Will collegiate education for the masses characterize the twentieth century? Already this century has witnessed an astonishing development of interest in higher education. The great universities of the country, institutions interested primarily in specialization and research, have found themselves swamped with thousands of immature youth, eagerly clamoring for college education. But transition from high school to university has been abrupt and student mortality in the freshman year has been appalling. Parents have hesitated to lose their children in the university mass. Does higher education *of* masses necessarily imply education *in* masses?

The answer is the *junior college* — a more widely diffused opportunity for two years of college education in smaller units, an institution educating a larger number of students at home in their less mature years, an institution where closer contacts are possible with instructors more interested in teaching than in research, an institution facilitating transition from high school restrictions to university freedom.

According to latest available information there are over four hundred and fifty junior colleges in the country with an enrollment of seventy thousand students. All but five states are represented. It is recognized that the movement is yet in its infancy or early

[1] Eells, W. C. "Fad or Fixture?" in *Red Book Magazine*, vol. 53, p. 6. (July, 1929.)

childhood. Many states are considering legislation to authorize and encourage the junior college. Its ultimate form and organization are not yet known, but it is beginning to occupy a unique position in the American educational ladder — unmistakably higher than a glorified high school; distinctly lower than the scholarly specialization of the university.

Many young men and women are finding they can secure adequate preparation for various life occupations in two years at junior college. Others, for whom college was only an unrealizable dream, are finding two years of cultural education possible for them at home. Still others are finding excellent preparation under superior conditions for later specialization in the university.

A wealth of evidence of a wide variety of types has already accumulated to indicate that the junior college, even in its early youth is certainly making good, scholastically and otherwise. There is no question that it is a permanent addition to the American educational family. It has many problems before it — financial, administrative, scholastic. Its form of organization is not settled. Its functions are not uniquely defined. Further research and experiment are needed. The professional educator finds here a fascinating field for study and investigation. The general public is beginning to realize that here is a really major movement for improvement in American education — the development of an institution which promises to popularize and democratize collegiate education. The junior college is not a fad — it is a fixture!

QUESTIONS AND PROBLEMS

1. Study the list of disadvantages of the junior college, as given by 3000 California students (see Eells and Brand, in Suggested Readings), to see which are incidental to a small institution in its immaturity, and which are more fundamental.
2. Compare the objections to the junior college, as stated by Holliday in 1920, with those stated by him in 1929.
3. Compare the objections to the junior college made by Sachs in 1905 and in 1918, with present conditions. How many of them could be urged against the junior college today?
4. Find the ratio of number of four-year colleges and universities to population in each state. Compare other states with California to see the need and probability of an increase in number of junior colleges in them.
5. Employing the technique used by the author in predicting junior

college population in California, predict probable junior college enrollment for a decade in some other state.

6. Select the five most outstanding fundamental objections to the junior college, and write an answer to one of them.
7. Select five outstanding problems in the junior college field, and outline a method for the solution of one of them.
8. What do you feel is the greatest opportunity of the junior college in your own state?
9. Is the junior college movement growing too fast for its own good? If so, what should be done about it?
10. Look up all the advantages claimed for either the six-four-four or the six-three-three-two types of organization, and see to what extent they would apply to the suggested eight-three-three type.
11. Look up all the disadvantages and dangers seen in either the six-four-four or the six-three-three-two type of organization, and see to what extent they would apply to the suggested eight-three-three type.
12. The following has been given as the definition of a junior college: "The junior college is an institution where students who can not get into a real university spend their leisure time"! Write an editorial for a college paper, or a local newspaper, using this definition as a text.
13. "I am satisfied that the junior college is a large part of the answer to the question as to what shall be done with our youth as we increase in prosperity and feel the need for more understanding and more training for a necessarily more complicated life." (Wilbur, Ray L. "The Junior College — A Message"; in *Sierra Educational News*, vol. 22, p. 147, March, 1926.) Just how does the junior college answer this question?
14. The president of a new junior college writes, "The largest danger we face today is the cramping of our program that will result if the senior college hedges us in with so much red tape that we can function only as feeders to their junior year." How can this danger be avoided?
15. Mrs. C. L. Graves, of New York, said at the Atlantic City Meeting of the American Association of Junior Colleges: "And I would lay one more possibility before this Association; the founding of a senior college in the east for junior college graduates. It will be many years at best before the eastern colleges recognize the possibilities in the junior college. It is a case of fundamentalism *versus* modernism in education. What the junior college can really accomplish will not be known unless an outlet can be found where its graduates may go on in kind. Suppose I could announce today the founding of a senior college, with degree-giving power, here in the east, a college which was especially interested in junior college graduates, what a sigh of relief would go up from all of us!" Outline a plan for such an institution, its advantages and disadvantages, and its value for the junior college movement.

16. In an address before the American Association of Junior Colleges, Commissioner Cooper, in 1929, thus defined the three-fold opportunity of the junior college: "These seem to me to be your opportunities. I have tried to put them in the order of their importance: first, to offer a liberal education to a new stratum of the American public; second, to train for certain semi-professions that have not been taken care of except in the private business college, and in the private automotive school, or in the polytechnic college; and thirdly, to do whatever the university wants you to do with about eight or ten per cent of the population who will go on in the law, medicine, and other professional lines." (*Proceedings of the Tenth Annual Meeting of the American Association of Junior Colleges*, pp. 92–94. Atlantic City, New Jersey, 1929.) Do you agree that these are the greatest opportunities of the junior college? Would you arrange them in the same order of importance?

SUGGESTED READINGS

Burnham, J. M. "The Junior College Movement"; in *The New Republic*, vol. 30, p. 315. (May 10, 1922.)

Criticism of the junior college because it lacks university atmosphere and influence of notable scholars.

Campbell, W. W. "The Junior Colleges in Their Relations to the University"; in *California Quarterly of Secondary Education*, vol. 2, pp. 97–101. (January, 1927.)

President of University of California says that "attitude of the university to the junior college movement is thoroughly friendly and sympathetic, but this attitude is not unconditional."

*Eells, W. C. "Trends in Junior College Enrollment in California"; in *California Quarterly of Secondary Education*, vol. 4, pp. 59–69. (October, 1928.)

Eells, W. C. "'This Junior College Movement' — Again"; in *School and Society*, vol. 31, pp. 598–601. (May 3, 1930.)

An answer to second article by C. Holliday.

Eells, W. C., and Brand, R. R. "Student Opinion in California Junior Colleges"; in *School Review*, vol. 38, pp. 176–90. (March, 1930.)

Lists disadvantages of junior colleges, as seen by their students.

Gibson, J. E. "The Public Junior College in Mississippi"; in *School and Society*, vol. 30, pp. 680–81. (November 16, 1929.)

Indicates possible dangers as well as advantages.

Holliday, C. "Junior Colleges — If"; in *School and Society*, vol. 11, pp. 211–14. (February 21, 1920.)

An early criticism of the junior college movement.

*Holliday, C. "This Junior College Movement"; in *School and Society*, vol. 30, pp. 887–88. (December 28, 1929.)

A later criticism of the junior college movement.

Kersey, V. "California Education: Significant Facts"; in *Sierra Educational News*, vol. 26, pp. 37–38. (February, 1930.)

Names ten places contemplating organization of district junior colleges in the state.

*Lillard, J. B. "Pitfalls of the Junior College"; in *Sierra Educational News*, vol. 26, p. 48. (April, 1930.)

Rebok, H. M. "The Junior College"; in *California Quarterly of Secondary Education*, vol. 4, pp. v–vi. (October, 1928.)

Trends in California and problems of the future.

Reinhardt, A. H. "Why is the Junior College?"; in *Sunset Magazine*, vol. 59, pp. 12–13, 77. (October, 1927.)

Advantages and disadvantages of junior college in American education.

Sachs, J. "The Elimination of the First Two College Years: a Protest"; in *Educational Review*, vol. 30, pp. 488–99. (December, 1905.)

A vigorous early statement of objections.

*Sachs, J. "Junior Colleges in California"; in *Educational Review*, vol. 55, pp. 117–25. (February, 1918.)

Junior college movement in the Middle West has not been successful and is not likely to be permanently so in California.

Wilbur, R. L. "Junior Colleges Free the University"; in *World's Work*, vol. 56, pp. 200–03. (June, 1928.)

"Within a short time, it is probable that as many will apply for admission at the junior year as formerly applied with the beginning of the freshman year. This is as it should be."

Wilbur, R. L. "The Organization of Stanford University"; in *School and Society*, vol. 29, pp. 286–87. (March 2, 1929.)

Suggestion of 50,000 enrollment in California by 1940.

Zook, G. F. "The Junior College Movement"; in *School and Society*, vol. 23, pp. 601–05. (May 15, 1926.)

General evaluation of the movement and suggestions regarding its future place.

*Zook, G. F. "Is the Junior College a Menace or a Boon?" in *School Review*, vol. 37, pp. 415–25. (June, 1929.)

"The movement seems to me to have more implications for good than has any other single proposal which is before us for consideration."

Kersey, V. "California Education: Significant Facts," in *Sierra Educational News*, vol. 26, pp. 17, 18. (February, 1930.)
[illegible] places [illegible] of [illegible] junior colleges in the state.

*[illegible], J. B. "Pitfalls of the Junior College," in *Sierra Educational News*, vol. 26, p. 16. (April, 1930.)

Rebok, H. M. "The Junior College," in *California Quarterly of Secondary Education*, vol. 1, pp. [illegible]. (October, 1925.)
Trends in California and problems of the future.

Reinhardt, A. H. "Why is the Junior College?" in *Sunset Magazine*, vol. 59, pp. [illegible]. (October, 1927.)
Advantages and disadvantages of junior college in American education.

Sachs, J. "The Elimination of the First Two College Years, a Protest," in *Educational Review*, vol. 30, pp. 488-90. (December, 1905.)
Vigorous early statement of objectives.

*Sachs, J. "Junior Colleges in California," in *Educational Review*, vol. 55, pp. 113-[illegible]. (February, 1918.)
Junior college movement in the Middle West has not been successful and is not likely to be permanently so in California.

Wilbur, R. L. "Junior Colleges Face the University," in *Nation's Schools*, vol. [illegible], pp. [illegible]. (June, 1928.)
"Within a short time it is probable [illegible] will apply the [illegible] of the junior year [illegible] with the beginning of the freshman year. This is as it should be."

Wilbur, R. L. "The Organization of Stanford University," in *School and Society*, vol. 27, pp. [illegible]. (March 3, 1928.)
Suggestions of [illegible] enrollment in California [illegible].

Zook, G. F. "The Junior College Movement," in *Educational Review*, vol. 31, pp. [illegible]. (May 15, 1930.)
General summation of the movement and [illegible] place.

*Zook, G. F. "Is the Junior College a Menace or a Promise?" in *School Review*, vol. 37, pp. 415-25. (June, 1929.)
"The seriousness with which [illegible] have [illegible] the point that [illegible] other [illegible] proposal which is before us for consideration."

APPENDIX I

BIBLIOGRAPHY

THE American Association of Junior Colleges, at its ninth annual meeting at Fort Worth, Texas, in December 1928, voted to ask the author of this book to prepare for publication as complete a bibliography on the junior college, as possible. This was recently published by the Federal Office of Education.[1] The bibliography was used as the foundation of the present volume, and is considered an indispensable supplement to it. Every reader should be supplied with a copy.

This bibliography is arranged for convenient reference, either by topic or by author, but it is too extensive for a class or student who wishes to become familiar with the principal literature of the field. The twenty-five titles which follow are, therefore, recommended as most important for early reference. Acquaintance with the material included in them and in the present text should make one reasonably familiar with much of the best literature in the field. Many valuable studies, however, will be found in other sources. Reference to many of these has already been made in the suggested readings, given in connection with each chapter. The most important sources are starred in the following recommended list.

A. Books and General Surveys

(Arranged chronologically)

1. McDowell, F. M. *The Junior College.* United States Bureau of Education Bulletin, no. 35, 1919, 139 pp. (Out of print.)

   The first comprehensive study which was made of the junior college movement in the country treats the history, influences, present status, and accrediting by states, for approximately one hundred junior colleges existing in 1917–18. Fourteen appendices contain questionnaire forms, detailed statistical tables, and a bibliography of 82 titles. Enrollment by colleges is given for 1914–17. The study was made by Dr. McDowell as his doctor's dissertation at the University of Iowa, in 1918.

---

[1] Eells, Walter Crosby. *Bibliography on Junior Colleges,* United States Department of Education, Bulletin no. 2, 167 pp. (1930.) For sale by the Superintendent of Documents, 25 cents. This bibliography is being kept up to date by the publication of supplementary entries, in the same style, in the monthly issues of the *Junior College Journal.* The original bibliography included 1600 annotated titles. Monthly supplementary titles to the number of approximately 300 had been added by June, 1931.

*2. Koos, Leonard Vincent. *The Junior College.* Research Publications of the University of Minnesota, Education Series, no. 5. 2 volumes, 682 pp., 231 tables, 100 figures. Minneapolis. (May, 1924.)

This monumental work is an exhaustive report, based upon an investigation financed by the Commonwealth Fund, in 1921–22. It is divided into five parts: (1) the scope and aspirations of the movement, (2) the educational functions of the junior college, (3) the forces of reorganization in higher education, (4) overlapping in high school and college, and (5) instituting the junior college plan. The appendix contains lists and statistical data on public, state, and private junior colleges, and a bibliography of 78 titles.

*3. Koos, Leonard V. *The Junior College Movement.* 436 pp. Ginn and Co., Boston, 1925.

A less technical presentation in summary form of the detailed matter and conclusions reached in the author's more extensive research monograph, *The Junior College.* It is an excellent general manual sufficiently detailed for many reference purposes, and more widely used and quoted than the author's research volumes.

*4. Proctor, William Martin (editor). *The Junior College: Its Organization and Administration.* 226 pp. Stanford University Press, Stanford University, 1927.

A symposium volume of fourteen chapters, ten, by California junior college executives, the others by the President and two professors of Stanford University. Due to composite authorship there is some overlapping, but on the whole it gives an excellent presentation of the development, status, and problems of the principal types of California junior colleges. Contains an annotated bibliography of 90 titles.

*5. Whitney, Frederick Lamson. *The Junior College in America.* Colorado Teachers' College Education Series, no. 5, 258 pp. Greeley, Colorado, 1928.

An extensive fact-finding study of the status of the junior college movement in 1927–28. Deals with development, objectives, laws, standards, curriculum, costs, and criteria for organization. Has valuable tables giving statistical data for 1926–27 and 1927–28 for 146 public and 236 private junior colleges. Unfortunately it is inaccurate and inadequate in some respects, and therefore must be used with care and discrimination.[1]

6. Bennett, G. Vernon. *Vocational Education of Junior College Grade.* University Research Monographs, no. 6, 244 pp. Warwick and York (1928).

A careful selection of 28 occupations for which junior colleges could

[1] For evidence to justify this statement see review by the author in *School Review,* vol. 37, pp. 388–91. (May, 1929.)

furnish suitable preparation. Considers necessary curricula, and stability, and probable increase in each occupation. The author advocates establishment of vocational junior colleges in cities only of 25,000 population or over. This volume is essentially the author's doctoral dissertation at University of California, in 1925. Unfortunately the statistical data represented the conditions in 1923 and 1924, and were not revised at time of publication. Therefore it cannot be relied upon, especially for the California junior colleges, but this does not seriously affect the general validity of the conclusions drawn.

7. Hurt, Huber William. *The College Blue Book*, second edition, vol. 1. Colleges of Liberal Arts and Sciences, Technical and Professional Schools. 576 pp. Hollywood-by-the-Sea, Florida, 1928.

A general reference book, covering a much larger field than the junior college. For the junior college it treats of development, distribution, and standards, and gives detailed statistical tables by institutions and states for 382 junior colleges (96 of them tax-supported), statistics of 9 negro junior colleges, and a series of state maps showing the location of each junior college.

*8. Eells, Walter Crosby. *Bibliography on Junior Colleges*. Office of Education, Bulletin no. 2, 167 pp. Washington, D.C., 1930.

The comprehensive bibliography described on page 805.

B. Proceedings of Associations and Conferences

*9. *Proceedings of Annual Meetings of American Association of Junior Colleges*. Doak S. Campbell (secretary), Peabody College, Nashville, Tennessee.

Proceedings of eleven annual meetings, including one at Berkeley, California in November, 1930, have been published, varying in size from 10 to 153 pages. Further details concerning them have been given in Chapter III. These contain a wealth of material on all phases of the junior college movement. The later reports contain not only the full text of addresses, but also stenographic reports of all discussions. *Proceedings* of the first annual meeting, and of the junior college conference held a year earlier (1920), were published together by the United States Bureau of Education as Bulletin no. 19, 1922. This bulletin is now out of print, but obtainable in many libraries. All other *Proceedings* have been published by the Association.[1] The *Proceedings* of the eleventh meeting appeared as the February, 1931, issue of the *Junior College Journal*. It is planned to continue this form of publication in the future.

*10. *Directory of the Junior College*. Published annually by the American Association of Junior Colleges. Doak S. Campbell (secretary), Peabody College, Nashville, Tennessee.

For 1928 and 1929 this was published in mimeographed form. The

[1] Several of these are out of print, but, in the spring of 1931, the following could still be furnished by the secretary: seventh, eighth, ninth, tenth, and eleventh.

March, 1930, issue was a printed pamphlet of 20 pages, containing the names, addresses, and a variety of statistical information concerning 429 junior colleges, with a reported enrollment of 67,437 students.[1] The January, 1931, issue published in the *Junior College Journal*, contained similar information regarding 436 colleges with a reported enrollment of 74,088 students. This directory is the most complete, recent, and reliable for general reference. Subsequent issues will be published annually in the *Junior College Journal*.

*11. Gray, William S. (editor). *The Junior College Curriculum*. Proceedings of the Institute for Administrative Officers at the University of Chicago, vol. 1, 261 pp. University of Chicago Press, Chicago. (1929.)

Contains 19 chapters, by different authors, dealing with many phases of the junior college curriculum. Emphasis is placed on reports of junior college courses as given at the University of Chicago, and at Stephens College, Missouri. An excellent annotated bibliography of 107 titles is included.

12. Bulletins of the Department of Secondary-School Principals. Annual meetings of the Department of Secondary-School Principals; H. V. Church (secretary), Berwyn, Illinois.

The *Proceedings* of the thirteenth annual meeting, at Cleveland, Ohio, in 1929, contains eighty pages, reporting the eight addresses given at two sessions of the junior college section. Similarly, the *Proceedings* of the fourteenth annual meeting at Atlantic City, in 1930, contains 75 pages reporting six addresses given at two sessions of the junior college section. The *Proceedings* of the fifteenth annual meeting at Detroit, in 1931, contains 58 pages reporting five addresses at two sessions of the junior college section.

13. *Seventh Yearbook*, National Education Association, Department of Superintendence. (February, 1929.)

This important Yearbook, devoted entirely to "The Articulation of the Units of American Education," contains much matter dealing with various phases of the junior college, especially in its relationship to other parts of the public school system.

14. Bulletin of the Pacific Coast Association of Collegiate Registrars. *Proceedings* of the Fourth Annual Convention, Riverside and Claremont, California. (November, 1928.) Published as an Occasional Paper (vol. 4, no. 1) of Riverside Junior College, Riverside, California, 120 pp. (March, 1929.)

Contains ten addresses by Pacific Coast educators, on junior college problems especially from the registrar's standpoint.

---

[1] Erroneously given as 67,627 in the directory summary, due to numerical errors in totals for Arkansas, Minnesota, and Mississippi.

15. (*a*) *Junior College Conference.* 66 pp. University of Southern California, Los Angeles, California. (May, 1928.)
(*b*) *Junior College Education.* 95 pp. California Society of Secondary Education, Berkeley, California. (1928.)

In May, 1928, an important junior college conference was held at the University of Southern California, on invitation of the School of Education. Eleven addresses which were delivered, were printed in the *California Quarterly of Secondary Education* for October, 1928 (vol. 4, no. 1). These were reprinted in the form (*a*) above, as *Junior College Conference.* With three additional papers from the *California Quarterly*, they were also reprinted as a monograph (*b*) *Junior College Education.* Both are now out of print, but will be found in many libraries. Their contents can be found in volumes 3 and 4 of the *California Quarterly of Secondary Education.*

C. State and Local Publications

16. Foster, I. Owen (chairman); Clark, Harold F.; Patty, Willard W.; and Chamberlain, Leo M. *Some Phases of the Junior College Movement.* Bulletin of the School of Education of Indiana University, vol. 4, no. 1. Bloomington, Indiana, September, 1927, 125 pp.

Contains results of a questionnaire investigation on extent and trend of junior college movement, and special studies of costs, standards, legal status, and curricula.

*17. *The Junior College in California.* Bulletin G–3, State Department of Education, Sacramento, California, 48 pages. 1928.

Contains history of the junior college in California, by Commissioner of Education, W. J. Cooper, text and analysis of junior college laws, and detailed statistical tables. Incomplete, since important changes in legislation passed in 1929 and later years are not included.

*18. Reid, J. R. *Texas Municipal Junior Colleges.* Bulletin no. 255, State Department of Education, Austin, Texas, June, 1929. 93 pp.

A very detailed and extensive analysis of the situation in Texas, including law, growth, location, standards, requirements, staff, student body, courses of study, buildings, libraries, finances, and extra-curricular activities.

19. Broom, Knox M. *Public Junior College Bulletin.* Bulletin no. 58, State Department of Education, Jackson, Mississippi, 1929. 43 pp.

Contains a study of the essential factors in the successful location of state-supported junior colleges; Mississippi statutes governing junior colleges; and detailed consideration of junior college needs and possibilities in fifteen different zones of the state.

20. Koos, Leonard V., and Weersing, Frederick J. *Secondary Educa-*

tion in California: Report of a Preliminary Survey. 128 pp. State Department of Education, Sacramento, California, 1929.

Contains a careful study of many phases of the junior college movement in the state, especially considered as a phase of secondary education.

*21. Ricciardi, Nicholas; Kibby, Ira W.; Proctor, William Martin; and Eells, Walter Crosby. *Junior College Survey of Siskiyou County, California*, 87 pp. Yreka, California, 1929.[1]

The most extensive individual junior college survey yet made. Considers questions of need, type, curricula, cost, and location.

D. Educational Journals

The four leading journals, from the standpoint of publication of material dealing with the junior college, are:

22. *The School Review.* University of Chicago, Chicago, Illinois. Monthly, except July and August.

The leading journal of secondary education. *The School Review* has published at least 70 articles dealing with the junior college, including many careful and significant objective studies.

23. *California Quarterly of Secondary Education.* California Society of Secondary Education, 2163 Center Street, Berkeley, California. Quarterly.

During the five years of its existence the *California Quarterly* has published over 40 articles dealing with the junior college.

24. *School and Society.* Grand Central Terminal, New York City Weekly.

At least 50 articles have appeared in this well-known educational weekly.

25. *The Junior College Journal.* Stanford University Press, Stanford University, California. Monthly, except July, August, and September.

This new journal, beginning publication in October, 1930, under the joint editorial control of the American Association of Junior Colleges and of the School of Education of Stanford University, is devoted exclusively to the junior college field. The first volume contained 600 pages.

In addition, junior college material of importance is often to be found in the *American Educational Digest* (now the *School Executives' Magazine*), in *School Life*, in the *Educational Review* before its merger with *School and Society*, and in many other journals.

The state journals which have dealt with the junior college field most extensively have been the *Sierra Educational News* (San Francisco, California), and the *Texas Outlook* (Fort Worth, Texas).

[1] A few copies are available from the author of the present volume at Stanford University, California.

APPENDIX II

SUGGESTED TOPICS FOR TERM PAPERS

BELOW are suggested a few general topics suitable for term papers, or in some cases for theses. They can be easily adapted to local conditions or special situations. In addition, it is suggested that the student read: Angell, J. R., "Problems Peculiar to the Junior College"; in *School Review*, vol. 25, pp. 385–97 (June, 1917); and Kemp, W. W., "Research Problems in Junior College Education"; in *California Quarterly of Secondary Education*, vol. 4, pp. 25–30 (October, 1928.) Many other problems suitable for term papers, or theses, will be found in the questions and problems suggested at the close of each chapter.

I. Historical and General

1. Development of the junior college in any particular state.
2. Present status and prospects of the junior college in any particular state.
3. Influence of University of Chicago on the junior college movement.
4. Influence of Stanford University on the junior college movement.
5. Influence of any state university on the junior college movement in the state.
6. Progress in separation of lower division in American universities.
7. History of junior college legislation in California.
8. Development of junior colleges from four-year colleges.
9. Development of four-year colleges from junior colleges.
10. Why the junior colleges in any state have been discontinued.
11. Development of junior colleges for any particular denomination.
12. Why junior colleges of any denominational group have been discontinued.
13. First uses of the term "junior college."
14. Should the term "junior college" be retained permanently?
15. Dr. Harper's influence on the junior college movement.
16. Dr. Jordan's influence on the junior college movement.
17. Dr. Lange's influence on the junior college movement.
18. Ten men with greatest influence in the junior college movement.

19. Courses on "junior college" in American universities.
20. What shall be the future of the four-year college?
21. Will junior colleges destroy "culture" and the "scholarly amateur"?
22. Development of junior colleges for Negroes.
23. Critical review of Whitney's "Junior College in America."
24. Critical review of Bennett's "Vocational Education of Junior College Grade."
25. Critical review of Koos's "Secondary Education in California: A Preliminary Survey."
26. Critical review of any other recent book in the junior college field.
27. Significance of the Stephens College experiment.
28. Significance of the Sarah Lawrence College experiment.

II. *Legislative and Organizational*

29. Criticism of existing junior college law in any state.
30. Criticism of a proposed junior college law in any state.
31. Proposals for new or revised junior college laws for any state.
32. Outline of a system of junior colleges for any state.
33. Relation of teachers' colleges to junior colleges.
34. Should a junior college be established in a particular community?
35. Minimum criteria for establishment of junior colleges.
36. To what extent is any university in effect a junior college for its own locality?
37. What junior colleges in a particular group or area should be discontinued?
38. Should there be a maximum junior college enrollment?
39. Minimum income for a junior college.
40. Minimum tributory high school enrollment for a junior college.
41. Minimum endowment for a private junior college.
42. What should be the policy of a national junior college journal?
43. What are the special problems of a junior college on the 6–4–4 plan?
44. Should the junior college be largely a terminal institution?
45. Should the junior college have ambitions to grow up into a four-year college?

III. *Administrative and Curricular*

46. Analysis of contents of a group of junior college catalogues.
47. Comparison of costs of junior college and four-year colleges.

48. How should true junior college costs be computed?
49. Should the state treasury contribute to the support of the local junior college?
50. Vocational courses for women in junior colleges.
51. Engineering, agricultural, commercial or other special vocational courses in junior colleges, or in a selected group of them.
52. Study of any special subject of the curriculum in a group of junior colleges; e.g., fifty or more.
53. Retardation, failure, etc., of junior college students.
54. Student survival in junior colleges and four-year colleges.
55. Teaching load of a junior college faculty.
56. Educational tests appropriate to the junior college field.
57. Should high school seniors be allowed to take junior college courses?
58. Advisability of Saturday classes in the junior college schedule.
59. Classification of students.
60. Differentiation of grading systems for different classes of students.
61. The junior college library: Size, contents, administration, support, use, etc.
62. Should the junior college be housed with the high school?
63. Should junior college instructors teach high school classes?
64. Should research be expected of a junior college instructor?
65. Does and should the junior college instructor have the doctor's degree?
66. Methods of improving and encouraging scholarship at the junior college level.
67. Should the junior college train teachers?
68. Inferiority or superiority of junior college instruction.
69. Proper relationship between state university and junior college.
70. Magazines desirable for the junior college library.
71. Comparison of junior college and four-year college faculties.
72. Essential laboratory equipment for any science in junior college.

IV. *Student Activities and Relations*

73. Should junior colleges have fraternities?
74. Student activity program in a single junior college.
75. Athletics in a group of junior colleges.
76. Dramatics in a group of junior colleges.
77. Journalism in a group of junior colleges.
78. Other student activities in a group of junior colleges.
79. Intelligence of junior college students.
80. Age of junior college students.

81. What becomes of junior college graduates?
82. Junior college transfers in university athletics.
83. Junior college transfers in other university student activities.
84. Honor scholarship societies in junior colleges.
85. Can school spirit be maintained in a two-year institution?
86. How much freedom is desirable for junior college students?
87. Desirable forms of student government.
88. Would you attend the junior college again, if repeating your education?
89. What traditions are desirable, and how best developed, in a junior college?
90. How can a college atmosphere be created in a junior college?

APPENDIX III

CLASSROOM METHOD FOR A JUNIOR COLLEGE COURSE

It may be interesting and suggestive to state the principal requirements for the course on the Junior College, as given at Stanford University, by indicating the way in which it has gradually evolved. Following are the six main requirements for a successful completion of the course, as given to the class, before a textbook was available:

1. Write a term paper. Due one week before the end of the course. Choose your subject within the first two weeks from subjects suggested, or otherwise.[1]
2. Choose two California junior colleges with which to become thoroughly familiar; from catalogues, interviews with students, etc. One of these must be a *District* junior college, the other some other type, public or private.
3. Choose a group of junior colleges in one state other than California, with which to become as familiar as possible.
4. Select one subject of the curriculum, from the list below, for comparative study in an assigned group of junior colleges:

English	Physics	Commercial
Mathematics	Chemistry	Agriculture
Latin	Biology	Engineering
Spanish	Other Science	Music
French	Orientation	Physical Education
German	Psychology	Art
History	Philosophy	Religion
Economics, etc.	Education	Home Economics

5. Read extensively in the periodical literature.[2] Keep approximate record of sources and pages read. At end of term, hand in a brief list of supplementary reading done in the course, with a short comment on its value to you.
6. Score three junior college catalogues.[3]

---

[1] A list of suggested topics was supplied, similar to those given in Appendix II.

[2] Mimeographed bibliographies were supplied, supplementing the one prepared by the author as Chapter XIV of the volume on the junior college, edited by Dr. Proctor.

[3] Copies of the score card, as reproduced in Chapter XXI, were supplied each member of the class.

In the future, when the course is given, the class time will be more largely devoted to discussion of the questions stated at the end of each chapter, since the existence of the text will free much time which has had to be devoted to the presentation of the material contained in it in the form of lectures. Written answers to one or two of the questions in each chapter may well be required of each student.

INDEX